The Final Colossus
In Battle Array
AD 2010-2012

by
William L. Roth
Timothy Parsons-Heather

The Morning Star of Our Lord, Inc. is a nonprofit, tax-exempt religious and charitable organization incorporated under the laws of the State of Illinois. It has been established for the dissemination of a miraculous body of work received through the supernatural intercession of the Blessed Virgin Mary under the titles of the Morning Star Over America and the Final Colossus. This organization is solemnly dedicated to all the principles delineated within these written texts in union with the spiritual catechesis of the Supreme Pontiff of the Roman Catholic Church, the Vicar of Christ on Earth. It is the intrinsic role of this Corporation to evangelize the Gospel of Christianity and provide pastoral consolation to those lacking in faith, the infirm, homebound, incarcerated, deprived, dejected and those who are otherwise suffering-humanity for the sake of the Glory of the Kingdom of Jesus Christ.

The Morning Star of Our Lord, Inc.
Springfield, Illinois
www.ImmaculateMary.org

Published by The Morning Star of Our Lord, Inc.
Used with permission.

Copyright © 2017   William L. Roth
All rights reserved.   Timothy Parsons-Heather

Publish Date: October 13, 2017

ISBN: 978-0-9793334-4-6

To the Salvation of men
and a King who lived that it be so...

The Final Colossus
In Battle Array
AD 2010-2012

Chapter 1
Miraculous Intercession
Say What?
1

Chapter 2
Miraculous Intercession
Now In Our Time
17

Chapter 3
Frames of Reference, Perspectives and Reactions
Our Interior Constitution
29

Chapter 4
Jesus the Christ
Truth Beyond the Ages
55

Chapter 5
The Fruit of Certainty
Faith Brought to Life
71

Chapter 6
How Do I Pray?
Fiat Maximus!
81

Chapter 7
Discernment and Man's Response
113

Anthology of Messages

AD 2010
143

AD 2011
309

AD 2012
469

The Final Colossus
In Battle Array
AD 2010-2012

One is my dove, my perfect one is but one, she is the only one of her mother, the chosen of her that bore her. The daughters saw her, and declared her most blessed: the queens and concubines, and they praised her.

Who is she that cometh forth as the morning rising, fair as the moon, bright as the sun, terrible as an army set in array?

> *Canticle of Canticles*
> *Chapter 6, Verses 8-9*
> *Douay-Rheims Version*

Let the Miracle Go On
Statement from the Seers

Anyone familiar with our *Morning Star Over America* apostolate knows that the Blessed Virgin Mary dictated messages to us from February 22, 1991 through December 28, 2008 intended for the whole world. And, through our love for Her, we have done our best to record, protect and disseminate them. During the final weeks of 2008, the Mother of Jesus Christ told us several times that it would be necessary to culminate Her messages to humanity in accordance with the Will of the Father. Our mission would become complete. And, as Her sons, we were heartbroken to hear this, even as Our Lady said that She would continue speaking to us privately, that the messages She would dictate thereafter would be solely for our comfort. So, we collected Our Lady's messages meant for the world into twelve published books and delivered them like heralds to Bishop Thomas John Paprocki of the Roman Catholic Church.

Our hearts were not broken for long. In early January 2009, Our Lady, in keeping Her word, began dictating private messages to us that were more uplifting and compelling than any mortal ears should have the liberty to hear. She invoked the spiritual romance of the Glory of God to draw us further into Her Immaculate Heart. Our Heavenly Mother spoke about divinity and deliverance in tones and measures that no mortal being could have possibly conceived. During Her private appearances after 2008, our messages from the Mother of God seemed as transfigured as Her Son on Mount Tabor. The entire Domain of Righteousness descended upon us like honey dripping from Her lips. We were indeed uplifted, consoled and renewed. And, it was here again that we fell prostrate not only in thanksgiving to God, but with humble supplication that She would give us permission to share with the whole of humanity the private beauty from Her Wisdom with which She has always comforted the forlorn.

These new messages would become the health of our spirits and the delight of our days. We begged, felled to our knees, to not let us be the only ones on Earth to see from the inside how brilliantly a Morning Star can glow. We poured ourselves out like Jesus in the Garden, promising our obedience to anything She might require – all that would bring Her to believe that the entire world should hear what She said to us after December 28, 2008 and rejoice.

We beseeched Her to remember the faith of the Saints, those who had called on Her during their mortal years for the same intercession that has thus far spared the world from the justice of Her Son. And, lo' and behold, this book, *The Final Colossus*, resting in your hands, is Our Lady's response. She could not wait to answer. She spoke brightly and fervently about what humanity means to Her Son. She lauded our eagerness to approach Him. She gave Him thanks with prayers of Her own, ones we could hear, with tears in Her eyes, that we had remembered His Sacrifice on the Cross. At the last, Our Lady, the Queen of Love, the *Morning Star Over America* and *Final Colossus* said YES to us the same way She invoked Her love for God upon the Great Annunciation. So, let the miracle go on! This manuscript is another gift from Our Lady to reflect everything She ever wanted and believed. It is as much a response to us as a grace for humanity itself. Let the doubtful step aside – in the lineage of the triumphs of old, this is a victory anew. Let there be no mistake, *The Final Colossus* is a linguistic new wine for the nuptial between God and His Church.

William L. Roth
Timothy Parsons-Heather

The Final Colossus

Basking, bathing, brilliant! Outpouring the Wisdom of God!
The Visage of Heaven, flowing freely the tears of pristine Glory.
Clothed in unerring, inevitable Light. The winds of change!
Eradicating, electrifying, compelling, beloved!
You teach the shedding of Earth amidst the corals of sin.
Go! Go into the world that knows no peace.
Greet, bless, call, embrace! Heal, sanctify, purify, caress!

You, the Virginal Shores of Paradisial Love.
Monogram and Monument to the Triune God.
The Trident, the Benevolent, the Salvific, the Bold.
You, the Sunlit Matron of God's Holy Ones, lost in the portals of bewildering Death.
O' Perfect Glory, Mother of Life Renewed. You, the Hands of Grace.
The Fair Maiden who birthed the pacific Pardon of fallen souls.

You, the Beatific Dawn of a Boundless Age.
Bring the solstice of Ecstatic Light to heirs and orphans.
To the Well of corpus hearts brooding in hopeless Dusk.
Seek ancient tundras and mystical parlors where mortals huddle amidst battle and waste.
You, the flawless Blessing and newfound Trust of generations lost!

You, Matriarch and Queen of the lifeless Daughter in the Harbor.
Your Son is the Torch of Life to the children of Earth.
His Light unifies the blessed, the grated, the wretched, the lost, the timid, the damned.
You! Summoned by the outstretched arms of Hope!
Stationed high above the stillness of invincible Freedom.

You celebrate the Destiny of man and beast, alike,
with Your Immaculate Crown of Stars,
to which the little Child in the Bay bows in deference,
her spiked chapeau heeled near her humbled feet.
She welcomes Your cultivating Touch to the unwitting masses,
the hopeless chest of inordinate pawns awaiting their passage to the Celestial Port,
while the Streams of Paradise reflect your glistening Mantle.

Yes, You step into the world to claim the Unknown.
Clasping errant palms that flail in the dark,
pulling to beat their breasts in the vibrant New Groves of the Land of God.
You are the Parasol of Infinite Bliss. Refined, Robust, impassioned Delight!
Where cities of angels moor to feast on placid temperaments.
Come this Day! Lift every age to Heaven's Door!

Chapter 1
Miraculous Intercession: Say What?

What is meant when someone refers to miraculous intercession? Well, it's probably best to point to the stories in the Old and New Testaments of Sacred Scripture such as when Jesus miraculously appeared to St. Paul at his conversion on the road to Damascus, or when Samuel heard a voice in the night and Eli recognized that it was God speaking to the boy and instructed him to respond, "Speak Lord, your servant is listening." There are also the examples when the Archangel Gabriel appeared to the Virgin Mary at the Annunciation, the angels appearing in the fields to the shepherds at Jesus' Birth, and when the angel "whose appearance was like lightning" was seen by Roman guards stationed at Jesus' Tomb on the morning of His Paschal Resurrection. The more notable, non-biblical examples are the apparitions of the Virgin Mary in Paris in 1830 to Saint Catherine Laboure; in Lourdes, France in 1858 to Saint Bernadette; and in Fatima, Portugal in 1917 to the small children Lucia, Jacinta and Francisco; this latter appearance being confirmed by the great Miracle of the Sun witnessed by 70,000 people, believers and atheists alike, on the 13th day of October that year. The mystical experiences of Saint Joan of Arc are another poignant example. She received miraculous intercession in the form of the mystical Voices of Saint Michael the Archangel and the great French SS. Margaret and Catherine. Saint Joan of Arc was mystically guided through this divine intercession to advance a military campaign for the successful liberation of France from the English in the 15th century. She was later betrayed and delivered up to be burned at the stake by corrupt ecclesial authorities who refused to believe that she was actually guided by Heaven. Today, however, she is heralded as one of the great patron saints of France while the legacies of her persecutors, prosecutors and executioners will testify until the end of time that they martyred a Saint. All of these examples, as diverse as they are, reflect the quality of breaching the boundaries of the world we normally see and experience. This is why the word "supernatural" even exists in our vocabularies. It is a word that has been created to describe something that is wholly beyond what nature would normally manifest as we understand it, realizing that we might eventually come to know more about how God has ordained nature to serve Him. Now, it is recognized that there are more nuanced theological definitions on the spectrum between natural and supernatural; and there are also the factors of deception and demonic influence that must be winnowed. But, to keep the point simple, history records that there are innumerable instances where God has blessed us with special occasions of grace where He has allowed us to apprehend the moment as being beyond the laws of nature, the consistencies of our senses or the timely progression of circumstances that surround us. Something does not have to violate the laws of mere physicality to be considered supernatural. All grace supercedes the sinful nature of human beings and is flourishing throughout our lives through innumerable facets and situations we encounter every day. Moreover, billions of people have testified to the stories in the Sacred Scriptures where it confirms God's miraculous intervention and interaction with His people, and none have done so in vain.

So, for all the historical evidence and testimony, it should not be a challenge for anyone to accept that He reached into people's lives in profound ways in past generations. But, what about miraculous intercession that He might wish to extend today? Would we not expect it to impact us on a wholly different level of reality when face-to-face with it than simply being asked to acknowledge a story repeated from history? When these extraordinary occasions of grace happen in the realism of the present moment, they become more than stories from ages past. They instead bring with them profound perspectives of God's presence into our contemporary psyche whereby we either acknowledge them or reject them, depending upon the formation of our disposition. In the present day, these graces meet the contemporary American mind-set, and there they often perish in the collision with the secular ideologies that are choking our society with a Godless interpretation of our existence. Similarly, they meet the impenetrable wall of facile religiosity in those who are terrified of the faith they are asked to invoke. Testimony to miracles often seems to lose at the moment of acceptance because we are usually unable to unveil to others the actual instant of the breaching. Vast groups of people and even entire societies find it very difficult to accept that God continues to help us just as He did in those great stories of the Bible because they are distracted by distorted and errant orthodoxies and ideologies that do not grant venue for God to assist them in obtaining the rewards of His Eternal Kingdom. The miracles never quite seem big enough to kick down the door of cynical skepticism and the fortress interpretations of theologies and institutional conventions erected in the path of God. Part of this seemingly insuperable phenomenon lies in it being very difficult to prescribe static boundaries where something may be recognized categorically as being outside the normalities of nature. Members of the Church have struggled with this demarcation in nearly every claim of miraculous intercession that confronts them because the confirmations of authenticity that God does give are rarely recognized or respected because they require an extension of faith in nearly every case, save the astounding events like the Miracle of the Sun at Fatima or the miraculously imprinted image on the tilma of Juan Diego at the shrine of Our Lady of Guadalupe in Mexico. This tilma is a perfect example. Mankind is staring directly at a supernatural miracle from God, and most of the intellectuals are still searching for any other explanation than the Almighty. Most want to see the miracles themselves and not just their fruits. The Most Holy Trinity has a difficult time overcoming our hyper-scrupulous human nature and our inordinate fear of being wrong. In truth, we are not so much worried about being wrong as we are of being required to change our lives and what we will have to sacrifice. Men demand material confirmation and signs when God is saying instead that He wants our faith and trust as a sign of our love and abandonment to Him; and He will use any instrument or circumstance at His disposal as a veil to defend that call for faith. The point being made is that the determination of supernaturality is inevitably a challenge to the scope of one's faith. For those with great faith, the signs of authenticity glare like beacons at them; but for the rest, a million suns might be beaming their way, and they will still claim the darkness. There are even some religious commentators and leaders who have succumbed to debating whether the Holy Spirit even acts in the world anymore in the ways we read about in the Apostolic age of Christianity. This says more about their faithless strictures of thought than God's abundant blessings. Truthfully, God has not quieted His actions; it is the clarion of faith that He would respond to that has nearly gone extinct. The universal voice of Christianity has been all but diminished to a haunting warble of a crying bugle lost in the distance which is trying to signal His faint-of-heart brigades to rise to conviction once again. He would rather hear a thunderous wave of battle cries like the ones Saint Joan of Arc commanded. She gave one mystical message to the Dauphin of France, and he surrendered his armies to God's service at the command of her visions. Thereafter, the miraculous victories commenced unto the liberation of his nation and his crowning as its king. This might be something we could ponder when assessing our own moral victories. The modern psyche always prunes occasions of divine grace into the frameworks of secular doubt. If we allow this, does this not bar us from being touched by God in the ways He wills, thus leaving humanity collectively lost in the suffering of a spiritual wasteland? If true, this would more testify to the extinction of Christian faith across vast swathes of the planet than it does about the fact that God is the same yesterday, today and tomorrow. For those whose thoughts are defined by the void of contemporary secular humanism or other radical ideologies, it transcends their pretentious sense of rationality that our Heavenly Father would consistently dispense prodigious grace and verifiable manifestations of His divinity all throughout history. The blessed testimonies of witnesses are discarded as delusional outgrowths of zealotry, religious myth and superstition in those cases that happen to pass before them. The spectrum of awareness of those immersed in the secular world, along with those who believe His every act must operate through their scrupulous approval, serves as a great opaque liability to the elevation of mankind in the truth as God wishes we would know Him. Several generations of American children in succession have now grown to be adults deprived of their birthright to know their Savior who loves them. And, the farther they wander into the forest of secularist excuses for life and the ideological materialism that wants their money at the expense of their soul, the more lost, blind and consistent in godlessness they become. Deeper they descend into unhappiness, deprivation and depression, famished for the true meaning of their existence, until their ultimate suffering arrives where they can go no farther. And thus, we see the evidence in the societal order and the lives of broken families, suicides, addictions, rioting, revolutions, and the decadence and injustices in our culture, not to mention entire regions of foreign continents laboring in absolute desolation, darkness and death.

  Let us consider a parable using the refraction of light. The refraction of light through a medium such as a prism or a sky filled with rain manifests the spectrum of colors we see. Worldly people, meaning those with no recognition of God's spiritual Kingdom, are ones who would readily acknowledge the visual colors of the rainbow; red, orange, yellow, green, blue, indigo, and violet, because they can see those colors. But, they are also the very same people who find it difficult to accept there are other wavelengths of light in the portions of the spectrum they cannot see. In other words, they refuse to admit that wavelengths of light such as ultra-violent, x-rays, gamma rays, or infrared, microwaves or radio waves even exist. Those are wavelengths of light too. They also cannot understand how these unseen wavelengths could have any effect on them. Yet ironically, they are unfazed by their inability to explain their sunburn which is caused by the ultraviolet light. Their approach instead is to convince everyone else that the redness and blistering of their skin has nothing to do with the light they cannot see. Can we recognize how intellectualism without a recognition of the unseen realms surrounding our lives might twist our perception of reality into misguided notions? It would be the same as a radio blaring music at them, but their not having the foggiest notion that invisible wavelengths of light, i.e. radio waves, are bringing them the sound they hear from distant lands. Now, this is merely a parable contrasting the seen and unseen realms using the wavelengths of light as an example. But, the allegory is revelatory. Secular-minded people have a very difficult time acknowledging a need for God because they cannot see Him; agnostics and atheists go even further to presume He is absent or does not exist at all. They will not allow the realms they cannot see to influence the world they do see, even though there are millions surrounding them who are testifying to unseen light. They wish to remain instead as skeptics who lie in the sun beside their backyard pools, cooking their skin, listening to the radio, ignorant of the greater dimensions of their actual lives. Secular humanists, relativists, agnostics and atheists exclude the most powerful light which is the spiritual Light of Jesus Christ issuing from His unseen Kingdom through all the physical and mystical dimensions of the Church, including the human heart. They dismiss the wisdom and grace that are trying to penetrate their soulful awareness, and thus, their conclusions on a whole host of issues remain uninformed, distorted, and in extreme cases even diabolical, such as becoming advocates for the murder of children in the womb. How morbidly deranged can one's intellect be if you believe the slaughter of an infant to be acceptable?

The Final Colossus - In Battle Array

The reason it is difficult to accept God's closeness to us is because He requires us to invoke our faith in order to see the truth. He wishes us to voluntarily use the senses of the heart and intellect oriented and imbued with His grace. For instance, how is trust displayed if one refuses to make an act of surrender? God rarely violates our faith by performing a great "ta-da" in front of us to conquer our cerebral misgivings. He could have come down from the Cross upon being jeered by the crowds at His Crucifixion, but what would Divine Justice have required then? What purpose toward eliciting our faith and loving surrender would that have served? What possibility for heartfelt change would have been left? It is instead like someone always following us, directly behind us, whom we are never allowed to turn around to see just yet. But, if we were walking on a sunny day and turned in the right direction, we would see their shadow on the sidewalk and realize they are behind us. This is how it is with Jesus in our lives. If we situate ourselves in the divine light with the correct disposition, we will see His shadow all the time, realizing that He is standing right behind us, just outside our field of vision. Imagine that thought. Always recognizing God's presence with us, even though we have yet to see Him face-to-face.

    My brother Timothy experienced this parable in the early days of Our Lady's miraculous intercession in the living room of his home in Beardstown, Illinois. That night, while praying before his devotional altar in 1991, he said the candlelight was projecting softly upon the wall in the darkened room when suddenly the pronounced silhouette of our Heavenly Mother appeared as if She were standing in front of the candles, blocking the light so as to leave Her shadow on the wall. He explained it as being a very astonishing experience, almost fearful, looking at the candles, then tracing the path to Her image on the wall, with his mind deducing that She had to be standing between the candles and the wall in front of him; but he was not able to see Her. This is the definition of supernatural. It was a mystical event generated by the Holy Spirit that had the physical effect of impeding light waves in the material world, causing a shadow on a wall by someone who could not be seen. And, to flourish this parable with a bit of deductive reasoning, those who do not see the world as the Catholic Church has from the beginning are people who are not situated in the light correctly, and thus, they find it difficult to see the shadow of God which would confirm His presence to them. They admit as much when they acknowledge that they cannot see many of the Truths that the

Miraculous Intercession: Say What?

Catholic Church professes or His divine hand in events such as His Virgin Mother's appearances throughout Catholic history. This is how all of us reject clarifying graces from God at different points in our lives. Many groups of people are intellectually hardened against accepting the most spectacular occasions of grace that God has ever given because their orientation never allows them to recognize that He is overshadowing them with such love. The Virgin Mary's miraculous intercession worldwide cannot possibly be believed, they say, simply because they have never personally recognized the shadow of God before through the silhouette of the Woman Clothed with the Sun. But, if they were positioned correctly in that light, they would see that the Original Apostolic Church of Roman Catholicism has been the definitive shadow of Jesus Christ on the Earth for the past 2000 years. And then, they would see the glorious splendor of their Heavenly Mother and recognize Her profound maternal love through Her many instances of divine intercession through the ages. From within the Catholic Church, humanity not only has the opportunity to see Jesus' sacred image most clearly, but to become part of the silhouette that reveals Him, knowing that our beloved Savior and Messiah is the blazing Light behind us. Now, it is right and just to admit that many Catholics are not in perfect alignment either. And for this, the Church not only apologizes, but labors within itself to make it right. All of us could be better focused upon the overwhelming nature of the spiritual Kingdom of our Lord. There is no dispensation for Catholics remaining in any way blind. We are not an exception to the sanctifying process of being brought into a deeper conversion and better imitation of our Savior. For example, there are many in the Church who claim the Virgin Mary as their Mother, and they are right in doing so. But, these same people are often unable to recognize the silhouette of God in Her miraculous appearances; and in this, they are no better than the most skeptical protester of the Church itself. They reject the "motiva credibilitatis," the motives of credibility of the Catholic Faith. [*Catechism of the Roman Catholic Church, 156*] Miraculous intercession exposes the immediate recipients to the Light in a way that often produces undeniable certitude about the truth being revealed and confirmed to them by God. It is not to say that they are given the complete compendium of mystical wisdom possessed by the Almighty Father. But, they are given an impregnable rock upon which to stand in their witness to the divine. The Catechism of the Catholic Church references quotes by Saint Thomas Aquinas and John Henry Cardinal Newman that state that "the certainty that the divine light gives is greater than that which the light of natural reason gives. Ten thousand difficulties do not make one doubt." [*Catechism of the Roman Catholic Church, 157*] This is true for many to whom Our Lady has transcended. Heaven and Earth may pass away, but the mark She leaves upon the soul will last forever. The Catholic Church in its Liturgies, Teachings, Dogma and Hierarchy is the prime motive of credibility that sustains this divine light in the world through the devotions and obedience of the faithful. Through this body of certitude, we possess the power to acknowledge every other motive of credibility that flourishes throughout the beatific realms of our Faith. The Catholic Church generates the potential that draws the lightning strike of the miraculous intercession of the Virgin Mary, along with the companionship of the Angels and Saints. Jesus loves His Original Church. It has been with Him in His Sacrifice from the beginning in the Mother who never failed Him. The Light emanating from the Church of Rome should be enough to make ten thousand difficulties not matter; it is enough to transform us into interpreters of the language of Creation and the supernatural impressions that God speaks through its sacred dialect. But, because faith is often weak and immature, this is not always the case. Thus, God consistently enlists the higher orders of His Church Triumphant—the Saints—and the Hierarchies of Angels to dispense special actions of His Word through miraculous intercessions that penetrate the mental fortifications of those who doubt in order to explicate the power of the truths proclaimed by the Church. And, sometimes those who are challenged to greater faith are members of the Church itself, even into the echelons of its esteemed magisterial Hierarchy. The Holy Spirit engages the weaknesses of men, no matter who they are, to ring out the truth in those ages and times when courageous faith grows cold. Those who then hear the testimony to miraculous intercession are blessed with the opportunity to accept indirectly through the parameters of the greater faith that Jesus was initially hoping Saint Thomas would offer before placing his fingers into the nail prints of His Savior's hands. We must remember that every authentic intercession of Heaven's Queen will stand in Eternity as inviolate truth because each occurrence is a manifest actualization of Marian Dogma that is bound in Heaven and on Earth. The outstanding question is what will each of us think about our own conduct toward those Marian truths when faced with their magnificence in those glorious realms. Is Saint Thomas the Apostle our scriptural admonition? It is really a simple and consistent motivation of the Holy Spirit. He does not want anyone merely saying they are Christian, but to herald that they are Catholic to the depths of their sacrificial conviction. He wants everyone to confirm it by how we live, move and have our being. It is a communion of souls who are glorifying the Creator and testifying to what our God does through the power of the Catholic Sacraments. By offering something unique by way of His miraculous power, He punctures our rhythmic awareness of secular existence to make way for the highest truths of His Kingdom to flourish with greater clarity and explication. He renews His splendor amongst men in the hopes it will spontaneously ignite conversion and transformation of heart in those who have the courage to listen and respond. Is this not what has occurred for millions of people through our Holy Mother's appearances in Medjugorje, Fatima and Lourdes, and a whole host of other occasions of Her mystical grace through the centuries? Is it not special what Jesus is allowing His Mother to do? Does He not expect us to acknowledge Her presence and heed Her guidance? It is His reverberating testament of "Behold your Mother," echoing throughout time until His Second Coming. Did He not say, "*Heaven and earth will pass away, but my words will never pass away.*" [*Matthew 24:35*] He has given Her the maternal commission to gather His children around Her within the Church that He founded in His words to Saint Peter who is His Rock. Yet, it has not faintly dawned on many that the miraculous intercession of our Most Blessed Mother in our present time is the reverberation of His Word orchestrating this divine purpose. There are many priests, and even a few Bishops and Cardinals, who are in need of a more precise orientation in order to recognize the full scope of God's care for His children; and most would humbly concede this to be true about themselves. They are good, and often extremely holy men of great sacrifice in the midst of a commission that witnesses unseen truths to some of the most stiff-necked, acerbic worldlings that human history has ever produced. Their Heavenly Queen is simply asking them to allow Her to help them. She can do very little without our cooperation because faith allows Her to transcend the veil with power. Oftentimes Jesus' Love is so great and His intercession so profound that it seems too good to be true. None of us should believe that we are not in the process of "fully-becoming." We are being inspired by the Holy Spirit at every moment to believe in ways that would move mountains. And, many times those mountains are none other than our own skepticism, cowardice and denial that we try to convince ourselves is only prudence. Our Lady says it is possible to exercise our cooperation without a hint of resistance, even to the magnitude of Her Fiat to the Archangel Gabriel and Her accompaniment of Her Son Jesus to the Cross. Fiat means "compliance with God." The Saints did not live in fear of being wrong; they trusted Jesus more than that. So, no one should see my words as an uncharitable admonishment of anyone for not yet seeing as clearly as they could; my words are not meant that way. Christians have been struggling with this perfection for millennia, and so do I. Rather, it is about recognizing and capturing this beautiful moment of opportunity that God has provided through His Immaculate Mother in our day. These are our times, a grand occasion for our faith to be inspired to great confidence and clarity wherein we will find the strength to cooperate with Her guidance and explicate the Holy Gospel to people who are having a hard time recognizing their deliverance is at hand. The truth we are asked to spread is the same Truth to which the Catholic Church has consecrated its existence in the Blood of our Savior and two millennia of Martyrs.

Now, many people might ask why don't we see miraculous intercession more often. Why isn't God's miraculous power openly apparent to us all the time? Well, it would seem that these questions are a little light on perspective if one will not acknowledge the evidence in our Blessed Mother's appearances every day in Medjugorje for the past 36 years, or Fatima in 1917, or to Saint Bernadette in Lourdes in 1858, or to Saint Catherine Laboure in 1830 in the beautiful Rue du Bac Chapel in Paris where the world received the Miraculous Medal. The historical list goes on and on. Our Holy Mother has been allowed to salt the Earth with Her miraculous intercession since Her Assumption into Heaven, predominately in nondescript and humble places reminiscent of Jesus' Birth in a stable. Instances of the intervention of the Angels and the Communion of Saints equally abound. The mystical lives of the Saints exhibit legendary miraculous prowess. Just because someone is not aware of these miraculous graces does not mean that they have not been readily apparent throughout the world to those who will look. God can only provide the grace; each of us has to make the individual effort to get close enough to partake of it. He is no more inclined to work a grand miracle in Times Square on New Year's eve than He was to succumb to Satan's temptation for Him to throw Himself down from the pinnacle of the temple so the Angels could catch Him to prove who He was. [*Luke 4:1-13*] Jesus has made seers, visionaries and evangelizers out of millions of little people, but they are routinely ignored and dismissed, delegated by Heaven to become the image of their crucified Savior, because other people's lives are filled with secular interests and oftentimes high doses of pride. Materialistic skeptics are distracted from discerning the more important events of their salvation, those that assist their eternal destiny, by all the seductions and pleasures of the material world that will eventually slip from their grasp in death. Speaking of miracles, sacramental Baptism is a moment of supernatural grace for every Christian; one that makes an evangelizer out of each of us. The administration of this initiating Sacrament may not be visually miraculous very often, but the change in the human soul is miraculous nonetheless. It is a supernatural moment that transcends and redefines the essence of the person. [*Catechism of the Roman Catholic Church, 1265-1266*] Those who are skeptical would mock us and demand that we prove our claims while simultaneously ignoring the fruit in the lives of baptized millions throughout the ages. It is like planting a seed in a field and someone immediately demanding that you prove to them that it will produce a plant that will one day give rise to a golden sea of grain. The seed is germinated through Baptism and thereafter produces the miracle of a harvest of fruit like unto itself. But, God cannot seem to encourage atheists and other doubters to either plant or cultivate their own plenty. They refuse the seed. And thus, they will one day starve. It is much the same destiny as those who were awaiting the bridegroom who forgot to bring oil for their lamps. [*Matthew 25:1-12*] The more important point is that God is determined to reveal Himself to us in ways that encourage us toward greater faith, not remove our need for it. While He gives the rains through great manifestations of miraculous grace, especially through His Immaculate Mother, it still requires the seed of faith to be accepted and planted for the rains to have any purpose. Miraculous manifestations merely give an impetus to invoke the assent of faith through a sacrificial act of the will. Everyone's faith is required, yours, the leaders of the Church, even from myself and all others who may have directly experienced miraculous intercession. We are still required to engage the requirements of the same Gospel, the same holiness, the same sacrifice, the same magnification of the fruits of the Holy Spirit, and to exercise the spiritual works of mercy, all while testifying to conversion and renewal through our obedience to the Divine Revelation proclaimed by the Church of Rome. That sacrifice is the same for each person; that acceptance is identical. We are all asked to live our lives as a humble fiat to our Creator and gather to embrace the Holy Sacrifice that makes us one body.

There are millions of people throughout the world who believe they have a vibrant faith in Jesus Christ, but in reality have very little capacity to respond to Him when He acts in special ways requiring the cooperation of their faith. He comes calling with graces to help convert their lost brothers and sisters; graces that they in fact have prayed for, and what happens? Their eyes remain blind to God's mystery, and the exercise of their faith falters. Their worldly interests veto the echoing of their heart. They are ashamed of the Son of Man in the moment of sacrifice. [*Luke 9:26*] Their allegiance, shorn by doubts and distractions, is revealed to be anemic and limited in substance and effect. They hold their autonomy in abeyance for themselves. Oftentimes, faith is diminished to being little more than a vaunted intellectual exercise of religious history, vain apologetics, and rote practices. This is how one can claim to have faith, but have very little in any operative sense that would respond to the Holy Spirit when He calls in contemporary ways. They do not imitate Our Lady's Fiat to the Archangel! For example, what is the number of people who profess faith in Jesus Christ in the United States? *(~250 million)* Why has abortion been permitted to continue by secular law for almost a half century? These two questions cannot be reconciled without admitting that people of Christian faith are not responding to the Holy Spirit in order to stop it. Neither are we being led to engage it in any meaningful way. Sometimes humanity, in this case the unborn, has to bear the agony of waiting for leaders who will finally rally a nation to engage the battles for truth, justice, and life. Satan is not sitting on the sidelines waiting for opposition through some sense of fair play. He sees his opposition as being nothing more than a tiny kitten whimpering a nearly inaudible "meow," while the Communion of Saints are pleading to Jesus to inspire His Church to roar like a lion that represents its King and inflict temporal consequences for the sake of the immortal souls of murderers. This lukewarmness is how Christian civilization has become extinguished in greater parts of the world, and we are well on our way to that epoch of abysmal darkness in the United States of America. The beauty that has been ceded to evil without a fight is astonishing. We are witnessing a diabolical holocaust on our watch being led by the devil himself, and we are still saying "please" to those who slaughter babies and sell their body parts. God sees this. So, He responds to the prayers of Saints and sinners in extraordinary ways to provide us the spiritual weapons to stop the massacre. Indeed, He grants His Mother's miraculous appearances, yet finds few who will respond with the abandonment that Abraham and our Virgin Mother displayed in the Bible as our example, let alone raising an army and surrendering it to Saint Joan of Arc's intercession. Christians cannot find the unity to cooperate and act because we are so afraid of being accused of not being meek. These same people would have wagged their tongues at Jesus the moment He raised His voice in righteousness, mocking Him on how He could not possibly consider Himself the Prince of Peace. In contrast, Abraham moved in obedience to sacrifice his son Isaac; the Mother of Jesus instantly accepted the testimony of the Archangel Gabriel, and Joan of Arc stormed with ranks of righteousness across the landscape of her fatherland. The miraculous efficacy of the Gospel, meaning "able to produce fruits," is still as powerful today as it was in what we read in the Sacred Scriptures from twenty centuries ago, if He could find the faith of Abraham and Our Lady, or even a Dauphin of France, in a critical mass of sacrificial hearts willing to respond with the courage of warriors for His cause. *"For the sake of the ten, He replied, I will not destroy it."* [*Genesis 18:32*] If we consistently invoke our faith and allow ourselves to be led by the Holy Spirit, not persisting in unbelief but believe, faith becomes a disposition of flourishing power perfectly in submission to the Holy Spirit that humbly makes way for the truth at every moment, no matter what God may ask of us. We become razor-sharp swords in His hands. No sacrifice is too great to dissuade our unity with Jesus in His Sacrifice. And, in this is His glory revealed through we who are His children...and greater things than this shall you see. [*John 14:12*]

    The purification of the soul allows us to see these things with the added benefit of obliterating any doubts that come from wilful intellectualism and pride. There's never been any intellectualism that could have survived the challenge of the Crucifixion in that original bloody moment on Mount

Calvary. All intellectuals and academics would have cowered and run at the horror and mystery of it, wagging their heads, unable to find strength in any way of thinking they ever possessed. Secular intellectuals and academics are weaklings, and so are many of those in the religious realms of study. Only the abandonment in the "Fiat" of Jesus' Mother sustained that faithfulness that is precious to Him. *"This is a great joy to you, even though for a short time yet you must bear all sorts of trials; so that the worth of your faith, more valuable than gold, which is perishable even if it has been tested by fire, may be proved -- to your praise and honour when Jesus Christ is revealed."* [*1 Peter 1:6-7*] Christ Jesus revealed the consequences of doubt when He called Peter out of the boat to walk beside Him upon the water. Peter got out of the boat all right, but his natural mind overshadowed his visionary heart and he began to fear, and then to doubt, and then he began to sink into the turbulence of the waves, crying out for His Savior. [*Matthew 14:29-31*] Likewise, there was Thomas who doubted because he was too proud to believe the pleading of his friends to accept that the Resurrection of Jesus had occurred as He had foretold. He had begun to believe that it had all been but a delusional fairytale. Obstinate to the moment of being humbled, Thomas was too intellectual, too natural thinking about the horrific events he had just witnessed. Too broken, too shocked to believe that there could possibly be a mighty Resurrection after the humiliating defeat in the Crucifixion he had just witnessed. But, upon appearing to them after being raised from the dead, Our Lord intoned to him the greater blessedness that He recognizes in those who will believe without seeing, without satisfying their intellect, without looking for worldly anchors, the way His Mother believed. He said to Thomas, *"You have believed because you have seen. Blessed are those who believe without seeing."* [*John 20:29*] And further in Scripture, it states when Jesus appeared to the Apostles after His Resurrection, *"Afterward He appeared to the eleven themselves as they were reclining at the table; and He reproached them for their unbelief and hardness of heart, because they had not believed those who had seen Him after He had risen."* [*Mark 16:14*] Consider again: why did Jesus reproach them for their unbelief and hardness of heart?—*because they did not believe those who had been sent to them bearing the truth of miraculous events.* Is it not the same today? Is not the reproach forthcoming if we stumble for the same reason? Jesus did not condemn Thomas; He did not send away the original Apostles. He simply wanted all present to consider what it was within them that caused them not to believe their brothers and sisters bearing such beatific testimony. Even these original leaders of the Church, our great Faith Fathers, were admonished for not believing those who were sent to them. Is this something that piques our present consciences in the face of Our Lady's miraculous intercession today? How many have presented themselves before us, testifying to the truth of Her miraculous appearances and interior locutions? How do we receive the blessing instead of the reproach? We are blessed in our unity in the truth, professed and displayed through twenty centuries of God's Word, articulated through Dogmas and Traditions of the Catholic Church, composed in the lives of the Saints, confirmed through the intercession of the Virgin Mary and the court of Angels surrounding Her, through our oneness of heart with all who have lived for Jesus, down to the last person in the last pew in the most remote country church on the last dusty plain of human existence. I have always believed this testament from the moment baptismal waters ran over my forehead and down past my ears. I am united in heart with each of these great creatures, each called a child of God. I know the Holy Spirit has lived in every one of them to the last breath of their beautiful lives. And, I testify that the spectacular "motiva credibilitatis"—the motives of credibility—effected by the Holy Spirit in our time through the miraculous intercession of the Most Blessed Virgin Mary are a great outpouring of Divine Mercy that the Almighty Father expects us to heed with the most sincere dispatch. We need to be stricken from our donkeys of doubt and hoisted upon the backs of stallions, rearing their determination to enter the battle for the conversion and sanctification of mankind.

The Final Colossus - In Battle Array

Chapter 2
Miraculous Intercession Now In Our Time

Holiness is an institution.
Memory is a day gone by.
Hope is something imagined.
Faith is a dream come true.

Miraculous intercession—this is what is occurring in mystical succession in our time. For our part, the grace my brother and I relate is that Jesus Christ has allowed His Mother, the Most Blessed Virgin Mary, to extend an extraordinary mystical relationship with us that began shortly after our pilgrimage to Medjugorje in the late fall of 1989. Medjugorje is a small village in Bosnia-Herzegovina where the Mother of Jesus began appearing to six young people on June 24, 1981. These mystical apparitions and messages have been in process every day thereafter into our present day. It is recognized that the ecclesial leaders of the Catholic Church to the date of this writing have made no official declaration regarding their final position on the authenticity of the events in Medjugorje, although the machinations of a formal ecclesial commission have been unfolding for many years. But, as faithful Catholics who have personally experienced the grace of Our Lady there, my brother and I are instructed by the Holy Spirit to declare our personal faith in those events so the Church may recognize the fruits of Her presence which are manifested by those who have the courage to believe and have responded in obedience to Her call. There have been millions of people who have made their own pilgrimages to Medjugorje since 1981 who have the same personal convictions of authenticity as we do. They had similar experiences that convinced them of the supernatural grace of the heavens there. On February 22nd of 1991, just over a year after our return from our pilgrimages, on the Catholic Feast of the Chair of Saint Peter, the Virgin Mary blessed my brother and me by magnifying Her miraculous presence to us in a concrete mystical and physical way. She manifested Her motherly presence in the United States as the

The Final Colossus - In Battle Array

Morning Star Over America through apparitions, locutions, and other mystical phenomena that occurred to us spontaneously from the unseen as we prayed the Most Holy Rosary each day. The Rosary is a devotional prayer of meditation that Catholics have been praying for centuries. It employs a contemplative expression where one meditates on events in the life of Jesus while offering the prayers attached to the Rosary, such as the Apostles Creed, the Our Father, Hail Mary, and the Doxology (the Glory Be). As we prayed, Jesus responded through His Virgin Mother by rendering the spiritual precepts of our faith to be recognizable realities for us in very profound ways that were undeniable. I was inspired from the outset to begin a personal diary, having the sense to realize that memories can fade and fail regarding specific details in any situation. I wanted there to be a memorable record so I did not forget the facts nor embellish them in the future, even though I was never certain that there would be a future of any significance. My initial intentions possessed no more extended dimensions than that. The mystical experiences were meaningful to me, and that was enough to make the record. My brother and I had no agenda, no expectations, and nothing to grasp for definition in our thinking. We resided in the smallest circle of understanding like being bound within the tiniest concentric growth rings of a sapling. Our Lady came and said you may be saplings, but you are saplings of a giant redwood that will one day tower to the skies and spread comforting shade during the blazing heat of the days to come. We bore a simple knowledge of previous apparitions by our Holy Mother such as in Lourdes and Fatima, and our experiences in Medjugorje just a few months before. A complete sense of wonderment befell us that circumscribed our lives on every level. Deep humility caused us to question how such things could be happening to us. Yet, there was an ecstatic excitement buoyed by an instinctive and intuitive knowledge of who She was. There was no guessing or wondering as to Her identity for my part, although Timothy experienced deeper levels of shock due to most of his early life being a Protestant in a Methodist denomination. A mystical recognition was impressed into my soul that to this day is unquestionable and impregnable. Our Holy Mother was fully apparent to my personal interior cognition as clearly as I would know my own earthly mother. No one could deceive me by presenting an imposter and telling me it was my birth mother, not even if she had some previously unknown biological twin. A sensation of insecurity was also present when anticipating the skepticism of others because I realized the phenomenon was so far beyond the acceptable boundaries of anyone's thinking that we knew. Who am I kidding, it was nearly beyond mine. My rational deduction contemplated that many responses would not be pleasant. It was to be a significant leap of trust for anyone to make, even amongst our immediate family members. My soul was afraid of losing the support of affirming friendships and familial bonds which I sensed was inevitable. Think about it, telling your friends and family in this modern world, "Hey, the Mother of Jesus is speaking to me." A great leap of faith was required into an ocean of spiritual mystery without anyone knowing the temperature of the water or the distance to the horizon. Neither did anyone expect to be asked to swim in water so deep. A beckoning occurred to step out upon the waves of mystery and revelation which proved to be too big a leap for most of our friends and families at the time. Very few people have the stature, credibility or composure to sustain the allegiance and approbation of others when relating the occasions of God's mystical grace. And, neither my brother nor I were worthy of that depth of deference. Most could not accept what we were declaring because they knew whom we both were. While looking for other plausible explanations, nearly everyone began to believe that we were making it all up with ill intention, zealous emotion, or worse, diabolical infiltration. No proof was available to stem the tides of doubt that swelled around us. Mutual support was out of the question. We simply possessed our honest testimony to what was happening and the initial messages that Our Lady was presenting to us in a daily fashion. This proved to be insufficient evidence for nearly everyone, including the priests at the time who counseled many of our friends to dismiss themselves from our prayer group. Through all the disturbance that arose, Our Lady finally brought my brother and me into a cloistered privacy with Her so that She could compose Her great Morning Star work. And, that is how we progressed for the last twenty-six years, beneath Her Mantle in silence before the world, to this present day.

  Our diary began through prayerful hope and a desire to remember details clearly in the future. I sensed that only a first-person record could secure the integrity of the events into the future protection of the Church. I sought to defend Our Lady in whatever She wished to accomplish through my obedience. I would suffer anyone and anything for Her. It was prescient to realize that I could not trust myself to remember the magnitude and multitude of messages, phenomena, signs and sequences within our Holy Mother's maturing relationship with us. Even today while reading our earliest writings, I am reminded of things that occurred that I would have otherwise forgotten. I was inundated with the Love of God in supernal dimensions from Her first immaculate words, and my soul savored each one. I committed myself to capture Her grace in every way that She shared it, in case She never spoke to us again, as if each moment of Her mystical intercession was Her last to us. I began the construction of a shrine to Her Immaculate Heart, where each word would be held sacred, every sentiment conserved with the dignity that it deserved. If She was to give me a single message in my lifetime, I would have hewn those words into a granite mountainside using only my bare hands if no one would have given me explosives or a jackhammer. As it is, each of these keystrokes is a strike upon that mountainside with my fingertips; and Her words are the explosions. And, just as Mount Rushmore in all its secular grandeur remains unfinished, so will the ultimate work of the Morning Star Over America remain unfinished until the last faithful child succumbs to Her grace. Recall that our leaders encased moon rocks in glass cases in museums all over this country after our courageous astronauts traveled and brought them back from the moon in July of 1969. What then should one do with the artifacts of an event such as the Morning Star Over America and the words from the Most Blessed Virgin Mary that are coming directly from Heaven itself? Are they not more precious than gold, let alone a rock from a barren world? Do they not deserve to be engraved upon the face of mountains in letters as tall as buildings?

  I saw a video recently where a young lady about 29 years old had been born deaf. She was receiving an implant in the video, hopefully to restore her hearing. The recording enshrined the moment of her hearing the first words of her life as the mechanism was turned on. She broke down in emotional tears at the magnificence of becoming complete in her senses. There are also other videos where people who are color-blind are given a technologically-advanced set of eyeglasses that allow them to see all the colors of Nature, just as we do who see normally. Almost to the person, these people well-up in emotion at seeing the actual colorful beauty of Creation for the first time. This is somewhat the phenomenon that I experienced when our Holy Mother revealed

Miraculous Intercession - Now In Our Time

Her presence to us. My soul shook at the dimensions of the gift, seeing and hearing as I had never experienced. I wept openly, and sometimes still do. Life was demarcated and broken open, like cracking an egg and splitting it with your fingers. I realized that life would never be as it was; the shell had been breached. Spiritually, I had been deaf and blind since birth, but suddenly was able to see and hear as never before. When seeing a flower of breathtaking beauty, you wish to capture it, protect it, and enshrine it so that everyone can witness its resplendence and share in its glory. The love that Our Lady gives in the Son that She bore is the final thing that each of us is searching for. Ultimately, it is the only thing. In Her arms with Her Son is where we were always meant to be; together, united, brothers and sisters of the same Mother and Father, siblings in a Kingdom of Everlasting Light saved by a glorious Messiah; a New Adam, a New Eve, a New Heaven and a New Earth. A portrait of what our Blessed Mother asked us to share is recorded in the books we have written. Our innocent reactions along with the facts of events and the many mystical phenomena that supported our faithfulness are inscribed there; all of which have led us to the place where we reside today with our Holy Mother, some 26 years later. *Here we stand!...not in a 500 years-old defiance of the truth, but in a two millennia defense of it in communion with the Roman Catholic Church and its faithful Hierarchy.* I ask everyone to invoke their faith and make room for this glorious mystery of the Virgin with Child who surrounds us with Her engaging Beauty. She explicates Truth to the entire world, here in our age through Her spectacular grace. Our Holy Mother's particular intercession to us is one inflection of the same universal intercession that God has employed throughout the storied history of human conversion. Whether one wishes to call it an elevation, magnification, cultivation, explication, articulation, or declaration, Her actions make clear the Truth of Jesus' Kingdom so that our faithfulness to Him would be reawakened for the sanctifying purposes that His Death and Resurrection sustain. One rose is not diminished in its beauty simply because there happens to be another blooming from the same bush. Our Holy Mother is not proclaiming a new Gospel, but instead, re-focusing the Original through its ancient origins in Her Son's Church and directing us toward the depth of its revelations, consequences and rewards. She is explicating, meaning 'making clear,' the imperative of seeking Her Son's Divine Mercy in our age before it is too late. The story of human redemption, if we would remember, is also the story of Her life. It is the story of conversion and sanctification that is unfolding from the origin of Her Womb to the epicenter of Jesus' great act of Redemption on Mount Calvary where He surrendered His Life to save the world. She is elevating the Gospel of Redemption that She began sharing in union with the Church after the first Pentecost in Jerusalem, whereafter Her spiritual sons, the Apostles as stewards of Her Son's Kingdom, fanned out into dangerous lands with the message of the Light of the World. She prayed then as She prays to this day that the Light of the King of kings would now be cultivated in each of us in like stead until the end of time which She says is swiftly approaching with ominous consequences.

For my brother and me, it has been easy to ratify our belief each day because we have continued to employ our faith after accepting from the beginning. There are no doubts that sustain themselves before Her presence. Everything was moved aside in order to accommodate all that She wished to tell us, then She fortified everything that the Catholic Church has ever taught us to be true. She awakened the verifiable life to Her Son's Kingdom within us. It was not simply an intellectual confirmation, but the bringing to life of our sacramental Confirmation in the Roman Catholic Church. It is so easy to listen to and obey Her because She is so beautiful in a fulfilling type of way, in a completeness of being. No distraction can compete with Her beauty. Not just physical beauty, but ethereal beauty emanating from Her identity as the Matriarch of Heaven, and how She achieved that title on Calvary with Her Son—Majesty, grace, sanctity and feminine poise personified on a level unequaled by anything created. If the world could see Her just one time, the entire planet would be transformed and renewed. Barbarians would fall to their knees in tears. Protestants would storm the Altars of the Catholic Church in tear-drenched waves of conversion. Conversion would flow from atheists like a raging river. And, perversion would be eradicated by purity like a flood dousing a match. So, it becomes easy once recognizing the overshadowing of Her immaculate presence. What has not been easy is to be united with Jesus' Sacrifice through it all, to be exposed to the glaring contrast between Heaven and Earth, between conviction and compromise, between sin and perfection, seeing the horrors of the world without excuse every day from such a pure perspective, pining for love to consume the Earth to a point where you would believe your heart might succumb to the agony of the ecstasy. Nothing is so opposed as Jesus Christ and His Kingship, except the station of His Virgin Mother in His Kingdom. Our Heavenly Mother desires that we grow in vision, in holiness, and engage our spiritual purification so that we might accept Her Son fluently within us and defer to Him in all ways. She is trying to make us strong and unapologetic for knowing the Truth. She wishes that we adopt the mind of Her Son in every way He wishes to touch us and become united with us. This is how sin is wiped from the Earth. First, sin is confessed, then it is forgiven, then the virgin thoroughfares are overwhelmed by newer rites of grace that will prevail. My presence here writing these words is one way the King of kings wishes to touch His children through the graces of His Virgin Mother. I do not believe that I could be sitting here after a quarter century without Her encouragement and assistance. She has sustained my brother and me, and encourages us onward.

Our faith in Our Lady's presence with us has been confirmed over and again through our acceptance of Her presence and obedience to Her wise counsel. We have known it is the Virgin Mary without a doubt throughout the years. We have felt the authority of Her Queenship and the gentleness of Her confidence. We have been speaking to the same Virgin Mother who stood beneath the Cross of Jesus 2000 years ago and watched Him die. Contemplate this for yourselves. Imagine what that reality means in a person's thoughts, speaking to someone still alive after two millennia, telling you how She felt standing there that day and what it has meant to Her and to humanity. It is an earthquake of revelation in one's thoughts, an explosion of Light, so much reality and truth, so many bonds breached. Once your faith allows you the realization of just how close She is to you, your emotions succumb to Her. She is here with us now as I write these words to you. She knows your thoughts, your difficulties, your reservations about your faith; even reservations you might have about what I am relating here. She knows every pain and heartbreak that you have ever experienced; and She has been with you through them all. She loves you unimaginably and is waiting for you to accept that She is with you now, as She has always been since you were conceived in your mother's womb. She has seen your every skinned knee, every tear you have ever shed on your pillow, every sorrow you endured in loneliness, every disappointment that has ever caused you to be sad. She has cheered your triumphs, wept tears of happiness alongside your joys, and has assisted the voice of conscience within you during your innumerable occasions of uncertainty. If She were to reach-out and physically touch you right now in the place where you sit, your thoughts would lose all composure and you would probably begin to cry at the explosion of the revelation and the reorientation you would feel. And, above everything else, you would feel special through a love so profound that it would seem you were a tiny child again. Your innocence would come flooding back to you like a tidal wave crashing upon the shore. A freshness of rebirth would inundate your soul upon realizing you were no longer orphaned from God's Kingdom, and that you mattered. This is the effect of our Holy Mother's mystical presence. Many of you are actually feeling Her presence right now, just as I have explained. To this day, She only interacts with me in ways that I can bear because it is so easy for Her to leave me speechless and in tears. It is too easy for Her to transport me into ecstasy. Her Son I can rarely speak about in a contemplative and heartfelt manner because my composure and emotions cannot sustain what He means to me. I weep. Standing in His presence and holding His outstretched hands, and looking into His eyes is a memory seared into my being that I cannot unveil without fracturing my emotional composure. I recognized our Holy Mother's presence this clearly in the beginning, although I did not have a grasp on it with the perspective I possess now. I realize it with tender conviction after a quarter century. She is with us, as is Jesus. They are one in the presence of Love. Our Holy Mother's statue rests beside me on the bureau. It is just a statue, but it symbolizes a wholly greater reality of Her presence in each of our lives and Her presence here with me now. There is no doubt or wondering or second-guessing for me. Belief was the order of my existence on February 22, 1991, and the monsoons of confirming graces have never stopped flooding into my life since that moment. Believe and respond, put your hand to the plow and do not look back, and these graces will likewise come to you.

    Our Lady asked me one day to think about how many hundreds of millions of Christians throughout the ages prayed from their hearts in their hour of need for just one audible word from Her in response to their prayers, but were never blessed with that gift just yet—*And they prayed anyway.* She declared that this is faith coming from a powerful hope and love for God. When I invoked my acceptance in that early morning in February 1991, it was enough for our Holy Mother to dispense a grace of solid, immovable knowledge into my soul of who was speaking to us, and in that came absolute obedience to Her because Her majesty perfectly reflected the undeniable glory of Her Son. I assure you every knee will bend in Heaven and on the Earth, and under the Earth, and proclaim to the Glory of God the Father that Jesus Christ is Lord! I was faced with the Mother of that Glory, and I knelt before Her in veneration and thanksgiving for the Sacrifice of Her Son. She, too, sacrificed everything for the redemption of humanity. She, too, is to be honored. Her maternal Majesty is to be venerated. Her Immaculate Heart was pierced for humanity in depths unimaginable. Her very own innocent Son and perfect Child became the Victim for the Salvation of the world.

As my brother and I progressed and matured, our faith was rewarded and confirmed repeatedly through Her mystical appearances and the miraculous signs and signal graces that She dispensed to us. She not only dispensed unheard of signs, but opened our eyes to signal graces and mystical cadences that flourish about our lives openly, but that our faith was too anemic to recognize. The content of Her conversations multiplied and deepened. Her parables and teachings bloomed. She revealed signs of providence within human history. It has never been our work. We became Her work. The signs of God's grace permeate all humanity. She encouraged us throughout to remain faithful, to persist in obedience, and promised that we would one day share Her presence with everyone "in future times." Well, we are at the cusp of those awakening times. The floodgates are being breached. Her messages have been made public; the Church has initiated its ecclesial commission for discernment, and we lay the splendid authenticity of Our Lady's appearance as the Morning Star Over America before everyone in our published works and the testimony of our lives. Every person who first hears of our Beloved Mother's work as the Morning Star Over America rests at that same initial moment of decision, the same spiritual state that both Timothy and I resided in when we initially faced Her grace so unexpectedly in the early morning hours of February 22, 1991. It is a moment of decision and opportunity; a pure moment. For us, we made room for the possibilities of Her miraculous intercession in our mental constitution, notwithstanding anything we had ever believed or experienced before or thought would ever happen to us. Nowhere in our wildest imaginings had we ever conceived such a possibility as Jesus'

Mother coming to us in any miraculous way. Neither of us ever prayed for such a miracle. Yet, we trusted and embraced that occurrence immediately without questioning or raising our heads to debate. We did not analyze Her; we just loved Her. The Virgin Mary is poised to gather you alongside us through your embrace of Her work that we have recorded. She will speak to you there with great clarity. The literary works we present are the residual artifacts of the spectacular miracle of Her presence in the United States as the Morning Star Over America. They embody the grace to immerse any human heart in a supernal communion with Her. From there, She will secure our sacramental repentance and escort our presence to the Sacred Altar to receive the authentic Bread of Life that we may become one in eternal life and live forever. Our writings are a transcendent agency that elevate the heart into union with the highest Truth. Our Holy Father, the Pontiff, has encouraged his flock to make use of modern technologies to share the Gospel, to communicate our experiences of Jesus' grace in our lives. This is what my brother and I are doing in unity with this call from the Church and in obedience to our Virgin Mother.

There is so much that She has said that it would take further years to relate its flourishing perspectives. This is why the detailed transcriptions of the original Morning Star works serve such a foundational purpose. We must begin somewhere. Our Holy Mother wishes to restore the innocent framework of Truth into everyone's thoughts in the same way She taught my brother and me from the beginning. She did not ask us to immediately understand everything about Heaven or the deepest genius of the Church's greatest Saints as if drinking from a fire hose. The suffering required to understand would be too great for anyone to bear. Instead, She molded us in sacrifice, each in our unique way, engaging our unique dispositions in a motherly fashion. My vision became dimensioned as much by observing Her interaction with my brother as through Her addressing me directly. I benefitted from the comparison of Her approaches to each of us, and why. It added another dimension and bound my brother and me together as one heart with Her. She has never spoken in what I would consider to be complex terms, nor has She been rhetorically scrupulous, but rather She has taught us with eloquent simplicity as children would understand. She wishes me to always remember this simplicity, even if I may be unable to replicate the eloquence. The reorientation or conversion that She seeks in us is a putting away of the old world and accepting the one that She tells us is coming so that we will be prepared for it when it arrives. Will you allow Her to touch you? Can you transcend your fears of Her? Can we begin together to resurrect all that is good and holy? Can we try to put the pieces of a noble humanity back together, restored to the image in which we were conceived, before the forces of the world blinded us from our true dignity and scattered us into adversarial persuasions? This is how our Holy Mother would have you begin, as She first touched us. Please grasp this opportunity to display your greatest faith; never doubt Her presence with you. She is as close to each of you as She is with us. She is simply a whisper of faith away from speaking to you. The world is so much in need of these prolific avenues of grace. This is why She is here, to show us the path long obscured that Jesus wishes us to place our feet upon with determined devotion. Our Heavenly Mother loves you, and will help you if you move closer to Her, speak to Her, ask Her to help you, and obey what She asks of you. I promise that She will respond in ways that you will recognize, all for Jesus' Glory. And, in this and through your faith, the world will be changed. Be of good courage, and the heroism of a Saint will come to the surface of your life.

The Final Colossus - In Battle Array

Chapter 3
Frames of Reference, Perspectives and Reactions
Our Interior Constitution

"I urge you therefore, brothers, by the mercies of God, to offer your bodies as a living sacrifice, holy and pleasing to God, your spiritual worship. Do not conform yourself to this age but be transformed by the renewal of your mind, that you may discern what is the will of God, what is good and pleasing and perfect."
[Romans 12:1-2]

Perspective is defined as being a way of seeing something through a frame of reference. Now, one might ask what that means? Perspective implies a viewer, in our case, a person who is observing. It also implies that something is being observed, an object and circumstances surrounding that object. An object inherently possesses substance, attributes and properties, and it exists in an environment that sometimes defines it and usually influences it. An object is not necessarily limited to being a physical thing. It can be something immaterial such as a concept, idea or situation. When any object moves into our field of awareness, we respond by invoking a frame of reference from which a perspective is generated, then opinions and actions follow. We, as viewers, invoke our unique reference frame by drawing upon our knowledge, memory of experiences, and the disposition of our heart. The question this should cause us to reflect upon is what things determine and influence our frame of reference; and, are they all good? How much knowledge does a person contain, and how numerous are the experiences that influence one's perspective? Is our supposed knowledge factual and balanced, or is it self-deception or maybe a lie told to us by another person that we have believed? How many memories color our responses, good and bad? What biases are associated with our memories and base of knowledge? How many experiences may have caused us to frame our viewpoints in unusual and inordinate ways? How pliable is the heart in mediating the interior engagement between good and evil, light and darkness, hopelessness and futility, pain and suffering, knowledge and ignorance, etc?

The Final Colossus - In Battle Array

What does a person bring to bear when invoking their response to the world? No doubt, each of us brings our preferences, hopes, biases, beliefs, conclusions and moral formation, if we have one. All the things that makeup our intellectual and spiritual identity as a human person are brought to the fore according to the priorities of our subliminal interior hierarchy of influence the moment we invoke our frame of reference. For example, one person could look at a 1969 Ford Mustang Mach I automobile and feel great nostalgia at having owned one when they were in high school, where another could feel great grief at being reminded of the loss of a dear loved one who perished while driving such a car. Both see a grand vintage muscle car, yet each draws upon their knowledge, experiences and heart in a way that creates a wholly unique frame of reference that influences their perspective, and thus their emotions, feelings and response. Our perspectives are innumerable and meticulously complex. They are mostly disjointed and often lack harmony between them. They are fluctuating by the moment, and frequently illogical and based on selfish preference and whim. Some have a dominant theme of grievance that colors everything about their world in a desolate negativism. Others have the affliction of "rose colored glasses" where they refuse to address the truth of human suffering. We have a dominant perspective prepared with the spontaneity of thought about nearly everything we believe or experience. And, from those perspectives, we generate opinions and beliefs that not only govern our conduct and attitudes toward what confronts us in life, but that also conscript us into patterns of existence, again, be they good or bad. How many cannot live down their mistakes before others? What patterns of conduct amongst many of the poor serve to enslave them in poverty? Oftentimes, it is as much a perspective problem as it is an aptitude deficiency or lack of opportunity. Opinions and beliefs, along with the repercussions of those beliefs, grow, solidify and exert influence upon us. They have become part of our intellectual human constitution from which we construct a frame of reference that either assists our beatific ascent into the high realms of moral goodness or thrusts us into a destructive descent into iniquity. In the darkest situations, unfortunate souls are incarcerated in frames of reference that are completely distorted beyond the reality of the moment because they are so influenced by the hauntings of their past. These are people whom we can refer to as lost souls; and we love them nonetheless, realizing they must be found.

Frames of Reference, Perspectives and Reactions

We wish for them to find the revealing grace of God that lies obscured within them by their pain. They are broken and burdened souls who live without a solution to their dysfunctional engagement with the world. And all too often, salting their mental constitution with a new perspective is met as an invasion upon their right to personal sovereignty as if all the world should instead embrace the carnage given birth through their pitiful mental framework of darkness. This is not just the materially poor; it includes the spiritually impoverished who may be the most successful and financially well-off human beings among us. Indeed, many on Wall Street have dead souls. They are nothing more than materialists who bring about great destitution, poverty and destruction, and are possibly headed for the fires of hell. Wealth is their hedonistic god, and him alone do they serve while all else is required to attend their lavish success or be discarded into oblivion. For some, the recognition of reality through their frame of reference is so obscured that they will passionately defend a position in one moment and argue against it in the next without any sense of hypocrisy. They are ships blown about without anchoring in the truthful frame of reference. [*Ephesians 4:14-24*] In fact, the concept of hypocrisy originates in the inconsistency between two frames of reference competing within a person that then manifests in conflicting stances they take on the same issue. A person has one frame of reference that positions them as being opposed to something, and another that tells them it is legitimate because there are benefits of profit that diminish their sense of the interior reconciliation of their beliefs. They are divided within themselves. [*James 1:8*] Their frame of reference has no consistency or strength. They can be easily blown about by the winds of self-interest and ultimately have their soul purchased for any small amount of coin. This is the basic mechanics behind our culture being driven into the pit of abomination by people who are demanding that we not only comply with their immoral agendas, but that we applaud them as well so they will feel better about their wickedness. They want us to applaud loudly enough that their indicting consciences become drowned out by the accolades they shame us into heaping upon them after donning themselves with false victimhood. They are living a state of spiritual cognitive dissonance, and they recognize it by the way they fight for the legitimacy of their evil ways. God will not give approbation to their existence until they repent and reform their lives, and neither should we.

The Final Colossus - In Battle Array

    This short description of the concept of perspective and frames of reference, although not clinical, should help us recognize not only their fluidity and uniqueness among people, but to assist us in realizing how they influence our personal recognition of the truth and our engagement with the world. We see things differently, and there are reasons why that need to be addressed to help us better understand ourselves and our lack of peace on the Earth as the family of man. And, we must accept that there is right and wrong, holiness and wickedness, and truth and lies. There are truths etched in the universe, both seen and unseen. In addition, there are innumerable examples of things that factually exist which people do not have a perspective about because these things have yet to move into their frame of reference. They are not aware of them, and thus have generated no perspective about them. You can have a perspective without forming an opinion. You can also have many perspectives, but never come to an understanding. Everyone should be able to see that interior lack of peace, as well as conflict between peoples, cultures and nations, originates in this swirling, turbulent battle between frames of reference fueled by each person's personal attachment to perspectives that range from selfishness to generosity, hatred to love, and atheistic secularism to beatific Christianity. Most people see the surrendering of their perspectives as cutting a pound of flesh out of their body or forfeiting an arm, instead of merely being asked to wipe their boots of the mud that they are tracking throughout the house that is going to have to be cleaned up before the Master returns. Jesus recognized this phenomenon in His scriptural admonition to cut off your hand or foot than allow it to impede your journey to Heaven. [*Matthew 18:8*] Others are consumed with amassing fortunes and building lavish empires that foment division and destroy the very fabric of human cohesion, thus making it nearly impossible for them to be either instruments of peace or enter into Heaven on the final day. There are going to be whole herds of camels passing through the eyes of needles before most of them ever think about embracing the Divine Mercy of Jesus Christ. The meaning of our existence on Earth is bound up in reconciling the individual reference frames of men into a single framework that actually reflects eternal truths. Only there will we find unending peace for this world. But, the question becomes, reconciled into what? Our Lady says the answer is the Mind of Jesus Christ. And, where does that Mind exist? It resonates within and throughout the Body of Christ, given structure and

Frames of Reference, Perspectives and Reactions

cohesion through Divine Revelation secured in the Sacred Heart of the Roman Catholic Church. There is no such thing as multiple conflicting truths, or others we can make up for ourselves. There is no truth in protesting the Original Apostolic Church and all She teaches. It is always a battle of reference frames, where the doubters have lost their bearings of what the overarching Truth of Christ really is and where He would lead them if they surrendered everything to be like Him. Consider the following scene:

"See a great number of children shrieking with happiness, crawling through brightly colored plastic tunnels and traversing the wooden trusses of playground equipment at a beautiful park. Their faces are covered with grins ear-to-ear. They are squealing with hair blown back, polishing the nearest slide with repetitive swipes of their posteriors; then spit-out into a pile like diminutive bobsled contestants careening to a stop in a cloud of sand. Others are spinning on carousels until sick, laughing in unison at being unable to walk a straight line to take another turn. Giggling torrents of childhood rush from one ladder to the next, to each swaying pathway or beckoning swing set seeking out hyperventilation as fledgling architects peacefully pat sand castles into shapes with meticulous artistry amidst the pandemonium.

Seated nearby on a sideline of freshly painted benches, two people oversee this recreational bedlam. With watchful authority, these two see sure that the littlest ones are not overrun, and that the eldest are not enticed into danger beyond their years. One of these observers seems to be a young babysitter, perhaps sixteen. She browses a cell phone while periodically lifting a disinterested gaze to maintain at least some semblance of responsibility toward her charges. On her right, a lady, still young, but somewhat older, gazes intently upon the children. Sorrowful memories are betrayed by shadows of grief deeply cut into her stately demeanor. Her eyes sparkle in attentive poise, surveying the innocent passion of the moment, appraising every movement and expression of childlike beauty playing-out before her as if missing an instant was the loss of life itself. And, the playing continues unabated in its innocence."

This scene is a microcosm from a vantage point from which you are observing as the reader. It is an object that has come seeking your awareness, ready to engage the frame of reference that will be laid upon it. I have another vantage point as the author. Both you and I reflect upon this scene uniquely. Within the scene is a collage of perspectives all occurring in unison; the epitome of a world in miniature, stripped down to its essence as we observe it from outside itself. The panorama in this scene presents to us a revelation of the pathways of communication, measures of openness and receptivity, activity, distraction, blindness and vision. Formation, perspective, shape of conscience, impediments and burdens, responsibilities and carefree liberty are all intertwined within its choreography, playing-out in spontaneity, soulful responsibility, societal conscription and habit. What is unique above all else is that those in the scene do not know that we are observing them, even as contemplative as this parable is. The characters are oblivious to the writer who conjured them; all except the heartfelt lady of stately appearance. Her heart senses something that permeates and transcends the microcosm where she resides. She looks upon the beauty of the moment just as we see it. She has the vision of the writer. Now, the question is this. Who's watching us? Who created the scene where we sit now? What does this Writer see as He observes the panorama composing our lives? And finally, do we see the world the way He does?

Simple observation of our American society would have us conclude that tens of millions of people are trapped in a single perspective of life, a flattened existence with no transcending vision. They are confined within the parameters of a secular scene, only affected by the strafing worldly impressions of the marketeers of the moment, whether they be those who manipulate for profit or ideological transformation. Never have any of these millions risen outside themselves to observe or accept who they truly are in the grander scheme of the Author's designs. They inhabit the social vistas that splay before them, but exist merely as slaves to their base inclinations as mortal creatures and the manipulations of others, unaware of what will be greeting their ill-prepared banzai charge when they pierce the veil into the next day, let alone the next life. They have never contemplated their true identity as children of God in the higher dimensions of moral virtue, nor have they encountered the prophetic perspective that would awaken them to realize that true life has nothing to do with the insecurities, emotions or impulses by which they are battered on a daily basis. Truly living has nothing to do with pondering what mobile device should be purchased next, what garments need to be procured from the celebrity rack at the local mall, what resources are needed to keep the carousel spinning, whose amorous affections are worth vying for, or what plans must be scored for the weekend, and with whom. In that narrow alley of darkened existence, there is no true life, nothing that will last beyond the ages; no affirmation, no accolades, and no reward for a life lived as God would have intended. Hopes go unfulfilled, dreams remain undreamed, broken lives abound, wisdom is snuffed-out, perspective remains locked in a nightmare, and vision never brings forth divine light. In this disconsolate gloom, the children of Light never ignite, but remain sopping wood never combusted, lost in a whirlpool of decadence and dereliction, unable to recognize a Savior they never bothered to know. Their direction and sound judgment toward any meaningful success as a human person is irretrievably forfeited to the worldliness, sensuality and materialism of the moment; and the actual chariot of life passes them by, weeping upon the winds of opportunity that the reigns of God's stallions never graced their hands. Inevitably, their banzai screams die on their lips as they step through that final curtain and take their position before the Writer where they encounter the panoramic aspects of their life from above for the very first time. There, they see the stately Lady and those others who were beside her who chose to passionately live out mortal life with an unconquerable devotion to human sanctity. And, the unyielding truth glares its testimony upon them that they did nothing more than sit on a park bench, burdened by undesired duties, with their nose buried in the latest materialistic fad of the day as the meaning of their life was lost to extinction, one material whim at a time. If true life is about finding a stage where everyone can sing along with us and hail ovations at the concluding strains of our performances, then let the perspective originate with the Writer in the heavens because we are all on the stage of human existence, our lives open and apparent before the scrutinizing gaze of the ages who watch us from the reckoning realms outside of time. Jesus has produced both a score and a dialogue for our command performance in His Death and Resurrection from the grave. The Heavenly Hosts sing along to our great devotions to God, should we engage them. They hail the heartfelt sacrifices that go unnoticed by the world. They weep ecstasy when anyone perks up and peers with the perspective of the heart upon the playing out of their lives, just like that Lady on the bench. This parable is not offered to impress a despondent view toward the failures or inadequacies of anyone's life. It heralds, "Arise and awaken!" It is about release and re-creation, focus and freedom. It posits the reality of a far more profound frame of reference than we might have contemplated before; one that will reconcile humanity into eternal peace across the palatial estate of all human affairs. And, it is to this reality that all miraculous intercession harkens. The Writer comes into His own scene as a participant, incarnate through a Virgin who revealed the reference frame of God to everyone exiled in mortal existence. The Incarnation of Jesus Christ is the earthshattering event that testifies to the veracity of our Creator's frame of reference and the credibility and motivations of the Matriarch who brought forth by Fiat His eternal perspective and laid it in the historical manger of the Roman Catholic Church. Yet, the heavens are faced with the dilemma of how to penetrate the self-will of men and the fortress mentality we have erected between our true identity and the facade we front to the world that supports the aliases that we wish everyone would venerate instead. Then comes miraculous intercession!

Each person has their own personal interior criteria that must be satisfied before they will accept anything from another person, especially if it is something as unique as a claim of miraculous intercession from their God. The original Apostles of Christianity encountered no less. It is good for everyone to realize that it is neither required nor possible that anyone artificially fashion themselves into different shapes in order to measure up to the unique criticisms of so many people of contradicting persuasions and steadfast whims, although Saint Paul did say that he tried to become all things to all people in the hopes that some might be saved. [*1 Corinthians 9:19-23*] Our Lady said it is humanity that must change one person at a time. We must seek our God while He may be found. And, this is why Christianity proclaims the need for conversion. Conversion of what?—our frame of reference, our perspectives and every action and intention that flows from the invocation of our will. Our reference frame must be the Sacred Heart of Jesus Christ, and our will must become His own. Verily I say, the secular humanist manipulators of our culture are lost attempting to reconcile for everyone but themselves the sea of reference frames throughout the diversity of the world because they refuse to testify to the Holy Sacrifice of the Lamb of God that would bring consonance and unity to us as a common humanity. They are no more effective than a traffic officer at a demolition derby trying to suspend the melee with a whistle and a few white-gloved hand gestures. The collection of drivers have no intention of not crashing into each other, and his statutory motor vehicle code is unenforceable to any meaningful end before a screaming crowd who is pining for the next pile-up. None involved have fathomed that the true function of their vehicles is to transport humanity to a beautiful destination, not produce a pile of wreckage that will ultimately be hauled away by wrecker and flatbed truck to the proverbial boneyard, never to be of any use again. These self-ascribed social engineers should be seeking instead to replace every reference frame with the eminent supremacy of the King of kings. The purification of the world through the sacrificial labors of belief is combusted through each individual at the ignition of their faith in the Messiah from Bethlehem. Fire lit upon the world, indeed! [*Luke 12:49*] World peace will come no other way in this advent or after it.

In the process of evangelizing this truth, little doubt remains that many will reflexively conclude that any recipient of miraculous intercession is delusional or an unbalanced religious zealot, or merely lying for personal gain, fame or attention. That's their frame of reference that must be amended with the truth. But, that amendment is their own sacrificial chore. Personally, I would reply that these conclusions are glaringly incorrect in our case if one engaged an honest review of recorded events. There has been no fame or gain, and whatever attention may have been lent to us has usually been accompanied by skepticism, ostracization and derision. Others sequester occurrences of the Virgin Mary's miraculous intercession into being a Catholic issue that is unworthy of any serious person's attention, simply because their frame of reference demands that they keep their fortress gates fully secured against all things Catholic. That, in itself, should be a revelation of their factual incarceration. In reality, theirs' is also an errant conclusion, and is probably a bit naive with so much mystical evidence to the contrary etched into recorded history. The reference frames and perspectives of these people will not allow them to realize that the Virgin Mary is their Heavenly Mother too; and that She is patiently awaiting their faithful allegiance to the Gospel that tells them to "Behold their Mother." They must stop allowing their egos to dictate the darkness that has eclipsed their more inspired contemplations. This is a completely foreign concept to them, although it is eternally true. Steady faith should better encourage them to be more merciful to themselves and invoke the courage and patience to take an honest look instead, because Jesus is offering them a great clarifying gift through the grace of His Immaculate Mother while challenging their lack of faith in the process. These are the ones who sincerely pray for God's help, but then protest the answer when it arrives. God is having a hard time determining what sign, message, miracle or grace they would pay attention to, since they will only give attention to that which affirms the cultish fraternity they have created for themselves. It is not hard to admit that the world needs every encounter with God that He might so generously dispense. The Bible says, *"If today you hear His voice, harden not your heart."* [*Hebrews 3:7-8*] Yet, He has spent so much effort proclaiming "Hear ye, hear ye" through His Immaculate Mother with such little effect that He has nearly grown hoarse doing so. And, if there is any impatience in Jesus Christ, we are surely straining it by ignoring Her great gifts. Hardening our heart means remaining locked away in our limited perspectives and frames of reference, and battling away anything that might penetrate, alter or season those perspectives. This is why Jesus gave the image of salt and light. [*Matthew 5:13-16*] Why salt? Does salt not change the perspective of what has been seasoned? For many people, they do not want salt anywhere near them, thinking it is an attack upon the structural integrity of their entitlements. They have been taught to hate salt by those who think an unseasoned fare is a delicacy. And furthermore, if our capacity to season has been lost by leaving our salt on the shelf too long, the effect is the same as having never seasoned anything to begin with.

    We are a beautiful human creation that is mired in a swirling ocean of perspectives as unique to each of us as our visage in a mirror. Yet, it remains a cause for wonder why anyone would forbid Jesus and His Mother to appear and speak to their children on Earth, and send them as messengers of what they wish the world would know. This is called discipleship and evangelization which He said He would send the Holy Spirit to assist. God is unique too, but His theme of redeeming His people has always been the same through baptism and the priesthood of believers. [*Catechism of the Catholic Church: 1268*] It is the same grace historically as the Apostles traveling into the pagan world and sharing their testimonial experiences 2000 years ago. The challenge to accept contemporary testimony to what the Holy Spirit is doing is as provoking today. The altercation between the truth and the reference frames of sinners is as stimulating. If we reject now, we would have rejected the Apostles then because it is the same worldly frame of reference that is the source of the rejection. It is the old wine skin. [*Mark 2:22*] These followers of Christ

Frames of Reference, Perspectives and Reactions

walked into the centers of heathen societies, unknown, unannounced, risking abuse and death, speaking of miracles and the Death and Resurrection of the promised Messiah to the most practical, pragmatic, prickly and pagan people of the age. My brother and I have endeavored to speak similarly about a miraculous relationship with the same Virgin Mary those Apostles knew personally and are seated beside now. We speak from a frame of reference with a transcending perspective that is difficult for many to accept as a possibility. The Apostles faced differing responses. Scoffers abounded. Danger lurked around every corner. Being called delusional was the order of the day. Most were martyred. But, they witnessed nonetheless to the truth they had lived. It was a truth based in miracles, supernatural events and the grace of a King that has now withstood the test of time, the rising and falling of worldly kingdoms, global conflagrations, wars, cataclysms, barbarism, despotic and tyrannical regimes, martyrdom, genocides and every intellectual movement and force that would attempt to either explain away their Gospel testimony or submerge it in the folds of time as historical delusion and myth. The Bible records how the Holy Spirit came down in special ways upon all those who made the sacrifice to believe and remained in communion with that original testimony. The perspective and frame of reference of those so blessed became altered to acknowledge that God was now present, and their identities were transformed by grace to become children of God. *[Catechism of the Catholic Church: 1996]* What changed at Pentecost was a complete replacement of the frame of reference of the Apostles at the ignition of the tongues of fire of the Holy Spirit. *[Acts 2:1-4]* Supernatural grace overwhelmed their beings and created a virgin reference frame that was so powerful that it would inform every perspective they would ever have throughout the last breath of their earthly lives. This New Testament has promulgated in as many ways and through as many people as would make room for the Truth and thereafter claim their inheritance in His Kingdom and become clothed with His sanctifying power. It is no different now in our contemporary age. The names of those who are sent may have changed, but the Holy Spirit is one and the same; and His methods of making disciples of all nations moves onward undaunted through the populations of the world toward the moment when He will arrive a second time and reward all who have repented of their sins and believed in His Divine Mercy. And, those who held the Queen of Heaven in their heart alongside the

King of kings will receive the highest Heaven, while the rest will wonder how they could have been so blind.

If you would grant me your forbearance, I would like to reflect further upon the differing reactions to claims of miraculous intercession in order to illuminate a wider perspective on our understanding of the engagement of our faith. Something being supernatural signifies a character of being beyond the chain of natural causation as we understand it from our purview in exile. This definition can also be applied to our essence as human beings and as sinners. We cannot hear the thoughts of other people; we cannot know what is going to occur next week; we do not know the day nor hour we will die, and we cannot know God unless He reveals Himself to us. Each of these would be beyond the "natural" state of our exiled human nature. Now, all grace is supernatural, meaning beyond our sinful nature as exiled creatures. The universe did not create itself; it was the Father who said let it be. A lightbulb cannot turn itself on, while intoning a heartfelt Our Father is a supernatural projection of Light. Ask any atheist to recite the Our Father from his heart. It is impossible for them. Every one of them will refuse; and if one of them might, they utter that great prayer outside their sinful nature by the power of God at your intercession, which in itself is the action of the Holy Spirit in them. This is why living in a state of sanctifying grace is a supernatural plateau of existence. Catholics invoke a supernatural identity that breaches the boundaries of mortal human existence in an ultimate way every time we celebrate the Holy Sacrifice of the Mass, while it is easy to recognize that the atheist can never transcend his mortal frame of his own accord. Those who reject baptism have no power to believe. Their rejection is the proof. They are incapable of generating anything more than bounded sinfulness. In reality, supernatural actions of God flourish far more apparently in the elevated attributes of the spiritual soul than they ever have through the breaching of the laws of physical nature, although the Miracle of the Sun at Fatima in 1917 is a pretty colossal exclamation point to the latter. It is much like Jesus asking whether it was harder to forgive sins than to heal a physical deformity. But, so we would know He had the authority to restore the soul, He brought the physical miracle of the healing of the body. [*Mark 2:9-11*] Hence, the concept of supernatural within miraculous intercession not only applies to the physical laws of nature that we observe, it can have a reference frame consisting of the

Frames of Reference, Perspectives and Reactions

"laws of the state of our being." Sinful human nature, of itself, can generate nothing beyond its lowly position confined in the mortality of sin. We cannot save ourselves or advance our human definition without divine grace. No act, thought or intention absent of grace can live beyond the grave. What is "natural" for exiled mortal creatures is to be limited by time, space, knowledge, vision, strength, the laws of physics, nature and death. This is why we needed a Savior. After Jesus' great Sacrifice on Mount Calvary, everything done in union with the sanctifying grace of the Holy Spirit is elevated beyond exiled nature. We become more than we were before. Our beings, along with our acts and intentions, become supernatural, meaning unconfined by the limitations wrought by sin because they are now God's work given life in full cooperation with His Holy Spirit. Nothing of everlasting goodness can occur in the mortal realms without the cooperation of the Spirit of God. It is all futile and subject to depletion and death. There could never be an earthly kingdom of absolute beauty without the supernatural grace from the Holy Sacrifice of Jesus Christ. This is why the Catholic Church is a supernaturally-divine institution on Earth throughout its Liturgies, Dogma, Hierarchy and Communion amongst its people. And, while Jesus bestows the unseen mystical healing to souls in the Church's sacramental forgiveness of sins, He confirms this healing agency in the Mystical Body of the Church by displaying the physical miracle of His Mother's intercession…*"that all may know the authority of the Roman Catholic Church on Earth."* It is the same testament as in Mark 2:9-11 and a verifiable action of the Holy Spirit down to the last bell that rings.

Now, it is obvious that each of us is impacted differently by these things as has been acknowledged. We mentally process and react differently according to the mental composure we possess. Most people have never had it enter into their consciousness the spiritual concepts that I just related in the previous paragraph. Yet, we are creatures far more blessed by our God than we may have ever conceived before. It almost goes without saying that most people have never encountered miraculous intercession in any way they recognized or accepted. Our framework of thinking, how we view things, how we assess situations; this amalgam of perception and mental adjudication has been forming and solidifying in us since birth; and, it defines what things we allow to affect us and what we repulse. And, the sorrowful part is, this forming process in many cases and for most people has been either distorted or lacking, leaving them confused about the actual beauty of their lives and separated from the possibilities that reign at the invocation of their faith. Look at the regions of the world that lie desolate and dominated, notwithstanding the greatest technological and humanitarian advances in human history. They labor in darkness simply because the framework of reference of these multitudes is without the light and wisdom of Jesus Christ that is needed to be united and sacrificial toward the highest possibilities of human potential. Perhaps one might consider the United States of America as swiftly regressing into being one of these places for which we mourn. Very few people are flexible enough where they can expand much in the way of faithful grace after a given age or without certain amounts of suffering where they find themselves required to take to their knees to seek out higher powers or alternate avenues of meaning. We become hardened in dispositions that require very little sacrifice of ourselves toward nobler ends. Unsanctioned intellectualism is usually impregnable to any cultivation by God, especially amidst secular progressive liberals. This dark mentalism circumscribes the pride-filled scoffers and gnat strainers who hide their faithlessness behind false claims of prudence, cerebral pontifications and their tony propriety. These ego-stricken individuals believe that their ability to manipulate worldly events, their skill in fabricating knowledge to prosper their agendas, and the degrees that enshrine their self-acclaimed privilege give them an anointing of credibility for the validation of their own personal will. Our Lady would tell them that Jesus' Will is the only thing that matters, and His genius is the source of all wisdom. She can do very little with an intellectual in many cases because their highbrow mental estates reek of pride at its zenith. And, oftentimes religious intellectualism is the worst. Their appetite for learning is both a veil for their insecurities and the soapbox upon which their fragile character and low self-esteem stand. In fact, there is such a thing as intellectual gluttony which is every bit the sin as engorging ourselves with food to satisfy our undisciplined appetites. Gluttony is a form of greed that violates the simple orders of Creation and obscures the wisdom that comes through those orders. Why so hard on intellectuals? Because they are the dungeon masters holding the keys. They create prisons and throw their brothers and sisters in them. But, did not God bring an earthquake to free SS Paul and Silas? [*Acts 16:25*] Intellectuals revel in clanking

Frames of Reference, Perspectives and Reactions

their argumentative perspectives on the crystal glassware of attention. They raise goblets of nuanced detail to toast their sophistication while peering down from their ivory towers upon the serfdoms of creation as lording overseers of those realms. They rarely come down on anything but the fence of the next criticism, conjuring debates as esteemed sorcerers of skepticism against anything that challenges their dogmas of secular indoctrination. They make disciples of their acolytes who are multiple degrees more wicked than themselves without realizing the animals they are feeding will ultimately turn and tear them to pieces. They dance on the rails of the intelligentsia like gymnasts on balance beams, never realizing the wood they are teetering on is a Cross upon which their Savior was nailed. Postulating their own contributions to the Beauty of Calvary is retrograde, archaic, and out of the question to their spiritual sensibilities because they have none. Their souls are dead. They scorn miracles and mystical events because they sense the looming responsibilities of Christian sanctification they wish not to engage either intellectually, materially or spiritually. They refuse to put their authority and their faculties at the feet of the King of Creation. Their frame of reference demands that all allegiances align toward them because they feel they know more than anyone else, which in reality is no obedience at all—for them. [*Matthew 23:15*] They consider themselves to be the center of the universe when God actually sees them as lost little asteroids hurtling through the lonely cosmos on a collision course with the Crucifixion come the end of time. By contrast, our Holy Mother has great success bringing humble loving little children to embrace the greatest beauties of the universe; those who are excited and grateful to get to know Her and do what She asks. Intellectualism is rarely, if ever, formed in such a way to allow the exercise of faith to the magnitude of Abraham or the Virgin Mother. Multitudes are peering at the world through a framework of delusion that is very difficult to see through, over, or past. The devil acts as the friend of travelers on the road to Salvation, waving his caution sign. And, when a rationalist sees the miraculous intercession of our Heavenly Mother along that road, the devil excites the ungrounded intellect and points to the off-ramps, claiming Her superhighway lacks the scenic ecumenical distractions he would better provide if we drove through the meandering countryside of collaboration, mediocrity and compromise. The Queen of Heaven is thus deprived their faithfulness, their allegiance, and all they could have accomplished for the conversion of the nations had they surrendered their venues and faculties to Her. It is not that the intellect is opposed to faith; it is not that spirit-imbued rationalism is wrong; it is the framework created with that intellect unhinged from Divine Revelation and the mystical imprints of history that becomes solidified by pride which will not make room for spontaneous obedience to the Holy Spirit when He calls. These mentalities will not travel a path in faith unless God satisfies their pride with visionary prescience as to the final destination and all the curves involved. But, it is the little children who will scamper down the road in obedience to their Mother, leaving the headstrong in a dither wondering why their shallow sanctimony was not revered enough to hold anyone's attention. Then, the doubters engage their pride in a fight for survival and proceed to counsel everyone within earshot that no one is required to believe that the spiritual food being devoured is really so delicious. I challenge anyone to tell me this is not the truth because Our Lady has told me better. Of course, those who accept the challenge will not engage this indictment directly, they will do what intellectuals do—nuance a response so seductively that the principle of the entire admonishment will be rendered obscure and meaningless. They slither off the hook with what?—yes, their rhetoric. This is the pyre where most moral truth has breathed its last in our contemporary age. Our Holy Mother admonished our original prayer group on April 22, 1991 amidst an occasion of early skepticism and turmoil, saying "*I cannot come while you are asking questions! If you want to ask questions, ask yourself why you are asking questions, instead of praying for peace!*" We can be humble and also of great intellect and deeply in union with God. Pope Benedict XVI is a giant intellect, but as humble as a child. No wonder the Holy Spirit found pleasure in him and elevated him to the Papacy. Each of us has a unique composure to our inner self that is either liberating, growing and flourishing, or confining, enslaving, and depleting. One elates, one terrifies. One nurtures a new day, the other deflects the dawn.

These veiled forces that cause such depletion influence numerous aspects of our being unawares, unless we are keenly observant of our interior composure. Very few people are as independent in their thinking as they believe themselves to be. Few allow the Holy Spirit complete autonomy within them. Vast collages of impulses and compulsions impact us interiorly and can enslave and dictate our thinking, our choices, and thereafter, our conduct in very spiritually destructive ways. This is why Catholics identify so ardently with the purification and sanctification of the soul, while Protestants speak merely of a verbal declaration of faith as being sufficient unto the perfections of salvation. Protestants rarely mention the concept of human perfection, sanctification and conforming to the image of Christ, although Jesus did say, "be perfect as your Heavenly Father is perfect." Sanctification of the soul sounds much too Catholic to their guarded sensibilities. Our Lady has said that while most every Protestant who loves Jesus to the best of their acceptance will ultimately achieve a place in Heaven through Jesus' Divine Mercy, each of them will nonetheless be faced immediately after their passing with the astounding spiritual supremacy of the Roman Catholic Church where purification and sanctification reached to the apex of divine life in Christ Jesus. And there, She said the Truth will ask them why they refused to unite with it as One Body at one Table of Faith. The question is, what will they protest then? We cannot break habits or change opinions if we are incapable of contemplating beyond our present selves. There is a great breath of freedom to be savored once one is liberated from the mistaken perspectives of ancestral players that we do not even know who scarred our lives with their willful arguments. How difficult it is to think independently from familial legacies, militant religio-political ideologies and protesting religious traditions. Some are led away to debauchery at the drop of a hat, while others are as impenetrable as concrete walls and slanderous as hellcats when asked to consider something that contradicts a protesting legacy they possess or belief they already hold. We call this "affected vincible ignorance" and a shame; and for most, not even the testimony to the miraculous intercession of the Queen of Heaven is enough to breach these insuperable walls of generational obstinance. But, Her Triumph will!

    Formative years notwithstanding, each of us has been molded and impacted continually with the ideas of secular culture, the things we've suffered, and what we have chosen to accept and reject. There have been many different people in our lives, even from the cradle, who have been impressing upon us what they believe, for better or for worse. The television with its advertisers and program producers are a stellar example. They are manipulating millions of people every day for the sake of their profits. How many idols touted as the ultimate have they created which they then destroy in order to market a newer version for profit? Empire builders spend billions of dollars every year for the opportunity to influence us through any medium before our eyes. What does a Super Bowl commercial cost these days? Which of these advertisers and media companies are not trying to configure our frame of reference by force of repetition, brand something into our psyche, create a fad, or seduce us into a materialistic way of life so they can profit from it, whether we are in need of their commodities or not? How many people did they get to buy a rock, calling it a pet? They rubbed their greedy palms together laughing at humanity with each dump truck they sent to the nearest gravel pit. Can you see the point? This is the materialistic consumerism that the Holy Pontiffs of the Roman Catholic Church have been counseling us against for decades for our betterment as a people. These themes of manipulation are open and apparent to us in the world, and we succumb to them as a matter of course. It comes from the material world we see. But, there is also the unseen world, and manipulations come from those realms as well through the antagonisms of demonic spirits. They are called temptations, compulsions, oppressions, delusions, and enticements, and they influence our frame of reference for the purpose of holding our perspectives hostage, away from divine grace. Consider how many people have been influenced to scar their bodies with hideous tattoos, radical piercings and surgical body modifications? It is an amazing phenomenon. One could posit that it is an example of mass delusion by a demonic force. Our Holy Mother told us that Satan works as a fine grindstone who hones away at our innocent holiness as imperceptibly as he can. He does not sleep. He can play the long-game with the days of our lives so as to better manipulate and mold our frame of reference to be of service to him for destruction without our being aware. He will work for years subtly stroking man's pride and clothing individuals with worldly stature, preparing them to be of service to him in the most opportune moments to obscure the truth from thousands, and thus destroy their hopes that life may have offered them something more revelatory, magnificent and beautiful. The evil one will affirm abominations, sow discord in perceptions, slander great traditions and rewrite ages-old tenets of moral propriety that impede his progress toward human annihilation. This is how he has secularized society. Secular humanism is his work. It is his blanket of darkness. And, he will not stop there. He did not bring America's soul into eclipse overnight and for no reason. He has been working meticulously for centuries in particularly extraordinary ways. Let's face it, secular means godless; but where did God go if most believe He exists? Satan divided Christianity most seriously 500 years ago in the western world through a few unstable men who incited a protest throughout a naive population against the original Apostles and the Church they founded. Our Holy Mother does not engage in all the posturing about who was at fault during those turbulent times. She simply says the protesters refused the sacrifice and walked away from the brotherhood of Peter, Paul, James and John. While thinking they were saving, Satan was sullying. Then, the evil one spent the succeeding five centuries downplaying amongst the populous every religious truth that was disagreed upon to where the original Truth was relegated to being just another version of intellectualism alongside every heresy imaginable. Human pride reigned! Thus, history records countless differing flavors of religious pluralism. Once Satan had sullied our unity with the Divine in the squabbles, he brought the supposed humanist enlightenment to claim secular rationality in the chaotic arena of human affairs and shoved the mystery and majesty of God's unseen Kingdom to the private realms of superstition, marginalization and irrelevance. He hijacked mankind's frame of reference and replaced it with bondage to the sinful egos of men who would now claw for the pinnacles of worldly power. In order to do this, everything had to become relative to the different reference frames and perspectives of blind individuals lost in sin who wanted each of their egos to be worshiped as being godlike. Satan thrived in this detachment from the Divine Revelation of the Original Apostolic Church. He began the persecution and prosecution of Truth through his jeering antagonists and agitators, rewarding with position, power and resources anyone who served his diabolical reign. He raised the supposed Enlightenment and instigated the murderous holocausts of the French Revolution where he attempted to slaughter the Church into non-existence in France, and the spirit of Saint Joan of Arc was never invoked. How she must have wept from on high. Thereafter, he raised Communism in Russia and proceeded to wipe the Church from the public face of their motherland for nearly a century. He inflamed Nazism which also implemented the diabolical design to eradicate the Church and replace it with Arian fanaticism, along with targeting the children of Abraham for extermination. And all throughout, Our Lady miraculously interceded in hamlets and boroughs amongst the simple, the heartfelt, and the faithful that Her Son's Church never fail in them. And now, Lucifer has raised progressive atheistic secularism, just as much a beast, to snuff out the Christian spirit of the United States of America and the fatherlands of western Europe. He has spent millennia draping and re-draping a veil of derision over the Rock of the Church to diminish its ethereal superiority. Thus, with the ideological assistance of unprincipled protesting heterodoxy, Satan has used religious pluralism, secular humanism and moral relativism to replace the singular supremacy of the Definitive Revelation nurtured by the Catholic Church in the minds of contemporary man. Our path toward salvation as a collective family has become all but lost to a supposedly modern civilization that has come of age in industry, science and technology, along with the sophisticated weapons of mass destruction, biological obliteration, and war. We have come to worship the diversity of frail human reference frames lost in the failures of sin, and the evidence is everywhere we look. The devil has employed this subterfuge through creative adaptations of his deranged sophistry in every age, and we are teetering on the precipice of conflagrations that will thrust us into a thousand years of darkness where the Catholic Church will be the only light left in the world. In fact, this is what the sexual scandal involving the Catholic priesthood has been all about since the opening of the new millennia; Satan throwing a veil of derision over the Rock of the Church by highlighting the failures and omissions of a few. Our Lady mentioned to us how ironic it is that unrepentant sinners would jeer Jesus' resplendent Church as not being holy enough. The King of this Church would tell them to reconsider their lack of mercy before He administers sentence upon them for their sins in equal measure to their jeering. She said that the injustice in the accusations against the esteemed Hierarchy of the Roman Catholic Church has been colossal, and will be adjudicated at His Throne on the final day. She posited that libertine secularists and other Christians-in-name-only unleashed sexual abomination through their licentiousness and are now wailing that a beast is on the loose while trying to blame it on the Roman Catholic Church. Is it any wonder that certain priests fell to temptation once the American culture ignored Pope Paul VI and became swamped with sexual perversion during the 1960s and thereafter, which spread like a plague into our present age through all the mediums of communication and entertainment that Satan has brought into allegiance with his diabolic reign?

Frames of Reference, Perspectives and Reactions

Need we warn humanity so emphatically of our vulnerability when so many are still oblivious to these dangers to their salvation? The answer is yes because the innocence of the human soul has become disoriented and blinded to this vulnerability. This results in the pure and consecrated being attacked anytime evildoers sense clarity or unity in our frame of reference, anytime there is the possibility to transcend back into the holy of holies, anytime we claim any supremacy for God, anytime we forward virtue as the mode for human life, anytime we bring clarity between light and darkness, purity and perversity, and sin and sanctity. And, why do these attacks come? Because those who are lost are having their frame of reference challenged, and they do not like having to admit their conversion might be necessary. We are vulnerable to depletion and destruction when any person who possesses a corrupt frame of reference assumes a position of power who can wield their illicit perspectives. The wicked and the worldly have no anchoring in the preservation of humanity in the grace of God, and thus we will together experience the flames of purification that will rise up and consume our societies, states and fatherlands. Yes, purification is coming! Satan rockets perversity to the pinnacle of prestige, power and publicity almost as if by miraculous means. He makes billionaires of his acolytes and gives empires to those who will serve him. Look at the culture of immoral audacity sold by Hollywood as entertainment and the heathen pop stars who announce bombast, blasphemy and impurity from their stages. Look at the hip-hop culture of misogyny, hatred, racism and violence that has corrupted an entire generation of our children. Look at our universities brainwashing our young people to serve as storm-troopers in Satan's next rendition of social upheaval, agitation and antagonism. Let it be known that our Holy Mother stands with Her Son's chosen people in the homeland of Her childhood and asks all humanity to respect and defend the children of the God of Abraham, Isaac and Jacob! Remember what the beast promised Jesus in his temptations if Our Lord would fall down and worship him—the kingdoms of the world. Look about! Who sits at the pinnacles of those material kingdoms now? He has groomed judges for years for his moment to use them to supercede the will of freedom-loving people to attack the societal construct of marriage being only between one man and one woman in the United States. He has blinded our nation to such an extent that our leaders have not the courage to discern between the biological sexes and defend little girls in the privacy of their bathrooms. They defer instead to people who are definitively under the influence and possession of the Antichrist. He accompanied seven Supreme Court justices from early in their careers, grooming their egos to be of service to his diabolical evil and vote to enshrine the slaughter of children in the womb into the parchments of our nation's charter in 1973. The devil has nurtured particular theologians through years of study, allowed accolades to be heaped upon their scholastic achievements, placed letters behind their names, and elevated them into influential chairs of distinction throughout the world, simply so his slithering voice would resound to dismiss and mock the Immaculate Virgin Mary's miraculous intercession each time Her presence comes to the fore—miracles, healings and the conversion of millions notwithstanding. These are only a few examples of his manipulation of our perspectives through people who have forsaken Jesus Christ and embraced the devil's wickedness for profit instead. And, sly and seductive they are. The evil one and his legions of demons have their hands in everything that is surrendered to them, every person who has not clothed themselves in the armor of faith as their reason for living. [*Ephesians 6:11-17*] Our Virgin Mother is the sign that contradicts them because She reflects Her Son with majesty and power. She is clothed with the mantle of truth, purity and grace, and petitions us with a pleading voice to gird our loins, return to the narrow path and believe in the ancient Traditions of Christianity once again. The devil is enshrouded with the tattered rags of religious pluralism, secular humanism, moral relativism and multicultural diversity. He washes out every conviction of holy excellence that is oriented toward faithful and committed unity based in divine and natural law, and he acts like the most merciful and generous person while doing it—the advocate for sinners from whom he will ask nothing but their souls. Satan is an activist, instigator, and agitator. He is an anarchist who violates with impunity every law of stability that impedes him because he knows righteousness has become so weak that he would never be put on trial. He foments radicalism, division, riot, revolution, hatred and war. The moniker "bigot" drips from his lying tongue like the rain, and his drool is spat upon anyone who rises to impede him. If he senses a realm of peace and brotherhood, he considers it a challenge; a place disinterested in his agenda of damnation; and he will stir discontent into a cause draped in false righteousness and call it progress. He will hail the fruits of the righteous as undeserved privilege while sneering at his own sacrifice. He has deluded entire armies of naive do-gooders into serving him. He acts as the most caring, considerate entity fighting for the rights of the marginalized. But, the only rights he cares about are for mankind to turn away from the Gospel of Jesus Christ into the bowels of sin. He asks for no sacrifice, but screams of liberation. And, liberation from what? The yoke which is easy and the burden which is light. It is virtue that he assails. He mocks sacrificial holiness and the selfless labors that enhance our unity as the Body of Christ. How many feuding factions does he have to raise up? How much of our politics must he poison? How low does the Catholic Church have to grovel to keep the possibility of unity alive? Satan takes life instead of giving it. He will inspire an abomination against the Almighty Father, form it into a social collective, clothe it in the moniker of progress, encourage it to be called a class, portray the class as being victimized, then manipulate the conscience of an entire nation into becoming defenders of this class of supposed victims, declaring we must honor their heinous dereliction, lest we be accused of bigotry and racism. And, he will tease, taunt and ridicule anyone who challenges him, cajoling our faith into doubting where Christian charity and love may truly be found. Jesus Christ is the only Victim worth emulating; and He became a Victim because He embodied the perfection of the human race in virtue, pure grace and obedience to His Father, and commanded us to imitate Him. The Prince of Peace and King of kings, he is called! If we believe ourselves to be victims for any other reason than to suffer in His likeness, for the same sanctity, then we are delusional. Christians filled with the Holy Spirit openly recognize this. Those who serve the beast believe they are bringing about a better world when they are actually surrendering themselves as demonic instruments to destroy it. Satan mimics God. He calls for conversion also. While the Lord of Heaven calls sinful men to holiness through conversion, Satan calls good men to wickedness through reversion. And, the way the evil one makes this possible and palatable is through the inversion of good and evil in the reference frames of men. [*Isaiah 5:20*]

    This entire appeal to recognize this evil in our lives should help us better understand what Jesus was saying in Matthew 6:22-23 when He spoke about if the light inside you is bad, your whole body will be filled with darkness. In other words, if our frame of reference has been formed, manipulated or transplanted with a corrupt variant absent the grace and wisdom of Jesus Christ, all of our actions and decisions are vulnerable to being of service to the darkness of the evil one with our consciences so dead that we will not even realize it. The darkness will be so deep that we will believe we are serving God and humankind by what we do. This is the demonic infestation that enshrouds Planned Parenthood and the abomination of the infanticide movement. Satan factually owns the perceptions of their souls, their frame of reference and every one of their perspectives; and they do his works of human annihilation. They are headed for damnation in the fires of hell. It is monstrous evil, equally as hideous as the Nazism of World War II. This is why the miraculous intercession of the Virgin Mary is such an apocalyptic weapon against this kingdom of darkness. Satan hates the Matriarch of Creation and is terrified of Her resplendent presence, while She could not care less what he believes because She has Her heel on his slithering throat—and he knows it. He spews at Her at every opportunity because She heralds as the Immaculate Repository of all Heavenly Wisdom that annihilates every reference frame where he might leverage his diabolical force. The forces of hell are powerless before Her Queenship, and the Most Holy Rosary is the chain that binds him. She has birthed the Truth of the unseen Kingdom, and has laid it in the manger of the Roman Catholic Church, there to remain illuminating human existence until the last day of the world. Then, this Universal Church will take its rightful place in the Glories of its Sacrifice united with our King. The immaculate presence of the Most Blessed Virgin Mary brings the entire facade of diabolical disorientation to the ground in a smoldering pile of humiliating defeat. Of course, the news media of the nations do not want to elevate Her miraculous intercession that they see occurring throughout the world. Recognition brings the responsibility for the reevaluation of their entire reason for existence. This is the agenda of authentic miraculous intercession, lightning strikes in the darkness with such spectacular brilliance that the devil could not begin to figure out how to extinguish the fires they ignite. It is the Light combusted on Mount Calvary; and the Most Holy Virgin was there being bathed in that Sacrifice. The miraculous intercession of the Virgin Mary removes the veil that the devil has thrown over the Rock of Salvation. Most in the Original Apostolic Church know that their witness to the truth of Jesus Christ is being obscured by rampaging secular ideologies at every turn, but most seem not to have the foggiest notion how to finally remove the impediment once and for all. Secularists mock the raiment of authority clothed about the Roman Catholic Church without compunction. We must begin to realize that Our Lady empowers all authority through belief and cooperation with Her miraculous intercession because it is in this obedience to Her that clarity and power will rise once again. The mystical power of the Church would be restored in our midst. She places the ultimate personal weapon in our hands in the form of the Most Holy Rosary. She is a gift that cannot be coopted by the Protestant world. Jesus Christ will not allow it. She is veiled from their eyes because they do not make themselves worthy of recognizing Her. They follow errant men who kicked the Queen of Heaven to the curb and sped away. Prodigal sons, indeed! Giving them a seat at the table of Truth is a sin against righteousness. They must return through conversion, repentance and their own humble assent within the Sacrament of Reconciliation. The Vicar of Christ is standing in the Jubilee doorway looking afar. He has ventured throughout the byways of the world. Cooperation with God always produces the effect of granting authority and power for the declaration and propagation of the authenticity of the Holy Gospel. He always rewards faith with great power. The lampshade comes off the Church when the world sees heroic faith from within its sacred midst. All intellectualism marvels at where that capacity for self-giving originates. What would entice a person to run against the grain of secular approbation in our time and slap the cheek of fashion with the rawhide leather of mystical truth? I tell you, the Queen of Heaven is placing these gauntlets on Her sons, lifting them to the withers of their war horses, and smacking their hind quarters for the charge into the final battle for Redemption! The Almighty Father is not asking for merely good works and noble habits because those manifestations can be imitated and marginalized as worldly by the most secular and godless. He is calling for full-throated testimony that the Virgin Mother of His Son has come to the United States of America in our time, and is standing in majesty and authority at the epicenter of Christianity in the heart of the Roman Catholic Church. From this original frame of reference, She declares that we must return to belief in this Original Sacred Church or the inevitabilities of Divine Justice will rain down upon every institution, and burn us into acknowledging the King of Heaven once again.

The Final Colossus - In Battle Array

Chapter 4
Jesus the Christ
Truth Beyond the Ages

His is the most beatific face ever set upon a man,
for whom marigolds dance and the winds accede,
In Him all things eternal find their new beginnings.
For He makes rich the paupers' broth, low their ire,
true their fathers' joy, and sweet the trumpet's song.
- The Dominion Angels
April 22, 2017

In the midst of the formation of our perspectives and frame of reference, and all the turbulence of information, ideas and claims that deluge us in an ever-increasingly secularized world, we should recognize that there are undeniable bedrock truths that are above anyone's manipulations or claims to the contrary. Opinionated critics, cynics and contrarians have no standing to contravene the truths of the ages. Hence, we must begin by respecting these bedrock truths as the anchors to our overarching reference frame or we will inevitably function with the perspectives of delusional renegades, fighting for legitimacy that will never be ratified by reality. For example, mathematically, 1 + 1 + 1 equals three. It will always equal three. On the other side of the universe, it equals three. In fact, in Heaven it also equals a Holy Trinity. But, for the moment, I would like to stay on this side of the veil. The composition of the number "3" is knowledge enshrined in natural law. If anyone tried to convince us otherwise, we would wonder what was wrong with them. Every toddler acquires this knowledge before their third birthday. Doesn't each one of them hold up three fingers when asked how old they are? Another example is gravity. Gravity bears an undeniable truth throughout our lives in this universe. If we jump off a cliff, we will most assuredly be injured or killed, depending on its height. Tiny children do not know this truth, yet it still has its effect in their lives, therefore every mother guards her child from high places where they can be injured. These are physical examples in the world we can see and touch. But, what about truths that are rooted in facets of an unseen world, in the realms of the heart and spirit, and in our recognition and relationship with God? What about the Kingdom of Heaven itself, an entire infinite realm we cannot see? What about all the healings rejoiced, miracles reported, visions seen, astounding coincidences experienced and impossible victories attained? Adding numbers is logical because they are apparent to us on the physical level of our five senses. Jumping off a cliff is obviously delusional because we know what it means to fall down; the higher the fall, the bigger the hurt. Physicists and mathematicians have examined the truth of gravity and determined the acceleration of our fall on this planet would be 9.8 meters per second squared. On the moon, it is less; approximately one-sixth that value. Mankind has delved into the physical truth of our falling and the forces that cause things to plummet to the ground in the world we see. But, do we realize that we can also plunge to eternal death upon reaching the unseen world after our passing? Do we realize that there is a force similar to gravity that will hurtle us into the abyss? Imagine how many objects have been thrown off high places in history with the observers wondering what unseen force caused them to fall. We call what they do science, or more specifically physics, in a world everyone can see and measure. But, what do we call those who seek to delve into the facets of the unseen world where our physical measurements have no relevance, where mathematics holds no subjugating values, where grace cannot be measured and the capacity of the human heart for love is infinite? What are the units of measure for purity of the heart? How long will an eternal Kingdom last? How can something be created out of nothing? Can we imagine the number of people in the course of history who have knelt before God and offered Him their love, hoping that His grace would fall into their lives? This is no less a search for answers than the physicist's material ponderings and calculations. But, unseen realms are researched and explored through prayer from the heart and the grace of God who reveals Himself in response to those prayers. Wisdom comes through conversion and sanctification of the heart and soul. Hence, one who does not pray knows nothing of the unseen realms, which leaves their framework of reference and their perspectives blind to the truths of God's heavenly Kingdom that would validate their dignity and reason for existence. I have always been astonished at why the godless presume so much authority to deride that which they know nothing about. Their lips are moving, but nothing they say will ever be heard in Heaven.

Jesus Christ - Truth Beyond the Ages

The point is, "truths" exist in both the seen and unseen realms that are beyond any person's command or authority to alter or claim otherwise. For example, the sun exists in the sky. That is a truth even for a blind man. It is so high a material truth that no human being dare utter the absurdity that it does not. But, think of the faith that the blind man extends to someone who tells him that the warmth he feels on his skin is actually a great ball of fire that hangs in the heavens which he cannot see? Imagine if the world were filled with people who were blind, and God came and gave sight of the sun to those who believed in Him. What if the sun was not common knowledge? Might all the blind laugh when you told them of a flaming celestial sphere 93 million miles away that emitted the warmth they feel? Similarly, the existence of God is a truth as well, and history has held sight of Him in His Son Jesus, and now in our contemporary world as the Most Blessed Sacrament of the Catholic Altar. He commands a truth that is even higher and more permanent than the existence of the sun in the sky. But, He resides now beyond our physical sight in the realms of His spiritual Kingdom, leaving it to seem, for now, that we are all blind men unless we invoke our faith to see. It is easy to acknowledge truths in the world we see, and far harder to accept them from realms where we cannot see. Miraculous intercession flourishes from these unseen realms of Creation; the realms that Jesus wished to reveal to us by His Life, Death and Resurrection. Therefore, it is predictable that more diverse and even animated reactions would be generated when one asks others to accept unseen truths because there is far less to anchor our listeners intellectually to steady their acceptance. The intellectual has no more advantage than the most uneducated child. In fact, the child has the greater advantage, and that is why Our Lord said that *"unless you become as a little child, you will not enter the Kingdom of Heaven." [Matthew 18:3]* This is the reason far more instances of miraculous intercession are experienced by children, paupers and peasants. They are receptive entities filled with humility that God does not have to banter with or convince. They have created far fewer obstacles for themselves in their frame of reference to instigate haughty debates. They have no oppressive ghosts to make them uncomfortable. Saint Padre Pio, the stigmatic priest and mystic from Pietrelcina, Italy once said, "The habit of asking why has ruined the world." God asks, "Would you believe My Son," and humanity asks, "Why?" Then, He replies, "Because I wish for you to be with Me in Paradise." And, humanity retorts, "Why would we believe there is a Paradise? We don't see it."

The Final Colossus - In Battle Array

God then says, "I will send Jesus' Mother to show you what Heaven looks like." And, humanity responds, "Well, we don't have to believe in that." And, on it goes.

As adults, we cannot imagine letting go of our worldly stability, even when it may not be the bedrock we think it is. This is where faith becomes operative and clothed in true power. Faith allows us to bridge that gap of uncertainty. God is on our side when He wants us to believe something. We just need to let go, make the sacrifice and cooperate. Our Lady told me that faith becomes knowledge to those who serve. I have always been inspired by the example of a tiny child standing on the edge of a pool for the first time, toes curled up at the edge, water-wings on, uncertain, afraid, glancing at the water, then to their mother with arms outstretched, beckoning them to jump—and they do. They do! Imagine what that means. It is an enormous act of faith by those tiny children. Think of the millions who have transcended that moment. You might remember the first time you did. Jumping into the unknown at the calling of your mother. This is the portrait of the miraculous intercession of the Virgin Mary who stands beckoning for our faithful leap of cooperation. Most intellectuals, including many religious leaders, never truly make the jump because they are paralyzed in their estimation of themselves and their self-autonomy, analyzing the consequences, the depth of the water, the noise and splashing of the other children, and whether they will ever again come up for air as if she might fail to catch them. A thousand reasons to be frightened, and afraid of being wrong. They never look into their mother's eyes and launch themselves, as if in mid-air, untethered, unbalanced for a moment, out of control until they splash down in her arms. They have never felt that complete helpless, dependent moment of total self-giving without their having a say in the outcome. They are terrified of that moment where they are no longer in control, where their authority and self-sufficiency no longer matter. But, there are millions of others who do believe, who have already jumped and are swimming around Her like ducklings paddling about their mother. And further, imagine those who are standing on the side of that pool, recognizing no mother with outstretched arms ready to catch them. These are the protestors, doubters and ditherers. Rare few of them ever really get wet. At best, they sit on the sidelines and dangle their feet in the water. They never swim like true Christians in the fathoms of everlasting life. The water is Jesus;

the body of water is His Catholic Church, and our Holy Mother calls us through Her miraculous intercession to jump into a more profound state of grace in Her arms. After alighting there, maybe after going under, maybe with a mouthful of water we spit out, She will further teach us to hold our breath, to put our face in the water, then to swim in it, and to even dive to the bottom where God has tossed His fairest coins of revelation.

    You see, God wants us to span that gap between the concrete physical world and the spiritual beauty and power of His unseen Kingdom. It occurs only through conversion, baptism, faith, acceptance, repentance, absolution, and the vision of our heart imbued with His divine grace, with the framework of reference being the Original Apostolic Church of Roman Catholicism, the Mother Church of Christianity. The Holy Spirit gives light for that vision to anyone who accepts Jesus Christ as their King; those who turn to His teachings of prayer, devotion, repentance and sacrifice. He wants to free us from the confining frameworks of distraction and disbelief so that we would recognize and be uplifted by both His Eucharistic presence and His redeeming actions among men until the end of time when He will come again. Let's face it, not everything we have been told by others or things that huge numbers of people believe are actually true. A majority can be a pretty lost group of individuals at times. We often see vast collectives of individuals drafted into delusional mobs advocating sheer lunacy, civil disobedience, lawlessness and destruction. It was the late Senator Bobby Kennedy who stated that the voice of the mob is madness. There is an abundance of deception, corruption and outright evil agendas in this world right now. I suppose there always has been. It is like being encouraged to climb into an airplane for a joyous ride, but somebody under the hood of the airplane is ripping out spark plugs, another is beneath the fuselage removing the valve stems and deflating the tires, and a third is syphoning gasoline from the tank. Each one is a mechanic who believes his actions to be wholesome, not even thinking about the purpose of the plane we are going to be riding in. You see, the one removing spark plugs really needs them for his lawn mower. The person underneath removing valve stems from the tires needs them so he can inflate the tires of his race car; and his pit crew member thinks nobody is going to miss the high-octane fuel that he is syphoning from the tank. Each of these things is not bad in and of itself, nor does each person not have talents for maintaining equipment, but in the context of greater things, which in our case is our flight toward Heaven, they are surely not putting their skills to good use so those who board might reach their destination safely. God requires us to voluntarily sacrifice the personal truths "we think we know" for the deific Truth He wishes us to actually know, all for the purpose of bringing us back into our original homeland of the paradisial garden after our passing from this world we see. This occurs through a sanctifying process beginning with conversion; and it is where the miraculous intercession of the Virgin Mary fits. It is part of the "how" that God is employing. He has commissioned His Immaculate Mother from the moment of Mount Calvary to assist the sanctification of those who will some day gain Heaven. If Jesus desired with such passion to save humanity that He willingly accepted Crucifixion, then the thing that He wanted to save us from must be ominously real and awfully horrendous. It is called Eternal Damnation. Think of all the people who fly in the face of that rational deduction. Jesus Christ with all power as God at the command of His Will chose to remain hanging on a Cross until death for a reason. He allowed Himself to be tortured and executed for a reason. And, it is a serious one; not for His sake, but for ours. It is an awful moment, one of horror, when a soul realizes that they have deliberately rejected this King and have dismissed their every opportunity for the redemption of their soul. They experience themselves plummeting; yes, the gravity of the unseen, forever into the abyss of Hell. Jesus said, "*You are my friends if you do what I command you.*" [*John 15:14*] And, He also said, "*And then will I profess unto them, I never knew you: depart from me, you that work iniquity.*" [*Matthew 7:23*] These two Bible passages show that each person has a part to play in the ultimate outcome of their own lives before His mighty judgment. What did He command us to do to remain His friends? To love as He loved in His Sacrifice for the redemption of humankind; to declare the truths of His unseen Kingdom as He declared them; make disciples of all nations, clothe ourselves in faith, hope, charity, prudence, temperance, fortitude and justice; to rebuke evil as He rebuked it and not to scandalize the children; and perform the works of mercy. And, what are the works of iniquity? All of them come from a corrupt frame of reference which seethes pride, envy, sloth, greed, gluttony, and lust; choosing the seen at the expense of the unseen, creating idols and ghosts that steal away our devotions, those things that destroy our purity and identification with Him. These are the things that will make Him say, "I never knew you. You have no identity in Me." Iniquity is violating the Ten Commandments and the Beatitudes. Iniquity is scandalizing the perspective and purity of children. Iniquity is assaulting the Catholic Church. Iniquity is reveling in the worldly at the expense of the truths of the unseen. Look at our American culture compared to these criteria. People by the millions are risking the flames of hell by how they are living. We cannot walk through life committing sin with reckless abandon and believe we are simply too precious a creature to be thrown into hell. We cannot purposely kill our holy conscience, then claim a merciful amnesty based in a claim of ignorance on the last day. In order to change this, Jesus wants us to make room for Him in every way He desires, voluntarily and faithfully, again "Fiat," compliance with God in the framework of our beliefs, and then that we would respond as graceful children and jump into His Mother's arms. From there, She will protect us, nurture us and fly with us to the Cross to be bathed in Her Son's Sacred Blood for the final absolution of our souls. We will be saved at our final judgment from eternal damnation. Jesus wants us to adjust, to accept, to make room, to convert our thinking and the movements and motivations of our heart, to be the image of His vision through the realms of faith inside us. And, we find all of this through prayer where He reveals what resides in the depths of that great ocean of His Love that He placed within us at our conception. If we do not pray, we will not find this beauty. It is a great sifting and sorting process for nearly everyone because we are distracted by a culture that gives far too much credence and precedence to worldly, physical things. Too few are the visionaries; too few the poets; too few the lyricists and composers, as Oliver Windell Holmes wrote, "Alas for those that never sing, But die with all their music in them." We can compose a Paradise within us by letting Jesus reside there, as the poet Robert Herrick wrote, "Christ, He requires still, wheresoever He comes to feed or lodge, to have the best of rooms; Give Him the choice; grant Him the nobler part of all the house: the best of all is the heart."

    We are distracted from these overarching truths of Creation flowing at us from the unseen by all the material things that shimmer and glisten before our eyes. If worldliness is our priority, the truths of Eternity are obscured for us as a result. We will never find our Home there. There is no way around it, the walls are too high and the gate too narrow. [*Matthew 7:13-14*] Clarity of thought in relation to our holiness is not hard to understand. Vision is relevant to our every action. The concept is accepted in every sports team that we watch. Each athlete we see on our television screens, or in the stadia or arenas where we sit, has adapted their thinking to see and believe they will triumph. And, we revel in the great feats of athletic ability that flow from their convictions and sacrificial habits. Well, the grace of God flows prodigiously from our convicted belief in Him as well. And, conversion gives us the alignment with sacrifice that will grant us victory in Jesus' Resurrection. Great feats of grace are manifested through the power of His Holy Spirit within us. Look at Saint Teresa of Calcutta or Saint John Paul the Great. In the realms of universal truth, their lives prove they were historic athletes of universal grace whom we now call Saints. It was their hearts imbued with the great knowledge of the unseen realms that confirmed the immensity of their sacrificial lives in the flesh. Their indomitable faith provided them a portal of reference that expanded into God's High Kingdom, and our same invocation of belief is the door of commitment we likewise open to this supernal land. The Virgin Mary is assisting in rebuilding our holiness through the supernatural dimensions of the Holy Spirit. God's benefaction flows like a raging river through the belief that we invoke that She is truly interceding for us throughout the world. One might ask why should anyone believe this? I respond—because it's the truth! The Morning Star is in the sky! I believe truth, whether it is two plus two equaling four or the Mother of Jesus Christ appearing in the fertile heartland of the United States of America. Two plus two is easy to believe. Accepting Our Lady's guiding presence and divine words of motherly assistance requires the sacrifice of faith, although it is just as easy to accept. We should collect truths inside our heart no matter what it requires, and our Virgin Mother's miraculous intercession is Heaven's Crown Jewel for contemporary man before the final day. The truth of the unseen realms of God's Kingdom is flowing upon us and purifying everything in its path. Is it a new truth?,..no. The Bible testifies to it, and the Catholic Church has been fighting with teeth, toenails and tonsures to keep the Divine Revelation of Jesus Christ vibrant and beautiful before humanity for 2000 years through the faith of those whom She nurtures through Her sacrificial disciplines. This is what 265 successive Roman pontificates across two millennia have been all about. What on this physical planet seriously competes with that? It is the genealogy of the Truth.

Jesus Christ - Truth Beyond the Ages

It is a Rock that cannot be thrown away nor excavated from the planet which is rumbling and tumbling through time. It is a thrice-blessed monolith etched into history that is indelible. It is the same truth that has been shared from the beginning, from the moment Jesus stretched out His hands and allowed Himself to be Crucified. Now, in historical succession, these words are but an authentic witness to the same raging torrent of Truth, with the additional blessing of being confirmed by the miraculous assistance of His Immaculate Mother. She gives the Morning Star Over America its power. She is affected by neither the skeptic, the cynic, nor the antagonist, no matter how loudly these goats bleat. If these fussy peddlers of mediocrity do not wish to believe, then I tell them to walk on to their destiny, but don't utter a whimper when the veil is pulled back and the unseen truth convicts your pride as the source of your humiliation. God gives humanity power to be very strong in great holiness and righteousness, to be like Him, if we would approach our conversion and sanctification in the way of our great athletes. Saint Paul himself spoke about running the race and claiming the crown of victory in the likeness of Jesus, the same Love, the same sacrifice in which we participate as His brothers and sisters. Beaten, shipwrecked, stoned, imprisoned, threatened, mocked and martyred. What a man! What devotion to the truth! The impregnable Spirit of God staring down the world! And, history is filled with these heroic evangelists.

It has rarely been conceived by the mind of men the glory beyond this life that is awaiting those who grasp life like a Saint. I have seen an abundant measure of this splendor which was enough for me to surrender my life to Our Lady to assist Her in any way I can, and with all the strength I can muster. It is a final tragedy for a person to ignore God their whole life long, or lie to themselves that there is a new progressive gospel to live by that is absent the Holy Sacrifice, and then realize that they were deluded by their own pride and left themselves out of eternal joy. We do not accidently stumble into Heaven, but instead through the narrow gate robed in repentance of our sins after having committed to the Holy Sacrifice that unites us in His High Kingdom of the Saints. Jesus wishes His people to meet Him at our best with our baptismal garments unstained, arrayed with the loving powers of the heart, where our great devotions reside within that intimate personal solitude that He shares with us. And yes, it is also true that He is reserving for Himself that fateful day when He will appear in Glory before every eye where the Truth will extinguish everything that held out against Him. Arrogance, obstinance, faithlessness, pride, protestations; they are all such weaklings, headed for their reckoning. God can testify to far more truth than the wicked have rebuttal. Impenetrable, permanent and eternal mean just that. They are like a house of cards erected on a coffee table in reach of a toddler heading their way. But, this Baby is a King from a manger who will scatter their playing cards like confetti in His victory celebration. He could win over everything to Himself in the blink of an eye through His sheer presence. I have factually witnessed this majestic bearing, and know that unrepentant humankind is not ready to face Him. What power does arrogance, obstinance, pride or protestation have before the omnipotent majesty of the crucified and resurrected Lord of Creation? They will lash themselves to death. Faithlessness will be obliterated by eternal fact; and ominous clarity will descend on what Our Lord expected each of us to have become. Likewise, the beauty of our Heavenly Mother will consume them like a flame-thrower that in itself could transfigure the world if God were to unveil Her grace to everyone a single time in these exiled realms. Evil will be mowed down like a blast wave from a galactic meteor vaporizing a continent upon impact or a fusillade of a million nuclear weapons detonating upon a nation. This will be the Triumph of the Final Colossus. On that day, my words will be complete, my race finished, my witness fulfilled, my message culminated in Her maternal glory, even if I am at Her side in Heaven when that day arrives. I will rejoice in it nonetheless. The entire story of human history, all the Truth of the sky-faring universes, will resonate from the compassionate reflection in Her eyes. And, what will we see reflected in those eyes?—the King of all kings dying for His people on a gruesome Cross in a salvific spectacle that has become the center point of all beauty in the universe. Her gaze has been sculpted by the Crucifixion of Her Son, and Her Immaculate Heart clothed in Triumph in His Resurrection. God restrains unleashing this earth-shattering colossus so evildoers are given their opportunity for conversion because He possesses the greatest Divine Mercy before He administers His ultimate Justice. [*Matthew 24:30*] But, Justice will be served. Victory and triumph will be heralded. The final and ultimate definition of "Conquer" will be brought to the battlefield and unleashed. Jesus Christ created the element of time to grant humankind the opportunity to choose, to voluntarily exercise our faith, to show the great devotions of the heart, to repent, to submit ourselves to Him in every noble and sacrificial way, and to display our love for our Savior in its completeness through the unity He asks us to embrace within His Roman Catholic Church. He wants the greatest possibilities of our humanity, the greatest capacities, the greatest movements of our free will to be freely and passionately surrendered to Him out of love, in thanksgiving for the Holy Sacrifice that He endured for us to be allowed entrance into Paradise once again. He wants us to believe without seeing, just as He told Saint Thomas, when He said blessed are those who have not seen but believed. [*John 20:29*] Why blessed? Because our love for Him becomes our act, our unique possession, our testimony to allegiance, our perfect gift, conscripted by no one, but a fully self-generated act of personal identity which is beauty in His image. This is why our Creator conceived our free will and dispensed it to the human soul. Our lives must become a great declaration of "I love you" to Jesus. And, you cannot truly love Him without loving His Immaculate Mother. Who has greater love? Someone who surrenders themselves to another without question because they trust in them? Or, someone who holds out until they are convinced that there is profit in it for them; whether the sacrifice is worth their while?

    The Truth of Jesus' Death and Resurrection, the Revelation of this mighty Love of God, has processed through the centuries through messengers of the Gospel sent by the Holy Spirit; sinners like everyone else, but different in that they have made room in faith for the highest truths of an unseen Kingdom. Each of them converted to make room for Him. They cleaned their interior house, conformed their framework of thinking to the divine, and received absolution and affirmation from the Holy Spirit. Then, they were sent to share the grace they had received and proclaim the Good News of forgiveness and redemption in the Crucified Savior through whom their words were given power. There is no one who has proclaimed the Kingship of Jesus Christ and testified to the Bread of Life from the sacred hands of Catholic priests who has not reoriented their thoughts to accept Him; and each thereafter has been fortified and assisted by the graces of the Holy Spirit. Every one of us is a sinner who is just a simple person who can stumble, but are nonetheless commissioned to respond and communicate the extraordinary graces that are personally given to us as members of the Body of Christ. And

The Final Colossus - In Battle Array

so it is here, at this moment, through this venue of the written testimony that we are laying before the world. So you see, if we function by only accepting what we can see, instead of further recognizing the great moral movements of the heart, the great devotions, and the vision provided by virtue for the refinement of the soul, those places where God does His finest work, we remain separated from all the Truth that propagates toward us from the unseen realms, leaving us to ultimately reject all Truth. How is this so? Because by rejecting the miraculous and mystical operations of the Holy Spirit, we thereafter sterilize all other truths we do believe, rendering them just words incapable of supporting our faith to respond to God when He calls. If we revel in our skepticism and pound our pride-filled chests, we will never have the footing to accept anything from the unseen, even to the point of unreasonably demanding miracles of confirmation before we will believe anybody trying to reveal the grace of God to us. It reminds me of a comical story I heard one time where a man was standing by a lake amidst a group of people when he took off running across the water. Everybody standing nearby was shocked at witnessing a seemingly miraculous feat of a person running on water, but not sinking. But, when the guy rejoined the group, he whispered to his friend, "I just knew where the rocks were." He knew the unseen truth of where his support lie, but to everyone else it looked as if it was an event that could not be believed. None of them could imagine walking out across the water as they had just witnessed. Our Holy Mother told me that it is much like two people witnessing the Miracle of the Sun at Fatima in October of 1917, and one turning to the other and saying, "Wow, did you see that?" And, the other responded, "I don't know." Then, the first says, "Neither did I." If we have ever contemplated for ourselves what our response would have been to Jesus had we been in the boat with Peter when He called him forth to stand beside Him upon the waves, then now is the time to face that beckoning call through the Most Blessed Virgin Mary. Come stand beside Her in union with the Church. Fear nothing and brave the winds of derision and the depths of hatred that will storm against your conviction.

Now, after all this discussion, can we see that if a person has been raised without the awareness to believe in the reality of graces flowing from the unseen realms, who has been left to wolves who have devoured their innocent frame of reference, that they would now also shut-out all the possibilities that

God might use to reveal Himself to them? Would they not be incapable of accepting any messenger of the Gospel, or what any Saint ever tried to share, or any miracle that was ever reported, or any mystical dogma the Church preserves, or anyone else who tries to convince them that God is real and is asking for their faithfulness too? Can we see how the mystical knowledge of God that they might have accepted has instead been overwhelmed by the worldliness of doubters who defined a confining prison cell as their frame of reference? Have they not had unholy ghosts welcomed upon their perspective when they should have had confident wisdom affirmed atop their reservations instead? We can see examples of this everywhere we look. And, how does God address this situation? Well, He allows miraculous intercession to pierce this darkness with such mystical audacity that it leaves even the esteemed hierarchies pondering the monumental nature of what might be occurring in the vineyard left under their stewardship. The Holy Spirit acts to jostle everyone to an awakening, knowing He will be greeted by multitudes who are prepared to do nothing more than process it through their thinking in a way to reject His gifts as easily as they can with the affirmation of an entire chorus of other lost individuals who are stumbling around in the secular darkness. I repeat again, a majority can be a pretty lost group of individuals at times. Jesus spoke about it as the blind leading the blind. [*Luke 6:39*] Take the appearances of the Blessed Virgin Mary in Medjugorje in Bosnia-Herzegovina which have been occurring every day since June 24, 1981. Nearly four decades, every day, and it is an irrelevant event to the media organizations on this planet and most people who sit in the pews of their congregations every Sunday. Sometimes I wonder what the purpose of media organizations is if this earthshattering news is not worthy of their attention. They would be more inclined to report space aliens communicating with NASA than accept that the heavens may actually be communicating with the Earth through the appearances of the Mother of God across this planet. While they are staring at the front yard, wondering when everyone is going to show up for their party, Jesus and His Mother are celebrating with the faithful in the backyard, feasting on finest fare. And yet, they claim to be guardians, disseminators and analysts of the societal truth of historical human events. They are instead self-deluded, living a profitable deception of their own capitalist making. They are the epitome of those who believe their own press, even when no one truly united with the Kingdom of

The Final Colossus - In Battle Array

Heaven would concur. Jesus Christ and His Mother would love to speak to millions of people every night through their television programming where they could resurrect a veritable paradise on this Earth if they were allowed to do so. But, the King and Queen of Heaven have found it virtually impossible to penetrate the secularized void of these media empires and whom these pontificating news idols believe themselves to be. They are distracted by the secular religion of politics. Many ask why God does not reveal Himself more apparently to them and force a recognition of Himself so their careers would display some morsel of eternal value. Our Holy Mother says, *"In due time...but, for now, are My daily apparitions in Medjugorje for over three decades not enough? Is My speaking to My two faithful sons in the United States for over 25 years not enough? Tell Me what sacrifice will be enough, and I will find a child to endure it for you in the image of My Crucified Son so that you may come to believe."* Nearly one thousand major media organizations in the United States of America were sent a beautiful pamphlet describing the momentous events of the appearance of the Queen of Heaven as the Morning Star Over America in their nation. Further, they were each sent a press release stating that the Bishop of the Catholic Diocese of Springfield in Illinois had created an ecclesial commission to study the works. But, what has been their collective response? The miraculous intercession of the Queen of Heaven is mere flotsam to them. Let's face it, it is not that they do not know, it is that the Truth was repelled as it attempted to scale the ramparts of their worldly frame of reference. They rejected outright and feel justified in doing so because they see themselves as being the esteemed gatekeepers of the American consciousness and the voice of the Republic. The Mother of Jesus says they truly have no voice of any significance before the Throne of God. They mistakenly believe they are the deciders of the frame of reference for His High Kingdom, along with the vineyard plot of this great nation which He owns. She says they do not speak for the Almighty Father; and She also believes that they should get off His Throne and let the real King sit down. They are posturing themselves for the Second Coming of the Messiah where they will be taken by surprise, thrown into terrifying disarray, wondering why such a celebrated cohort as themselves was not notified in advance. They will plead, asking why someone did not alert them to the signs of the times. Oh yes, they will find themselves scooped on that day...into the coal shovels of Saint Michael and His Angels, and heaved into the blazing furnace of God's judgement where they will be either purified or condemned. It will be their decision, and oh what a difficult one it will be. The phrase, "We were not required to believe..." will have a terrible ring that will be drowned out by the sound of their sizzling souls. Those sentiments will be revealed to be nothing more than indifference from a lukewarm minimalist whom God declared He would spit from His mouth. [*Revelation 3:16*] But, the just will rejoice in *John 3:16*. I have always wondered what kind of person lets the words "we do not need..." pass their lips, be they from pagan or Prelate. It pierces the Immaculate Heart of God's Queen like a searing sword. But, She is compassionate, long-suffering and understands how difficult it is for Her children to have faith and to believe against so many influences of darkness, deception and doubt. If the world cannot believe a child sent to them by the Queen of Heaven, there is not a Christian with the standing to be believed by anyone. And, in that, the Great Commission is dead. God is apparent before everyone in His works and in the faith we see across the holy realms of our culture, truly in the Mystical Body of His Church. He resides here, but He is willfully relegated to the backwater by the secular world, to the barren stable so men do not have to engage the battle for the truth of an unseen Kingdom to come, but whose truth is already here.

The Final Colossus - In Battle Array

Chapter 5
The Fruit of Certainty
Faith Brought to Life

"In all ages, men have been divinely instructed in matters expedient for the salvation of the elect...and in all ages, there have been persons possessed of the spirit of prophesy, not for the purpose of announcing new doctrines, but to direct human actions."
St. Thomas Aquinas
Summa: 2:2:174: Res. et ad 3

Let's go back now to the reason that one would offer the frame of reference ensconced in this manuscript. Personally, it is easy to recognize that the miraculous intercession of the Virgin Mary might seem like a rather tall tale, like a lake that can't be walked on. Most people have never engaged this possibility before, being influenced as they are by a secularized framework of thinking that is barren as a desert and impenetrable as a miser's wallet. They don't consider God or anything unseen, let alone anyone from unseen realms actually speaking to anyone. God is a fanatical delusion of weak-minded people, they say. They've acquired this void of thinking from others through life, from many whom they might respect. They're firmly disposed to reject the possibility of miraculous intercession being true because it hasn't happened to them. Well, so much for their faith. They have too much to lose because they know most people will begin to look upon them in the same way they look at those who are openly committed to their faith. Vast majorities of people are enculturated to react this way in our contemporary day. It is easy. It is a safe approach that requires no faith whatsoever. Who needs faith if you're never going to jump? Who needs to endure the mocking as a religious zealot or a delusional nut? Who needs to be laughed at as a naive dolt? Who needs to risk respectability and influence? It is ironic to realize who the weak-minded truly are. Saint Paul recognized the phenomenon of being a fool for Christ; and he reveled in it, knowing that he would be vindicated in an ultimate victory that would last forever. Faithlessness requires no adjustment, no accommodation, no conversion of thought or expansion in the mind. It requires no courage, no devotion, and no sacrifice. Faithlessness is worthy of no merit. It commands no respect, offers no loyalty, reflects no heroism and cowers before the challenge between life and death. Summarily rejecting claims of the miraculous intercession of our Virgin Mother, especially when they glaringly possess the attributes of authenticity, never leaves one interiorly with the peace of God, although Our Lady did tell me that the solitude in a dead soul is often mistaken for peace. Doubters and skeptics sidestep the sacrifice of themselves when their faith would better winnow their reservations to reveal the authenticity where allegiance takes on its sheen of worthiness. It is the soul that comes to know through the powers of the heart. For my brother and me, our declarations represent truthful resolve because we were allowed to experience the unseen that came to us in all its purity from behind the veil. We testify truthfully to the wisdom of our maternal mentor, knowing with whom we speak. I could say that the sun is in the sky or that if you jumped off the nearest cliff you will either be seriously injured or die. And, those statements would possess as much certitude as our declaration that the Queen of Heaven Herself has dispensed and nurtured our work, despite our weaknesses. If in the midst of our work there are mechanical errors or lapses in our descriptions caused by the frailties of human communication, surely ascribe them to my brother and me; but be awakened and even astonished by the beatific content woven into our witness that no man could have generated; and surely again, not my brother and me. We recognize the dilemma between believing and being duped that haunts others, and we have great empathy for that vulnerable position. We realize that there are far more cases of people claiming connection to the unseen who are mentally ill, delusional, seeking celebrity, lying for profit or who are possessed by evil. Satan created this dilemma with the very first lie he ever told in the Garden. He manifested the first quandary, the first decision between truth and falsehood. He generated the initial moment of indecision between goodness and evil. Before that moment, we were innocent and trusting as the tiniest children because only God reigned. Nonetheless, as unique as our claim may seem, this is not one of his deceptions through any method, force or accident that he might employ. Not this time. Not through the Morning Star Over America. This time, there is certainty. Indecision has been banished, and obedience is the order of our response. Our witness is rooted in the veracity of God; and the works that my brother and I have recorded over the past quarter century are the evidence, the best we were able to foster into a contemporary communicative style and the written word. We have attempted to describe the indescribable. Our literary testament is the confirming fruit that anyone with an honest conscience can review to help them bridge their own gap of faith into the body of unseen truths that God wishes them to know. We are scientists, per se, of the spiritual realms who are telling the world that the Earth revolves around Jesus Christ and the Roman Catholic Church in which He is seated as its King in the Most Blessed Sacrament of the Altar.

The truth remains—a very precious gift has been bestowed by Jesus upon us, for all of us. We have been given the gift to recognize the priority of the unseen through our open communication with His Mother, the Virgin Mary, so that everyone may hear what She believes to be distinctive between truth and falsehood. Likewise, I have been taken to stand before Our Lord in an incontrovertible way. He is... There are no words. It is impossible for me to put such consuming love and omnipotent majesty into syllables that would describe Him worthily. The closest I can come is to hold up a Crucifix, say nothing, and allow you to gaze upon it until His Majesty dawns in your soul. Mount Calvary is the moment of the "All." It is the best one can do. Our Blessed Lord told me to listen and obey His Immaculate Virgin Mother in all that She would relate, to be strong for Him, and that He was proud of me. Thus, I have simply tried to learn from Her, retain Her wisdom, and conform to everything She has ever said to me, and then record it accurately for everyone else as I was asked to do, with purpose and inflection. Being no more than a child with a paint set of water colors, I was asked to reproduce a Rembrandt whose original was painted by the hands of the Master. And, it happened miraculously like those coloring books that only need water applied, and the colorful picture mysteriously appears to the child who giggles at their accomplishment. Yes, that is the analogy. My brother and I only applied the waters of our baptism, and the picture of God miraculously appeared as Her artwork. She is our Heavenly Mother, the Matriarch of Humanity. She is the Queen of Heaven and our Morning Star Over America. She is the Final Colossus. The Almighty Father wishes us to honor and obey Her, just as any father wishes his children to obey their mother. This is part of the family of

God; it is part of the mystery of our redemption. Jesus spoke to all the ages of humanity from the Cross before He died. He knew His words would be recorded in Sacred Scriptures and disseminated throughout time. Some of His most important and valuable sentiments He left for His final moments to place the capstone on His salvific legacy. And, what did He reserve for that moment? He asked us to recognize His Mother as our own. He said, "Behold your Mother."

During the course of our Christian responsibilities, my brother and I expect the entire spectrum of reactions from hostility to childlike acceptance. We have seen it far too often already. We recognize the human condition. We recognize that faith is a challenge. We are also prepared for there to be far more rejection than acceptance. The propagation of the Holy Gospel inevitably engages us in a profoundly personal way. The Truth confronts us like an immovable rock that we cannot circumvent. Human pride abhors definitive statements because they confront us with only two options: to surrender or fight; accept or reject. It is a battle between the flesh and the spirit. Some believe that maintaining a stoic indifference is a prudent third option, but Our Lady says that this, too, is a conspicuous act of rejection. The definitive truth inconveniences us and shakes our world and the estimation that we have of ourselves. It alters our path if we are not moving in union with the One it represents. Negative reactions are expected. It would be like expecting a baby not to cry the first time they hear the concussion of a thunderclap of lightning or the report of exploding fireworks. Sometimes it is hard to have faith because we have to sacrifice something in order to come into communion with what it declares. And, that something is usually the way we see life and ourselves positioned in it—again, our frame of reference. When the truth presents itself before us, no matter the way, it usually wrenches us around, makes us sit up and take notice, and allows us to see ourselves in a wholly new way in a land that has now become somewhat out of our control, and even foreign to us. When God shocks us with the clarification of the truth, there are as many responses as there are people. It is inevitably this way; He is God, and this is not Heaven; and we are not Saints…yet. It's been the turbulent nature of the propagation of the Gospel Truth from the beginning. We are required to change, to convert, to accept the highest unseen truths so that we become more like Him. He wishes that we would have fluently learned these truths from our cradle, but societies and human sin have caused this not to be the case for many. Nonetheless, He wants our transformation into the children He created us to be. But, if we are not yet oriented to accept how He works, His interventions to awaken us will be shocking. We will be caught off guard much like believing we are alone in a darkened room when the lights suddenly come on and all of our closest friends shout, "Surprise!" Who would have dreamed up a burning bush that wasn't consumed or a virgin bearing a son, not to mention the irony of the Crucifixion of an unrecognized Messiah becoming the greatest triumph ever known to human history through His Resurrection a couple sunrises later? Or, leading the Israelites out of Egypt after miraculous signs before an Egyptian pharaoh, the parting of the Red Sea and destroying his armies in those fathoms. Or, a shepherd boy with one smooth stone striking down a goliath warrior and saving a nation. Talk about shocking. It is awesome to consider what our God has done. But, what if David's courageous zeal for the God of Israel had not advanced into the tides of destiny before his king, commanders and countrymen who were trembling in fear; a simple shepherd boy stepping forward amidst seasoned warriors to meet the enemy of God's Chosen People head-on while the rest were dithering in fear? We should be able to recognize from just these few things that it is really not a great leap to believe that Jesus would allow His Mother to speak to humanity in miraculous ways down through the centuries in order to help us become the intrepid children He wishes us to be. King David, pray for us. No one should deny Jesus the right to work miracles in someone's life through His Virgin Mother. Our lives are a confirmation that He does. How would it be otherwise? Who would possess the power to convince an entire world walking in darkness to come into the Light if not validated by divine wonders? The Bible does say that the Holy Spirit would be upon us and grant signs. The question is what will we allow the Holy Spirit to do that will matter? Both my brother and I have seen the Immaculate Virgin and have spoken with Her for years as a way of preparation and maturation. She is alive and breathing. We have seen the light of beauty by which She is clothed. She is not some ethereal misty vision of vague mysterious poise. But, rather a living, breathing Lady of unimaginable grace who is more alive than any of us. She lives in the part of Creation that is awake, while we are either groggy or fully asleep. She possesses an unequaled station in Heaven above every other woman, above every other creature. This Woman Clothed with the Sun is the Mother of our Savior. She has suffered as no other woman has suffered while participating in human redemption from the depths of Her beautiful soul. The true Mother Church of Christianity has always manifested the truth about the station She possesses and the veneration She deserves. And, I intimately know why after seeing Her maternal glory. Those who relegate Her to being nothing more than another sinner are blasphemers, plain and simple. And, I am unconcerned whether they are offended by my words. Defend my Mother, I will! Rebuke them, I must! Their radical delusions are a cause for sorrow, and much suffering is heaped upon the innocent by their error because the truth remains—the Virgin Mary is the Queen of Heaven and the Matriarch of all humanity; the most gentle, beautiful, pure, and compassionate creature that God ever created; blessed above all women as Scripture says. All generations shall call Her blessed, at least those that will be saved. Calling Her insignificant in human redemption is a mighty big error to swallow at one's final judgement.

With that said, all of this is probably shocking for many; that is unless you are familiar with Christian history and the extraordinary lives of the Catholic Saints throughout the ages. Not everything is a pious legend as many Protestants and pagans like to boast. Too many like to claim that everything they don't have the faith to believe in is a myth, or they diminish it to mere symbolism of some sort, just as they do with the Bread of Life actually being the real Food of Salvation from the Catholic Altar. My brother and I would never consider ourselves equals with any of the great Saints. We are far more sobered by our weaknesses than that. We are just like everyone else, moving through life exercising an orthodox faith passed to us from the Saints trying to show Jesus that we love Him, and that we wish to obey Him in the things He has asked of us through His Immaculate Mother. We have conceded with joy to every sacrifice that She has asked us to engage. We recognize the Great Commission, as every Christian must, to strive for the holiness that every Saint has exhibited by example and to share the same message of the Holy Gospel that they shared, come what may. We can petition the assistance of the Saints every day. They are allowed great leeway to assist us in our needs. Catholics call it "intercession." They can reach and console anyone they wish they could have touched when they were on Earth. They love us. And, the devil cannot impede them now. They pray for us. They petition God for the graces and gifts we need; and God responds because He loves us all. Some of those responses are their being allowed to appear and speak in special circumstances to their brothers and sisters who are still on the Earth. The testimonies to miraculous appearances of angels, Saints, departed loved ones, signs and coincidental events are evidence too conspicuous to dismiss. The Virgin Mary's many miraculous intercessions are the crown jewels of this assistance from the Communion of Saints in the most prolifically supernatural ways. Catholics even select a special patron Saint upon the day of our reception of the Sacrament of Confirmation as an extraordinary advocate whom we can call upon throughout life. This is not to diminish the great companion that each of us has in our own unique guardian angel who is charged with the commission to assist and protect our soul in every way we might allow. These dimensions of angelic and saintly intercession help us understand reality more clearly through the true essence of our lives, not only through the legacies left or the writings deposited in history for us to read, but through the pure intercessory prowess of these benefactors who live now in the realms of glory, perfectly united with God. While we are separated from them by a veil due to our sins, they are sinless, and thus have no veil. They are no longer subject to the consequences of sin in a mortal exile which they have conquered. I refer to how God chose to interact with the Saints during their age so we might better accept what He continues to do in our times. Miraculous intercession has very little to do with anything any person has done. It is far more about sacrifice than it is reward. No sinner deserves it. None of us can summon it at will; we cannot demand it, nor self-generate it. It occurs as a gift from a loving God who dispenses His generosity where He wills. He sees the world in need of special grace; He sees the conversion that needs to occur; He hears the petitions of His Mother whom He loves; and Her miraculous intercession is His response to Her. He goes looking for a soul with the love to receive the burden of the Cross. He then fortifies the faith of that soul to sustain His gift the best they can amidst what is usually terrible opposition, derision and suffering because it is hard for people to believe. God looks throughout the world and says, "Where is my rock that I can throw in humanity's path?" And then, a faithful child receives miraculous intercession and the rock is manifested; the rock of Saint Peter's Faith.

The Final Colossus - In Battle Array

So, we are back to the concept of how the truth engages people in their soul. Our Lord is looking for this engagement to be an eclipsing phenomenon or overshadowing that fluently permeates and consumes our soul, rather than a collision of destruction such as two planets colliding. Nonetheless, Jesus said, *"Everyone will hate you because of Me."* [Mark 13:13] The world hates the Rock placed in its path. It hates Truth. Jesus' Mother has one purpose. Every act, every sentiment, each of Her movements is intended for one outcome—To glorify Her Son. And, that glory is in every redeemed child who will give their life to Him in faith. We are the spoils of His Victory; everything He died for. His Mother advances Her Son's Glory by helping us accept Him as the Messiah and gathering us around Her in prayer in preparation for the colossal storm that will close out the ages. From there, She will escort us to Him in repentance to receive His final absolution. She will teach us to love Him, and will unite us at One Table of Faith so that we may be saved as one family into everlasting life. This is the great truth of the unseen that cannot be stopped, which is being consolidated into oneness at this very moment. Everyone is being called to this great convocation of deliverance through the words of the Gospel and the beckoning of Christ's successive Vicars. Jesus and His Mother love us with the same love, and their Love is infinite. They proved it on Calvary, and I have seen it and experienced it, and I'm asked to share it the best I can. It is beyond linguistic ability to describe, or any of our capacities to fully encompass. But, it is not beyond the power of the heart to experience, to imitate and to share, if we would orient ourselves according to the teachings of the Roman Catholic Church. Uniting with the Original Apostolic Church and accepting all Her salvific truths is required in order to come to that full perfection and ultimate unity with Christ Crucified. Only in the Catholic Church do we meet "Macula non est in te,"—Stain is not in Thee! We must accept the Holy Sacrifice of the Mass and receive the authentic Bread of Life. [John 6:53]—or we will not have life in us. It is better to believe these truths now because we will most definitely believe them later, or we will never see Heaven's golden streets. Even the demons believe the Dogmas of the Catholic Church, but they hate them and obscure and slander them at every opportunity given them. Our devotion to the Truth of the Church is not necessarily about submission, or discipline, or obediences, or penances, or conversions although each of these is a sparkle twinkling from the diamond of our convictions. It is

The Fruit of Certainty

about sacrificial love and spiritual purification so that we can maintain composure in that love, and unity in the Body of Christ where we share that love. One of the greatest acts of sacrificial love is to tell humanity the truth; we must proclaim the supremacy of the Roman Catholic Church, declare the responsibilities of the Holy Gospel, and effect the corporal and spiritual works of mercy. If there is sacrificial love and an ultimate desire for unity in that love, there will be conversions, and self-discipline, and harmony brought by fraternal faithfulness. And, there will be penances and sacrifices offered until all become one in Him. Penance and sacrifice are nothing more than the openness of the heart to suffer for the salvation of men. If we do nothing else, it would behoove us to remember all those throughout the world who are suffering horrible lives because humanity remains unconverted to the Truth of Christ Jesus. If we have an ounce of Love in our heart, this body of suffering humanity should be the mortifying sign that beckons us to greater faith, heroic abandonment, impenetrable confidence, full-throated evangelization, and unyielding hope—and true belief that the Morning Star Over America has come into our midst. We are witnessing across the globe the single greatest outpouring of maternal grace that a broken humanity could have ever envisioned. Let us give the heavens our reciprocal fiat in the image of our Heavenly Mother. Then, God's visible Kingdom will come to the Earth once again.

The Final Colossus - In Battle Array

Chapter 6
How Do I Pray?
Fiat Maximus!

A common English rhetorical idiom, "elephant in the room," is often employed in situations where something that is uncomfortably apparent goes unaddressed by everyone involved due to the inherent risks and discomfort that have to be endured if one acknowledges the obvious. Case in point, fanatical secular socialists have perpetuated the greatest "de-structuring" of Christian virtue in the most profoundly blessed nation in history, and the "elephant in the room" is that they believe the social chaos of the last sixty years has nothing to do with them. If there has ever been a time where one might have found it implausible that Jesus would be unable to find faith on the Earth when He returns [*Luke 18:8*], this might be the bone-chilling "ah-ha" moment of realization for them. Grand social architects, delusional progressives, political publicans and the materialistic empire builders unleashed by secular humanist self-glorification refuse to acknowledge that nothing in their failing void measures up to Roman Catholicism as the ultimate sustainer of human civilization. Not just some generic christianity, per se, as it has been splintered into thousands of ideological factions by those who protest the Sacrifice of Unity, but Roman Catholicism alone. It remains one, united, universal and holy in every culture of the world through the Chair of Saint Peter and the Succession of Pontiffs who have taken their seat on that Throne. All the progressive revolutionaries and their vacuous ideologies, each in their time have failed, just as the current naive utopian rendition slips from their fingers through the terminal failures they have wrought upon the hallowedness of our country. Perhaps the great Pulitzer Prize winning historian, Will Durant, said it best in his massive 11 volume work entitled, The Story of Civilization. He summarized with concise honesty what he had studied regarding what lie in the wake of the Protestant Reformation when he wrote:

"Your emphasis on faith as against works was ruinous...for a hundred years charity almost died in the centers of your victory...You destroyed nearly all the

schools we had established, and you weakened to the verge of death the universities that the Church had created and developed. Your own leaders admit that your disruption of the faith led to a dangerous deterioration of morals both in Germany and England. You let loose a chaos of individualism in morals, philosophy, industry, and government. You took all the joy and beauty out of religion...you condemned the masses of mankind to damnation as 'reprobates,' and consoled an insolent few with the pride of 'election' and salvation. You stifled the growth of art, and wherever you triumphed, classical studies withered. You expropriated Church property to give it to the state and the rich, but you left the poor poorer than before, and added contempt to misery... You rejected the papacy only to exalt the state: you gave to selfish princes the right to determine the religion of their subjects... You divided nation against nation, and many a nation and city against itself; you wrecked the international moral checks on national powers, and created a chaos of warring national states... You claimed the right of private judgment, but you denied it to others as soon as you could... Every man becomes a pope, and judges the doctrines of religion before he is old enough to comprehend the functions of religion in society and morals... A kind of disintegrative mania, unhindered by any...authority, throws your followers into such absurd and violent disputes that men begin to doubt all religion, and Christianity itself would be dissolved...were it not that the (Catholic) Church stands firm amid all the fluctuations of opinion and argument...the one fold that can preserve religion." [Durant, Will, pp. 936-937, The Reformation, (volume 6 of 10-volume The Story of Civilization, 1967), New York: Simon & Schuster, 1957.], [Dave Armstrong, The Protestant Revolt: Its Tragic Initial Impact, 2007]

This describes much of the contemporary American society, does it not? The beast continues to devour. Godless people are not very good architects of a Kingdom for human hearts, while our culture labors beneath the fracturing forces of their conflict theories that they wield to satisfy their passions for proletariat revolution. This destructive pluralism that gives venue to division and immorality over unity and virtue has flourished from the divisions of Christianity in the 16th century. Faith and fraternity faltered in the midst of pride and sin. There are elephants in all kinds of rooms proving this to be true. Secular ideologies do not possess the framework of wisdom that humanity can build upon because its adherents are oblivious to the plans of their Creator. The misfortune, sadness, inequity, hopelessness and suffering, along with the greed, opulence, and elitism that we see, is the tangled old-growth result of wild human souls who have been deprived the cultivation and nurturing of the Eternal Truth. The resulting spiritual vacuum, void of any hierarchy of virtue, self-restraint or sacrifice, becomes a post-apocalyptic wasteland where the perceptions, perspectives and principles that would prosper a nation's righteousness are extinguished before they can ever be laid in the sacred cradle of the human heart. Meaning, purpose and fulfillment are then lost in the typhoon of wilful immorality that is scratching and screeching with the wild selfishness of a feral cat. Absent the spiritual light of Jesus Christ, havoc and desolation consume our social circles, societies and nations, leaving us face to face with the specter of war that would bring suffering to a crescendo in the annihilation of continents. Be not fooled, for this is where humanity is racing. This is why the Most Blessed Virgin Mary has been allowed to step into the arena, onto the battlefield in beatific array, in the pause before the dogs of the final war slip their chains. She says that the elephant in the room is that human civilization will be healed only through conversion to Jesus Christ the Messiah who will restore the human heart from where all goodness, peace and eternal identity flow. And, we know it! Two things serve the reorientation of the heart, and Our Lady speaks to them both. Prayer and suffering. The act of prayer signifies hope in one who prays. And, not just any prayer or incantation. Prayer and spiritual contemplation must begin in the Heart of the Greatest Love, which is the Sacred Heart of Jesus Christ. Intoning mantras and processing in circles hurling rocks are irrelevant, absent devotion to God's Only-Begotten Son who is Christ and Messiah for all mankind. And then, there is suffering if we forsake this meditative conversation with the wisdom of God through prayer. His wisdom would tell us that we are far too enamored with ourselves, and that our high self-estimation is more of a delusion than a tempered fact. So, the process of self-awareness must commence in earnest if we are to find peace.

  Engaging humanity in our age requires clarifying admonishment and rhetorical altercation because brash contemporary egos are dominating the discourse in our pressure-cooker humanist society. Our culture has been bolted down by its hypnotizing gatekeepers with the lid of secular atheistic intellectualism. Additionally, the protesting biblical exegesis of the past 500 years has extorted the grand bargain of ecumenical compromise, absent unity in the Sacrifice, and locked in a simpleton ideology of pastoral ego worship. We have moved into a time of outright apostasy where too many believe Christianity means everyone simply "getting along" in the pseudo-peaceful simmer of mediocrity while condoning self-possessed hedonism, rather than engaging the righteous battle for our elevation as a species worthy of being united with the perfections of Heaven. "Get along" simply means accommodating petty delusions, lest the protestors and persecutors throw a tantrum and dismiss themselves from any fraternity in grace. Our Lady says, fear not, proclaim the Truth and let them decide their destiny! Jesus did not allow the Truth to be held hostage by threats of walking away. He simply asked whether the rest were going to leave Him too. [*John 6:67*] Christ the King is not the unprincipled effeminate coward that the many androgynous-minded renegades in our day would have everyone believe. He testified to the heroic Patriarchy of the Father who sent Him to engage the world for its deliverance from sin and darkness. Delusional sinners have assumed the audacity to define the King of all kings in their own wretched image by stealing the historical integrity of His Sacred Life, Death and Resurrection and twisting it into rancid narratives to justify their sins, hailing a Divine Mercy that, on the final day, they will never accept. Satan could burn every Bible on the planet, and Roman Catholicism would not even blink on its march into the eternal embrace of God because the beauties of Christ burn as the very Heart of His Original Church where they were ignited in the beginning, while Protestantism would die in the holocaust of those pages. Brotherhood does not mean placating agitators, activists, and antagonists for fear of being chided as divisive or unmerciful. Every one of these people would have hated the authority of the Holy Spirit invoked by Saint Paul. And, this great Saint would have taken each of them to task with even greater fervor. Our spiritual ascendance as a human species has stagnated because we are pandering to a critical mass of sinners who are too selfish to make the journey. There seems to no longer be an authentic evangelization of the Truth of the majesty of Jesus Christ because we are afraid of the Cross that our detractors will attempt to place us upon. We are afraid of their scowls and taunts. We are terrified of the storming rhetorical terrorism and public defamation that they will hail against us as their weapons of retaliation. What more could the Son of God have done to reveal the perfection of humanity than to engage the darkness, loving us so much that He would unleash the Light of Truth in the face of all odds and authorities, knowing His horrific execution was inevitable? The moral story of Christian civilization has been hijacked by liars who want the Savior of Humankind to be one among many so they do not have to proclaim the singularity and sovereignty of His Kingship and the imperatives of human sanctification; and thus, they will never enter Heaven. I tell you, no one comes to the Father but through Christ the King. [*John 14:6*] Christianity will always contain the central requirement of spiritual conversion and sacrificial love because people are sinners from the womb. Warped ideas about human justification have been pile-driven into the innocent psyche of our modern culture, leaving little room for the authentic articulation and emulation of the perfections of Christ that used to flourish as foundational maxims of our societal cohesion in the earlier times of cultural simplicity. Amidst the resulting turbulence of swirling ignorance and pontificating egoism, His innocent wisdom lives its passion enduring the throes of secular humanist relativists who try without authority or legitimacy to convince everyone that they have not produced the chaotic nightmare in which we find ourselves presently submerged. There's that elephant again. The United States of America is gasping for the Truth to be spoken with authority. Jesus Christ wants us to hold our heads high in grace. We simply need our cowardice to get off the seat of influence within us so that the King of kings can sit down. Relativism means no principles, no honor, no devotion, no sacrifice and no life. Humanist means worship of the human ego above all spiritual principalities and powers. And, secular means godless. What a hellish broth of damnation and fire! Jesus Christ is truly a foreigner in a xenophobic land of proud and accomplished sinners. But, Christianity thrives too mystically to be destroyed, and the Cross stands too impenetrable and unimpeachable to be removed from history. Yet, the undeterred march of fanatical evildoers in the likes of J.R.R. Tolkien Orcs advances nonetheless to construct in vain a new paradigm of deliverance, absent Christianity, thereafter selling their delusions through every communication medium they are allowed to dominate. They are attempting to brand the Sacrificial Lamb of Christianity with their new gospel of atheistic inclusion. A progressive, Godless ideology vacated of the Holy Sacrifice is being preached that is an insult to the Crucifixion of Jesus Christ. [*2 John 1:9*] Indeed, if their supposed social justice credo for dividing up material possessions is all that really matters, then let them get on with trying to throw Jesus Christ's Sacrifice out of the world. They will then stand in horror at their hollow victory and what a mistake they have made in the darkness that will be brought upon the Earth! Then, the Resurrection will come with mighty power, deliverance and Glory! Sacred Scripture is eerily prophetic to have questioned, *"But when the Son of Man comes, will He find faith on the earth?"* [Luke 18:8] I tell you that we are staring the Crucifixion of the True Faith right in the eyes. It is being stripped from the world in the name of worshiping the corrupt humanity of sinners, lest they be offended. What a time for the truly Offended One to return!

Our beloved Virgin Mother has asked me to be as descriptive and open as possible with the thoughts and sentiments that She has matured within me so that others can find stable identification and amplification with what She wishes to accomplish in them. She told me that there would be multitudes who will want to know what my brother and I think; most for the purpose of attacking us when we refuse to validate their errors. But, it will bring Light! She said that we will stare the world down together. There will be others who will wish with all their hearts to know Jesus and Her better. She said that multitudes will be inspired to compare their sense of awareness with the plateau of vision by which She has taught my brother and me to engage the world every day. Many will find great solace and affirmation upon realizing they have been in holy communion with the heavens all along through their faithful allegiance to the Catholic Church, while others will be shocked at just how far away they truly are. Most of the rest will do no more than raise their protests, shaking their fists and their Bibles with cursing and blasphemy dripping from their tongues against Heaven's Queen and the messengers whom She asked to announce Her introduction to them. In truth, my days are not composed of worrying about what ground seems to have been ceded to evildoers or what material success any cultural idols believe they are achieving. I instead engage a deep sense of urgency for their awakening. Very little time is left for them to effect their conversion, where in its absence or omission they will face a reckoning that will annihilate their pride and thrust them before the eternal judgement of their soul. *"And if anyone hears my words and does not observe them, I do not condemn him, for I did not come to condemn the world but to save the world. Whoever rejects me and does not accept my words has something to judge him: the word that I spoke, it will condemn him on the last day."* [John 12:47-48]

How Do I Pray? Fiat Maximus!

There are millions who are going to be taken by surprise by a Truth that is going to gouge heresy out of their souls like their fleshly organs being ripped from their bodies. Their arrogance will meet the "immovable" which will lay waste to their obstinance, leaving them prostrate upon the ground with their lungs heaving the dirt as the Majesty they rejected passes them by. They will pronounce eternal judgement upon their miserable lives. And there, face-down, naked and unconverted, they will consume the ultimate failure of existence wrought by their own selfish insolence. But, until that time of jubilation for us when all evil is defeated, I am sorrowful yet hopeful, knowing they still have a chance to be delivered from the scalding bath they are going to endure and the eternal justice they are going to reap; justice that they will have sown for themselves by lives of wanton and wilful sin. I live every day petitioning the Father that they be given the grace to convert their hearts and join the ranks of those who will live forever in Paradise. But, that grace resides in the proclamation of the truth and in conversion of their hearts into a state of communion with Christ. The Heavenly Hosts are pining to announce their jubilation should the conversion of a sinner come. There is more rejoicing in Heaven over one repentant sinner than for all the righteous who did not need repentance. [*Luke 15:7*] I pray daily and make my small sacrifices, keeping my thoughts upon them before the Throne of God, asking for the light from Christianity's Sacrifice to be enough to make them squint their eyes in wonderment at the beauty, and then, have them realize it is for them. I experience amazement at the magnitude of wilful blindness demonstrated by humanity before so much heavenly grace through our beloved Virgin Mother. Yet, there is nothing that would ever make me believe that the preceding decades of my life have been futile. I pray in hope that Our Lady will reach each wayward soul with Her immaculate grace, and that they would succumb to Her beauty. The Morning Star Over America will shine! Humanity has no more recognized Her beauty and power than it recognized the Savior of the world when He walked the Earth. We give intellectual lip service to this beauty and have never shed a tear over it. With God's grace, nothing can deter us from our responsibility to complete our lives in honor of Jesus and His Mother. Their beauty and love are just too great.

Our Blessed Mother engaged a contemplative exercise with me one day where She asked me to complete the sentence, "I hate..." My heart did not know what to write because the words "I hate" were so foreign to the relationship that we shared. I could not summon those two words in Her presence. In fact, She presented me with the sentence without audibly speaking the words Herself. After a bit, and not knowing how to finish the sentence, She completed the phrase for me. "I hate...nothing and no one." In other words, the very formation of the concept "I hate" has no place in us, even toward our enemies. This does not mean that one fails to feel colossal disdain or indignation at unrepented sins, flagrant blasphemy or horrific acts. Nor does it preclude a recognition of sinfulness or our rebuke of all that is unholy. No, rebuke is not hate, nor is it unkind. Our Lady is unconcerned about anyone's self-righteous entitlement to sin or the feelings they promote to deflect responsibility and otherwise manipulate others with their false victimhood. She knows that rebuke and admonishment are holy acts of love, the fruits of righteousness, and that too much suffering is occurring in the breach. We must never offer friendly affirmation to false fraternity at the expense of guiding another person out of their wickedness. Fear no one walking away. Case in point, my brother attended a job interview for a position within an ecumenical Christian council in our city in October 2010, being one of the final three candidates to be reviewed. During the interview surrounded by a boardroom filled with supposedly Christian council members, it became clear that the integrity of the organization's ecumenical bond was maintained by sacrificing their commitment to defend unborn human life because certain members of the board were pro-abortion. Timothy unilaterally concluded the interview, stating that such a position was beneath the dignity of any organization claiming to be Christian, and proceeded to dismiss himself. And, the Catholic Priest seated at the table who was a member of the board simply hung his head; probably more for being embarrassed that a fellow Catholic had insulted his colleagues than the fact that he had compromised his faith away for the opportunity for a false fraternity in a pale ecumenism. This priest met courage and conviction for Christ face-to-face, and he found himself wanting. We know righteousness when we see it. Hate is an altogether different state of darkness that is manifested from helplessness and impotence. Hence, one who hates has lost their communion with the power of Jesus. Our Lady does Her best to maintain and mold our dispositions in the vaulting strains of His Triumph and Resurrection through the magnificence of Her Queenship. I have experienced both in Her. Those whose names are written in the Book of the Living have never lost a battle. Evil has suffered such a humiliating defeat that there is only cause for joy. This is why we can laugh in the face of our oppressors. We may suffer, but vindication is ours. Once we embody the passion to love Jesus, fear of the Cross is diminished, even eliminated in His Divine Light. Lift high the Cross. Endure its sweet burden. Remember the Bible states that perfect love drives out fear, because fear has to do with punishment. And, if we conquer the fear of our own suffering, or what we will lose, or how the world will indict us, or what exile will be sentenced upon us, then every breath of our lives will be transformed into the spoils of our victory in Him.

   The key to the transformation of the soul and the elevation of the human spirit is prayer to Jesus Christ in union with His Mother, the Angels and the Communion of Saints. There is no such thing as plurality of religions in the Kingdom of God, but there is a definitive faith. Heaven is all unity in the Beatific Vision of one Sacred Heart. When we pray to Jesus during the Holy Sacrifice of the Mass, we are all the same. Our hearts are united there in the same Absolution. When I enter into prayer, my heart is raised upon a plateau of impenetrable confidence. Amazing confidence! It is as if the flesh is shed, indeed the whole mortal and physical world becomes overshadowed by the supernal realms. Our Holy Mother taught me not to grovel, but prepare to meet Jesus in humble adoration, as a warrior entering the throne room of the King, ready to give complete allegiance and stand at attention alongside the Archangels. My priorities are completely aligned; He is God and I am His beloved creation, an image of Himself as He sees me in His Divine Mercy. I actually feel a sense of invincibility in my spirit as if my soul extends beyond time itself in command of the attention of the heavenly hosts. I speak to the ages with a realization that the entire Church Triumphant hears me and loves me, while they know I love them with all the devotion I know how to give in that moment, such as it is. I greet them all, to the last Saint, with subordinate affection and admiration because the least in the Kingdom of God is greater than the best of this world. [*Matthew 11:11*] I reverence the Saints with the esteem they deserve beyond all ages. If one would look for the definition of heroism, look to each of them. I withhold nothing from them. It is a feeling of mutual reciprocity in the same Sacrifice of Jesus. And, this is humbling, sensing the majesty and recollecting the pure personas of so many giants who surrendered their hearts to the Sacrifice of the Cross of Jesus; they who have suffered in dimensions beyond my simple discomforts and obstacles in a nation of such prosperity. I receive everything they possess through their allegiance to Christ whereby they assist me. I admire every palette of saintly divinity from which they applied sanctity to the canvas of human history. My weapon of choice is the Most Holy Rosary that I carry into the arena where they stand. I pray the Rosary because this is what Our Lady asks. Neither She nor the Church need submit any other justifications to me, although Saint John Paul II encouraged us in his Apostolic Letter, *Rosarium Virginis Mariae*, saying, *"The Rosary has accompanied me in moments of joy and in moments of difficulty. To it, I have entrusted any number of concerns; in it I have always found comfort. Twenty-four years ago, on 29 October 1978, scarcely two weeks after my election to the See of Peter, I frankly admitted: "The Rosary is my favourite prayer. A marvellous prayer! Marvellous in its simplicity and its depth. [...]. It can be said that the Rosary is, in some sense, a prayer-commentary on the final chapter of the Vatican II Constitution Lumen Gentium, a chapter which discusses the wondrous presence of the Mother of God in the mystery of Christ and the Church. Against the background of the words Ave Maria, the principal events of the life of Jesus Christ pass before the eyes of the soul. They take shape in the complete series of the joyful, sorrowful and glorious mysteries, and they put us in living communion with Jesus through – we might say – the heart of his Mother. At the same time, our heart can embrace in the decades of the Rosary all the events that make up the lives of individuals, families, nations, the Church, and all mankind. Our personal concerns and those of our neighbour, especially those who are closest to us, who are dearest to us. Thus, the simple prayer of the Rosary marks the rhythm of human life."* These words of this great Saint are enough for me. But, even if he had never spoken them, even if Our Lady had promised nothing throughout history to the many mystics and seers, even if its strains convoked no signs, graces, strengths, or even a scent of recognizable benefit to me or anyone else in this life, I would still pray the Most Holy Rosary because She has asked us to do so through Her many appearances in this world. Requiring any other explanation or justification before tendering our obedience to Her reeks of pride. Why is the Rosary so powerful? Because Jesus Christ responds to this offering of our submission with plenteous beatitude in as many different dimensions as can be

How Do I Pray? Fiat Maximus!

contemplated, simply because our littleness and our humility before Him are proven through our obedience to His Mother. It is "Fiat Maximus!" Why pray the Holy Rosary? Quite simply, because it changes who we are. It blossoms holiness in the soul; it restores our framework of reference; it makes Saints of sinners, which is the sole reason for our lives here in this world. More specifically, during the moments of our communion with its mysteries, the contemplative nature of the Rosary wipes away this world and opens our eyes to the concrete dimensions of our hopes that are fulfilled in the Holy Sacrifice of Our Lord. In the Rosary, spirit meets Eternal Spirit and is consumed and changed by that Divinity as it eclipses every sense, both physical and spiritual, that a human being could possess. When one imbibes the cadences and contemplations of the Rosary, the realms of Heaven expand from within and transcend the exilic veil to consume man in his mortal existence. The Heavenly Hosts take notice; the Angels and Saints turn their attention toward the world with renewed intensity, and all assistance and succor descends the ladders of Heaven through the hierarchies of Creation, seen and unseen, to reach mankind in his need. This is grace; the human soul animated by the greatness of the beatific realms of Divine Love flowing from the Sacrifice of the Lamb of God. As we contemplate the magnificence of Our Savior's presence in human flesh, the sheer brilliance of God is manifested within our interior vision. We see with the eyes of Angels and experience with new senses the highlights of a Kingdom which is coming again with the clouds and thunder that will rupture the celestial vaults. The Rosary possesses transforming power because it establishes, cultivates, and nurtures an authentic beatific relationship with the Virgin Mary who was recognized as the Matriarch of Creation by Her Son while He hung on the Cross. It purifies, focuses, and unites our purposes and sentiments with the perfect intentions of the Mother of God, which opens and inaugurates the flourishing power of God within us. There is a difference in the nature of a soul that prays the Rosary compared to one who does not. The magnitude and breadth of sanctity is augmented to degrees unattainable without the interior spiritual accompaniment of Our Lady. The soul receives spiritual gifts of enlightenment and assistance that it will not receive anywhere else. That is a part of Heaven's gift to those who respond. I can prove this statement. To wit, the soul who refuses to respond to our Heavenly Mother's request to pray the Rosary will never feel the glowing warmth of Her appreciation for doing so.   This mystical sense alone is enough to secure Salvation from the faith of any creature at the Throne of God. Our Lady says, "This one is My special child. This one obeyed because they loved Me." One Rosary prayed from the heart renders this affirmation to any soul on the final day. This is why the praying of the Rosary is a great sign of ultimate destiny in Paradise in the spiritual life of any person. Our personal prayers do not possess such standing in Heaven because they are as imperfect as we are. We ask wrongly and petition for our passions and whims. We pray from a corrupt frame of reference. We remember the Apostles asking Jesus how they should pray. [*Luke 11:1-13*] Our Lady has been teaching the Church how to pray from centuries ago through the Saints who advanced the Rosary into its present form. Pontiffs and priests have acclaimed the spiritual merits and the salvific fruits of the Holy Rosary into the Church universal. Saint Louis de Montfort, pray for us. The Most Holy Rosary is perfect prayer! It embodies our opportunity to perform a request in the service of Heaven which possesses the definitive certainty of its approbation by virtue of the miraculous intercession of the Most Blessed Virgin Mary.   Heaven asks, we respond. This is the perfect order of Creation; to do the will of God. The recitation of the Rosary is our proof to Jesus Christ that we will respond in the testing moment; we will tender our allegiance at the calling of the ages, and we will submit our lives to the yoke that will identify us as His heroic brothers and sisters who accompanied Him and His Mother in the squalls where human Redemption played-out their most spectacular beauty. No other personal prayer possesses such synchronous perfection with the Communions and Dominions of Heaven. The mind of Heaven resonates the mysteries of the Rosary, and every knee bends to its Fruit.

When anyone takes up the frame of reference that Our Lady possesses in their prayers, we become permeable to one another. Empathy is not just some emotion of imagination. It is an extension of the power of the heart into the realms of God. We can eclipse, diffuse through and permeate in spirit the members of the body in manifesting our oneness of being as Christ's Mystical Body. As I offer the prayers of the Rosary, I recollect the simple dimensions of each mystery and apply the spirit, virtues and power of the mystery with ordered passion wherever the Holy Spirit directs my thoughts into the world at that moment. All of this happens with no direct intention of my will. I do

How Do I Pray? Fiat Maximus!

not orchestrate my thoughts and contemplations, nor my intentions, in any way. I surrender the direction of my interior attention to the Holy Spirit while providing my heart in sacrifice. It is a sacrificial journey into the Heart of God where I accompany His vision across the landscapes of continents, nations, events, and times. I go into the darkest places in the world sometimes, into the most desolate and despicable recesses of human existence, and from there I bring that suffering and ruin into full relief before His Sacred Heart. Neither the boundaries of time nor the barriers of location impede the reach of my prayers. I pray for people suffering their final agonies in past ages, knowing they were given comfort by my prayers of today. I have been on battlefields beside the mortally wounded, seen the aftermath of disasters and the human misery, observed the solitude and torture of gulags, sat on planes plummeting toward the earth, and shared the darkness of those lost in the night. Throughout the human experience of history, I unite the vehicle of my heart in the depths with those prostrate in suffering until I can sense their grief, their torment, confusion, and pain. Then I ask, sometimes plead, to our Blessed Jesus, recognizing Him as both my King and my Brother, Conqueror and Savior, to deliver the world into the beauty and safety of His Kingdom. I say, "please save them, please redeem them, please give them comfort and strength according to your will." I ask for courage for warriors, freedom for captives, wholeness and uprightness of spirit for those broken and bowed down, new beginnings for those who have squandered their opportunities, and healing for the afflicted by asking for the conversion of the wicked who inflict such intense suffering upon their brothers and sisters. Our Lady always tells me not only to pray for the end of suffering, but also to pray for the end of the need for suffering. At one time several years ago, my heart was given a vision of those who had been kidnaped, especially children who had been thrown into dungeons, cells, and circumstances of outright diabolical subjugation; into slavery that everyone had long forgotten about; those lost to their families without a hint of their whereabouts. Thereafter, I began to unite with them often in my prayers. Suddenly, I began to notice repeated instances on the nightly news of people throughout the world being freed from captivity at the hands of wicked people after extended lengths of time; those hidden in terrible situations where all hope had been lost. It somewhat startled me by the apparent coincidence of it all because I was not disposed to ever search for evidence of the answers to my prayers. But, Our Lady said that Our Lord wanted me to apprehend directly His response to my prayers in order to strengthen my awareness of their authentic power. Each Hail Mary feels like sensible thunder from my heart now. The spiritual realms of the Earth tremble and rattle like china in a cabinet during seismic tremors. I was sitting on the porch one evening during a late summer thunderstorm, and I noticed that the rain was intermittent; sometimes pouring down rather heavily, then dissipating to a gentle drizzle. After a particularly loud thunderclap that shook me in my chair, Our Lady spoke to me through a locution and asked me to notice that the rain would momentarily increase in heaviness. And, sure enough, in less than a minute, the rain began falling in very heavy sheets as if someone had turned on a spigot. She told me the concussion of the thunder shakes the water droplets from the clouds, and I was seeing the result in the heavier falling rain. She said that this is the same concussion that the Hosts of Heaven hear at the recitation of the Hail Mary. The Rosary dislodges the blessings and graces of God from the clouds of His Glory. We have a simplistic view of the prayer of the Rosary as if it is just the recitation of a formula or holy words spoken per rote memory that have some unknown benefit. Prayer is the "extension of the passions of the heart" into the realms of God. And, within each heart is the power to which He succumbs when we embody the Cross and are united in love with Jesus, especially through the Catholic Sacraments. Those who pray but have no unity with Jesus' Crucifixion through the Sacraments have very little power. They command no respect from the heavens, neither from its Throne nor its Communion of Saints because the one who prays absent the Sacraments has not surrendered themselves to the Sacrifice, no matter how faithful they believe themselves to be. They hold out, boasting that their light is shining when the lamp is not even plugged in. It is like whimpering at the thunder-heads and expecting our voice to have the concussion to shake the rains. Christ testified to true power when He commanded the seas and the winds to calm themselves. This is the Voice that He gives to those who receive the Bread of Life from the Catholic Altar. Our Voice, the Voice of the Original Apostolic Church, is amplified with the power of the Sacred Body and Blood of Jesus, the Eucharist, and our liturgical petitions and supplications resound throughout the Kingdom of His Holy Spirit through the Rosary. When we pray the Rosary with our Blessed Mother, She makes our prayers Her own and magnifies them throughout Creation and into the Sacred Heart of Her Son with the empathy of Her immaculate Voice. Her Voice brings Jesus' Sacred Heart joy and relief. He loves to simply hear Her Voice, no matter what She says because He knows it will always be beautiful. Her Voice is the voice of the Original Church before any Apostles were ever called to testify. Her lullabies were the first canticles to the Savior. And, He smiled then and seeks to please Her now. Can we imagine the colossal concussion of the prayers of the Queen of Heaven and Earth throughout time and eternity, and the graces that She has dislodged from the Sacred Heart of Her Son? Her Fiat dislodged the Second Person of the Most Holy Trinity from the vaults of Heaven into Her immaculate womb.

The Catholic Church has professed for twenty centuries the amazing graciousness of the Holy Virgin toward the children of God, while recognizing the verifiable manifestations of Her mystical relationship with Her children. The Encyclicals, Exhortations, Letters and writings of Popes and Saints throughout the ages have directed the attention of the Catholic faithful, indeed all humanity, to call upon the Immaculate Mother of Jesus for divine assistance, to be our comfort in times of trial, and to extend to us the graceful benefaction of Her Son as at the wedding feast of Cana. And in this, the Church has helped generations of faith-filled people live the Holy Gospel to the letter. The Scriptures testify to the benefit of approaching Jesus' Mother with our petitions; and in doing so, we solicit Her compassion and invoke Her great intercessory influence with Her Divine Son. Is this not what was done at the wedding feast of Cana when the supply of wine ran dry? [*John 2:1-12*] Why would the story of this wedding feast even be in the Bible if it was not to assist our understanding of Our Lady's graceful and efficacious benefaction toward us? Therefore, to hail this great Mother of Heaven with more worthy affection, it is fitting to reconsider any sentiments that devalue or obscure Her maternal dignity and intercessory power. Many errant opinions exist that declare the Mother of Jesus to be of no more relevance in salvation history than any of the sinful Eves of this broken world. Balderdash! This is no more than ingratitude. We honor ourselves at the drop of a hat, erect shrines in honor of our mortal achievements, and place our names upon any edifice that our pride can etch into its cornerstones. We honor presidents and prime ministers across the landscapes of nations, and recognize and respect their first ladies with the deference becoming of subjects to their secular royalty. We honor fathers and mothers of warriors, athletes and achievers, and search out ways to impress their legacies into the historical record that they always be remembered. We enshrine stars in walks of fame for people who do no more than make us laugh with salty humor. We show respect to the most menial of human accomplishments and tout the shallowest sacrifices of the most rogue partisans by engraving their names across any facade that might serve as a marquee for their political legacies. Yet, it seems that we somehow cannot find even the most humble of pedestals upon which to honor the Lady whose stately affirmation to an Archangel initiated the salvation of us all; the Mother who bore, raised, and taught the perfection of Love to the greatest Man ever to have graced human flesh; and then watched Him crucified. The feeble foundation upon which many stand to reject the great gift of the Most Blessed Virgin Mary's miraculous intercession and the maternal care She offers to Her Son's brothers and sisters is not worthy of Her bearing. These lost souls have little difficulty acknowledging that Christ is King, the New Adam, for the Bible tells us so. They accept His Kingdom, His Father, His brothers and sisters, His Crown, His Throne, His Scepter, His Angels, and the family of man, yet cannot find within this great Dominion or in any corner of their devotion the courage to accept His Mother and Queen, the New Eve who reigns at His side as the Matriarch of the family of the Redeemed. Since Jesus is the first-born Son of God, who is the first-born woman? If Christ is the New Adam, who is the New Eve? If Christ is King, who is the Queen? If the Father came to Earth as His own Son, who is the Mother of Heaven? And, if the Virgin Mary is of little relevance to our salvation, why has She appeared and produced spectacles and wonders throughout history; why is She appearing across nearly every landscape of the globe; and why has She appeared here as the Morning Star Over America, wielding the power of the Holy Spirit with healing, revelation, miracle and prophetic warning?

There is no doubt that embarrassment and more is the future lot of all the detractors and protestors at their presentation before the Hosts of Heaven. Their rejection of the Most Blessed Virgin Mother is nothing more than a product of their feeble faith and their historical hatred of the Catholic Church. For should they accept Jesus' Queen, they know the inevitable conclusion that must be reached: The Roman Catholic Church is truly the Church founded by

How Do I Pray? Fiat Maximus!

Jesus Christ 2000 years ago; still here, triumphantly processing through the ages with stately eloquence, enlightening the world with its endurance of suffering and derision, and fulfilling its commission with each passing of the keys to successive Pontificates. Hail, indeed, the Kingdom on High, Thrice-Blessed Domain of the Living! Hail all paradisial royalty and pageantry; the pomp of divine circumstances! All humanity must hail the Scars of Paradise! Those of the Sacred Body of our Savior, and also those of His Saints and Martyrs who died in emulation of His divine greatness! And, from the most grief-stricken depths of they who have filled up what was lacking in the sufferings of Christ stands the blazing beacon of the majestic Lady of Mount Calvary, the Fairest Dove of the Earth's liberating Holocaust, She who knew suffering to its grieving depths and stood alone without stain or imperfection amidst the wailing typhoon of evil that broke upon the shores of this mortal age! Our Lady is the Sign of the End Times. She is the Mystical Testimony to the Eternal Truth that all humankind must embrace to find favor with God once again.

For those who eschew the Most Holy Rosary, I ask you to imagine standing in a completely dark room whose size you cannot discern. In that darkness, you offer your personal prayers. You do not apprehend if anyone can hear your prayers; you have only hope when faced with the silence. Surely Christ hears your whispers, but for the children of Mary who pray the Rosary around God's Queen, we do not stand in darkness; nor is there silence. All is light where we stand. The Holy Spirit reveals that we grace a colossal theater where One Body of billions intones our prayers in unison with our hearts. We are one Voice; a deafening chorus of affirmation and supplication rising from the sea of the Communion of Saints in whose midst we glory. Yes, who are these who are dressed in white, who have made their robes clean in the Blood of the Lamb? [*Revelation 7:13-14*] From the distances of God's Kingdom unbounded, the roaring thunder of this united Voice reverberates in Heaven as if it was the rushing wind of voices unleashed across the cityscape from a frenzied stadium upon the crack of a bat, sending a walk-off home run into the seats ending a World Series. Hearing the roar in the distance from worldly athletic stadiums has always been a great grace for me because it is such a premonition of what is occurring behind the veil between Heaven and Earth. The only difference is magnification and intention. Our Holy Mother allows me to mystically hear this roar in a sensible way on occasion to remind me of the greatness of the Kingdom. And finally, in the reverberations of this infinite theater, the amplified voice that rings out above all others is the gentle strains of the Most Blessed Virgin Mary who leads us all in giving Glory to Christ, the Child of Her Womb.

These sentiments lead us to conversion, to something wholly greater about our existence. We discover through the spontaneous outcomes of authentic faith that you can change your mind much more easily than you can change your heart. The human mind and rational intellect are much more shallow and passing; they are not as deep as the winsome excellence of the spiritual heart. The mind more quickly asserts our personal and individual identity on a social level, depending on what we say to others based on our thoughts. There is no real passion in the human mind compared to the values and emotions that we safeguard inside the heart. This is why our submissive acts of obedience to God involve feelings that include sacrificial self-denial, translocation, dynamic spiritualism, cognitive purification, reparative sanctification, humility, passion of the heart, Messianic invocation and the abandonment of personal desires. I have the sensation when looking into other Christians' faces that the vision before my eyes originates from beyond the vaults of the unseen dimensions. There is a magnification of confidence that comes from outside my being that impacts my self-perception and where my physical composition is located in the context of the evolving tangible world. In other words, my consciousness is transferred to the outer limits of my corporeal existence as though someone is able to see through a mirror and view the surface on which the mirror itself is attached. If there were a photograph behind the mirror, I am able to see both my own image reflecting back at me as well as the photograph on the other side. The self-denial that comes through this contemplative exercise is one of innate sanctification — my identity containing all my fears, faults and weaknesses is reoriented, and I can see myself cleansed of every flaw. I feel enriched when being enlightened by the teachings of the Church and other Christians in the same way that I hand over my self-will to God. The Church standing before me becomes God's instrument through which I am able to connect with Heaven in the same way that I see the photograph behind the mirror. This vast complex translocation occurs at the exact moment when my mouth first utters the words, "...not my will but

How Do I Pray? Fiat Maximus!

Thine, O' Lord." My senses overload with a power that seems stronger than the two of us combined. This is where the passion of the heart feels almost like an explosion in my chest at the same time that a tremendous sensation of peace overwhelms my inner-being. Almost immediately upon entering contemplative prayer, my conscious awareness is transported into the spiritual identity of the Holy Paraclete, and I cannot even imagine what it would be like to suffer anxiety again. I feel as though my childlike innocence is being restored; time itself is reversed, the whole universe in which I am situated becomes engulfed with heavenly light, and the entire definition of myself is rewritten. I sense a universal connection with all the stars and moons that God ever created. When I am offering acts of obedience, I can sense the rhythm of the Father's divine heart beating more vividly within me. It is as though the words of my mouth and the confession on my lips are knocking-down invisible walls that are keeping humanity from seeing the fullness of the Crucifixion of His Son. I could never pretend to appropriate any equality between what I experience and the suffering of Jesus on the Cross, but I can see in three dimensions the actual healing of broken-humanity while I am immersed in prayer. When I feel myself breathing in silent petition, I have a certain sensation of inhaling the warmth of Jesus from His Sacred Heart like a backdraft from a humongous kiln. It feels as though the unseen realms are responding to my cry for help. The gentleness that I experience seems to defy the crudeness of daily life, and it gives me an insight into the kindness of the Kingdom yet to come. The Holy Spirit is as identifiable as God's dominion, and I can feel the sensation of answered prayers raining down upon me. I know that God can deposit Himself within His creatures, and I also know that discovering the origin of human life is one of the most primal joys that man can ever acquire. This is, in a sense, my motivation for offering reparational obedience. I feel united with the Cross by satisfying the primal needs of the sick and impoverished in the same way that God Himself suffices those needs for us. There is a reciprocal feeling that God is handing the world the essence of Jesus through humanity's charity in a measurable and manifest way. The Church can see, touch, smell and taste the eternal being of love through our protection of the innocent and providing for the poor.

I do not see success or defeat in worldly terms as if human events or actions have any influence on the hopes that I ask Our Lord to bring into being. This leaves me undisturbed if immediate answers to my prayers are not forthcoming in a way I can recognize, although they often are. All answers are surrendered to the will of Our Lord with confidence in the power of my love issuing forth, no matter whether the sensible answers boomerang back into my sight. For me, it is never a matter of if, but when; and when is not important when our vision is anchored outside of time. There is no will directed toward God demanding answers in any particular way, even though my heart may passionately grieve specific intentions for those who suffer. In fact, I never demand anything from Our Lord. I never have. I simply say "please" and ask to share the suffering until He delivers His answer. I display to Him my love and trust to do with my heart as He pleases because I have confidence and knowledge that He is doing great things with the small things that I offer to Him. Our Lady gave me many parables to this effect, and has offered me many confirmations to prove it. I never diminish myself in any way before Our Lord. I never make those assessments. It is a waste of thought and time because it is already a certifiable fact that I am diminutive before Him and have failed both Him and myself at times. When He is trying to lift me up into His embrace, I do not invoke my will to try to convince Him how heavy I am. He knows. Our Lady said that Satan spends too much time accomplishing our diminishment, and that we should not assist him. We should simply be of humble gratitude that the King of all Creation looks upon us so fondly. This is where true thanksgiving is manifested. Humility is not diminishment; it is very powerful love. If we fall, have the honesty and integrity to confess the momentary misstep; trust in God's great Mercy, know that He understands our weaknesses, and be confident that He will grant the grace to protect us from these slights against His dominion in the future, but only if we are committed to being watchful against these stumbles and never intend to indulge them again. We may fall again, even to the same weakness, but we must always set out in repentance with pure intention. Does a mother become dejected if her infant collapses on his backside when trying to walk the first few times? Of course not. But, she will call the father of the house if her teenager repeatedly stampedes her flower bed through horseplay. Never wilfully choose to do that which is wrong. Never surrender through laziness; never desire a brief respite from the sacrifice Jesus asks us to endure with Him. Never love the things of this world more than Jesus. Never hurt His Sacred Heart by a flippant choice in the moment. Do not mock or abuse His Divine Mercy. Fight the good fight, run the race all the way to the finish line and through the tape. We must not allow the currents of the world to carry our thoughts away where we lose our recollection of Jesus being with us. In every situation, at all times, selfishly possess the ability to recollect Our Lord's presence into your dominant perception in the mere flash of a thought, and maintain a life where you are not ashamed when you do so. Never leave Him saying, "Oh, there you are. Where have you been?" Let your frame of reference be defined and dominated by His wisdom.

When I wake at night, the instant I have conscious awareness, I invite Jesus, Our Lady and the Heavenly Hosts to the fore of my thoughts in a very simple way. I immediately ask whether I am being called to pray for a specific intention that requires my deeper meditations of the Holy Rosary. And, even in this example, I refrain from igniting any scrupulosity by thinking every time I awaken in the night that I am being called to completely awaken myself, omitting my rest and entering into prayer. Lack of rest causes many sins. Sometimes, our Holy Mother merely wishes to extend to us the knowledge that She is watching over us, as if a mother were checking on a child to make sure that he has not kicked off his covers while asleep. Every parent who has placed a tiny child down for a nap has witnessed the same phenomenon that Our Lady experiences with us. As the small child dozes off and is nearing complete sleep, they suddenly raise their head fighting off their exhaustion to see if their mother or father is still sitting beside them. Then satisfied, they drop their head again on the pillow, and fall farther asleep. Most of my interaction with our Heavenly Mother at night, She sees this way. Yet, there have been times where I have been called directly to pray for specific situations that were imminent. One such incident was a fire that was to break out in the residence of someone I knew. In fact, this was confirmed soon after by the very people who experienced the fire who caught the blaze quickly enough to be delivered from it. Another was the early morning I was awakened before dawn by a terribly ominous feeling of disaster. The feeling scared me because it was so intense and unique. I knelt to pray with Our Lady, knowing something was occurring at that moment, although I did not know what. Later that morning, the news media reported that a National Guard F-16 deploying to Denmark had crashed only minutes after take-off from the nearby air base at the very time that I was kneeling with our Heavenly Mother praying. The name of the pilot was not immediately reported, but the instant I heard this news, my soul experienced a mystical perception of the identity of the airman who had perished, for whom I had been praying. I saw him clearly in a vision. This was a striking moment of grace for me, albeit a sorrowful one, when his identity was ultimately confirmed to me through the news media. This airman was present at an air show the previous fall at the local airport. He was a man filled with life whom I simply observed from the anonymous crowds. We never met; I did not know his name, but I always remembered him when I thought of the aviators at the fighter wing. He stood out that day in his flight uniform amongst the group of his fellow airmen, excited and animated about his participation in the air show and how he loved flying. He was moving his hands through the air as if they were jets, gesturing formations and how he observed things from his cockpit. He talked about "hugging the deck" as he called it, then lifting the nose of his aircraft and rocketing skyward. Everyone around him loved listening to him. Oh, he was humanity at its best the day I saw him, and I am blessed to have been praying for him as he passed through the veil to see His loving God. His name was Captain Donald Leckrone, and July 31, 1992 was the day he did pierce the vaults of the heavens. Another heart-warming example was the time I was traveling westward to see my family in Ashland. I was watching the sunset unfold as I drove, praying the Rosary. It was a particularly spectacular sight to behold. I asked Our Lady to make sure that my family looked outside so they would not miss seeing it. When I arrived at my sister's home, she greeted me and asked if I had seen the sunset on my drive out to see them. I told her that I did. Then, she said that they would have missed it if my four-year-old nephew had not been going wild trying to convince everyone to come to the window to see it. I knew that his excitement was due to our Heavenly Mother touching him in a special way. She had answered my prayer by inspiring a tiny child to recognize the beauty before him. These are simple examples of my life of prayer with our Virgin Mother, and the mystical overtones that have inundated my life in Her presence. There are hundreds more, perhaps thousands, and it is the same with each person who prays the Most Holy Rosary in unison with the Catholic Church.

    Our Heavenly Mother made the following statement to me one day

How Do I Pray? Fiat Maximus!

when I was pondering these mystical gifts and what causes God to act in particular ways. She said, "*Mystical gifts always come through the diminishment of the flesh.*" She helped me understand that diminishment of the flesh means a discharge of the framework of reference that the mortal world has impressed into us, dismissal of our wants, desires, needs, pleasures, passions, our sensual nature. It does not mean that all of these sentiments and appetites are eliminated, rather they are subordinated toward extinction in the moment in their proper positions beneath the glory of our beings. It is like a liberation from slavery where the slave now has his foot on the neck of his former taskmaster. Diminishment of the flesh allows a new creation, or the heightening of something that will grow after it is given room; new wants, needs, passions, and an ordered possession of our own senses, even physical ones. The diminishment comes through self-discipline, reorientation, the sacrifice of our worldly ego, which may mean discomfort through self-denial, suffering in union with those who suffer, holy thoughts and aspirations instead of sensual or material ones, the sacrifice of material comforts and pleasures which blind us to the higher spiritual joys. It is an ordering, a purification and sanctification of our frame of reference that allows the resurgence and resonance of divine grace. God is permitted to reach us through the divine hierarchies of His Kingdom and the orders of Creation. Will an athlete who seeks nothing but his own comfort ever train hard enough to someday feel the exhilaration of ultimate victory? Diminishment of the flesh means being able to accompany Jesus in every moment over and above any other force or temptation that would have you look away from Him. It means allowing nothing in the world, nothing, to tempt you to choose the world over Him, and sacrificing yourself to help Him bring about the conversion and sanctification of the entire world. It also means the diminishment of our personal sovereignty, the surrender of our will in obedience to His Will, all in union with the love manifested in His Holy Sacrifice on the Cross. Diminishment of the flesh is the sacrifice we make. And, when we engage that sacrifice with love, Jesus in all His great power and glory becomes manifest through us. Thus, mystical gifts may flow as we describe them if it be His Will. In Him, we live, move and have our being. He becomes alive in us because we have His mind. There are so many dimensions to this that have their ultimate meaning in the hierarchical Church of Roman Catholicism and in the Holy Sacrifice of the Mass. All mystical gifts flow from that Holy Sacrifice. It is a deep ocean of understanding, while we are merely standing on the shore talking about it lapping at our feet. In other words, have we put away the seductions and distractions of the world to an extent that we see love so clearly that we will sacrifice and embrace suffering so that others may be redeemed into that love? Laying down our lives for those whom Jesus loves. Will we surrender our framework of thoughts, our disbelief, our manipulation of the Gospel into a preferential prosperity gospel, and allow Christ's sacrificial reign of revelation to dawn within us? Will we serve Christ, and to what depth? Make disciples of all nations, He said. Our Holy Mother has given me an understanding of the composure of the Saints in Her lessons to me. Many people counsel others to maintain "balance" as if it is a mixture of the spiritual and the worldly, as if we must adopt a miscellanea of worldly opinions amongst our spiritual genius to be healthy in our constitution. They are actually counseling others to remain part of this world when Our Lord spoke differently in John 17:14-18. I have learned instead from our Virgin Mother that the balance should be between Heaven and Earth where the fulcrum is at the veil of our exile. In order to possess the "balance" that God desires, it is our responsibility to balance the Earth to the identical composition of Heaven so that both ends, the seen and unseen, are equal in stature and perfection. And, this occurs through our emulation of Jesus Christ in His Sacrifice. Our Lady wishes to help us engage that type of love. Then, the Holy Spirit will be near with the gifts that help us to become like Jesus more fully, to make room for the master of the house, that it not be we who live, but Christ alive in us. The path to this relationship is found in putting away the world and engaging prayer from the heart fueled by great love and devotion, not only to God in His unseen Kingdom, but to the Catholic Church and our brothers and sisters. Ultimately, mystical gifts are irrelevant to us by way of any reward in the present because they are sustained by great sacrifice and suffering. Poverty of spirit is the great companion of mystical gifts, and the dark night becomes our day. One who prays to receive mystical gifts usually does not realize what he is asking. It is like James and John asking Jesus to sit one on His left and the other on the right in His Kingdom. Jesus said, *"You do not know what you are asking. Can you drink the cup that I am to drink?"* [*Matthew 20:22*] We too often take for granted the stability and peace of our thoughts and the

How Do I Pray? Fiat Maximus!

composure of our lives being a result of the sustaining grace of God who is inebriating us with His protection. It is only when this composure is taken away that we recognize the supernal care we were under and the universal power of God's Divine Kingdom that sustains us. It is the power in the Crucifixion of Jesus Christ.

Jesus, my spirit was created for greatness in you, to experience divinity and success and consolation and peace. My heart knows what it needs. It needs love! It needs affection! It needs Heaven! It needs you. My emotions need to be saturated in your light. You created me to know and recognize you. And, I do recognize you, but I am being told 'no, not yet' at every turn, on every occasion. The world is saying 'no' to love. I am begging you, remembering the grief you endured in the Garden; please deliver us into Thy Light! Only you can change the days that will appear tomorrow. And, this I ask you to do. Please I beg you, make tomorrow beautiful. Open the hearts of humankind! I know nothing of how to effect this change because it only comes from you. You are the world changer, you are the Amender of human history, you are the Creator of the future, you are the Maker of our dreams, you are the Hope of the world. O' the contrast between the dreams I see in Your Mother and the nightmares propagating in this life are so stark that I cannot bear opening my interior sanctuary to the desolation of this exile. O' Lord, don't leave us this way. I pray for Heaven to come to Earth because the pain of it not being here is so heavy a burden to bear. Please come and close this last age of the valley of our tears, these times of pain and suffering. I could go on burdening you with my pleading, a hundred more hours and pools of tears petitioning you for your divine assistance to change the world for us. I know there are millions who are lifting these same prayers, immersed in their own suffering. I lift all my brothers and sisters to you in union with my prayers, especially the heartfelt petitions of my beloved brother Timmy. No one could imagine what he has suffered, but they will one day see, and they will marvel and take unto his heart in thanksgiving. We have been one, he and I. Jesus, hear us anew and respond to our needs. Please inspire humanity to see this exceptional light, that we would be drawn to you over any other one. Let knowing and seeing this be my gift for the rest of my life. Please create my dream where you are loved totally and unconditionally by humanity. I have never asked this in such a pleading way before. Help me know how to progress in helping bring it into being. What sacrifice does it require? I know not the steps. Give me wisdom and understanding. Allow me to see my way. Give me the confidence a saintly man should possess. Make yourself radiant before humanity's eyes, where their hearts are as pained as mine until fulfilled by you. This is the kind of love that I wish to find within humanity, blazing and burning everything in its path. I pray for the world to recognize that humankind was created in the beginning for you, to complement you, to know you, to be your satisfaction and your love, and to worship you in the Light of the Sacrifice you suffered. I know you can do this for me, Master. I trust in you; I have hoped so many things in you, but none as deeply powerful as this. Allow humanity to personify the grace and composure of your Immaculate Mother. Allow the world to see Her. Then, your people would possess a strength that nothing could destroy; nothing could strike it down. Your Holy Mother's undying support can make me stand atop the world and face any onslaught. This is what Her love does. This is what She does for your people. You saw Her beneath the Cross, holding you there in your Glory. I pray for this divine blessing upon the hearts of humanity in exile. I call down the heavenly court to adorn your Creation with miraculous grace. And, even if I am deprived of seeing all this in my time, if I am to travel this subterranean mine while so knowing the daylight of the green meadows above, my heart will see this life through to its appointed end in you. If this be your Will, I will carry the cross prepared for me; you know I will because I love you, and I love humanity. I will imitate you like a redwood seen in a sapling. But, the pain hurts me, even though I know I can endure it and rise again with you. Living the rest of my life without seeing this love made manifest is a barren path up a terrible mountain. I do not say no, but I wish the pain would cease for humanity, as I wish it would stop for me. Heaven seems so far away, and the path so disheartening to tread. But, if this be the path you wish me to tread, I must ask you for your strength because I cannot forge the path on my own; it is too difficult for me alone. I have to know it has meaning. Please let me see the meaning as you have shown me before. Let me see the signs. Let me be confident in your miracles. O' my unstable heart needs the solid rock of your affirming Will. I need to know that you are with me, and that you are fulfilling the prophetic vision of my heart. I need to know you love me this much to fulfill my heart, and that you hear my needs, and are moved to respond. My Lord, these words pour out of me like molten metal from a forge. Inside me they burn everything until they find fulfillment from you. Please quench this fire of unrequited love. My God, please so simply turn mankind's thoughts to deeper meaning, please, please, please. When my brothers and sisters are alone in their rooms, open their hearts to my pleas; allow them to feel the movements of my heart

How Do I Pray? Fiat Maximus!

lifting them to you. Give them fond memories. Break their hearts open to these dreams, bring tears of understanding and clarity to roll down their cheeks. Let them set out upon the world looking for their brothers and sisters. I know you can do it. I know you have the power. You have willed this throughout the Earth and the ages in every divine romance and spiritual movement ever experienced by man. You have brought warriors home from battlefields, sanctified in victory. You have placed the reigns of civilization in the hands of mighty champions. You have restored and recreated over and again with the noble powers of your Kingdom. It has been you who have done this in every case and in every time, through every act of love. None have been effected without your divine touch. Please pass your divine hand over humanity in all corners of the globe as they commune alone with you. As they lie in their beds each night or on the ground beneath the stars, send the divine fires of your love, send them miraculous light and heart-rending visions, send them locutions; speak to them, work miracles of transfiguration in any way that will startle their hearts as you have mine; inspire them to make a decision to seek out the depths of your Sacred Heart, to yearn to find that something which they have always dreamed of finding. Send them your Mother! Send them the Royal Queen! Roll out the Glory of Her Immaculate Heart before all humankind! Let Her preciousness shudder the Earth like a meteor strike. Please do this for me – I want it in the Name of Jesus Christ, my Lord and King; in the Name of the Heavens, the Saints and Angels, in the name of every sufferer in union with your Most Merciful Heart. Father, in Jesus' Name, I ask for this kind of love to explode upon your Creation. I ask for it pure and holy, unending and everlasting, resilient and powerful, steadfast and unbreakable, ocean deep and high as the stars. I pray for it to flow across the ages like a torrential tidal wave of light from our union, from this prayer in this place and time. Create a vision from the unification of humanity at the Catholic Altar and my heart sanctified in yours that will electrify this age with you as its centerpiece. Please touch the world with your inspiring truth, and place your face upon the marquee in the hearts of your people, so humanity will lay its precious head upon your breast, and hear the breath of life from its origin. Please, please, please.

Jesus, by your divine grace, make this relationship between man and God appear in the beauty that you have ordained for your people, yet have seen only in your Saints. Give it the miraculous assistance that it needs to be everything you have sought from this world throughout the mortal ages, and wish to see before you call time complete. I am asking for the ultimate miracle from your limitless compassion and divine power. I believe in you, I have dedicated myself to you, I live in solemn consecration to your Immaculate Mother, and I trust in you. I ask you to dispense this seemingly impossible gift in response to my love for you. Bring the New Time of times! I know that neither I nor this humanity you look upon deserves to be so blessed among the ages, yet I still believe in you because I know that you are good, and that your Sacred Heart grieves and pines as does mine for this union of your Creation with you. I know of your help for your people because I have seen your beauty, your majesty, and I know that it could come from nowhere but the flames of your Most Sacred Heart. I ask that your wisdom not be impeded, but to be set loose without restraint to assist in bringing this glory to its appearance, no matter the cost. Bring us the Cross, if it be the only way the bonds may be breached. Bring forth Calvary, and seat man before your glory. How many people have gained grace for me that I could neither summon nor accept on my own? It is you who condescended to me at their behest, you who overcame my willful disposition; it is you who stooped to conquer the walls that separated me from the happiness you had while waiting for me; it is you who delivered me. Now, I ask you to deliver this same humanity; these beautiful people, my brothers and sisters. Deliver them from their lesser selves, and let them rise again. Raise them to grace at your side. I plead with loving supplication in recognition of your powerful love. O' how they would one day be so sorrowful and tearful if they were to see that my prayers at this moment were not enough, that their stubbornness required more than my heartfelt pleading, that you declined to extend your uplifting and liberating hand to raise them from the muddied pit to which they had been thrown by the sinister darkness of the netherworld. I stand beside that pit from which I was extracted by your Mother's grace, asking you to reach to this humanity, to this age, to this beautiful spark of new life, and allow them to see your hand; allow them to understand their decision, and to choose the greater destiny in Thy Light with your Immaculate Mother. If prayer has ever influenced your Sacred Heart and miraculously changed the hearts of men or the course of human events, influence and change their destiny now. Give them the grace that my soul wishes to dispense to them. Share with them all that you have given me. Grant them the composure, wisdom and grace of your precious Mother. I want them to know upon their entrance into your divine Kingdom that I loved them too, that I fought for them, and that my sacrifices in union with yours obtained for them the blessings of redemption. I wish them to know that I gifted them with my love as your brother. Let them realize that their lives became beautiful because I loved them, and came

How Do I Pray? Fiat Maximus!

before the God of the Universe and begged from my knees and with my tears in my eyes that they be given a life they would never find on their own. Let them know one day that I expended the highest petitions of my heart for them, such as they were, and you answered them because you are the love whom I knew you to be. Dear Jesus, I know that their most derelict wills cannot withstand the supernal attraction of your Divine Love, if you but show it to them. Reveal yourself to them, and deliver them from the darkness that human exile and unmitigated pain have thrust upon their broken hearts. Dear Lord, I know that if they were to have been given the miraculous graces that I have received from you, they would be smartly abandoned to your Mother, and would find comfort in the heart that your Mother has matured in me. There would be no mortal impediments then. Beauty would thrive. I wish to intimately share with them all that I have known of your Mother, slowly, day by day, minute by minute, to the ultimate goal of manifesting divine love to the ages as one heart beating in love with you. My Jesus, you overcame my will and made me obedient to your Will because I was so blessed from the beginning, the beneficiary of so many petitions and the prayers of other men. I am not to credit for my deep love and allegiance to you; I am not to be lauded or praised for the faith that you have so miraculously and generously instilled in my soul. It has always and everywhere been you who were triumphing over my lesser being with complete magnanimous grace – undeserved, unearned and free as your gift because you wished me to know that you love me. You saw my better self before I ever looked into my soul to divine that I am your adopted brother. This is why I ask that you accept my request as humanity's own voice. I intone their prayers for them that they do not yet know how to utter. I ask for their baptism in the miraculous as their sponsor of good intention. I speak for them to invite you to unveil their eyes to the sublime supernatural. And I tell you, should they stumble in accepting, give them even more graces as you have given me, and charge their missteps to my tally. Blot out their offenses with thy Divine Mercy. Do not fail or be unrelenting because of the weaknesses of human nature. Empower it with the same Holy Spirit that you have brought to a raging fire within me. Please triumph over the darkness for me, for humanity, and for the entire record of our humble origins. Please allow them to return to love, to transcend the human tit-for-tat and the hideous jousting for sinful supremacy. Allow them to recognize these moments that are quickly passing away, that they may never see again. Allow them to see the beauty and possibility in their submission to your Divine Love. Please do not let them pass this opportunity by. Please do not let them lose the years, but instead begin anew. Let this be the day when the souls of men break through the soil of this world and begin their ascent into the bliss that you in the Most Holy Trinity have shared with them. Dominus, please hear me now! Please grant this miracle of fortification and transformation upon humanity's being. We will surely thank you when you overwhelm us with the vision of your Face. I am praying for their strength to say 'yes' to you in response to your graceful call. If the world can be changed by my prayers, please play out this dream today. I wish to touch your Heart with my love. Destroy the devil as quickly as you have pushed the clouds from the skies. May a pleasant breeze waft across the union of humanity with its God. O' Great Dominus, rescind the curse of Adam with thy Most Sacred Body and Blood and thy Divine Word; roll back the darkness and lay fortifications surrounding the dream thou has placed within my grasp, and enshrine humanity within these ramparts, raised by your Kingdom. All these things I pray for every human heart, that the vision of your love overwhelm our will and make it perfect in conforming to you who are Love Incarnate. I am love too, O' Master, as you have redeemed me in you. I call to your bountiful Heart with strains of your own voice. And, in the generous bond where we share everything that is good, I ask from you miraculous deliverance for humanity from the darkness, from diabolical subterfuge and demonic distraction. Let humankind wholly understand the transcending beauty of love; let them see it, let them know it as theirs, assist them in choosing it, yearning for it, striving to find it, stopping at nothing, no sacrifice too great, leveling their most determined will to arrive in full communion with you, and let them see you vibrant and amazing for all the nations and ages to come. All you Holy Angels of Heaven, I beg you to come forth! Light-bearers, healers, evangelizers, visionaries, luminaries, courageous heroes, romantic dreamers, dispensers of wisdom, soul-soothers, conscience-rousers, and heart-restorers. My heralded friends, my compatriots and guardians, my beloved Dominion Angels – Blessandarie, Octavius, Flavius and all the rest, descend upon the place where humankind rests; enter their souls and caress God's beauty to beatific light; bring it into their day, adorn them like the pauper plucked from obscurity and called before grace to be elevated to his throne, bearing diadems and a crown at the right hand of the Lord.

O' Dominus, I do not know how to say with sufficient words that I love you, and I love them too. I come to you because I adore you, and because I know you are the fulfillment of our dreams. My only hope is in your word which I ask you to utter for me with confident happiness and eager expectation. O' how joyful

How Do I Pray? Fiat Maximus!

I am to be your brother! O' how I wish to be evermore like you. I admire and worship you beyond the skyscraping stars. There is nothing for which I cannot praise you. Even your decision as to the dispensation of my petition, I praise, because I know that there is nothing in the universe that would stop your granting it, except that one soul who would require the darkness of my sacrifice for their entrance into Heaven. I understand, I agree, and I submit to this wisdom in union with your Divine Will. I too see the granting of my wishes as being subordinate if the soul of my brother or sister hangs in the balance between the abyss and the vaults of Eternal Paradise. I choose to save them if this be the case; I choose the darkness to go on. I choose the Holy Mass to continue. But, I pray that that one broken child would say 'yes' and that the awakening of the millions would commence by your granting of my request. I bring before your Sacred Heart the vision of the collapse of the protesting nature of man and its transference into allegiance to your Mother. Scorch 'I do not need...' from the vocabulary of men. I beckon that you will see my petition as the portent for the defeat of our enemies, conquered by the maternal grace of your Most Immaculate Queen. Make my petition a radiant force in the transformation of this final age. My prayers speak to your greatness, to your mighty choreography of our lives. I ask you to manifest my desires in the beautiful ways that I envision them. Can someone be so blessed as to have such dreams realized through thy divine consent? I will praise you all my days, notwithstanding the finality of your Will, because I love you, and I will follow you, and I trust in you. The salvation of humanity resides in your Most Sacred Heart. Place us all there now, and deliver us to your perpetual light.

In nomine Patris et Filii et Spiritus Sancti. Amen.

The Final Colossus - In Battle Array

Chapter 7
Discernment and Man's Response

"Do not conform yourselves to this age but be transformed by the renewal of your mind, that you may discern what is the will of God, what is good and pleasing and perfect."
— Romans 12:2

Prideful naivete often circumscribes discernment of the works of the Holy Spirit, particularly instances of miraculous intercession. Most everyone has boundaries to their faith where they will ultimately say "I don't believe that" to truly authentic manifestations of God's Love. Perfect surrender to the Holy Spirit is extremely rare, while the arrogant willfulness of those who wish to decide for everyone else is not. Very few have ever exhibited the ability to immediately invoke the faith of Abraham complying with the sacrifice of his son Isaac or the Most Blessed Virgin's perfect assent before the Archangel Gabriel. This is why God made a covenant with His chosen people based on the first, and saved the redeemed through the second. God can present His Will to humanity with perfect clarity, knowing in advance that rare few will believe as He desires. This is evident in Jesus' Life, Death and Resurrection. The Father knew that humanity would reject His Son and crucify Him, although Jesus had the omnipotent faculties to convince them of His true identity with His miraculous power any time He desired. The Father wants allegiance without bounds, a perfect act of the will, uncoerced. We must realize that no criteria exists by which we can prevail in putting God's works on trial. Even inflicting death upon the Truth is of no permanent effect. He will do whatever He desires without consulting any human being if He so chooses, while still expecting us to grasp the opportunity to display our obedient response to His sanctifying grace. His methods and motivations reside in realms that render our intellectualism irrelevant. Why? Well, for the explicit purpose of giving us an Abrahamic moment of faith where we would offer Him our ultimate fiat. This is why the criteria we humans often employ to discern whether situations and events are of His Holy Spirit are misapplied when they are oriented toward ruling Him out, instead of ruling ourselves into the operations of His grace. We should never have the disposition of requiring Him to convince us before we respond. He turns His back on such audacity. We should rather invoke our personal circumspection, and a bit of fearfulness, that we not reject Him in any way. [*Psalm 111:10*] You see, our sagacity can be employed in two ways. We can employ stern incredulity in defense of our self-autonomous pride, or we can call upon the cardinal virtues so as not to offend the truth with our reticence and denial. It is simply whether we consider ourselves to be gods, or whether we testify that Jesus Christ is the true King. Saint Augustine in his work, "Of the Morals of the Catholic Church," invoked "virtue to be nothing else than perfect love for God." And, prudence being one of the forms of virtue, "...is love distinguishing with sagacity between what hinders it and what helps it." If we approach Our Lord to place His works on trial, our efforts will be futile. We will find ourselves holding the hammer that drove the nails into His hands because He will endure the sacrifice by remaining outside our intellectual grasp, calling us to abandonment in the highest reaches of His grace. He will not capitulate to the extortion of those who refuse to believe by conceding to their demands for miracles that would ultimately destroy their need for faith altogether. Although, He will triumph with power that every living soul will understand in the end. Until that glorious day, He will allow the doubters to walk away and create as much havoc and division as they can willfully generate. He will allow sinners to treat His messengers exactly as He was treated. In fact, the Scriptures testify to this. Does not Jeremiah 20:7-11 say as much? This is the sacrifice of love that His messengers and evangelizers offer. Further, multitudes of people perceive private revelation as some anomaly which only a deluded eccentric would claim. There are others who see it as assisting their personal divining process where they hope to catch a glimpse of their future which they can then begin to manipulate. Our Lady would tell us that the Holy Spirit is often seen as unconventional to worldly people; and secondly, She would say that the future is not yet written, although She knows what it contains. She is here because the free will of humankind possesses the power to mold our destiny and render it holy through our repentance. She told the world at Fatima in 1917 that absent humanity's response to Her, God would send a great chastisement upon the world. And thus, most of the planet endured the horribly destructive

Discernment and Man's Response

burden of World War II. Well, so much for the opinions of the pastoral parsers who keep telling the world that it doesn't matter whether or not we respond to our Holy Mother's miraculous appearances. Notwithstanding Her knowledge of the future according to Her Son's will, nearly all that She relates is conditional upon mankind's response. This is no different than God declaring to Jonah the destruction He meant to inflict before relenting due to their repentance in sackcloth and ashes. [*Jonah 3:10*] Our Lady's scrupulous detractors hail these occasions as false prophesies, while She instead sings the triumph of the prayers of Her children that have altered the course of history that She was warning about. Many times, She states things to impel humanity's response, knowing if we would but listen and obey, Her declarations of our future will be amended. And no, She does not have to overtly declare Her prophecies as conditional just to satisfy someone's scrutinies. She expects greater faith than that, and trusts that Her children would seek the higher wisdom. She knows what She is doing. Her miraculous intercessions have always been about the amendment of our lives and the impending future She knows is coming, should we ignore Her. None of this perspective is offered to give legitimacy in any way to delusional soothsayers, charlatans and unbalanced dreamers. All credible prophecy and mystical events come through the frame of reference of the Catholic Church and are discerned therein. Any other examples have almost no power for conversion. What good does it do to prophesy horrible future events if the prophecy does not provide the prescription for altering those events? Our Holy Mother has told me that if there were no hope that She could inspire the conversion of men, She would never have come.

    I have read many personal opinions professing how one should discern the substance and motivations of those who claim to be sent by God to dispense His message of salvation. Most are nothing more than missed opportunities to have encouraged people to greater faith, where instead they have been shown the off ramp into skepticism. The few that were substantively written only provided very generic guidelines on where to begin our personal discernment, presuming one has a mature, well-formed, mystical Catholic framework of reference to begin with. For those who do not, these simple guidelines are usually contorted into a cudgel that they wield to pummel everyone else's faith into compliant skepticism alongside their misinformed fears. The first skeptic with an opinion personally decides for everyone else what God is doing as if they are the infallible ones; and they usually do so claiming that they are in complete conformity with the mind of the Church, which oftentimes couldn't be further from the truth. Nearly all who believe themselves to be experts, or who are acclaimed to be, actually are not. While the Church's wisdom is arrayed in layered beatific nuance that is open to the spontaneity of the Holy Spirit, their dispositions reflect sound-bite disorientation that rejects the Third Person of the Most Holy Trinity altogether, not to mention scowling at their Heavenly Mother because She creates difficulties for their ideas of a pluralistic ecumenism. Then, there is the disordered frame of reference of the Protestant mentality. No significant act by the Holy Spirit in the present day, especially through Jesus' Mother, can pass the ridiculous exegetical stringencies that these terrified individuals employ to level judgement upon anything that tweaks their pharisaical biblical rigidity. They are lost deceivers quoting Scripture who are unhinged from the frame of reference of the Roman Catholic Church, which their religious traditions and interpretations of the Bible inform them to hate.

It is from an unbalanced sense of discernment that one stakes-out disparate actions and words of a seer, judges them with one's own naive intellect and lack of mystical understanding, then spreads personal fears, misperceptions, and misconceptions as the factual information that was supposedly received directly from the seer. This occurs consistently in the atmosphere surrounding our Holy Mother's appearances. We must realize that none of our opinions, nor most of our analysis, really matter to God. He wishes not for His Mother to be analyzed and critiqued, rather, He wishes for Her to be faithfully obeyed. He knows most people judge mystical things with a worldly mentality, and are poised to reject Him at the drop of a hat because He did not show them a miracle. Commentary related to Medjugorje is filled with a maelstrom of this drivel. Worldly opinion is mistaken as prayerful discernment; and wilful pride presumes to speak as a surrogate of the Chair of Saint Peter. The possibility for confusion grows even further when no one of ecclesial grace with a mature mystical sense accepts the responsibility to protect the work of the Holy Spirit by offering faithful affirmation to one who is experiencing these mystical gifts. Jesus says, "Go show yourselves to the priests," whereupon these authorities shudder, saying amongst themselves,

Discernment and Man's Response

"This person is a mere uneducated leper. How dare he come into our midst and challenge us with a claim of his healing by the hand of God. Healing is only what we say it is. Satan could have been the one who healed this vagabond." And, the Gospel continues its march toward the Cross. Ecclesial affirmation, when legitimate, serves to quash Satan's opportunity to generate turbulence and division ginned up through the undisciplined personal interpretations of the secularized laity who fill the vacuum left by ecclesial indifference. The devil descends upon the mystical atmosphere surrounding every authentic instance of miraculous intercession where he is given an opening through the lack of faith of any spectator. He interrogates crowds looking for aggressive personalities that will sow division and derision. Those who believe they know the most about the Church he targets to become his instruments of slander, if he can. He looks for pride. How many false witnesses appeared before the Sanhedrin, accusing Jesus absent the facts? Of course their sensibilities were offended when Jesus challenged them to destroy the temple, where after He would rebuild it in three days. [*John 2:19*] Think about it. For that statement alone, no normal worldly thinking person at the time could have continued believing in Our Lord—and people would do the same today. But, our Lord did not pander to them by trying to explain the mysteries of His Majesty that they did not understand. He knew future generations would see the error they were perpetrating that day, and why. Where did their discernment falter? He did not throw the pearls of His Kingdom before the swine. He did not appeal His Crucifixion. He did not plead for His Life amidst their stubborn ignorance and pride. In fact, it stuck in their craw even to the pinnacle of Mount Calvary where they jeered Him upon the Cross, "*You who would destroy the temple and rebuild it in three days, save yourself, if you are the Son of God, [and] come down from the cross!*" [*Matthew 27:40*] And, every one of those scoffing bystanders was ultimately chastised by their own consciences after their deaths for having so offended the authenticity and integrity of His Sacred Life. The beliefs they held in the hour of darkness were revealed in the fires of the Truth. [*1 Corinthians 3:13*] We should not for a moment think that this exact phenomenon has not been occurring throughout Christian history. And, it occurs today. Oh, how much divine grace has been rejected. How filled-up with justice is Jesus for our rejecting His Mother's overtures!

The Final Colossus - In Battle Array

Let us now go back to the original point. A sea of people usually surrounds the events of miraculous intercession who do not have the heart to offer their own fiat. But, these same ones have an unrestrained penchant to obscure any difficult truth that challenges their self-identity by invoking their wilful pride against it. They exist in a state of uncertainty and fear that something is going to be asked of them in the way of Christian sacrifice. They are terrified of life being anything more than how they have conscripted it in their mental and emotional conjuring. And, from that churning sea of self-estimation and doubt, the scandal commences against the blessings from Heaven. Very few intercessions in their potential magnificence survive the process of discernment from a human perspective because of the faithlessness of those surrounding the occasions of grace. Is this not the case in regards to all evangelization? The Scripture parable of the seed sown in the thistles, on the rocky ground, or onto fertile tilled fields is evident and accurate even here. [*Matthew 13:1-23*] Think of the destruction that thistles, rocks and a parched landscape can impose upon delicate, peaceful beauty. My earlier description of frames of reference and perspectives is completely applicable in this process of revelation and discernment, especially in those who are not the immediate recipients. And, those frameworks of reference, mixed with ego, are unique to each person involved. Among how many faulty perspectives can miraculous intercession survive discernment for the benefit of mankind? There are millions of deluded authoritarians who are scandalized that I even used the word "mankind" instead of the androgynous term "humankind" in my previous sentence. Imagine what the wilfulness of men can do in their critiques of thousands of pages of words from our Heavenly Mother. It is shortsighted to say that every authentic intercession will survive if it is indeed authentic. In truth, each of them has already succeeded in glorifying our Lord Jesus Christ outside of time. Great vindication is forthcoming for every authentic seer and messenger at the final judgment of the nations. The question is, did each of us grasp our Savior's merciful overtures for the sanctification of our soul in the time of the green wood, or will our suffering be the catalyst for our purification when it becomes dry? The smallest things seem to scandalize many, while the more principled are left wondering how the sea grew so choppy. We see the same dilemma throughout political campaigns in the relationship between the candidates, pundits, partisans and the public. Candidates who try to portray their views clearly must endure partisans salivating for any series of words that comes from their lips that they can twist, misconstrue and stuff back into the candidate's mouth so they may hail to the ill-informed public just how grotesque the candidate truly is, using their own manufactured interpretations as evidence. Thereafter, the hopeful public servant is left wondering how anyone would believe he would say something so outrageous. Then, pundits and news anchors, partisans all, report on the scandal of character that has just been manufactured by this twisting of the truth by the candidate's enemies. This is all truly the work of the devil in the political and media processes of our republic; and it is the work of the devil in the discernment of occasions of mystical grace. Both recipients and believers of miraculous intercession must be very prudent, anticipating Satan's wiles and the weaknesses of sinners. In the case of my brother and me, Our Lady has offered us great insights and assistance at times in navigating subterfuges that the devil planned against us. Others, we were asked to engage with our courageous faith in order to grow our strength in defending the truth. We can refer to Jesus' wise guidance of His apostles, *"Behold, I am sending you like sheep in the midst of wolves; so be shrewd as serpents and simple as doves."* [*Matthew 10:16*] If any messenger of the Gospel does not respect this wisdom and naively divulges information to people who sow scandal, Satan will enlist those who mistakenly believe they are being righteous as his wolves to tear them to pieces. He will send waves of skepticism throughout multitudes at the slightest opportunity given him. The Holy Spirit is peaceful, prudent, patient, and steadfast in sacrifice, but is well-equipped to admonish and thunder the Truth of Christ Crucified. The devil agitates, slanders, is impatient, boisterous, aggressive, and exclusionary. He incites fears, arouses egos, sows doubts, and portrays himself sanctimoniously as the authority over all things while holding a Bible wrapped in the robes of any denomination where he is given a seat of influence upon which to sit.

    My contemplations, even from childhood, have always renewed a challenge within me. Would I have believed Jesus and been His follower if I would have been alive 2000 years ago? Not knowing what I know now or having the foundation of the Catholic Church as my contemporary confirmation, would I have been swallowed up in the arrogance of the Pharisees, thinking I was obeying God while attacking His Son? Would I have accompanied Saul or been on the run from him with the Apostles? Would I have been scandalized by Jesus stating that He could rebuild in three days a demolished edifice that took 46 years to build; or would I have been intrigued by His spiritual presence and words, searching for meaning and understanding in them? Would I have walked away when He spoke of eating His flesh as actual food, or would I have asked Him how so that I could have moved forward in my allegiance to Him? Would I have recognized five thousand people being fed with virtually nothing in the middle of nowhere as being a miracle, and then astonished at the overflowing baskets of leftovers? Would I have been scandalized by Jesus restoring a man's withered hand in the middle of a synagogue in a high noon showdown with Pharisees on the Sabbath? Would I have considered the shepherds at His Birth to be delusional when they spoke of the miraculous intercession of the Angels singing before them in the fields? Would I have believed the Most Holy Virgin when She said that the Child in Her womb was conceived by the miraculous intercession of the Holy Spirit, absent a man? Would I have been ashamed to stand with John and Jesus' Mother at the Crucifixion, unable to summon the faith that Jesus' Life had not been in vain and that He would rise again? Would I have been scandalized when the Prince of Peace was making a clearing in the Temple of all the merchants and their livestock with whips and cords, had I been there? Would I have slandered Him in private amongst my friends after hearing Him publically admonishing the chief priests as whitewashed tombs whom I would have been taught to respect? Would I have believed instantly when my friends barged into the room saying the Son of Man had risen from the dead? Would I have believed without placing my fingers into the wounds of our Savior's hands? Would I have believed the miraculous works of the Apostles; Peter and John, Paul and the rest, the risings from the dead, the healings, the calling of the Holy Spirit upon their congregations, and their miraculous deliverance from imprisonments and shipwrecks? Would I have believed the prodigies of the Holy Spirit that were shared throughout the early days of Christianity? The only people who can say they would have met the challenge of these things and testified to the Truth are the ones who invoke their faith and believe God's great works today!

  The challenge to faith leveled by the Holy Spirit is identical. Not just acceptance of dogma and doctrine, that's the easier part, but an open-hearted and full-throated allegiance to Him "in Person," a cooperation and belief in

"God with us" today. Otherwise, our doctrines and rituals are dead as doornails and will wither within us without bearing a morsel of fruit. Scriptural apologetics absent the experiential mysticism of the Holy Spirit becomes an uninformed bludgeon of parsing and exclusion. Arrogance thrives in position, power, and worldly authority. And, university sheepskins profess nothing more than ill-gotten flesh from the Lamb of God, filleted from His esteem; self-acclaimed sentries at the gate who declare that no one may pass, while the miraculous assistance flourishing through the Holy Spirit is sent to crucifixion in the way of the Messiah in cadence to their sanctimonious mockery. The King of kings dies in all who do not believe because men kill Him. The Crucifixion is being effected nearly everywhere we look, but no more poignantly than in the rejection of the miraculous intercession of the Most Blessed Virgin Mary in our time. Must She die in the hearts of men too in order to validate the compromises of a pale ecumenism? I tell you, Her Son is not going to allow it to happen. The Triumph of Her Immaculate Heart is imminent! And yes, if I were alive 2000 years ago, I would have been cheering Our Lord as He was purifying the Temple because His Mother is doing it now, and I assist Her. Hear my voice hailing Her miraculous intercession! Hear me declaring the beauty and supremacy of the Roman Catholic Church! Hear me elevating the priesthood! Be convinced that I defend the Papacy! Never doubt my hope that Jesus will find the True Faith fully-vibrant and in command of the full attention of humanity when He returns! Our age and this nation will be converted and saved! All you cowards and doubters, consider yourselves rebuked!

    Everyone can readily see that it is very difficult for the body of humanity to collectively embrace what the Holy Spirit does without astounding miracles to prove each occasion. The human reference frame will not make way for revelation, and obedience is far too great a sacrifice for unchecked pride. We are skeptical to a fault of any sinner being worthy of belief, leaving each evangelist to seemingly walk the lonely road to Calvary. Again, see Jeremiah 10. It is a miracle in itself that the evangelization of the Holy Gospel has produced so much fruit through two millennia by virtue of the witness of sinners. Actually, it has occurred through the horrific suffering and sacrifices of the Saints and Martyrs in the image of their Savior. Yet, no matter how derisively humanity reacts to the miraculous intercession of the

Holy Spirit, God is triumphant nonetheless. He manifests His power either through the obedient fiat of those who believe and convert or through the sacrifice of His messengers in the face of all those who do not believe. So yes, God will be successful through every authentic revelation. There will be success in faithful obedience invoked by the hearers or triumph in the sacrifice of the soul who imitates Him in His Sacrifice. But, woe to those who cause the sacrifice, should it be required. There is a day of Reckoning for all injustice. He will not allow the world to gloat over the worldly defeat of those faithful ones who were put to derision, shame and death for spreading the Holy Gospel. The Saints will have their day. There are entire galleries of supposedly discredited evangelizers, visionaries and martyrs who are waiting for their moment of vindication in the Glory of His Second Coming. Our Lady calls it with sacred emphasis, "When Legends Rise Again."

Sinners who allow themselves to be guided by their pride naturally set themselves up as judges from thousands of miles away, or next door for that matter. Opinions are actually no more than that. Pseudo-experts are self-acclaimed and commonplace. They are non-sanctioned adjudicators of realms they do not have the authority to breach. They often base their discernment on news articles and books that are written by other people who are themselves frail and faulty. They establish their incredulity on the traditions of skepticism that Satan has anchored in the orders of time, while disregarding the testimony to the faith enshrined in the Scriptures that they should be invoking. Let me repeat: *They establish their incredulity on the traditions of skepticism that Satan has anchored in the orders of time, while disregarding the testimony to the faith enshrined in the Scriptures that they should be invoking.* Their doubts and fears get the best of them. They look for the slightest anomaly that might disturb them and hang their faithlessness upon it, thereafter becoming better evangelizers for their doubts than they ever were for the Gospel of Jesus Christ. Things are rarely how we initially perceive them at first blush or after the crowd of doubters has crafted the narrative and scorched the landscape. I have watched this scattering process stir for over a quarter century as Our Lady's Morning Star Over America work has unfolded; and I accept that neither my brother nor I were polished vessels that allowed others to see the reflection of the truth clearly in our lives at the outset. Yet, it is also true that those who are educated and well-read about every apparition and mystic in history seem rarely

Discernment and Man's Response

disposed to surrender their skeptical criticisms when faced directly with the beatitude of Our Lady's miraculous intercession. Ah!—it is then that the test of faith arrives. They believe they are more the experts than the recipients. They have a vast body of knowledge as an observer, but rarely any as a sacrificial participant. There is no virtue in being simply an analyzer forming critiques when Our Lady is looking for obedience, sacrifice and communion in order to understand. She is looking for a band of brothers, heroes who will launch salvos of sacrifice in honor of Her Son Jesus. There is no Christian brotherhood, charity or common sacrifice in being a persnickety bystander. There is no bond of father and son, or brother and sister. Yet, the hemming and hawing often continues for years and decades in the face of Her converting grace. The doubters never quite place themselves into the perspective of actually being the one whom God expects to believe and respond. Discernment usually flounders and ultimately stagnates for decades or centuries before the response that Our Lady was seeking is ever forthcoming, if at all. Ironically, no one will understand until they believe. It is a paradox. One's frame of reference must come into clearer focus, become "inspirited," into becoming a participant in the redemption of the world through a sacrificial faith that is in communion with the heavens and the Original Apostolic Church. We are staring directly at indistinct blurry images of the truth, and become disconcerted when Our Lady snaps any of them into focus. We like blurry images and believe they are the end-all to our faith because they give us leeway for the mediocrities we desire. It is much the same as someone needing glasses. Oftentimes, a person does not realize his eyesight is radically out-of-focus until a pair of spectacles with a clearer prescription is placed upon his nose. Until that moment, while in the indefinite realm of uncertainty, latitude is given to our pride. This is where our Heavenly Father calls us to be like unto His Son instead. Of course, conformity with the Gospels, the teachings of the Catholic Church, and sincere efforts toward a holy life while manifesting the fruits of the Holy Spirit are to be conscientiously sought by any seer. But, are not these the basic requirements of faith for everyone, especially those who wish to discern? If the discerner does not manifest these things in their own life, how are they able to discern any work of the Holy Spirit in the life of another? Does not the ground have to be fertile for anything to have a chance to grow? The Truth of God has its verifiable signature in all that He does.

And, that signature is the Cross. Both seer and discerner have need of the Sacrament of Reconciliation, and each should readily admit it. Climbing into the vaults of perfection is a humbling, yet courageous, venture. Even Saint Paul ruminated over his battle with the flesh. What you will rarely hear critical observers concede is that maybe their human perception of events is not the way one should discern the mystical actions of God. People stand where the worldly crowd is and follow where it leads. And, if it is a crowd of doubters, it is rare courage that stands forth and declares belief, knowing that rocks will be hurled, and Saul will stand over a pile of cloaks until the mob finishes the job. The world has too many self-acclaimed autocrats who offer nothing but frail human opinions about the supernatural intervention in the life of another, most having never responded to an authentic supernatural "light" in their lives. I think it might have been Saint Teresa of Avila who said that the authentic nuances of mystical phenomena are hard to distinguish unless one has received them personally. When someone says, "Well, I don't think so and so's messages are authentic...," we should counter their boasting by asking, "by what criteria?" Invariably, the intellectual obfuscation by inundation will commence. And, with the confidence that they are one of the Church's most prescient minds, we will hear them offer the reply, "Based upon the teachings of the Church," while we realize that their understanding of the depths of Catholic Truth is truly not all that dimensioned. Anyone could line up one hundred Christians and gather one hundred different perspectives regarding any religious truth, and the serious contradictions among them would be innumerable and astounding. The fractured nature of Protestantism tells us as much. There is a denomination on every street corner because those who became unhinged from the Original Apostolic Church cannot seem to agree on anything. Does this not show how personal opinions can be formed and influenced by both ego and attitude over the course of our lives? How many people does the devil form subtly their whole life long to use as his instruments to scandalize Our Lady's miraculous intercession when the season arrives? Each of us is vulnerable to being radically scrupulous when determining whether the deceptions of Satan are present in the life of another, but rarely admit that very perception may be his lies in our own. There is an entire movement of unprincipled scrupulosity assailing Our Lady's long-suffering presence in Medjugorje by individuals with nothing more than worldly stature;

and they are wrong. Their discernment has failed them, and their pride has taken the seat of their humility. What irony! The Scriptures witness to humanity's normative response to the grace of God when the authorities assailed Jesus' power as coming from the devil. It is an easy deception to place ourselves into a mental state that requires God to convince us of His work instead of extending the faith that He expected from the beginning. Do we not say, "Show us a miracle, and then we will believe?" Jesus was haggled repeatedly by spectators to prove Himself with miracles. And, the dozens He did work were never enough. The resurrection of a man lying dead in a tomb four days was not enough. Now, do we really wish to be identified with that skeptical crowd of insolent doubters who jeered Him on the Cross? How does that help encourage our openness to the Holy Spirit? We risk snubbing His beatific gifts while thinking that we are being the obedient ones. *In no way am I suggesting that one should be gullible and believe everything within earshot. The frame of reference is the Roman Catholic Church, and it is an imperative companion to our discernment. We must always solicit the discretion in the wisdom of its esteemed Hierarchy.* All of us must simply be open-hearted like children, and as wise and perfect as Our Lady when the Archangel Gabriel came to Her. Occasions of mystical phenomenon must be discerned for their purpose, elevation, universality and possibility. They all flourish to their intended magnification through faithful trust, or are squelched into the obscure backwaters of history as lost opportunities, only to be regained by future ages that might prove more worthy. We must ask ourselves instead what is growing, then till, nurture, fertilize and cultivate the good to its ultimate magnification with the Holy Spirit being our guide. Our times are more radically oriented toward disbelief of anything Our Lord does than they are toward our being hoodwinked by demonic fantasies. We should be far more confident in our ability to recognize our Lord. I say unleash Our Lady, give Her the venue of our hearts and the rostrums where truth is proclaimed, and let the holy turbulence of worldwide conversion begin. Cultivation, indeed!

    The devil does not need mystical phenomena in our contemporary secular era. Ol' Scratch has already run the table, and is ready to sink the eight, having all but blinded humanity to the supernal reverberations from Jesus' Crucifixion and Resurrection. The devil has hidden himself so effectively in the fads of our time, making the expedience of our lives absent the cultivation of moral virtue. In truth, most do not understand that Satan actually exists as a real demonic personage, a hideous spirit, who is the instigator behind everything that humanity suffers. Why would he remove the camouflage provided to him by humanity's lack of faith? He thrives there, nearly unopposed. While tens of thousands sing the "Ave Maria" in a sea of veneration to Our Lady each year at Fatima in the Cova da Iria on grand Marian feast days, multiple hundreds of our children were singing in unison, "Kiss the Devil," in a nightclub in Paris prior to a mass slaughter, inspired by the very one they were kissing. Why would the devil ever need to mimic miraculous intercession? He performs his work outright in full view of the entire world. He has workers for his cause. And, to complete the spectacle of moral inversion, the rock band U2, fronted by the international humanitarian and supposedly Christian, Bono, legitimized the satanic evil manifested in Paris by hailing the Eagles of Death Metal band and sharing his stage of popularity not a month later. I say—*Hail Our Lady's miraculous intercession from your stages, Mr. Bono, and you will truly obtain the changes to the world that you seek!* We never seem to recognize the obvious, and descend from our holding pattern of discernment in order to land on the tarmac of the Truth of the Ages. It is like a plane flying in an epic thunderstorm with visibility being a few feet, and lightning cracking and turbulence buffeting the cabin and all its occupants. Danger and destruction loom. Vulnerability terrifies everyone aboard. The pilots are unable to see the ground, and are afraid to begin any descent toward land. Then, they hear Our Lady's landing beacon pinging on their flight console and Her Light strobing across their windshield calling them to their rescue, and they are too paralyzed with fear to call upon the courage to steer the craft in Her direction and follow Her home. I tell you, they will ultimately be taken down by the storm.

  Doubts circle above those with cowering faith like buzzards targeting a kill. Consider how many of the citizens of Lourdes and the surrounding countryside in 1858 wagged their tongues and scoffed, turned their backs and walked faithlessly back to their homes as if in the glow of vindication as Bernadette began digging through the mud and wiping it on her face when Our Lady told her to wash in the spring. Who stood with this Saint in that moment? Who sensed the supernal truth? Was not all intellectualism mortified by the pure obedience of a small child executing circumstances that they were not remotely prepared to embrace? Where did faith survive that day? What happened to worldly judgment and ecclesial discernment in those moments? They were in the back row skulking when God shamed them by replacing humanity's insufficiency with an astounding vision of the power of faith, all embodied in a young child with a dirty face who had just done public penance for those who were too filled with pride to believe her innocence at the outset. The Almighty Father placed a rock in everyone's path named Bernadette, and everyone but the most faithful stumbled over it. Our Heavenly Father repeatedly manifests His converting power in situations with themes such as these. He always has. Did He not allow Jesus to be crucified as the ultimate example of superceding mankind's darkened intellect once and for all? It has been the same from the beginning when Abraham heard the God of Heaven asking him to sacrifice his son. What a moment for this great Patriarch! O' how I admire him and praise the heart that generated the faith to believe something so contradictory to the sensibilities of his affections. He loved his son, yet he surrendered his heart, his progeny and his future to his God. We must ponder our faith becoming like his because then the Almighty Father smiles at finding something worthy on the Earth upon which to heap His blessings. He provides the opportunity for our allegiance to eclipse the mundane and proceed to the stratospheric heights of His Throne. He takes us to the proverbial end of our rope, and then advances onward past our intellectual reach to see if we will follow Him beyond this world into His beatific reign through a sheer act of supernatural faith that will imprint the ages. Then, He saves us! He unleashes Heaven's power in miracles of conversion and healing. It is like watching Hoover Dam collapse before our eyes, and life-giving water storming down, out of the mountains of His Kingdom. We traverse a thousand miles in holy practices tethered to our intellectualism as if they came from the Mind of God Himself, then let the most trifling gap between ourselves and His unseen reign scandalize us into throwing away the moment when time could have transcended Eternity. We do this simply because we are faced with that line in our being where supernatural faith truly takes flight; and at that precipice, we skid to a stop and refuse to launch ourselves into the arms of God and take flight across the chasm.

The Final Colossus - In Battle Array

Consider the Crucifixion. Of the multiple thousands who witnessed Jesus' healing power and heard heavenly wisdom from His own lips, how few stood at Calvary. And, those who did, save Our Lady and Saint John, had their faith annihilated. John was innocent enough to believe; Our Lady was pure enough to know. The rest could not span the breach into the Resurrection. Belief died with Him, just as it died in a Grotto in France on the day of an innocent, dirty faced child. Why? Because it is natural to comprehend events according to the flesh of human understanding, bound by the architectural reasoning of a world where suffering and death reign. They did not yet love Jesus with the untethered, supernatural, world-conquering faith that was to descend upon them at Pentecost; and neither was the faith of the spectators of Lourdes reignited until the verifiable healings began to flow from the miraculous spring birthed by Bernadette's obedience unto humiliation before the masses. But, my friends, look at our Virgin Mother, so beautiful, so confident, so powerful, yet so stricken. She was unbounded in allegiance to Her Son. She knew at the moment of Her Son's Death on the Cross that the story was not complete; there was to be a new day, just as He had foretold. She believed in the Triumph of Her King while the rest would consider Her faith in Her Son as delusional, believing the power did not exist to triumph over the Cross. Surely upon seeing Her grief, She was chided by those near Her to let go and accept the inevitability of Her loss. Her faith instead echoed Her Son, "Get behind Thee, Satan." And today, the miraculous intercession of Jesus' Mother is mocked as liberally by our detractors, not outright, but through the pathetic drool of reasonableness that drips from their fanged incisors. Too many scoff, too many turn their backs, too many immerse themselves in worldliness, hoping to outrun fate. Any one of us would now wish in hindsight that we would have had the courage, insight, and composure to believe precious Bernadette when very few would on that revelatory day in Lourdes, France. Would that we would have said before the miracle of the healing spring began to flow, "This young child does not lie. It is not her will being done, but Our Lord's as she obeys Him. Blessed is our God!" It is a wholly different person who invokes the courage to declare Jesus Christ in those grand moments of the greatest faith. Imagine the joy and vindication that God will place in our heart after the miracles commence. Our display of faith prior to the miracle is the fuel that generates our ecstasy afterwards. The

Discernment and Man's Response

heavens will eternally record, "This servant believed before placing his fingers into the nail-prints of His hands! This child ran to the Tomb in joy at the first declarations of, 'He is Risen!'" This is the unending joy that Our Lady's children are going to experience at the Triumph of Her Immaculate Heart where the entire Earth will experience the culmination of every Marian prophecy ever pronounced at Her many shrines and places of appearance throughout the world. Our fists will fly into the air as we shout again at the top of our lungs, "Yes!" You see, we believe the miraculous intercession of the Matriarch of Heaven at this very moment in the realms of our everyday faith and trust. We cry, "Mother!," with a voice that brings tears to the eyes of the Archangels. We recognize the signs of the closing ages and declare them to a failing world. Our love is large enough to let God be God, and we follow where He leads. We have the courage to participate, to publicly profess to pastor, parishioner, pagan, Protestant and publican what we know to be true amidst Her gentle grace. And, that Truth is the Roman Catholic Church and the Bread of Life from Her High Altars! It does not necessarily matter where the Queen of Heaven is appearing because "where" is a worldly dimension that She supercedes. She is with us and miraculously interceding in this world, powerfully and vividly in the lives of every child who will listen and obey, with the miraculous intercession of seers and messengers being the glaringly apparent "motives of credibility" that are testifying to this truth. And, it is these same visionaries who endure the sacrifice, recalling everyone to prayer from the heart, to seek once again our God while He may be found, to embrace the Kingdom of the Saints who have gone before us, and to unite at the Sacred Altars of the Roman Catholic Church. Yes, Saint Bernadette pray for us now and at the hour of our death! You, blessed creature of seraphic love.

The wiser course when confronted with the mystery of God and the testament of messengers and evangelizers is to discern the clarity of the orthodoxies and animations of our own faith from within. We must allow the Repository of Faith of the Catholic Church to become our framework of reference, detach ourselves from our worldly druthers, insulate ourselves from the choirs of skeptics that will no doubt congregate around honest faith, balance our prudential caution so as not to offend grace, withhold judgements based upon our offended sensibilities, allow God to do things we have never dreamed, accept the challenge of a deeper faith, test the spirit within us, desire to sacrifice ourselves to every end, be poised to believe, watchful for the voice of confirmation, patient to the unfolding, and ready to cooperate with the full measure of our faculties with both hands upon the plow the instant our courage grows large enough to respond. Then, plow deep and wide with eyes on the horizon of Glory! No one has the faculties to discern mystical works who does not have an extraordinary capacity for humility and interior self-sacrifice. Satan attacks honest discernment like a rabid wolverine. He sows doubts and whispers, "prudence." He is a deceitful and cunning beast who knows our individual weaknesses, and employs diabolical strategies to disorient the clarity of our perceptions. He will disturb sleep, create depression, instigate fears, foment mental torments, infuse terrors, leverage selfishness, generate insecurity, inflame ego, inflict sickness, cause accidents, multiply doubters, twist facts, manipulate narratives, and overall create confusion, all for the purpose of getting someone to conclude that the work of the Holy Spirit does not bring peace, and is therefore illegitimate and the source of all the disturbance. He will give people riches, esteem, validation, temporal peace and contentment in this world, if they surrender and reject the truth, just as he promised Jesus while tempting Him in the desert. He implements any confusion possible against Bishops and other clergy who are called by God to the responsibility of affirming and protecting Our Lady's miraculous intercession, knowing their ecclesial cooperation with the Queen of Heaven is a death blow to his agenda of evil. The devil searches to leverage any weakness of faith or inordinate appetite held by one who discerns. For example, he will attempt to hold hostage the discernment of a Bishop, if that Prelate possesses any career ambition for ecclesial appointment or elevation in the Church. He will whisper to him that he will lose the respect and esteem of his more skeptical brothers, and lose his chance for the magnification of his ministry in the hierarchy if he affirms the miraculous intercession of the Most Blessed Virgin Mary. He will torment him into being hyper-scrupulous if he can. He will encourage indifference and reticence as the safe alternative to faithful surrender to the Mother of God and cooperation with Her Queenship. But, a Roman Catholic Bishop with a pure heart who has bathed his life in personal sacrifice and self-denial is lethal to the devil. He is rock who can unleash the transformation of the Earth. These Bishops, and there are many, are the heroes of the divine Kingdom whom God tenders the power to bend the course of

Discernment and Man's Response

human history toward the beauty of Salvation in extraordinary and miraculous ways, all through their heroic faith which they stretch-out across the chasms of doubt. Authentic discernment of what is right and true rests in the unity of any discerner with the Crucified Christ. There can be inquiry without doubt, and faithfulness that accompanies patience. We must never force God to convince us by annihilating our faith with the final definity of miracles. In fact, He rarely does so, allowing instead for men to simply walk away of their own free will, leaving seers and messengers to embrace the suffering of the Cross for the purification of the Church. If we approach the supernal interventions of God with the humble disposition of a child of Mary, He will invoke the blessings of a proud Father upon us for standing so open-hearted before Him. And, the victory will not only be His within our souls, but a great gift of Light upon those walking in darkness. We will be standing in awe when this happens because He will reach down and reveal Himself to us.

Imagine the sorrowful indictment in the hearts of those who realize they fought against the Immaculate Queen of Heaven by doubting a messenger of God who was doing the best he knew how. Recall the response of Bishop Zumarraga of Mexico in December of 1531 when confronted with a peasant named Juan Diego who proclaimed he had been sent to the Bishop by the Mother of God. Bishop Zumarraga was a very saintly man who had displayed great devotion to his vocation by building hospitals, libraries and universities for the people. He was also called the Protector of the Indians in his defense against their enslavement in any form. Yet, as the story is recorded, after turning away Juan Diego's entreaties twice and delaying his attention a third time, he fell to his knees in apologetic tears when Juan Diego's tilma was unfurled before him, and his eyes fell upon the miraculous image of Our Lady of Guadalupe. Why tears of apology when he was not "required" to believe anyway? Because he had doubted this simple child whom the Queen of Heaven had sent to him. He saw his pride. This is the pride that needs to be recognized; the pride that rejects the miraculous intercession of the Most Blessed Virgin Mary because we are not "required" to believe. A pride that we too will one day see in ourselves, and weep. We have been dismissing what is holy in Christ for two millennia, and are presently waist-deep in a crisis of faith that Our Lady is attempting to rescind. Each of us is called to the perfection of our soul, no matter what anybody says about how, why, or if it is even possible. We are called to perfection in trust, abandonment, light of the heart, contemplative belief, and unity of purpose and wisdom, fortified by knowledge of the Gospel and the angelic Dogmas of the Catholic Church. Our vision must become inflamed by the hope of Our Lady, our strength forged by the endurance of martyrs, transcendental courage held aloft by mystical trust, and grace polished to the golden glow of a radiant Kansas wheat field so as to succeed in every holy endeavor as human creatures conceived by God. We are called to a radicalism that is the only realism, that of the perfection of our faith whereby we ratify and concur with every morsel of grace that God so deigns to bestow upon His people. Our beings should resonate the beatific grace of Jesus Christ in union with the supernal essence of Creation that is sustained at every moment, in every molecule, atom, and scintilla by His Divine Mercy. How does the concept of skepticism even have meaning in the midst of such a beatific communion? The doubter has nothing to offer. We should be cheering sunsets and babies' births, instead of passively numbering abortion body-counts as each dusk comes upon us. The gifts of God are abundant and unique among His faithful through the power of the Sacrament of Confirmation. "Come forth!," He says. We must be brothers and sisters among them all. Jesus' Life on Earth, the Public Revelation of Perfection, is the example of our human potential, here and now, through the Sacraments in union with the motivations of His Holy Spirit in our modern day. Our Faith is one great Construction and Progression of that Divinity, displayed to humankind and the ages. And, this Christ prayed, "Be one with Me. Be like Me. Love Me. Trust Me. Offer the Sacrifice upon the altar of the Cross. See the Father whom I reveal to you." The Son of God died proving the redefinition of our lives. He brought Redemption upon His people! Now, upon every sacramental Confirmation until the end of time, He proceeds in dispensing the full measure of His Holy Spirit into the very fiber of every soul who will let go and allow Him to guide them from the inside, cultivated with the good sense of Catholic Dogma to know its conception, responsibilities and consequences, and how with honest intention we enliven it in our flesh for the Glory of God. Why? Not so much that we will see and applaud His great Sacrifice, although we ought; not so that we would be found as having been obedient to His Kingship, although we must; but that we might be transformed in being, restored and ignited as a new creation in the flame of His Spirit, and risen to the perfection of love that He passionately embodied so that our redemption may be assured in the highest heaven in our own eyes. [*Matthew 7:1-2*] He wants us to be happy, not only with Him, but with ourselves forever. He wants us to feel His power flowing through our veins, children of honor and distinction in the ranks of the Saints. He wants us to humiliate Satan. He wants us to be raised out of the confusion brought by the veil of our exile, wrought by the sins of Adam and Eve. He wants us to forsake that which diminishes us. He wants us to portray the beauty that is beneath the scales of sin. Did not scales fall from Saint Paul's eyes after Ananias laid hands upon him that he be filled with the Holy Spirit? [*Acts 9:17-18*] Why? That he might testify to the Glory! This is the fruit of miraculous intercession. Sight to the blind! Insight into the wisdom from on high! And notice, it was the ecclesial affirmation of Ananias that unleashed Saint Paul to begin his evangelization of entire swathes of the pagan world. Initiated by miraculous intercession and ignited by ecclesial affirmation. The Lamb of God was united with the Will of His Father unto death, through a horrific Passion into the bowels of Hell and back into His Creation Triumphant. Oh, what a conquering this King has inflicted upon this mortal world and the realms below it! And, He is coming in Judgment of His Kingdom on Earth. The Owner of the vineyard is on the way! The stewards are going to be held to account. Entire packs of angelic sheepdogs are going to be set loose upon the wolves for daring to enter the meadow where the True Shepherd watches over His lambs. His Holy Spirit obliterated death and now resides peacefully beside our soul at this moment with the benisons of His Triumphant Reign. He simply asks that we open our eyes to the Light that streams from the Heaven that we can see with our hearts, in the vision of our holiest selves, our greatest imitation, our oneness of being with Him. We cleanse both the lepers and the holy places. Whips and cords or tears and gentle touches, it does not matter if it be for the glory of God. Here and now, this grand Holy Spirit waits for heroes to accept the charge.

But here we are; His genius not allowed out of the books of our Bibles, obscured behind habitual manners devoid of passion, sincerity and gratitude. Oh, the stories of the Gospel are common knowledge; nods are given to the teaching and the Dogmas of the Roman Catholic Church, yet argumentation and intellectualizing dominate the parameters of how far we must reach-out with our heart to God and where our faith should take us. Intellectualism is rendered dead if faith does not take flight into sacrificial actions of the heart. Even the best often posture in opposition of the final steps that would set them free. The Heavenly Father allows the Most Blessed Virgin access to our terrestrial domain, but their mentalism turns them away from the sacrifice required to embrace Her assistance and become instruments in Her hands because it requires their faith. Truly, one cannot achieve the likeness of Christ if we reject the station of the Most Blessed Virgin Mary in Heaven. The Mind of Christ holds Her elevated as His Queen because He saw Her tears as He hung on the Cross. And, He will never forget it. The poseurs of faith mock us when we strive to emulate the breadth of this communion. There is always a boundary that they cannot seem to pass, whereafter they assail those who outdistance them in faith. They knock every baby dove out of the sky that they see fluttering toward our Holy Mother's arms. They become instruments of the devil by inciting fear into the hearts of God's children so that they will not answer the call of their Heavenly Mother. Was it not said that the devil attacks those who are discerning by sowing confusion and doubt? The Holy Spirit is present and working with undeniable power in the world, and little children see this Light and giggle with happiness at having a Heavenly Mother so beautiful.

I say repeatedly that there is a difference between knowing the Faith and having some, between reading the Bible and embodying it. There is a raw difference between observer and participant; between one who speculates about the Cross, and another who joins Jesus upon it that He not suffer alone. We know very clearly the example that Christ set, which He expects us to imitate to the best of our faith. This is our potential. This is our duty; and it is our destiny. Nonetheless, it remains difficult to look into our hearts and follow where the Holy Spirit is guiding in this 21st century because faith has been vacated from the reference frame of our culture. The world ever descends into darkness until we return to the Light. Our Lady says the sacrifice is not too great, our opposition is not convincing, our suffering is for glory, Jesus is the Way, and our reward will be Resurrection in eternal Paradise. Knowing who Jesus is is not enough. The devil knows exactly who He is, as well. Suffering for the purification of humankind will continue until every soul comes into full communion with Christ as a family at One Table of Faith. That Divine Faith

Discernment and Man's Response

has been deposited in a succession of Pontificates of the Roman Catholic Church as the source of this salvation across 2000 years. The Original Apostolic Church has performed its Sacrifice well. The world is suffering because of the lack of faith in Jesus Christ, and nothing more. Multitudes numbering in the billions are not up to the task of the righteous fight. Dispositions are trembling before the altercation between light and darkness, deceived into believing the world will be as peaceful as a millpond if we simply allow evil its reign through some hollow pagan worship of humanist diversity in sin. Those without heart will stand and fight for nothing of eternal consequence. They will bury their righteousness and speak nary a word when staring into the abyss of the conflict. They capitulate to a false peace on the devil's terms. They reject the Cross and refuse to allow anyone to place them upon it next to their Savior. Where are the willing warriors who laugh in the face of the threats of Calvary? Who are the righteous ones who will tell secularists that their day is over; their experiment in darkness has miserably failed? Long past obvious does truth testify that we worship comfort at the expense of those who are suffering; we feel entitled to self-worship and luxury; and curses we hail upon anyone who calls upon our moral conscience to impede our impending damnation. How long will the false accusation ring that we are nothing but "moral scolds?" We are doing nothing more than asking that love be allowed its reign; and purity, truth and justice given their day. I may be no more than another thief hanging next to Jesus, but I will be a sinner who tells everyone who is watching that the Man beside me is the King of kings. When the truth is spoken, it is Satan who throws a conniption. It is he who causes the altercations and lack of peace. He instigates the riots and mayhem. He foments the wars and disagreements. He trashes great traditions and taunts for progressive revolution. He screams for Christians to remain silent in their quarters. He demands to be treated equally alongside all that is holy and majestic. He kills children in the womb. He attacks the Roman Catholic priesthood. He is the diabolical one who accuses the righteous of being uncharitable and destroyers of dignity and peace. It is he who assails us as xenophobes if we declare the looming separation of the sheep from the goats. He is the liar. He is the antagonist and agitator. Jesus said that if the world hated Him, it will also hate you because you are not of this world. [*John 15:18-19*] My brothers and sisters, be of Heaven! Thunder righteousness even if you have only the capacity to whisper! If you can't whisper, sign salvation with your fingers. If you have no fingers, blink your eyes in Morse code. When you can no longer run, you walk. When you can no longer walk, you crawl. When you can no longer crawl, you scoot. When you can no longer scoot—You conquer the world from where you sit! With anything and everything, glorify Jesus Christ and His Mother, and move into unity with God's Catholic Kingdom!

Our Lady is appearing in our generation across the cultures of the planet; She is the Morning Star Over America, and we should be saying, "Blessed is our God for such a Mother!" Our responsorial allegiance should be that the entire world kneel as one collective heart in prayer of the Holy Rosary as a preparation for the Holy Mass, just as She asks. But, what does the contemporary chronicle testify? Indeed, one successive dispensation of grace after another discarded with indifference and skepticism, consumed into the fabled lore of history because discernment and devotion faltered in the most powerful among us. Leadership cowered, and the faith that has raised its honorable head in the moment was turned away sullen because the heavenly taper found nothing combustible to set the world aflame. It is Jesus' Divine Mercy made manifest that the Most Holy Virgin intercedes in these dark times of our contemporary era. The light of Lourdes is still shining. The premonitions of Fatima still loom. A miraculous image on a tilma still hangs majestic in a Mexican basilica. Medjugorje yet stands proud. And, Miraculous Medals and Brown Scapulars are adorned about the necks of millions. Yes, Our Lady's voice rings with a truth so sweet upon the appetites of simple men. She repeats and petitions undaunted in the face of intellectual arrogance, pride, stiff-necked indifference and derision of Her generosity. She knows that faithlessness informs the coward's prudence, and dithering debates scatter the devotions that She calls to order. She speaks of salutes and postures and composure and comportment before our Crucified King, in whom we will see what was meant to be. Our Lady is the colossal evangelizer of human history, indeed the Final Colossus, who appears in union with the Deposit of Catholic Faith to these closing ages of uncivilized chaos. Given venue, She will vaporize evil through Her majestic grace and bearing. Jesus Christ the King will be glorified in the Triumph of His Immaculate Mother! And in it, He will come again with Power and Glory, just as the Apostles saw Him taken up into

Discernment and Man's Response

Heaven from the Mount of Olives. But, this time, He will be accompanied by Legends in their glorified flesh! Maybe we should plant enormous olive groves on each of our mounts to beckon Him to return as our welcome to Him. Maybe then, He will not feel that He has had to wait so long for His people to adore Him.

    We must do more than stare directly into the Face of Divinity and offer conscience-soothing excuses for our lack of obedience to Heaven's Queen. When God asks for our abandonment and full-throated declaration of His Kingship through His Immaculate Mother, and we do not respond, is this King not justified in thundering, "What is the meaning of this? Bring these skeptics before Me!" Our hearts must be extended sacrificially in obedience to God, here and now, at the closing twilight of the mortal ages. Our faith must be intrepid in order to break past the reservations that cordon these lukewarm and trembling souls. We must invoke the holy audacity to laugh at the intellectuals and theologians who glean every tidbit of caution that they can sift from the wind that blows from the flapping lips of their college of skeptics. They are all irrelevant and anemic. They place one hurdle after another in the path of the truth, and then exaggerate the height of each one. God works miracles in front of them to elevate their souls away from their acedia, and they invoke the temerity to look Him in the eye and say, "We've decided your miraculous intercession is unnecessary. It's not biblical. We don't really need the appearances of the Virgin Mary or Saints and Angels. We're not required to believe that anyway." Christ thunders, "Cowardice by any other name!" He has not sent Angels to spread the Gospel; He sends repentant sinners who have soft hearts, who are asked to claim great things in His Name. If the world would abandon itself to Our Lady in deed and truth, and obey Her, we would see both religious pluralism and moral relativism wiped-out by Universal Catholic unity in a matter of months, if not days. But, it must come with the full-throated allegiance of every member of the Original Apostolic Church. Then, everyone will want to be a part of the supernal Love that the Virgin shares with Her Son. It is rather foolish to believe that God is allowing Her mystical presence as only a spiritual novelty for the few. Evangelization has never been personal, but universal. Jesus Christ is not preaching to the chorus, but asking everyone to sing along with His Choirs. He grants miraculous graces, such as His Mother's miraculous appearances, as an inflection of His

Divine Mercy because He knows the world is lost and failing with the Day of Reckoning bearing down upon us like an approaching shockwave of an earthquake that will rattle mountain ranges into rubble around our feet. One day, Jesus was presented a sinful woman by His enemies who were nothing but a crowd of gnat-strainers. Yes, justice stated that she be stoned according to the law. But, Jesus bent down and wrote on the ground. Then, peering at them with His forthright gaze, He asked for the sinless one among them to step forward and cast the first stone. [*John 8:1-11*] He does likewise when faced with those who claim that the miraculous intercession of His Immaculate Mother is dismissible as merely an unbiblical distraction. He reaches down and writes the history of Her miraculous interventions upon the Earth, the sins of men mitigated, the healing that flowed, the conversion that was ignited, the Light that shined, and the suffering of the innocents that made it so. Then, He likewise stands and says, "Let he who is without sin step forward to dismiss My sinless Mother." The only person who can say "I do not need..." is one who has already reached the pinnacle of spiritual perfection and is torn with ribbons of suffering, after which, the statement becomes nonsensical blasphemy because no person who has displayed such passion for God and love for His Mother would ever let such a brash statement of pride pass their lips. Anyone who does so is lost in their intellectual dictums, proscribing to God what He will have to do to secure their obedience.

Yes, the Deposit of Faith is the motherlode of knowledge that points to spiritual Christian perfection through our union with the responsibilities engendered throughout its Divine Revelation. The Deposit of Faith testifies to a trinitarian theme: Definition, Manifestation, and Assumption. This is the ladder of salvation by which the Author of Life came to Earth, and by which we must return to Him. The Godhead of our Creator is the Definition. He is Three Divine Persons upon His Throne in His unseen paradisial Kingdom. The Life, Death and Resurrection of Jesus Christ is the Manifestation. The Lamb of God is the Messiah who came into the mortal world, all that is ultimate made visible as Man. And, the Assumption is a reciprocal action between God and man through the Holy Spirit where Jesus lays claim to every generation of humanity, while man takes upon himself the yoke of faith to believe in the Manifestation. We are assumed into the Manifestation through faith as Christ assumes us into His Divinity. This is the operative thesis of the

Deposit of Faith that is consecrated into humanity's soul as a gift of Jesus' Divine Revelation of Himself, sent by the defining Father. And, this Messianic Revelation has been impressed into intellectual form for transmission through the ages until the end of time. But, it is only intellectual for the sake of the initial dispensation, after which the assumption of the soul into unity with God occurs through repentance, prayer, sacrificial devotion and suffering in unity with the Great Sufferer of Salvation. We must remember that the operation of the Assumption can occur perfectly, absent all theological knowledge through the intonation of one Our Father, uttered from a penitent heart who receives the Most Blessed Sacrament. The Definition prompted the Manifestation, who in turn testifies to the Definition and offers the Assumption. The Definition was perfectly articulated in the temporal realms by the Manifestation of the Second Person of the Most Holy Trinity, assuming flesh to sacrifice His Life for the Salvation of humankind. The Deposit of Faith manifested itself within those who had been assumed through the Great Sacrifice of Calvary into companionship with the Manifestation, who is the Definition. There ever after, the Definition has been present where the Manifestation flourishes; and to this, the Deposit of Faith testifies. The Manifestation of the Definition is present through the Holy Spirit through that which Jesus has assumed, be it nature, the baptized human heart, the liturgies and orchestrations of the Catholic Church, the assistance of the Communion of Saints, the protection of the choirs of Angels, and the intercession of the Virgin Mary. Did not Jesus say the stones would cry out? Why? Because they had been assumed by His Kingship. And, does not the Deposit of Faith which records His prophecy testify to those cries, should they rise up? The stones of the Church, the little ones, are crying out in testimony to the miraculous intercession of the Queen of Heaven, She who was first assumed. The Deposit of Faith lays claim to the entire history of Christianity; the Earth that has been sanctified by His Blood, the faith in every person, the tides of history choreographed by the Holy Spirit, every miracle and grace from above, every voice that says, "Jesus and Mary," and each gift for which we have suffered and prayed. This entire compendium is "Manifestation," it is "Christ" and is the confirmation of the presence of the Definition testifying to the veracity of the Deposit of Faith. It is in Him that we live, move and have our being. This grand Revelation is the product of a unity between the all-encompassing

Definition and its Manifestation through Him who is the Holy Spirit. We are one with the Most Holy Trinity through faith because He has assumed us into His Definition through His Manifestion by the power of Assumption! And, the Queen of Heaven is the embodiment of the Assumption of Creation. This is why the works emanating from on high, including the miraculous intercession of the Most Blessed Virgin Mary, cannot be simply dismissed without bringing discordance, not only to our testimony to that great definitive Deposit, but to our unity in it as well. This is why human dignity is held in such esteem by the Deposit of Faith, for the baptized human heart is "assumed" and is therefore a Manifestation of the Definition.

Ultimately, the Most Blessed Sacrament is the supreme Manifestation of the Definition; it is Christ Himself in His Flesh and Blood who cannot be ignored or rejected without offense to the Definition. One cannot reject the miraculous effects of the Sacrament of Confirmation without generating a dissonance toward the Deposit of Faith, and thus the Definition. One cannot dismiss the Hierarchy of the Apostolic Succession without offending the Definition. One cannot reject the consecration and manifestation of the Bread of Life during the Holy Sacrifice of the Mass without impugning the Manifestation and slandering the Definition. And, neither can one be in communion with the four great Marian Dogmas of the Deposit of Faith and thereafter reject the divine intercession of the Most Blessed Virgin Mary. It is like saying that you believe in the Dogma of the Most Holy Eucharist, then claim that it is incidental whether you attend the Holy Mass and receive the Most Blessed Sacrament from the Sacred Altar. In other words, "Do you acknowledge the Manifestation of the Definition you claim to embrace?" And, the martyred Legions of Heaven roar, "Oorah!" Two thousand years and counting of God manifesting His grace and power through manifestations of the Holy Spirit prove the Roman Catholic Church's supremacy in its Deposit of Faith. Indeed, the motives of credibility abound! Jesus Christ allocates and apportions the converting graces of the Holy Spirit upon His vineyard because He still works to save this generation by helping us mitigate the atrocities from the previous. He sends His Immaculate Mother as an effusive procession of the perfect Spirit of Pentecost. Therefore, we must accept and magnify Her miraculous intercession to lost souls who would then be converted and caressed by Her motherly affection, that they be assumed into salvation alongside our

Discernment and Man's Response

love for them; that we may be one. And, then the King of kings will come and make all things new because we are all pleading in unison, "Come Lord Jesus!" The ladder of revelation is extended from Heaven in the order of Definition into Manifestation, leaving an imprint called the Deposit of Divine Revelation for the Assumption of the Earth into its rightful place in the vaults of His Kingdom beside Her, who was first Assumed. Our return to Heaven is an ascension upon the same ladder beginning with the Deposit of Faith which tells us to take on the yoke of perfection through the Sacraments of the Catholic Church, that we may recognize the holy manifestations of God that would guide us Home. We accept the Deposit of Faith for the absolution and sanctification of our soul, and for the purification of our vision, that we may see the full spectrum of the Christological Manifestation who has assumed Creation in the Holy Spirit, whose esteem effects the return of sinners to the Father who is the Definition. There, the definition of sinful man will be expunged from our own memory, leaving us in the glory of a Kingdom that we will believe we never left.

The Final Colossus - In Battle Array

The Final Colossus
In Battle Array
AD 2010

Saturday, January 2, 2010
12:44 p.m.

Introspection - psych. the observation or examination of one's own mental and emotional state or cognitive values.

Introversion - psych. the direction of interest inward, as in preoccupation with one's own thoughts and feelings.

Extroversion - psych. the direction of interest outward or to objects outside the self, as toward the external environment.

>Conscience and confession - introspection
>Faith, hope, and prayer - introversion
>Charity and compassion - extroversion

"My stately sons, the miracles you have inherited from the Lord which began in your youth have now continued into the second decade of the twenty-first century. I clearly know that you are dedicated to the refinement of human life because of your devotion to Me and dedication to the Church. And, your obvious consecration to My Immaculate Heart has stationed you inside the Most Sacred Heart of Jesus where you will always be comforted and raised, no matter what happens to you mortally. You should be thankful for this; you should reflect upon what this means to people worldwide who have been touched by the Crucifixion and Paschal Resurrection of My Son. We will begin 2010 with a mixture of pedagogy and mysticism as we have in years past. I wish for you to learn that your speech and writing, indeed your very psyche, is shaped by your relationship with God. The Holy Spirit works in you and also for you by your own conscience and confession. This is your introspection. And, your faith, hope and prayer are manifested by your spiritual introversion, not that you look at yourself as the means to the ends of human redemption, but that you come to know yourself as you are and must become. Your charities, compassion and sacrifices on behalf of others are fruits of the extroversion of your belief system, in this case and as always Christianity, so that you are known to others and the greater world by the outward expressions of your inner-constitution. Humans tend to be expressive based upon their ability to communicate. If they know that words come easily, they will use them oftentimes to excess. Neither of you are like this; words do not come easily for you because you are yet scrutinizing Creation. You have not come to all the conclusions that you will eventually embrace. And, this is as it should be. People who are unsure of themselves tend to be verbose in ways that are illogical, as they attempt to conceal the deficits in their knowledge inside the facade of undue garrulousness. You have both met people like this; they tend to speak a great deal about nothing. They tend to speak whatever comes into their minds at the time without careful forethought. Others employ language skills and phraseologies to cover up for their weaknesses and failures, or to cite the weaknesses and failures of others whom they do not like. This is what it means to speak in hyperbole, to exaggerate conditions and circumstances to make a point. This is not the way I have taught you to communicate, but it is the way the enemies of the Church do.

My Special son, your writings and that of your brother are precise and cogent. You make a point clearly and defend your arguments with sufficient scriptural and doctrinal documentation. If anything, most homilists speak clearly the strains of Truth without the flowery excesses inherent in most secular and political speeches. I have taught you how to think, speak and write with the conciseness of the Holy Spirit. There is a term used for this kind of communication that is the antonym or opposite of hyperbole, and it is litotes. (Greek word meaning "simple.") This is pronounced in such a way as to emphasize all three syllables. Lie-toe-tease. And, the accent is on -toe. What this means is to speak in understatements. If I were to suggest that something is all good, I would simply say it. However, if I wished to understate the same thing, I would say that something is not bad at all. In other words, I take its opposite and accentuate the negative of that opposite. 'Bad' is its opposite, and 'not' is the negative. Do you understand? *"Yes."* This is how moral circumstances are rephrased into questions, such as Pope John Paul II was known for. Another example would be to say something that is 'the same' as actually 'not unlike.' Do you see? How do you think this affects the reception of speech and writing when it comes to the radically imperative persuasion of evangelizing the Christian Gospel? *"It does not have that definitive element to it."* Yes, and most important, it does not sound overly accusatory. If you wish to convince someone that a moral position is the only one acceptable to God, you simply ask the question as though the alternative places them at odds with Him within their mind. When arguing for the end of abortion, one might ask somebody who is against ending abortion whether the unborn child should have a choice. This directs the focus of the argument toward a creature whom you are suggesting has the capacity of self-will. In effect, you are stating that a fetus is a human being capable of judgement before they have the chance to tell you otherwise. This is called premising or circumventing the false arguments of the enemies of the Church, effectively reducing the alternatives they might employ to distract the conversation into something else. Is this clear? This is a technique that is used by politicians every day. What was the concept used by Vernon Merle Kays in his dissertation? Obfuscation by inundation. This is what seculars try to do when they are faced with the immutable teachings of the Catholic Church. They use hyperbole and exaggeration to issue baseless opinions and proclamations. We do the opposite. We speak succinctly by citing the dogmas and doctrines handed down by the Holy Spirit through the Church to uphold the foundation upon which a blessed human life must be stationed. This is how you are writing now. It is the way you speak when you wish to make a point. I am telling you these things because I wish for you to not waver from them. You are doing well, and I want you to know it. *"Your words help me to know the temperature inside me."* And, that temperature is actually your collective consciousness about the way the world ought to be. I ask you again as 2010 opens to believe that it is on the way to being that kind of world. There is no question that it has a long way to go. There is sin of all kinds eating on the spirit and flesh of exiled humanity. Mortals are corrupt creatures who are searching for a renewal of their very essence, whether they are aware of this search or not. We have something they all want, and it will be their big surprise."

Saturday, January 9, 2010
9:22 a.m.

natural virtue — any moral virtue of which man is capable
cardinal virtues — prudence, justice, fortitude, temperance
theological virtues — faith, hope, and charity

"The leap of faith that the Holy Mother describes is preservative and predestining. Falling in love with God is never a fatal schuss."
William L. Roth

"How better to wile-away the winter blues than to hear the voice of the Mother of God? My children, it is always fair when we speak, when we proceed to whittle the resistance of nonbelievers into shreds through your miraculous faith. You have known that My intention to upbraid those who reject Christianity is based on their own judgement of themselves when they see their Savior one on one. My Special son, My speech today is about the upcoming reward that you and your brother will have because of your faithfulness to Me and your loyalties to Jesus. I can imagine that you have forecast what the rest of humanity will endure, those who pursue the flesh and materials that blind them from seeing what you and your brother have known for decades. You are compassionate when you pray for them in private and condemn their selfishness in public. I have introduced today the concept of virtue and the Virtues that are written in the Catechism so you can use them in your memoirs. It is imperative that you make your memoirs goal-oriented toward the theological virtues, but you may if you like place them in the context of the idea of virtue itself. Every creature is capable of natural virtue; it is the way that the Lord gave them life. This is especially more true with the human species because you are also connected directly to God through the Holy Spirit and the Church. In case anyone asks, animals and fishes do not attend Church. This is My sorrowful attempt at humor. Anyway, humans are capable of intelligence in manipulative things, the term 'manipulative' not connoting anything negative in this case. And, humanity has the gifts of innovation and ingenuity on more than a practical plane. Beavers are creative because they can impede the flow of water, but humans are ingenious because you know that water is actually $H2O$. The point I am making is that you should when writing your memories remember that you are addressing a species about faith, about the urgency of being connected to the origin of life and not simply its practical facets. That said, it is appropriate for you to describe your youthful connection with the material world so you can better detail what transformation took you into the realms of the religious. Do you know how and when this occurred? No, and this is something that you should ponder, a matter for you to examine so you can explain how someone lives in the physical realms concurrently with the faith required to transcend those boundaries before you leave this life. Your quotation at the beginning of this message is quite relevant in this case. I am speaking about the phenomenon of faith as a noun and a verb, the same way that love itself is both. Faith and prayer are interchangeable terms in that you urge God through your active belief, your living faith, to change the world as you see it. This is likewise the definition of prayer. Without your prayers, I could not have come because the Father would not have allowed it. He knows that you speak to Him when you pray, even when you ask for My intercession.

Let us speak about the virtues again. The Cardinal Virtues that you will find in the 1994 Catholic Catechism that was published by then-Cardinal Joseph Ratzinger make clear that the 'content of the character' as you have called it shapes the verity of a Christian's faith. Again, if you prescribe the motivations of your own maturation in Christianity this way in your memoirs, it will have more universal appeal. It will help non-Catholics understand what it means to grow in allegiance to the Pope. It will make the Catholic Church appear more clearly the religion of Eternal Salvation to those who have never believed it. You and your brother have written many books together in the past ten years, but your memoirs, specifically yours, when written with the power of your own experiences, stand to be more converting than all of your previous books combined. Why? Because it is you who were called to believe. You were asked to trust that God was working through Me and through your brother. These are separate tasks, as you know. Once humanity makes this connection, they will more readily accept that the Pope in Rome is infallible, for example. There is a host of other fruits that can come of your memoirs in this respect. The point I am making about trusting should not consume the entire thesis of your first memoir, but simply be an opening to it. After you have made clear that you were required to enlist your deep religious faith, get on with the message. What has become the mainstay of your endurance, for example? What goals have you set for your family and friends? Did they accept them or reject them? What obstacles did you see in their way that perhaps even you could not have overcome? What have you learned from Me about the mysteries of life, about the lifeblood of your allegiance to the Crucifixion, about the role and influence of the Angels and Saints, about the phenomena of sacrifice and suffering, about individual responsibility in the collective Mystical Body, about the relationship between religion and secularism, about the countless theses that have been written regarding the concept of forgiveness, and the list goes on. Whether you believe it or not, you have an innate opinion about all of these, and your judgements and conclusions can be extremely converting for those who are lost. You wrote on the back cover of your last book that your only motivation is to transmit My messages to the world. Citing this objective casts the focus away from yourself and more toward My messages. This is a welcome sight for those who would only see you as another faulty human being. Give them reason to judge the messages instead of you and your brother. Do you understand? My goodness, I could give you a list of 50 to 100 more concepts to discuss in your memoirs, but I will not list them here. *"I would appreciate it because it helps me generate my thoughts."* Well, I have given you enough earlier in this message to keep you focused for the next two years. I am speaking about writing in intense detail about what a given subject means. Take charity, for example. It certainly means more than carrying water or giving two cents to the coffers. There are such things as charitable admonitions, charitable forgiveness, charitable almsgiving, charitable sacrifices and the like. You should ponder what an outline of your book might be composed of and what title you would use.

You are different from your brother with respect to wanting to know exactly where you are going. In other words, you do not need to subscribe to a given number of pages before you begin. Your brother does. You do not require advance knowledge of how much writing you will complete in one day. Your brother does. Neither of these approaches is wrong. Thus, you see that natural virtue is inherent in the Cardinal Virtues, and the Cardinal Virtues are inherent in the theological virtues. Each of these is described in detail in the Catechism around the 1803 mark. Indeed, you must realize that at least some virtue must be present before anyone ever begins to pray for faith itself. One cannot have deference to theology unless he is capable of natural virtue. Every person is born with this capability. I believe that I have given you at least an introduction to what I will speak in full about your upcoming memoirs. I also believe that your prologue for your next book is sufficient in length, and that it covers the topics that you need for the text. Remember that it is supposed to be mid-sequence in your anthologies, so you do not wish to give it the appearance of a crescendo. Now, what are your comments and questions for today? *"I didn't know how to chronologically put together my first memoir. It is an autobiography, but I did not know what autobiographical information to include."* This is because you are dwelling too much on you. You should not begin your memoir as though it is based on the passage of time. The idea of chronology is not the point. Let Me see. Please take in hand the Jimmy Carter book behind you – Keeping Faith. Now, this is an example of a memoir. And, he includes how he fell into politics and his earlier roots, but he does not do so according to dates and times. I am not suggesting that you should exclude every facet of your childhood that links you to My present-day manifestations, but you should also write about how you look back at yourself and your assessment of life while you were riding your bike for donuts and delivering the newspaper around town. What I mean is that you should describe how God saw you then, and how you as one person represented all the children of the Lord who were cast behind Adam into exile, innocent as you were. What were your struggles to comprehend the connection between labor and self-preservation, the seeds of service and reward, the shadows of capitalism you learned before you were ten years old, and such. What could you have possibly learned about those who are bound in hospitals and nursing homes when you broke your leg? What about the moving story of your surgeon from 1972 and the man whom I have described as another Doctor of the Church in your New Millennium anthologies? These are the kinds of things that pique readers' interests. Indeed, it would be the place to describe how your earthly mother overcame her obstacles in the face of giving birth to so many beautiful children, and working full-time, getting you ready for Church, cooking the meals, washing the laundry and every other such matter. Always remain positive when speaking about others in your memoirs unless it is to address the behavior of an entire class or group of people who have attempted to impede the mission of the Church. I sincerely appreciate your permitting Me to speak to you on this bitterly cold January morning. You will one of these days read this message when it is 90-degrees outside and wonder where time went. Thank you for your humble prayers."

Sunday, January 17, 2010
9:13 a.m.

Some standard identifiers

range - distance	value - quantity
altitude - elevation	rank - priority
attitude - slant or level	order - sequence
bearings - position	grade - inclination
heading - direction	degree - intensity

"My dearly beloved sons, I come to you today after you have seen a difficult week for western humanity as the earthquake has killed tens of thousands in Haiti. This is not some punishment from God, it is the result of a geological fault beneath the mortal earth. It was destined from the beginning of time. The casualties could have been averted because the geological survey indicated two years ago it would occur within the ensuing 24 months. They were warned; the government of the United States was asked to help relocate these poor people, and nothing was done. Now, the supposedly heroic United States is giving sparse aid to the region, and its people are patting themselves on the back for being so charitable. The stock markets will continue to climb; Americans will still purchase million dollar homes and luxurious automobiles; they will still fly to foreign nations on holiday, and they will do everything they have ever done to ignore the plight of the poorest of the poor. It is heartening to see the gigantic transport airplanes landing on the island of Haiti, but why must it come after the fact? The United States has given billions of dollars to the thugs and thieves in Haiti as a bribe to leave the common people alone, but with all the force of the American military, it is not used to enforce goodness and fairness in its own hemisphere. The military has been sent to fight for vengeance in far-off places for pride and profit instead. The plight of the Haitians is the direct result of the greediness and selfishness of the United States government. This is My assessment. *"I wish the United States could have great leaders."* I agree, but those who wish to lead the United States regularly plead to the electorate with their conscience wrapped around the American flag instead of the Calvarian Cross. There are tens of thousands of deceased Haitians who could have benefitted from the latter. Today, My Special son, I have given you some standard measurements of distance and degree. These concepts are criteria that help people discern where they are now and where they are headed. They can see location, intensity and intention by such things as these. The reason I have given them to you is so you can ponder them in relationship to the location of the human soul in exiled Creation. I have told you that Heaven is infinite, that it is not measurable in any context understandable to man. However, there are certain scales by which you can weigh the holiness of someone's soul before the Cross. Do you remember the virtues that I spoke about recently? These are the identifiers that allow someone to know where they are located in time, where they are headed, and to what intensity they are given to the Crucifixion on Mount Calvary. While the virtues I spoke about before assist in the determination of holiness, the standard identifiers I have mentioned today relate to the location of the soul in physical space. The point I am making is that they cannot be mutually exclusive because as long as the spirit remains within a man, he is affixed to the flesh into which he was born. Hence, a connection can be drawn between the two. If you speak in ethereal terms, you can make correlations about the Church and humanity that composes it.

      The Church is a spiritual creature. Let Me repeat – the Church is a spiritual creature. How can something be spiritual and also a definite creature simultaneously? This is the seeming contradiction, but it is actually no contradiction at all. The collective souls of humanity are the Mystical Body of Jesus Christ, and one that is spiritual in nature. Hence, Jesus is the 'creature' that all humanity must become. Do you understand? Let us look at a couple of the identifiers that I have named. Let us consider range and elevation. These terms are common to aeronautics, but they can also be applied to the conversion of the human soul. I see that you have already predicted where I am going. A person is a given distance from the Lord based upon his level of elevation. In other words, one is directly relational to the other. Let us look at the lower list of identifiers. Consider the ideas of rank and order. These tend to show position. You have heard these used when describing the Angels and Saints, for example. One can be a Saint and also a Doctor of the Church. There is a certain level of distinction here that refers to one of the earlier terms – attitude. Do you see how they are all interconnected? The reason I have issued this conversation today is to reveal another means to indicate that the beatific realms are altogether more connected to the world of men than most people are willing to recognize. When the Holy Spirit is shown metaphorically as a dove, does it not have altitude and direction? Yes, is the answer. The following is the crux of My point. The distinction that I am making is that it also has beauty. It has mysticism and all that comes from Heaven to which the inner-spirit is given. An airplane has none of these. What is the inner-beauty of a flying machine? It makes no sense. All the attributes of Heaven are present on the Earth; they eclipse and interconnect with the Earth, but the same is not always necessarily true of the limited physics of the mortal Earth. In other words, they are interchangeable only when men make it so. Do you understand? (*Air Force One SAM 26000 from Dallas became more than just an airplane because it bore the body of a martyred Catholic president, and is now enshrined in the National Air Force Museum in Dayton, Ohio.*) Yes, but you should understand that Heaven must be invited to fulfill this role on the Earth in Creation. Let us repeat. All the attributes of Heaven can be manifested on the Earth, but not all the aspects of the Earth are present in Heaven. What are some examples? There is no death or suffering in Heaven. There is no deprivation there. However, when men build great Cathedrals on Earth; now listen carefully because this is important, those same Cathedrals are built in Heaven. Their exact replica is standing in Heaven at this point in time. Hence, when you go to Holy Mass, whenever a priest pronounces the consecration during the Eucharistic Liturgy, God supplants the Cathedral in Heaven with the one in which you are standing on Earth. When the priest asks the Father to 'take these gifts' to His Altar in Heaven, He does so. That Altar becomes the one upon which the presiding priest is offering the Holy Sacrifice.

Hence, you see that the Church itself has standing in Heaven as a physical being without having measurable dimensions. It has beauty, self-worth, holiness, faithfulness, love, charity, light and all the other aspects that can measure its magnitude in the eyes of its Savior. It has value and direction, elevation, peace, joy and all the Fruits of Love and of the Holy Spirit. Since it has these things, they coexist on Earth and in Heaven. Is this simple enough for you? And, this is how many other matters are shared between God and mankind through the power of the Holy Spirit. It is how the Sacraments are given relevance. They are seen by the Lord the way you see inside your heart. In truth, you can see that holiness itself is given flight, measurable identification, by how well humanity trusts and interacts with Heaven in all ways taught by the Holy Gospel and the doctrines of the Church. Let us look one last time at the terms I have provided. These are also the measure of things by which you can transmit your feelings about the list you have drawn for your memoirs. It is more important that you describe what these things have meant to you universally, spiritually, than what they actually appear to be. For example, we spoke about your having broken your leg. What did I do, what did I say about your kind of suffering in relation to the ways human suffering worldwide is interconnected? How, for example, have I discussed the crashing of the airplane in the Andes with relation to your own fractured life while lying in the hospital? These are the matters to which I am referring – not so much the time sequence or the practical application of what has happened to you, but the broader scope of how they relate to humanity at large and the evangelizing of the Church. What is the immediate connection between your broken leg and the falling of the airplane? I will give you the opportunity to see, beginning with when they happened. What is your early intention for the list you have compiled? *"It was just a list of things that were poignant in my thoughts that I could work into the description of who I am and how you have taught me to see the world."* Yes, you have done well; you have created an excellent beginning to your outline. Just for My own apprisal, what would be some of the examples of a title for your memoirs? *"I haven't thought of any yet."* There are infinite choices, but only certain ones that will help define your heart through your vast experiences with your youth and through your relationship with Me. Your life has never really been about driving yourself into riches. Even the institution of marriage is not that important for men on Earth. After all, Jesus never married. What you should focus upon is driving home the message of clarifying the role of humanity in the finishing of the Earth according to the mandates of the Gospel. You can mention something that was at one time completely foreign to those who lived centuries before. No one has ever seen God. The idea that He would be born on the material Earth was so distant from the consciousness of mortal men in earlier centuries that it was laughed-off as cynical humor. But it happened! And, the prospect that a person could die and not cease to exist was equally unaccepted. The body dies, but the spirit lives on. My Special one, these are still radical concepts to millions of people today. This is how far I have to go to convince My children that eternal life is real. Whenever a new generation is born, the process must begin again. However, there will be many who will not be converted when Jesus returns in Glory, but works like yours and the many other shrines of the Church and My apparitions will be hailed before them to prepare their souls for judgement. There is nothing new to add to the Holy Gospel. Everything that was written for it had been done. I am the last hope for the conversion of lost sinners because I was there. I birthed Jesus into the world. I am a firsthand witness of His life, death and Resurrection. This is why My appearances and messages have been ongoing for so long. The Lord is merciful, and My life and intercession hail from that same Divine Mercy."

Sunday, January 24, 2010
8:58 a.m.

"The soul living in us now, here on this Earth, has the same eternal qualities that we will take into Heaven. What changes is our worthiness; we must become more holy through our prayers and the Sacraments of the Church. We belong to Christ's perpetuity despite the waning hours. The spiritual conversion of man is an amalgam of our faith and our soul's redeeming love—always absolving, infinitely shining, and forever bound to righteousness."

"I called you to Medjugorje for the purpose of revealing Myself as the Morning Star Over America. I called you there; this is what I do for all who travel to the Saint James parish. It is curious, however, that some go there and refuse to believe, even though I have summoned their acceptance. This is a function of their human will. It is also the impact of their pride. Some say that if I were appearing in Medjugorje, I would say more, I would make more emphatic gestures about the condition of the world. Others maintain that My only role in Salvation history was to give birth to Jesus in Bethlehem. The latter is correct to an extent written in the Scriptures, but I come now not only to urge My children to accept the Cross, but to overcome their own humanness, to bridle their opposition to the teachings of the Church. My role in Medjugorje and here in America is not so much about redeeming humanity, but converting humanity. Jesus has saved humanity outright. There is nothing I can add to His Sacrifice. Remember that I told you that Jesus did not ask Me to carry an ounce of the Holy Cross. It was completely His to bear. I never shed blood for the redemption of lost sinners.

Therefore, you see that My role as Mediatrix is to ensure the cultivation of the hearts of mankind either with kindness or the rawness of the cold facts. I speak with impassioned overtones when I see My children straying from the path of holiness, and this is the way you have learned to speak and write. I am not suggesting that I am not still the gentle Mother sung about in those pretty melodies, I am saying that gentleness comes in many forms. How could God allow Me to sit idly by and watch His children walk such crooked paths? How could humanity, all born from motherly wombs, not grow in enlightenment by the Wisdom of the Immaculate Womb that bore their Salvation into the flesh? There is an obvious correlation between being born into the flesh and being reborn in the Spirit. There is a great heaviness that attends the mission of teaching lost sinners right from wrong, and you have felt that weight upon you at times. I wish to make clear what I said before. You have the faith, love, and will to remain calm in oneness with the Holy Spirit. You have the power to tell evil around you that it has no authority to shape your thoughts, actions, and feelings. I realize that this sounds easy when it comes from Me because I am already in Heaven. However, think about My sorrow in seeing the Son of Man tortured and crucified before My very eyes. This is a grief that no one should ever have to suffer again. I have said on many occasions that it is replicated by mothers and fathers everywhere, those who lose their sons and daughters in the battles of war, accidents of all kinds, diseases, and outright carelessness. These losses unite the sufferers with the Cross to immeasurable degrees.

How many words have I said to you in almost two decades? It is nearly unimaginable. You should be pleased with yourselves, even righteously proud, for caring enough about your brothers and sisters to help Me convert them to the Cross. There are moments in history that account for thousands of years of change, and your lives here in this place are filled with those times. What humanity will see the most on this side of the veil is not the dailiness you have invested, but the earthshaking product of that investment. While you have lived hours at a time, they will see an eternity of beatific grace. Why? Because they could not have lived your agonies. Someone had to be called. A certain soul or two had to be touched by the miracles from afar, where the Angels tread and Saints repose, and you and your brother are these fortunate and yet unfortunate souls. Your sorrows have been real, your burdens toilsome, your suffering intense, but your hopes remain alive. The Lord will reward you with the presence of your friends beside you at the foot of the Cross and the gate of Paradise. You must realize that you have been chosen because you are capable. You are worthy because of your compliance. You must know that the Holy Spirit is consoling and advising you and that you are doing well. You have given your life for the Church and to the Church."

Saturday, January 30, 2010
1:01 p.m.

"We must remember that God does not create corrupt souls, but that we were corrupted by Adam. We are cleansed of that stain upon our baptism, and we remain pure by avoiding sin. Let us focus on the root of the problem. Exiled humanity is not inherently evil, but is constantly influenced by it. Unseen forces can oftentimes cause visible destruction. After all, it was not the iceberg that first doomed the Titanic, but the deathly cold temperatures that froze the North Atlantic."

William L. Roth

"During the awesome beauty of this winter, we are speaking about thawing human hearts, softening them to the Holy Gospel, tenderizing their meaning and direction, and preparing them for the admittance of the Holy

Spirit. My dear sons, I am truly grateful that you have decided for God your whole lives, and that you have again today come to pray with Me for the conversion of the lost. You know that these are historical times for the Church and for you. We must be careful to not lose sight of the majesty of your consecration to Jesus' Most Sacred Heart and to My Immaculate Heart as you greet each new morning. You have become accustomed to hearing and seeing the sarcastic cadence of the secular world that infiltrates the minds of those who are not predisposed to the spiritual realms. My Special one, your writing continues to awe the heavens. You have become capable of pouring-out your intellect about the Truth and your feelings about the way humanity ought to accept what the Kingdom of the Lord has to offer. You are so much like Jesus during His ministry, and your heart reflects the innocence that He never lost. My wish is for you to know that whatever the future brings, whatever blessings and obstacles come, I will always be with you. I have never lost sight of your desires to see the defeat of the wicked in your time on the Earth, and God the Father is completely aware of what this means to you.

My children, you are capable of becoming the pristine likeness of Jesus here in this world. If this were not possible, the Sacred Scriptures would never have been relevant. We have seen what prayer can do to change them, to enlighten the ignorant and correct the errant course of those who deny the existence of Heaven. My intention all along is to prove through you that those who cannot help themselves are aided by the intercession of the Church to learn their true inner-being. You have created a bibliography from which they can choose where to begin in discovering themselves. "At the Water's Edge" opens the door for the discussion that compares the Light of Heaven to the darkness of the Earth. "When Legends Rise Again" contrasts spirituality and realism. "White Collar Witch Hunt" reverses the slanderous attack against the priesthood. "Babes in the Woods" reminds all Christians everywhere that one must be mature in faith but childlike in nature, retaining the innocence of children who approach God openly and willfully. "To Crispen Courage" demands that human beings everywhere stand for something, to pull themselves into the acknowledgment that Jesus requires more than passive faith, but active spirituality that interacts with all the dimensions of the created world. It uplifts the Roman Papacy and reaffirms its infallibility before those who protest. We shall not forget "Supernal Chambers" because it consists of some of the deepest poetic theological thought ever committed to the page. Now comes My anthologies and the advent of your memoirs that will encapsulate the beauty of your entire deposit of works. All your books and writings advance the mission of the Church and the awakening of wayward sinners to the 'conscience' of the Gospel.

    I am in the company of Saint Francis of Assisi, and he is praying for his namesake apostolates, just as he prayed when his church was felled by the natural disaster. There are issues and themes that the Lord commends and allows that further His Kingdom here. If we attempted to apply human logic to this, we would surely fail. I wish to thank you again for taking such good care of your brother. He loves you endlessly, and he wishes you to know that he is working as hard as he can for the success of your mission. He heaps great praise upon you during his prayers and petitions. He asks Me to induce Jesus to make all humanity just like you. It is a gift to him that you are his friend. "*He is my gift too.*" I reassure you that I have not given you My messages in vain. "*Thank you, I have always believed this.*" This is why it is important for you to finish and publish the AD 1997-1999 book about My intentions for the world. This book also makes a more direct connection between Medjugorje and My appearances here as the Morning Star Over America. When I speak about a second Diary in those messages, which I have told My Angels to leave in the text, this gives humanity the impression that you are still writing at My behest. This second Diary is actually your book of memoirs. I am honored and pleased to be your Mother, and My Heart is filled with admiration for your mature spiritual faculties with which you perceive the mortal world. The genius of God is deeply seated in your being."

Sunday, February 7, 2010
Thomas Heather Sr ✞ 1988
9:14 a.m.

"*We recognize the cyclical nature of human life, the repetitive errors and accidental yields, the reassuring days and enviable nights, the shy phases of the Moon, our comedies borne and skirmishes lost, the love and loathing, the keen and outlandish, the scarce and opulent, and everything else that bridges the gap between our tallest mountains and deepest dreams. All things come and go; we either hand them to our descendants or commit them to the past. Nothing but our soul in Jesus lives on. Indeed, even the town mortician is eventually laid to rest.*"

> *"Our refuge is Christ Jesus the master griever, the succulent fruit, immortal rector, comforter and consoler, bewilderment of the learned, Abraham's eye, the shoot of Jesse, perfect sufferer, anointed one, keeper of the flame, compass for the lost, servant of paupers, virgin brother, key to the heart, banner for the people, spirit of wisdom, King of kings."*

William L. Roth

"My dear little sons, what we are doing here together creates a higher threshold in the annals of heraldry that can only be matched by the Annunciation of Saint Gabriel. You and I are giving new meaning to the concept of messaging (miraculous intercession). We are connecting the present and the future in an ethereal way, one that cannot be discarded by those who yearn to see the Face of God. I bid you good morning on this Sunday, the anniversary of the entry of Saint Thomas the Patriot into Heaven 22 years ago. It was a cold and blustery morning the day he died. I promise that you will see him and all the Saints when you come to Heaven. My Special son, you already know that your brother loves your new prologue. He has read about one-third of it. You are seeing the miraculous infusion of the Lord's presence into your new book through your heart and mind, and humanity will be holier for it. I often tell you that I am humbled for your obedience to Me and companionship with the Holy Spirit. This is how you should present yourself when describing your connection to the Deity and your Mother. You and I have a relationship, and you and Jesus have a companionship. You are brothers, comrades and compatriots in the conversion and redemption of humanity. Some have asked that since Jesus died and was raised from the dead – two grand accomplishments – for the Salvation of men, why does He not do the easy thing like making Himself more prevalent to ease the obligation of converting the world to Christianity. The fact remains that faith is the key to human Salvation. Why would lost sinners place any effort in becoming holy through their own repentance if they knew that the Son of Man was going to simply hand their perfection to them on a platter? It is a matter of meeting God where He calls the world to encounter Him at the foot of the Cross.

I am pleased because you are pleased. Your meditations, descriptions and narratives in your new prologue are inviting for the many who will read what you have to say. Let Me be clear. I wished for your book of AD 1997-1999 to have an elevated prologue and contain the eloquent references and dedications that you have incorporated into its text. If I had asked you to write this prologue that you are completing back in 2000, you would have lacked the spiritual insight that you now have, and the content and impact of the prologue would have been lesser. This is the reason I have asked you to publish the Twentieth Century Anthology last. Even as you yet cannot see the outcome of your apostolate and the completion of your mission as we speak today, you should feel confident knowing that I have guided you well. And, the two quotations that you wrote this week that are mentioned earlier in this message are ones that will tweak the hearts of those who wish to know God. They can be imbedded in an existing or future text, or they can obviously be used as stand-alone quotations in the beginning of a book or elsewhere. I am also elated that you are pleased by My messages for that three-year period. Their rhythm, style and content provide an excellent seam between your first Diary and the New Millennium messages. The transition will be comfortable for everyone who becomes deeply involved in reading your deposit of works. Indeed, you have chosen to rededicate humanity to two holy Popes! It is clear that history sometimes fades the memory of current-day Saints because of the tides that overshadow their legacies. It is appropriate that you have cited the two historical dogmas that are so key to the Church. Your brother sometimes sits in a chair in the livingroom and wonders how he could have been so fortunate to have been given you as a brother. He weeps with his hands on his face not of sorrow, but of thanksgiving that you are his friend. He has now turned another year older, and with this comes a fair amount of reflection. It is natural to all men. He looks at his younger years in college and briefly thereafter. He knows who has stood by him, with whom he has discussed and dissected the days, and who has given him friendship and advice. This has been you all along. You have satisfied the needs that his elder brothers refused to provide. You brought him into the Church. You have defended his character against his detractors. He has tried as have you to control his temper against those who have abused him physically, mentally and emotionally. It has been difficult for him because of the aggressive personality that he inherited from his mother. Timmy is much milder now. He has mellowed because he sees what is worthy of pursuit versus the things that are in vain. When he chooses his battles, it is never ones that will be ultimately futile. This is the reason he had the debate with the newspaper reporters last week. Above all things, newspaper personnel are curious souls. They know where there are veins of knowledge and wisdom, and they have seen your writings and those of your brother. You have engaged them and taught them, shared your concerns about suffering humanity with them – both born and unborn – and you have allowed them room to discuss their own views, even when they have amended those views because of your faith. After all, they are employees who are paid to do a job by a monstrosity called the American media conglomerate, one of the most evil entities on the face of the globe. The reporters will never forget their experiences with the two of you here in this home. It was their decision to publish your essay about the last hope of humankind."

Saturday, February 13, 2010
2:11 p.m.

"When we speak about the origin of Christianity, we are referring to the Holy Roman Catholic Church, "Sanctae Romanae Ecclesiae," an eternal institution that itself has been maligned through the tropes of atheists and secularists since its beginning, that has never once conceded to its detractors or persecutors, and that will prevail in triumph forever beyond the extinction of the created world."

"We often wonder why Christ had to make obligatory something so appealing as human love. Why is it so difficult to wrap our minds around the very catalyst of world perfection? We understand that compelling inner-beauty is its origin; our best nature always blooms from there. The sheer definition of universal divinity requires that we recognize spiritual love as having texture, color, sound, technique, and situational context. It also consists of degrees of consequence because we feel differently when a friend says he loves us compared to hearing it from our relatives. It is as though we appropriate a certain dynamic of expression; we make it a privilege for someone else to love us, even though we hold no such dominion over the feelings of other men. We can see the effects of the love in our admirers' eyes, but we can only imagine the architecture of its origin. Hence, our capacity to internalize the lives of others allows us to assimilate their suffering and sacrifices as our own, much the same way that Mary, the Mother of God, adopted us on Good Friday. We learn from all this that love and affection are not necessarily interchangeable. Love is an authoritative mandate; affection is a prevailing emotive desire."

William L. Roth

"Let us be thankful that the good Lord has given us this time together to pray before the Son of Man Returns in Glory and concludes the progression of the ages. We can still make a difference in the lives of the lost and brokenhearted, those who have grown bitter against the thought of God, and the billions who have not yet accepted the Holy Cross of their Salvation. My little sons, we speak together today at an advantageous time for Creation because you know what I have to offer them. It is amazing that you lack the capacity to realize the power and beneficialness of the works of your hands. This is as it should be, however, because you have no time for resting on your laurels and taking pride in issues that are only now beginning to be effective. There is no question that you can see how lost your brothers and sisters are; all you need to do is look at their opinions in the daily newspapers. When the unitarian pastor calls for the legalization of the 'marriage' of two people of the same sex, wrongfully basing it on the designs of Nature and the Will of its Author, he is speaking for the devil. He is an instrument of the Antichrist in the same way that Adolf Hitler and all the brutal dictators in world history incarcerated, tortured and killed millions of innocents. In fact, people like the unitarian pastor are more malevolent than other fascists because he is hiding his evil in the cloth and cloak of a reverend.

My little ones, we are making amends for lost sinners like the unitarian pastor. It is not something that we take lightly. We do not happily suffer for what wrongs other people commit, but we do it because we already know the outcome of the Earth. At no point in the Old or New Covenant does the Lord allow for the 'marriage' of two people of the same sex. It violates the basic tenets of righteous order. It ignores the wise counsel of the language of Creation spoken by the Holy Spirit. Even on a broader scale, we must pray and act to nullify the catastrophic damage that people like the unitarian pastor have done to the self-image of impressionable children who are still developing their own sense of identity. It is one thing to boast of knowledge of God when one actually knows His Will, but it is another to claim to know the Will of God when someone lives, preaches and acts in ways that are diametrically opposed to His Truth. These are among the reasons we pray here together, and you will this month begin your 20th year. There is no way that you can judge from your vantage point in exile what this means to Jesus. What else could you have been doing? Pursuing your dreams in secular causes? Begetting children upon your wives? Traveling the globe and couching with influential magnates? Yes, you could have been doing all of these things, but their effects would have died in the grave. You have joined the Land of the Infinite with your devotion to Me, your labors for Jesus, the vision you are sharing with your brethren, with the prayers that are sustaining the Church, and the profoundly important writings, prologues and prefaces to counteract the ghastly history of humanity's error. Your hearts, souls, minds and lives are unified with the Blood of the Cross that has obliterated human sin and every vestige of its impact. You are partakers of the Divine Love that is healing your land one day at a time. You know this to be true because Satan is fighting against you. As I have told you on many occasions, Satan is dead outside of time because Jesus killed him on the Cross. He is drawing his final breaths and suffering his last throes. Surely you understand by now how these two conditions can coexist simultaneously. Satan is dead because he can never win. He is in his last throes because the Holy Spirit is rescuing lost sinners from his clutches. Unless Satan has human souls on which to feed, he can barely breathe his last to any extent. Indeed, it is the very souls that we are trying to claim for Jesus on the Cross that are imitating Satan's evil lies, destruction, impurity and recklessness. He cannot win; and in the fullness of time, you will see that it was only the unholy sinners around you that kept his evil alive. It is clear that you already know this.

My Special son, you have again prepared another book for proofreading by yourself and your brother. As he has stated, you must always tell him what is happening at your workplace. You must never conceal your pain or loss of dignity there. Your brother does not like what they do to you, but you must share it with him. I know that each of you is building your own strength and vision against the evil in the world, and I assume that this process of construction led you to say that you do not always have the capacity to fight against the things that harm you. I pray that you said this only in a mere moment of weakness. I have said many times that you are not being singled out for this treatment in the grand scheme of the American workplace. It is the same all over the country. I ask you to see this for what it is – temporary and passing, but important enough for us to counter with every utterance of our prayers. I speak about the Sacraments in the context of knowing them from the beatific side of the veil. Please be assured that your heart and happiness will be resurrected with tremendous joy when My messages are circling the Earth in full. It will be the same feeling that you had seeing Secretariat running full force around the racetrack. Many will declare that the Mother of God descended on humanity with ethereal ferocity, speaking and admonishing Her children like a tremendous machine. They will know that I am trying to reverse the damage done to the Church by collective women around the globe and the men who have exploited them. There is much to look forward to, but you must be patient. I have always called you to this. I am deeply touched by the quotations that you have written recently uplifting the Catholic Church and celebrating the Resurrection of My Son. The deep and abiding respect you have for Jesus' Crucifixion runs predominantly through your writings, and this is the hand of God operating through your eloquent faith. What happens after you have completed your books will come as His response, and you must stand prepared for the onslaught of naysayers that have been heckling My visionaries for twenty centuries. As long as humanity gets the message, it will be worth the price of suffering. I am not saying that your life will be grievous to bear, but you must know that there is horrid opposition to anything holy these days."

Sunday, February 21, 2010

"If we are not attuned to the Holy Spirit, we see but have no vision. We plot our future, but are lacking in foresight. We hear the chimes, but cannot decipher their message. We stand in the breeze without sharing its fragrance. We die without ever having lived."

William L. Roth

"My sons, we resume our international and universal prayers for humanity that you know will achieve their desired effect. We are here in this little home where you have been harbored for so long, and yet only a brief period in the grander scale of life. All that humanity hungers for is found in Jesus; every morsel of divine peace and lasting life are gained through His Crucifixion. My Special son, this is why your quotation to begin today's message about remaining open to receive the Holy Spirit is so overwhelmingly profound. You know about the nourishment of the soul that is as important as food for the body. We have for many years kept quiet as the world 'brawls and bubbles' in ignorance. We have been working to build-up a miracle so large that the world cannot cast it away. Let Me be clear. The miracle is larger than anyone's books or diaries, but it is the exertion of your effort that humanity will see. The dedication of your life to the Church and to Christianity is the miracle. This does not mean that the content of My messages is not crucial to retraining the conduct of the lost. It certainly does not imply that your own personal writings are not beautiful to behold for every creature living and deceased. The point I am making is that the investment of your life and the loyalty that you have shown My Son with your brother are what the world will focus on most. You have asked the rhetorical question on many occasions. Who would give so many years of their life for something that was untrue? Thus, you will celebrate tomorrow a full 19 years of work on your books and writings, and you have already entered 21 years since your pilgrimages overseas. Do you and your brother not see that the impact of your generosities, your months and years of hard labor are as important as the content of My messages? This is what I wish you to dwell upon even as much as what I have said. If there are times when you believe that My messages are not moving around the globe quickly enough, know that this is a process. Your dedication and service in preparing the manuscripts in which they appear is practically complete. That effort cannot be erased from history or expunged from the record. You speak in grand terms and often summarize difficult circumstances in a single phrase, but never forget the daily moments that have led to this tremendous period in time. *"I won't forget."* I gladly remind you that there are innumerable souls who will inherit their new life in Jesus because of your love for their future. I hope this gives great peace to your heart. You and your brother are now proofreading your next book of messages, and you will be on to grander things. The Holy Spirit will touch you with new Wisdom to help you comprehend the meaning of 'divine intervention' and supernatural intercession. You have written eloquently in every book about the assistance and advocacy given you by the Most Sacred Heart of Jesus. You have spoken about enlightenment, suffering, sacrifice, compassion, admonishment and all the elements that compose the viable traits of living holiness that should make all Christians grateful. Your writings and warnings will not be lost in this world. You have helped Me fashion a description of what the future holds and what it should become. As you have appropriately placed in the preface of your next book, I came to you and your brother because someone had to be called.

Today, therefore, you know that I have come to speak to you not to necessarily bring new lessons and teachings, but to allow you to witness My presence in the same way that I have to hundreds and thousands in centuries past. You correctly described My role in the redemption of the world, and more importantly the conversion of the wicked. When you have completed and published your next book, you will have all the years in the future to describe what your books filled with My messages mean. *They are more than a collection of literary religious works, they are en masse a means that God has touched the people He loves. They are as alive as the Gospel itself. Even if nary a single soul ever took one of your books in hand, they are food for your own redemption. They are sustenance for your own joy, knowledge for your understanding of God, and help during times of trouble. We know, however, that they will not be held back from those who need them. My messages are meant for a humanity that is parched for compassion. This is why My decrees and reprimands are dripping-wet with beauty. I have stated the obvious in special ways, in themes and cadences that stir the heart of man to realize that Christianity is a vibrant cause. It has been said that there will always be new generations of men, but I say that this will someday not be the case. There needs to be a means to that end, and the means is the Will of God for His creatures to repent, to ratify what Heaven and Nature have done, to fall on bended knee and recognize that the inevitable passing of humanity is coming near. What we have done together here in this place will grow that repentance; it will speed-up the day when everyone alive will come to the conclusion that there is no life, truth, or resurrection without Jesus on the Cross. (Section paraphrased in AD 1997-1999 manuscript as allowed by Our Lady.)* No matter what the future brings, please never lose sight of the grand and noble gift you have given humanity in the name of God."

Saturday, February 27, 2010
8:57 a.m.

"*I had a vision of the last day, and Jesus said, 'I sent you fires, deluges, upheavals and insurrections. My disciples were subject to starvation, disease and violence; and their hearts were lanced by insults, sorrow and rejection. I made the foothills quiver and the valleys echo. I gave you signs and wonders, and manifested miracles untold to help you believe. I brought you through the darkness with faith as your lantern, and in this you shall always rejoice. But, I beg to know, which of these things brought you closest to Me?' I pondered deeply and then replied, 'None of them, My Lord. It was your suffering that I remembered most.'*"

William L. Roth

"My dear little sons, you are the flower needed by God because you make His Kingdom beautiful. You are sightly to the brokenhearted, and you attract those who are looking for a semblance of beauty and fragrance of peace. You have comprised a collection of works that will allow humanity to reach out for God. We must await their acquaintance with the Holy Spirit by what they suffer; this is the way of the Cross. When you pray for the conversion of the wicked, you are indeed asking God to destroy all that is unholy in them. This vacuum is then filled to the brim by a righteousness so awesome that they forget their former selves. This wipes away their feelings of guilt and prepares them to say 'yes' to Jesus when He asks for an accounting of their lives and whether they will go with Him to Heaven. It is written in the heavens and on the Earth like megaphones sounding liberating strains. It is in the architecture of the universe like the name JESUS etched into the woodwork. And, it is touchable and reachable through your faith. My Special son, it gives Me great hope and happiness to know that you are taking your time on your new book, and that you will work with your brother to ensure its accuracy."

Sunday, March 7, 2010
8:58 a.m.

foodstuffs	- sustenance/nourishment
sexuality	- procreation/gratification
religion	- morality/redemption
politics	- governance/ideology
education	- intelligence/aptitude
employment	- solvency/stature
entertainment	- aesthetics/relaxation
travel	- mobility/culturalism

"Here I have come again, My dear children, to pray with you this Sunday morning for everyone needing the Lord's intervention. It is obvious that everything you have done for Him in the past 21 years has been the forerunner to the conversion of millions in the United States alone. My sons, the enemies of the Church can blame God for a lot of things, but they cannot lay the blame for their own evil ways upon Him. They do this of their arrogance, obstinance, pride and materialism. They ignore the signs that Heaven provides for their fate, for the insignificance of their agendas and preferences; and it is without merit that they speak of life after death without preparing for their own demise. We are asking Jesus to help them now, and every time we pray, because He is their Judge whether they know it or not, whether they accept and believe it or not. My Special son, you have heard My many hopeful oratories about how the world could become whole. You have wept at the beauty of the Holy Spirit inspiring your hope through the strains of My speech. This is as it should be. It is the same all over the world where hearts are open to receive the Truth of Love as spoken through the Gospel and from the tongues of the modern disciples of the Church. I tell you that only the Lord in you makes you weep in happiness when you sense the victory of the Cross over the death knell of the ages. I have given you a few examples of the institutions of men at the beginning of My message today to which humanity is oriented. The list is not exhaustive, and it is in no particular order. Of all these categories, you see that 'religion' overcomes and supercedes the rest. It is the beauty of the origin of life, the arts and all others that spring from the Father in Heaven and man's faith in Him. This proves that you and your brother, and all who believe in God, have given your lives to the fullest to its origin and its destiny. Instead of focusing on a subpart or subset of the fullness of life, you have looked at the broader picture of the meaning of human existence on Earth. We have in effect made your lives and those of your fellow believers a mission in growing into eternity from a timed framework in which you have lived and worked. As I have said many times, this makes you part of eternity already; it creates for you a link to the Afterlife that is missing in those who refuse to believe. And not only that, you have believed and properly acted on your beliefs. This is the operation of the conception; it is the movement of the inanimate, the genesis and the reason for your judgements and decisions. It is crucial that you remember that these things come to you from the outside to the inside, but not as one would walk into a room through a doorway. The Holy Spirit comes into the heart of men from the outside to the inside, but also from the center-point of all knowing and being in Heaven, which is not set apart from the absolved creature himself. You are uniquely united with God through the paradisial center of the love you have for Him and all who have walked this life with you. No one goes to the marketplace to purchase this unity. They cannot requisition it through another sinner. They have no power to create it on their own. Hence, as you proceed into the endearing future that God has planned for you, it is appropriate for you to disregard the comments and criticisms of those whom you have written about in your books, prologues and prefaces that do not subscribe to all things miraculous. It is as though anything or anyone you encounter that attempts to impugn or discredit My messages and all the Lord's intercessions are void of both natural and supernatural life. They are like spiritless robots making noise. This is why I ask you and your brother to disregard them; do not stone the devil's dogs or chase someone down a dark alley for your own justification. I have said that all who will eventually reside in Heaven will come to My work that you have done. You need not defend or justify what I have said.

Let us take another look at the institutions at the beginning of My message today. Thinking about life in the United States, where do you suppose most people spend their lives? Think about personal versus social needs. *"Most people in the United States are involved in sexuality and entertainment, and worried about employment so they can keep those two going."* Very good. And, do you see either of these two things leading them to the Church? *"No, and some churches are trying to make their services entertaining to bring people into their congregations."* Yes, and I have said that the Church provides for the poor, their foodstuffs and medical needs, and the like. What about the politics? *"I don't know what it's good for."* You have made a good point. If you look at nearly every form of information and entertainment in the United States today, they are consumed by either carnal desires or politics. There are now well over 300 million Americans, and the gap is even wider between the percentage who place value in the benefits of spirituality. And, what is the cost? Horrendous greed, violence, degradation of social values, abortion, depraved sexual conduct, poverty, social neglect, and on and on. This is a nation that aspires to be called the greatest on Earth. We have discussed this many times, and you have sufficiently admonished those responsible in your books. The point I am making is not just that the condition exists, but that there is negative momentum here. There is movement away from spirituality that can be measured in the direct actions of people. There are identifiable effects. I am not saying that this is a hopeless case or that nothing is being done to change it, I am only asking you to realize that the further destruction of the moral fabric of America is occurring while most everyone goes on with their lives. All the while, capitalism attempts to own and make servants of the common people who are doing their very best to keep their lives afloat.

When you consider all that you have done with your brother, is it not clear to you that you have been living within the circumference of life's true mission? It is obvious as I have said that you have been forced to interact with secularism because of your need for the first of the institutions that I mentioned today. You have had to eat and be sustained. However, this has been to your credit because you have not been cloistered in an environment where you have not known what is actually going on. With this, you have been able to write directly to the problem, to address issues and conditions that you have experienced firsthand. This is what makes your faith more panoramic. Most people are either deeply involved in secularism to the exclusion of spirituality, or they are the reverse. You have been deeply involved with both because you have had to base your criticism of the world on what you have seen with your eyes, shaped and evaluated by what I have taught. You are extremely fortunate that you have not chosen to do this while living in matrimony or raising several offspring. That is an entirely different vocation itself. It must be clear to you now, at long last, that I came to you and your brother because no one else in the United States could have devoted the time, effort and resources. Priests are too busy with what they do. Wives and husbands could never have given their lives to Me in the way of you and your brother. Multiple millions of others lack the intelligence and communication skills that you and your brother have. The list of reasons goes on. And, you are exceptionally not addicted to or distracted by travel and entertainment to a degree that would have inhibited your work for God. And yet, you can speak of marriage and the American culture as well as any pope. Why? Because you have surveyed their parameters with the measuring instrument of the Gospel. Two-thirds of marriages in the United States fail because the partners lack the keen love for the Church and human Salvation that you have known all along. Young children curse their parents and teachers, engage in unchaste behavior, commit awful acts of violence; and they think nothing about it. No one has told them that it is wrong. They use drugs and chemicals in place of purity and prayerfulness because they have been reared in an atmosphere of heathenism. All we have done here in this country since 1991 addresses these things, and I will succeed in letting them know it. As for circumstances as they unfold, I have always wanted My children to have a road map to direct them to the entire body of works that you have created; and this map is the list of these works in your next book. In other words, when they read your Diary and the remainder of My messages from the last part of the twentieth century, they will know where they are going and when the messages will end because you have included them at the beginning of your next book. It would have been absolutely impossible for you to create this list and include it in the 1997-1999 book if I had not asked you to wait until last to publish it."

Sunday, March 14, 2010
9:14 a.m.

"Here I have come into this blessed and holy dwelling place to speak to the children whom I have touched with the brilliance of Divine Light. It is My intention before I finish today that you realize how special you are, the intensity in which Jesus loves you, the gratitude of the Father for your lives, and what your faith has done to rectify the terrible wrongs that evil on Earth has done. We must never lose sight of the fact that you, My little sons, are the principals of our relationship. You are yet mortal; you still live in the same world into which you were born in the flesh. My part is easy; it has always been this way since I entered Heaven. I wish you to know that I understand your worries and concerns, your fears and reservations. I lived them Myself. You must remember this, My sons. Today, we have reached another Sunday on which humanity rests from its labors, but few attach to it the meaning of the higher calling of the Lord. Your entire lives have been given to Him. I think today about all the priests, sisters and brothers, deacons and all the rest who gave their whole lives for the success of the Catholic Church. The mission of their hearts and souls was for the redemption of lost sinners. This is why they are with Me in Heaven, alongside Jesus and all the Hosts who for many decades prayed for them. I simply ask all who live to remember the Saints, and I know that you both will do so. When you ponder what all this will mean in the ultimate climax of Creation, just remember that it is too large to describe, and that you have been equally as loving and sacrificial as the greatest Saints who ever lived. My Special son, My love and hope greet you on this day as always. We have come to another week, and this one apparently reveals that you have completed proofreading your next book. I am so proud of your wisdom and efforts in the Preface that you have written. It is a fitting introduction for this new book because it reveals your own vision of holiness in accordance with the teachings of My Jesus. I wish you could know how the Father has blessed you for all you have given Him during your life. So many ills have been mitigated, so many sins remitted, so much pain alleviated. Now, you are staying with your brother who is battling another illness, and you again will reap the rewards that have been given to the mightiest Saints. It seems that Satan has attacked him again with sickness and worry, and you are trying to console him and comfort him as you always do. You realize that thoughts enter his head much the same way as they sometimes do you. This is a terrible battle in an often horrifying world. Thank you for being at his side and showing him such tremendous love. You and your brother have a holy brilliance that is unprecedented in these times, and especially in the country in which you live. Please be prudent while listening to those who predict the early demise of the United States' economic system, although it is certainly not on sound ground. There is great resilience in the American people. I have prayed that the capitalist empire that has been so selfish would crumble, and this is what is slowly occurring. However, I do not wish for anyone to starve or the weak and vulnerable to be cast aside. A simple view of your country indicates what happens when financial stress arises, and it is not at all auspicious. The number of abortions has the potential to double during hard economic times. Brutal crime, theft and violence occur at exponentially higher degrees. This is the product of desperate sinners who have nowhere else to turn. Consider the looting and violence amid the destruction of Haiti and Chile. It is always the same when there is a struggle for bare necessities in difficult times. America is not immune. But, you and your brother are living well. You have planned ahead with intelligence and by simple means. Your brother said yesterday that he was as comfortable here as if he was living in a million dollar home. This is because he is with you. And, you can see why the simple means is more holy than the extravagance of materialists and nonbelievers. You are not distracted by physical possessions. Do you realize how blessed you are? You have made this happen because you have given your life to God.

As you can see, I have not come to give you any new terms today or a specific spiritual lesson. I ask you to remember that I am with you always and everywhere, whether I am speaking to you or not. Will you remember this? Jesus is always in your heart. Heaven is always living vibrantly in the holiness of your heart. These are basic issues that I pray that none of My children ever forget. What are your comments and suggestions today? "*I pray for Pope Benedict XVI to be protected from the demons in the media who are trying to destroy him.*" Now, wait just a moment here; who on Earth has the power to destroy the Vicar of Christ? "*I mean lay burdens on him and soil his credibility before everybody.*" Do you mean to tell Me that you believe this to be possible? "*There's a lot of people who have their souls damaged by these people. They believe lies.*" God will never allow lies to bring harm to the Pope in Rome. I commend you for caring, but you must realize that you are speaking about the Rock of the Church. Against this Rock, nothing will prevail. You will hear plenty of hate speech and rackets, but this is only the palaver of sinful men.

We know that we wish only good things to be said about the Pope, and I agree with you that nothing ill will be uttered against his dignity or the integrity of his office. I wish for you to take the Holy Father under the wing of your heart and ask Jesus to keep his reputation safe. This is the main issue, not that anyone has the power to somehow destroy him. "*I understand. I misspoke.*" My Special son, you were simply asking Me to protect the Pope from scandal, and I accept the accuracy and sincerity of your wish. Thank you for caring so much. When you take your books in hand after a long period of not reading them, you can see how moving and shocking they are to behold the first time. Before I close, I would ask that you take your brother for additional medical care if he takes a turn for the worse. I will close for now, but I will never leave you. I am always at your side. I am always with you, wherever you are in this world."

Saturday, March 20, 2010
1:48 p.m.

scrimshaw - (*n*) a carved or engraved article of whale ivory made by whalemen as a leisure occupation; (*v*) to carve or engrave whale ivory or whalebone into scrimshaw.

"There are infinite reasons for the suffering of the Church, endless avenues through which humanity might emulate My Son's Passion, and overwhelming opportunities in the mortal world to do so. My little sons, you are seeing these venues come and go; they have made their mark on the history and consciousness of the exiled world since the beginning of time. I come to you with great joy today because you are creating another reason for lost sinners to change – the miracles you have fashioned here in this home are your dedication to the Father in real life terms. I pray that you will always remember His thankfulness and My gratitude for your hearts given to the Holy Spirit so Creation might be remade into the images of perfect love. My Special one, it is almost the month of April 2010. Where is time going, you are prone to ask. I have said that it is you who are traveling through it. By now, you understand what this means. You have inherited the wisdom and genius of Heaven by your years of holiness. The Cathedral you entered today welcomed you and your brother as its own. Yes, you went there to see the modernization of the Cathedral, but the essential super-structure of sublime character is still intact. This is due to the prayers of the faithful and the lineage of Saints who prayed and served there. Today, I come to ask you to ponder the mission of the Church in practical terms, even as those miracles about which I speak are making their way around the globe. I do not speak of practicality like deciding what color to paint a room, but in the way of growing the faith and charity of believers by seeing and recognizing the supernatural presence of Heaven in ways to which they might become more accustomed. One of the reasons why My apparitions are not embraced more than you see is because many view them as excessively elusive, not meant for those with common faith. We know better. Your books, all of them, speak to the fact that miracles form the basis for the faith of the Church – the miracle of the Annunciation, and all the Sacred Mysteries that you celebrate in the Holy Rosary every day. It all begins in the heart, as I have said, that feeds the mind and spirit the nourishment of Holy Love and sacred pardon that each sinner yearns to receive. I have told you that this is a process; becoming holy is not like flipping a switch, but turning a rheostat. All the gifts that humanity has given to God, every initiative that glorifies His name, all the prayers, prayer groups, speeches, priestly homilies, blessings, tithes and gifts – these are the making of the practical presence of the faith of the Church. Again, it all begins by accepting the Will of the Father in the heart and activating everything in the human will to comply. It is a process composed of seeing 'something' from an invisible bounty. Let Me see; how shall I say this? I wish you to tell Me what I am speaking about when I ask you to think of something. Imagine a circle of dots in your head. Now, see a single dot precisely at the center of this circle. See now a line connecting the center dot and the one that is highest above it. See another line connecting the center to the rightmost dot. What do you see? Yes, you see a clock that says three o'clock, even though there are no numbers. You made an assumption based on your knowledge of what a clock is. And, you were more importantly able to discern identifiable information based on the description I gave you. You not only told Me that I was describing a clock, you told Me what time it was. What you have experienced is that something exists; you are able to determine the physical attributes of an inanimate object. You determined its form. That is the first part. The second part is that you determined its function. You utilized your basic instincts to apply the concepts of form and function to something that you did not see with your eyes. This is exactly the role of the Church in leading the Mystical Body of Jesus to Heaven. While this may seem overly simple, it is actually a pretty large leap for those who have never seen or heard of an object called a clock. You employ mental images to discern the identity of something only after you have internalized what it means to you.

This is the essence of conversion. It is the effectiveness of the Gospel. Christians are capable of seeing the Crucifixion in their hearts because the efficacious Truth of the Sacred Scriptures teach you what you must know to be saved. In all the predictable and not as foreseen reactions by the secular world, they refuse to accept this basic foundation. I am speaking about a framework of belief that is unprecedented and unmatched in the history of all worlds, and yet it is as simple as a clock on the wall. This, My Special son, is how those who read your prologues and prefaces along with My messages will know that it is truly the God of their Fathers who sent Me. "*I understand.*" And, you know that there are limitless ways to apply this concept in describing the influx of Grace from Heaven. Indeed, you have already done so in your two decades of writings. Can you see that My messages were only a catalyst for the creative energy you derived from My presence that allowed you to write with such proficiency? Your writing has become eternal because your heart has always been eternally Mine. "*I understand.*" Now, please give Me something to think about that would be an example of the clock. I promise that I will suspend My ability to know beforehand. "*Okay. Imagine a vertical line. And, on the left side of the vertical line are two tiny circles, one above the other. And, there is an arrow that goes from left to right from below the two circles past the line to the right. That's it.*" I told you that I would not use My ability to predetermine what I should see, so I need you to draw it on a page. *(I drew the image in my mind on a nearby piece of paper.)* Now, let Me try to guess what this is. Are you permeating the veil of your exile with your eyes? "*No, it's not the veil.*" Are you looking out a window? "*No.*" Are you walking or seeing through a wall? "*Walking.*" You are walking through a wall. "*Not a physical wall.*" But, these are your eyes? "*No, they are symbolic of something else. I didn't want to give it away.*" I am still trying to figure this out. Jesus did this to Me as a boy all the time. All right. I give up. What is it? Is it you and your brother passing through the veil? I confess that I do not know. Is it you and your brother passing through time? "*Yes.*" Well now, that is very good. It was difficult for Me because I never showed you and your brother walking through walls. The point is still well taken. You did just fine. As a matter of fact, your drawing makes My point easier to make. How many good people in this world know absolutely nothing about their redemption in the Holy Cross? "*A lot.*"

Yes, millions. They are not necessarily under the influence of evil, but are simply unaware. They have been waiting for the proper miracles to prove to them that the Lord is speaking to them with urgency. I have done this in Fatima and Lourdes. I have called My children in Garabandal and Medjugorje. I have solicited My children's attention through the Church and here in this home. All of this will have its desired effect.

Indeed, it is difficult to even persuade Roman Catholics to see their own Church the same way. How can it be true that Shawn Hannity and Michael Moore are both Catholics? They seem to be polar opposites. This is the point I am making about teaching them. This is part of the diversity of secular America. Secular choices often influence how people look at the teachings of the Church. It is a matter of interpretation for them in the institution of Catholicism that is not subject to debate. This plays out in many ways in this country; you are seeing it with the stirring of so many Americans in Washington in preparation for the Congressional vote about health care. There are enough Roman Catholics to end legalized abortion in the United States, but they allow their sense of secular liberalism to overshadow their vision of the Truth. I need not repeat that they will be held accountable for it. I have told you this for 19 years. Again, this is why your example of a mental image is so appropriate. Do you know how many ways your drawing could be interpreted? *"A lot."* And, this is what the Church is fighting against. As I said a few moments ago, all the gifts that humanity has given to the Lord, all the melodies and lyrics, the architecture, the scrimshaw, the poetry, the infinite intricacies of the heart – this must be accompanied by a hard and fast devotion to the Gospel Truth. This is the essential meaning of My messages, and it is clearly the purpose of your own writing."

Saturday, March 27, 2010
12:17 p.m.

"Yes, you are adorable and venerable; your hearts are pure and perfect, and your souls are shining brightly like the sun. I thank you overwhelmingly for praying the Holy Rosary today for the conversion of the world, and particularly for the American Church. As you know, we have a surprise waiting for them that will upend their arrogance and materialism, and Jesus is anxious to set it into motion. My little sons, you must continue to be patient while this process is unfolding. As you read My AD 1997-1999 messages, you see the simple beauty that connects the beginning of My appearances here with the concluding world-message in December 2008. There are measurable parameters that the Church and all societies can see, directing them with sureness toward the lessons and teachings that I have given you. While My apparitions here are included in the worldwide phenomenon of the miracles wrought through My Queenship, they are directed toward the prodigal United States. It is an effect on the western mentality of freedom at any cost, including scandal and the compromise of moral principles. Those in the United States have gone to the Moon, as we know, and this has made some generations to believe that they are like gods. Why do they not learn the lessons along the way? How do they not see that when one attempts to domesticate the panoramic universe, it suddenly changes and abandons them; it turns against the very logic with which they have earlier approached it? What has been the cost of caging lions and tigers, gorillas, bears and whales? Yes, these wild creatures have turned on their trainers and killed them. This is the lesson of the wild to exiled men. You can feed, nurture, groom and pet the realities of life all you want, but it will win-out in the end with the Providence of God as their Maker intact. Men were instructed in Scripture to hold dominion over the Earth, but it should have been done righteously! Even the animals can discern the unholiness of men! This is how civilized beings must learn to approach their legacy in a world that cries out for healing and decency. My sons, we have spoken about this at length for several years; we have addressed the need for your brothers and sisters to be humbled before God and dutiful and deferential to His earthly Vicar. God the Father will not condone any insubordination directed toward the Pope. You are seeing a lighted candle leaning far too close to a powder keg here. I simply ask you to watch how the Holy Spirit reclaims the moral high ground from the opportunists who believe that they have found a weak place in the Church. All attempts to impugn the Roman Catholic Papacy will fail. Those who throw epithets against it will die horrible deaths. This will be their lesson. They will be slain by the untamable wrath of the Father in Heaven. This is a good day. Your prayers, and the prayers of all the faithful, have already preserved the integrity of the Holy Father in Rome. Today, My dear sons, it is My pleasure to say that I continue to watch the progression of your next book. Nothing you do is ever wrong. Now, you have composed and submitted a letter to the editor on behalf of the Holy Gospel message of repentance and forgiveness. This is the simple, basic message of true human love that the secular world chooses to disregard. This is among the many reasons why secularism is already damned. I have asked you not to feel pity for the many people who are responsible for creating animus against the Church. They will get what they deserve. I beg you not to feel sorry for them. And, when your brother called the newspaper columnist on the telephone asking for further reconciliation and friendship in Jesus, his request was denied. This says a great deal more about the columnist than it does your brother. It must be known that your brother has done all he can do in this matter. The rest is up to the obstinate columnist whom he contacted. As you know, America is not alone in the nations filled with these kinds of sinners. It is a joy and pleasure to tell you that you are on the winning side; you are with the Angels and alongside the Saints who are in good favor with the Lord. It would seem that I consistently commend you for living such a holy life, but this is My most important message to you. You are becoming more peaceful inside because you have placed things in perspective at your office; and as long as Satan sees you doing this, he will leave you alone. If he knows that he can rattle you by attacks against your sense of pride and self-worthiness, he will do everything he can to take away your peace. We also must look beyond the next two weeks when your brother will complete his proofing. You both know what you need to do to finish formatting your next book and submitting it to the printer. Your brother needs to relax after that for a few weeks, knowing that a decompression will come for work that has lasted over 19 years. And, you and your brother can plan some travel days or a vacation if you would like. I am saying that there are no other mandated books by Me. What you write in the future, your memoirs, essays and the like are totally yours to decide. You are seeing the importance of having a good job that pays a fair wage, and your brother can later this summer see about finding one. You have been princely and holy to help him through many difficult times, to sustain his peace and sense of purpose, give him the practical support he requires, and remain one with him in heart and soul. The faith you share with your brother will mean the conversion of untold numbers of wayward sinners. We have discussed this before. I also have said that I will return to giving you longer, detailed and deeply spiritual and theological private messages around Memorial Day that will make you wonder why I have been holding back all these years. These will consist of images and parables that will lend beauty, purpose and poise to your memoirs. I would like for you to begin realizing what it means to be in your place in God's Kingdom. Try to internalize what it means to Him that you have given the past 21 years of your life solely to the propagation of the Church. These are intense thoughts of eternal victory that should begin to saturate your consciousness, not in a prideful way, but in a thankful one. You have gained a stature and dignity before Jesus that is rarely known to men. *"I understand. I value this as one of my greatest gifts."* You should always regard yourself highly as God sees you with tremendous gratitude."

Saturday, April 3, 2010
1:08 p.m.

"We consider these days miraculous from dawn until sunrise again, and you rest through the night in peace, knowing that your days' labors have made the world a better place. My children, I have come on this Holy Saturday to give you the blessings that you richly deserve because you have fashioned a mode of spiritual conversion that will serve the Church until the end of time. My Immaculate Heart is consoled by your obedience; your love has made Me the delight of the remainder of Creation. Yes, you are seeing My messages around the globe, as brief as they may be, to enlist My adopted children's prayers. You are also seeing the persecution of the whole Church for what a few have done. The radical enemies of the Holy Cross are only doing themselves in. You must not feel sorry for them when they fall. My Special son, you have seen the publishing of your letter to the editor supporting Pope Benedict, and you have also heard from some of its seers. I promise that for every one that has contacted you, there are 5,000 more. This is the charity of the Holy Spirit in you; it is your means of admonishing the secular void for speaking ill of the source of human Salvation. Yes, I wept with thanksgiving along with you. We must be sure to remember your letter in your memoirs or any other book that you may write of your choosing. It is clear that nonbelievers are lost and blinded by their own bigotry and indifference. They are held in chains by the thralldom [slavery] of their own sins. It is our mission to reach them, to enlighten them about their path of errors. Let Me be clear. You and your brother have already done enough. Imagine in your future writings, your letters and reflections, your postings and essays – you have all My messages from AD 1991-2008 and the private words we have spoken to support your views. No matter how long the world will last, men can cite excerpts from My messages to you and your brother to explain how God the Father and God the Son feel about certain matters of faith and morals. You have seen My Medjugorje messages excerpted in many places too, and now My words here in this place can assist the conversion of those who do not yet believe. I am in endless joy because of this sacred deposit, these strains of beauty that I have given you to share with humanity. If you wish to look at it this way, I have handed you an arsenal to destroy the evil ways of wayward men that took us 19 years to amass. You have crossed over the top of the hill and are taking the easier course down the other side. Congratulations to you and your brother for having reached this auspicious pinnacle in your lives. I have told you that the spiritual aptitude of humanity is all about the heart. The past upon which you reflect and your future plans are all formed in the heart. You can have no happy memories without the heart. The Lord speaks to you there. The human heart is the voice box of the Holy Spirit with which Jesus speaks to His people. This is one of the ways that you have become the instrumentation of the Gospel in your time. You live and breathe the Truth of Salvation into a dead world; and with this, you all live in the light of peace. Now, I have come today to share with you the Easter joy that should live in everyone's heart. It cannot be properly placed into words any more than Jesus' Transfiguration could be explained in the Gospels. If I attempted to describe Heaven to you now, we would have to depart the whole of the languages of the Earth and enter a fourth dimension of communication. Yes, a fourth. You and your brother are extremely fortunate to know the redemption of humanity in paranormal terms. I have said that this makes you more responsible than other men in keeping yourselves pure, chaste and upright. However, you are willingly accepting of your commonness with the fullness of your being. You know that you make mistakes that you correct as you go. On the other hand, you have already become perfected in the ways that Jesus has spoken. If this is too difficult for you to believe, try persuading the people who called on the telephone and sent you mail thanking you for your editorial letter that you are not capable of the perfection of the Spirit of God. There is tremendous heroism living in you and your brother. It has simply been shrouded by all the mechanical labors that you have had to accomplish in recent years preparing your books and tending to your daily employment.

Now that My mandated books are almost finished, you will have more time for reflection and travel, relaxation, the formulation of your memories to be shared with your friends, and all the things that you decide spontaneously that you aspire to experience. I will be here speaking to you all the while, as long as God allows. As for your next book, you see that your brother will complete his proofing a week from Tuesday, or perhaps Wednesday, if it is of his choosing. This will not be an ordinary day. It will be the moment when the eternal clock strikes high noon. All that your brother was born to achieve in his mortal lifetime will have been accomplished at that hour. Whatever he does after this, wherever he goes, what he achieves and accomplishes – all of this is the extra time that the Lord allots him to live in the moment of joy. There will be setbacks and problems that everyone alive sees and experiences, but he will have done what he was called to do. You both have clung to each other with miraculous love, with devotion and friendship because of the Love of God living in you. We shall allow the Church to proceed with the inspection of My messages, and they will be touched deeply by Me. It would seem that the darkest hour that we have spoken about is nigh at hand. I have tremendous hope for your new book that contains My messages from the last three years of the twentieth century. I wish to close with a brief discussion about the serial killer program that you have been watching on television. You have said that such mortal sinfulness is rooted in the way these men and women were reared from childhood. You are correct, and then some. It has not been so much about what was perpetrated against them as much as it has been about what was lacking. They had no love from others to compare their dysfunction to. What I am speaking about here will sound somewhat strange. It was not so much the abuse they suffered when they were young because, at the time, they did not feel offended. It was experimental and permissive on their part as well because of their innocence. It was only when they were abandoned that they felt a sense of violation. They were the subjects of curious attention when they were being abused, and it was not until the attention left them that they felt useless. Do you understand? This is where the sense of power comes in. They feel the need to regain their footing that they lost when they were abandoned, and it oftentimes results in such frustration that they abandon the ones they later abuse, even to the point of homicide. It is not genetic or self-inflicted. Those who become serial murderers are always like little children inside who are controlled by Satan. The father of lies tells them that if they will only listen to him, they will have the world and all in it. They will have their power back again. This is the same tempting that the devil plied against Jesus in the desert. *"Jesus felt the rejection of humanity that was to come?"* No, it was not that He felt rejection, but that humanity would not accept His Holy Sacrifice, not Him personally. It was not His humanness or dignity that mattered to Him, but His Crucifixion for the redemption of the whole world.

Do you see the difference I have drawn? *"In other words, He was not upset that He would be offended, but that His gift would not be accepted."* Yes, you are exactly correct. And, the way this differs from humanity feeling abandoned is that mortal men know that there is no redemptive gift in them. This is why the Holy Spirit must be allowed to assimilate the 'being' of man. When a person converts to Christianity, their life becomes a gift to the Father in the way that Jesus is a gift to them. Let Me be clear; no one who is a sound Christian can take another person's life. You clearly know about this. The fact that Jesus carried in Him the Gift of Redemption is what made Him the Deific Victim. His humanity was crucified, but not His Will. *"I understand."* I simply wanted to speak about this today, and I will add to this discussion in the future. *"I would like to know the difference between a sound Christian cannot take another person's life and the Pope calling for Crusades to reclaim the Holy Land."* You have made an excellent point. The answer is that the exception lies in the propagation of the Church. This is why Saint Joan of Arc and all the Saints were given the right of reclaiming the Earth for the Glory of the Church. Certainly not all homicides on the Earth today strengthen the mission of the Church. This is the point I am making – Thou Shalt Not Kill. *"Contemporary people would never accept the idea of the Church aggressively defending its earthly domain. It sounds too much like other faiths spreading religion through the sword."* It will be done on behalf of Catholics by the Lord's avenging angels. All the Church's enemies will be felled in time. Thank you for your attentiveness today. Thank you for your love."

Sunday, April 11, 2010
3:18 p.m.

"The Holy Spirit drafted the articles and calibrated the instruments that validate our redemption in the Kingdom of Heaven through Jesus' Sacrifice on the Cross. Human exculpation resides in this."

William L. Roth

"Today, My darling sons, I speak to you with intense reflection and appreciation, and you know the reasons why. It is with the spirit of hope that you live because you now have sound reason for hope. You have seen the despair in which others are living; their suffering, faults and oppressions, their sickness and illnesses, and all the burdensome responsibilities they have inherited by virtue of their chosen paths. You too have decided upon the difficult path, the avenues of holiness down which you travel for the sanctification of lost sinners. You have done this willingly and graciously. You have made available to the world My messages that will cause great upheaval in the secular void. You are assisting Jesus to turn their world upside down. We have many issues to address in the future that will continue your work for God. You are not even close to being finished with your prayers for the amendment of conditions that take humanity so far from His Grace. Will you please continue to pray with Me for this? *"Yes."* I realize that you are tired because of your work outdoors yesterday. It was difficult for you because you have been inside so long during the hard winter months. My Special one, I once spoke to you about your brother's close friend. He has no ill intentions toward any person. He is sharing and caring; he has the heart of a child, and he wishes to express to your brother his own pains and guilt that he cannot share with others. He has seen your own writing, and he has finally reached out to your brother because he is somewhat more available during the daytime. His communication with your brother is about Christian friendship, and he is hoping that your brother can teach him about the workings of public institutions and the politics that accompanies working for tax-supported agencies. No one in this city knows more about this than your brother. He will be able to help his friend through these rough times. You know that the man has suffered the loss of his niece and sister, and his two best friends at St. Joseph Church; and his parents are also growing very old. With the indignity that he is suffering at his workplace, the politics of the world, and the loss of his relatives and friends, he has prayed and decided to approach your brother for help. This will take your brother no distance from you either spiritually or physically. You must realize that there comes a time when people become so desperate that they do not know whom else to call upon, and this is why this person has called on the assistance of your brother. In this case, it could mean the difference between his better health and his own self-destruction. I am prompted to remind you that you have done this for others in your acts of friendship at your office. It is clear that you have a much better reputation than you know. The Lord truly appreciates your comforting words to those who work for the Hospital Sisters.

    Let us refer again to your quotation that is cited at the beginning of today's message. You rightly speak of articles and instruments. This of course refers to the Holy Gospel Word and the Sacraments, but also the many essays and issues that are brought from the heights of the heavens when people turn so lovingly and pleadingly to the Father that He cannot help but respond. When I first approached you in Medjugorje in August 1989, you seemed almost desperately inquisitive to know more about Me. Why? Because you knew that I would take you closer to Jesus, closer to God. It is as though you were like a tiny child in a manger. I placed your hand around the Father's thumb, and you squeezed. You squeezed because you felt secure there, because you realized that your soul was on solid ground. And, when you squeeze something, especially another person's hand, what do they do? They respond by touching you even more affectionately to let you know that they are with you in all ways. The dictating of My messages to you beginning in 1991 was the grasp of the Lord's hands around your heart and soul, around your whole life with your brother. Heaven has not let go of you since. Do you realize that it was your first impulse that initiated the response of the Father? He reacted to you because you approached His Grace with your own faith. This is the point that I wish for you to make clear to the American people when you write your memoir later this year or next year. It is the fact that God avails Himself to humanity; humanity must respond, and then God enters men's lives even further. This is the whole idea about Jesus knocking on the door. If you open the door, He will enter. This is what your brothers and sisters need to remember. And, you know that it began when the Lord sent the Archangel Gabriel to Me upon the Annunciation. When I affirmed that it should be done to Me, God reacted with this same affirmation. This is part of the chain that connects Heaven and Earth. This is what the Father meant when He said that whatever Peter bound on Earth would be bound in Heaven, and whatever Peter loosed on Earth would likewise be loosed in Heaven. This promulgates the gift of absolution between warring men. Peace leads to greater peace. Indeed, when Jesus was born a Man in Bethlehem, He brought with Him in human flesh the identity of God to reign among His people. When Jesus saw someone in need of healing thirty years later, He healed them in response to their faith. It is as much about faith as it is about Jesus' love for the suffering. This is how the faith you offered Him in Medjugorje has bloomed into the awesome deposit of holy works that you now have in your possession. You gave more than a mustard seed, and this is why you have the workings of miracles under your name that will last until the end of time. I cannot overstate the opposition to all this that will come from those who refuse to believe. You have been known to be one who wears your feelings on your sleeve, and you must somehow change this. It will be patently impossible for you to sustain the opposition to your works if you do not. This is one of the reasons Jesus did not allow most of My messages to take hold until the receivers had already entered Heaven. He simply did not want to see them suffer the rejection of My works. After all, it is Me who came to you. It was not you who asked Me to begin speaking to you. *"I am getting so much more confident than I was ten or 15 years ago."* I am grateful that you are placing things in clearer perspective. This will serve you well when the times become extremely difficult for you. I must say that your brother is not any better at accepting criticism than you. In fact, he is even worse because he commands others' respect. *"It's like there is a whole different level of that ability when it comes to people criticizing my claims of your intercession, compared to criticism at my workplace. I don't expect them to accept or grasp your work in any kind of instant way. The last 20 years have taught me that."* It is clear that you must maintain this compartmentalization if you expect to have any degree of dignity at all. And, you have also seen the opposition of those who are higher up in the Church.

I am simply saying that your critics will come from all directions. They will attack and mock you. They will claim that you are mentally unstable. They will say that you are under the influence of the devil. All of these things must roll off you like water from a duck. *"I have had great preparation in experiencing things like that with my family and other people already."* I am simply warning you that it will be dozens of times more intense than you now realize. *"If there is no suffering, there will be no success. If I am not scorned, I will not claim the crown."* Yes, please remember that you have said these things today. Thank you immensely for staying at your brother's side all these years and believing his claims. You have seen from your own writing what it means when someone compliments you. Imagine a world in which the Morning Star Over America was never allowed to become real. I have told you that we will have many other messages to share in the future about the Church, the Sacraments, about the principles of theology, absolutionism and many other topics that will assist your understanding of the place of man in Creation and the foyer of eternity. I told you this in December 2008, and I gave you some of those messages in 2009. If you look back at your messages through the years, I have had to spend a great amount of time addressing you and your brother's anxieties and fears, your burdens, worries, adversities and emotions that you have had to deal with as your lives have grown. I am not suggesting that this is negative in any way, I am simply saying that this is what happened. I am extremely pleased by the way you and your brother have lived, how you have shared your personal burdens with each other, and how you have supported each other with tremendous spiritual love."

Sunday, April 18, 2010
8:21 a.m.

"My dear little sons, it is with deep delight that I come pray with you today for the conditions in the world that led Me to visit you in the first place 19 years ago. I have hope, My children! This is the hope that you must embrace. I have hope even though I have already seen the consequences that will bring the Earth to perfection; even as My eyes have already feasted on the outcome that the Lord has fashioned, I have hope. You live in an environment surrounded by heretics and miscreants; and your writings, especially your most recent prologues and prefaces, say what must be said to warn humanity about the dire effects of their rampant pride and arrogance. However, this is not what I came to speak to you about today. I have visited you here in this place again to tell you what a meaningful presence you had at the Holy Mass at Christ the King parish church yesterday afternoon. It is clear that the Holy Mass is of the Sacred Mysteries that Jesus has deigned for your redemption; you above many others know this entirely. However, it is clear that you must begin to look beyond the physicalness of the moment because your position in exile makes the Holy Mass seem somewhat less miraculous. Your faith has increased to such heights that you are expecting others around you, even the clergy, to touch and move you the way I have moved you. Indeed, when you attend the Masses of priests and parishes that are as close to Me as you and your brother, you will not sense any physical or environmental distractions. The Masses at grand cathedrals and at the various beatific altars in Rome keep those who attend in the same elevation that I have taken you. Here, you live in the middle of cornfields and common folk. You and your brother are so far advanced in the mysticism of the Church that they do not even know what they are missing. See how far I have brought you! My point is that you must create in yourself the willingness to realize that the Holy Mass is the same whether the altar is located in Saint Peter's Basilica or the top of a suitcase in the countryside somewhere. Please do not misunderstand My intent here today. I am trying in an almost awkward way to compliment you. I am thanking you for recognizing the beatific miracle of the Holy Mass in the way the Lord wants all of His people to see. You see best because you have given your entire life to Me, and to Jesus' ministry and Crucifixion. You have the heart of seers and dreamers because you have seen and dreamed; you have imagined greater than veritably everyone around you. Today, I have also come to pray for the conversion of the many who are leaving the Church in America and around the world because of the 'perceived' scandal involving the weakness of the priests. You must have greater hope, you and your brother, about the conditions in America and on the other continents. I am pleased that you have the energy to be so excited about keeping track of the public debate. You always weigh what you see and hear against your knowledge of the Christian Gospel, and this is always beneficial to you. It spurs you into deeper thought and provides additional avenues for your personal writings. On balance, you and your brother are doing extremely well. You are realistic but not cynical, visionary without being melodramatic, and hopeful when others live only in despair. I am pleased and proud of you. I will always embrace you in everything you do for Me. I am saying that the future is yours to speak and write whatever you wish. The foundation has been laid; you have adequate resources in the messages I have given. There are no more mandated works for you to do. You can get married and have children if you desire. *"I don't think that will be happening."* I am simply saying that, as children, you are free to go outside and play. I will always be here speaking to you as long as the Lord allows."

Friday April 23, 2010
3:11 p.m.

> *eschatology - theol.* any system of doctrines concerning last or final matters, as death or the afterlife.

"Now, I have come to speak openly about your wonderful lives and the dedicated devotion you have given to Me. You are praying today because of everything I have told you through the years, all the needs of humanity, the pain and suffering, the lacking and overages, and the real agony that innocent children feel. We have made the world a better place because the Father is listening and Jesus is tending to His sheep. It is His Love that has done this,

My sons, and your promptings, your reminders that your brothers and sisters still need Him. My Special one, you are reminded every day what these things mean to Me because you and your brother still pray the Holy Rosary. You seek the invocation of the Holy Spirit to touch humanity, to soften stony hearts, to heal and bless them, and to unite everyone who has drifted apart because of indifference or interpersonal conflict. We have averted wars that would otherwise have cost thousands of lives. We have been the resuscitation of dying hopes and the restoration of dreams that many had thought were forsaken. Today, we proceed with all this glory into the Earth and around the globe. I hope you realize that we do this freely. I wish to uphold My oath as your Mother, and you lend your free will to the Kingdom of God because you shall inhabit the spacious awesomeness of Heaven someday. Your prayers have been answered in that you now have been given a new Bishop by Pope Benedict XVI. As you can see, he is young and vibrant, and he is open to all that the Holy Spirit has to offer. I wish for you to listen to what I am going to tell you now. For him, no matter what he encounters in the fields of religion and theology, presentation is everything. He will not have seen anything in the world where presentation has been refined as you and your brother have accomplished it. He knows that the world needs miracles. He has found one here. You are in possession of a massive, absolute gargantuan deposit of Marian works the likes of which the Church has never seen. Who sets out on a journey who does not know the destination and the distance involved? Only the wandering and lost. These people wish to know the expanse of their mission to carefully discern My messages in this diocese. I wish for you not to worry; it appears that you have never been very worried about the success of your mission. Thank you for trusting Me so well. Ah! My son, when I read your books of messages, My Immaculate Heart swells with gratitude for the gifts of you and your brother to the Church! You surely must realize what I mean as you reflect upon the messages that I have given. Your brothers and sisters will respond to Me, I promise. This is the way it was always meant to be. This is indeed why I am speaking to you now. It seems as though you and your brother lose sight of the miracles you have brought into being; and this is not a negative thing, it simply means that you have grown accustomed to expecting no less from God. When such people as the Bishops and others read such messages as the ones you just received, how can they not believe? It must make you feel satisfied knowing that you have accomplished the work that Jesus has asked you to do. *"Yes, I feel like I have much more work to do, which is good.*" Thank you for honoring your brother by taking such good care of him. This is after all your greatest legacy to the Church. I am proud of both of you for taking seriously the need to release a good final book for your collection. You are giving it special attention as I have asked. Please pray for all those who are working underground in mines and the poor who are begging on the street."

Sunday, May 2, 2010
8:48 a.m.

superficial - (adj) of or pertaining to the surface

"Now, we gather inside the Light of Love to bask in the noble achievement that we have accomplished for God. My little sons, you have done it. You have finished the work that the Lord has given you to do. Congratulations. Well done! No matter what else you choose to do in this life, nothing can reverse the impact you have had on the Church and the mission of Christianity. I beseech you to think about all the contributions of the Saints throughout the ages. They have of their own accord written and spoken the strains of self-sacrifice and redemption according to the mandates of the Gospel. And, they did so according to the available tools in their time, their pen to paper and palms wrapped into megaphones. They left a deposit of genius to those who succeeded them, and all to the glory of God. These modern times are different because there are more distractions luring people away from the Cross. We have turned the tables on the wave of modernism by utilizing the same advancements in technology to spread the Holy Gospel. No greater number of souls in exile will ever hear more about Me than you have just allowed them to receive. This is a monumental achievement that you must not take lightly. While I have always asked for your patience, I have not taken you into the future; I have not preempted your lives one day at a time as though there were no purpose in their passing. My Special son, there is no question that you had dignity long before February 1991. Now, however, you have distinguished esteem and ranking membership in the lineage of Saints that was not there before. You came to know Jesus more in the heart than on the page. You and your brother have seen from the inside what it means to suffer and struggle for the Gospel that has so effectively converted millions before you. When you speak about secular Americans, you refer to the enemies of the

Church and adversaries of the message of the Messiah. We have addressed them with a miracle of your obedience that will not go unrewarded. The Lord has already ratified your compliance, and it will have waves far into the future and around the material world. You have pierced the veil in ways known only to few mortal men. Your faith is deep and abiding; your love is strong and gentle, your vision is deeper than the oceans, and your sympathies are as authentic as the stars. Again I ask you to not take these gifts to humanity lightly. You should not feel so alone anymore because there are billions of souls with Me in Heaven who are aware of you and your brother's commission – all of them know that you have joined their cause in purifying and sanctifying the lost on Earth through your faith and trust in Jesus. While secular men live shallow lives, while they focus only on the superficial, you have penetrated the deepest meanings of human life and joined the utter source of divineness in your response to Me. Thank you for having responded to My call. Today, it is My honor and pleasure to remind you that there will be more years ahead, more opportunities to display your talents in teaching lost humanity, hours and moments to tell the world about the gladness that is yet to come. Of course there will be trials and tribulations. It is inevitable that you will see more intense suffering. However, unlike 20 years ago, you now know the reason for this suffering and the efficacy that it entails. Where there is no love in Creation, suffering fills the void. Where hatred prevails, condemnation is the result. This is the way it should be. Where the Holy Spirit is prohibited to enter, there will only be corruption in that place. This is why you and your brother are different. It is the reason you are beautiful and superhuman, espousing the paranormal aspects of inhabiting the flesh. You understand the eccentricity of people like Saint Francis. You comprehend the lightheartedness of mystics and servants who all have lived and died in the multidimensional arena of miraculous Truth. We have seen the record of human weaklings, and we know that life need not be this way. I have spoken and you have written about larger-than-life prophesies that began as no more than mere hopes. The Son of Man will prosper them into reality. Hundreds of years hence cannot destroy the impact that we have made on the physical world. Where could anyone go if not for the Mother of God? Where is the advocacy that humanity requires if not for the nurturing Mother of the Man-God Most High? Whom would call upon His Mercy? Who else would ask Him to relent? Who would remind Him that there is no more wine for the wedding? I am here as I have always been, still invoking My Motherhood, still asking My Son to remember the repentance of His creatures, still walking softly and speaking boldly about the errors of sinful man.

I hope and pray that you and your brother remember everything that you have learned from yourselves, not just from Me, but what the Holy Spirit has brought to fruition at the center of your conscience. If you were not baptized in Jesus; if you had never approached the Sacraments of the Church, you would have remained only on the surface of life, only superficial, like so many millions in your homeland and around the globe. You are more united with the Will of God than you really know. You are engaged and wedded to the Divine Truth more intensely than most any other mortals who ever lived. I cannot claim credit for this blessing. I have facilitated your union with the Wisdom of the Father because of what I have said, but I am only the cook and seamstress. You have been raised of your own accord into Saints, into human beings who have superceded your own presence in the flesh to capture the meaning of life. I have sewn your garments for your presentation before Jesus, but you are the incarnation of His sacredness to whom Heaven is speaking. Please remember this new dignity that you have found; recognize the higher stature to which you are now devoted in ways that are rare to any other men. Even as God's priests who bear the mark of the High Priest on their souls are unaware of their divinity before the Throne of the Father, you cannot see your greatness that has been bestowed upon you. It will never leave; it cannot expire over time, and it will be with you as you take your place alongside the Saints and Doctors you have celebrated in your writings. This is a time for reflection and memorializing the grand holiness that you have shared with the Faith Church, the Church Militant, with whom you have prayed for the redemption of the world. Humanity of which you are a member is more pious and more deeply in love with Jesus because you are proving that it is possible to be perfected in His Blood. I repeat My solemn oath that every time you and your brother stroked a key on your word processor, another soul has been saved into Heaven. Indeed, ten times, a hundred times more souls have been redeemed!

These are grand and glorious moments you are sharing here and now, as awesome as those you lived on the summits of Medjugorje. The dailiness of life would have you believe otherwise. The pressures of your workplace would tempt you not to care. I am stating openly and directly to you today that the world into which the Son of Man was Incarnated will never be the same because of your love. You and your brother have retread His steps. You have reechoed His message. You have reaffirmed His ministry. And, there is no question that you have shared His pain and internalized His sorrows. You have seen time and again the potentials of mortal men go soft and unrealized. You have been disappointed in the ignorance of intelligent people who looked more toward their own achievements than those that would have advanced the mission of the Church. You have witnessed egotism and selfishness, violence and incivility. You have wondered why the Father has not rained hellfire onto the enemies of the Cross, and you have asked where your support has been from the Most High Lord who owns the entire universe. These are the things of The Christ. These are His questions and sentiments. These are what made Him the Perfection of Divine Love in a wholly imperfect world. You must remember that the Father did not answer Jesus during His Agony in the Garden. The Father did not provide any lengthy dissertation as to why His Son was about to die. Do you remember? *"Yes."* And, why do you suppose this to be true? *"So that it would be an act of the Son, and the definition of who He was."* Yes, this is the very reason. It would be an act of the Will of the Messiah that humanity would be saved. The Will of the Father and the Will of the Son were united only because the Son agreed to make it so. This is His call to all creatures on Earth. You live and let live, share and heal, supply and reward all because you 'will' to live in the likeness of Jesus. There is no coarseness in this. This does not imply that the Father does not love you. It means that He knows all men are stronger than they really know. He understands that humanity's search for the Truth must begin from within, where the conscience resides, where true issues having to do with life and death are resolved, where discretion is born, where Holy Light originates, where reason and decency grow, and where the door is situated through which the Paraclete of Heaven enters to refine the very essence of the soul. This is what it means to be deeply in love with God, not superficial, not crass or cold, not barren but spiritually fertile for the forests of genius to bloom skyward. This is how Jesus lives, and it is how you live as well. History and eternity have both proven this to God. I realize that you recognized this historical moment when you sent your final book to the printer yesterday. It was not an ending, but a defining commencement of momentous joy. It completed the origination of your companionship with God that began long before you were born. I wish for you to remember all of your books this way, that they were given to humanity through you and your brother not to raise you up in any way, even though they have, but to change the world in which you have lived. This shall be done. My messages to you will have their desired effect as I have told you all along. The next months will be slow in moving because your new Bishop will have to take time for exposure to My presence in this diocese. You will have plenty of work to do, perhaps writing briefer essays and beginning the opening of your memoirs. As I have told you in past weeks, you have sufficient messages from Me now to teach your brothers and sisters about the intentions of God if you lived another 500 years."

Monday, May 3, 2010
6:47 p.m.

Rededication of Personal Messages
to the
Sacred Heart of God

I was required to endure the sacrifice of surrendering back into the vaults of Heaven hundreds of pages that I had recorded of my personal conversations with the Most Blessed Virgin Mary. They were factually incinerated and destroyed by the Angels at God's intention. It was crushing to my heart losing such a physical anchor to our Holy Mother's intimate relationship with us. For all that we have received, it was devastating to feel this loss of beauty, wisdom and comfort that I would draw from frequently in difficult times. I had been treasuring this accumulation of words, as I have all the others, as if they were the very meaning of my life since the very first day She began speaking to us. My life was to conserve and transmit them all in order to leave them to the history of the Church after my passing. I was grief stricken for hours without relief. Then, our Holy Mother came and spoke to me.

"My dear sons, I alluded to this message in the past, a happy and glorious one, a time of renewal and opening of the heart to all that is possible with the Lord. My Special son, if you wish to have those personal messages back, I will return them to you. However, I wish for you to think about a few matters first. I ask you to ponder My message yesterday morning in which I told you that you have in your minds, hearts and consciences the genius of Holy Love, of mystical and charismatic characteristics that transcend time and space. I told you that you would see from God a blessing, that He would share with you the Passion of Jesus. Nowhere and at no time have you ever been this close to Him. While not specifically mentioning those messages just yet, did you actually believe that you were going to end one of the most righteous missions in the history of the world without some sort of renewal in the likeness of My Son's Crucifixion? Did you believe that there is no sacrifice in the victory that is assured? I will tell you more about My intercession that, at least for this issue, has been for the good of you and this holy life that you have chosen. First, does it seem a coincidence that the disposition of these personal messages came on the very same day that your AD 1997-1999 work has been created by your printer? I feel your grief, I know your sorrow, and I understand your sadness. I simply ask you to place this message and God's Will into perspective. Surely you would have known that the completion of your mandated books would have brought something historical? History was to include two things. First, your messages were to end on May 2, 2010. That has been rescinded. Second, the one with whom you have shared this vast experience, your brother, having finished the work he was asked to do, was to be called to his heavenly reward in his sleep last night. Your brother was to pass into the arms of God on May 3, 2010. This is why he was crying in 1992. This is the date that was given him on March 15, 1992. Do you remember? He is still with you because I asked My Son from the depths of My Immaculate Heart to teach you about grieving in another way. This is what happened to you today. I promise that I understand your sorrow. God has His ways. He does not punish people by allowing them to know how I felt on Good Friday. This is precisely what I felt then, what you have experienced today. While this is little consolation, I hope that you know how much I wanted your brother to remain here with you. Yes, he is tired, and his reward is waiting. Jesus asked Me in return if there would be increased fruit from your continued union, and I assured Him that I would make the most of the future with you. It is true that you are united with Jesus in more ways than you know. He does not want you to grieve. You have lost no more than relics and sentimental keepsakes of which you have sufficient number in the first years of your messages.

I pray deeply that you will look away from your sorrow and know the Sacred Heart of Jesus better, to see what He experiences every day of the world. "*I will.*" I ask you to think more critically about what I am saying. I am saying that yesterday was to be your final message, and today you would have been calling Timmy's family to tell them that his race was won. I ask you to place this matter in perspective. You are so wonderful to understand and advise others who are grieving and sorrowing, but can you practice it yourself? We have more work to do because there is time, there is more momentum and effort than you can possibly realize in our mission of converting humanity to the Cross. Have I given you any consolation this evening? Will you be able to sustain your hope in the future? *"Yes, that hasn't changed."* On behalf of Heaven, the Triune Father, the Angels and Saints, and the Church Triumphant, we are deeply sorry that we caused you such pain. *"I just want you to see what all this has meant to me."* I have known this all along. This is what your books are about. It was your books all along that we have been pursuing, yes? *"Yes."* Something good will come of this, My son. *"Thank you Mama."* I have hope that you will stand tall and give everything to Jesus that He has given to you. We have discussed what a blessing you have been in the mission of the Church."

Sunday, May 9, 2010
8:48 a.m.

in aeternum - *Latin.* into eternity; forever

"God knows that a mother needs fortitude and courage and tolerance and flexibility and patience and firmness and nearly every other brave aspect of the human soul. But, because I happen to be a parent of almost fiercely maternal nature, I praise casualness. It seems to me the rarest of virtues."
Phyllis McGinley
(d. Feb. 22, 1978)

"Here we are, My dear sons, on this Sunday in May 2010 when you are on the course of joy in the Resurrection of Jesus. We share the indivisible Grace that has made the years worthwhile for you, that has given you Light and Love amidst the world of darkness and hatred, that has kept you aloft in the hope of God's peace, and that has saved you from condemnation. My children, I have spoken numerous times about the Grace that 'has brought you thus far' as being your union in Jesus with the Father, and it is likewise the discreet kindness that I always espouse in My messages to My seers and locutionists. I beg you today to remember the joy that I have brought you, even in your saddest hours. We have together forged for you a stately conscience with which you engage other men. We have allowed you to see Creation from the other side of time. Yes, we have taken your spirits to heights that few have ever known. Why? Because you have faith. You live and breathe

the liberty of faith in ways that others refuse to espouse. I need not appear to them as I have here to you for My children to approach Me. They should do as much even so. After all, did you not come seeking Me in Medjugorje? And, you have discovered that I have been with you your whole lives. You discovered that we have a 'relationship' that you have written so finely about. And, this is the reason I have cited the celebrated Phyllis McGinley at the beginning of today's message. I am indeed a Mother of all the attributes that she mentions, and I am also human, so much so that I understand your weaknesses and temptations in ways many might not know. Even as the Mother of God and Queen of Heaven, I have compassion for humanity's smallest pains. I realize the forces of mortal life that cause you such agony and angst, such fear and self-doubt. I would not say that I am a 'casual' Mother as dear Phyllis has said, but that I am approachable as your Mother in a way as to wish to create, foster and maintain the relationship that you have described in your books. Thus, with this in mind, I have come again today to speak about My Son.

My Special one, I am confident that you will never cede your heart to someone who will not care for it. You have been chided by your detractors for believing that Jesus would dispatch His Mother to your side, here with your brother, because there seems to be no legitimacy in such interaction. What fools they are! The Lord can do anything He pleases. He bows to no man and takes no advice from the wicked. He can place a miracle anywhere He chooses to situate one at His simple whim. This is what makes you and your brother so special to Him; you believe that He maintains this far-reaching power. As you have written and spoken, most people who refuse to believe in miracles base their opposition on the record of the past. They simply do not understand how a modern miracle can bring anything new into being. They believe that they have seen and heard it all. I tell you that no eye has seen nor ear listened to the glory that has yet to fall into the lives of these souls. You know yourselves that anything is possible with God. Hence, you have taken your gifts to the Bethlehem manger long beyond the night Jesus was born, here in your time and place. He has received you as though you were there that day. He has looked at you as you have sought His peace, and He is your legitimization. His Love is your strength and vision where few others will believe. His Kingdom is inside your heart where the Angels have seen the Fire of Truth, where the summit of all human potential is reached. It is in this that you will have life to the fullest into infinity. You will reside with Me and all the Saints in gladness for longer than eternity has ever known to be. In aeternum will your soul bask in the Glory of God from whence your Salvation has come!

Today, you are pondering what will come next for your apostolic mission. You should always remember that time is your friend. Once a mansion is built in Heaven, it cannot be destroyed. Once a notion is placed into the minds of men, it will live long beyond the echoes of their own progeny. Such is the nature of human beings. I give you My assurance that I will always be here with you. And, I will be there with you. I will be everywhere your Matriarch in the Messiah whom you have emulated in this life. We must be careful to nurture this promise in all who are only now coming to know who I am. Next month, your new Bishop will be seated. The Commission on Medjugorje is also developing during this time. Your final mandated book is being released. The Holy Father Pope Benedict is preparing the Church to believe in miracles more potently than ever before. The Shroud of Turin that the Vicar of Christ has venerated has surely been that of the Son of Man. You will find scientists and forensic researchers who will doubt. They will scoff about threads and time lines. This is as was always expected. Did they not reject Jesus, Himself? As I have said, the Lord God can place a miracle anyplace He chooses. However, the conversion of the world has little to do with the Shroud or the first Ark. It has hardly anything to do with history at all. No, the bringing of lost humanity to the Cross is about what happens here and now, how I direct them to the contemporary signs that My Son has deposited in His path. Great speakers and religious servants are ignoring the present-day evidences that lend credence to the unfolding of the centuries-old New Covenant Gospel. This is why I am still speaking in Medjugorje and elsewhere. I wish to take My adopted children to the Blood of Jesus that has been brought from the first century into this one, always dependent upon and believing in the Original Apostolic Church that has foreshadowed the events of these latter days. I do this by proving that Jesus is again alive by the gift of His Paschal Resurrection. Without this miracle, there would have been no Pentecost, no Spirit that still speaks to you today. It is one thing to kill a man and repose his remains inside a grave, but what about a Man who has been given life again on the third day? How can this be explained? We have shared for nearly 20 years the fruits of this inexplicable miracle, and your prayers with Me here now are further proof of its blessing. You have voluntarily taken your Rosary beads in your hands today, but it is because your 'will' and the Will of

God are sewn together and united at the center of your heart. This is the Glory of His Providence shining in you. It is His Omnipotence incarnate in your physical acts. It is your hope to be like Jesus actualized in 2010 the same way that it was actualized by the First Apostles. You are their comrades, you and your brother; and they are your friends who have seen the ornate architecture of your respect for them. Time cannot separate them from you, neither can life or death. You know that this is true because you wish for the best the Church has to offer to come to pass. You preach and pray; you ponder and meditate, you sense and evaluate – all to the satisfaction of Jesus' Commandments and Beatitudes for the whole world of men. You shall be honored for all this! I am not saying that such honor will come before times of darkness and sadness, but you will be lifted into the realms of the beatific before the world is through! There, you will see the identity of the wholeness and fullness of human sacrifice as it must be known. I kindly ask you to believe Me because I am speaking the Truth. *"I believe you."*

I have spoken My piece today, with your prayers as the background music for My words, with your heart wide ajar in reception of My Grace that keeps your hopes alive. There is no greater peace than Jesus; there is no other Salvation, this is what you have told humanity for Me. You often wonder what God does every day. He waits. He watches and sees. He builds where His creatures lay foundations. He forgives and purifies. He basks in the affection of the Saints. He dispatches the Angels to Earth. These are things that you can conceptualize, but there is so much more that God 'is and does' that you cannot place into discernable ideas in your head. You will get there as sure as you are alive. You will one day perceive with the adeptness of the Hosts who bless and support you. I wish for you to always remember that the days are long, but the years are short. No matter what you see or experience on this Earth and in this world, never forget that Jesus is with you and was there before you. You cannot tread a path of suffering down which He has not walked. He did not savor most of the victories that you have already won, but this is why He has given them to you. When you win a battle, you do so for the consolation of His Sacred Heart. When you endure a loss, you do so for the Glory of the Cross. When you look at your life with your own future in mind, you are elevating Jesus' Resurrection on Easter. These are all incorporated in the Sacred Mysteries that you are praying right now. We have much more to speak about this year and beyond."

Sunday, May 16, 2010
9:24 a.m.
(*reference* Jan. 17, 2010)

"Herein this beautiful presence of Light, your hearts are enlivened and elevated beyond the parameters of your physical being, past your imaginings, and further than your hopes can reach. I offer you today the congratulatory blessings that are due you for having completed your final book in the series containing My Morning Star messages. This is truly an accomplishment that supercedes the ages. I promise My loyalty and Love as your Mother, as I have always shared; and I give you My Immaculate Heart as your gift from Jesus. My children, there is no means by which you can comprehend the majesty of this moment. Why? Because you go about your lives as you always have, rising at the break of day and tending to your chores, taking-in the emphasis of the world, tendering your attention to that which approaches you, doing your labors that sustain your lives here in this land, wondering and hoping about the future as it unfolds, and never surrendering to the despair that the devil would heap onto you. The moments when you see champions cross the finish line is not sufficient to express what your work for the Lord means. Commencements and ceremonies are too weak to display what is being done. If you encircled history with meta-history, with an overreaching and far-flung vision past the strains of extraordinary life, you might be able to see a small slice of the victory you have won. Indeed, it is more than the human senses can appreciate. I ask you to believe Me as I speak here in this place, as I employ My frail attempts to describe the Glory that you are unleashing on the unsuspecting world. My sons, I do not tell you this to build up your pride. I do not raise you above all the others. I have not come to show that you are supreme over the suffering or to offer you any kind of favoritism. I am simply saying that there is no flavor of speech or writing that can express what it means for America and the world to know what I have said to you. You have truly given your lives to this cause, but it is God who has taken advantage of the same faith that He gave you as a gift. This makes you instruments and standard-bearers for the Cross and human redemption, conversion and reconciliation. Looking at the world right now, one would think that this would be an exercise in futility. Not Me. I believe wholeheartedly that we can together wipe the Lord's vineyard clean! You have said it properly. We can pave the way for the Second Coming of the Son of Man, and we can assure Him that it was a worthy wait. We were not wasting our time here; we were not merely speaking and conversing because we had untold idle hours to pass. I will make of My appearances here more than you can imagine. Thank you for responding to My call.

My Special son, I wish for you to think about some of the points I made in My January 17, 2010 message about certain identifiers because it will lend more understanding to what I am going to say today. I wish to draw your attention to the inclinations of humanity, the properties and priorities of the created world. I wish for you to think in terms of hierarchies and orders. They transcend nearly everything you have ever seen and heard, in fact lived, about human life. You are born as infants, dependent upon elders and more mature creatures to feed and protect you. This is your primal hierarchy; that is to say, it is the place where you are the most helpless, even less self-sufficient than the plants and trees. You have no idea what life you are born into; there is no instinct yet in you to know that your life has form, function and reason. These are attributes that come to you as you age. Thank God they do! Now, you are nearing your middle years, and you know full well what life is for, not only because I have shown you, and that the Church has taught you, but in that you have a greater sense of your own role in the existence of man. As you have been taught, not everyone shares the same purpose. Some are teachers, others are learners, and still more are simply living and breathing in bland indifference. The point I am making is that the hierarchy from which you are born expands and diversifies as man grows in years. And, what else does he discover about this hierarchy? That it is everywhere, that it is the entire essence of the slow construction of societies and faiths, of nations, governments, economic systems, and the whole inexplicable architecture of the thoughts of intelligent men. It is reminiscent of the food chain, the solar system circling the sun, the preeminence of the beasts and Nature, of the civilities of God, His own choice to birth and destroy, and the entire scheme by which men and Creation interact with character and spirituality.

Do you understand what I am saying? *"Yes."* And, this system of hierarchies is innate to the very conscience and consciousness that compose and comprise the interaction between all that is organic and inorganic. Humankind throughout the centuries has understood this; although most were incapable of discerning its origin, many at least accepted that they were helpless to do anything about it. As I have said, even democratic governments are hierarchical in that they have different levels. They have multi-tiered capacities of legislation and enforcement. They can tax and control, define and extract, and determine the culture for generations beneath their charge. Likewise, fighting forces are inherently hierarchical. There are captains and privates, generals and lieutenants, and on down the ranks. Even the littlest creatures have hierarchical structures, the birds and insects; everything that can be sustained by the Earth is dependent upon, superior to, and inferior to everything else with which it coexists. Geniuses and ignoramuses have understood this with equal emphasis since the beginning of time. And, they have taken it as the Will of God, as the way things are and ought to be. Historical actions and the record of the acts of men have proved this to be true. There are sects and social classes, noblemen and rogues, princes and paupers, and kings and servants. There are millionaires abounding in the United States of America, and they are free to exercise their elitism. All of this, My son, is ingrained in the psyche of man. It seems natural and predictable, right and foreseen. This is the way that men are born; they are secular in nature from the moment they begin to breathe. However, what happens when the Vicar of Christ stands before the nations and says that there is a Hierarchical Church? The secular masses scream bloody murder! They claim that there is no such thing. They say that all are equal under Heaven, that what was written into the Constitution proves what God would have them do. They say that Churches cannot be like governments because there is too much involvement in the unseen. And, what they cannot see, they do not believe. They are surely victims of their own corruption, their own conspiracies, that keep them in the dark. Some people are blinded while others see. Is this not too a hierarchy? Some Americans believe in God, and others do not. Again, they place themselves as subservient to the Church Hierarchy by declaring their disbelief. They are pagans and heathens, far down at the bottom, near the dungeon of humanity, fit to be used as kindling to keep the fires of Hell aflame. We know this, but they seem not to know it. This is their huge surprise, My son. It is what we have been working and waiting for. They must eventually come to know the Catholic Church as the network in which servants are classified by their dedication and benedictions, by their prayers and good works. Never mind that non-Christians do not understand; they cannot even see their own feet to know their standing in the spiritual domain. They are hanging from their necks by the ropes of their own pride, nearly strangled, starved for air, wondering why the Church has left them in the darkness. This is the origin of their demise. We know it, and the Lord knows it. Even the little creatures beneath your feet are capable of understanding. But, the subjects and focus of our prayers are too self-ingratiated to help themselves. They are the lowest form of human life – lost, unchastened, selfish and doomed. We can help them if they are willing to assist themselves. As I have told you all along, this is what Jesus is waiting for. Somewhere deep inside these sinners is the desire to survive. Buried far beneath the rubble of their obstinance is a seed of righteousness begging to grow. We believe, you and your brother and I, indeed all creatures great and small, that they will allow that seed to live beyond their own error. Everything I have said on the Earth since My Assumption into Heaven has been for this reason. I am trying to reach the innermost facet that will redeem them in the Catholic Church. This is the power and purpose of My messages to you.

Continuing to speak of the Church Hierarchy, you are quite aware that it is not a democracy. There are stations and vocations that differ. There are Cardinals and Bishops in service beneath the Pope who have declared their allegiance to His Pontificate. There are deacons and servers, all who realize that the Godhead has come to Earth in the Holy Eucharist. This is the Situated Hierarchy. It is the Perpetual Hierarchy. All men and women are subservient to the Son of Man, and yet also His beloved brethren. They are not His equal in excellence and poverty, but they must aspire to be. They have the capacity to become His perfection. This is the Hierarchy of the Soul. And, men and women of all walks must understand the suffering of their peers; they must know that Jesus is present in them. This outwardly extended compassion is the Hierarchy of the Heart. One must care more about a suffering man than a mouse who is caught in a trap. This is the Hierarchy of Creatures. It goes on and on, as you can see. The summation of My message today is that allegiance to the Holy Father in Rome is as natural as human life itself. It has been this way since the Year of Saint Peter. I will add a great deal to this discussion on another day. I am thankful, My Special one, that you are taking such good care of your brother – the extraordinary love and devotion you are affording him. You are brilliantly united with Jesus! I pray that you will proceed with joy in the knowledge that your having taken such good care of your brother will bring multiple blessings into the world. "*Yes.*" You will soon need to think about what you will write to Archbishop Lucas when you send another book to him. It must be clear that this is the book containing messages that he has not yet seen. Tell him that I asked you to complete this book last because it contains the syllabus of works that needed to be listed in the front. I have concluded My message for today. "*Thank you Mama. I loved your message. It could inspire a hugely powerful book.*" This is what I was hoping to do!"

Sunday, May 23, 2010
9:12 a.m.

portmanteau -   (n) blended words, hybrid or amalgamated syllables

flare	=	flame and glare
motel	=	motor and hotel
splatter	=	splash and spatter
squawk	=	squall and squeak
chortle	=	chuckle and snort
Internet	=	international network
Illiopolis	=	Illinois and metropolis
Technicolor	=	technique and color

"My dearly beloved sons, with intense joy and elation I come into your presence once again with words of love and encouragement from the heights of Heaven. I have the authority and expertise to speak for the Lord through the power of the Holy Spirit with as great intensity as the Son I bore. Be assured that I will accomplish the favorable goal of reaching all My lost children, all who are embattled in secularism and materialism, all who are steeped in sin and indifference, and every last one who has never known the name of Mary. Thank you for aiding this cause, My little ones. You are blessed beyond all telling. You have heard and read the Sacred Beatitudes; you are aware of Jesus' Passion and Sacrifice on the Cross. He has created His brothers and sisters anew for God. Surely it is true that all good men have entered deeply into His Crucifixion for their redemption and the purification of the world. Do you remember the Holy Spirit speaking about the righteous being the salt of the Earth? It was Jesus' pain that brought such holiness to those who love Him. He asked them and continues to request that all who yearn for Salvation to enter His Sacred Wounds. But, how can this be? What happens when salt enters a wound? Yes, intense pain. Terrible, profuse and agonizing pain. Still, this is how the world is made righteous. The salt of the Earth becomes so because they are cleansed in Jesus' Wounds and at His behest, inflicting horrible pain upon He Who Is. This is the Will of God and the Grace of the Savior. It is by this Grace, these Wounds, this Bloodshed that broken men are made whole. Matthew 5:13 remarks about this mystical phenomenon, and goes on to say that these righteous ones are the light of the world. Indeed, the salt of the Earth and the light of the world – taste and vision, preservation and focus. My sons, I have given you an example of several blended words at the beginning of My message today. The reason I have done this is to seek your contemplation of the blending of hearts to create consonance, the combining of ideas to manifest reason, the marrying of Heaven and Earth to culminate in redemption. All absolution and forgiveness is the unity of penitence and pardon. All new beginnings come from shedding the past and welcoming the future. It is by matrimonial unity that wedding banns are sealed. It is through conjugal truth that young children are begotten. All good things on Earth are manifested by God, given to humanity for his reception and absorption, for inclusion into his life in exile. Think about all the concepts and ideas that are brought from the communication between men and God and between societies and nations. These are all portmanteaus because they include parts of each whole. And yet, each whole must sacrifice and defer, a compromise as it were, so that there can be a new face and new order in certain matters in life. However, there are no compromises when it comes to obedience to the Truth. What men must do is offer the good in themselves and eradicate the bad. This is not a compromise, but a sorting of priorities and values so that all men live in accordance with the teachings of the Church. This is what must be done to change the minds and hearts of those who are its enemies. For some, they have nothing yet to offer and everything to surrender. They must essentially discard their whole self and begin again. This is the radical reorientation that is spoken about in the Catechism. This is what I have been trying to accomplish throughout the ages with My appearances and messages. It is the focus of much human suffering. It is the reason the winds blow on certain plains and around the mountain foothills. The reorientation is the reason why skyscrapers fall and avalanches roll through gorges. You realize by now that all is to the changing of the world. All you have done for Me in the past two decades has been for this purpose, to exalt the Cross and celebrate the Paschal Resurrection of Jesus from the Tomb.

    I have spoken about Jesus' Agony in the Garden. He knew that He was about to die for the sins of mortal men. How could He have known any sense of welcome to the suffering He was about to know? Because He knew that it would pay the price; it would satisfy the call of the Father for the repatriation of all lost souls into His presence in Heaven. This was Jesus' blended thoughts and feelings, His portmanteau in the Garden of Gethsemane. It was the combination of the human and the Divine. It was agony and ecstasy in one Sacred Heart. This, My children, is what God calls out to each of His disciples. He asks all Christians, especially those devoted to Me, to recognize that there are blessings and crosses along the path to conversion; and not only your conversion, but the cleansing of the prodigals with whom you live. It is both terrifying and heartening to know that you will someday join in Jesus' death so that you can be raised in His Easter Resurrection. These are parts of the whole of man, unifying and yet distinctly different emotions that comprise the beliefs you espouse. This is why people can cry through their tears and laugh in the face of certain demise. The point I am making here today is that although there is no compromising the principles of the Holy Gospel and the way you must live, there are amalgamations of feelings, thoughts, emotions, approaches and conclusions that compose your experiences in exile. Do you remember that when you are strong you are strong, and when you are weak you are also strong? This is the refusal to compromise, but there is no doubting the coexistence of weakness and strength. You are concurrently human and divine in the way of Jesus. If this were not so, He would have already given up on the lost. There is stasis and kinetics, example and potential, and a far-flung hope that all issues dealing with the conscience of man will fall at last into the loving arms of God. This is the point; that no matter how cold and callous men have been, no matter the depth of their sins and their unloving thoughts, they have the ability to be perfected in the Blood of the Cross and in the Cup. No matter how sarcastic and unfeeling someone has been, there is renewal in the Church. This has been the message of the New Covenant and the essence of My messages to you. I reassure you, My Special son, that you have done an exemplary job making this clear in your books. You have shared abundantly everything I want humanity to know. This is the deposit that you have placed before the world to receive. And, as you told little Mary Jane Kerns last night in delivering your final book, there are reasons aplenty to see that humanity is in need. They may yet be unprepared, but social and economic conditions are making them aware. It is crucial that you make your appealing memoirs available to the Church and all who have yet to enter it in the ensuing years. Why? Because your testimony about your years of experience are imperative for them to know. Your writings can help humanize a seemingly intangible event, that of My Maternal intercession. Many years have come and gone, and who knows how many more there will be? I am stationed in Heaven and on Earth outside the boundaries of time, so the years are irrelevant to Me. Even though you are yet in the mortal domain, you are fortunate to resound your knowledge about the Afterlife through your own writings and meditations. I wish you to be humble about this, and righteously proud. Not filled with human pride, but proud of the faith you live. It is clear that there is a difference, and you must address these differences in writing head-on. You must remember that it was accusations of pride that felled the Apostles at the hands of those who despised them. This will not happen to you, but you and your brother will certainly be maligned for stating your case in your books. I have completed My lesson for today, and I will finish My message by reminding you that I am always with you. Jesus is forever your friend and strength. He is perpetually beside you; and the Holy Spirit reigns eternally within. These are the founts from which you draw intense strength and perseverance."

Saturday, May 29, 2010
9:34 a.m.

Various Implications of Power

lordship	-	subservience
sovereignty	-	subordination
superiority	-	inadequacy
aggression	-	resignation
dominance	-	deference
command	-	obedience
control	-	submission
discipline	-	compliance

"Welcome into the brilliance of My Immaculate Heart on this new day that the Lord has brought. My sons, you must be thankful that you are living in this age of awe and wonder where you know not what miracles that Jesus will avow into your presence, where the Angels have embarked in entourages the world over, and where you have ignited from this place and time a means by which the souls of men can be converted to the Holy Cross. Indeed, you have enkindled the divinity in human hearts that has been ignored too long, and you have provided Me the means to chastise the unbelievers and bless the faithful. I know that you are seeing the Church through admiring eyes because of the Glory that has engulfed all who have come to the Altar of Sacrifice. We have imagined and you have dreamed of untold benefaction to come to all who stay the course of Christianity. My Special son, you have said many times that the Catholic Church has stood firm for twenty centuries, and rightfully so. You have also acclaimed that nothing will prevail against the Church of Saint Peter. With this confidence, I promise that we may see the dawning of the purification of the world through hellfire and chastisement. I have not made a great haste of these issues in your messages to humanity because there are enough prophecies of doom already in the public domain. I have always given My sharing Heart, My Heart of hope and redemption, of loftiness and dignity, My Heart of peace and tranquility. This is the way that I ask you and your brother to live. I request that you maintain your composure at all times, that you realize the beatific logic of Divine Truth, and that you understand that Jesus has already rectified what is yet lacking in those who cannot presently see. He has made amends for them through you. He has filled the void where they might have been working for God through your alliance with the Holy Trinity and your loyalty to Heaven. You must understand that it is in this grander beauty that you have always lived.

    I have come to speak more to you again today about the concept of hierarchy. I have said that it entails certain levels of authority, and now I wish to address its implications of power. You realize that power can be used for good or for ill intentions. The kind of power that is granted by the Lord is always a benevolent one, always utilized to lift-up the lowly and slay the wicked. Too many times, humanity sees power errantly. It is not power that creates sin, but weakness. When any man surrenders to the temptations of sin, it is not because the powers against him are too strong, but because he is too weak. This speaks to the difference between power and force. I have always told you that Satan uses force against mortal men to drive them away from the Cross, but I have been reluctant to say that Satan has power. Yes, I have said it to other visionaries and locutionists, but in a much different tone. I wish for you to remember that force is not to be equated with power. I have given you today a list of implications of power, not an exhaustive one, but some varying degrees. Here, you see a type of cause-effect relationship between the concept of owning and wielding power and those who are affected by it. The kind of power that I am speaking about today is righteous power, that power that serves to cultivate avenues for the Truth to grow in places that are otherwise barren of Eternal Light. Prideful men must be at times taken to their knees in order for them to see beyond their own arrogance. This is the power of the Holy Spirit setting them free despite their own penchant for remaining detained in their own darkness. You must remember that one would not recognize darkness if there were no light with which to compare. This is why God's authority seems so oppressive to men of free will. It is not that He wishes to incarcerate them, but to liberate them from a captivity of which they are unaware. This is why the Apostles spoke as they did. It is the reason the Saints wrote with such seeming contradiction to the facilities of the day. They drove a saber of light into the dark consciousness of men that was unwelcome. It was not requisitioned by the masses, and it certainly was not allowed to penetrate the places most needed for the betterment of the world. I am not suggesting that this is what happened to those who eventually chose Christianity, but the many who waited until they died to embrace the Cross. It would seem that one might be speaking figuratively about Divine Light piercing the consciousness of mortal men, but it is an actual eventful fact. It is a manifestation that cannot be seen with visual faculties, but it occurs in the same way that spiritual love is shared. It is a liberating emotion of awareness that takes the human heart and marries it to the Kingdom of God high above the skies. You should remember that the soul will always follow the heart. If you give your heart to Jesus, you will also place your soul in His hands. Therefore, when speaking about the implications of power, this is why prayer is so efficacious. When you ask Jesus for something in His Holy Name, you are appealing to His sacred power to change human life as you know it. When you invoke His Will to aid your friends, they must be deferential to Him in order for this to occur. When you read the Commandments, you see that the implication is that human beings obey. This is the concept of power and response. Do you understand so far? "*Yes.*" I have touched today on the phenomenon of power in a way that I have not spoken to you about before because I did not want this discussion to come from Me to the created world, but from you as a participant in it. The ideas of lordship, control and discipline are clearly explicated in the Sacred Scriptures, and I did not want anything in My messages to preempt My children from learning about holy power there. They must read and learn from the Bible as a matter of course. It is the Gospel read by untold numbers of souls through the centuries, but everyone from every walk of life must come to the same comprehension of the writings of the Gospelers and Saint Paul. You probably realize by now that this has been an extremely tall order. There are as many personality types and opinions in this world as there are the number of people who inhabit it. Imagine this. The Holy Gospel of Jesus Christ has been the most common focal point over any other persuasion in the history of man. This is because each infant boy and girl is born with the desire to return to the perfection from which their conception was derived. If not for Adam and Eve, they would never have left it. The key point is that there are endless judgements that people make before they come to the same conclusion that all human life comes from the Father, and every soul returns to Him through Jesus' Crucifixion. This is the crux and nexus of understanding the experience of exiled human existence. It is a life that begins in the womb and continues beyond death into the endlessness of eternity in Heaven. Thus, it does really matter what happens in between, regardless of what Miss Daisy told Hoke that day in the cemetery. What occurs between one's conception in the womb and shedding their flesh upon their death makes all the difference as to the shape of infinity to come. This is the reason why everything we have done together will have such impact on the architecture of Heaven. We take souls to Jesus by our prayers and your intercessions. We hold true to the mandates that the Father has established through the Church. Make no mistake, we recognize the benevolent use of power through the Church hierarchy that cedes nothing to its enemies, not even the mere mention of a negative word that might impugn its good name.

Some personality types that are shaped by genetics, experience and the environment are better prepared for leadership roles than others. They are more capable of utilizing power for the advancement of good than their counterparts who are not. This is how God knows whom to vest with the authority of the Church. Almost any Cardinal who votes for a new Pope would himself be a Pope if not for the Lord's perfect discretion. He knows who is weak and who is strong. This is why males hold the power of authority in the marriage. They are stronger like horses and not weaker like lambs. This is also the reason that milder souls seek-out those who are sufficiently confident to guide them on the right paths of life. I am saying that holy power, righteous power, must be protective and nourishing; and this is the reason that Christ, the Head of the Church, has kept the faithful united for so many centuries. This is the reason some people seem more capable of leading public institutions and governments. It is not that they are inherently more intelligent, but that they are not as prone to cower from criticism or outright attack. Inward and outward personalities determine who becomes famed writers and performers.

There are psychological mixtures of all kinds between these two poles as well. However, when it comes to power, the kind of power that brings peace and justice, the kind that slays evil and upholds righteousness, those who wield it must see human life the way Jesus desires it to be. This is best communicated through the Roman Catholic Church through whom humanity is given to God, and God gives Himself to men. This is the power of the Holy Spirit to create and re-create, to absolve and bless, and justify in the Messiah, binding on Earth and in Heaven whatever is deemed and deigned righteous in the eyes of the Father. This same kind of power makes unions strong, national and personal, so that societies of all walks and attributes join as one in the purposes under Heaven serving the King of kings.

Some people evolve in and out of assertiveness and timidity. It is not something that they do intentionally, but a phenomenon that is controlled by the elements of daily life and the cares and worries that arise. Others are literally taken in hand by the sheer necessity to lead, and this is the kind of power that was given to Saint Joan of Arc. All throughout the centuries, it is imperative that humanity recognize these leaders as chosen for whom they are, that their acts and decisions are ratified by God in Heaven. You already are thinking of many of these people now, the great Popes and Saints, the romantics and lyricists, playwrights, and all who have touched the human heart with the ethereal love of God. This is power, My son. It is good and well-placed in mortal men when you see them eventually defer their own offices to the Glory of the Father. What did the battlefield leader say when he attested that his body was broken? 'I will now go to my Father in whose presence I shall not be ashamed.' My Special son, the Father was always present in this man, all men who fight for righteousness and lend their entire selves, even unto their death, for the shaping of the mortal Earth into the likeness of Heaven. Your brother is a man who was once a good leader, but is not at this time because he was asked to remain alongside your command. He needs you like a flower needs the rain. He clings to your words like honey. He admires you as one would see a mighty king feeding his subjects and safeguarding their lives. This has been brought to your brother because Jesus needed your companionship with him in order for My messages to come. I have told you that this was ordained in Medjugorje. This is the reason your brother receives his daily bread from you. You are the origin of his dignity and the sharer of his spiritual love. His soul is comforted and his heart enlightened by what you do for him. This is his way of seeing the Love of God the same way the battlefield soldier knew that it was the Lord who sustained him from his youth. This is the way your brother sees you. This is the reason he needs you. This will never change, even as the whole world is consumed by the beauty of everlasting life. Do you understand what I am saying? Humanity is on course for Salvation. The plans and hopes of the Church are being fulfilled. Do you have any issues to discuss today? *"Does it mean when you see people fail in their charge, like in my office, that they have been placed there because of their personalities, or because they are failing to manifest the power that they have venue for?"* No. They were not placed there in power, they were placed there by force. *"But, in the Church, they are placed there by power."* Yes, you have it right. In the case of your workplace, these people were installed as forces against good, and you know who they are, in that they do not espouse or propagate the Will of God in His quest that righteousness should prevail. This is extremely critical for you to know. Are you sure that you understand the difference between the two? *"When people violate the hierarchies of grace, they forfeit their power within any framework, and resort to willful force."* The key concept in this discussion is that the Lord dispenses and recognizes the power of goodness in souls whom He knows belong to Him. Thus, you see that it is not power that the United States president is now wielding, but brutal force. Anyone in office who works against the teachings of the Church is not using power, but their own transgressions to promulgate public laws and effect social policies. They are not powerful in the way of Divine Truth, but effectively corrupt in their abrogation of it."

Sunday, June 6, 2010
9:31 a.m.

"Our truest calling and outward signature must be to indwell the genius of Christianity into the framework of our social conscience, a deposit of righteousness so profound that it brings the wicked to repent of their sins and give their lives to the Cross. Messianic Salvation. It is all about the irreducible troth of human holiness dictated by Christ's Crucifixion, imbedded deep within the heart of man."

-William L. Roth

"You are made of the substance of utter brilliance, the awesome Wisdom of God that repairs and amends the broken and bent, and that carries you through life with the knowledge that all things will be reconciled in Him. My sons, you are fortunate not only because of your faith, but by virtue of your willingness to bring faith alive for others, for the lost and brokenhearted, for the whole nation spread before you that anxiously awaits its deliverance and worries about its next crisis. We hold their answer, My little sons. It is in the Gospel of Christ that you have lauded in your opening quotation today. The concept of 'social conscience' must be a spiritual one, not something based on earlier founders who knew only little about the Roman Catholic Church. This conscience must be shaped and nurtured, and this is what My messages here in Illinois have been about. I know that you are accustomed to hearing such themes from Me, but I wish for you to remember how I am truly invested in refining the souls of men in this land for the conversion of the whole world. It is true that countless inventions and innovations were begun in the United States. Your people have refined the art of art itself, of interrogation, investigation, travel, communication and learning. America has lent its knowledge and discoveries in science and medicine to the citizens of entire continents thousands of miles from its shores. You have seen, My little ones, that America has also found new ways to sin. It has manifested whole venues through which the worst of human conduct can be spread. Yes, you have seen this, and you will likewise see its demise. This is the good news. And there is no bad news, only better news. You will see the constant dribble of spiritual lethargy be incinerated in the Flames of the Sacred Heart like a house afire. Out will run all who have been causing the problems and wreaking havoc on the innocent and impressionable. I ask that you never lose sight of this future because it was meant to be, whether I ever appeared to a soul in exile or not."

Sunday, June 13, 2010
8:34 a.m.

O Lord, be my light, and be my shadow.
Be my flight o'er the depths below.
Be my breathing and my dying,
In the sacred peace your love bestows.

The sunsets call and daybreaks beckon
The hearts of men to your healing bread,
The Holy Cross that all must welcome,
The blood of Salvation you bravely shed.

William L. Roth
June 8, 2010

"Duty to humanity calls Me here, My little children. The awesome reconciliation between God and man illustrates the need for My presence as these months and years continue to pass. I wish you could know how much I truly enjoy speaking with you this way. It is the delight of My Immaculate Heart to relate to you the emphasis that Jesus places on living faith in His disciples and followers, in the Church Militant, those whose lives have been touched by the kindness of His Spirit. My Special one, these are the days that you will remember your whole life; these are the hours that are changing the direction of the world. What you have written, attested and heretofore published will mean the greatest to those who are far from God, but it will also instill in those who already believe in the Church to reach out with bolder trust and heightened senses. I see that you wrote a poem last Tuesday that you have presented to Me today. It is a wonderful gift that you have written it. It is mystical and miraculous. It is divine and appropriate. Oftentimes the simplest poetry is the sweetest, and this is what this one clearly demonstrates. I shall repeat; this poem is not only eloquent, it is beautiful in its brevity. It ranks among one of the most profoundly awesome writings that Jesus has ever seen. I pray that you will someday publish your new poem in a place that is reserved for the mightiest of pledges. Today, I have come speaking to you about the issues that are important to the Church and to humanity in the secular void. It is obvious that there are deep chasms dividing humankind from its utter destiny in holiness. My messages in Medjugorje and elsewhere have made this quite evident. What can I do as the Mother of God? What would inspire a whole world of unbelievers to come to the Cross en masse? Surely this is the calling of the efficacy of miracles and chastisements. It is the promulgation of new disciplines and Dogmas by the Church. Yes, I am the Co-Redemptrix of lost humanity, that I have known My children from the day My Son was Crucified. I adopted a broken people who are made whole in Jesus' Sacrifice, and I wish to lead them mended and well to the Light that has fashioned their healing. Please know that I am not so naive as to assume that all will come running to Me based on My apparitions alone. They must have a change of heart that is of old, that inspired Israel to heed the call of Moses, that made the marketers and tax collectors stop in their tracks and consider the consequences of their actions. What bravery brought the first Saints to open their eyes and voice their witness to the Gospel of the Son! What courage and deference they employed to lay down their lives to sustain the holiness that they eventually came to know. What gifts they accorded lost sinners by standing fast in the Truth to which their hearts and souls were dedicated! It is no different in the world today. There may not be as many martyrs as there was once before, but that same intense passion for love must always be there. The focus and movement toward human spiritual perfection must never be lost; it must be forever the direction that the mortal Earth is traveling. This is the initiative that I have come to instill. It is the awakening that I have desired to begin. Thanks to you and your brother, to all who are consecrated to My Immaculate Heart, to all the spiritual heroes who call themselves Christian, I am succeeding to inspire the globe. You may not be able to see it from where you are positioned right now, but it is happening. God knows that the refinement, cultivation, fertilization and seeding of His vineyard are ongoing now, but so is the harvest. We take great hope in all of these things.

  Also today, I bring you the good news that My priests and bishops are growing stronger. They are purer and holier because of your prayers. Their days are long and their nights are longer. They are lonely in the world, but surrounded by the Hosts of Heaven. It is clear that secular humanity does not realize the gift of the Lord's priests to the sanctification of His people. Indeed, you will soon receive a new Bishop here in this diocese. He is a man of intense intelligence and protracted ecclesial instruction. He is a priest of sacred honor, of trust and congeniality, and someone who has given his heart and soul to the Cross. The most important aspect of his character is that he is approachable.

He is open to receive the Spirit of God and all His ways. It will take him some time to become acquainted with the country-like atmosphere that is apparent here in central Illinois. This is why your books do not seem to fit-in here in this rural area. They are of a much more urbane, distinguished and sophisticated tone that is obviously the gift of Heaven. I pray that you and your brother will be patient while this holy man takes his rightful place among you. And, there will be a blessing come upon him to rival that of the Resurrection should he respond to My call to elevate My messages here in this diocese. He has a free will, and I have said that he will react to your messages as the successor of Bishop Lucas. We know that the Lord will provide. Why? Because there is so much need here. There is so much fertile ground and great need. There are so many untapped spirits and sleeping hearts. The Catholic Church is hungry for more souls, more Christians, more disciples, more affection and dedication, more ways to grow The Faith into the far corners of the globe. We know that all things are possible with the Lord. I ask that you and your brother proceed in your daily chores with reassurance that Jesus is taking care of you; the Father watches over you, and the Holy Spirit gives you rest and confidence. My Special son, yes you know. It has been a long 19 years. You and your brother have been so holy that it has brought Jesus to be encouraged about the rest of His flock. You have shown obedience when others were not disciplined. You sacrificed your time and talents when men of greater means turned away. You prayed while they played. You have given your hearts to the Son of God, but others gave theirs to their habits and vices. You have been charitable when they were unwilling to share. And, you will inherit the victory while they are left out in the cold. This will be their lot, chosen by themselves, once their lives are laid alongside the gifts of the Saints. You have known this since you were first aware that there was a Church. The Holy Paraclete has been imbedded in your heart and has hovered above your every action to inspire and guide you. This is the way of all who believe."

Sunday, June 20, 2010
8:49 a.m.

Six Suitable Definitions

space - *(n)* the unlimited or indefinitely great three-dimensional expanse in which all material objects are located and all events occur.

matter - *(n)* physical or corporeal substance, whether solid, liquid or gaseous; distinguished from incorporeal substance, as spirit or mind, or from qualities, actions and the like.

energy - *(n)* the capacity for vigorous activity; vitality; available power, forcefulness of expression. *Phys.* The property of a system that diminishes when the system does work on any other system by an amount equal to the work so done.

thought - *(n)* the capacity or faculty of thinking, reasoning or imagining; the intention, design, analysis or application of cognitive instincts.

action - *(n)* the principle or power of operation; a state of realization as opposed to potentiality, as in function, exertion or production.

spirit - *(n)* nonphysical, incorporeal, unseeable essence or existence; often contrasting good versus evil, light versus darkness, love versus hatred; the genesis of belief, often animated with courage, zeal, ardor.

"Good morning, my stately sons, on this warm summer's day here in the heart of your nation. It is My unbridled joy to pray with you and be able to speak in terms that you can understand. It is true, you know, that My Immaculate Heart encompasses all the hopes and prayers of the faithful from all walks of life. It is good that you have decided for God because your prayers from your youth are helping shape the world of today. We remember today the poor, the sick and dying, the impoverished and incarcerated, those who are contemplating self-harm; and we pray for the end of abortion, and especially that the poor souls in Purgatory will receive the prayers of the Faith-Church on Earth. They are parched for the quenching petitions of those yet in exile, the darlings of faith who know Jesus and the Father only through the power of the Holy Spirit. It is fathers day today, a secular observation, but not all whose fathers should be with their children are doing so. It is clear that we still have much more praying to do. Thank you for responding to My call.

My Special son, at the beginning of this message is a series of concepts that have been in place since the beginning of time. When you ponder the meaning of space, matter, energy, thought, action and spirit, you notice that you do so without the consideration of time. Time is not one of the concepts listed here. Neither is eternity. However, there are certain concepts that are more prevalent in time than eternity, and the reverse is also true. Certainly space and matter are facets of the material world. But, do you see energy, thought, action and spirit as being of both realms? *"Yes."* And this is true because the Afterlife is a viable state of perpetual peace. It consists of the energy of the heavens, the thought and mind of God, the action of the Saints, and their spirits in union with the Holy Paraclete. This kind of thinking is not widely employed in the material world. It is clear that anything that assists humanity in understanding the consistency and constancy of Heaven is from the mind of the Father. This is how your prayers are formed in your heart. They are fashioned by the Holy Spirit and placed in your consciousness when it is in perfect alignment with the Will of God. You are there. You have attained this unity with the Most Blessed Trinity because your heart is right. Your meditations reflect the amendments to Creation that the Father desires to see. And, with this seamless state of being, you are already one with the Salvation that no one can see with their physical eyes, at least no one whom has yet to die. We are together again today because only few understand what I just said. I am asking you through your contemplations and writings to express to your lost brothers and sisters the critical emphasis that should be placed on the process of changing not for the sake of simple change, but being radically reoriented to the coming Kingdom that will right all wrongs and then begin anew human life as it has been known. You and your brother believe in miracles as did Sister Faustina and Saint Bernadette, as did the Fatima seers and all who have witnessed the extraordinary gifts and graces of the unseen Kingdom. It does not take miracles to have faith in the Holy Gospel, but believing that it is the New and Everlasting Covenant of human redemption is itself the most important miracle that the people of God will ever know. I am but a portion of that event.

Therefore, what can be said about the concepts of space and matter, and of energy and the like? Whatever it is, it must be to highlight their obedience to the God who created them. What is written of the stars and skies must always reflect due deference to the beauty of their Maker. Whatever songs come and lyrics are penned, they surely must herald the Truth of the Cross in every way, in all aspects and intentions, so that the single focus of a nearly incalculable number of mortal human beings can be drawn to the one Sacrifice that has absolved them all of sin. Men speak of space and matter; they even draw references to time and traveling through it, but they fall short of the omnipotent sight they require because they will not look at eternity from their position in time through the lens of the Messianic Crucifixion. This is the message that the secular societies have yet to discover. Without this single focus of which I speak, peoples and nations are splintered. They cannot overcome the barriers of language, customs, habits and ideals. They are blinded by their own prejudices because they lack the vision inherent in the Sacrifice of Jesus on the Cross. Nothing anywhere in Creation can be seen sufficiently or accurately unless it is laid alongside the Crucifixion, and then it becomes eclipsed by the Bloodshed of the Son of Man, thereby refining and reorienting both the sight and beliefs of all who live. This is why all become one in Him. The greatest fear known to man is death. Surprisingly, its imminence is also the greatest source of freedom. This must appear to be a paradox to many, but not to Christians, especially those who are obedient to the Pope in Rome. The Vicar of Christ is called the Pontiff of the Holy See for a reason, that all will be able to perceive the teachings of Jesus through the mind of God in one infallible being. Here, you see My point that all avenues and mind-sets are unified under the blessing of the Pope, the one who has the Heart of God on behalf of all who love Him. I realize that I am not telling you anything you did not already know, but I am attempting to urge your thinking to include the whole consciousness of men, not just their faith beliefs, in the panoramic constituency of their view of Heaven. There is nary a soul who does not wonder from where they came. They issue ultimatums to Nature and themselves and vow to discover the meaning of life before they die. The answers will not come unless they defer to the Cross. The Cross is both the speaker and the message. It is simultaneously the text of the narrative and their ability to understand it, the beginning and the end. This is Jesus the Alpha and the Omega. It is concurrently the road and the destiny. The Cross is the hunger and the food, the thirst and the drink, the suffering and the healing, the dying and the living. You can again see that I have not dwelt on the concepts of time and eternity. Why? Because time is irrelevant, and eternity is self-evident. Again, do you understand? *"Yes."* And, it is not so much that simple or not-so-simple death is the greatest factor in the accomplishing of eternity for mortal men, but whether the soul adequately prepares for the 'correct' eternity, the redemptive one, the wholesome and peaceful one. These are contingent on the whole host of influences that are met during mortal life, how the person encounters them, what they take with them into the future, what they discard as being meaningless, what graces they accept, and in what miracles they believe. And in this, space remains a factor. Matter and energy are factors because people must physically participate in the Church to perpetuate the faculties of their faith. Thought is a deeply unique aspect of prayer, and the spirit of men must reflect and accept the Spirit of God for the clarity of the unity about which I have spoken. My Special son, think about the implications of this unity. What changes would come to the minds of men if they knew that their physics and sciences spoke directly to the existence of God? How they would see that they too are unified with the Lord in the same way they feel united to the universe they are dissecting! There is belief on all levels and all forms in this sacred proposition. Men and women who examine the aspects of matter are capable of sensing the Creator who made it out of nothing. This is a discussion that has not been sufficiently covered, an argument that has not been clearly made. There is no need to believe that matter and space are divided from the presence of God any more than the souls of men. Whatever He deigns to be His possession certainly remains so, regardless if it is matter, space, energy or anything else conceivable in the minds of men. The Father owns anything that can be drawn into contemplation, but He condemns everything that is evil and casts it into Hell. This is a sovereignty of which no mortal is capable. And, as you have written, this is due to the division between men and their Maker caused by sin. While this seems like a simple discussion to you because of your closeness to the Church, it is widely unknown to 80 percent of the citizens in the world. Does this not sound like good reason to place it into print? *"Yes."* I agree. And, we agree because of the final concept that I have offered at the beginning of My message today. Spirit. The spirit is the whole thing. All things can be created, conquered, vanquished, restored and resurrected in the spirit. Now, I will speak of the Holy Spirit. The souls of men must give themselves to the Holy Spirit as though the latter needs them for food. The Holy Spirit is a Bird of Pray. It feeds on the good will of all humanity who yearns for the liberation that they cannot find elsewhere. It calls from On High to a lowly humanity who lies lifeless and helpless without the Spirit of God. We must ensure that all within our reach and without hope respond to Me, to answer the call of the Mother of God, to reach upward and take the hands of Jesus in their faith, and to remain suspended there with their feet dangling off the ground. This removes the effect of gravity from the equation, and it supercedes space and matter. I am certain that you understand this to be metaphorical speech, but it helps you comprehend the supernatural aspects of what I am saying. Lost sinners must become tendered and tethered to Jesus in a way that reveals to them that they are even incapable of walking without His direct intervention. These are among the issues that I wished to discuss with you today. Thank you, My Special son, for listening to Me and for praying about what I have said."

Sunday, June 27, 2010
9:21 a.m.

"Precious is what you are, My children. Honorable and gracious, holy and humble. Indeed, I love you. We have come this far because you love Me too, and you love Jesus and God the Father through the power of the Holy Spirit dwelling within you. I insist that you accept My accolades and gratitude because they are your gifts here in this time and place. You have retrieved for God the humility that your brothers and sisters lost long ago; you have brought it back to Him from the far corners of Creation where lost men went wandering. I pray that you will proceed in your beatific recognition of your righteous place among the Saints, with the Angels, your hearts hovering beyond the stars, and your souls polished finely and prettily for Christ the King. Today, I come briefly to touch your lives with tangible speech about the Kingdom to come. My Special son, you seem to never relent in your tireless work for Jesus, and for this you will be crowned a Prince in the arena by the God of your fathers. The document upon which you are now working is utterly stunning and priceless. I need not tell you this, however, because you are aware of your connection to Heaven through your faith and holy works. You know your talents; you know your ability to relate the Will of God and the salience of the Holy Gospel through the wisdom you have gained from Me. It is all for the good of the universe, My son. Yes, you must be careful to not appear to be filled with personal pride in your presentations; but righteous,

holy proudness of your position in the Lord's Kingdom is due and appropriate.
 Now, we are on this glorious Sunday speaking about the future of the Church and the lives of sinners everywhere because we can make the difference that we set out to achieve. You have become more holy than even you are aware of knowing. As you have reached these higher peaks of perfection, you have changed your view of the created world. You are not as critical of the failures of men because I have shown you why they come. You are more patient and less apt to surrender the fight for change. All of this is for the good of the Church and to the detriment of anything that opposes the Salvation of the human race. You have vision that has grown not only in what you see, but how you see. You have turned a hearing ear to God and shut out the clamoring world. My son, we once spoke about what it would be like to be either deaf or blind, and your brother once asked if someone was one or the other, which would they choose. This is a difficult prospect to ponder because there are certifiable blessings of sight that differ from the gift of hearing sounds. If asked on a martyr's stage, which would you choose? *"I would choose to be deaf."* And, this is because you would not be as dependent on others? *"Yes."* This is a significant decision because it renders a portrait of you that the whole world should see. You would not want to be a burden on anyone else. How noble. Your brother should become as noble as you. He would rather be able to hear the world, the voices of those he loves, his songs and melodies, and the words of the Mass. However, this would make him wholly dependent upon others for food and all the physical aspects of being human. It seems that those who are deaf can at least see the Body and Blood of their Savior. You are correct; this is the greater blessing. Sight is better than sound.

Let us take this to another level. Would the question or someone's response change if they were told that they were going to lose only part of these senses, meaning lost hearing in only one ear or lost sight in only one eye. How would this alter someone's decision, do you suppose? *"I would imagine that most people would rather have hearing gone in one ear, and mostly for cosmetic reasons, should they lose an eye."* Let us focus mainly on the functional aspects of the issue. *"They would rather lose hearing than sight because of the loss of depth perception."* Yes, your answer is absolutely correct. But, there is more than this, something more practical. Does an eye or ear have the greater chance of being lost due to injury? *"An eye."* Yes, an eye. This is an aspect that is rarely weighed in the proposition. The world injures the heart and soul. It attempts to remove the vivid dimensions of the whole Truth by causing men to stumble, by sending their vision reeling into the darkness by the onslaught of evil works. Your point about depth perception is the crucial one. You retain the faculty of the third dimension with two eyes. And, this same third dimension is retained when someone loses his hearing in one ear. The latter proves that sight is best, just as you say, but for other reasons than self-preservation. *"I understand."* What then do others mean when they would rather walk by faith and not by sight? *"It means they would rather engage their pilgrimage on Earth through the tenets of the unseen Kingdom."* Yes indeed, and this is the kind of sight that must be protected because, and here is the point, hearing the voice of God is as much a vision as seeing itself. When you hear the voice of God, it is with the faith and insight that you are given through the silent Spirit of Love entering your heart. You effectively see and hear simultaneously. The sights and sounds of Glory are implanted in your heart and imbedded within your soul as though you could at any time open your physical eyes and see the Face of God. Please know that I am not trying to be too difficult in this discussion, but I would like to take this one step further as a conclusion. When you see and hear the presence of the Father in your life of exile, what does this mean for the future of man? What is the origin of the all-appealing redemption of the souls of humanity when pondered through the facility of the senses of sight and sound? *"The Crucifixion."* Yes, and where do you see the Crucifixion? *"At the Holy Mass."* Verily, you are again perfectly correct. The Holy Eucharist is the Body, Blood, Soul and Divinity of Jesus Christ, seen with the eyes. The breaking of His Body is heard with the ears. And, yet, what difference is seen before the consecration and afterward? None, and this is called the accidents of the Bread of Life. The accidents make way for your ability to see, touch and consume the Body and Blood of Jesus Christ under the appearance of bread and wine. *"I understand."* Their substance has changed; they are gone. The elements have become the Body and Blood of Jesus, while the bread and wine no longer exist. This is the sight of faith that you employ, the execution of your own beliefs made manifest in the physical world. My Special son, do you see where our discussion has gone? *"Yes."* In other words, when the Father takes the gifts to His Altar in Heaven and places Jesus on the Altar of Sacrifice, He simultaneously transforms the sight and hearing of all believers. This is the gift of faith. It is possible to reap ethereal fruits of love and sacrifice in each person through this faith on behalf of those who are weak and helpless. You effectively become one with the Victim of the Mass. Well done – you have understood this nicely. And, it must be remembered that there are no orts to this Sacred Meal. Nothing is left over to be discarded. The Tabernacle gladly stands as a carriage in waiting to transfer this Sacrament to the hearts of all who come. *"And, all the beatitude that is over and above the needs of each particular soul, the spiritual orts of the Mass are dispensed to humanity as their benefit from the Catholic Mass."* You have spoken the Wisdom of Jesus whose Spirit lives within you now. *"And, this is how all redemption occurs within the Roman Catholic Church."* You are correct again. Thank you for giving Me your heart."

Saturday, July 3, 2010
9:12 a.m.

"It is the goal of contemplative Christians to make their dreams more than just vague nighttime images, but to give them identifiable meaning and the capacity for life in the framework of the physical world. They represent the marriage of the Spirit and the hope of the human heart that is plush with divinity, that electrifies the whole Faith-Church with passion. This is the magnification of fruit-bearing supernaturalism that would remain otherwise undiscovered and unharvested within the realms of everyday existence. It is the freedom to pursue real perfection through the Holy Gospel without feeling pretentious."

William L. Roth

"There are genius works abounding in this world, but yours stand above the rest because you live in devotion to Me. I am your help and guidance through the darkness of the Earth because I bear the Light of My Son always and everywhere. I care for humanity as much as any creature ever given the breath of life. My little sons, you have arrived on the weekend of the year here in the United States that I have spoken about many times. I suppose that it is a worthy celebration when examined against the backdrop of so many tyrannical governments in the world. It is all about pride after that. My Special one, you and your brother are continuing to build on the awesome work that you have laid out; here where it is almost 19 and one half years into your mission, you have not given up. This is why you and your brother are giants among men. You hold Jesus up before the nations as the standard for human life. You live according to the Gospel as the measure of your faith, wide and far-reaching into the massive legislature of human thought and action, and your hearts are given to the Lord; your souls ooze the Divine Love that has brought you out of the cold. I am so pleased that you are still focused on the outcome of the Earth as well as the daily details. This is true. You must live one day at a time. You must heed the call of everyday existence one person, one event and one word at a time. You must live specifically each day that comes, every dawn that breaks. You must not let your minds go too far into the future because you will lose track of the goals at hand. You must never say that the next ten or fifteen years will be here and gone before you know it. Your life is for living; it is for seeing the length and breadth of man's exile for what it is. Remember that the days are long and the years are short. My Special son, you are working on a miracle itself as you change, build-up, enhance and refashion your apostolate. It is obvious to you that you know your talents, that you have the capacity to realize what impressions about My Queenship and the Kingdom of God will gather the attention of your brothers and sisters to a greater degree. I am elated that you are adding the drawings and excerpts from My messages that are a living model, that can touch different people in multiple ways. This is the first summer during which you have not had another mandated book planned for editing during the fall. This gives you and your brother a vastly more redeeming period of time when you can look at the scope of your work inside certain parameters that were never available before. This is what your thoughts are about these days, growing and manifesting everything and anything that will spread the news of My intercession. In effect, you are harvesting the crop that you planted years ago, taking the sweet fruits of your labors to those who are spiritually famished. You must always remember that you are admired for this; you are loved beyond all telling, and you are blessing the poor in spirit and the brokenhearted in the way of the Sacred Heart of Jesus. You give Me reason to weep happily, not with sadness. You know the difference between the two. And, I have told you that there would be signs and wonders to accompany your faith. In fact, I have told the whole of humanity that there would be signs of God's presence everywhere you turn, large ones and smaller ones. I am saying that you are mentoring humanity by the fruits of your life, and the Lord is saying that He agrees by showing signs of His actions. And, when you speak of making another placard with My titles thereon, it makes the heavens shudder with joy. Please look at the date of August 5, 1992 in your first diary, and you will see some of those titles, along with the many others that the Church already knows.

We pray together, My little children, because we realize that it makes a difference in the constituency of Heaven. People who go there do not simply depart earthly life, they have access to both. This is what most commoners in exile refuse to see. There is one Church in three parts – Militant, Suffering and Triumphant. You have known this for years. Some people, mostly Protestants, believe that the Church-Suffering and the Faith-Church are one and the same state. You know better. You know that Purgatory is a real condition of the departed human soul. It makes sense that the Church kept alive through the Blessed Trinity would itself be composed of three stages. It is not to dwell on these kinds of divisions and distinctions that I have come, but to assist everyone to focus on the Original Apostolic Church under the Pope in Rome. We have been discussing this for as long as your messages have come. There is nothing new in this, but you must remember when you construct your future works that only one in six human beings on Earth knows about the Catholic Church. It is clear that you must never be ecumenical in your dispensation of My messages, but never assume that someone else is going to understand exactly what I have said in the context of the Church to which you know the Lord is drawing all men. World harmony and simplicity come through My beauty and the ability of all the world to comprehend what the Cross has to offer inside the Holy Mass. You are making this clear so far. Thank you for responding to My call. And, it appears that your brother's recollection of his early years is helping lay the foundation for his thoughts regarding his memoirs. He has spoken about certain themes that run concurrently throughout those times. Such things as education, occupation, family and friends, politics, religion and entertainment run pervasively through his life. He is more able to discern his own role and self-identity in preparation for his memoirs by creating this ledger. Such is not true for everyone. This would probably not be the appropriate way for you to ponder your memoirs because you are less an archivist and more a meditative, contemplative person."

Sunday, July 11, 2010
8:43 a.m.

"We ought to spend more time dignifying other men by living more parallel to the sacred divines that Christ Jesus has established within us. Our hearts should be more endearing, our motivations more conciliatory, our actions more appealing, and our proclamations more attuned to the

great hosannas declared by the heavenly hosts. Such pious love is the making of legacies and legends; it primes the teardrops at our weddings and wakes; it is the triumph in our pageants and our birthright in the new nativity we have inherited in the Cross."

"What makes Christians such excellent little creatures is that we are willing to forego the known for the unknown; we stake our fortunes on the faith of a billion anonymous fathers; we speak and conduct ourselves in ways considered awkward by practical men, and we have founded our future on the coattails of a Covenant that was etched in stone and ratified in blood long before we were born or had the opportunity to shape it. The enemies of the Cross are tinkering. They are no match for the Roman Catholic Church; they will never reach a formidable mass; their undertakings are unequivocally futile, and they will ultimately convert and die as martyrs in the battle for lost souls while feeding the flames of righteousness or remain as they are and be consumed as heathens by the inferno of justice themselves. This is the crux of the message espoused by Pope John Paul II the night he was elevated to the papacy, imploring humanity, Do not be afraid. Believers have a whole history's worth of engorged promises fulfilled by Popes, Cardinals, Bishops and visionaries proving that our efforts are never in vain."

William L. Roth

"This is extremely visionary writing, My Special one. It is of the high extremes in divinity and holiness, and it is true. You have the capacity to write this way because Jesus gives it to you. Please do not be confused. You should always know why you are so present in the mind of the Father, because you love Him. You are sacred as the Angels to His Heart because you have given your life to the Holy Cross, to the redemption of lost sinners. Does this not seem crucial enough reason for the Lord to bring miracles for the whole of humanity into being? *"Yes."* You are the author to whom Jesus turns. Your vision about Christianity and Catholicism is clear. You are developed in the Wisdom of God because you have been absorbed by the Thanksgiving Meal that you have willingly received in faith your entire life. You have consumed the Truth that has reciprocally consumed you. Do you now understand how it is you who can write of the fruits of the Church where others are incapable? *"Yes."* I pray for all who have been converted to the Church because they have another past that haunts them; they are required to discard their previous beliefs that protest against the Most Blessed Sacrament. While this was not a problem for your brother, it is what keeps millions from coming to the Catholic Altar of Sacrifice. This is how someone's heritage can be quite damning for them. If they believe that pride and history are that important, they will fall with them into the Abyss. Thankfully, we are reaching them in time; we are helping America decide for God in ways that you cannot yet see. This is why you write so prolifically about courage and Wisdom, about new beginnings and happy endings. I have always told you that those who do not believe in the Catholic Church make a mockery of their own intentions when they attempt to serve God outside its jurisdiction. It is leaping beyond the normal that makes people take notice. It is touching people whom you have never met. It is the element of surprise about seemingly normal events. It is making friends and building bridges over miles and meanings that causes humanity to awaken from its sleep. You have seen these things in your time. This is the essential impact of your brother paying the fine for the man with the statue of Me who is being abused by your city officials. This man, Charles D___ is a child of Mine since long ago. His loyalty is with the Pope in Rome and the Church Hierarchy. He placed a statue of Me in front of his home so the world would know My Motherhood. And, he was persecuted for it, even ostracized by the city and his own family. The story about his difficulties with the city over the statue needed an ending. It needed closure that would make the people of this city and statewide area take notice. And, with the help of your brother, the ending is a happy one. The timing of events was ripe for a tremendous impact to be made on many fronts. It most importantly called off the secular dogs from My little son. It proved that My children help and defend one another. It made the local government look outright evil. You can do no wrong when you elevate the Mother of God! Men can do no wrong by venerating Me and showing intense devotion to My Most Immaculate Heart. It is for all these reasons that Jesus never gives up on His people. It is why He defends His flock and encourages His Church. What you do for Me and the Blessed Trinity stands in such stark contrast to the rest of the world. All of your prayers, your writings, the example you leave others, your kindness to the common people, your simple way of living, your hope for the coming of the Grand Glory of Redemption; all of these things keep the world moving in the direction of righteousness. You are not alone; there are untold numbers of holy people all around the globe praying for everything I have mentioned here today. There are even many who are enduring physical suffering, punishment and incarceration because they refuse to deny the faith they have placed in the Church. Each person has his own role, and you have seen how you and your brother have left a mark in Creation.

My Special one, when you give a Cardinal, an Archbishop and a Bishop reason to smile, to well-up in their eyes with pride that you are their sons, then you have had a good day. It is your kind generosity that has made this possible. You do not realize the goodness you have shown. The photographs of My statue on South Fifth Street in Springfield cannot be removed from Creation. The nighttime arch of light around My likeness will glow through the darkness of the Earth until the end of time. It is not that the Lord is unaware or that He declines to elevate what He sees My children doing, but He awaits the proper moment to make an impact so enduring that it takes everyone else by surprise. This is the effect of you and your brother paying this poor man's fine. Imagine being the ordinary citizen here in Springfield or someone reading the story about this man with My statue a half-country away. How does it look from a distance? *"It has all kinds of dimensions to it."* What are some of them? *"It shows that the person who stood-up to engage the situation was receiving miraculous intercession from the Virgin Mary Herself, and had written books about it."* Do you believe that most people think that Mr. D___ should have moved the shrine when he was asked by the city to do so two years ago? *"Yes, even Christians, because they have been taught to just lay down to this kind of evil, as the standard way for a Christian to act."* What is your personal opinion about the matter? What would you have done? *"I probably would have left it there to prove a point, the greater point of how our government is becoming oriented toward outright religious persecution."* Yes, and I would have supported you in that. The parcel of land on which My statue was located belongs to God, not the governing officials of a municipality. As long as these shrines are reflective of Catholic Christianity, of the God of Abraham and Isaac, of the Father of Jesus Christ or the Messiah Himself, Heaven will ratify it. *"The government does not hesitate to erect shrines to sinners all over the states by placing legislators' names on highways, bridges, buildings and anything else they choose. The state hierarchy believes it is a religion to be worshiped."* Yes, you are speaking the truth, as though they believe that secularism is a form of organized 'religion' itself. They worship the right to reject the Catholic Church and its teachings, and they use Catholic taxpayers' private money to do it. All of this is being addressed by the Son of Man right now, in My messages worldwide, in your writings and your greater apostolate, and in the signs that are occurring every day. Your patience has been praiseworthy in waiting for these things. Thus, you have come to another new week in the summer of 2010. You are making excellent progress on your work. The hour is drawing closer when you will visit your new Bishop. You are aware that all things are moving toward the culmination of human events in the Crucifixion of My Divine Son. Thank you again for taking such good care of your brother. He is experiencing tremendous exhaustion brought on by 20 years of satanic attacks for the work we have accomplished. Please allow Me to state this more clearly. No person who has received even a tenth of the messages from the Mother of God as you and your brother has been able to return to mainstream society. Many have died years earlier than they normally would have. It is all in the mental, physical, emotional and spiritual exhaustion that they suffer, the feeling of missing years of their lives, of being left out, of being impacted by draining forces they cannot see, and not knowing how all this will end. This is where you both are now. Let us close with one last thought about the roadside shrine of My little son. Imagine the view from Heaven when the Angels and Saints, all the Hosts who bask in the Light of God's Glory, watched the trucks and machinery arrive at the location of My statue and began dismantling it. It is of the same character as the soldiers who nailed Jesus on the Cross. There will be intense redemptive power coming from that day for all to see, for the world to know exactly what those who refused to accept the Kingdom of Christianity were thinking."

Saturday, July 17, 2010
9:13 a.m.

"One of the most ironic aspects of having spiritual faith is that it proves so many things; we are able to discern right from wrong before being forced there by a surplus of untimely mistakes. We can envision the prescience of the Creator through His enviable capacity to foresee our next moves, that He is willing to nullify our transgressions if only we will invest ourselves in Him. Christians learn to recognize not only the roots of human sin, but its effects deeply seated in the corruption of the physical world. In Christ Jesus, we are bound here by little more than the element of time, for surely we have already superceded our posthumous frames in the sanctity of the Cross, ascending like angels to deposit our sheepish spirits inside the heart of the Messiah who was crucified there. In truth, nothing

can bring harm to anyone bequeathed to Him on the occasion of their passage from this life. To be reborn and regained in Our Lord's Crucifixion is the ultimate definition of joy; for now listless cities can thrive again, and fallen heroes can rise. Babes can sound the strains of Tchaikovsky, and the barren can birth their first sons. Organs can shake dust from the rafters; the skies can be strewn with jasmine, and things without luster can shine. God has spoken through the Trinity, and all who believe Him can hear. Anxiety has been rightfully destroyed; and humanity should not fret seeing cracked rainbows, fraying moonbeams or dulled mountaintops anymore because the whole universe has been created anew."

William L. Roth

"My dear Special son, you have written so prettily that it makes the Hosts weep in joy. I must assure you that all this will come to fruition in the transition of the whole Earth into the Light of Paradise. Thoughts, symbolism and metaphors as sweet as those you speak and write are too awesome to leave concealed beneath the random physicality of the world. I realize that you have been working diligently for Me and also at your workplace, and it is clear that you are duly faithful and responsible in all your duties. You and your brother have achieved a remarkable force for goodness because you do not concede to the material world. I have come today to tell you that these are the days that this diocese, the Church in America and the Universal Church have been awaiting, not simply because of your work, but because time has now come into the second decade of the twenty-first century. It is obvious that new Cardinals and Bishops are assuming pastoral positions of authority, and the older ones are retiring and entering Heaven. We have discussed on many occasions the heavy burden that is placed on the leaders of the Church. There is a grand amount of speech about the heritage of the Church, the seemingly countless numbers of episcopal coats of arms, and the practical issues of parish affairs and operations. It is all about finances these days, you know. This is not as it should be. Prelates and clerics should be thinking as you think. They should set aside their radical pursuit of pragmatic issues and think more conceptually and operationally about Divine Love. To this you have dedicated your entire adult life. You have a vocation as Marian visionary and contemplative, mystical, meditational Roman Catholic that is the envy of the Old Saints. Do you realize that this is true? "*Yes.*" Even your brother lacks the awesome capacity that you have for reaching the Spirit of the Lord in all cases and circumstances because, even though he is a visionary, he is a practitioner of public policy and an archivist of human events. He learns from you the things that must be known about spiritual excellence, just as he followed you into the Church. You have led him to Jesus in the Holy Eucharist, and it was you who directed his attention to My appearances in Medjugorje. If you had not done this, I would not be speaking to you now."

Saturday, July 24, 2010
1:29 p.m.

"If Saint Paul taught us anything, surely it is that we should not cast aside as beasts and barbarians those who do not believe in redemption, for they are still lost creatures in search of identities, vessels waiting to be filled. But for all their eightpenny opinions, they might already know the truth. It seems that faithless men stand summarily alone, idle-toothed and hungry along Creation's margins, wondering why their brazen arrogance and prudish isolationism lead only back to themselves. They squint to see life's meaning through dung-shuttered eyes, ignoring everything catechetical that lends humanity Our Lord's transcending wisdom. They ingest a daily regimen of secular crassness and queer indiscretion lapping at their shorelines with tasteless pursuits, and still they starve. They invest in perishable goods instead of viable hopes; and they rely on clockwork, crankiness and kilometers to survive, but seem to go nowhere from there. They seat themselves at delectable banquets with exquisite fares and quaff the finest sloe gin, all the while impugning the heritage of Godfearing men, mocking the miracles that refurbish the Earth, and turning deaf ears to the dogged tenacity of Christian disciples who are warning them about their fate. It would please the heavens if we sheathed our indignation for now, for the slow piercing arrows of time will eventually strike them in the knees, pilfer their youth, cripple their pride, and expunge their last scintilla of doubt."

William L. Roth

"My dearly beloved sons, it is My delight to break the silence of the airwaves and heart-waves to speak to you again. I bring the blessing of Jesus to you because you are so deserving of His care. We speak at a time of transition when you are galvanizing and utilizing My messages in a most profound way.

It is true that they belong to you to quote and display as you please. My Special son, the whole Church Triumphant is admiring you for the care in which you are creating new presentations for My messages, the recrafting of your other exhibits and the entire host of new ideas that you are pondering for disseminating My messages. This is why you are loved; it is the reason that Morning Star Over America will do what was planned from the start. Today, I would like to speak to you about this grand experience that you are undergoing. It is true that you have seen many signs that your work is of God, and I am mightily touched by your efforts to succeed. As in the days of the earliest Saints, you cannot yet see the monumental gifts you are tendering to the Church. You cannot measure the converting power that is inherent in your acts. You are yet too blinded by the material world to see the astounding beauty that you are creating on your own. These are for history to know, for what is left of the mortal world, for all that is true and graceful wherever the Holy Spirit goes. You and your brother have created a path down which lost sinners can walk to find conversion because you have listened to Me. You have embarked on a long journey that will culminate in My Immaculate Heart. You have blazed trails that will never grow shut; there are too many souls to walk behind you, and there is far too little time. I have promised that every passing year has seen you running through time toward your great redemption; all the faithful have done this with you. The Church Militant is living toward the great and awesome *annus mirabilis* (the year of wonders) in which the Son of Man will return. It may not follow the calendar in its beginning to end, but transcend and include partial years. The point I am making is that a year is presently underway that is not unlike the year of Pope Peter or Pope John Paul the Great or Pope Benedict XVI. You are living the Year of Wonders as we speak because it is the period succeeding Jesus' Paschal Resurrection on Easter. The whole history of the Church has lived in the Year of Wonders. My appearances around the globe have occurred in this same Year. What you must recognize, however, is the seasons. What season you are presently living is the matter at hand. You have seen the long winter before Jesus' Nativity. You also have seen the long winter of the cold hearts of men. They are around you now. The springtime of conversion melts their indifference and helps them blossom into disciples of the Messiah. This is where their true time in the desert begins; this is the summer of the soul. Can you see that I am speaking about the turning of the seasons in the Church as well as within each and every heart? "*Yes.*" And, the autumn harvest about which I have been speaking to you for more than 19 years is a vast undertaking of collecting the lost to be found in Jesus' Sacred Heart. This is what your mission with your brother has been all about. You are planters, cultivators and harvesters for the Lord here in this place. You touch other souls by your own reflection of the Gospel, but you cannot alter their hue. You cannot ripen them on your own. It is themselves who must do this. If this were not an achievable goal, I would not be here speaking to you now.

Therefore, I wish for you to imagine that magnificent time about which I am speaking – the harvesting of human souls before they are caught outside in the stark, cold days of darkness. We have every intention of completing the Will of God. I ask that you recall the perceptions to which you have always been drawn, the ones that make you so aware of your own interior beauty. Indeed, please look at your writing from the beginning of this message, and you will see more evidence of My words. How do you do this? – you are prone to ask. Because above your heart is a valance that helps you shine and a foundation over which you are hovering to teach humanity right from wrong. You have been here with Me. You have been in the world, but not belonging to it. It is beyond descriptive words; it is too difficult to explain to you where you are stationed in space and time. This is true for all who are consecrated to My Immaculate Heart. With the Holy Spirit as our guide, we are sharing the Truth of the Gospel and the language of Creation with the world. I am appalled that so many around you choose to close their eyes. It is their pride that makes them do this, just as you have written today. When those arrows of time about which you speak impact blatant disbelievers, they will assuredly fall. It is with a heartfelt compassion that I look at them because, as you say, they are in the process of becoming alive. They are empty vessels waiting to be filled. I had not planned to give you a particular lesson for today, but I assuredly want to thank you for everything you continue to do to galvanize My intercession to you and your brother for the rest of humanity. The whole deposit belongs to you first and the Church secondarily. *"Thank you Mama."* It is imperative that you always remember this. Will you please remember how you are so greatly admired by Me, by the Holy Trinity and all the Saints? Yes or no? *"Yes."* It is imperative that you internalize what I am saying. I am not posing a simple passing prospect. *"I understand deeply how grateful Heaven is for me participating in the completion of the Heart of Heaven."* Thank you; that is better."

Sunday, August 1, 2010
9:22 a.m.

"*The Lord ordains for humanity abundant new dawns pouring copiously over the horizon, a fabric of life that dries the weeping willows' tears, friendships that never die, hope for the despairing, overtures yet unwritten, cantatas still unsung, stallions in the wild, infants bound for knighthood, timidity outdone by heroism, apathy slain by wisdom, steely moral courage, immeasurable depths of righteousness, the fascination of the Cross, freedom of the spirit, clarity of sight and sound, sustenance for the poor, strength for the frail, counsel for the wicked, truth that never wanes, confidence for the unsure, honor for the upright, stability for the wavering, fathoms for the shallow, dignity for the despised, faith for the lost, comfort for the mourning, victory for the honest, and grace for all things redemptive. It is here that the world must begin to live again, to feel the texture of life from the inside out, grasp the handhold of genius, and expand the vision of human love brought to perfection in Jesus' Sacrifice, leaping toward the future untethered from our fears. We thereby satisfy the cravings of Heaven and the eternal ages with our own sweet holiness. We gain access to the grand ballroom of Salvation en masse and Jerusalem restored by making our volition compatible with the obedience of the Saints and the excellence of the universe that touches the face of God. We die gladly in His Son because the Crucifixion takes our breath away and hands us back new life.*"

"*Those who believe in God understand that spiritual virtue has measurable effects. Things like order, friendship, charity and good will have both motion and direction; they are goal-oriented even if unseeable with the naked eye. We all have different prayers, penchants, aspirations and talents, but these are part of the same contemplative daring that unifies the whole Church as one collective faith to seek the origin and purpose of life. Personal piety is even capable of discerning intent when given access to reviewable input. A photograph of a crescent wrench laying beside an apple means very little to us, but the scene of an automobile sitting on the shoulder of a freeway stimulates our relational thoughts to envision a larger comprehension of objects and actions. The car is a well-known method of conveyance belonging on the pavement inside a system of highways and intersections in a world and universe that sustain their own presence. It is somewhat akin to the parameters of the Holy Mass within God's boundless Kingdom. This is the way our entire religious ascension should be, a measurable expression toward an infinite destination with a specified outcome. In order to do this, we must ask Jesus to give humanity individually and as a single body of creatures a sacred heart like His, one 'corazon sagrado' as Our Lady of Guadalupe might say, that is inclusive and yet verifiably distinct, the way syllables and verses constitute the Sacred Scriptures. All of our holier attributes, peacemaking, positive energies, and constructive emotions are derived from this same indivisible goodness.*

Let us pray - Lord Jesus, heal our broken hearts and feed our hunger with the fastness of your everlasting truth. Be with us when our temples fall, our warriors die, our cities burn, and our bodies break. Bless us today and evermore. Remind us that the human will is never deity-prone but pride driven, power seeking, blinded by the flesh, selfish when tempted, and stubborn in the face of outright sacrifice. Remain forgiving of your people despite our repugnance; be relenting when convicting us of sin. Rhyme our words with your Gospel commands; chime our simplicity with the Church of old, and pluck our heartstrings clean of the dust of good men's silence. Guide us to clear your pathway to the Earth; help us charm the angels, broaden our vision to see right through the crusty walls of human arrogance, to break them down and trample them underfoot. Give us the sheen of righteousness that will make our faces glow with unfeigned loyalty in the way of the Apostles who first walked with you. Preserve the souls of stouthearted Christians and pull us into the fires of your Kingdom, inflamed by your holiness, fanned by human suffering, felt by prisoners, and carried in torches the size of sky-scraping summits, closer to you now than ever before. Instill our spirits with harmony's peace through Creation renewed, with Nature emboldened and redemption assured. You can make one voice speak an orchestra's song, and nations pray in symphonies. One last request should suffice our needs. Dear Jesus, be there when we die in you! Come again in glory wearing your martyr's Crown, shining like a castle afire, taller than the oceans wide, Scepter held high and arms outstretched; Lord Jesus come again! Benevolence adorned and beauty beyond all imagining! Light like never before beheld with the eyes of mortal men, trumpets blasting and melodies aloft, Vatican choirs raising Judgement Day prayers, the sunup of the Blood-drenched human soul, the resurrection of undeniable love, and old hearts born again into new! This is where you have fought to be. Always absolving; forever blessing, restoring, revealing, retrieving and redeeming the humanity you died to save by your agony on Good Friday, by your Sonship with God, with your Sacred Heart moved by what you've seen us do with the Earth you hold in your hands. You raise it high and hold it steady; you bid your Church to bless it here and feed it there; you warm one precinct with the blazing sun while cooling another when the nighttime comes. This is why we pray, O Lord, to you who are worthy of the sanctity of your brothers dying in honor of the Cross, of your sisters beating their breasts, bewailing the casualties of this life, given to you from the foothills of the world to the heights of Heaven where you live and reign with God."

"Life is always more about how we feel than what we know; and our thought-lines are often calico and restless, unstable and disquieting, inquisitive, and sometimes merely faint. Many of us have not yet figured out what the Bible means by spiritual ingenuity. It certainly implies an explicit belief that someone eternal is watching us, whoever started this whole thing, whatever Creator fashioned the world so beautifully and anonymously, with such reciprocal simpleness and complexity, intricate detail and incalculable design, allowing the coexistence of such harmony and discord, discretion and error, inequality among its species, and such far-reaching extremes of sharpness, intelligence, dullness, and ignorance. Humanity is separate from other creatures in that we are communally aware of what causes our own demise; we have the capacity to know that we are not beasts in the wild, and we have the venue through orthodox faith to will into being our transition from this life through a network of parallels, morals, and conclusions that permeate organic flesh and help us reject illicit impulses. When we speak about prayer, we refer to the intersection of previously existing outer-limits, infinite and inexplicable, unseen and undying, with our measurable social and individual desires. It is the coalescence of our needs and preferences with the forces of dominion empowered to satisfy them. And, we know what to pray for based on the aforesaid ingenuity we have inherited from the deific hierarchy that gives us license to practice the principles and revelations aligned with its laws and doctrines relevant to our final redemption. In short, Heaven allows us to establish and ordain the protocols and metrics that best reflect the heart and teachings of its King. This is what prayer is for; we remain consistently connected like a lifeline to the Godhead we cannot yet see, instilling in us the ability to fix what is broken and suffice what is lacking in His eyes."

William L. Roth

"Good morning, My children, I love you beyond your comprehension. My goodness, My Special one, you were certainly a prolific writer last week. And, it is a good thing because your brothers and sisters are voraciously awaiting the wisdom that you have accorded. I have said in other places that spiritual faith is attached at a right angle to the human heart when awareness first comes to those who believe. It impacts like the arrow you speak about at times. It is an eternal implant that permeates the surface of mortal life and takes the bearer of this new purpose into another dimension of living. We have much to be thankful for that so many are the beneficiaries of this gift. Today, I wish to readdress My previously extended blessings and graces, to reissue them with more power and beauty. You are doing more than the ordinary Saints would accomplish because you have looked at the tools that Jesus has given you, and you are building a Kingdom with them. You are aiding the fineness of human perfection in the Holy Cross and Sacred Heart of Jesus because you are innovative; you possess the spiritual ingenuity that you wrote about last week. I must remind you that all these purposes take time, and time that is well spent and intensely worth the wait. You and your brother are living and growing in faith, service and trust because you are seeing the power of My messages through the brief passage of time since I first delivered them. Once you are away from anything for a period of months or even years, you look at it a subsequent time through seemingly different eyes. You are more able to look at My messages in the way that all in the world will see them for the first time. You see more power than you could prior to today because they impact your faith and hopes anew. How pleased you must be to know that most all the work of receiving My messages is behind you. There is nothing more to this statement than to reaffirm that all My messages for the world are finished from the date of December 28, 2008. I will continue to speak happily to you and your brother as long as the Lord allows. I would like to turn back to the concept of the right angle in which the Holy Spirit enters the human heart. It fosters and leads to a conversion and consecration that is irreversible. Imagine that you are standing beneath a huge cantilever, feeling its strength and magnitude overhead. The center of this power is the point where the cantilever is connected to the vertical surface from which it juts. There can be no true projection or extension of the cantilever if that intersection is not strong in structural integrity. In the case of the spiritual heart, this means that there can be no flaws in this connection; the person of faith must be willing to sustain whatever pressure arrives, as though huge weights of life will come rest on the top of the cantilever. Hence, you are protected by your own faith at the same time you are able to bear the weight of the world on its surface. This is where the graces come. One might ask how long is this cantilever that so prominently connects the human soul with Heaven. The answer is dependent upon the intensity of the gift of that heart to God. It is a function of the degree of surrender that the believer tenders to what he believes. It centers around the concept of giving oneself to unseeable forces that impact, affect and direct seeable forces that are fashioned and controlled by the converted spiritual heart. Do you understand? *"Yes."* This is the origin of your ability to write with such beauty. You have given yourself to God; and as His apostle, He has inspired you with Divine Wisdom and ecclesial knowledge that can be applied in the grander analysis of all that is mortal, laid alongside everything supernatural. You are preparing and presenting to the world a magnified rendition of the yet unseen Kingdom that has sustained with gladness the joy in the heart of all who have ever believed. This may seem somewhat a contradiction. How does one magnify something that cannot even be seen? And yet, this is what you are doing with your brother in companionship with all the priests and clergy, the Saints of old, the Church at large, and in tune with all the holy acts of kindness and blessing that have ever been extended in the history of the world. You are growing the faith of the whole Church by your own knowledge of its tenets, by your willingness to practice what the Holy Gospel has taught you and deposited in your spiritual intelligence, the ingenuity that you say humanity gains through prayer. Indeed, you have added to the writings of Saint Thomas Aquinas your own perception of prayer in such a way as to strike humanity again with another arrow of awareness. He and Saints like him handed you his quiver and arsenal of arrows that you have pointed toward the destinations you know to require the impact of the Holy Spirit. What shapes the tips and length of these arrows is how well you know to craft them, meaning your ability to pray in the way you have been taught. This is all connected to the world miraculously through biblical works, the acts of the Apostles and disciples, through the divine intervention of the Angels, and My messages and appearances throughout the ages.

    There is symbolism of this connection of Heaven and Earth, the heart and the Spirit, and the Truth with the human soul all over Creation. This is the purpose of My telling you so many times that the fruit of your own life seems to run perpendicular to the everyday actions of the secular void. You do not live parallel to it, but contradictory to it in an extremely blessed way. One of the physical cantilevers that most impacts the Church is the loggia on which the Holy Father in Rome stands once he is elected, or when he offers his blessings to the world. Your books and electronic website are cantilevers in another distinctive way, one that is more than symbolic. You literally have in your hands arrows and daggers than can slay the enemies of the Cross. You have been vested with this charge, commissioned in the army of true believers, and dispatched by the Holy Spirit to do the bidding of Heaven while you live on the Earth. As you know by now, this does not mean going door-to-door with religious literature. It does not imply that you must build a physical church. The whole concept of Christian evangelization is more connected to the beatific and sublime than the pragmatics of physical travel. This is why you have done so much to purify and cultivate the world from right here in this home. While secular crowds are building their facades and empires, you have been erecting another cantilever upon which the Truth can stand and be projected, and you have been building-up a Kingdom that cannot fail and that will last forever. Here is another seeming contradiction. The Lord God is infinite, and His Truth is boundless. The term 'kingdom' implies measurable places and states, even nations and continents. In the case of the Lord's Kingdom, however, it is without parameters. It is also separate from the element of time, yet it includes the whole of time. The Kingdom of God is perpetual and infinite, and yet you and those who work for Him are doing your own building that is capable of being perceived in its full deposit. You have assisted in the erecting of a cantilever of faith and trust that is attached to a supernal Kingdom that is both vertical and horizontal, and yet neither of these. Yes, it is neither of these and simultaneously inclusive of both. If you are not confused by now, you are more blessed than you really know.

I hope that you understand My intent here today. I am not giving you doublespeak, but I am attempting to indicate that your work in this place, while in a physical location and time specific, is limitless in date and order. *"I understand. It is as if it has wings that fly in supernatural realms throughout time."* Yes, and these realms originate from the Throne of the Father, dispensed throughout history and space to encircle and incorporate the epoch and region in which you live, where your forbears built their lives and countries, where so many have lived, suffered and died, where the Good News has been propagated; wars fought, won and lost, and the dignity of the human species restored by the Messiah who has overseen it all. You and your brother have often asked why God allows certain things. The answer is more simple than you may have believed. He is the Creator of life and issuer of the human will. He is a Master of ingenious freedom. He yearns for the affection and loyalties of His creatures according to their own designs, their own capacity to be raised from the mire into the beauty of all that was perfect before the Fall of

Adam. Do you remember the question that God asked Adam and Eve? 'Who told you that you were naked?' What is the true implication of this question? After all, God already knew the answer. It was that He wanted Adam and Eve to be self-aware of their condition before Him, in His presence and in the wake of what the past may have held. As soon as God asked this question, the future was invented. What was once indivisible eternity was paired by Adam and Eve into time and eternity. How? They were disobedient. This was the 'creation' of Adam and Eve. They had the power to create something good, but they used it to create something bad based upon their inability to resist the temptations of the devil. Nothing has changed about fallen humanity since then. Jesus came to offer the alternative, to give humanity back its ethereal vision before Adam and Eve were blinded by their exile. That sight has been restored, and you are helping lost mortal men open their eyes and deploy it. This is what the Church is for, prying open the eyelids of the material world for the awe-striking view of Creation renewed. We know this is happening; the Church hierarchy knows it. You and your brother are intently aware of it. Sadly, modern secularism remains blinded by their own diversions and distractions, greed, isolationism, materialism and lustful tendencies. My purpose today is to assure you that My work here since 1991 has been not only to stem the tide of opposition against the Church, but to utterly reverse it, the way one might cause a river to run uphill. *"After an earthquake (chuckle, chuckle.)"* By all means, we are shaking the ground beneath the feet of humanity that will leave their legs dangling in midair. What will be there for them to grab hold of? That is correct, the cantilever that I have spoken about here today. This is the interior vision that all men must come to know. It is the power, beauty, honor and sanctity that are gained by those who already believe. I sense that I have not told you anything new today, but served to reaffirm your present knowledge."

Thursday, August 5, 2010

Apostolic Love and Matrimonial Love
By Timothy Parsons-Heather

"Christians are anointed with grace and become identified with God through the apostolic love they inherit upon their sacramental baptism. Through this love, '...Man participates in the wisdom and goodness of the Creator who gives him mastery over his acts and the ability to govern himself with a view to the true and the good.' (Catechism, Sec. Ed. 2000, #1954) This, in my view, gives us the capacity to recognize trueness and goodness in other people. It is one of the criteria by which we identify our companions and, if it be the will of God, our own spouse. Hence, matrimonial love is a fruit of apostolic love; and like the children that marriage begets, it grows to be as strong and viable as the apostolic love from which it is born. The sacrament of holy matrimony must follow the natural moral law laid out by God through the teachings of His Son, through the teachings of the Church. This is why marriage is between one man and one woman, to comport with the 'divine and natural' that the Scriptures command. Marriage can be in no other way valid because '...The consent by which the spouses mutually give and receive one another is sealed by God himself. From their covenant arises an institution, confirmed by the divine law, even in the eyes of society. The covenant between the spouses is integrated into God's covenant with man. Authentic married love is caught up into divine love.' (Catechism, Sec. Ed. 2000, #1639) It is obvious that matrimonial love cannot survive unless fed by apostolic love. A husband must shed his independency, become head of the family the way Christ is head of the Church, and guide, serve, nurture, console, shelter and protect his spouse and children. A wife must honor and respect her husband deferentially and bear his children according to her sacramental vows and physical ability with an open heart, accepting the yoke of motherhood willingly, sharing mutually and equally her divine affections with her spouse and children. Through these gifts, apostolic love remains the thread of counsel as the Holy Spirit teaches and sustains all believers according to their station in life. During the sacrament of marriage, apostolic love and matrimonial love become simultaneously wedded and spouses of each other as do the husband and wife, not to dissolve their identities, but to support the family in the service of Christ."

Sunday, August 8, 2010
9:18 a.m.

"*The marketplace concept 'economies of scale' means that manufacturing costs per unit are reduced as the production rate increases. This must be what the good Lord was thinking when He showed some 70,000 people the 1917 Fatima Miracle of the Sun, touching so many lives at once with such intense converting grace in a matter of minutes. It would have been difficult for that many witnesses to deny what they saw. This reinforces the fact that Fatima was perhaps one of the greatest miracles of the 20th century because most supernatural events are seen by one or two visionaries at a time over a span of months or even years. It was one gargantuan blessing meant for the entire population of the Earth. And, knowing the reciprocity between Heaven and the Church in exile, the reverse must also be true. We should accept the Crucifixion as one humanity, even though we are over six-billion strong, because we are all one body in Jesus. This would be our own miracle for God. If we think about how people suffer in this world, that they often feel forsaken, exhausted, depressed and abandoned to themselves, it must be difficult for them to believe that there will ever be a single purpose of life under any particular cause. Christianity is the exception. In Jesus, no one ever suffers alone. We are all broken as one body the same way that Christ is one body broken for us. This is the reciprocation of the Cross and the efficiency of eternal redemption, the way the whole economy of human Salvation is invested in a collective Church so socially diverse and continentally far-flung. We must be the spiritual merchants who ensure the solvency of our own beliefs; not through some democracy of ideas, but in the sacred principles guided by one Gospel Truth.*"

"*The Lord wants us to believe that He speaks to the world through the Spirit and Creation, that there is little difference between hearing His voice and actually feeling His presence. The latter is more ardently the way Jesus solicits our avowal. And the Scriptures say, 'If today you hear His voice, harden not your hearts.' [Heb. 3:15] Here, we are reminded that Christ speaks through life's circumstances about our inner-feelings and the prospect of facing certain setbacks, crises, and even death by infusing deific Wisdom into our consciousness. There is no doubt that we are hearing God's resonance, counsel, consolation, and advice. He often requires from us mutually shared sacrifices to knit us together, not through some kind of staged theatrics, but by endearing faith; not by secular sentimentalism wrapped around populist politics, but by genuine holiness grounded in the Church. The real* question is what will be our response. What will we give or lend to our own redemption? How does our faith translate into pious works? Jesus gave us an entire Crucifixion with which to prepare our answer, but God will not wait for an eternity. In Christ we have the means to overcome the burdens of sin. We have through the Cross the ability to rise in dignity where Adam once fell in shame. So, let us anchor our destiny to that lodestar, come to our feet again, begin laying tracks toward the immortal horizon, and prepare to wrap our arms around the Kingdom that knows no end.

    Let us pray - Jesus, without your love we would be like ships out of water; with no foundation, no purpose or direction; our lives would be lightless and seedless, shed of hope and shorn of innocence. Our memories are but brief outlines of the way life used to be, while we scribble the margins with regrets about the way it should have been. We are still young foals and fledglings in your arms, little foxes gnawing at your door; and we search for moments that make things right, all the arts and elements that soften the hardened, smooth the gritty, square the corners, and round the edges. Our years in exile pass too soon, as if clicking through a turnstile; they slip away, so bereft of sanctification, they tend to blur into one. We pray that you will score us clean of whatever tarnishes our souls without leaving too many scars, without allowing our faith to become fodder for the world's worst cynics, without giving us apprehension that we have not done enough. You manifest our completion in all good things. You finish us finely and set us out like kindling across the Earth so in need of the fires of your love. Let us never resist your advances, come what may, during hours of joy or sadness, whatever clouds our eyes, whenever we are feasting in joy or fasting in hope. Help us remember you just as the Father has never forgotten us. Reap from our prayers a fortune of real redemption, and feed the hungry from the work of our hands. Most of all, dear Jesus, make us holy; make us pure and simple, pretty as flowers, fragrant, sweet, gentle, encouraging, satisfying, and sincere. Hear our confessions and cultivate in us everything that Heaven wants us to be. Rescind our dying and bless our living. Call us back to you when we are wandering; render us lame should we go astray; mute our voices if we speak in error, and give rise to the Kingdom taking root in our hearts."

William L. Roth

    "My dear little children, there is a vast difference in being able to see across a chasm and having the ability to focus upon one thing. It is the difference in having conceptual knowledge compared to operational knowledge. I have come to build a framework of wisdom upon the foundation of faith that My Son has given you. My messages to you and humanity have been to provide definition to the terms of your absolution. I hope that My appearances here and elsewhere have served to reignite the flame of righteousness in places that have grown indifferent. Indeed, I have given you the tools to build the Kingdom of Love in your hearts and around the globe. This is the reason I said to you last week that you are helping build this Kingdom only hours in time different from saying it to another visionary in Medjugorje. It is the building-up of My Son's Kingdom that the whole Church has been doing for 2,000 years. Therefore, when you look across the chasm of the ages, you can pull focus on certain acts and gifts that complement and replicate everything the Gospel teaches. As I have said so many times before, thank you for having responded to My call. My little Special son, you are intently working on collecting My messages into collation, into a certain order that will best allow the world to grow accustomed to My Motherly instructions. As I said last week, you have at your hands the ability to do whatever you feel necessary to take My messages to the world, as long as you do not get in their way. You and your brother are just alike. You have a driving will to get this done because it has taken you more than 19 years to record what I have had to say to your friends, companions, enemies and all the nations. I am not faulting you for this; in fact I am complimenting you, but you must remember that we are approaching a secular structure that is not accustomed to My intercession, if it were ever to be welcomed at all. Jesus will ratify your acts if you maintain your poise and composure, if you do not push too hard. I accept and bless you for desiring the Kingdom of Heaven to overwhelm the Earth as soon as possible. We have spoken about this many times in the past two decades. We have also spoken about the concept of patience. You have listened and learned well. You are far more patient than little Jesus ever was. He always wanted to set the table an hour before meals. He wanted to clear it within two minutes of finishing. He would cleanse His face first thing in the morning so as not to give the impression that He was unkempt. All of this is fine, but I told Him that there was still sufficient time for these things, that it was the inward person that everyone should address. Yes, He would turn and tell Me that He already knew that, chuckling as He spoke. I give you My firm commitment that we shall enter the hearts of the lost and hurting with Jesus' Holy Spirit as our guide. You pray finely and live peacefully. It was clear by your tears when the priest from the Philippines spoke about being the only pastor for 25,000 people that you care deeply about the condition of the Church. I was appalled that so few parishioners in the pews beside you listened with any sense of compassion. This is a message for another day.

Today, however, I wish to speak to you about the profundity of your own writings and the means by which you are taking to heart the calmness in which I have asked you to live. My Special one, you have received the writings of the past two weeks into your heart from the Seat of Wisdom because you are continuing to give yourself to Me. If I may offer My personal attestation, I believe that what you are writing is profound. You link the persuasions of the Cross to everyday life. This is something that I wish your brother would do. You noticed that he wrote about the topic of apostolic love and matrimonial love, but almost everything you saw and read was dictated to him by the Angels. He knows about the concept of apostolic love wedding matrimonial love during the Sacrament of Marriage, but he did not have a vision of how to put it into words. He did not know which parts of the Catechism to include. All this was done by the Angels for him. When he hears you tell him this in the next hour, he will be comforted and consoled because it will reinforce the fact that Heaven is this close to him. You must be sure to always remember that the same is true for you. If one priest can pastor 25,000 Catholics in a far-off land, surely you and your brother can remember that the Savior of humankind can hold you dear to His Sacred Heart from within. I offer My congratulations for your victories in Him. They flow from the motivation that you have received from the Spirit of God flourishing from deep inside your faith. I have guided and taught the whole of humanity for centuries about living peacefully with this Spirit until Jesus comes again. This has provided ample time for the Saints to complete their missions and bless, heal, build and unite. You are in their ranks already because you are setting your deposit of works upon their footings. This is how the Church remains one unity from this life into the next. It is the reason that My children are such exemplary disciples for the modern world. It is the reason why people call upon your brother for advice. They have no agenda of any kind; they simply wish to hear what someone has to say who is close to the Blessed Trinity and Me. It happens to everyone sooner or later. Those who come to the vineyard late will receive a full day's pay as well. It is the prerogative of God to make these decisions based upon the heart of the penitent."

Sunday, August 15, 2010
Feast of the Assumption of Mary
Medjugorje Pilgrimage – 21 Years Hence
9:06 a.m.

"My little sons, the battle for lost souls began long before you were born, but has heated up and raged on since then; it has waned and grown into fullness again. We are on the verge of seeing one of its most grotesque crescendoes now because the Son of Man is closer to returning than any time before. The simple flow of years reveals that this is true. You have indeed seen a bomb threat at the Holy Shrine of Lourdes, and this is among the unprecedented evils that are lurking where My children gather to honor Me. All Christians have the capacity to overcome perils such as this because you have the weapon of prayer. It gives humanity power that you do not know you have. It is not unlike the concept of being able to compute intricate mathematical equations in your sleep that you are unable to do while awake. My Special son, you and your brother have been sheltered from the attacks that have taken the lives of priests and nuns, that have martyred them and the other disciples who have fought to propagate the Gospel of My Child. It is good that you have lived in this safety because it has allowed you to peacefully complete the books that you are looking at today. You have done a yeoman's job preparing a bookcase in which to present them to your local diocesan Bishop. It is neat and conservative. Your ability to build it reveals your innovative craftsmanship and desire to ensure that your presentation is excellent. It has been 21 years since you stood on the mountaintop in Medjugorje, praying while I spoke to the pilgrims there the way I am speaking to you now. Theirs were simple messages, small ones, concise and brief intonations of My Wisdom that would lead millions to return there for prayer and conversion. The girl whom you greeted on your second pilgrimage, the one walking along the road near the eating place, the one who seemed filled with doubt; do you remember her? Your words took hold; she is an extremely devout Christian. These are among the friendship conversions that you wrote about in 'Babes in the Woods.' It is all about witnessing, counseling, prayer and living in the knowledge that the Lord hears you. Thank you for always attesting to the power of prayer."

Sunday, August 22, 2010
Feast of the Queenship of Mary
8:51 a.m.

"Thank you, My darling son, for singing of My beauty on this grand feast. You are cherished, loved, admired, honored and adored as My child, working so intently to spread the Holy Gospel of Jesus around the world. I feel so welcome here, so embraced. I yearn for the day when we embrace in the Light of Heaven. It will come so soon that you will wonder where the years of your mortal life went. This is why I have invoked your patience so many times. You truly do not realize the miracle of your life, your great contribution with your brother to the Church and the redemption of souls. For My part, I have always been one with you in the Love of God. We have existed where He has always eternally preexisted. You must remember that even though human life in exile is stressful and burdensome, it is precious and beautiful. Why? Because it is a time of preparation, a preparatory experience for all who live yet in the flesh for your encounter with the divine. I have always had a sense for the failings of humanity, even as most of them are unintentional, from the time I walked there with you. My Immaculate Heart has always been filled with positive emotion and high hope for the amendment of humanity's ways, for the healing of all that has broken men and women on Earth. I was assumed into Heaven and crowned its Queen; this is what today's feast is all about. What does this mean to your lost brothers and sisters? How does My Queenship affect the conversion and Salvation of sinners worldwide? You already know the answers, and you are embarking on the issue of advising your friends and enemies alike that I have the power to unite the nations under the Cross. It is in this sign that men shall conquer their own deaths. My Special son, we must be sure to pray for all men's understanding of My intentions, to pray for them and seek them out in others. You and your brother have been given marvelous faith with which to live, a vision of this life and the next, a means to endure the pains and agonies, indeed the mundane aspects of everyday existence, because you are keenly aware of the mission to which all Christians are called. Jesus the Christ has taught you this through the painstaking ways you have lived through Him. The Holy Spirit has been your fire and your light, your inward focus on the external aspects of the Kingdom of the Divine. You touch your brothers and sisters in ways that motivate them from the inside, that lead them to the warmth and vision they acquire from their own conversion into the Church.

Jesus' teachings have become your teachings. His example has become the way you and your brother live. Imagine all the places on Earth that have been discovered, developed and destroyed again by the hands of man. Ponder all the rest that have never been discovered or explored, all the virgin soils and untouched beauty that God has fashioned into being. Yes, and think about the incalculable beauties that lay there now, that shine and glow, that emit supernatural resonances to unhearing ears. This kind of beauty, this type of innocence still resides in the human heart, and it must be protected and matured. This is what the mission of the Church has done. Throughout the past 2,000 years, the Holy Spirit has subtly instructed believers through the regions where men live to turn outwardly in love with this interior perfection. It is not a mainstream kind of thinking in the secular void because there is no deific romance there. You have touched on this divine essence, this innate connection with God in Heaven, through your prayers and writings. You are manifesting it now in the work you are dedicating to your public exhibits, and all the preparation of your manuscripts for presentation to the world. These are part of your connection with the unseen but seamless unity you have with the Father of Creation. This makes part of you one with that first moment when He decided to create something out of nothing. He knows you specifically and personally. He knew what and whom you would be and become from the instant He deigned to imagine what priceless love you would return to Him. It is this way for all who believe in Him, for all who love Him in the way of you and your brother. Imagine this. Even though you are but 48 years old, you are as timeless as the mind of God. He knew every word I would speak to you in AD 1991 until now. He realized that you and the rest of His creatures would be touched by the beauty of the Angels, the teeming seas and towering forests, by consoling art, poetry and music, by the sunrises and sunsets, by the charity of men of good will – everything that can be measured, believed and espoused by humanity on Earth was seen by Him an eternity before they ever began.

    This is also the limitlessness of My own Queenship. I was Queen before I was conceived. You were theologian, disciple, apostle, pontiff and Saint long before you were conceived. It is as though the past, present and future flow from the same waters of time over one waterfall into the basin of eternal life. Who knows from where they come on any given day? What does it matter that Christ was born 2,000 years ago or yesterday, or a hundred years from now. It is all unaffected by the element of time. This is how the Lord can sift and strain the impurities and imperfections from the existence of men. He has the power and authority to slow your pace through time or stop it completely. He possesses the power to reshape the Earth, reverse the history of His creatures and rewrite it, give new life where there was none to stir, resurrect what has been deposed, and instill in any heart the desire to be united in Him. All this He accomplished by being incarnated through Me onto the Earth as a Son of Himself. Oh, My goodness, the undescribable paradox of the Holy Trinity! The point I am making is that no one who is bound for Heaven can deny that Jesus has been their redemption and their own identity, yes their very own self as His Mystical Body. Jesus has been trying to give Himself a bath since the hour of the Crucifixion. He has cleansed His creatures of sin in the Blood of the Cross. He has given Creation a clear perception of what the Father expects from those who will see His Face in Heaven. The Sacred Scriptures have explicated His Will for all who live. And, the sacred miracle of the Holy Sacrifice of the Mass that you attended at Saint Aloysius parish last evening is another example of the elegance and pageantry that must become the soul of every living man. The Eucharistic celebration is the begetting of prayer for redemption. It is the unification of all peoples beneath the Cross. It is the hearing of the Truth through the ageless counsel that God has given the world still locked in time. All who pine for Salvation must come to the Original Catholic and Apostolic Church, not that they will be necessarily sent to perdition if they do not, but so that suffering on Earth will finally end. You have made this specifically clear in your prior writings and polemics. Therefore, it is to this awesome task that we have dedicated ourselves. I come today in humbleness, but also in righteous pride that I am stationed on a plateau where there is no more sorrow. I remain with and beside all My children in exile, but I must reassure you that nothing can harm Me here. I am immune to the shock that befalls mortal men when they are introduced to repugnant impulses because I have seen the end of time. This is why I ask you to be both happy and careful during the same conditions in which you are afforded the guidance you require to see beyond the perils you often face. Let us pledge today, My Special one, to stay above the fray, that we ignore the distractions and clamoring ignorance of those who oppose the teachings of the Church. Let us pray for its persecutors and do right by those who support it. We can accomplish great things by just asking God to make things come true. This is what I have been telling the modern world in places like Lourdes, Fatima, Medjugorje and here in Springfield, Illinois. You have judged men's characters for yourself, and properly so, based on what they have said and done. Your prayers and petitions have preserved the life and health of untold numbers of souls. We must continue this mission and stay the course of pity and mercy for all who are forsaken and in pain. Turn your prayers toward those who mourn the loss of loved ones by random acts of violence. Remember them to God. Ask Him to void their grief and heal their hearts. Most of all, pray that He renders assistance to them, that they realize that everything they will ever know, see, decide or judge will slide over the waterfall that I spoke about earlier, that all time is one. There is deep consolation in this, and there is predestination too.

My Queenship is your comfort because I deign to you the Son of the Most High from My Immaculate Womb. I offer you His guidance and Wisdom, His dignity and poise, His patience with suffering humanity, and His childlike demeanor when you might otherwise be tempted to become embittered. You are so much like Him. You and your brother have perfected in yourselves the identity of the perfect disciples. The accolades that accompany this gift are too high to phrase; they are too numerous to explain in the limited resources of the human mind. I ask that you esteem each other with the assurance that you have done the Lord's work faithfully and beautifully. We pray that you will have many more years together to continue what we have begun. I give you My promise that I will watch over everyone for whom you have asked Me to pray. I realize the scope of My power as the Mother of God, and I do My best to intercede for everyone who is consecrated to Me according to the dispensation of His Will. The Lord God loves His people! He reigns over His Kingdom. He holds dominion over everything He has given life. Please accept My profound gratitude for giving your life to Him, for listening to Me and recording My words, for using all the venues and technologies at your disposal to disseminate My messages, and especially for taking such good care of your brother. The latter of these has been the manifestation of the conversion of the masses. And, thank you again for singing the pretty song when I came today. I give you My solemn promise that I will utilize the power of My office as Queen of Heaven and Earth to make all creatures great and small the living image of My Son."

Saturday, August 28, 2010
9:29 a.m.

"Little children, you must remember that I am a sinless human being, and I have dreamed in ways that you have dreamed. I have laughed and wept. I have imagined and tread the long paths down which your hearts go, seeking the light that makes hope shine; and not just any light, but the brilliant Light of God that overwhelms the human spirit with hope. I have in these precincts and around the foothills of the greatest nations on Earth walked with pity for those who suffer. My hands have touched the lowly, lonely and afraid. I have listened to the testimonies of the innocent about to be handed over to their executioners. Yes, I have looked upon and shared the beauty of a nation once cradled in the arms of their own faith in the Father of Love. But now, too many Americans have rejected Him. All that was once holy has been traded for expedience and disdain for the singular Truth. Men have exchanged their potential for greatness in the ways of the Apostles for another way of life, a lower one, a degraded form of existence that compares them with the beasts of the wild. My sons, we have together watched over the past four decades the corruption of the United States that can only be reversed by the Roman Catholic Church, not just any religion, not just Judaism or Protestantism, not secular humanism. Only the most crucial form of Messianic Truth can redeem America from its years-long slide into the material abyss. These are the words that should be spoken at the Lincoln Memorial today. *(Glenn Beck Restoring Honor rally at Lincoln Memorial)* You will not hear them because secular America would begin burning their own country to the ground. They are blind and ignorant of the medicine they require to cure them of their error. They have given themselves to evil, at the same time they are asking My Son to deliver them from it. The prayers of the faithful may be no more powerful than those who pray for the first time, but they are the most consistent. Those who hold the tenets of the Holy Gospel dear to them; those who apply the teachings of the Son of Man to the intricacies of daily life are prone to heroic acts because heroism comes to them naturally. They do not see themselves as such. The many who have dedicated their lives to the conversion and purification of humanity are the yet-mortal saints whose future is already in the hands of Almighty God. My Special and Chosen ones, we must pray for those who live otherwise. We must never allow them to take their eyes off the destiny of the human soul. They will impact the Holy Cross when their eyes are shuttered in death, and the Holy Cross will reciprocally impact them. They can neither see nor touch the Kingdom of Heaven without passing through the Crucifixion of Jesus Christ. And here in this place, in America and around the globe, they will never taste the sweetness of true victory until they have consumed the Holy Eucharist of everlasting life. My Special son, we are praising and lauding the Father for your having published your new website yesterday. Your service to Heaven is unprecedented. You must realize that everything to be known by mortal men about the redemption of the soul has come to you; it is still growing in your heart. Saint Benedict and all the Saints are leading you through their own prayers on your behalf, for your piety and good will, for the seasons of the years that seem to pass so quickly, for the untold numbers of sinners you are leading to the Church. My messages have always been about focusing the attention of the world on Jesus' life, death and Resurrection. This has been a broadening mission with a concise purpose. It is not unlike the motion pictures you see of the Earth in outer-space, focused more and more closely on its surface, then to a particular continent, then a nation, a state, a city, a block and a residence. This is not the way the Holy Spirit comes to men because Jesus arises in the human heart from the inside. But, it is the way My messages have attempted to focus the responsibilities of converted Christians upon themselves. Do you understand the difference? *"Yes."* And, it is not like focusing the entire view of a photograph at once. For example, if you see a blurred picture of a house that is slowly brought into focus, you begin to discern the size, shape and colors of the windows and doors at the same time. My messages have been more dimensioned than that. As I have focused the faith of humanity on their faith in Jesus, I have been able to clarify certain elements in the same picture while other elements remain in the background. It is like focusing and making clear the entrance door of a house while the remainder of the home is still blurred. It is as though each pixel in a photograph is its own picture. *"I understand."* I have told you this, My son, because this is also a way of viewing human life. Time is too brief, daily and repetitive to refocus one's attention on all the elements of earthly existence, all the acts, statements, impulses and reactions that occur on any given day. We have spoken for almost 20 years in increments. Priests and other homilists portray their vision of the Kingdom of God in daily increments. However, each of these is a pixel in the picture of righteousness that God sees from His Throne in Heaven. Every time you pronounce Jesus' name, the heavens respond in kind by attesting to your faith before the Cross. Every Rosary bead, every blink of your eyes, every step you take, every thought that nourishes and uplifts broken humanity is a prayer for the Kingdom to come.

My message today is specifically about your greatness in company with your brother and all who labor on behalf of the Gospel in remaking the face of the Earth, redressing it in the Glory that you know to be true. And, My words speak volumes about the success that good men and women like you have had throughout the ages. This is why My Son still lingers in this place. He yearns for disciples like you. He savors your obedience and hangs on your every word that pronounces His esteem. My Jesus is your Jesus. You and your brother must long remember that you have been enlisted for this mission because of your determination to succeed. Verily, you have already done so. Longevity is said to have its place, but you are now accomplishing what the Lord has asked you to do. It is My prayer that you and your brother are given longevity to proceed into the last bastions of earthly life with My messages of conversion and Salvation. It will not require your own longevity for this to occur, otherwise you would be under daily attack by evil forces to procure your death. My Son has provided for you long lives, so Satan knows that causing your death will not stop what I have done here with you. Hence, there is no need for evil to bring you fatal harm. Do you understand this too? *"Yes."* I still require you and your brother to live prayerfully, to keep yourselves out of harm's way, to keep away from unsanitary places and conditions, and be on guard against those who might bring you injury. This is My message from Saint Augustine, Saint Ambrose and all the Saints. I know that I need not keep repeating this same request. I ask you to pray for the many who have lost loved ones in wars and the inordinate number of accidents that you are seeing in the news every day. People who drown in street sewers? My goodness! Hay bales falling on their heads? Young men suffocating in grain bins. Motorcycle accidents. Falls from tall buildings. Every day, it is utterly a dramatic shame how people refuse to live prayerfully. And, they must protect their children from vicious dog attacks and drowning in ten-inch pools of water. On and on. We in Heaven will safeguard the lives of the praying faithful."

Sunday, September 5, 2010
Blessed Teresa of Calcutta
9:09 a.m.

consequences - (n.) the effects or results of earlier occurrences; the conclusions reached by lines of reasoning or inferences; importance in rank or position. *Syn.* outcomes, ramifications, implications, sequels.

"For you, My dear little children, I have come again to pray, and I have enlisted your aid for the conversion of lost sinners. How could it be true that we have been so brilliantly successful thus far? Because you are obedient. My Special son, you must remember that it is the Holy Spirit in your heart that helps you write such beautiful strains. You have come into complete unity and full communion with My Son here in this life, and this is why your gentle heart knows what to say. You and your brother have capitalized on your friendship for the good of the Church, the advancement of your faith, the propagation of the Gospel, and the preparation of the world for the Second Coming of Jesus. You must remember that you and your brother's first weeks of close companionship began in the fall of 1977. In September and October of that year, you spoke of the tragedies of the world, about living in America, about the issues gripping the spiritual realms, and of the ideals that you hoped to actualize in future years. I heard all of these conversations, and especially those you enjoyed beginning on October 8, 1977 in the little Formula car. You and your brother were laying the groundwork of your relationship upon which Jesus has built your apostolate, and you have in your own divine way remained one inside His Most Sacred Heart. Here we have come to another fall season exactly 33 years later, and your mission has been accomplished. You have published your global website; your public deposit of Marian works is complete, and you are prepared to meet with your new Bishop. Indeed, I will speak about that meeting now. You should know about Thomas John that he is a practical man, one who believes that spiritualism and secularism can work together for the advancement of the Church. He has a childlike heart. I must impress upon you that few bishops in the history of the Church are as pragmatically intelligent as Thomas John Paprocki. He can see in someone's eyes their motivations. He knows by what speech enters his ears the dedication of the speaker to the mission of the Catholic Church. He is witty and charming. He has an elevated sense of humor, and this is coupled by his deeply engaging approach to those with whom he deals. These are the traits that make his service to Jesus so valuable in that he is a staunch defender of the teachings of the Gospel. With all these admirable attributes, he also is divinely inspired by miraculous gifts. This is why he runs and sings. It is the reason he can relocate to the countryside diocese in which you live and matriculate into the culture you have known. Bishop Thomas John will take an immediate liking to you if you are unassertive and deferential; if he sees you pleading rather than demanding, he will welcome you with open arms. This stands to reason. He will embrace you if you do not ask him for any decisions or actions in a certain time frame. If you approach him as a prelate, he will respond to you as his son. You are well trained in these things, and I believe that I have sufficiently made My point. The books will speak for themselves. And, even though your brother will not attend your first audience with Thomas John, he should write an extremely brief letter for you to deliver, along with your usual donation. Do you have any questions about this matter? You are free to meet with Thomas John at your leisure, at your earliest or later convenience, according to the alignment of your schedules. Jesus and I will be there with you. Knowing that your Bishop is an avid reader, he will absorb My messages, recognizing their beatific content and Matriarchal essence. You are fully capable of presenting yourself and your works with ease.

I gave you and your brother the term 'consequences' when I first arrived today. This is the ultimate reason we began together not only in 1989, but in 1991 and all the years until now. By all means, it is the reason your brother was relocated to Ashland with his family in 1956. The consequences of the Earth, men's actions, the failures of the mortal experience, the opportunity to purify the nations – all these things have yet to be finalized because there is time remaining. The Salvation of man has been finished by Jesus' Crucifixion, but the composure and constitution of the identity of His Mystical Body are still being defined. This is why I first came to you. It is the reason I have spoken so fluently and prolifically about the moral status of humanity in exile. Let there be no mistake. We will accomplish the goals that we laid out from the beginning, all the way back to 1977. Yes, all the way back to 1973. There has never been any indication that you and your brother's friendship would do anything otherwise. You are so much alike that it is remarkable. You have reached the requisite 33-year plateau that you began ascending in September 1977. I attest that it has been 33 years for reasons according to the providence of My Son. Does this mean that you and your brother's friendship will now be crucified? Not even in the slightest. Your union will never be tested or accosted from the inside. Not even the outside. You and your brother have ultimate control over your friendship. Thus, let no one ever tell you anything to the contrary. No relative, no friend, no pastor, no pedestrian. Do you understand? *"Yes."* I will continue to bless you in every way that God deigns, and Jesus will remain with you and in you according to the promises He has made. You describe human life correctly when you say that humanity does not do very well in internalizing other people's suffering. The more time that passes, the greater impact this vision will have upon humanity. For instance, many have extreme difficulty reconciling their opinion that you and your brother are mentally unstable with the intense success your brother has had at the local university. His accomplishments there speak in direct contradiction to their voices. Hence, if they believe that he is unstable, then they must also believe that My messages have come from an unstable origin. Therein lies the problem. My messages are as eloquent and shining before humanity and the world as his educational successes. Here you see the genius of My request that your brother procure his second master's degree. Detractors have great difficulty accepting because they refuse to heed the Gospel. But, it does not matter. This record of history remains. How can anyone justify thoughts of disdain for you and your brother when now seeing what you have lived? This is how all humanity sees the prophets and evangelists. You and your brother are piquing their consciences, even from miles away. You are helping humanity see their faults, when all they want is to be left alone. They feel comfortable with their own level of spirituality, but Jesus does not wish for them to hand over their lives to Him at the end of time in such indifference. This has been the purpose of My messages since they began centuries ago. Thus, no one is being singled out for undue treatment. It is not about them, and it is not about you or your brother. It is about what Jesus seeks from those with whom He will share the blissfulness of Heaven. My whole purpose here is a spiritual inquiry. Does humankind wish to be like Jesus or not? This is the question. This speaks to and feeds the concept of 'consequences.' There are consequences for not knowing Christianity. There are consequences, and good ones, for accepting it. There are different consequences for knowing about it and rejecting it. There are even other consequences for the degree in which one's acceptance is practiced. Why would one build a tower without knowing the cost in advance? Why would one follow Jesus to the gate of Heaven and refuse to enter? Why speak the Gospel only to those whom you know will readily believe? Why enter a battlefield and never approach the front lines? These are the questions that I have asked throughout the ages, that Jesus has placed before the modern world. These are the inquisitions of the heart whose answers stabilize one's capacity to suffer and endure for the good of the Cross. What is happening in your nation is applicable to all regions everywhere. And, it is good. It is productive to the extent that the Lord does not wish anyone to become lax or complacent in their belief in Him. It might be different if the world of men were not on the road to perdition.

Thus, as you said only two days ago to your brother, 'Life is good.' You are living the precise moment when the Earth is being changed. You and your brother and all the disciples are changing it. You are proffering a proposition not only here in this place, but to the archive of the ages, that Jesus' Crucifixion and Resurrection are as relevant now as ever before. This is what makes you all such heroes. As I told you previously, you are all small lights on one grand marquee of divine inspiration, toward the goal of the redemption of men, no matter the generation in which you were born, by which you will ultimately reside in the Kingdom of Glory. When you were writing yesterday in your room, you garnered Jesus' attention because your glow became brighter than all those around you. You were like a star in the heavens that suddenly twinkled with somewhat more power. Your heart gleamed with holiness as it always does, and this is why you shine the Light of Love in which you have been bathed. You must remember that it is through your gift of your days to My Son that He will bestow His blessing and forgiveness upon those whom you have never known. I have said this many times before. I hope you will ponder the principle of 'consequences' in the future as you remember the motivations behind My messages."

Sunday, September 12, 2010
9:14 a.m.

language - (n.) communication of meaning in any way
antemundane - (adj.) - before the creation of the world.

"The language of Creation speaks volumes about its maker."
"Unity at the expense of morality cannot withstand the test of virtue."

William L. Roth

"My sons, we speak again because our work is yet ongoing. Remember that Jesus said that 'It is finished' on the Cross, and we are assisting this finish. Men have often thought about the life of God in the infinity of pre-Creation, known as antemundane eternity. How could the Father make something out of nothing? When Jesus hung on the Cross and pronounced Creation complete, note that He did not say that the world or the Salvation of men were 'refinished.' While this may seen a subtle difference, it has a great deal to do with the modern thinking of those who refuse to believe. The Messianic redemption of humanity was completed; it was finished by Jesus' Crucifixion. It will never need to be repeated. His Holy Sacrifice has absolved all sinful mortals. Thus, humanity must understand that what the Lord God created out of nothing was the protraction of His Will of Love. Imagine what this must have felt like to Him, a bodyless Spirit of Truth, in that the wholeness of what evolved to be the physical realms resided at first in His eternal thoughts. Our mission here together is to refer the world to those thoughts, to the meditations, to the excellence and ecstasy that He enjoyed knowing that He had the power and willingness to forge into being anything He pleased. My Special son, what did God say after He began the creation of the world that you know? *"It was good."* Yes, that it was good. Thus, does this not provide the genesis of the definition of goodness? *"Yes."* Therefore, anything that pleases the Father is good. It pleases the Father when His creatures live according to the 'language' in which He deigned to make all good things. This language is expressed not only in the natural sounds of the world, but in its appealing beauty, in its function, in the sight of every facet of the Earth that makes the heart feel warmed. This is why men feel consoled by the sight of a rolling stream or field of sunflowers. It is the reason the sunsets seem like happy endings. There is focus, motion and intensity in all these things. There are metaphysical images and parables, and analogies and metaphors. When you see a tree bent over from the winds blowing against it, you are capable of seeing language with your eyes. Meaning is expressed by what you see, and you perceive a message. You can see the effects of the winds, and you can hear them roar, but you cannot see the air. Thus, humanity is capable of discerning the antemundane aspects of the Love of God. You know that He created the world through His Will because you are kneeling here now. Thus, every man, every living being with the capacity for reason, understands that there is not only a cause and effect for the existence of the Earth, but force and direction. The Lord is leading you to redemption through the Gospel of Jesus Christ. The Holy Spirit is the unseen power that brings believers to see what cannot be detected with the eyes. The Spirit is the force, and conversion is the direction. You have known about these attributes of human existence for many years, but those for whom My messages are intended are still unaware; they are blind to the transcendental power of human love that brings them to the foot of the Cross. Even certain Protestants are blind. What I have spoken to you about thus far today is that God is so apparent through everything He has created that few can deny that He exists. However, the main reason that so many refuse to believe in Him is because of the behavioral aspects of believing. In other words, there is a stark difference between knowing that God exists and behaving the way He commands. While this is rather elementary, do you understand so far? *"Yes."* The point I am making is that nonbelievers have more difficulty with compliance than the capacity to see the work of God's hands. This reflects the fact that every created being has the ability to believe in Him. It was imbedded like a lifeline tethered to their souls in the womb. What goes wrong as the person grows and matures is the distraction of being reared in the material world. Moreover, men have throughout history distorted and perverted the meaning of life that is handed down through the Holy Gospel and Jesus' personal teachings when He walked the Earth. This is where pluralism came from. It is where relativism got its beginning. Logic follows that you know their effects.

The single Truth of Jesus Christ, the Man of Virtue, cannot be diluted. If anyone tries to alter or amend what Jesus finished on the Cross, that person strays from the Virtue that lived in the mind of God before He fashioned Creation into being. There is but one God with a single antemundane mind. This is where Jesus has been trying to take humanity since He was born of My

Womb. This is the summation of My discussion today. Jesus' role as Savior included teaching His followers that His Father created everything of men and conceivable by men through the Love in His Divine Being. It has never been seen by any mortal man. As I say, its effects have been seen through Nature and all the thoughts and actions of Jesus' disciples that reflect and reiterate that Love. This is the source of your quotations at the beginning of this message. There is no such thing as human unity under God unless all men congregate there through the Cross. It does not pass the muster of virtue if they refuse. Secularism does not agree with Me, as you know. We care not what they believe! And, your second quotation today refers to the volumes spoken by the Father in His created works, including the architectures instilled by the Church through which He lives and reigns. In other words, the great Cathedrals that you so admire are the artworks of human nature in the same way that the Father created Niagra Falls. The prayer chapels and holy shrines that are constructed by the mystics and other devotional believers are the actual products of their love for God and His for them. Are you with Me? *"Yes."* The pillow on which you are kneeling to receive this message is an artifact for the conversion and redemption of the world when it is used for the purpose of receiving My messages. The Rosary beads passing through your fingers right now are also relics. They were first seen in the minds of men and fashioned into being, and the Holy Spirit of God has conscripted them for His own use. This is part of the antemundane process through which the world and its humans are moving toward their final destiny in Heaven. While this is a broad prospect, it is difficult to discern for those who will not allow their thoughts larger range. They are too busy conjuring ways to make more money, or traveling to places that have nothing to do with the refinement of the soul. They are steeped in partisan debates that have little to do with holiness. They will argue fist and foot about the difference between an antenna and an aerial. It is all irrelevant to God. This is why you and your brother, and all who have remained close to Me, have lived such meaningful years. No matter what happens in the future, no one can undo what you have accomplished for God. As Jesus said, it is finished. You must feel elated knowing that you have come this far, that whatever you accomplish in the future will resound your already stupendous victories. This is the reason that I am happy far more than I am displeased by what I see in the world. Human potential is being transferred into finished works every hour of the day and night. There is bitterness everywhere, but not in Me. There is cynicism and cries for vengeance, but not in you. Thank you for listening to My staccato discussion today. It is the pretty month of September, and your favorite time of year has arrived. It is a time for reflection about the spring and summer, a time not unlike the review of one's earthly life. It is the time of harvest. You are seeing in the news where there continues to be so many people harmed and killed by neglect, negligence and accidents. They are not living prayerful lives. This is why I always ask you to be careful."

Sunday, September 19, 2010
9:31 a.m.

"My dear little sons, this week will bring the beginning of the fall of the year, and you will feel the briskness of the changing seasons. I ask you to reflect on the great accomplishments that you have made so far in 2010, and remember with confidence every gift you have given to Jesus in years past. My Special one, tomorrow is the marking of the anniversary of your own birth, and it is likewise a time for you to look forward as much as you indicate internally that the Lord has blessed you for 49 years. It is much warmer in the heart of humanity because of your faith. There is a great deal more holiness around the globe because of your willingness to receive Me here. The winds blow more mildly; the sun shines brighter, and the Sacred Love through which you were conceived can be seen more manifestly by those who suffer. I have loved you, and God has blessed you. These are the making of a sanctified soul. Yes, when the fall comes; when you perceive that the heated degrees of summer give way to the peace that you always feel this time of year, I pray that you will remember the finely designed rest that the Father gives those who have labored for Him. We in Heaven see you on Earth. We acknowledge among ourselves those who belong to God, and those who do not. We see where His sheep are comforted by others in His flock. It is imperative that you look upon yourselves with gratification that your lives mean something, that you stand for something greater and grander than ordinary life provides. You hail the Saints aloft to intercede for you. You imitate their lives. I would be remiss if I did not thank you with My whole Heart, My Special son, for everything you have given Me in response to My Love. There are a great many more gifts that we can give to the world, and I know that you and your brother will help. This is the essence of My message today, that your awareness of the blessing that you are to the Catholic Church becomes imbedded in your consciousness. We have together assigned your life to the Cross in the way of the first Apostles. Yet, we have also given you every new beginning that you could hope for in Jesus' Paschal Resurrection. When I think of the term 'happiness,' I am reminded of all the moments when I have looked at the Earth knowing that My Son did not die in vain. If not for the history of the world's faith given freely by the Father in Heaven, there would be nothing righteous to record for all the generations that ensued. The Holy Spirit is the origin of your happiness, here and in the afterlife, because you are the holy vessel containing the Wisdom of His Word. I wish for you to think about your age for a moment. It has nothing to do with the passing of time, but of your own maturity in the matters of supernatural composure. You have come alive in the past 21 years in ways that you never realized in the years before. And even in the light of this, you have never lost your innocence. You have never shed the sheen of glory that was spread over your inner being when you realized that the Salvation of humanity was more than a Kingdom on a page. It is living, giantly striving and courageously struggling to bring peace and justice to a world lost in its own distractions. Your sheen of holiness is pretty and guiding; it is overwhelming to the Angels. It is a gift to you from God and your gift to your brothers and sisters. Your sheen of goodness cannot corrode or dull with time. It cannot wane or erode like the rocks beneath the falls. It grows ever larger in countenance by the hour, not just the day, but each hour you remember that you are loved. It is thrice pronounced by the Most Blessed Trinity before those who do not yet understand the purpose of the Church and its redemptive mission. I have come to lift up your awareness of your station in life, your sense of elevation before those who have yet to meet you. The Father has placed you and your brother in elite company with the Saints at His side and with those who are still battling for His Kingdom here where you live. Your armor is the faith that you have been accorded. It is untarnishable because you have committed yourselves to the Church for the remainder of your days. I ask that you look with pity on those who do not know God, for He does not know them. This is the ultimate chasm, a fatal breach that cannot be closed unless those on Earth make it so. It is their will that we are attempting to amend. This is what My messages have been about all along.

Thus, I have no specific lesson for today because I come only to admire you. I have no English terms to describe your goodness. It is from your holy heart that your brother's faith has grown. He learned it from you on December 24, 1977. That was 33 years ago, and the world has truly been changed since then. With the assistance of Saint Augustine and Saint Monica, you have caused your brother to fall in love with the divine excellence of Roman Catholicism. He has promised from the center of his heart his allegiance to the faith, to the Holy Father in Rome, to defending the priests who serve so dutifully in the vineyard of the Lord, and to all the miracles that have been handed to humanity from the bounty of My Immaculate Heart. I will not require any more sacrifices from you like those of the past. Everything you give to God from now through the end of the ages is yours to choose. I promise that I will be with you and all who are consecrated to My Immaculate Heart through the end of time and into the Eternity of Heaven. I know it is difficult to do, but I ask you today to ease your thoughts and take kindly the counsel of the ages. Make peace with the fact that the Church is at war against the secularism of the material world, but this war need not diminish the spirit in your heart. Learn wisely the teachings of daily life so you will not become bitter in future years. Discard and ignore those ideologies that run contrary to the Holy Gospel. Do not dwell on the persuasions that bring you grief; do not stop to stone the devil's dogs. Remain at peace in Jesus through Me. Jesus has already fought the good fight, and yet He still fights for humanity's holiness through you. You are battling the errors of the world for Him, for God, with the Holy Spirit in your heart. These things I ask you to remember as the future unfolds. Your brother is grateful to be here with you. He is vigilant so that no unforeseen accident or other kind of evil will bring you harm. He reminds himself daily to protect you. *"I am just simply happy to be where I am. My heart is at peace."* This is because you have remained close to Me and unified with Jesus in the Most Blessed Sacrament. Thank you for your holy prayers. I will bless you again on your birthday tomorrow! I love you!"

Sunday, September 26, 2010
9:34 a.m.

The Seven Liberal Arts of the Middle Ages
(Template for modern American intellectualism)

trivium (3 paths) lower division
grammar
rhetoric
logic

quadrivium (4 paths) advanced division
arithmetic
geometry
astronomy
music

What is lacking?
volitional personal self-denial
orthodox theological instruction
social/interpersonal reciprocity
mainstreamed supernaturalism
mystical/spiritual romanticism
chastity-oriented social morality

"My dear little children, it is to reflect upon the virtues that are lacking that I have come into this world; it is based on the teachings of Jesus in His days on Earth and into Eternity. What is lacking? This is the focus of the Church and the Supreme Deity that has chosen you to voice the Truth of the Gospel in your time. We must remember that the liberal arts of the so-called Middle Ages did little to enhance the Kingdom of Love that Jesus urges humanity to embrace. Even mathematical calculation does little that affects the spreading of the Gospel message. Grammar is the construction of speaking and writing, and you have seen where rhetoric has taken the modern day world. It is rhetoric that is such a reprehensible distraction from the mission of the Church. What humanity needs to know has already been recorded in the Scriptures. There are echoes and reverberations of that Gospel, and good ones.

This must be translated into the orthodox teaching of Christian Truth in every venue, and often with supernatural overtones. My apparitions and shrines are evidence of this. You have seen the list of what is lacking; the one I wish to concentrate on today is 'mainstreamed supernaturalism.' I do this because this is the origin not only of miracles, but of men's belief in miracles. I have said that faith itself is a miraculous gift from God, a blessing that cannot be derived from the troves of the Earth. It is given to those who seek it in prayer. I have also told you that everything before you is about the battle between light and darkness, good and evil, and religiosity versus secularism. You need not look very far to see that your spiritual religion is regarded by the secular void as a private matter for superstitious individuals. At least the individuals who espouse Christianity have life! At least those who embrace the Holy Cross have a belief system that grows righteousness, that cures and heals, that feeds and esteems, that uplifts the lowly and cares for the poor. You see that chastity and morality are two main fruits of those who practice their faith in Jesus. What can be said of the liberal arts? What of natural science and the philosophies? What of extracurricular competition and the teaching of championing the celebration of the self? Are these indicative of the mainstreamed supernaturalism about which I speak? The answer is that they can be. Do not mathematicians strive for the unknown quantity? Natural science can actually testify to the existence of God. Philosophy can provide the necessity for belief in a higher being. Championing the self is a good thing when the focus is to refine everything in accordance with the person that Jesus has taught humanity to become. Therefore, the liberal arts are not inherently evil, but they are distracting when not utilized to propagate the Kingdom of Heaven. If someone has a five-gallon pail and uses it to carry explosives instead of drinking water, he is perverting the purpose of the pail. This is a metaphor for what men must do with their intellect. Saint Thomas Aquinas proved that keen intelligence need not be a barrier to a devoted Christian life. Here, you and your brother have worked for two decades debating the virtue of Christianity with the secular void. Editors and writers have both lauded and assailed you, when they were not ignoring you altogether. You have given your city and central Illinois food for thought about Christian moralism, particularly Roman Catholic doctrine, but the media with whom you have worked have taken little stock in what you have said. It was more a business proposition for them. It was filler for their columns, a way of touching another facet of their reading subscribers. We have fooled them! We have taken advantage of their greed!

We have used the devil's money to lead lost sinners to the Cross! The newspaper is completely unaware of the number of children who were allowed birth because of your subtle and sometimes not-so-subtle messages written from your heart. You know that these blessings occur behind the scenes in the intimacy of the human heart, but you also realize that they are seen by Heaven nonetheless. This is the reason why I always tell you that your victory is ever-growing inside the bounty of the Triumph of My Immaculate Heart! I show you the list of virtues that must be grown, specifically chastity and self-denial, because the former eradicates a whole host of problems, and the latter defuses conditions that lead to theft and war. My dear little children, I try the best I can to think of words, tones and phraseologies that attest to the happiness that you have given Me. It is clear that you have lived up to your promise to never leave Me. Many before you have done so when faced with the sacrifices of the fight. We must enter an agreement that you will never forget that you are a blessing to this world."

Sunday, October 3, 2010
9:23 a.m.

fructify - (v.) to bear fruit; to make fruitful or productive; fertilize

primacy - (n.) the state of being supreme, paramount, superior in order, rank or importance; a conceiving essence or principle

constant - (n.) something that is permanent, invariable, unchanging, ceaseless, uninterrupted, persistent, unwavering, steadfast, resolute

pre- (-) an element occurring in Latin applied to modern language as a prefix meaning before, prior to, in advance of

pre/amble	=	preamble	=	walk in front
pre/cede	=	precede	=	come before
pre/dict	=	predict	=	tell in advance
pre/view	=	preview	=	before seeing

"This, My dear children, is My first message for October 2010, and it is always My honor to welcome you to your favorite month. We remember the concept of 'harvest' every day because this is the key issue of the spiritual conversion of humanity. They must come to the harvest of the vineyard in which you are working. They must ripen as do the sweet fruits that the Lord savors when you pray. We have come to fructify their lives in this world, to turn them over to God for preparation for entry into Heaven. You must always remember that it is the harvest that leads to the springtime of redemption. Today, My Special one, I refer again to a message that I gave weeks ago about the primacy of the Church, the conceiving essence of the Holy Spirit in the human heart. I will not repeat that message today, but add to it in a way as to allow you and your brother to relate to My other children the natural consistency of religious faith. It must run as a thread through the lives of all believers. The Love of God is the constant that makes all mankind one here in this life and in Heaven. I have given you an example of an element that is taken from one language and added to a different one. It is pre-. Such terms are called 'loan words' because they are transferred from one language for use by another. There are many other essential elements that help humanity understand what is constant in the world. Consider the syllable 'graph.' You know about the phonograph, telegraph, monograph and such things as these. Then, there is the paradox principle where one element is used to describe its own definition. An example is the word 'prefix.' You have to use the prefix pre- to define the word. You see how these constant elements are utilized to create common themes. Subordinate. Submarine. What is the constant element here? Sub. What we are attempting to do through your language, through your books, My messages, your prefaces and prologues, through your upcoming videos, through everything else at your disposal is to communicate the common yet extraordinary theme of Divine Love. This is the constant to which all Creation must be drawn.

 The Roman Catholic Church is the living, viable definition of Christian love and Salvation. It consists of all the stages of human purification and redemption. The Faith Church sustains you during your mortal years. The Church-Suffering purifies the imperfect. The Church Triumphant is your eternal home. The constant theme in each of these is the deliverance of the human soul into the presence of God. *'Humanity can be perfect on Earth and go straight to Heaven.'* The three facets of the Church are distinct parts of one entity, much the same way that the Father, the Son and the Holy Spirit comprise the Most Blessed Trinity. Indeed, the Father has come to Earth in the Second Person of the Trinity, and the Holy Spirit, the Third Person, calls every human soul into beatific presence in Heaven. I am not telling you anything that you do not already know, but it is keen to think in terms of The Word. Jesus is called The Word for a reason. God knows that human beings communicate and interact through words, spoken and written. Do you know how many different words are spoken in all the earthly languages combined? *"No."* I do not have room for the number here, and that is the point I am making. Jesus is the personification of the Gospel. The Gospel is composed of words. He is the collective Word of God that is discernable to all peoples in every nation. Do you know what best describes The Word? Love. Then Truth. What else? The Way. The Life. I have listed The Truth before The Way in this message because one must see in Truth to find the way. Yes, Vision. There are hosts of other virtuous terms that describe The Word, and each of them is synonymous with righteousness; each is constant as the constancy of the Father who created them. You and your brother have inherited through Me that constancy of God to whom you are drawn for eternal Salvation. This is what I seek of the whole world. You have learned through the Church and in My messages that you were created in the primacy of God's Love, that you are directed by His primacy to remain in the Original Catholic and Apostolic Church. One can visually see in the Church Hierarchy the primacy of the Papacy, much the same way that the Lord God holds supreme primacy over the entirety of Creation. It is both symbolic and real. You can take this concept, this living faith that you have been given, and create a whole vision of human love that exists inside and in communion with the Sacred Heart of Jesus. Do you remember last week when I spoke about the liberal arts? One of them deals with numbers. Yes, mathematics. You are familiar with mathematics and algebraic expressions from your studies in high school and college. Can you think of an equation that shows a constant? *"Pi. A ratio of a circle's circumference to its diameter."* Yes, and what is constant there? *"It is the same number for any circle, no matter how big. It has an infinite number of decimal positions."* Do they ever repeat? *"The decimals never settle into a repeating pattern."* Let us take another example to discover two sides of an algebraic fulcrum that have a constant. The fulcrum is the equal sign.

$$A + B + C = D + E + C$$

What is constant in this equation? Yes, C. This means that no matter what A, B, D and E are, their sum is never affected by C. Is this true? *"Yes."* One can then say that C is the unchanging principle of this equation. "*Uhmmhmmm*" Do you see any correlation between what I have identified as C and the Truth of the Holy Gospel? C is also never affected by the sum of the other values. "*Yes.*" This is the point I am making. People see Christianity as unaffecting their lives, all other things being equal. God sees Christianity as the imbedded command that provides constancy to the greater world. It always seems to be there, sometimes when not wanted. What else do you know from algebra? If you were going to reduce this equation, what would you do? You would simply remove the C from both sides. This is what secular men have done to spiritual faith in the material world. Now, here is the crux of what I am saying. All the other values in this equation are determined by the alignment of the world's thoughts and actions with the constancy of God. His primacy is the hand-hold that all fallen creatures must reach for in order to equalize the faith of men with the Glory of their Creator. The primacy about which I speak is Jesus Christ, His Incarnate Son. When the whole of the world is converted, cultivated and redeemed, everyone will see the following equation:

$$C = C$$

All the matters of history, internal feelings and unleashed expression will give way to the equation of the Earth's divinity with that of Heaven. In this, we are trying to cancel-out everything that is not C. God has put His own handiwork on some of these things. They not only include the extraordinary actions of men, but the spiritual genius of Heaven that will meld everything righteous that is not C with C itself. In other words, pretty paintings and iconic statues will become imbedded in the Sacred Scriptures the same way you see pictures beside words in a dictionary. It is the inclusion of everything divinely created by man with the beauty of God's Eternal Love. This is how the Saints recognize their own gifts when they arrive in Heaven. And, instead of saying that it was their work, they say that it was Jesus' work in them. Is this all clear to you? "*Yes. But, how do the A and B and the D and E relate. Are those all the good and bad actions of men, or just symbolize the worldliness because all the good has been united with the C?*" Anything that is not C includes all the actions of men, good and bad, that are examined with the human conscience through the prism of the teachings of Jesus. In other words, whatever is not C that stands in contradiction to the Gospel is eradicated by the new union of redeemed souls and Jesus, His own Mystical Body. Jesus acts through all redeemed people as Himself, even before He comes again. Let Me be clear. There can be F, G, N, P, W, Z and on and on. Anything that is conceived by man is made part of the equation and sifted in the process of shaping the Earth into the likeness of Heaven. Does this answer your question? *"Yes."* I have given you this metaphoric example so you know that there is the C, the constant, that is sometimes unable to affect exiled men, but also unchanging and unavoidable. Here, I have also used only the alphabet in this equation. Imagine now that we add numbers that reach into infinity into the equation. How many actions, how many thoughts and opinions expressed and silent, how many movements and innovations are there in Creation? Do you see? I am not suggesting that anything exiled humanity does solely for its own advancement is infinite, except for all that is in alignment with the Gospel Covenant. All human actions there have immeasurable effects. Any apology cannot be located on the numerical scale in Heaven because there are insufficient numbers to cite it. Sympathy, charity and forgiveness – each of these is infinite, although manifested by mortal men. They are distinct and separate acts that meld with the constant C to enlarge the sacred nature of the Kingdom of Heaven, much the same way that Jesus' Mystical Body grows with each newly converted soul. It is all quite simple, really. Therefore, we have discussed today the concepts of primacy and constancy, of being able to fructify the lives of men by looking at its deeper individual elements. We have achieved what I came to do today. *"Thank you Mama."* It is always My honor to speak to you and your brother because you listen intently and take to heart what I come to say."

Sunday, October 10, 2010
9:11 a.m.

The Pet Rock Animation Theory

"Many things are attributable to human nature, My children. People are attracted to the odor of gasoline because it means they can get from here to there. They like the smell of new tires because it means they are unlikely to be forced to stop and change a flat. We speak about such human nature in the context of needs and preferences because that nature is oftentimes shaped by lifelong habits. Today, My Special one, you know that the Lord wants both of you to prosper in His Love, that you should become enlivened with joy in the new opportunities you have been accorded through Me to evangelize the

Holy Gospel. You are taking on the practical matters too. All your weeks and months, your years really, have contributed to establishing an atmosphere where you can propagate My apparitions and messages to the Western world. It has to begin someplace, and the Lord has chosen this humble home and the friendship origins that you and your brother manifested long ago. I began this message about a matter called the Pet Rock Animation Theory. You are familiar with the Pet Rock from the 1970s American culture. What can you tell Me about it? *"It was a novelty for people who did not have time for the responsibilities of a pet to say they had one, and it was a rock that did not require anything from them."* Yes, they gave organic identity to an inorganic matter. And, what goes along with having a pet? What feelings and emotions? *"Affection and protection."* Yes, both of these. From what you are saying, the Pet Rock Theory was a way for Americans to 'enjoy' something without adopting the responsibilities that accompany it, even though it was a tongue-in-cheek gesture. Remember that there is a kernel of truth in all good humor. In this case, there is a much larger vision to be gleaned. Does not the Pet Rock indicate a more vast description of human nature? *"Yes."* And what is that? *"We want to indulge ourselves without responsibility."* Exactly correct. And, many people wish to declare that they have or own control over something else or even other people without accepting the relevant responsibility. The concept of the Pet Rock is more about animating objects to fit the inner-desires of its owner than satisfying their need for a pet. If they really wanted a pet, they would adopt one. On the larger scale that I have indicated, this is how they view the rest of the world. They elevate material items into an almost animated state. On the other side, they reduce other people as though they are physical objects. This is the converse of the Pet Rock Theory. Do you understand? *"Yes."* It is toward the converse that the thesis of this message is based. All human degradation and social deterioration is based on the fact that people refuse to become acquainted with others' spiritual needs. There is secular interaction aplenty; this is obvious from all the news issues on any particular day. However, what will you tell your brothers and sisters about what the Mother of God has said about reducing their peers to material objects? This is something else that you might think about. If animation in any way occurs, it must be the personification of the Holy Gospel by exiled sinners. They must make living the writings on the page. If they wish to objectify anything; if they wish to diminish the living elements of any matter that comes to the fore, suggest that they declare their own desires and temptations dead. Remind them to throw aside their whims and eccentricities that have nothing to do with the Church. Tell them about what I have said regarding the elevation of the suffering and the dignity of the poor. If they will only look around, through and within the walls of the institutions that harbor the ill and frail, those who are not sound of mind, the many who are incarcerated because of their conduct, they will see more than constructed structures and isolated institutions. It is for humanity to pierce the bricks and mortar of these places with their prayers and practical actions that the teachings of Jesus are personified in your day. You can animate such things as good will and charity. You can give a recognizable face to healing and happiness. The Faith Church can erect and celebrate the Living Christ in all who suffer by centering on their identity as beneficiaries of the Cross. We speak about the Pet Rock as being a symbol of humanity's slothfulness. This is an accurate accounting. I speak conversely of a boulder that was once removed to open the Sepulcher of the resurrected Son of God. This is to whom all men are called. It is against this rock that the pride of man has been shattered. And, it is upon The Rock, Saint Peter, that the Roman Catholic Church has been built. I speak of boulders that have sanctioned the conversion and redemption of the human soul, while the 1970s cultural Pet Rock speaks of the lazy side of men who employ humor to hide their own sins."

Sunday, October 17, 2010
9:10 a.m.

Poised Intuition
Presence of Mind
Pureness of Heart
Earnest Conviction

Eternal Knowledge + Spiritual Faith = Transcending Vision
Steadfast Confidence
manifest ignorance + secular disbelief = obstructive blindness
rampant uncertainty

"My dear little children, I arrive today flanked by the Archangels and Angels as usual, not the glass figurines that your friend Mary Blackburn brought you years ago, but the vibrant, living Angels from Heaven that intercede for humanity on the Earth. I wish to speak today about the prospects of your own knowledge about the conversion of the many who do not yet know Jesus as you do. We must change their minds, hearts and lives, and offer them something counterfactual to their errant discourse, something that will bring them to turn about in thought and action, thus rendering them open to the Holy Spirit. For a great number of Americans, their welcoming of the Spirit of God cannot come too soon. I have provided four virtuous conditions of the human heart and mind to open My message today. I refer to intuition and conviction as they relate to the ability of men to realize the internal intentions of the Father as He sees them working for the redemption of humanity through the Church. Conviction cannot exist until this intuition is in place. It is natural for men to open themselves to receive the Paraclete as much as it is natural to breathe. While the latter sustains the physical functions of the body, the former generates and sustains the life of perpetuity in the human person that begins at the moment of baptism. I speak of eternal knowledge and spiritual faith as giver and receiver. Spiritual faith is a product of the Lord's eternal knowledge, and faith is a gift to those willing to believe from this same eternity. One cannot have faith without living according to the Eternal Word. If someone claims to know God, and yet they preach and act contrary to His Truth, they do not contain authentic faith. They are liars and hypocrites. You know that this is where vision and confidence are procured. My Special son, it is due to your openness to the Holy Spirit that you have received My messages for so long. It is your brother's openness that has driven him to remain with you for the cause of the conversion of sinners. You both agreed to do so in Medjugorje in 1989. By this date in that year, you had already returned from your first pilgrimage, and you were captured by the Spirit of My Son in ways that you had not realized since you were also baptized. The blindness and uncertainty that are rampant in secular America and nonbelievers everywhere is a product of the reluctance of so many millions to accept the Gospel Christ. It would seem that I am preaching to the choir here, but I am attempting to instill in you and your brother the capacity to underscore the obvious when speaking in deep theological terms. You and your brother were destined for Heaven long before you ever knew that I was speaking in private revelations around the globe. You have pondered and examined My mission for many years, especially since I have come so profoundly to you. It is not necessary that you think in abstract terms about My resiliency the way most other Catholics do. I have Wisdom. I expound upon the Wisdom of the Father through the Son with My voice of beatific reason. I have the duty and authority to challenge the conclusions of all mortal men. I own the ability to reshape the human heart, to amend the course of mortal history, to bring light into the darkness, to summon the healing hand of Jesus where people are frail and broken, to cause the waters to run uphill, and to clear the skies of blotting darkness. While I am certainly not capable of all the powers of God, I am given the strength of their benefit to reach all My children to whom I was chosen as Mother on Good Friday. This was not something that I requisitioned. I did not have to; it came naturally to Me. I bore the Son of Man in My Womb, His Soul and Body, and I beckon fallen humanity to take refuge in My Sacred Womb as Jesus' Mystical Body. There, all men will be born into the likeness of Jesus through the Church, and all will live as one in the Love of My Most Immaculate Heart. Indeed, since I am the Mother of the redeemed, and I am the Queen of Heaven and Earth, I vow to protract My office into the deepest recesses of the mortal world where God's lost creatures are hiding. It was not beyond the scope of Jesus' ministry to enter places where the worst sinners would congregate. I have gone everywhere He has entered except the gruesome burden of the Cross. I have never been asked to shed My blood for the salvation of the world. The whole Trinity of the Deity shed blood for the redemption of humankind. Even the Holy Spirit. These are matters of theological relevance that can wait for another day.

  I also wish to commend you for creating an atmosphere where you can best transmit the message of conversion from your prologues and prefaces well. What you have thus far created is brilliant, to say the least. You know what needs to be accomplished to touch the hearts of the intellectuals steeped in mortal sin. I assure you that there are venues aplenty for you to share your views however you decide. The manifest ignorance and secular disbelief that have obstructed the spiritual view of untold millions to the ways of the Christ, you are now producing a means to open their eyes, to clear their way of seeing by utilizing a venue that is not unfamiliar to them. I also wish to thank you for being so kind to the poor, the ones who will benefit from your recent gift to the Padre Pio Foundation. You know that Saint Pio is a great and benevolent intercessor for whomever reaches out to him. It is with high hope that I give My children over to the prayers of the Saints along with My perpetual help. You and your brother have established an air of holiness surrounding you that is unprecedented by anyone in this area who does not have a religious vocation. I have taught you well. I hope that you never tire in realizing the blessing that you have been to Jesus in service of the Church. You will be satisfied that you have committed your whole beings to the Father when you see His precious face. Thank you for your prayers."

Sunday, October 24, 2010
9:02 a.m.

chemistry - (n) the science dealing with the composition, properties and transformations of substances and elementary forms of matter

chemisis - (n) the final composition of the created world; the completion of all chemical, biological and natural reactions and phenomena relating to organic and inorganic matter

"Good morning, My dear children, on this bright and beautiful day that has broken for you! I am joyous and gratified because you are yet working in the Lord's vineyard for the conversion of souls! We have created a venue to reach them; we have fashioned a way to open their eyes and soften their stony hearts. My Special son, there are endless strains of poetic beauty that run through your written books. 'At the Water's Edge' is elevating to the heart. 'Babes in the Woods' consists of extended segments of outright levity. 'Supernal Chambers' is versed beauty in linguistic form. All of these pages contain sufficient material to prove that there is happiness and hope not only in the Kingdom of God, but in your works that reflect it. Remember the first days, weeks and months of My appearances, and all the romantic wonder you have come to realize since then. Recite My quotations from My messages. Be happy and joyful that I have come to you, that you are participating in the conversion of men, that My messages here will grow and blossom around the globe, that you have touched the lives of the lost and lonely – all of the reasons you should be airing gleefully all that I have taught. There is beatific romance and divine hope in your mission. This is also a suitable definition of prayer. There is no end to the joy that you can bring the world through Me! You and your brother possess the latchkey, the passkey that will allow untold numbers of souls access to the Will and intentions of God. This latchkey is your deposit of works. Knowing this to be true, any hopelessness that you might have about your future is utterly inexplicable and without foundation. You will succeed in the things that I have asked you to do. You hold a latchkey that will open the outer gate for millions to come inside. I am proud of you and your brother. I admire you beyond linguistic description. I only ask that you do not take your gifts for granted. Remember the gifts, blessings and graces that have come upon you here in this home.

This brings Me to the discussion of the topics that appear at the beginning of this message. I have given you a new word with which to describe to your readers and listeners about the consummate state of the exiled world. You are all moving toward the 'chemisis' of the Earth. It was pronounced this way by Jesus on the Cross. As sure as the Salvation of men was assured upon the Crucifixion, Jesus fixed all Creation in time to be perfected with the heart of the redeemed. It is not unlike the photograph of the perfected soul that I spoke about years ago. When this Earth is supplanted by the New Earth, there will no longer be a need for chemistry as you know it. All that is physical will have been permanently refined into the ultimate chemisis about which I speak. It will be complete, but still alive. It will be fully prospered and grown, but not subject to the reversal known to mortal seasons. There will be spring, summer and autumn simultaneously. And, there will be winter only for those who want it. Do you understand this new concept? *"Yes."* Its derivation is the Resurrection, and it will be affected when Jesus returns again in Glory."

Sunday, October 31, 2010
8:57 a.m.

"Thank you for remaining here with your brother for so long, from whom you are inseparable and indivisible. Remember that the Lord holds sovereignty above all His creatures, great and small. He binds your suffering to the Cross. He benefits your righteousness by His Paschal Resurrection. Whatsoever you do should exalt His holy name. Christ Jesus has been companioned for your healing; and whomever else you befriend in spirit and faith, all your charitable gifts and daily petitions, your humble means and endearing sacrifices, the principles you commend to the good, and whatever else you do to soften men's hearts and salt the earth, when consecrated to this sacred love, shall be blessed by the Father."

- The Dominion Angels

Seven-part Structure of Our Lady's messages
1. A personal sentimental greeting
2. A spiritual preamble or premise
3. Notation of today's feast or other observance
4. Something is wrong in the world
5. I would like to discuss the way to fix it
6. Tell your brothers and sisters what I said
7. Receive a departing Marian blessing

"My darling little children, the secular elite are too busy smithing words, turning phrases, and spinning yarns to pay any mind to the reality of Christian conversion; they are headed for the demise that is rightfully theirs. We have implored them through much greater eloquence than they will ever know to open their lives to the sacred mysticism by which all blessed men thrive. I have spoken to you about your unity in Jesus, and therefore in the Father, through the Divine Love in which you were created. I bring you grand benisons that portend good things, that foretell of a future that is wrapped in the Glory yet to come. It is My joy today, My dear sons, to remind you that you have been set upon the pathway to redemption because you have always believed; you have always grasped the concept of the reconciliation of the Father and His creatures through the Crucified Son. Why must this be so? Why so much suffering? Why such true fashioning of grated feelings to reach a land filled with such peace? Because you will know that peace through your own fellowship with its Prince. All men must follow the footsteps of the One Who Is, the one 'I Am' of all that has been given from the limitless Heart of God. This is the reason we pray. It is all about reconciliation that is founded upon confession and forgiveness.

My dear Special son, it gives Me great delight that you have seen everything holy for what it brings into the world. I have spoken to you about the Earth reaching its chemisis, about the finality of the world in the Sacrifice and Resurrection of Jesus. Surely you know that we are working toward this now. As I have said, this does not imply that the world is traveling toward an ending, but a transition, a new beginning that will bask in the victory I have foretold. Jesus is the personification of that victory inside the Triumph of My Immaculate Heart. How can someone be both a victor and the victory? How can a path also be the destination? How can it be true that agony is also eternal ecstasy? Because the imperfect body of humanity is being perfected. It is being purged of the poison of its own sins, purified and cleansed of the stain of its own inequities. I have spoken about this as a process with a discernible outcome. There is a before and an after. There are recognizable attributes to a world that is corrupt and one that is perfect. The whole purpose of the Gospel is to elucidate these contrasts. It is to assist the vision and understanding of human creatures in knowing that it is purposeful to look away from the self in pity for all others. It is self-sacrifice that empties the human soul, making it fit to be filled with the Holy Spirit of God. Never mind the calling of the flesh, the pains and torments, the wounds and ills. They come and go as the wind blows. Steady the human heart, and all else will prevail. All goodness, all those principles that you are giving to the good, as the Dominions say, are blessed by the Father because He has always recognized them. He is their origin, and He wishes to look upon them again as though He is seeing Himself in a mirror. You and your brother are polishing the world, setting it in shining armor to fight against the evil works in which it is yet embroiled. We strive for the awakening of the sleeping. We call out like a collective clarion to cause an upheaval in the ordinary workings of the secular void. We attempt to shock them, like My miracles and apparitions have brought intense enlightenment to so many souls throughout the centuries, in the hope that they will perceive God and their relationship with Heaven as a goal too crucial to ignore. By all means, they must see it as their only lifelong goal! We pray for these things because the Lord will manifest them through faithful hearts like you and your brother. If you do not give up on them, neither will Jesus. He looks to you for continued signs of valor and endurance, here in this simple place, because He has always known that His Kingdom is grown by His followers with the greatest commitment. My Special one, you are too self-examining. You are counterproductively too self-critical. I ask you today to be more confident in what you believe, even if you never say another word to anyone else. Everything you believe about yourself must be invested in your own certainty that the Holy Spirit is thriving in you. I am not suggesting that you not be thoughtful. I am not saying that you should blurt out words and feelings without thinking them through. I am only suggesting that you recognize God's own genius inside you, in your words and deeds, in the product of your faith in Him. *"I understand."* It is for everything that He believes that you and your brother have lived. *"I can feel my oneness with Him."* I say this today because you must impress upon all who hear you that this unity, the unity of God and man, is frequently tested. All suffering and tribulation must be seen in this light.

Verily, it is not that the Lord is putting you to the test, but the evil in the world that is trying to steal you from the redemption you have accepted. This is the point. This is the question. Do modern men have the wherewithal to withstand the fight against the distractions that have come upon them? Is the burden of mortality too heavy to carry all the way to the horizon of certain death? Do good men surrender the fight solely upon the persuasions of the easier paths? Is there genuine stability in the tenets of their own proclamations? These are some of the questions that men must ask themselves while in the 'process' of pursuing the Promised Land. And, My Special son, we already know the answers. They are common to every man and relevant in this day. It is rather simple, really. I know that I have said this before. There is nothing complicated about keeping faith in the destiny of the human spirit. It does not require a battery of psychological tests or discovering the limits of physical agility. The whole concept is encapsulated in whether mere mortal men are prone to universal love. Do they tend toward the divine? Do they believe in the miracle of their own Salvation? If their responses to these inquiries are affirmative, then there is yet hope in their lives. If those answers are negative, they are already dead. Please remember the depths and heights in which you and your brother are loved. When you look back upon your twelve finished works, you often wonder how such a miracle could have been given to you. It was you who manifested the miracle! It is you who believed. It is your faith that has fathered these gifts. You have reached a new decade in time, a new series of years that will bring intense fruition to My own appearances here. What I have brought into this world is beyond the scope of ordinary faith and morals. It is beatifically divine. It is higher than the human soul can reach from inside the mortal frame. My messages and apparitions are supernatural even to the supernatural. They are sewn to the Glory of God and draped across the landscape of Creation like a fine blanket. And, upon this blanket, I shall lay the Mystical Body of My Son, born into that Glory, fit for presentation to the Hosts of Heaven. All will come again! From east and west in the whole of the universes, admirers will come paying homage to the newborn humanity that the Mother of God has delivered to their Savior. It will be the glorified summons of Jesus' Nativity again. It will mean that all that is seen and unseen will hear the first cries of men who escaped their own flesh and damnation itself because they believed. It will mean that all men will someday walk again, someday speak the strains of Truth so loudly that their syllables will echo across eternity. No more lies and half-truths, no more broken promises, no songs and sonnets unfinished. You have gained a foothold on this Truth here in your time. You have been handed the foyer of divine awareness as though it could fit in the palm of your hand. My Special son, I envy you. I envy everyone who has stayed fast in the struggle to understand what Jesus desires for you. I place My hand on My Immaculate Heart and thank God for what you are about to receive. I honor Him as My Creator, our Creator, because He did not leave Adam and Eve without an everlasting future. The Lord has given to men their redemption, one that you have already procured through Jesus, one that you have augmented by your faith, prayers and good works, one that you have prophesied to your friends and brothers, and one that is a mere thinness of a veil away. Never mind the time. It will take care of itself. It is humanity that is passing through it."

Sunday, November 7, 2010
Genesis 1:3-5
8:14 a.m.

Eternal Light and Created Light
A Compelling Concentricity

"My dear little sons, it is the dawn of another brilliant day, and we have come together in God's Love to speak about the struggle between goodness and evil. I am with you always. Jesus is at your side through your whole lives, and the Angels and Saints bolster your vision through the graces they represent. You have learned of the concepts of human rights and civil rights, and they must be protected at all times. There are individual rights, personal rights, that must be accorded to all peoples. However, through the Church, there is such a concept as 'situational rights' that are particular and unique to a person's gender, capacity to understand the genius of the Church, their station in life, and the opportunities accorded to them by life's conditions and circumstances. The protestors who are criticizing the Holy Father's visits in Europe are claiming that they should have the individual civil rights to unite in same-sex unions, to abort their own children, and to take greater leadership in the Church as women. There are no such things as rights such as these. What they are demanding is entirely repugnant to the Lord. The concept of 'situational rights' is both inclusive and exclusive. Some of the inclusive rights about which I am speaking are those dealing with the Sacraments. For example, it is a right to enjoy all the privileges that accompany the Sacrament of Holy Matrimony. Those who are unmarried must abstain from certain goals and activities that are given through that Sacrament. Hence, the situational right in this case, in the case of marriage, is that those who are married do in fact engage in these actions. The whole world should be ordered through the Sacraments of the Roman Catholic Church. All human self-deigning and self-actualization must be lived according to these gifts. Those who are protesting against the Holy Father are wrongly appropriating personal, individual rights that do not belong to them, and in some cases do not even exist. I have told you that there is no such phenomenon as a union between two people of the same gender. There is no such thing as same-sex marriage. It is the most contradictory suggestion that the peoples of the world could conjure. When you are delivering speeches and recording videos, you might mention the concept of 'situational rights' as I have described them here today. My Special son, do you understand the concept as I have presented it? *"Yes."* Thank you for being so open to My lessons. The situational rights to which I refer speak precisely to that. They are rights that are granted to individuals and groups according to their station in life and the calling of the Holy Spirit for humanity to comply with the mandates of the Sacred Scriptures. Today, I have also come to speak to you about Eternal Light and created light. You have come to understand that light is descriptive of the Love of God, and darkness is suggestive of the hatred of evil. It is also the contrast in the temporal world between day and night. One can see in the daytime because of this light, but it is functionally impossible to see in the pit of the night. Light and love allow someone to see. Darkness and hatred foster utter blindness. You have known these basic ideas since you were a boy. The point I would like to make today is that all light has a spiritual connotation. It sheds great light on a topic of discussion when true facts are presented in a conversation. This light is obstructed when someone tells a lie. When you consider the collective actions of men, the Church is the source of light, while secularism is the manifestation of darkness. This you have also known for many decades. Let us turn to the origin of this idea. When God spoke in Genesis, why do you suppose He said 'Let there be light' instead of 'Let the darkness disappear?' *"Because light was the object, where the darkness was a phenomenon."* You are partially correct, not in error, but needing additional information. He said that there must be light because He has always been Light. He was saying 'Let Me come here.' He has always been Light, and He has always been the origin of vision.

Once light is introduced, it is obvious that darkness goes away. Light is the reflection of God's Holy Love, which is the origin of this same light in the material world. Please hear Me clearly. Billions of people throughout the centuries have never drawn the connection between the Salvation of creatures yet to be born and the concept of Divine Light placing and instilling created light in time and space. *"By created light, you mean physical light from the sun, or spiritual illumination of what is true?"* Well done. I mean both. I am suggesting to you that the first chapter of Genesis foretold the birth of Jesus Christ, Light into the world. *"I understand."* The whole efficiency of human redemption was placed in the world before the world was ever finished. This is the foretelling of the entrance of the Light of the World coming in the Second Person of the Most Blessed Trinity. Jesus first, the world second. This proves that Jesus lives outside of time, that He has always existed, even before the birth of His Mother who is speaking to you now. *"And you existed before your birth in the same way because God spoke to Isaiah about who you were."* And, what did the Lord say to Isaiah? *"I will give you this sign, a Virgin shall be with Child..."* Hence, you are learning today that Jesus and I are perfectly united in the Eternal Light of God that has always existed. Now, you can also make the dichotomy between earthly sunlight and the spiritual light of Love and Truth living inside the human heart. And, this is good because it leads the human conscience to equate love and light as I have indicated. You know all the stories and parables about light conquering the darkness. I am simply making the case today that Christianity dates all the way back before the full creation of the world. You can make this case simply by telling your friends, your listeners that the verse from Genesis that I cited at the beginning of this message portends the Birth of Jesus Christ. The Father knew all along that His creatures would fall. He knew from the beginning that there would be an Old Covenant and New Covenant. He did not make anything up as the world moved along. This is an important element in the discussion of Judaism and Christianity because billions of people worldwide believe that the God of Abraham has not been consistent, that He has been flighty and uncertain, if He ever existed at all, about how to maintain His fatherly dominion over His Creation. Their argument dies in the description about the concentric nature of Eternal Light and created light that I have given you here this morning. The Light of the World should be as welcome here as the first dawn, the first sunlight was back then. Do you understand? *"Yes."* And, this begs the question, welcomed by whom? In the first days of the world, welcomed by whom? Had Adam and Eve been given life yet? *"No they hadn't."* When were Adam and Eve given life? *"On the sixth day, He created man."* Thus, the Light preexisted man. *"Yes."* And, this is the evidence that the Light of God has always preexisted all human beings. Now, back to My question. The light was welcomed by whom? *"By all that would succeed it."* Yes. By every creature who would need it for life. By all who could see its Creator interiorly and exteriorly. By every creature with reason and even those without it. By anyone who would see only dusk when their greatest dawns were breaking. By men and beasts, birds flocking, predators preying, Churches singing, children weeping, mothers birthing, old men dying, springs rolling and so on.

This is the Light about which I am speaking, one to which all the suns in all the universes must bow. No blast or explosion can supercede the Eternal Light of God. No fireworks can replicate it. It can only be captured by three simple words – I love you. With 'I love you,' the whole world is made fresh again. Newborn cries are heralds of glory singing in yonder skies. With 'I love you,' sons and fathers are reconciled. With 'I love you,' the whole of Creation was formed, given function and spirit, and converted and redeemed. Indeed, it was with 'I love you' that God raised Jesus from the dead and proclaimed to all who were, are and ever shall be that He will never die again. This is the essence of that Genesis verse that I cited when I arrived this morning. My Special son, you have the capacity to reduce whatever you perceive to be stressful conditions and circumstances to things that will not bother you if you will only do it. The intense pressures and emotions that exist around you and the whole secular social community are unfortunate. The Light of the World is also the Prince of Peace. Please remember this always. I am elated by the progress and near completion of your first video. It is heavenly and admirable. *"Thank you Mama."* It is uniquely holy, filled with Light and Love, professionally presented, clearly articulated, artistically produced, and as eternal as the Glory of Heaven. You have embraced beauty, Truth, Providence, sacredness, peace, justice – shall I go on? All of these gifts are present in your video production."

Sunday, November 14, 2010
9:00 a.m.

Roadblocks and Gatekeepers

denotation - direct meaning
connotation - inferred meaning

"Yes, My Special son. Your video is a miracle for the ages. It has taken-on the mysticism that you have seen throughout the years, and it will be noticed and accepted as such. You must remember that Jesus told the world that the Holy Spirit will fill the air with strains of righteousness through the voices of true believers. This is what is occurring. Do you remember what I told you about righteousness given venue? *"Yes."* Well, you have created the venue through My intercession for the spreading of the Holy Gospel. You will be rewarded greatly for this benefit to humanity, toward the advancement of the Church for the conversion of lost sinners. When you say that you do not recognize that it is you speaking in the video, it is because the Lord has inspirited you in every way a person can be inspirited. You are His instrument. For you to live is Christ. The whole manifestation makes sense. It is the fulfillment of what the original Apostles and early disciples believed and preached. It is what Saint Paul recorded. Your hope is well-placed in the dynasty of beatific faith that you have coopted as your reason for life. Today, I wish for you to remember that there are many issues that are inherent to this mission, the most obvious is the Holy Gospel. The Scriptures outlay the clear and stated purpose of the Church and all its many apostolates. Now we have to interrupt our message because you would not wait for the laundry to finish. *(The dryer alarm had sounded from my basement, and our Holy Mother acknowledged it. I departed my prayer room and collected and folded my laundry, and put it away. Then, I returned and continued with my prayers of the Rosary.)* Thank you. Anyway, these apostolates are like satellites communicating with the Mother Church. This makes the Church the denotation, the direct meaning of the faith of men, and the various apostolates like yours the connotation of the Church. They are inferred institutions and children of the Mother Church that reach-out to instruct, heal, admonish, and elevate all that must be touched. You can read these kinds of things in your mission statement. Each apostolate has its chosen mission according to the Will of God through the Holy Spirit. Do you understand the difference between denotation and connotation in this context? *"Yes."* I knew you would! And, this leads us to the primary discussion of today's message. I wish to speak to you about roadblocks and gatekeepers. While these things may be self-evident, you know that they are a constantly changing, ever-flowing framework of good and not so good forces that attempt to shape the way you interact in the world. Do you know about them? What are some of the roadblocks that we might mention? *"The lady whom Tim is dealing with at UIS. She is both a gatekeeper and a roadblock."* Indeed, you are really helping Me. You drew that connection between the two before I ever got to it. I think you will not require the more elementary things I was going to say about this. *"And the Bishop is a gatekeeper whom we are praying to keep from becoming a roadblock."* Yes, you are correct again. What secular forces do you see that are roadblocks alone? The newspaper? *"Yes, because they just cause problems. They don't keep you from doing anything."* Are you sure about the latter? Did they not refuse to publish your last three essays? *"That's right. And Protestant people."* In what way? *"They are a roadblock to those around them moving toward the Eucharist, but they are not a gatekeeper to the Eucharist."* You are correct again. Are there occasions where you or your brother's lives have been negatively affected by Protestants? *"Tim could not get employment at their school."* That is a good example. Would it not be proper to suggest that certain Protestant beliefs run contrary to the teachings of the Catholic Church? Many of them espouse homosexual unions, abortion, and capital punishment. One would not know that they believed in God.

So, you see that there are roadblocks and gatekeepers everywhere. *"People work their whole lives to become gatekeepers on as many different levels as they can."* And what is the reason? Power. *"Because they are afraid of the sacrifice if they do not have power to avoid it."* What sacrifice? *"To become in union with the poor."* That is true, but it is not the key reason. It is that they do not wish to become bridled by the wishes of any superiors. I am not suggesting that they are wrong here, I am only saying that it is the reason they seek more power. This power is more about freedom than being unduly influential. The point in all this is that you should speak about the elements of power in the material world in relation to the mission of the Church. You can include this in your videos. This discussion has far-reaching and deeply emotional implications for people everywhere. Secular power is one of the worst roadblocks to the mission of the Church. Does this not make secularism the 'default' gatekeeper of what is allowed to be heard through the airwaves and in print? *"Yes."* It has been said that the airwaves are public domain. Then, why does it cost so much money to exercise that right? It is the other head of the beast. Profit. Yes, power and profit. These are the symbolic horns of the capitalistic beast. They are the root of many other evils here in the United States. Would many people submit themselves to becoming subordinate to others if they were unpaid? Would they sit in unlit rooms and allow people they do not even know to exact judgements against them? Would men and women perform sexual acts for motion pictures if they were not paid? Would they refuse to do so if they knew that no one would purchase these wares? Where does that market come from? Evil works. This makes power and profit the tools of Satan in America. A multitude of sins grow out of these temptations. This is what your work and My messages have attempted to reverse.

Let us continue the discussion about power and profit. Many people will approach you and say that without profit, large companies would not be in business. Without that business, they would not hire any employees. Without employment, millions would have no wages, no means to purchase food, clothing, and housing. There are American corporations that are sitting on trillions of dollars in wealth because they believe that they will reap insufficient profits if they spend it now, in this particular financial atmosphere. Does this not prove that profit is directly related to self-ingratiation? Self comfort? Penthouse living? *"Yes."* So, profit as a concept is not inherently evil until those who hold wealth demand an unreasonable profit? *"That is true."* And, have you ever met or heard of anyone in the United States that has said that they do not believe they should accumulate any more than a given level of profit? *"No. Corporations become larger and extend their power as far as their profit margins will allow, and then say they are making only 8% on their investment."* The point is that there is no limit to the amount of social or international wealth they are willing to control. Does this not imply that 'profit' is always a source of evil here in this nation? *"Yes."* But, you can see that it need not be this way. The concept of 'profit' can be realigned to be more inclusive. The profits of American wealth and industry can be shared. The wealth can be redistributed to be more fair to those who work hard and follow the rules. The statement I just made is key to the matter. Those who work hard. Those who follow the rules. *"Who determines who works hard and who follows whose rules?"* The Gospel of Jesus Christ. Men and women must give their greatest effort, their best and most honest labor for a fair living wage. This is not always the case in America either. You see here that the concept of profit is also affected by the relationship between the business and its employees.

I believe that you have internalized My discussion here today. Who are the gatekeepers in America? Those with power and wealth. Who has the responsibility to keep fairness and equality alive? Those who are holding-out their wealth until conditions occur whereby they can earn even more profit. It is a two-way street. Those who are dependent upon the public coffers for sustenance must be truly needy. It is uniquely easy to claim that one is incapable of offering a day's labor when he is just being slothful. The guide is the center of the heart, the deeply-held view that what is proper must always be sustained. What is proper is that business owners must be willing to live in the same place their workers live, not in places such as Panther Creek. The whole blame for the deterioration of the American financial system is the greed of those who were already rich. It has been about nothing more than power and profit. The Holy Gospel has been shunned. The wealthy have been blinded by their own assets. This is not the definition of freedom. It is de facto thievery and corporate collusion.

I have concluded My discussion about roadblocks and gatekeepers for today. I will speak about it again in the future. You see that there are so many frameworks and institutions that are interconnected in the secular void. Public institutions and private entities are often commingled and inter-dispersed. They share the same goals with different drives and directions to reach them. They are comprised of people who are only looking out for themselves. There is extremely little societal compassion. Where is mine? What is in it for me? And, millions of souls go to their graves every year believing that this is the proper way to live. We are working to reverse this awful trend. I still believe that we shall succeed. What are your comments and suggestions for today? *"I don't have anything in particular. I like your message."* Thank you. I found all of this information in the Holy Spirit living in your heart. You and your brother shared Holy Mass at Saint Agnes Church last evening. Do you think the priest was rude to you? *"Yes."* This is the state of affairs of many priests in America today. They act like that because they believe that their vocations are soiled by their peers who have fallen to the sins of the flesh. The priesthood itself must be vindicated by the same secular fiends who have soiled it. *"How can we make that happen?"* Do the work that Jesus has given you to do. This is what you are accomplishing every day. Pray for them. Be their advocates to the Hosts of Heaven. Get your rest. Keep positive thoughts. All of these things can reverse the laws of Nature. Most of it occurs in the unseen."

Sunday, November 21, 2010
The Presentation of Mary
8:58 a.m.

When judging a human act – by what virtue has this been done?

The mountain could have refused to be hewn into four stone faces.

"With warm, holy wishes, I come into your presence through the joy of the Lord. I offer you My congratulations on your successes in Jesus' Name, and I bring His Light to keep you apprised of His Will for humanity. My sons, there is much for you to be thankful for this year; not that others have not been this way, but particularly now because you are about to reach into another new year, another new decade of service in your sacred works for the Cross. It is all about the Cross, and it is moreover about the Resurrection. All of your friends and neighbors will benefit from your lives here; all the denizens who are the residents and occupants of the homes across America will know of My miracle here. This is the Feast about which many have spoken, and on which I would like to speak about human action, all of it. Of what origin do the intentions of holy and unholy men come? This is the question. Everything you say and do is based on intention. Even your accidents. Even words spoken hastily or in anger. The human person is comprised of all the emotions that you have seen during your years, all the goodness and gallantry, the human daring that has made such a vast nation as yours, the imagination and innovative lures – everything that can be measured and all things infinite are products of the origin from which they come. We must speak of virtue today because it is this that draws you into the spirit of the holidays. There are cited virtues in the Catechism, and you can review them as you will. I am speaking today about the great umbrella of Virtue from which all other virtues have come. I am telling of the Glory of God who has fashioned the universe, the heavens above, the love in your own hearts, your faith and loyalty, and your drive to succeed in all that the Gospel commands. This is an over-arching desire for righteousness that has lived prior to the establishment of the Earth.

It was the subject of a message just weeks ago, one in which I referred to the essential Being of our Creator, and now grown, blossomed and dispensed in detail in and around you in all spiritual and physical being. Here is the question again. 'By what virtue has this been done?' When anyone offends another person, this is the appropriate inquiry. There is hardly any virtue in offending someone else unless it is to lead them into a holier state. All public laws and decrees must be measured by the question of virtue. Why could not the Lord have entered the room on January 22, 1973 and asked the so-called supreme justices why they condemned so many millions of unborn children to die? Because it was their responsibility to preserve them. They exercised their own human will for evil purposes. The Lord God already knew the answer to His own question. So why come? My Special son, you are watching play out before you the destruction that has ensued from such decisions. Abortion is just one of them. I have seen so many grotesque and unjust actions and motions of men in exile that it has become difficult to count them. They are blind to the Virtue that hovers over and permeates all created things. They are lacking in beatific luster because men's souls are stained with sin. They reject the Holy Man who has cleansed them. Jesus has given His Creation the ability to fight back. He has sent gushers and geysers. He has caused the winds to twist trees into knots, shooting splinters into far-flung timbers. He has flooded the valleys deep, fallen the motives of the hard of heart, brought pain and death to the unsuspecting, and given every reason for mankind from all walks and centuries to turn only to Him. And still, they resist. The Lord God could have asked the mountain to say 'no' to the four faces, demanding that America turn to the Saints instead. He did not do so because He wants the world to understand the power of the human heart. He desires peoples everywhere to remember the concept of freedom and those who taught it. He thought to Himself that if the citizens of the United States could get this right, and etch their heroes of freedom into rocks towering into the sky, then they just might have a chance to connect the dots. They had the potential to acknowledge that human beings everywhere can become as great as the peaks, to be memorialized for their focus on order, and to be remembered fondly in death as they were in life. The mountain about which I speak bears the faces of men gone-by, and this alludes to their fate outside of time. Yes, it fosters human thought about the Church Triumphant, and this is not a bad thing. This is why the mountain did not refuse to be hewn with four faces. You know, My Special son, that I speak more than symbolically about the call for higher vision. I am crafting the imagination of men to think for themselves about human existence outside the flesh. There is grand potential for changing the whole of the nations from there, but this does not imply that it cannot be done from here. When history speaks of heroes and legends, it refers to the many who have made a difference toward the good, so that when someone asks by what virtue their acts have come, the answer is the virtue in their hearts. It is their connection and identification with the God of their fathers, the God with whom they have supped and prayed for the refinishing of their mortal souls.

There is a certain personality type that is best displayed by discreet people, ones who are stoic but not rigid. It is called 'staid.' This is a word that can describe an orderly housekeeper. Prim and proper. Well established. Decorously traditional. It need not imply a negative thing. Those who are staid are poised in the long-held stately manners, like someone's well-treated adviser or servant. This is how many believe that all Christians should be – reserved, conservative, holding their true identities close to their breasts. While such is not a liability to the Church, Jesus is far more human than that. He admires a raw willingness to reveal the heart to the masses. He is the greatest romantic in the world. He is touched when He sees powerful men weep on the world stage about holiness and goodness, about making pious issues the talk of the day. Jesus holds hands with other men. He internalizes their suffering by allowing them to see. This is what is missing in so many people who are reluctant to be like Jesus. One cannot be like Jesus if he does not tell other men that he loves them. One cannot be like Jesus if he does not weep himself. Only those true heroes and legends that I mentioned moments ago understand this. Battlefield warriors, great generals, leaders, visionaries and holy people from all other walks of life understand that emotional conviction is not the same as baseless emotion. The latter is a product of insecurity. So, anyone who would mock a man who would weep in victory is likely an errant person, someone who might do something as mortally sinful as support the abortion of unborn children. *"The question is, from what virtue does your emotion flow?"* Well stated. This is the reason I keep telling you that holy men are not weak. When their hearts train their eyes on the victories of the Cross, they are brought to righteous tears. This is more the ushering of victory than an admission of defeat. Men who do not cry are ashamed of God, and they fear all other men. They doubt their own motivations. They are missing out on the greatest part of life. If they do not tell others in voiced words that they have love, then they are unworthy of the Kingdom of God. It has been My honor to teach you about holy devotion, about dedication and romance, for nearly twenty years. And, you are reflecting it in all you say and do. It is inherent in your speech, in your sentiments shared with others. It has become your defining moment for each new dawn. This is not associated only with you. It is the purpose of being self-aware that permeated the thoughts of every Saint now in Heaven. I do not speak of helpless sentimentalism, but of power-filled romance; the kind that can change the world. It is friendship that extends beyond the ages, showing a unity with Jesus that cannot be found in typical words. This is the way you have always written. It has been the tenor of My messages. It is the content of the sweetest strains of the Gospel."

Sunday, November 28, 2010
9:03 a.m.

Does everything on Earth have a primordial facet?
Does every impulse or action have measurable effects?

Clarity of content is always more important than length or quantity.

"Deep-seated faith runs pervasively through your lives, My little sons, where you can see with eyes both closed and open the meaning of human love. You are seeing well. You have learned well. It is part of your destiny to recognize the status of world affairs and the particulars of personal lives simultaneously. The privacy of one's personal life dictates how one views global affairs. Thank you for praying with Me today on this special opportunity to bring continued change, to foster greater holiness here and around the globe, and to seek Jesus' healing and the Lord's blessings on those who suffer alone. My Special son, I have stated two questions at the opening of this message, and the third issue I have addressed is a simple fact for your records. Quality is also more crucial than quantity in matters of heart-to-heart communication. You have known this for years. Someone can end a war with the words 'I love you.' A whole Creation can be brought to justice by the phrase 'It is finished.' Indeed, it is affirmation and approbation that hearts filled with love seek from the heavens. You find it in your own awareness that you have been inspired with the Wisdom from which justice comes. I know that Jesus has given you a heart filled with the genius of human sanctification, and this is what you have revealed in your writings and recent video. Bishop

Paprocki was overwhelmingly impressed by your presentation last Monday. What could this man have possibly said to you when given such a massive deposit of Marian works? You have handed him more than any other Bishop has received in the history of the world. As you are prone to say, 'think about it.' He realized that you expected him to be poised and reserved, to be stately and mature. This is what Bishops are supposed to do. He will do as you asked. He will read your deposit of works. He will call for additional advice. He will apply the criteria generally accepted for discerning private revelations. Your Bishop was humbled by being given these volumes. It could have been any other man, he thought. A long line of Bishops worldwide could have been sitting there with you, all the great Catholic Prelates who have graced the landscape of human endeavors. But, it was him. There is reason for pause in this, he sees. And, to look at the preparation that you and your brother have made. You recorded My messages. You offered your own diarist reflections. You have presented your manuscripts as professionals. Your digital website is stunning. Your credentials are impeccable. And, all for what? You even created a nonprofit organization to prove that you are not seeking monetary gain. Your Bishop sees that you have everything in place, from top to bottom. What he saw most predominantly is that the president of the organization had the managerial humility to remain behind. Your brother put your best face on My messages and your corporation by sending you as the perfect envoy. You were humble and simple, cautious and wise. You did not offer knee-jerk answers or flighty retorts. Again, as you have said, 'think about it.'

    The Chancery is a difficult place for Bishops to go. They hear about all the discrepancies, the disturbances and heresies. They are up to their eyes in fund-raising. They worry about their priests. Are they upholding their vows and protecting the image of the Church? Are they administering the Sacraments according to their pledge? And, once in awhile, a miracle comes by. This is what you brought Bishop Paprocki upon entering his door. He saw the November 22 date on the back of your book. He has accepted with grace your admonitions in the video you handed him. He realizes the gift of My messages to the Church. I only ask that you put yourself in his place. Could any man honestly declare that he will have time to read and review everything you gave him before the expiration of a year? "*No.*" He now gets the great joy of reading what I have said and you have written. He will someday wish he had rephrased his question to be '...on what date do you want my approval?' This will not be easy for him because of the sheer nature of the Church. There will be opposition by the devil's advocates. He will be urged to remove his emotions from the process. Others will remind him that many romantic writers have been able to 'channel' certain spirits. However, no one will find any corruption in My words. There is no new dogma, no particular dates certain, nothing that will lead them anywhere but to the Cross. This has been My intention all along. I can best convert My children by setting afire the Hierarchy of the Church. While this has never really taken hold, nobody has seen any works such as the Morning Star Over America. I will not affirmatively state that your Bishop will offer a public affirmation of My messages. This is what your lives into the future will reveal. Work together for human reconciliation. Feed the poor. Pray for the conversion of the wicked. Attend the Holy Mass as often as you are. Give your heart to God in every way that He has mandated through the teachings of His Son. Then, the grand things will come. Remember that it is a process, a day at a time, a moment at a time.

    I call you to ponder the concept of the primordial facets of the thoughts and actions of exiled men. Think about the two questions I have given you when I came this morning. Does everything on Earth have a primordial facet? The answer is in the definition of 'everything' compared to nothing. Everything consists of the eternal things, of the relevant impulses and actions that bring about the common good, that address the issues and matters important to the mission of the Church. All that is of God is part of this 'everything.' All that serves no beatific purpose is nothing. While I do not mean to be parsing words, I am saying that whatever is good and just, whatever is beautiful, whatever manifests the conversion of unconverted men finds its primordial origin in the Love of God. Anything that stands in contradiction to these things cannot exist beyond the end of time, and they therefore are lifeless now. Whatever is not in alignment with the Truth is a lie, and lies have no life. There is nothing primordial about fallacious things because they are not based in the eternal. You already know the litany of matters that can be classified as lies. *"It is as though fallacious things are aberrations or phantasms."* Yes, but there can be good aberrations too. It is according to how the term is defined. The point I am making is that whatever does not reflect the Truth has no primordial origin. Anything anyone says or does that provides the evocative sharing of Divine Love is founded in God – it is as timeless as Him. Thus, the answer to the first question is that not everything on Earth has primordial facets. The second question deals with human thought and action. Does every impulse, every act have effects and consequences? The answer is again negative because not every impulse is acted upon, and not every act is shared. The concept of interaction has effects and consequences, even if barely measurable. This is why it is important that the Gospel be spread to all peoples, to all nations. It would not suffice for someone to read the Scriptures and then fail to act upon them. Remember that the book does not say the 'Thoughts of the Apostles.' It says the Acts of the Apostles. This implies communication, thoughtful discourse and accord, sacrifice of the self to the advancement of the poor, consoling and defending, and the like. Each of these things speaks to the offering of the person on behalf of the whole. This is the basic element of the life of Jesus. Back to the question. Does every impulse or action have measurable effects? This question is answered repeatedly in the New Covenant parables. And, what is one of the first things I told you about the greatest waste? *"A prayer left unsaid."* This is true because the Lord declines to respond when He is not invoked to do so. One cannot retrieve water from a well unless a pail is lowered or a pump is primed. If somebody wants a drink without doing these things, does his parched state have a measurable effect in quenching his thirst? *"His parched state does not quench his thirst."* Correct. His impulse tells him to find a drink. There is no effect because he declines the action that will satisfy his need. There are impulses all around the globe that never lead to action, but sometimes this is good if those impulses will lead to harm or malevolence. Here again, it is according to the human will of exiled men. *"It depends on by what virtue do the impulses originate."* You are exactly correct again. You have repeated My question from a previous message; you have shown that you can apply the concepts of My messages well, and you have learned that inaction can oftentimes be as harmful as action itself. A governor who declines to stay an execution of a convict on death row is one such example. Whenever you think about the actions of mortal men, measure them according to the product of goodness, whether they are founded in the Primordial Truth to which all human thoughts and actions must be compared. Remember the idea of 'something' compared to 'nothing.' The answer to these questions is what leads to the third concept that I gave you this morning. Clarity is always more valuable than length or quantity. In the case of Morning Star Over America and all its relevant works, you have given the world both. There is nothing superfluous about My messages. Before I close, I wish to commend you again for your profoundly wonderful presentation to your Bishop on Monday. You were worthy of the grace by which you live."

Sunday, December 5, 2010
9:06 a.m.

"Finally brothers, whatever is true, whatever is honorable, whatever is just, whatever is pure, whatever is lovely, whatever is gracious – if there is any excellence, and if there is anything worthy of praise, think about these things. Keep on doing what you have learned and received and heard and seen in me. Then the God of peace will be with you." (Philippians 4:8-9)

The Ultimate Paradox
Solving one problem creates another

"Now, My dear sons, I have the honor and privilege of praying with you for all the intentions that we have discussed. You must always remember that it is for the consolation of My Most Immaculate Heart that I speak to you, for My comfort is knowing that the Earth is changing because of your love. We have within our grasp the conversion of all the souls I came to touch, all the hearts Jesus desires to open, all the lives in need of amendment. I chuckled as well when I saw the 106-year-old man who recently decided to quit smoking. *"It will probably kill him!"* Unfortunately, there are many others like him. They wait until their libido completely dies and then call on others to see how chaste are their lives! They should have given themselves to the purity of the Holy Spirit long before. Anyway, My appearance here today is a gift to Me, and yours as well, for the cultivation of everything known to human existence, all that will take the world closer to the Sacred Heart of God. I have spoken about the paradox of solving a problem just to create another one. The side effects of medication are one such example. Making peace between warring enemies is always good and righteous, but then what is done with the remaining spoils? Who presides over the distribution of the profits? My Special son, can you think of any other such paradoxes today? *"Two people being married."* This solves what problem? *"Of them wanting to be together at all times."* Indeed, and we know the whole host of other problems created by the satisfaction of this desire for companionship and intimacy. The point I am making is that these are worldly examples, ones that indicate the problem of stirring a whole environment when only its sub-parts are changed. What happens when termites are exterminated? Old dead wood and trees do not decay as quickly. On and on the examples go. However, what new problems are created when the Holy Spirit converts another soul? *"They become a thorn in the side of the worldly."* Yes, precisely, but this is not a problem. This is My point. There are no new problems arising when sinners take to the road of sainthood. Reaching for the Eternal solves a problem with no adverse side effects. This is why I have cited the reading from Philippians today. Whenever the human heart engages the good and honorable, the true and beautiful, the holy and sacred, there are no new problems created. Whatever is lovely, gracious and excellent when sought by those who know their origin becomes the food for the heart the way the Holy Eucharist is food for the soul. You must remember that all things holy are acquired from the power of the Holy of Holies. This is the unity of the Holy Spirit in which the Father and the Son reside. They live and reign in this unity, and Christians are with them in that power, not as gods, but godlike in love and righteousness. We have discussed on many occasions the awesome prospect of evil people being converted from the lies of their own actions to the Truth of the Holy Gospel. These are the souls that have the farthest to travel. This is why Jesus came to convert them, not the righteous. You know that this is a statement that begs the understanding of the person. Of course Jesus came to redeem all human beings. But, to reach deeply into the framework of the human heart, the Lord must be prying and excavating. He must awaken them through the clamoring of human suffering, of the diminishment of the flesh, of the radical reorientation of their awareness of life and the future through some inordinately striking thoughts and actions. The Scriptures are filled with these things. Go out and kill your son Isaac? Who in the world would believe that God would ask that? Cut birds and animals completely in half and lay them out on the ground? These are the precursors to a logical approach to opening the heart to anything the Lord seeks of His disciples. Who was speaking in the reading I presented earlier? *"Saint Paul."* And, there are two words in his letter that are more striking than anything else he says. What do you suppose they are? *"In me."* Yes, in me. Why do you believe these two words to be the most crucial? *"Because it is his witness of his oneness with God."* Altogether true. It proves the possibility that the whole Kingdom of Heaven can live in a single human being. Everything that is excellent, and all the other things, can live inside the heart of man. And, this implies the communication of everything righteous from one person to another. Everything that is learned, heard and seen in Saint Paul. Imagine that. The entire atmosphere of human redemption, the whole verse of human exculpation, the infinity of God's forgiveness was present in one man, Saint Paul. And, where did he get it? *"From Jesus"* Indeed, through his acceptance and propagation of 'I AM' to the masses. This is what the New Covenant has been trying to convince lost sinners to accept for 2,000 years. For all the clouded parables and clustered conclusions inherent in the Bible, it comes down to this one point. *"It is no longer I who live, but Christ in me."* Yes. And, looking back at My earlier point about creating and solving problems, do you now see that there is no problem in Christian conversion because the one being converted is gone? The will of the Christian convert has been absorbed into the High Kingdom in the way that death is swallowed up in the victory of the Cross and Resurrection. *"Yes. I understand."*

The only thing that remains which appears to be a problem is the issue of death. This seems to be a problem for many. We know that it is the extension of a life already begun in the hereafter. Jesus asks His followers to see death as the ultimate gift to those who believe in Him because it delivers them through the veil into His presence. There is life to live and much more to be done on His behalf by those who welcome His Commandments. This is why everyone who is still alive as we speak woke up still in exile this morning. It is the reason people speak to one another about more benevolent things, about issues that are relevant to the Church and the refinement of the soul. This is why there is forgiveness for the penitent and grace for the absolving. I wish you good fortune in meeting countless other souls who accept this as their mission in life. Back to the Saint Paul reading again. True, honorable, just and lovely. You do not see many of these things where you live. There are hardly any of them anywhere else in the world. But, Paul asks the Church to think about these things. He does so because, as I said last week, thinking leads to doing. Intentions and impulses lead to physical action. Washing leads to cleansing. Conversion implies the elimination of evil. The whole matter is a process that begins, as Saint Paul said, 'In me.' I have brought this point to your attention today because I ask you to remember that you are also filled with this righteousness. This will lead you to greater peace in your days, to seeing with clearer perception what should matter, what you should dwell upon as important. It teaches you to prioritize what you encounter through the days and weeks so that you will not feel the need to address every problem. You said in your introductory video that not every disagreement needs to be reconciled. No truer words have ever been spoken. Jesus will give you better peace if you allow Him to respond in you, permit His thinking to be the basis for your reactions. I am not just speaking about you here. I am referring to all men of good will everywhere. I am simply using you as an example. *"I understand."* This is the main point that I wished to address today, and I believe you understand it well."

Sunday, December 12, 2010
9:07 a.m.

fatalism - the doctrine that all events are predetermined or subject to fate

idealism - the cherishing or pursuit of high or noble principles, goals, etc.

exceptionalism - the theory that a nation, region or political system is an exception and not subject to the norm

triumphalism - excessive celebration of the defeat of one's enemies

resurrectionism - the doctrine, belief or theology espousing rising from the dead, the posthumous resurrection of life

"My beloved sons, My sacred love for you transcends and permeates this world, this room, and your souls through which we are communicating our prayers, intentions and desires for the Salvation of men. We have come to this day by no accident. It is the Will of God that we should speak here about training the eyes and souls of lost sinners on the Holy Cross. We have spoken about feelings and institutions before, about the myriad of beliefs that mortal men espouse. Nothing we have addressed is more crucial to the conversion of the world than our simple meditations about love. You have known this long before I came speaking to you, even before your pilgrimages to the hills of Medjugorje. Yes, at your baptism, you were given love as your own, as your sacred peace and reason for life. My Special son, you and your brother have made untold numbers of commitments to Me throughout the years because I have required much from you. There has never been a moment when you let Me down. There have been uncertainties and accidental mistakes because of your humanness. But, it is no accident that you have come to know Jesus better by way of your love for Me, of your devotion and consecration to My Immaculate Heart. If humanity would come to Me en masse, there would be no other so-called religions on the Earth, save Christianity. Today, I have listed some '-ism' concepts that represent what other people do and believe. You obviously know that the Resurrection of Jesus beyond His Crucifixion is My purpose here. I have listed each '-ism' so you can ponder them and perhaps place a discussion about them in your writings and videos. Some of them are not mutually exclusive of Christianity. Certainly idealism and triumphalism could be used to describe various measures of your faith. Other beliefs and institutions are of no import; they are part of that long walk into the dark night that your brother mentioned yesterday. We have the asset here of speaking from the purview of absolute Truth because I am the Mother of Truth, and you are Truth's incarnation in your imitation of My Son. You must reveal to America that the ages have been bewildering to them because they have been blinded by their own sins. Their only successes have come because of their patriots' blood and the common good of heart and spirit of those who sent them onto the battlefield. This is what great leaders do; they see the victory before the war ever begins. Indeed, who would build a tower without knowing the cost in advance? Jesus knew that He would die on the Cross. It was the price He was prepared to pay. It was the infinite height of the measure of His Love and the depth of His willingness to save you. It is clear that no man has since known what it was like for Jesus, unless that man walked perfectly every step in life. Many have suffered like Him. Countless numbers have emulated His compassion. But, none other has been perfect; no other would know the Father who was in Him until they shall come to the fullness of life.

    I have said that we speak volumes about the charities and harmonies of human life here on Earth. There is no doubt that the Lord is appreciative of these things. He accepts everything that is given to Him and those who believe in Him with kind adulation. He archives them in the Book of Goodness and moves on. He does not dwell on them when there is so much to pray for elsewhere. You have been told that Jesus did not come to Earth to convert the righteous, but to rebuke and cleanse the wretched. This is the mission of the Church. It is the focus of all the apostolates around the globe that have taken-up their crosses and the goal of healing the sick and feeding the poor. Jesus is alive in and through them. We have the popular task of sharing our blessings with them while they work, while you and your brother work. Your years of dedication to the Cross, to the Church, and to humanity and Me have been like artistry to God. You have consoled Him while He has looked upon His Creation with appalling pity. How many more insults and desecrations must He see before the wicked will change? What keeps Christ Jesus from incinerating everything that mocks the Church of Rome? You have said it before; it is His Mercy and patience. It is His desire that all men come to Him of their own volition. It is that He has allotted time for them to change their stony hearts into soft, open ones through the facility of My Maternal intercession. This is the reason I have been speaking to you for so long. It is why My messages here have been so urgent and filled with life-giving images. The urgency of which I speak is not necessarily about quickness in terms of accomplishing something in linear time, but urgent in the sense of their content. Millions of souls would have benefitted from your messages long before they were ever given. And, thanks to the handiwork of Eternity, they will still be able to see them. Many souls in Purgatory who never read the Bible are reading it now, memorizing it like you saw in a motion picture several weeks ago. Others who scoffed at the measure of My participation in the redemption of humanity are reading the whole twelve-book deposit of works that you handed your Bishop on November 22, 2010. Which do you suppose is surprising them most? I also must tell you how it feels for Me to know that a soul is going to be relegated to Purgatory upon their death. I have mixed emotions about it because I know that they will not immediately join Me in Heaven, but that they will, pending their time of purgation. Thus, there is hope and even more hope when someone dies and does not condemn themself to Hell. You are told that there is no more need for faith in Heaven, and this is absolutely true. You also know that there is no more need for hope in Heaven, and this is indeed a fact. However, we will have the option to hope because mortal men are still making decisions on the Earth below. We pray and then hope that they will decide for God, that they will open their hearts and receive Him like little children at their First Communion. We have the fortune in Heaven of seeing disciples like you and your brother on Earth who also hope in this same way, knowing that you have the venue through your participation in the Church to effect the changes, to bring the lost to the Sacraments and unite them with God. You help Jesus find them because the Holy Spirit in your heart is their compass to Him. There has never been any doubt that you will convey all of these sentiments to your brothers and sisters someday. I have spoken throughout the ages and hailed the heroism that has brought such dignity into this world. I have spoken of courage and might, of compassion and sharing, of commitment and enlightenment. My Special son, I was talking about you all along. We have great benefits to bestow upon those remaining in your midst and far-flung around the world. If you pray that it be done, Jesus and the Father will hear you. They have seen impudent sinners inside and outside the Church trample on My messages before. We must not allow that to happen this time. There is too much at stake in the age of such terror, rampant with faithlessness, lust, debauchery and outright disbelief. I have asked Saint Juan Diego to intercede for you and your brother today, and also the assistance of all the Saints."

Sunday, December 19, 2010
9:13 a.m.

Where heroes walk, societies will migrate.
When holiness is preserved, peace will prevail.
When love enters the heart, life begins anew.
When sinners convert, death breathes its last.

William L. Roth

The Complex Meaning of the Spiritual, Cognitive and Physical Worlds

Genesis [creating] versus Synthesis [combining]

"Here now, My children, we have assembled at the opening of Christmas week to pray for humanity, to envision ways to make it like it ought to be, and to ask the Lord God for the venues to accomplish it. I admire and exalt you, My little sons. This is not an easy task, all we have taken on. It is for this reason that it is efficacious, that it will bring the lost and blind to the altars of the Church. I have spoken to you intelligently about a world that is ignorant of its future. Today, I would like to share your lives more deeply by pondering the beginning of all created things in the mind and heart of God. First, however, I wish to thank you, My Special one, for writing the sweet little poem that you presented at the opening of My message today. 'Where heroes walk, societies will migrate.' Imagine that. You came upon this writing because of your openness to the Holy Spirit. Because of the duties of your office, you did not have time to write it down, so the Angels did it for you. This is the way it has been sometimes; and others, you have forged into print the sabers of love that will defend the Church and drive out demons. These are your prefaces and prologues. Your heart is found in them. I offer you My blessings and gratitude for standing firm in the battle to preserve the reputation of the Church. I wish for you to imagine the concepts of the spiritual, cognitive and physical worlds. I use the term 'world' as a plural here, even though all three are prevalent on the Earth where you live. You know that everything is based on the spirit. Love and Truth are from the Holy Spirit. Evil and hatred are from evil spirits. Human beings fashion their lives and build their physical surroundings based upon their cognitive condition. This leads to the second subtitle that I have posed beginning today's message. Genesis is the creating or making of something, and synthesis is the making of something by combining two or more elements, concepts or substances. Everything you see here in this room with your physical eyes was manufactured by combining two or more substances. Can you find an exception? *"Like natural wood (and also sunlight)."* There, you have opened the doorway for Me to connect the spiritual and physical worlds. This is rather elementary in that you know that God created the trees from which the woodwork was made, but it was man who shaped it into the articles you see. Man took in hand the natural growth of God's Creation and made something that protects you from the elements. This indicates a process, a sequence that has resulted in the world you see. This sequence is all founded in the beginning when the Lord 'created something out of nothing.' I wish for you to remember the contrast between Genesis and Synthesis this way. God is capable of Genesis. Is man? *"No."* Man is incapable of Genesis if one defines Genesis as making something out of nothing. It is obviously available to men to define the origin of many things here on Earth as their genesis, but they do not find their beginning in the ethereal Genesis. Do you suppose that the Catholic Church was founded by Genesis or Synthesis? *"Genesis. And, Synthesis too because God provided the Holy Spirit which inspirited the members that were synthesized by Christ into its body."* Yes, but what you have said is only part. The other part is the will of man. It is the faith of man. God created the Church through the Holy Spirit about whom you speak, but His Spirit needed someone to open the door and let Him in, not just Me. The faith of men. Hence, you see that Genesis and Synthesis cannot be separated when describing the origin of the Church because it required the intercession, the intervention of God and the consensual will, the faith of exiled humanity. *"It is the same with husband and wife conceiving a child. Both provide pieces of the Synthesis, and God provides the Genesis of the soul."* Were you aware that you already knew this? *"No, I have never thought about it before."* I already know the answer to My next question, but I am going to ask it anyway. How did you respond to My presentation of this concept with such quick intelligence? *"I synthesized the Genesis that you offered."* Yes, and with what elements did you do so? *"One of the Sacraments. I looked for the difference between what man assembles and what God provides, and applied it to the Sacrament of Matrimony."* Yes, and now I am speaking in general terms. Think of all the Sacraments collectively and the prospect of Genesis and Synthesis. Why did you have such quick intelligence in using the example of the Sacrament of Marriage? *"I simply looked for a place where God gives life."* Correct answer. Eternal Life is given through the Roman Catholic Church through the marriage of the Divine Spirit and the exiled human soul. The Blood of Jesus impacting the human soul resurrects life; it restores and reinvigorates life. It purifies, cleanses and saints life. *"It is like giving life to deadwood where trees begin to walk and talk."* Yes, and what would these dead trees in the woodwork of this home have to say if given new life? *"They would cry-out as would the stones that Jesus spoke about in the Gospel."* What did they say? *"I do not remember for sure."* It is sufficient to assume that the wood in these walls and doorframes would come alive and go out into the world and declare, 'My God! You would not believe what we just heard in the last 20 years in that home!' This is how the Holy Cross speaks of the Salvation of man. It is the reason the Cross is venerated during the Good Friday prayers. It speaks of the redemption of the exiled human soul.

You must remember that the Genesis that you have learned in the Church is from of old, predating Moses and Abraham. It is the intent of God's Divine Love in created form. We spoke about this in recent weeks. It came to man that he was capable of perception and judgement – of keen perception and sound judgement. However, it also came to man that he could utilize skewed perception and flawed judgement for nefarious purposes, lust and financial gain. It is to the latter that we must force all the power of Heaven to subdue, annihilate and destroy. Recall the Synthesis again. The Will of God is prepared for the prayers of the Church and believers everywhere. It is this Synthesis that will restore the pristine nature of all created things the way the Father wanted them to be. The Holy Spirit gives the human heart the proper words to pray. Thus, the Holy Spirit and the human heart must meet in the perfection of God. This is where His Kingdom is found. Genesis meets Synthesis at the line where the faith of men is perfectly joined to the Will of God. You therefore understand that the spiritual realm affects the thoughts of men, the cognitive conscience of those who believe; and this translates into tangible, temporal, physical manifestations of goodness on the Earth where you live. This is the conclusion of My thoughts about it. It is not difficult to internalize; none of My message are. I continue to give you suggestions about how to present the unity between Heaven and Earth in and through all venues capable of the human mind. I have used the word 'complex' to open this message because it is not simple for those who do not believe in the existence and presence of God. There is another dichotomy we will discuss on another day. Some people believe in the existence of God, but they do not believe in His presence. Do you understand the difference? In other words, there are people and groups who do not believe in the Most Blessed Trinity. They believe in God, but do not believe that Jesus was the Father in the Incarnate Son. Others do not believe that God can inhabit the hearts and consciences of sinful creatures as the Holy Spirit. And, billions do not believe that God can be present in a communion host. This goes on and on, you know. We have the Truth at hand and in our midst, in our hearts and with all men of good will. This is one of the true meanings of Christmas.

There are many forces, as you know, that work against good men doing great things. Remember the rule! Live one day at a time. *"I am happy that the Bishop wrote the article about your appearances in Wisconsin."* Yes, it proves that he is open to all the prospects that the Holy Spirit has implanted in him about My intercessory works. Please pray for all the poor souls in Purgatory, and remember the blessings of Christmas for all who are suffering there. I ask you again to be careful driving where you go, and be wise in protecting your safety in all neighborhoods. I hope that you will remember to pray for all unborn children too!"

Sunday, December 26, 2010
St. Stephen the Protomartyr
8:57 a.m.

> *"The Virgin Mary would have us believe that there is a pontiff in every man, perhaps a Pope Anthony Magnificat or a prelate or doctor, a teacher or writer, a philosopher or poet. What we make of what She sees matters most to God, not whether we cede our potential to our weaknesses or fail to recognize the grace in our own humanity."*
>
> William L. Roth

"My little sons, two years ago on this Sunday, I completed My messages to humanity, and I have in fact increased My private messages to you manifold. I told you two Decembers ago that I would speak more about the composition of the structure and spirit of the Church, and the Spirit who gives the Church life. You can see that I have kept My word, and I have done so because you are so precious to God. You have been both prayerful and obedient to Me, and your goal is to remain loyal to the Cross, even though times have been difficult. You know that I would never downplay the extent of your suffering, but I urge you to look around at those who live in poverty and neglect. Consider those whose family members are terminally ill at such young ages, and those who have lost their loved ones in war and acts of their own doing. There are certain degrees of suffering, and yours has not been the kind that others have endured. You are more tired than tormented. You are more disgusted with American secularism than abused by it. My Special one, I pray that you do not think that I am dismissing your suffering. It is never appropriate to consider one's suffering in the context of another person's if there is no faith, but there is faith here. You are aware of the levels of grief, sorrow and neglect that are occurring around the globe. I am only asking that you place yours in this perspective. I need you and your brother to recast your perspective of what you are doing or you will not have the inner-spirit to proceed. You will lack the willpower to hear Me into future years if you do not see My messages for what they are. They bring you strength and vision because they are gifts of the Holy Spirit. We have spoken before about your role in the Church, that of you and your brother; and we have addressed in detail the fuller mission of the whole Church. It is affected by the faith of its members. And, it is effected by the faith of its members. We must be sure to let your brothers and sisters know that they are loved at the same time we are warning them about the error of their ways. What you have said at the beginning of this message is true. Inside every person there is the power and majesty of hope and love, prepared to be launched into the rest of the world. The Church is like the gantry scaffold next to a rocket. They are taught and tendered; they are shaped and filled, and they are made upright and given direction by everything the Roman Catholic Church teaches, by the Sacraments and in the grace about which you speak. You and your brother are aware that the world about you has changed in the past twenty years since I first came calling on you. It has been given more power and enlightenment because of everything I have said. It is clear that you have remained steadfast in your devotion to Me. I will always love you. Nothing will ever take that away. My mission is to somehow let everyone else on Earth know that I love them too, that I am their Mother, the Mother of the Church. I am the Mother of the lost and wandering. Yes, I provide the answers to the questions of the wondering too. You have seen that My Queenship is universal to all peoples and nations. I implore My children to invoke and employ the power of the Holy Spirit. I pray for all lost sinners. And I teach. This is what I have done more with you and your brother over the last two years than any of the prior eighteen. You are extremely good listeners! You have heard what I have said about the changing of the world, what seems faddish and trendy, what comes of age and what passes into history. More and more human interaction has turned away from interpersonal, interfacial speech to electronic modes of conveying thoughts, feelings and information. Do you remember that I once spoke to you about the cost-per-inch of shelf space in department stores? We spoke about them as being dollars-per-inch, but now they are becoming obsolete. Instead of physical space determining the presentation of goods and commodities, it is the electronic storefront that you use most often. And, you never have to leave the house. This is progress. I am speaking in terms of something that has not had a negative impact on the American societal morals as I am speaking about increasing isolationism. There is no sin in this, but it grows the need for neighbors and friends to meet in the Church and other such venues. Even the phenomenon of email communication is not sinful, but it reduces the amount of personal time that can be spent with others. Things like this are progress, and the Lord is not against them. However, there must be more venues created for mutual interaction and communion in the spirit of shared humanity.

Please do not take this too critically. I am only making an anecdotal point. Young people used to go to prayer groups and Catechism to meet their peers, but now they just use their fingers on telephone key pads and transmitted pictures. I am not saying that this is wrong, I am only making an observation. It is that there must be something done to increase mutual physical presence to accompany these new ways to communicate. Lives have been saved by these new devices. Parents and children have kept in contact. People have found directions to churches and confessionals. It is a unique mix of technology and willpower that has generated a whole new framework of social and personal interaction. As the Mother of God, I am only saying that these things should be used to advance the message of the Church and its mission.

I will be speaking to you and your brother into the new year 2011. This is what God said shall be done. He loves you in ways that men have not begun to comprehend. He gives you peace in Jesus, and the genius of Creation that only holy men can know. He is the center of all the universes combined, and yet He cannot be restrained or constrained by any physical space. His designs are replete with new beginnings. His Truth is overwhelming to the soul. You have known all these great attributes in others you have met, great men and women who have espoused His teachings and advanced His Kingdom. It is in your heart that you have loved them and the God in whom they have believed. This is My intention as well. You and your brother have been touched by the lives of living giants, of pious servants who have fed the hungry and ended the poverty of millions. It is for them that I have given so many graces to the undeserving, because the ones who have been steadfast in faith have asked Me to. We have spoken over the past two years about the very essence of Divine Love. We have spread the mission of the Church like a tapestry on a tabletop. And, we will continue to do so in the future. I ask only that you rest and take life one day at a time. This is the seeming paradox about being a Christian. You keep your eyes trained on the Glory of Heaven by living one day at a time. Yes, even a moment at a time. We have much more to do here. We must ensure that you are restful and peaceful, or we will not be able to do more than anyone else who might have accidently fallen-upon a treasure in the sand with no idea of its worth. Let us pray for humanity, and let us serve them as Mother and friend. Let us be Jesus for them. Are you absolutely sure of the depth, height and immeasurable volume of My love for you? *"Yes, and I love you too."* I thank Jesus for giving you to Me!"

The Final Colossus
In Battle Array
AD 2011

Saturday, January 1, 2011
Solemnity of Mary, Mother of God
9:39 a.m.

Discerning the Message of Creation

"You are beautiful children of the Lord, adorable sons of the Father and brothers of Jesus Christ. You have been through great suffering and tremendous sacrifices to see that My messages have been given to your brothers and sisters on Earth. My children, it is true that the arrival of new years is irrelevant in the grander scope of eternity, but it marks another segment of mortal time during which you have fought faithfully for the Cross, for the mission of Christianity, for the conversion of lost sinners. The five simple words with which I began this message are what must be accomplished by everyone who wishes to know God. Discerning the message of Creation. What does this mean? It is certain that you already know. It is obvious that you have learned that Creation leads back to its Creator. We spoke often in 2010 about the constitution of the Church in its livelihood through the Holy Spirit and all its members. We have for nearly twenty years agreed that the success of the Church depends on human prayers, on the prayers and intercessions of the Saints, and everything I can rightfully do as Mother of the Church to enhance your standing with God. My little ones, nothing will change the fact that the Church must comprehend its place inside and outside of Creation. You know that dying to the flesh and entering the spiritual realms does not end your membership in the Church, it takes you to its Triumphant heart. What I have been attempting to accomplish throughout the centuries with My messages and apparitions is to support the miraculous nature of Catholicism, to ensure that all peoples in every nation understand that the Church is a supernatural institution composed of natural creatures. In its fittest form, the Catholic Church is representative of humanity at its best. This is why the true test of your religious faith is to accept your place inside the Grace of God that is made manifest there. Yes, this Feast is dedicated to Me, to the intentions of My Immaculate Heart, and to Jesus, the Fruit of My Womb. My Son asks all the holy to open their hearts and lives to the tremendous opportunities that He is giving this modern world to come closer to Him. My Special son, you and your brother have taken advantage of these gifts. You have confirmed your love for the Most Blessed Trinity by remaining here together, praying and working for the good of all you know to be Truth. You have seen the months and years come and go, and this is why today I ask both of you to remember that life is a daily process. Do not lose sight of the simple moments that compose larger segments of life. Even though you have your eyes set on the awesome prize of Redemption, remember to absorb the moments of life as repeating gifts of joy. This is how you can pray and do the Lord's work. Remember that those who claim to be high and mighty around you, all who appropriate for themselves some station that appears to be elevated and glorified, are only fooling themselves. When they fall, they will land on the foundation of faith that has kept you stable and confident your whole lives. You have seen that they are not so elevated after all; they are only vaunted. And, their impact will not fracture their consciousness so much that they will be unable to comprehend what we have been trying to tell them. They are already lower to the ground than they know. A man cannot fall very far from a basement window. It is in the shadow of these thoughts that you must be happy for their future, knowing that they will someday espouse everything that Jesus has ever taught and exemplified.

My Special son, this is why I do not regard the arrival of this new year as anything other than the passing of another annum. You have seen that My mission is greater than all the sums of years and decades. What matters, as I have said, are the moments. Live with love, and be patient with those who do not understand. Your brother has chosen as his new year's resolution to try not to be so combative. This is a worthy goal, but it must be done without compromising one's principles. I remember how Father Chester Fabisiak plotted this same resolution, and he was tremendously successful. He charmed more people into the Church with his kindness, civility, charity and wit than any shepherd could collect untold numbers of sheep. This became his nature after a lifetime of more aggressive interaction. Let it not be mistaken. There are a great deal of other influences in creating the way someone speaks and preaches. The emulation of other strong personalities plays a role, as does simple genetic inheritance. While these things are important, they cannot outweigh the power of the Holy Spirit to bring peace and confidence to any soul seeking to speak the strains of Divine Love. As I told you recently, I will offer you My prayers and intercession your whole life through. I intend to do this for the entirety of humanity. I hope that you and your brother see the world for what it is, that it can be a holy and greatly consoling environment if you do not get caught-up in its secular battles. You have a huge gift at your hands for the wretched souls on this globe! I have known it all along. You are clearly aware of the gifts that Jesus has given you for many years. Let it not be said that the Mother of God was not willing to try to persuade Her lost children to come to the Cross, to enter the Church and become united with Jesus, and to accept their Salvation. Indeed, you and your brother handed to your Bishop your Marian works in 2010. No one in the Church has ever in history seen anything like the deposit of works you have completed. We shall see what the months bring toward the further absorption of My messages by all to whom they have been given. I would tell them the same thing as I have told you today. Live one day at a time, one moment at a time. Keep your perspective, but do not place your mind too far into the distant future. Remember the progression of faith that grows inside the heart. Discern the message of Creation. This is My advice for today."

Saturday, January 8, 2011
1:04 p.m.

"Perhaps one of the most remarkable things the Blessed Mother ever said to me was after I had been to confession and reminded Her that I was deeply sorry for my sins. Our Lady responded that She had no idea what sins I was talking about. The Sacrament of Penance had wiped them out, rewriting the record of my past."

William L. Roth

"My dear sons, you are yet unaware of My admiration for you. Even in all I have said through the years about your adorable spiritual nature, the integrity of your faith and the obedience you have lent Me, you have not grasped the comprehensive adoration I have for your dedication to God. This is what I wish to proclaim to all My children, but I cannot yet tell them. They are much too straying, too brash and ignorant, too offensive and arrogant. They care not about the Kingdom of God that has come into this world. Please help Me pray for them as you pray for yourselves. I realize the difficulties of mortal life. I am aware of the tensions in your exile. You have seen My messages around the globe intensify about the failures of humanity. I have issued strong condemnations of secularism. Yet, we have remained united in the Love of the Blessed Trinity because we know that this is the essence of God. I have borne this essence into the physical world from My

Womb. I ask you as this year unfolds to proceed with patient assurance, and know that the Lord sustains you. His ways often seem too mysterious for most men to gather, but it is the self-will of those same men that often runs contrary to the Will of God. Today, I ask you to pray for those who are entering the Church around the globe. Pray that their faith will never waver. My sons, you are destined for the grand Salvation to which you have been drawn. Yours is the imminent victory already shared by the Saints in Heaven. You will both have as many years on Earth to accomplish the Lord's work as He commends, and then you will be brought into Eternal Triumph. Please do not dwell on the brevity of the years, but remain focused on the work of today. My Special son, I thought it would be appropriate to recount various quotations through the next weeks and months that would be fitting for your written memoirs. Do you realize the power of the one for today? *"Yes."* This leads to the obvious question. How could the Mother of God not know what someone has done in his life? It speaks to the power of the Sacrament of Reconciliation. If you frame its efficacy in the context of this quotation, those who are asking God's forgiveness will indeed know that it has the expunging capacity proclaimed by the Church. It is only through the Blood of the Cross that the Sacrament of Penance is possible. Its origin is in the Crucifixion. This also speaks to the grace of the priesthood, that all priests who are loyal to the Vicar of Christ possess the faculty to forgive sins and pronounce absolution on behalf of the Great High Priest. This is a manifestation of pardon from the Holy of Holies. It is the miracle for which men hunger when they know not what to do with their guilt. You have known this all your life, but I repeat it today so you will be sure to remind those who are unaware. I assure you that the Lord is with you! It is clear that you are sound in faith and stouthearted. It is the Will of God that you be this way. Please let yourself believe that you are in His good graces.

    Thus, I have come today to speak to you and your brother again because I love you, and the world requires it. Humanity is broken by its own fractured nature. The indifference of the masses is almost too awful to describe. There are mortal sins too many to calculate in America alone. I have told you that your dignity is important to God. It is important to Me. I love My children with compassion and power, with intensity and even ferocity. My global messages are building-up to one massive presentation of peace and faith that has been intensifying throughout the centuries. By all means, there is such a thing as righteous ferocity. There is grace in the destruction of the material world. There is light in flushing-out the darkness. There is pardon in contrition, and healing in suffering. One of the reasons that the Gospel is disavowed by so many intellectuals is because they see it as one giant contradiction. How can someone criticize the actions of another person when they still have a beam in their eye? The answer is that even those who know nothing about theology can teach the holy how to love. The Sacred Scriptures were written by Jesus Christ through the power of the Holy Spirit. Remember that they did not exist until years after His Crucifixion, Resurrection and Ascension. They reflect His perfection, the perfect Love of The Word in words. They classify the order of things; they give wisdom and perspective to those who believe. They are the charter for the Church, the means for understanding the plight of exiles and the Will of God to redeem them. My Special one, you know that the New Covenant is filled with sacrifice and sacredness. It is not shorn of moments of sorrow, but it is replete with gladness and hope. This is why you should refer to the Scriptures often in your videos and writings. Provide substantiation for your proclamations and Mine. We have been given by Jesus a means for touching lost lives and mending broken hearts. We have the capacity through the Holy Spirit to awaken them from their slumber. What is the origin of this sleep? Their daily habits and distractions; their seasonal chores and secular rituals. Year after year of competitive sports. They see the waxing and waning of the accumulating months not as the opportunity to become more holy, but to be more adept at what they do for themselves. My Morning Star messages will help break this cycle. They will, in time, strike the contrast between their short-lived victories and the all-encompassing Triumph of My Immaculate Heart. This is why the text you have shown at the end of your first video is so relevant. It indicates the brilliance of My Queenship and the invincibility of My Grace. When words like 'torrents' are used to describe the peace of God, human minds are taken into another dimension. They show that the Lord will do most anything to soften stony hearts. It amazes Me that only few pay any mind to the urgency of the Gospel message until thousands of birds fall dead out of the skies. One has nothing to do with the other. This is why My children must be called to prayer. It is through prayer that wisdom is gained, not through science or astronomy, not in the inexplicable tragedies of Nature, not in the billions of guesses that untold people have applied to the motivations of God. The whole matter comes down to simple prayer. This is what you are doing now. You and your brother, and the whole Church, hold to the Truth of God through prayer, through faith that God is listening and Jesus is answering. Even a little child can understand this.

I am still holding-out hope that the United States will awaken from its deadness, from its stagnation, from its obstinance against the teachings of the Church. It is only through My intercession that your previous governor, George Ryan, was taken to see his ill wife from his imprisonment. Do you remember what I said? 'Wait until you see what they do to him now.' He did nothing to warrant such imprisonment. He did not take the lives of six children. He was conducting himself the way every other governor in history has done. It has become part of the fabric of the office. It is true that there is very little clemency in the public domain. This is why his magnanimous pardoning of the death-row inmates stands in such stark contradiction in the history of the world. I ask you and your brother to be patient in your judgements of the actions of men. See them for what they are – acts of ignorance more than cold malevolence. Sinners surrender to their own temptations and harm and violate other people. It is improper for them to do this, but rarely is it premeditated. We shall pray for the recapturing of the innocence of those who have walked down these paths of darkness, those who have tread heavily and not lightly."

Saturday, January 15, 2011
2:01 p.m.

"*The Blessed Mother wants us to believe that we are all visionaries in a beatific sense, that we can see our victories through Jesus on the Cross, and classify and categorize our priorities so prayer is the focal point of our lives. Our Lady has made clear that humanity is ill-prepared to take on our most wrenching challenges without spiritual love nourished by the Holy Eucharist. She speaks clearly about the sanctity of our faith in God. Any ambiguity we feel about our mission here on Earth is unfounded. Our thirst for holiness is not an unquenchable desire, but the wellspring and purpose of life.*"

William L. Roth

"This is well said, My Special one. It is indeed My ardent desire that My children come to Heaven through the Holy Eucharist, by accepting Jesus' Sacrifice that has expunged their sins. My little children, you know the meaning of the Church. You are aware of the sacred anatomy of human redemption, the grace and peace inside you that have wrapped your souls in Salvation. This is the message that we must take into the whole world, where the Mercy of Jesus is spread from shore to shore and mountaintop to valley. What designs and architectures you create to manifest this message to lost sinners is your identification with the Salvation you have accepted. When you speak of the world's growing and dying, you are referring not only to its present condition, but what it will eventually become perpetually. My Son said that 'It is Finished.' Was He referring only to the redemption of exiled souls? Was He speaking about completing the creation of the Earth and skies as though the first six days were not enough? He was making sure that the Faith-Church would be aware that the Holy Trinity is One God in Heaven and on Earth. The Church would from that Good Friday be united in its three distinct parts, the Faith-Church, as you know to be the Church Militant, the Church Suffering in Purgatory, and the Church Triumphant in Heaven. The whole basis of human redemption is begun here in this militant age of men. The holy and righteous must prevail over the indifferent and atheistic. Whether mortal men go to Purgatory and Heaven, or whether they are sent to Hell instead is determined by what happens in the created world. I have given all My Heart to the cause of conversion, for the building-up of My Son's Mystical Body. You have seen the beneficiaries of My Love for My children in all who have been led. You have served as emissaries for the Lord, taking the Gospel message to the masses in writing and through your prayers. Your witness for Jesus is noble and noteworthy; it is blessed and sanctified. This is the thesis of My messages to the many who have stood beside Him in good times and bad.

Today, I have come to pray with you for all the intentions that I hold dear. I ask you to remember the Church Suffering. They are worthy of the petitions of the Faith-Church on Earth. They hunger for the taste of freedom that only Heaven can provide. I have told you that it is not necessarily an expanse of time that they are situated in Purgatory, but a length of prayers. There were tens-of-thousands of souls who entered Heaven from Purgatory during Christmas this year. It is important for you to tell everyone that I have told you this. Jesus has planned a celebratory conclusion to the times of Earth. He has in mind the elevation of all who have spread His Gospel during the most difficult times of any. My Special son, you and your brother are in that number. It is yours. The blessings and benefits have come to you and all who have fought the good fight for Jesus' Most Sacred Heart. It is in this Heart that you have lived, that you shall remain forever in the presence of God. I ask everyone to remember the words of Pope John Paul II and Saint Padre Pio. Among the Pope's first words on October 16, 1978 when he prayed before the pilgrims were 'Do not be afraid.' And, Saint Pio said many times that faithful men should be strong, pray and do not worry. What was inside them that caused them to make these proclamations? What vision? What prophecy? It was that they were united in the Holy Spirit with the Wisdom of Truth. They knew that Jesus had already conquered the world's evil on Mount Calvary. They were both aware of the outcome of time. Yet, they suffered deeply and egregiously. They wept for lack of love from their peers. They wondered when the Light would chase away the darkness in the hearts of evil men. They asked God when righteousness would prevail over impurity and materialism. And then, it came to them. They were given the Wisdom they sought in their own vocations, in their awareness of the faith given to everyone. It became obvious to them that men and women from all walks of life would eventually realize what had inspired them to proclaim that fear and anxiety have no place in the Christian heart. They were like Blessed Mother Teresa in that they desired to heal broken humanity in order to console the Crucified Christ. I am saying to you that the popes and martyrs, the stigmatists and servants all have in common with Jesus the same thing that everyone else has who believes in Him. It is hope! It is the interior assurance that whatever comes in this life has already been addressed by the Son of God in Heaven. There has already been a reckoning there of everything that will happen here. If one believes that Grace lives in Heaven, and if he believes that this same Grace lives on Earth, then the only thing left in the equation is the element of time. The common denominator is this Grace; it is the origin of peace and satisfaction that is lacking in the physical realms. These realms in which you live and to which I come speaking is a hotbed of competition, of warring and slander; but it is not beyond repair. Jesus did not come here to destroy the Earth, but to renew it. The remnants that will make it shine on the last day are the parts and particles that have been contributed by such great men and women as Pope John Paul II, Padre Pio and Mother Teresa. They are moreover the prayers of the faithful, the little things that no one else sees. These remnants are the millions upon millions of words and syllables that seers like you and your brother have recorded for Me. They consist of the flowery oratory of Saints like Father Meehling and Archbishop Fulton Sheen. This makes every man one of the same kind of Saint, one in the lineage of goodness that is taking over this world a moment at a time. This is why I have asked you to live in the moment with your eyes on the prize. The whole world shudders with every Hail Mary you recite before you go to work in the morning. Your concern for the poor, the disenfranchised, the ill and forsaken – this is the substance of grace for those who need the intervention of God. When you go to work and make it your life's purpose to pay those who tend to the sick, this is the mission of the Cross. All is connected; everything that uplifts those who cannot fend for themselves is part of the same Divine Love through which the entire universe was fashioned. You live this in minutes and hours, as you should. The real question that most of the faithful ponder is not whether the world is still growing or is rather dying, but where is the fulcrum. Where is, or where was, the point where the created realms took a turn for the better or worse. That fulcrum was the Crucifixion and Paschal Resurrection of Jesus. By shedding His Blood on the Cross, Jesus staunched the bleeding of the whole world. He saved humanity by destroying the evil in which it was gripped. This is why you celebrate every Good Friday, Holy Saturday and Easter Sunday as the fulcrum of the Earth. The faithful have the right thought, but they often fail to place it into its true context because the answer is altogether too obvious.

My Special son, we have shared already together the unification of Heaven and Earth. You feel it when you attend Holy Mass. You are touched by it every time you pray. I have said that Jesus is entering His Kingdom on Earth now and presently, by inspiriting your hearts and minds with His Wisdom and sharing His Sacred Body, Blood, Soul and Divinity in the Most Blessed Sacrament. These are not extensions of some promise that has not yet been fulfilled, they have already been given to you in advance of the Salvation that has been rightfully won. This is the message that the world has yet to understand. And, it is the message that I desire them to know. Jesus won the fight. He asked all mortal men to tender their self-will to Him, to accept the victory that is theirs. It is all about a thing called Glory. What is Glory? What is it that makes something glorified? It begins by realizing that all things can be made perfect. All creatures great and small, all the seasons and climates, everything that comprises what men see, think and feel. Glory means that the Will of God prevails over everything else. It becomes seeded in human hearts when those hearts let go of their own agenda, of their own preferences and prejudices, when they say, 'Speak Lord, and I shall obey your commands.' Glory is about climbing to the summits of primordial excellence inside the human heart, where everything that was ever meant to live in eternity has its origin. God created humanity from the heart, to the heart. He asked Adam and Eve to be one inside His Sacred Heart, inside the perfection in which they themselves had been given life. He asked them not to break their oath of living in and through the heart, not by scattering their temptations to the winds or listening to one fallen angel. The Father has been consistent in every way. He has mandated the clarity of the heart from all who have breathed, everyone who has had the capacity to know about His Eternal Love. This year 2011 need not have a wasted moment when it comes to the actions of humanity, but it will. There will continue to be devil's advocates and reprobates of all kinds who do whatever they can to impede the mission of the Church. This is the way it has always been. I am not saying anything new. However, I am suggesting that those who are faithful to God can take seriously the admonitions and proclamations of good men like Pope John Paul II and Saint Padre Pio. You and your brother live in their commemorative light. You reflect what they hoped to see in those who embrace the Gospel of Christianity. I have not conceded any one of your brothers or sisters to another course of life. I know that I can touch them, and we will together accomplish what we have set-out to do. It is encouraging for Me to say these things because all the Saints in Heaven concur."

Saturday, January 22, 2011
1:41 p.m.

"It is what we do for others that shapes our lives in Christ, whether we recognize His calling in them or not. Our Lord is quite adept at depositing His presence in those who suffer; and we do well by listening to them. Here, we are taught fruit from prejudice, piety from indifference, truth from lies, and acceptance from rejection. There are incalculable ways to inherit this wisdom through the faculties of the Roman Catholic Church, many facets to the crown jewel of redemption, but there is only one Divine Love, one Holy Spirit, one Cross to which our own crosses are affixed like railcars to a train. This is the essential message of the Woman meek and mild who has come to America seeking the demise of both atheism and secularism."

William L. Roth

Humanity's Progenetic Lineage

"My dear children, thank you for remaining loyal to the faith given you by the Lord. Bless you for manifesting from that faith the conversion that has come in your time of many who have called on Me. Yes, I indeed thank you for remaining faithful to the Faith. We here in this home are calling on Jesus to enter His Kingdom nighly, to bring with Him the redemption of all lost souls and the found ones too. I am here again to remind you that you not only have a past in the Church, one filled with the workings of all the Saints and missionaries, all the servants and clergy, but that you also have a present-day origin that you yourselves are fashioning. It is founded in the Faith of old, and yet it is still new. This will take you to the future that you need not be concerned about right now. I am calling you in 2011 to live in the moment; live for what you can do in the here and now. I am not asking you to lose sight of the future about which I speak, for it is forthcoming as God would send it. Instead, I am calling you to see each moment and each morning as your time in the sun, even as dark as it sometimes gets. Be the glorious warriors with your brother-and-sister Christians. Do everything that the Holy Spirit inspires in you, and live in peace. Live in the way of the Apostles who prayed quietly in their rooms and in outdoor shaded places. Pray that the Cup not come to you. We shall forever know that you are capable of winning the greatest battles for lost sinners ever known to man, but perhaps those in distant trenches can let this be their service to the Cross. You have become fighters in the lineage of the Martyrs, and you must remember that you have shed your spiritual blood already for the Church. These are the days and weeks that are given to you to protect one another, to be present as it is said, to think and speak peacefully and politely. I am not suggesting that you have not been doing these things, I am only highlighting that you need to continue.

My holy sons, I expect that you perceive your labors for Me much like a sheet of music, each of you plays a distinct part, sounding a specific melody of your own making in harmony with the Father. All Christians, especially Roman Catholics, are playing in this symphony of holiness. There is still so much work to be done by those who have yet to lift an arm. They will be reached by the Church in droves someday. They will run forward, down the hills and through the valleys to answer the call of Divine Love they hear echoing now. They will say as many before them have said, Rise: Let us be on our way! They will sing the anthems and chant the praises of the Messiah whom they have always wished to know, but whom they were distracted from knowing by the throes of this world. They will see that everything they were clinging to was slowly fading away, wearing at the seams and destined to disappear. They will search for the permanence in human destiny, that it is meant for eternity and not for the Earth. I have said here and many places around the world that suffering need not be! It is a product of the lack of love of humanity for the God who created them. We must recall everyone who has written about this. Remember the legacies and handwritten testimonies on parchments that are now barely legible. They all had one thing in common. They tried to connect it to the Will of God, and they saw that this Will was effected by His Son on the Cross. Many who believe in Him are given lives of less suffering than others; some walk on palm branches having never tasted the brine. However, they will all touch the Cross before they die. You have in your hearts the same character of sublime discovery that has come to every Saint who is now in Heaven. The content of your thoughts is connected to this. I am not one to envy another earthly creature, but I congratulate you for seeing firsthand what has been seen before. The writings and confessions of many Saints are available to you through the inspirations that have composed the substance of your speeches and writings. You are united with them in your allegiance to the Church. You have made true their hopes and dreams in your time because you have been obedient to Me. My request for you today is to remember everything you have learned from your own experiences, connected to what I have said in My messages, combined with all you have gained in your belief in the Gospels. This is a glorious mixture of beatific grace that has been seeded in you.

My Special son, I honor you and your brother always and in all ways. You are stationed in a life that is blessed; you have seen how it is blessed. And, you live in a country that does not prohibit the exercise of your faith. Some in America may not like it, but they will not put you in detention for what you believe. You are free to share and increase your faith to whatever measure and degree you desire. This in itself would be considered a miracle in some nations overseas. I have looked upon and watched My children across the United States fight for righteousness, for the lives of unborn children, for the sanctity of their conception and birth, for the end of capital punishment, for the feeding, clothing and housing of the poor, and for the preservation of the piety that once absorbed and enshrined America. You already know what caused these things to be such topics of disagreement – such movements as pluralism, relativism, secular humanism and atheism which are attempting to dismantle America's scaffolds of greatness. God would rather have governors who believe in Him that own slaves than have nonbelievers in this country who have enslaved no one. It comes down to whether faith in Jesus is accepted or rejected, for the degrees to which He is accepted can always be increased. Many Americans have heard the concept that you must destroy a village in order to save it. While this seems such a contradiction, it is precisely what Jesus will do with the United States and other democratic nations around the globe. Freedom is always precious, but not a freedom that permits the very fabric of a republic to become frayed from indifference. I am committed to seeing the mission through that brings all the Americas, North, Central and South to the realization that I am their Mother. I am not only their Patroness, but their Immaculate Mother. This is why it is so crucial that you understand the breadth and height of the love found in your heart. It is this love that will win over all. It is this love that will help you forget whatever you believe afflicted you in the past, in your youth and at times when you seem so out of control. Indeed, it is this love that you and your brother have shared; you have shared it with all who believe in God through the Roman Catholic Church. I commend you for retrieving your dignity from those who have tried to steal it without seeking revenge against them. You are the living reflection of the resurrected Christ. It is your progenetic lineage with the Saints of old and your service for the Church today and in the future."

Saturday, January 29, 2011
12:53 p.m.

"We have always known that Christianity brokers the coalescence of all souls beneath the Cross to be immersed in the Sacred Blood of Our Lord's Sacrifice, but many are still uninformed about how that mystical experience translates into tangible spiritual action. It has everything to do with effecting our brothers and sisters' conversion through our knowledge and understanding of the redemption of Creation. And, it has even more to do with placing our own suffering into that same context as we commit ourselves and our families to the purification of the world."

William L. Roth

"Nothing makes Me happier than to speak to My children who have devoted themselves to the intentions you have just stated. This is the writing of someone who understands the mission of the Church, the calling of the Holy Spirit throughout the nations and generations, one who is guided by Sacred Love instead of infatuation. My Special and Chosen ones, you are still undergoing the beautiful wintertime where you live, and the lands are yet asleep. As you have seen many years, the spring will come forth budding the freshness of new life; your hearts will open like the flowers to welcome the warm breezes. It is not enough, it would seem, that this parable represents the resurrection of human hope from the dustbin of the material world. I have stated this metaphor around the globe more times than one might care to imagine. But, why do they not understand? Because they have no hope in their hearts; they cannot conceive a world in which the present and future can live simultaneously. They are starved for knowledge about the workings of God's ideals inside them because they turn deaf ears to His callings; they ignore His benevolent signs. They do not seek what you search for, My Special one. They are not motivated for the exact reason you have said – they are distracted by the physical world. To many of them, entertainment is the meaning of life, their way of expressing their talents and demanding their preferences shorn of awareness that they are walking useless paths. Only what is done for God matters in this life. Whatever lifts Him up and brings comfort to His creatures. Whatever sings His praises before the nations in ways that clarify the mandate of the Gospels. How many times have you heard someone say that they are going someplace simply because, 'It is something to do(?)' How many of your neighbors and acquaintances enter the stores and theaters not thinking about God or how everything they encounter must be encompassed by His Love? The thesis of life is becoming united with Him. The outcome of life is to join Him in Heaven. What happens between the birth of a man and his death should be a salutation to the Father; it should echo what He wants from that life. The man walking the Earth should realize that the all-sustaining Grace of God is the sole reason for his redemption, for his awakening in matters of faith and morals.

Let us look once again at the writing you offered Me today. Many are still uninformed about the mystical experience with My Son's Crucifixion. Has this not been the reason for My apparitions and locutions for so many centuries? It is clear that the Holy Spirit provides the Wisdom, and I am here and all around the world asking My children to receive this Spirit. I cannot succeed in this task unless they comply. I have told the Medjugorje seers and visionaries elsewhere that the sacrifices of man are meaningless unless those who make them understand why. It is more than simple self-denial. It is not immolation for its own sake. It is to touch the hard-hearted with the genius of Heaven. It is to transform the actions of the practical world into the beatific resonance that inspirits all men of good will. My little son, if you should live to be 100 years old, you will never lose sight of this goal. No man who is destined for Heaven will ever reject the gifts that God pours-out for their benefit, including the means to procure peace and justice wherever they are not fully formed. You and your brother have been saturated with and conscripted by this genius about which I speak because you asked for it. You prayed to receive it. You asked the Lord to come get you, and Jesus complied with your request. Little do many others know what sacrifices this has meant, not only for you, but for the hundreds of millions of other servants and believers who have preceded you. I speak today of a joy that cannot be stopped, and the source of this joy is that you have been prompted by the Holy Spirit to stay the course. You and your brother have not strayed or wandered from your place inside the Sacred Heart of My Son. You have not rejected what so many others should have believed; and for this, history will treat you kindly. I am telling you today that there will be much to suffer for many in the future, much sadness and darkness, much deprivation and depression. This need not be the way you perceive your journey through life. Please consider what Saint Padre Pio wrote. He said that he envied those who suffer! What in the world could he have meant by that? It begins in the realization that the Body on the Cross was sacrificed for the Salvation of men, and the Mystical Body is suffering for the exact same reason. If it is for the redemption of souls that this suffering comes, how can it not be joy? This seems to be a perspective that many do not understand, and I have told you that if all souls would come to Jesus of their own accord, they would be saved; there would no longer be any need for suffering, no more need for time."

Sunday, February 6, 2011
1:32 p.m.

"Before a conscience can be stirred, it must first be formed, built on the foundation of moral excellence. Exiled humanity cannot become good until he becomes aware, not through the dialectical frameworks that promote the world's practical knowledge, but by the genius of the Christian heart."

William L. Roth

"My dearly beloved sons, you are bringing great light into the world by your suffering; you are tending to the lost sheep and indeed forming the Christian conscience about which you speak. It is My delight to be here with you as you pray for the Earth that is rife with sin and error. You know that you change these things when you pray every day, when you tender your presence to Me for those you love. I must mention the beauty of your written memoir thus far. You are reflecting and analyzing the world and the spiritual realms with tremendous depth, as well as delineating the practical, historic events that have brought you through the years. You will be able to make clear all you wish humanity to know. You have a wonderful capacity for transmitting the content of your heart onto the written page. This is something that is lacking around the world today; there is so much content-clipping, electronic snippets, sharp tongues and closed eyes. Whether you and your brother realize it or not, these are wonderful times to be living on Earth. No matter what you see happening in the Arab nations, in Egypt and other places, please believe that it will ultimately make way for the eradication of beliefs that run contrary to the Holy Gospel. This is the way the world must be, and no one ever said that it would be easy. There have been acts of violence and movements of insurrection, and this must come for there to be change. The Truth of the Cross will rise from among these ruins! I have spoken to you before about the fall of Communism, the destruction of materialism and idolatry. You watch these things happen every day of the world, and so does everyone else. What it portends for the future is somewhat unclear to all the seers, all who perceive it. I have been with Jesus, watching from close and afar. You are seeing the purification of the nations that was told in ancient times, the gutting and clearing of buildings and lands. I ask you to join the Holy Father in Rome and the whole Church in praying for My Son's intervention everywhere, where there is both peace and unrest, where there is eloquence and vitriol. Even the United States of America is not immune to these things."

Saturday, February 12, 2011
2:13 p.m.

"Therefore, I am content with weaknesses, insults, hardships, persecutions, and constraints for the sake of Christ; for when I am weak, then I am strong." (2 Cor. 12:10)

"We are constantly bombarded by different levels of commonness every day, against which we contrast what ultimately become the more extraordinary moments of life. We reserve the right to defend whatever we wish as being more beautiful than most, higher than the rest, and better than anything else based on the value we place on our own insights and actions. If we saw ourselves before the backdrop of the Earth as Jesus sees us, perhaps we might more clearly understand that every person fashions and transcends his own thoughts and tendencies to reach those heights in ways unmatched by any other creature in the world."

William L. Roth

"Now I have come, the Mother of Jesus, the Mother of God, into your presence with joy and appreciation for your obedience to Me and to the mission of the Church. My little sons, it is rare that I might be so elated to speak to mortal creatures with this joy when there are such gross sins and injustices in the world. However, I speak with you openly about My inspiration gained through your trust in God and response to My call. I have spoken to you and your brothers and sisters, your comrades in Christianity for many generations. As you watched in the motion picture 'The Song of Bernadette' last evening, I did not come to her to pronounce doom and gloom. I simply said that it would not be possible for Me to make her happy in this life. It was her understanding of human suffering and its purpose in purifying humanity that made her happy. Her joy was a fruit of her faith, of her realization that the Holy Spirit has come into the midst of men to give wisdom where there is ignorance, to offer the Lord's warning about what shall come if lost sinners do not adhere to the teachings of the Gospel. You have seen that your messages are much like this, and you have likewise taken to heart My messages; you have inherited the same meekness and courage that brought Saint Bernadette to the summit of God's embrace. While this was a good motion picture, lost in the cinema was the content of My messages. Surely it was clear that innocence, self-sacrifice, prayer, service, and suffering bring the hard-hearted to let loose of their obstinance. You saw public officials stand in disbelief, even to the point that they would incarcerate someone who stood so soundly on the facts of what they saw. Yes, they stood against Saint Bernadette until the miracles began to flow. It was then that they started to believe, and as unbelievable as it seems, their belief at first centered on the profits reaped from the visiting pilgrims. The suffering eventually turned to Me because of the suffering of the innocent Bernadette.

My mission throughout the centuries has always been clear to you. It is the same as the mission of the Church. I have heralded the value of prayer and prudence, of humility and self-immolation. Popes and Cardinals abound who have taken seriously My call for greater holiness; and they have preached that the purpose of Christianity is not only for the Salvation of lost sinners, but that they would work together to cure the sick, and to exert their efforts for all the Spiritual and Corporal Acts of Mercy. It is all about this Mercy that the Lord was crucified. He set out to unite Heaven and Earth by His public ministry, and His Crucifixion was the capstone above this Foundation of Love. History has shown that redemption follows the path of purity and righteousness. One can find the Promised Land by denying himself and taking-up the crosses in life that are laid upon him. The converted human soul can be discovered beyond the parameters of this Earth by living with the expectation that the whole of Heaven sees his every act. This is not necessarily a predestination of the soul, but its journey, its walk of life toward the Land of the Living. My Special son, you and your brother have been fortunate to know these things for many decades; and you have not been alone. You have shared the same faith and knowledge that billions of Christians before you have known. Would I as the Mother of God not be remiss if I did not celebrate them, raise them before the exiled world as Saints so many times in My messages to you? Would it not be unfair if I had not hailed them as heroes and conquerors in Jesus when they lived preeminently in His Divine Light for the whole of their years? I stand with them now as they bask in this Light! You have pondered universes never discovered; the history of men has proved that this is the one that matters most to God. You are living what will be revealed as awesome times of miraculous revelation because this is the way it was written. You and your brother, and all who believe in Jesus have been given vision that is widely unknown to those who refuse to believe. This is not something new that I am telling you. It is far and above what most mortal men are willing to embrace. They are oftentimes their own obstacles. They wish to walk with the sight of new birth in their minds, but they are unwilling to open their eyes. This has been the way of the world for thousands of years.

My Special one, this is the reason it has taken so long to bring humanity into these times. It has required the history of the ages, the birthing and development of throngs and choices, the teaching of the chosen ones who would create themselves a record of human achievement according to the Gospels that must be seen by those who are living now. The millions who have traveled to My shrines have come for many reasons, to know their Savior better, to procure physical and mental healing, to lay before their Mother their cares about those they love. I intercede for them and ask Jesus to answer their prayers; and He does so according to the Will of God. We have spoken about books and manuscripts, of poetry and music, of sonnets and reprises, and these are the renderings of inspirited men. They are all good when they lift-up the Son of Man in a way that dignifies His Glory here on Earth and sustains the faith of the masses. Hence, it is in this age of new devices that such people as you and your brother have composed and presented your Marian works to humanity. It has all been a stage of development and attainment, of pondering and reacting. You have walked with faith the same way the Original Apostles agreed to accompany Jesus on His sojourn from place to place. There was tremendous selflessness in what they achieved. Its echo is still heard here in your day. They knew that they needed to embrace what Jesus told them, even to their own mortal demise. As this is not the calling of others who serve in His Holy Name, that they would be martyred in the flesh, it remains true that anyone who suffers or is persecuted while preaching the Gospel is spiritually martyred for the good of the Cross. You have known personally untold people who have offered this gift to God. Remember them with gladness and thanksgiving in your heart, because each of them was special. They decided in their hearts according to their value of holiness what was beautiful. Each of them created beauty; each one measured the beauty of their faith and its resultant actions according to their degree of understanding of what God wanted from them. A beautiful song or heart-touching lyric is unique to its author, and it becomes part of the sacred culture that the Church espouses and teaches every day. Indeed, it is this sacred culture that helps every Christian carry on. All who believe and work for Jesus contribute to this larger culture. They are building the Kingdom that I have spoken about so many times. If you will permit Me to say so, these are the same gifts that you and your brother have laid at the manger and the foot of the Cross with such gentleness, with such care and generosity. The whole world is filled with gifts from faithful men and women to the Christ Child, their Savior Sacrificed on the Cross.

I am pleased by the opportunity to have spoken to you here today about what you have written for your memoirs because we think about the same hopes for a world that seems to be drifting away. I assure you that it cannot drift so far that it cannot be found again. The whole of the seas can be placed into one teardrop of the Son of Man. He realized the pressures and distractions of the world. The Lord God has embraced the same beauty that you have written about, the same individuality of His creatures, the same tenor of confidence by which you live. He knew about the courage of the Martyrs before they ever laid-down their lives. Through the Holy Spirit, He provided for what they would say. He penned their final speeches and valedictory addresses. Jesus has elicited the applause of the Hosts of Heaven from God-loving people here and now. He gives them the inspiration and holiness to achieve their goals on His behalf. This is what He has done for you and your brother through Me."

Saturday, February 19, 2011
2:02 p.m.

"May the Lord God bless everyone with His Sovereign Love. May the Angel Choirs usher the Holy Spirit into the lives of hard-hearted men. May our faith be good and strong, authentic, true and loyal, that we pay homage to Christ the King through His missionary Church on Earth, where the just and sanctified venerate the Cross by which millions have already been redeemed, a sweet and timeless clemency that can never be annulled."

William L. Roth

"It is consistency in this love about which you speak that makes you strong in faith. My children, I pray that you never surrender the vision that Jesus has given you to see the Will of the Father in all His works. My Special son, your writings and reflections are lovely. They are filled with your own renditions of the beauty of Heaven that you have summoned through your prayers and kindnesses. You and your brother are still united in this holy place to ask My Son to bless your work and your lives, to sanctify and purify all around you, to seek from all others the knowledge that you have been given. I also pray that My children from all walks of life will find their way to the Cross and to the Altar the way you have, the same way that your fellow brothers and sisters in Jesus have found peace of mind and heart in His Wisdom. You must remember that the Holy Gospel is the record of Jesus' life here on Earth as told by those who loved Him. His advice and counsel are found there, even His words. Jesus as the Holy Spirit wrote the Sacred Scriptures through His chosen apostles and disciples in this world, thus making the New Covenant somewhat of His own diary. You are fortunate to know Jesus the way I have taught you, but you must remember that everyone who accepts His Salvation knows Him as you. There is mysticism and the miraculous seeping from the Gospel too copiously to go unnoticed. There are warnings and reprimands for humanity too replete to ignore. The whole redemption of lost sinners is encapsulated in the Holy Gospel, and yet so few turn there for help and guidance as they awaken each new day. You know that Jesus is the Living Word, the Son of the Most High in whom the reason for living is found. Strength in the way of the great Martyrs is located there for the millions who suffer in their own repetitive ways. Light pours forth from the pages of the Sacred Scriptures, as it did from the burning bush, and yet those pages are not consumed. My children, we seek for all souls who wish to know God that they will turn to the Gospel, to the Church, to the Sacraments for the refinement and reconciliation they require to be reunited with the Father. I find intense happiness knowing that there are so many Christians in the world. There is consolation and hope in them as there is in Me. There is obviously deep hatred against the Roman Catholic Papacy, against the Hierarchical Church. This is happening because Satan knows that the Church will ultimately win all the souls meant to inherit the Kingdom of Milk and Honey, the holy place in which eternity will welcome them.

  Today, I have come to bless you at the fore of the week that will complete your twenty years of messages. I will continue to speak to you into the future as long as the Father allows. Please do not make a great deal out of this 20-year milestone because it is just another number toward the grand reunion of Heaven and Earth. We have our sights on things much larger than a two-decade span or measure of weeks and months. We look forward to events that are timeless and immeasurable, that cannot be captured on a calendar or a continuum of chronological records. We have been speaking and interacting in a relationship, as you say, that is unaffected by the hours on a clock. You live inside time because of the sin of Adam and Eve, but you are ultimately set free because of the Sacrifice of Jesus on the Cross. There is no way that I can too often make this statement of acclamation around the globe. I have reminded every seer and visionary to whom Jesus has ever sent Me that the Cross is the Way of Life, the Way of Salvation, the handhold you require to be lifted into the gladness of absolution. This is the Good News that so many on Earth have yet to grasp, and this is why the quotation you presented to Me today is so relevant. It is indeed proper that you and all Christians everywhere and in every age should ask Jesus to bless you, to bless your prayers and sacrifices, to enter the minds and hearts of those who are cold and stony, so that all who shall at last remain with Him will know why and how they got there. You speak of a sweet and timeless clemency because the Holy Spirit has revealed this to you. What is this sweetness? It is the opposite of the bitterness of the world. What about this clemency? It ends and overwhelms the guilt of the Earth and the daily indictments that are issued by sinners against those they despise. It has been said that America holds many truths to be self-evident, but the truth of forgiveness is lacking all over the world. It is missing here in the United States because of the competition for worldly things and the exacting of vengeance that belongs to no mortal man. My Special one, please do not be disconcerted about the theme of matters in your country because Jesus will guide the righteous around the obstacles in their way. Those who are responsible for the terrible atrocities in America will be forced to admit their errors; they will be rebuked and punished as the Bible quite clearly states.

Here today, we are reminded of the good people who are ministering to the poor and helpless, of the holy workers in the Lord's vineyard who are feeding His sheep, clothing the naked, sheltering the homeless and healing the sick. These are the souls that I choose to dwell upon; these are God's heroes and champions. You know who they are, and most of them are unsung by the secular void. The further rebuking of the many about whom you have spoken, the media executives and moguls of capitalism will fall hard; they will impact the floor of the Earth on their bellies with a thud. I have asked you not to pity them because I have no pity on them. They are fully aware of what they are doing wrong. They choose to do evil instead of accomplishing good. They are defiant against the teachings of the Church in spite of knowing what those lessons are. You have been watching biographies of sinners on television whose judgement will be much more lenient than those moguls and executives about whom we have spoken. I know that this is difficult to believe. *"It is not difficult to believe at all. I understand how that can be so."* You know that the Judgement of God has a great deal to do with assessing the nature of the hypocrisy of man. 'What did the President know, and when did he know it?' These are the historical words from 1973 that have echoed throughout the centuries for so long before. While this distinguished Senator was speaking about your President that year, it is a prime example of how Jesus will judge the actions of men. The level of culpability is based on the capacity of a sinner to know right from wrong according to the definition of 'right' that was issued by Jesus during His life, through the Holy Spirit in all the Popes, in the greatest homiletics of humble priests, and in the writings and reflections of lay people such as yourself. The Truth transcends all vocations to voice the Will of God in the statements of those who speak it. Even the little ones, the small children and adolescents who have not learned to cheat and lie, whose hearts have not yet been darkened by greed and hatred, are capable of speaking this Truth in the way of the great Doctors of the Church. You can see it in their eyes, in their innocence, in their hope for good things to come, in their maturing eloquence that will fill their future with sound teachings from the center of Heaven itself. Jesus' first blessing came from His hand in the manger. God knew what He was doing. His first assignment to those who heard Him was to go out and tell the whole world about His Birth in Bethlehem, about His admonishments in the temple, His blessings on the Mount of Olives, His healings and advisories – all to make the point that He was and is the reason for human life.

My Special one, when all sinners come to Jesus the way you have described in your books, the way I have spoken about in My messages, the way the Popes have proclaimed, you will see the gaps between the human conscience and the Glory of Heaven begin to close. I spoke to you about forming the conscience before it can be stirred. It is formed by hearing and listening, by responding, radiating, resonating, praying, living in perpetual expectation, trusting in the values of peace and mercy, and not caring what the rest of humanity thinks of you. This is the conscience that is fashioned by the urgency of Heaven's call and not by the whims of unbelieving men. This conscience is the basis for the true changing of the material world. Once this conscience is manifested in the converted heart, it cannot be reversed. It is like the clemency that you have said cannot be annulled. It is permanent, and it cannot be repealed. This is the origin of My joy from the day Jesus rose from the Tomb. I knew at that moment that the Light of the World was here to stay. It has come from under a billion bushel baskets to set the Earth aglow in new brilliance and eternal wisdom. It has warmed hearts left out in the cold by the hatred of other men. It has revealed the faults and cracks in the judgements and actions of mere mortals. This is the Light by which you have walked for almost 50 years. This Light is all humanity requires to know God perfectly, for this Light is a Spirit that has come into the fullness of the Church Militant to live with sureness in the redemption of men."

Saturday, February 26, 2011
12:54 p.m.

"Jesus has set forth a priestly calling to every soul on Earth, a command to protract our holiness into the world so we can overcome our pride and prosper the Gospel of Heaven and the Sacraments. The whole idea of reading between the lines surely must have come from the Sacred Scriptures; not that we are allowed to infer anything from its text that God does not intend, but so that the chapters and verses become the heartstrings we pluck with our prayers, playing-out the melodies of righteousness, relying on the strongholds of love with which our faithfulness is upheld. The Lord forms our thoughts with lyrics about the way life is meant to be, and the Holy Spirit endows us with wisdom rolling off our tongues like honeydew in the midday light."

William L. Roth

"My children, you must tell humanity that they are given faith when they tell God that they love Him, and they are able to say this when they have the seed already planted within them. This is the paradox; this is the timelessness of the gift of faith that transcends the hour and engulfs it. Some might ask which came first, the chicken or the egg. Faith comes when one believes, and one believes once the gift of faith has been inspired within them. This is one of the sacred mysteries that human logic cannot explain. Your faith is fashioned and ordained by your awareness that you are capable of loving God. This is the root of the whole manifestation of accepting Him, of investing in the power and practice of Christianity, and of giving oneself to Jesus' Crucifixion not only for eternal Salvation, but for wisdom and guidance through the worldly exile of men. My Special son, you have written about the miracle of the Father's intercession, His intervention in the affairs of mortal men in a way that creates the foundation of love based on Divine Love. You speak about the life of man as he is given life through the Holy Gospel and by the power of Heaven as it is revealed to the Earth. You refer to the love by which you are one with everyone else who loves God, all who have placed their entire being in Jesus' Most Sacred Heart. It is not the world that has led you to do this. It is by your sacrifices that you have been given the words to say, by your belief in the Sacred Mysteries of human redemption in the Messiah hailed as King of kings by your predecessors and forefathers. You are reading the Gospel account of Jesus' life and ministry, of His teachings, His enemies, and also about His persecution, prosecution, condemnation, Crucifixion and Resurrection. Indeed, you are reading about the process of life in which all who believe in Jesus follow. Again, these are not mere words to which you are called, they are not simple images of history as though those times have passed away. You are deeply involved in the record of immortal times that have been scribed into discernible terms for those like all with whom you have lived for five decades to absorb. I speak about the paradoxes of the Sacred Scriptures as though there are contradictions in what the Father has deigned. It is all a matter of context. The more His people respond on Earth, the greater their knowledge about the fullness of Creation as it has unfolded and will someday conclude. I have said many times that eternity has already begun, and all who are bound for Heaven are at this moment a subset within it. Hence, Jesus has come the second time, but not yet. Another paradox, indeed.

Today, I have come to teach you and your brother about what it means to realize with seamless joy what My intercession has meant already to the Earth. It is not that your mission and your messages will have no bearing on the outcome of this world. I wish for you to recall My own motivations at the same time that other mortals question yours. My reason for appearing throughout the centuries is about the conversion of lost sinners to the Cross. This will always be the main thesis for speaking to so many seers and visionaries. It is the reason the Holy Spirit has instilled words and images into those who have welcomed the voice of Heaven. The whole concept of 'locution' implies that the person denies the preferences of the self, that he or she is open to treading into new dimensions that cannot be seen in mortal time.

We have often discussed the prospect of suffering, that it makes amends for the sins of the world. Having said this, you must remember that suffering is not punishment for sin. Jesus was crucified to eradicate the sins of humankind, but He was not being punished. He was not being chastised or executed for anything He may have done wrong. Remember that Jesus is incapable of sin. No matter what else He may have done in His earthly life, regardless of how it might have been seen by others, it could never have been construed as sin. My point is that it is through suffering that Holy Light is revealed. This can never be a punishment. Those who suffer usher this Light into the dark material world. They are not being punished either. This begs the definition for the difference between suffering and chastisement. The answer is that chastisement is assigned to a particular meaning of human conduct in order to stop it. Chastisement can be related to a specific event or series of actions, but suffering in the context of purification and conversion is not always assignable this way. There is some overlapping in what I am saying, but I know that you understand My point.

This takes our conversation to a completely different level with significant new meaning. When good people suffer, does this imply that it is mitigating the sinfulness of others? Yes, it does. When unholy people suffer, is it because they have refused to live according to the teachings of the Church? Here again, not necessarily. It is possible that unholy people can suffer for the conversion of other unholy people; and in the process, all who are unholy join Jesus on the Cross (the good thief and bad thief) in reparation for the world's collective human sin. Suffering is suffering, no matter who is asked to endure it. The mainstay of what I am saying is what the person who suffers chooses to do with that suffering, whether they offer it to God for the sins of the world, or whether they turn against God for putting them in such pain. This is the doorway that leads to the judgement of the heart and soul before the Son of Man. Do they enter-in or turn away? Are they accepting, or is their callousness too great to permit them this vision? Satan attacks people from all walks of life, the good and the bad; and it is what these people choose to do with their own will that decides the effectiveness of their response. It would be easy for someone to be bitter about losing a loved-one to murder. One might question the motivations of God when a parish church is burned to the ground. Here again, faith rests in the response. While buildings cannot suffer, their meaning certainly can. The spirit of purpose they carry for believers is certainly a living thing. This is why you and all the faithful believe in and embrace holy relics and holy ground. They are part of the collective faith of those who realize and pay homage to the history they represent. I again mention the concept of motivation. The motivation of God is that you come to Him, that all men come to Him by treading the ground where His Son was born, lived and died, where I have appeared to visionaries and seers, where Popes and Cardinals have issued decrees straight from the heart of God, where anything manifesting the grace of Heaven has been given origin and lasting fruit. These thoughts stream from the words you have written at the beginning of this message. As you think about it, you will sense the connection.

    We must ensure that we pray for that final understanding of human love and Divine Love to come to everyone alive. It is already clear to those who have died. This is what judgement before Jesus is about. Does the definition of human love and God's Divine Love agree in the heart of the person? This is the question. Making sure they agree is what the mission of the Church is about. Throughout the ages, priests and all clergy have tried to clarify the meaning of human love in the way Jesus practiced it. For the purpose of human excellence and the brilliance of life after death, that love must become one with the Love of God. It must encounter and unify with the Love of God in the Holy Spirit through the heart and by the actions of all who believe. This is why when someone asks for faith, it is given to them. They cannot procure it from any other source, and they cannot steal it or inherit it from a friend. It cannot be borrowed and put back on the shelf. This is the other side of the equation, the motivation of exiled men. We have spoken on numerous occasions about the exchange of spirits between Heaven and Earth, that is to say, the engagement of the human heart with the Sacred Heart of Jesus, the unification of the human will and the Divine Will of God. It is a convergence of the goodness of man and the majesty of the Church. This is the road to Truth, and Truth is the ultimate destiny. Let us again refer to the passage that you began with today. Reading between the lines means knowing that not all the actions of the Messiah could have been written down. The world could not hold all the books. It means placing the self inside the history of the recorded Word as though someone twenty centuries later was there as that history played-out. It means knowing one's self, and comparing that knowledge with the genius of God that is recorded in the Gospel accounts. Mortal men everywhere and down through the ages have done this, wondering what they would have said to Jesus if they had walked and talked with Him during His earthly ministry. Now, it is obvious what all good men would have said and done. They would have deferred to His every wish, while seeking from Him every speck of sacred knowledge He had to offer. This is also the purpose of invoking the power of the Holy Spirit in your day and time. *"What causes Jesus to ask people to suffer by way of chastisement?"* This is the dichotomy that I spoke about. Chastisement is always clear. The reason for the suffering can be assigned an origin. The reason Jesus asks people to suffer by way of chastisement is to procure a means to an end, to take those who are not behaving according to the Will of God into alignment with what He would have them do. The point I am making is that chastisements have roots. General suffering, meaning suffering that appears to have no punitive purpose, is of the same agony that Jesus offered the Father through His Passion and Sacrifice on the Cross. *"In other words, Mercy characterizes general suffering, where judgement is manifested by chastisement."* There, you have your answer. I know that you will have no difficulty explaining this to humanity in your own words. Tell them that the Holy Spirit implanted this knowledge in your heart."

Saturday, March 5, 2011
12:19 p.m.

"It is said that persistence in prayer is as great a virtue as prayer itself because God is pleased by our determination to stand by Jesus and invoke the Most Blessed Trinity. It seems that this is the only way to purify the world, by beseeching the King who reigns over it, turning to the spiritual realms to effect change in our physical life. We must trust that what we cannot see is as curative as anything we can touch with our hands. And, we need to recognize the value of rhythm, learning not only to hear the sounds of the world's daily charms, but to live by the echoing silence of the off-beats as well. We can in this way envision the face of Heaven in our prayers and imagine in these dark times what it means to rediscover our lost innocence."

William L. Roth

"The blessings and graces of the Lord are with you always! Today, it is My happiness and fulfilment to speak to humanity through your love for Me, through your devotion to Jesus' Most Sacred Heart, through your determination to prevail in the Holy Sacrifice that has made you aware of the

Love of Heaven. My Special and Chosen ones, you have been praying for the end of abortion, for the feeding of the hungry, housing of the street-bound, the conversion of the lost, and all the other matters that I have asked My children to remember. We have reason to believe that God will answer these prayers in His own good time. I have told you this before. It is true that no one goes through life without learning at least something about God, even if there are those who disagree with what they learn. The fruits of spiritual faith are everywhere. They blossom in the hearts of men and feed those who do not realize what a blessing life truly is. We must continue to pray because this is the way the Father responds. It is the reason He sends His Son by the Holy Spirit to mend what is broken and awaken the sleeping. I call both of you today to remember to pray for all who are brokenhearted by lost family members, sickness, disengagement, civil strife, international wars, the diseased and forsaken, and for little children who pine to see their parents. Pray for those who are incarcerated in prisons, especially the ones on death row; and pray for all who lay paralyzed in their beds with nobody to heal them. It is by the prayers of the world that medical science will ultimately know how to raise these souls from their sick beds. I also ask you to pray for all leaders of governments, for spiritual counselors and clergy, and for those who serve in menial roles. This obviously leads to My call for your prayer for the Holy Father Pope Benedict XVI in Rome, for all the Cardinals and deacons, for nuns and sisters, indeed for all who bear the burden of religious vocations. Pray for everyone whose role is to serve the poor, to tend to hospital and nursing home patients, for the great ones who teach little children about God and how to pray. It is all about prayer, My Special and Chosen ones. This is how humanity is purified and preserved; it is the way to reach the center of the Heart of the Father with your petitions and desires.

My Special son, it is clear to you by now that you and your brother are being attacked by Satan for all the good you are doing. I have asked you this question before; do you believe your brother is doing physically all right? *"Yes."* He is enduring a particularly brutal series of attacks because of the progress of your books. This is Satan's anger being thrust against another person who is working for Jesus. Although My messages are meant to bring great peace into the world, those who commend My messages to societies that need them are regularly attacked and assaulted by evil for doing so. Is this not the reason that the Son of Man was Crucified? *"Yes."* I know that you and your brother pray often, that you ask for My intercession and the same of Jesus every day. We do as the Father wills; we tell all who will listen that to suffer in Jesus' name is to be blessed in every way possible as humanity continues to be purified. There are untold happy times too. There are moments when My children, My messengers, remember how fortunate they are. For example, you and your brother live here in the United States where it is legal to believe in God and tell others why. It is a place where you can display your faith openly and profess what you believe without being sent to prison. You have plenty of food to eat, a nice place to live, capable means of transportation, friendship and neighbors, sufficient health care, entertainment, and an outlook for the future of positiveness because of the promises Jesus has made. These blessings, these happy gifts are the ones you should dwell on. Thank God for His merciful Heart! Realize the heritage of your faith in this country where a lasting impression has been made not only in your mind and hearts, but that of millions of American children. You rarely hear about them because this is not what the public media dwell upon. You referred to this phenomenon when you said that it was barely reported that 400,000 people marched in favor of the birthright of every unborn child, for the eradication of abortion. I always ask you to remember that even the issues you learn about every day at work, those you see and hear on the television at night, the ones on the news websites – all of these focus on the negative, competitive and divisive subjects. These antisocial contexts have a way of seeping into the consciousness of millions of your fellow citizens, and this translates into hatred and violence everywhere. The Internet has become a hotbed of lies and sensationalism. It could be used more for spreading the Holy Gospel, but what secular profit is there in that? There are millions of sites on the Internet that peddle impurity, devil worship, cannibalism and materialism to the ultimate extreme. The themes of negativity that you see and hear every day from the workplace to the television screen are vexing to the human spirit; they do little to allow the heart to enjoy the peace that is given through the Spirit of God. While I realize that you and your brother do not allow this phenomenon to affect you in any way, others are not as founded in faith as you two are. You are peaceful here in this home because you recognize social negativity and violence for what they are. You do not internalize the propaganda you hear because you are given to Me; you are determined to remain fast in the peace of the Lord.

I realize that you have written about the substance of My message today in your prior books, but the issue about which you have written and I have spoken seems only to be getting worse. Even prior sources of reliable news have been diminished as trustworthy sources because they have sold-out to relativism and the fallacious idea of diversity. They have done this because it is making them rich. They are remaining silent about the abhorrence of sin because they are being paid by the same industry that is leading so many away from the Church. Please do not believe that this is a hopeless matter. I would rarely tell you about something that cannot be resolved. I would not discuss a problem that cannot be reversed. While it seems as though a call to prayer lacks a substantial or provable reason to speak to God, it is what I must do for man. I call My children all over the world to turn to Jesus for help because so many of them are walking on the road to perdition. This is not a statement of hyperbole. I am giving the messages that Jesus wants Me to relate. I have spoken in Medjugorje about the vexation of the human spirit that comes from the callousness brought on by the barrage of violence from the world. I have said that Jesus has destroyed the effects of evil on the Cross, and all humanity must believe this. Those who are already committed to Jesus must tell the ones who have yet to decide. This is the reason I am speaking to you now. It is the same reason I approached the young maiden in 1858 and the many thousands who would reap the benefits of My extraordinary intercession in 1917. Everyone must remember that Jesus came to Sister Faustina out of Divine Love for His flock, and at times this means offering warnings and early judgements about the current state of man. You can see that many matters have gotten worse since the 1930s. *"Yes."* I do not intend to dwell on the negative in My message today, however. I did not come to do that. I have appeared to ask you to remember that you are blessed with goodness and happiness in your heart, in your companionship with Jesus, and your sharing with all the Saints the knowledge that God is in command of His Creation. These are important issues to remember for the consummate Christian."

Saturday, March 12, 2011
1:56 p.m.

"While practicing what we know to be mystical faith, we are oftentimes tested by the hollowness and difficulties of everyday life. What we accept in faith is always laid alongside what we desire the world to become. This is the connection between faith and genius, knowing they are one and the same gift for the consciousness of man. We cannot say that we walk by faith if we just stand idly by, flatfootedly holding it. We must become alive

in it, inhale and exhale its fruits, and reach-out with courage to those who might chide us for embracing what the Holy Spirit has inspired us to believe."

William L. Roth

"My little sons, you have become integrated into the genius about which you speak because you have invested and immersed your whole beings in what you believe. This is what I have been trying to teach the world since the first time I appeared before exiled men after My own Assumption and Coronation. We here in this place, this earthly place; all who are My children, the ones Jesus has chosen as His own are worthy of the brilliance that comes to us from the Sacred Heart of God. I wish for you to always remember that no matter what the future holds, you are geniuses in the Kingdom of Heaven, and your fate and fortunes that are allotted to you are products of His Sovereign Love. I have come today to pray with you for all the things I mentioned last week, and also to lend My support to your efforts in praying about your writings. I have for you today My undying Motherhood in which you have been wrapped during the coldest days of the world. I wish for you to imagine two concepts today, beauty and alliance. When you think about beauty, it is with this that your soul wishes to become allied, to it that your heart desires to be tethered. When Jesus spoke about those who would enter Heaven when He was walking the Earth, He was referring to the men and women, and yes even children, who would live with Him inside themselves as the Holy Spirit, sewn to but seamlessly united with the Father in the Divine Love through which all good things are made. Beauty consists of obedience in whatever He asks; it is a portion of your own consistency that makes you like Jesus. If you respond affirmatively to whatever comes to you, whatever besets or befalls, whatever advances and glorifies redemptive Truth, you cannot help but be unified with Jesus in His ministerial teachings, in His Passion, Crucifixion and Resurrection. If the Lord comes to you upon your requisition, it is not solely because you seek the means to an end, but because His Love is made of this. He is motivated by your summons because you recognize Him as your God. We have spoken time and again about the cause and effect relationship between Heaven and the exiled world, but nowhere is it more clear than when He answers your prayers. You see in Nature and the composition of the universe the effects of His creative power, the loving evidence of His desire to keep on begetting beautiful things. This is why Jesus was born the Son of Man. He was birthed from My Womb to make you as beautiful as Me. He has offered you a Promise and a Plan that will take you to a fuller understanding of why Adam and Eve were given life, why they were separated from Him, and why they have been regained. There is welling up in Jesus an anticipation of humanity's collective acceptance of His Glory because He manifested it through the Sacred Mysteries. And, He waits for His lost sheep to respond. It is not as though He is lurking in the shadows or preying on those who are unaware. He is not a predator looking for victims of His power. Jesus desires only to save you as one mass of creatures; this He has made completely clear. It is also clear that not all will be saved because they refuse to believe.

My Special and Chosen sons, there are theological reasons why all men must believe, and philosophical and practical ones as well. Yes, they are too numerous to count in the span of a lifetime. One would suspect that there is a greater urgency than to take that long to collect one's thoughts about the reason the Lord creates life and deals death. It is not that He has nothing better to do. We have spoken of the conversion of sinners as a process and an outcome, and the former is as important as the latter. Why? Because the former is the means by which the world is purified, the suffering comforted, and the unholy made righteous inside the confines of time. The process allows for the Word to be spread from one continent to the next, from heart to heart, from friend to foe. We have also in our grasp the realization that this process can be extremely painful because of the influence of the human will. I speak of beauty in the context of everything arriving at last at the foot of the Cross to be rectified and reconciled, but not without the alliance about which I speak can this occur. Is it possible that an alliance can be forced to be forged? Not in the case of the human will. Alliances are forged when two or more parties agree on the same issues, working toward the common good, looking in the same direction, reading from the same text, and anticipating the same outcomes. If the human heart is not given to the Holy Spirit, which is the antithesis of righteousness, there can be no alliance between that person and the God who created them. It is all according to what the heart does, whether it is receptive or closed, soft or stony, loving or calloused. I have said these things to you in other contexts, in other messages, that certainly bring this matter into focus. However, I reemphasize them here today because it is what I do. I have in multiple ways and across various themes given you the single-minded message of human love brought to bear against the vices of this world and those who will not exercise that love.

It is obvious to those in Heaven that the Earth is yet in turmoil because of the many problems that I have discussed here today. One would also assume that if these problems were previously alleviated, the Earth would stop groaning and retching; it would stop convulsing from the pain of human error; it would relax and never heave another tsunami against another shore. Its winds would lay down into soft, subtle breezes. Its volcanoes would stop erupting their fiery wrath and stand there hollow, waiting for the breath of God to cross their tops and intone the peace that a converted world deserves. There would no longer be twisters and gully washers that try to reverse the mistakes of the world's troubled lands and cleanse them of their stubbornness. Indeed, the Will of the Father speaks through Nature because God and Nature share that alliance about which I speak; and this is a beautiful union. He calls the people of the nations to join in this beauty by taking the Gospel in heart and hand, spreading the Good News where people are now agonizing and dying, and settling down in the confidence that the future has been assured by what Jesus taught in His day. There are wide and various excuses why humanity will not comply, but none of them is a viable reason for the way they behave. Just as the Book of Genesis reads, something of manifestation occurred, and it became the first day. Another event followed, and it was the second day. Humanity in exile should take a message not only from what this Creationism says, but how it was written. It is not a theory because it never had to be proved. Such is the same with the New Covenant of Redemption. The Holy Gospel has never been a theory; it has never been a subject for debate. Someone either accepts or rejects it, but they lack the mind and authority to interpret anything else they wish to include. There is no doubt or question in faith. This is the essence of what I have told all My seers and visionaries throughout the world. My Special son, one of the Medjugorje visionaries asked Me in early 1982 if I ever appeared to someone who did not already believe in God. What do you suppose was My answer? *"It is like the answer between faith and belief; how can someone receive you if they don't have any kind of belief, and how can you have an alliance with something that is not already prepared to be united."* Yes indeed, an excellent response. It harkens to the question about the chicken and the egg. My answer to that visionary was that I have appeared to many people who have had varying degrees of belief in God, but some of them were scarcely there, almost undetectable pulses of belief. These were the seers who fell to their knees hard because they had the greatest distance to travel. They needed more proof, clearer evidence that Jesus' Crucifixion was applicable to common people, those who were not practicing religious vocations or otherwise predisposed to engaging a relationship with God. They became able to see His beauty because they became allied with Him through the manifestations and suffering of Saints like Francis of Assisi. There are untold other Saints and Mystics throughout the centuries who have been marked with the signs of the Crucifixion for all around them, for miles and centuries, to grasp the idea that Jesus lived for more than the reason of faith, but to invite and foster its exercise for the betterment of the world, in this one and the next. Therefore, whenever I have spoken to unsuspecting hearers, they have taken as their role the mission of proving that they themselves were not deluded. They wished all who were high and low, far and wide to share with them the miracle of the beauty of God and the potential of man, the alliance that to this day has been the cause of so many blessings for the poor and holy alike. God will never abandon His people. It might seem like He is light-years beyond the extremes of infinity away, but this is only the perception of men. The Holy Spirit is now living inside all good men and women. The Divine Paraclete is the messenger of the Wisdom about which I have spoken here today. The Love of Heaven forges this alliance; it feeds and nourishes it like water and sunshine for a seed. Although this seems rather simplistic, it is yet unclear to the secular masses. It is a blessing that you are so attuned to the truth of righteousness, and it is even more a blessing that all who do not yet know will eventually see as you and your brother have envisioned the mightiness of the Kingdom of Love."

Saturday, March 19, 2011
8:39 a.m.

"Sacrifice is not so repugnant to those who know what redemption is, what it requires from us, what it foretells about the fulfillment of Christianity, what Jesus seeks through His own desires, and what miracles can be begotten if we trust in God. We share more than faith in the obedience of His love, but an identity that overcomes and overwhelms the undertakings of the world. When we speak about righteousness giving endurance, this is what we mean. If we spend our whole lives making judgements about the immensity of our suffering, we will become so disconcerted by it that we will miss the blessings it procures. Not all things facilitate the kind of changes we need, and this is why we must focus on how best we can see. World affairs and circumstantial events must be weighed

according to how they positively affect our faith. It helps to know what to expect, and what we are searching for. If we see wood shavings scattered on a workbench, we can safely assume that there has been a carver there, and that he has just crafted something. We likewise connect the world and Heaven by what Jesus taught us throughout His life and by the Table of Salvation He has spread before us."

William L. Roth

"Those are beautiful words, My Special son. You write them every time you pray the Rosary; everyone composes their own symphony whenever they speak to God, and their strains are expressed in many different ways, multiple ways by each individual. This is called the 'license of faith' that you are granted by the Most Blessed Trinity, and it is tactile evidence that Jesus is alive in you. When you speak of a carver or a craftsman or a carpenter, you refer to particular skills. You must remember that newborns generally lack these kinds of skills; they are matured in someone who is devoted to a particular art or ability. It all comes from the experiences of life, what moves the inner-spirit, what reaction a person receives, and how that same person looks upon himself in the greater kingdom of human life. We have all done this. I was brought up as a child knowing that I would play the part that I have offered the Lord ever since. I am not saying that I was born with the knowledge that I would bear the Son of Man in My Womb, but that My life was different from others. It is the Lord who determines and defines the scope by which His apostles and disciples live, and you have seen that I am blessed. I have always been blessed. I come today in response to your calling because this is what God has allowed Me to do. Thank you again for giving your wonderful donation to Father Ted in Kenya. Your assistance will allow many to benefit from the Love of Jesus in your heart, expressed and manifested through the life of this holy priest. I wish to say something that is of key importance. Father Ted feels the call to live and preach among the poorest of the poor, and this is what the Lord has ordained for him. As has been said many times before, those who follow Jesus do so in their own way. You have a great deal of work to do for Me, and you must remember that what you have done has brought endless blessings and waves of graces across space and time that will last until the end of days. I also told you and your brother that the greatest waste is a prayer left unsaid. This is an awkward notion because of the way I said it. How can a prayer even be a prayer if there is no one to say it? What I mean is that the Holy Spirit gives humanity the words to say, the thoughts and impressions that connect the world and the Father in Heaven. Those who belong to Him, those who will spend Eternity with Him, are already communicating through the submission of the human will and the power of the Holy Spirit. A prayer left unsaid implies that the Holy Spirit has done His part, but the person on Earth has not. This is why I am still speaking to you and your brother. We have more praying to do, seeking more prayers, pushing and lifting, moving and inspiring, dedicating and consecrating. You are living on a Saturday morning in March 2011, and Saint Joseph is interceding for you especially today. I wish for humanity to remember Saint Joseph today more than they might recall the initiation of a foreign war. (War in Iraq officially launched today in 2003.) I have said to My visionaries worldwide that historical anniversaries should be held deep inside the heart for the way they assist the propagation of the Gospel, not whether they advanced any peculiar causes of man, especially secular ones. My messages this year have been of projection, reflection, hope and inspiration. When you look upon all My messages throughout the years, they have all had these same themes. Projection means that you advance Jesus' teachings to your brothers and sisters by everything you do, all that My children accomplish around the globe every day. Reflection means that you live in a state of gratitude for the gifts the Lord has given you. This means that you, all of My children, pray for whatever you need to complete the work He has assigned to you on His behalf. Inspiration is what we are doing right now.

    We are inspired to speak this way because the Father's Kingdom is completely alive. There is nothing dead in Heaven. There is nothing on Earth belonging to Him that is dead. All life springs from His Love, and all thankfulness is generated through His always-living, never failing sanctity deposited into the heart. You have life to the fullest according to the ways you have been taught, the means by which you have been reared and sustained throughout your life. I am speaking now about all people. If not for the Love of God given through parents and guardians, little children everywhere would not grow into the mature adults who have taken the reigns of leadership in nations far and wide. This is the message, the legacy especially of Saint Joseph. You have written today about a carver and his wood shavings. Do you suppose that Saint Joseph taught little Jesus how to work with wood? "*Yes.*" Of course he did. My spouse was a man of unique character in that he was as simple of heart as Jesus; he offered himself and his talents to someone who already owned all the talents in the universe. I have said that this is the reciprocation of the

Second Person of the Trinity. I saw these things with My own eyes. Jesus is present in this day not only in the masterful homilies of great priests and Cardinals, but His innocence can be found in a baby in a crib. You know that My Son's life spanned from Conception to birth, from adolescence into adulthood, just as all men do. There is nothing you have ever thought, nothing you have ever feared, nothing that ever tempted you that Jesus did not experience before you. His vision as a 12-year-old boy in the Temple taught the others who would listen that there would come a world fraught with peril and embattled in materialism. He told them that there would be terrorism and impurities, machines and artifacts that would distract the masses from reaching-out to the poor. He said that there would be centuries in which humankind would all but turn their backs en masse on the teachings and doctrines that were meant to purify and enlighten those who are far from God. Priests and nuns would be impugned and martyred. The sacredness of the Cross would be expelled from educational institutions. Does this sound familiar? *"Yes."* I am telling you that Jesus' lessons in the Temple were reflective of what He saw in His day, and this continues to be His day. He is still teaching the world about the Kingdom of God through the Church and Me. You see that I have relied on many visionaries throughout the centuries to be My help in relaying everything the Father wants humanity to know in multiple places and languages. I hope you realize that your prayers are your most powerful gift to God. Although your acts of kindness, your writings, and your good intentions are important to His Kingdom, it is your prayers that He desires most. I have tried to make this clear, especially in My Medjugorje messages. While they are simple in their text, they have resounding meaning when taken seriously in the heart. Your brother is taking his approach to his labors the same as you, one day at a time. You are given life this way because it is simpler, more capable of being grasped by the heart and mind, and more efficient in making small steps toward meaningful strides. I bless you and your brother for the way you live. You cannot possibly know how admired you are by Myself, Jesus and the whole of Heaven. There are times when the great Saint Joseph weeps thankful tears because you and your brother love Me and My Son with such devotion."

Saturday, March 26, 2011
2:43 p.m.

"The qualities of holiness, honor, fairness and kindness are attributable to the thoughts and actions of those who understand virtuosity as magnified by the New Covenant Gospel. Cognitive intelligence does not necessarily imply true wisdom, but beatific vision sure does. Although the consequences of random genius sporadically changes lives, it cannot reinvent them the way human love renews. Not all knowledge advances this reconciliation, and therefore cannot be equated with true universal power. The highest honor we can render Jesus Christ is to live His love with dignity and announce His presence before those who are walking in error."

William L. Roth

"My dear little children, it is indeed My honor as well to come bestow My blessing on your lives and works, your hearts and holy meditations. What you have written here above, My Special son, is reflective of the genius that we have spoken about, not the super-intelligence of the world, but the true Wisdom of Truth that created the Earth and established the framework by which it has been redeemed. It is true that a mother can be proud, and your Mother in Heaven has righteous admiration, gladness that is of old, that you adhere to the principles by which the first Apostles lived. I likewise come to you because we must continue to earnestly pray together for those who have not yet grasped the urgency to convert; not to live fastly or move so quickly that they fail to invoke the beauty of Nature and all that is sublime, but urgent in the sense that they will not be able to reverse their own damage if they decline Heaven's offerances now. Today, I have come to speak to you about the world of which I see, one that is lacking in the eternal beauty that lives inside the heart of Christians. Especially here in the United States, people, societies, mediums and governments make a fortune in wealth peddling fear. They say, 'Look out for what is going to happen to you next!' in the hope that people will invest their money in whatever they believe will alleviate their fears. There is taunting and fear-mongering about what poverty might come, or what wars or dark impressions will take away their freedoms of life. There is so much fear being marketed in America that there is hardly any spiritual stability left. People are being told to be afraid of their neighbors and strangers down the block. Day after day, the television coverage and newspaper articles are rife with frightening stories about what ills will befall the innocent and unsuspecting. Please do not mistake My motives; there are certainly things that you must be wary of, but you can see the everyday peddling of fear that drifts across the airwaves any time of day. This fear sells. Fear gets people's attention. Television producers troll your world wide web and local press lines looking for frightening news that they can spread across their screens and headlines to get people to take notice. Why? So they can boast to their advertisers how many people they reach, what age and ethnic demographics are watching, and where the most effective markets are found. Again I declare, it is prudent to be on guard against things that will harm you, but the media executives that you have spoken about so truthfully in the past are only making things worse.

My Special and Chosen ones, this is nothing new that I am telling you now, but I implore you to not get caught in this web of hype. The celebration of fighting and division by nearly every venue in America and around the globe is troubling, to say the least. Where is the truth? It is in the Peace of God. And, the Peace of God is everywhere that the American media are not. They are loath to speak about this issue because their viewers and listeners might not be afraid anymore. I ask you to keep your hearts aloft with Jesus, with Saint Joseph and Myself, with all the heavenly hosts in whom your lives are invested. Oh! I do enjoy a good debate. This is not what I am talking about. When admirable public people and advisers take to the airwaves and debate the issues of the day, this is good interpersonal discourse. When someone 'in the know' writes a new book about the political landscape in the United States and speaks intelligently about it on television, that is a good means to discover what is really going on. This is not creating fear as such, it is simply allowing you to see what issues are being distorted to create that fear. It is oftentimes difficult to discern the truth from the lies because there is so much dialogue going on simultaneously. Do you remember the early words from the lips of the newly-elected Pope John Paul II? 'Do not be afraid!' What did he mean by this? He was referring to invoking the power of the Holy Spirit against anyone who peddles fear. He meant to trust God at all times. He prayed that if God does not Will to have suffering to be removed, then please give the sufferer the courage not to be afraid. He was speaking about shouting-out the Gospel from the rooftops without being afraid of being mocked and ridiculed. Pope John Paul II knew what I am going to tell you now. It is not unnatural or an indication of a lack of faith to fear some things in this world. However, the invocation of the Holy Spirit should give you inspiration to know that at least suffering is changing something wrong into something right, wiping-out darkness and shining The Light. It is proof that simple people can become those gladiators that we have often spoken about. It was John Paul II himself who had to overcome so much fear in his young life and in his Papacy that made him the prime example of courage incarnate. Here today, My sons, all around the world, people are accorded the opportunity to disavow fear in whatever they do, wherever they reach-out from their homes by wire and letter, by prayer and petition, to instill in their brothers and sisters the vision about which you have written earlier today. It is not necessary that every Christian become a martyr, but overcoming fear is a form of martyrdom itself. It means that no matter what happens to me – suffering, persecution, prosecution, execution, whatever; I will face it because the Spirit of the Lord lives in me. There is too much meekness in a way that was not spoken about by Jesus in the Sermon on the Mount. It is not ethereal meekness to refuse to rebuke Catholics who have turned away from the Church. This takes courage, and courage that shall be rewarded on the last day. The lessons and teachings of Jesus Christ are all humanity needs to see from here to there. We have spoken about the power of prayer many times, and it is the only way to connect to the Will of the Father.

My Special one, there are so many hasty decisions made by the Church elders and others who are in positions of power that should have been given more time. Roman Catholic parishioners whom you have met have led innocent people astray by speaking about such things as neutral inclusive language and falsely appropriated rights to choose. This is a case where they should have feared what the Lord would do to them, but they did not do so. It was not that they are unafraid, but that they do not care; they have a fallacious sense of what the Gospel teaches. They have lost sight of the fact that Satan can influence them and others through their thoughts and actions. They adopt premise after premise that is not stationed in the foundation of true Christianity. They have allowed relativism and collectivism to skew their perception of what the Kingdom of God should look like. This is truly what they should be afraid of, not any kind of physical or emotional suffering they might endure. Every one of the prefaces you have written for your books makes this point clear, and I am highly pleased by your taking the effort to do so. A good man once said that, 'Now we are engaged in a great Civil War.'

This same man lay dead because he sought to end it. I am speaking to a world that is engaged in a war against itself, the splitting of the good from the bad, while the good should remain imbedded with the bad to teach them right from wrong. Even if they are shunned, they should not be afraid; they should ask God for the miracles they need. If this engagement does not occur, the good and the bad will lay dead together. In closing today, your brother is still under horrendous evil attacks that he is dealing with the best he can. You are his harbor and strength during these moments because you have allowed Jesus to enter your heart. It is not only your brother who is enduring these attacks. It has occurred over the centuries to many good souls. We must ensure that we pray for all who are enduring hardship, disease, poverty, wars and suffering of all kinds. This is the same renewal that you have spoken about in your opening writing today about the power of human love."

Sunday, April 3, 2011
8:37 a.m.

"We are poised for Salvation because God's Holy Spirit gives us hearts capable of faith. What does this mean? How do we focus on all things eternal while exiled yet today? Surely it is the combination of an inward and outward vision that helps us see invisible things like divine love, hope, peace of mind and a holiness that unifies us with all true believers around the globe. It is a redefining impulse that says that our lives can be beatific in the here and now. This is what Jesus told the Apostles. Live the message of redemption at dawn and anticipate its fulfillment before nightfall arrives. This is not too much to ask of a world whose completion was wrought by the Passion and Crucifixion of one Immaculate Man."

William L. Roth

"Hello, My dear little sons. I come with joy and compassion for all you are giving Jesus and the Kingdom of Salvation. You know more than anyone else the sacrifices you have made to arrive at this day. We cannot avoid whatever else you must endure to promulgate this redemption because this is the way sinners are converted. My Special son, I pray that you understand the grotesque intensity of the images your brother has described to you. They are visions so abhorrent that no human should ever be forced to endure them. However, your body of work is more than human. It is the greatest deposit of messages from the Mother of God that humanity has ever seen. This is because of your love for Jesus, for Me, for the Church, and for your desire for the Salvation of all exiled men. It is due and proper that you tell your brother that his suffering creates an atmosphere where good can be accomplished in other places. I have said that the attacks against you and your brother are doing this. I am so happy that you have taken such an interest in your little motorbike because it makes you think of those innocent days in America that seem so far gone. You are doing with the mini-bike what I am trying to do with the souls of America. They must be dismantled, cleaned, repaired, replaced, resurfaced and reassembled with the care that Jesus has for all whom He has healed. This is the preface to the Salvation that you spoke about in your writing earlier today. Let us look at it again. 'Poised for Salvation by an inward and outward vision.' Imagine what the great Doctors of the Church would have given to be able to create a quotation like this one; and yet you have. There are so many dimensions to this quotation that they cannot be covered with the pen. In order for someone to be poised for something, it must be offered to them, and they must accept. The possibility must be there. You and I know that all possibilities have come through the Grace of God; there is nothing impossible with Him. It is written in the Scriptures. And, the inward vision means that the Holy Spirit has cast the shadow of Truth deep within your heart and soul, and you are able to reproduce this vision by your words and actions. The latter is the outward vision. It is righteousness given venue by the human heart. We have also said that this is a process, not a single event. It implies the consumption, the passing of time. This time is available in the world, and humanity's journey through it is what is ongoing now. It makes for a logical culture in which the conversion of lost sinners can be achieved. The atmosphere and environment required for God-seeking people has been provided in this world by the Holy Spirit, by Jesus' life and legacy, and by the mission and effectiveness of the Roman Catholic Church. Too many souls to count have made the best of this venue, thank God; and they have inherited their reward of Heaven as a result. We have spoken about the element of time, and one should also consider the concept of timing. Scripture also says that there is a time for everything under the sun. You know the Ecclesiastes verse about this. Timing is important for the work that God set out to do when He first dispatched the Angels to the Earth in days of old, when the Archangel Gabriel came to Me, and so forth. This same aspect of timing applies to the propagation of My Morning Star messages around the globe.

You and your brother must begin to see life more a day at a time. I wish for you to know that you are blessed in more ways than are easily recognized. When I say that 'you' are blessed, I am referring to humanity entire. I ask you to think about what terrible conditions have been faced in places like Haiti and Japan. *(The disaster at Fukushima Daiichi Nuclear Plant in Japan occurred on March 11, 2011. The Haiti earthquake struck on January 12, 2010.)* Please assist Me in praying for all whose lives are broken and in shambles. There is so much destruction, poverty, disease, lack of food and shelter, and every other kind of deprivation. You can see the terrible prospects of the nuclear disaster in Japan as a result of the tsunami. Compared to all this, the people in the United States live in elevated comfort. You still have running water, plenty of food, medical care, and all the other blessings you are afforded because you are citizens of this land of plenty. This is what most Americans are reluctant to see. You have never shown that you are blind to what I am saying; it is those who are powerful and affluent, the people who walk down Hollywood boardwalks and night-club ramps who are ignorant of the suffering in the world. All of these matters are being addressed, My Special son. Jesus knows what is happening. He is aware of the distance so many millions must travel to be close to Him. You and your brother are to be highly commended for already being one with Him in all the ways the Father wants you to be. Even though there are awful things happening around the globe, there is peace and sublimeness here. You have pretty hearts of love and hope. You have taken-up your weapons of war against Satan's evil. You have the Cross, the Holy Rosary, your Holy Water, and plenty of icons and relics of the Saints. I applaud you for not surrendering the fight. *"I ask you to remember the lady at work who lost her son."* All of Heaven is sending her condolences and spiritual strength. You can imagine that such a loss is one of the most gruesome kinds of suffering anyone can undergo – you know that I understand what she is enduring. Thank you again for your pretty prayers. I will be with you always with the Child Jesus in My arms."

Sunday, April 10, 2011
8:50 a.m.

"Dear Lord Jesus, you are the Incarnation of infinite goodness having come into the physical world for our reconciliation. You have chased away the darkness with your Heraldic Light. You have awakened and purified your people to whom you have dedicated your life. Let our prayers reach your ears from our lowly place in exile, where you watch over us and make way for our entrance into your Eternal Kingdom. We ask that you remember us when you come again, and never allow us to stray from your side. Keep us forever holy; be our beatific conscience as we walk this narrow path. We pray for all souls who have found you, for the millions who are still seeking, and especially for those who turn their backs on you. It is only through your heavenly grace that we can guide them into your sacred presence. Amen."

William L. Roth

"My dear little children, you cannot weigh the Glory of God, but the measure of good men is taken by how well they respond to Him. It is during moments and hours of prayer that God and man are most completely united, especially during the Holy Sacrifice of the Mass. We have found together a special purpose. Myself and humanity are united with the Most Holy Trinity through our love for God. Jesus has made this possible by His Incarnation. Please know that He is always beside you; the Holy Spirit is inside you, and God the Father is watching from His place in Heaven. Today, I wish for My words to be a prayer like the one you, My Special son, have offered to begin in greeting. Here, you have cited the origin of human peace and forgiveness. You are hailing the Plan of Salvation that the Lord put into place centuries ago. When you ask Jesus to keep all men holy as they walk the narrow path, it would seem that you are putting constrictions on their conduct. However, we know it to be completely the opposite. You ask My Son to set the world free from sin, keeping them from wandering aimlessly in places that have nothing to do with the righteousness to which they are called. You are asking Jesus to keep your brothers and sisters from needlessly expending their energies on the distractions of life. The Father commends those who pray to keep humanity on the right and proper course. Remember that whatever is true, just and excellent must be pursued by exiled humanity on Earth; and this is never easy.

We have spoken about everything that tries to inhibit the progress of lost sinners to the Cross. Satan attempts at every turn to keep them away, to drive a wedge between the holier sights of people around the globe and achieving those sights in a span of a life. The punishment and defeat we have imposed upon Satan is a vast victory for those people and the Church. It would not appear that we have done so, but we have nullified untold numbers of evil acts that would have come. I believe that all My children should follow your lead; they should see Creation not only the way it was made, but the way it ought to eventually become. My Special son, you should be thankful that you have a courageous spirit, that there are only few things that you actually fear. This, in itself, is a gift from God.

I would also like to speak today about priests who every day must keep their eyes trained on their vocations. They are even more assailed by Satan than anyone else in the world. They are victims of his assaults that would drive them from the priesthood. He tempts them with pleasure of the flesh and taunts them because they decline. Evil works impose horrendous physical and mental suffering on priests all around the globe. Why? Because Satan is their enemy. The Consecrated Host in their hands is his nemesis. If humanity only knew what priests endure in their years of life, they would fall to their knees in pity. The priests are the most suffering ones. No other person from any walk of life carries the burden of the Roman Catholic priest. Sadly, some of them do fall to temptation because they are human as well. The devil's wicked ways capture them off-guard during their weaker moments, and even as they sleep. Jesus helps them as much as they will allow. The fight rages on through the day and into the evening hours, while they still tend to Jesus' flock. You have written in 'White Collar Witch Hunt' everything else I might add to their story. This is why we must continue to pray for them. My Special and Chosen ones, the priests need us; they need our support and intercessions. You have seen how they are mocked and ridiculed. They are held to standards that are incapable of any other men. They are lonely at times, even despondent and devastated, because they have given their lives to the Cross, and they then see so many millions of people who refuse to recognize that the Crucifixion of the Son of Man ever occurred. We have spoken about impulses and priorities before. Long have been our discussions about what good men must do to engage the bad. The Holy Spirit assists where this goodness is allowed, and it is propagated best when holy people turn to prayer for help. When you pray the Rosary, you lift-up the priests. You rededicate their lives to the Church;

you mend their divisions and heal their hearts. Your prayers make them shine in the dark, dreary world. This is what I am asking from all My children today, no matter where they live, whatever continent is their home, no matter if they are black or white. Prayer is the answer to all the problems of man. We have known this since we were all conceived. Let us thank God that this is true.

My Special son, Satan is poised to strike you and your brother as punishment for your 'Morning Star' deposit of works; the most comprehensive, persuasive, converting and enlightening series of written documents to be placed into the hands of humankind. The Gospel is the Truth; it is the magnetism to which all men must be drawn. Morning Star Over America is a compass that will lead them there. This is why Satan has been trying to punish you since long before My messages ever began, years and two decades before that. I will pray My best to ask God to preserve you. You and your brother must dwell on the positive, on the greatness that you are showing the rest of the world, on the joy that the Hosts of Heaven are having seeing you work. You should remember that you live in the most prosperous and free nation on the globe. You have the right to propagate your faith and My messages without fear of being arrested and incarcerated. Few other Americans feel strongly enough about what I have to say to stake a claim on your lives. Only Satan is that angry; it is he who works through faithless people. Please do not feel as though your brother is not strong because of his reaction to these attacks. The attacks on him are real; they do exist. They are as three-dimensional and fiercely intense as anything a human being could experience. He has this ongoing at the same time he is enduring his physical injuries and the stress from his homework for college. I am happy even in light of all this. I am elated because Satan is so afraid of what we have done. He knows its power as well as anyone else because its entire purpose is to defeat what he might do. In fact, your works can actually reverse the previous evil acts that Satan has committed. That makes this a very good day."

Saturday, April 16, 2011
2:36 p.m.

> *"There is so much goodness unfolding around the world, so much hope and inspiration, if we know where to find it, and so much potential for joy in all things comely and beautiful. We are God's gift to one another, with helping hands and consoling hearts; we are friends of spiritual confidence and the extension of everything holy that humanity has the foundation to become. There is nothing maudlin about this. I have always said that if you show me a man who never weeps, I will show you a man devoid of compassion. In this sense, innocence does not imply vulnerability."*
>
> William L. Roth

"Welcome to the joy of My Most Immaculate Heart! My little sons, love in the way of human compassion is what holiness is all about; it thrives in you by way of the Holy Spirit and instills in you the desire to make the world right according to the teachings of Jesus. I wish for you on this birthday of Pope Benedict XVI that you will pray for him, and please also remember to invoke the intercession of Saint Bernadette and Saint Alta, who was born 90 years ago today. It is true that you have a grand procession of Saints who are seeking the Lord's favor on your behalf. I need not remind you that your prayers are never in vain. I trust in you because you trust in Jesus. This is why I have come to convey to you in comprehensible terms what your daily lives have become, as have all who follow in the footsteps of the Messiah. My Special son, the words you offered at the beginning of this message are particularly heart-touching for Me because I have constantly called My little children to seek-out the good, strive toward the joy that is given to you in My Son. Indeed, the innocence that you are called to embrace is likewise the image of genius that you imitate every time you think about what Jesus would do if in your particular situation. Righteous innocence means that you are wise beyond your years in the knowledge of prudence and temperance. I have watched all My little children grow and mature throughout the ages, century by century, generation to generation, and day by day. It is inside the expanse of one day that you can glean what you must know to touch your lost brothers and sisters, not that it is a window large enough to capture the fullness of Eternal Glory with one thought, but that you are capable of adhering every moment to the Wisdom that teaches all men right from wrong. It is in these moments, My sons, that you ponder what you must do to satisfy your own expectations of yourselves in reflection of the lessons and teachings from Heaven. This is, therefore, another good day. I have consistently told you that you are gifts to one another, just as you have written today. This is the message that men should reveal to each other in prayer and throughout the interaction of the everyday world. Life should be a constant reminder that people are special; they are God's creatures that are still broken and fearful. I have been trying to teach them to find their healing and consolation in Jesus, and you have assisted Me in this task.

My sons, you are about to enter Holy Week 2011. I wish to make specific My intentions for you today, and I declare that you are fit for the blessings that Jesus gives every soul at Easter. You are to observe the Easter Triduum by way of the Vatican. You know that I have given you special blessings because of the awesome suffering you have known on behalf of Jesus through your years of recording My messages. At the same time, you should feel free to attend the Easter Mass at St. Joseph Church not very far from here. You endure the burdens of Lent the whole year through! You sacrifice daily for the work you have set out to do in healing the sick and praying for the masses. You are working diligently in your goals whereby you are forced to engage secular leaders. This is never an easy task because they do not think like we do. Do you recall what has been said? 'God's Kingdom is not of this world,' but we are trying to make this the world of His Kingdom. This is what I meant when I once told you that people should not look glibly upon one another. They should seek peace and pardon; they should rely on the credentials of the suffering-poor who are closest to Jesus; these are the ones who are vested with the power to bring down mighty kings! And, they will. I assure you that they wield tremendous and stupendous power before the Great High Priest because they are beautiful in His sight. Those around you who walk by sight do not understand the faith that you have embraced. They are fumbling, stumbling and bumbling through their lives, ignorant of the Truth that will set them free from the chains of their sins. They use quips and quotes to explain-away the most awe-striking miracles that humanity has ever seen. They resort to their pragmatic frameworks and haughty imperialism in an attempt to reclaim the composure they have lost when laying the record of their lives alongside that of Jesus Christ. They will eventually find themselves whimpering about what might have come to them if only they had listened. This is why I ask My children to be so filled with the joy about which you have spoken in your opening writing today. The ones who have already beheld the Grace of God inside their hearts are those who will be filled to elation with His beatific Truth. When I speak about potential for you today, I reecho what you have written as well. It is the joy that you have already found. You are envied by those who are far from God because they cannot understand why you are so happy walking toward a Kingdom you have not yet seen. Oh! – you have heard and felt this Glory already! You have tasted its sweetness in the Bread of the Altar. You have touched the Face of God in your suffering, just as Jesus suffered and died on the Cross. These are the ultimate foreshadows of your destiny in Him, and you are to be envied for this. It is true that those who have yet to accept Him are lacking everything they require for attaining the joy you have known.

I do not wish to dismiss the deepness of your suffering. I never want you to believe that God takes for granted your acceptance and bearing of the crosses you have carried. There will be more; this is true for all who are yet in exile on Earth. And, it is not so much what comprises these crosses that matters, but how you react to them. Here again, I say 'you react' when referring to all humanity. I watched My Son suffer and die for a world that rejected Him in every sense of the word, but He did it anyway. Why? Because He knew that it would please the Father. Does this not openly reveal that whatever pleases the Father must ultimately be good? Common people everywhere would be extremely surprised to know what actually pleases the Father. Is this not the same God who called for strict punishment, executions and all other kinds of vengeance? And, is this not also Him who has asked for pardon and mercy? Why is there a contradiction? Because the Father is the ultimate source of the judgement of man. He knows the hearts of all who live and die, of everyone who breathes and exhales his last, of all who are close or much too far from Him. He decides the degrees of sin that are actually forgivable, and through whom His justice shall be meted out. This is the same Father who gave life to all of us, and to His Son, and to the Earth and Nature and all the universes. It is for the Glory of the Father that the Son was Crucified, Died and was Buried, and was raised from the dead on the Third Day. This is the Deity in one Savior, and it is to this Godhead that all men must come to be given life eternal in Heaven or otherwise be felled by the Sword of Justice and sent to the flaming inferno of Hell. My Special son, your memoir is taking form beautifully. I am overwhelmingly pleased by your innocence; and not the vulnerability that comes with other innocence, but the kind of innocence that makes your spiritual purity observable to all who will read what you have written. Do you remember the paradox that says that some things are so obvious that no one notices them? *"Yes."* What makes this paradox come to pass? How can something be that obvious, and yet no one see it? Let us consider an example. What percentage of the world's population looks at the sun every day or the moon at night if there are no clouds? *"Most."* You are saying that they actually take time out of their day to look at the sun? *"I guess many just take it for granted."* Yes, hardly anyone bothers to look to see where the sun is located in the sky. They just know that it is light outside. The point I am making is that it is not until it becomes dark in the middle of the day that they notice that it is not there. They see clouds in the air instead of shadows on the ground. They come to expect that the sun is up there, though. It is the middle of the day in symbolic terms for many who have yet to find their way to the Cross, and they are unsure whether there is any light beyond the clouds. This is why I have come to so many seers and messengers around the globe. I have said in many of My messages that the night is coming, and the dawn will follow. Do you remember the quotation you once recorded about this? 'Go ye all of you into the darkness and conquer the night. Bring back the morning sun.' This is what you and your brothers and sisters in Jesus have been doing, and it is always more prolifically expressed during the celebration of Holy Week. I ask of you and your brother that you remember in your hearts, deep inside you where your thoughts rarely go, that you are loved by God in ways that cannot be described. There simply are no words to help you understand. The Father calls upon you through the Son to be assured that the Holy Spirit will never leave you orphaned. This is what your memoir must make clear to the secular world."

Easter Sunday, April 24, 2011
8:59 a.m.

"It is possible to see how bountifully we are blessed. All Creation makes it known. The limitless brilliance of our Christian faith tells us that this is true, as does the eloquence of the heart and the laudatory meditations we submit to the Father by way of contemplative prayer. Everything we do in Jesus' name resounds His divinity within us, extolled and projected through our pious reflections begotten by the undying wisdom that the Holy

Spirit deposits inside us. Humanity could not escape the veracity of the New Covenant Gospel if we tried. Whether everyone accepts this truth is quite another matter."

William L. Roth

"My good-hearted sons, the Easter Joy that has come belongs to you because you are the disciples of the Messiah whose Paschal Resurrection you celebrate today. All the world is shining in this Love, in the Sacred Peace and knowledge that Jesus Christ indeed rose on the Third Day. You gain more than you know by recalling what this victory means. You also realize what Jesus had to endure before He was laid to rest to rise from the Tomb on Easter. Today, I come with a simple blessing and a few words of good will. I have no lessons or grand eloquence to add to your overwhelming knowledge of what Easter means to humanity. This is a heraldic day, and yet a simple one. It implies that all who are lost can be found; everyone who is hovering in darkness can stand tall in the Lord's Divine Light. You have seen and heard the homilies of Pope Benedict XVI about the subsistence of Creation beneath God's eternal reign, and he has made clear that you have achieved the status of worthy servants in His Kingdom. This is most of all a prayer for thanksgiving, to remember all the blessings you have received. As I have said in the past, human beings are gifts to one another because you sustain the whole communion of goodness as one body. This is why those who are lost in darkness must be brought into the Light. It is the reason that all people must renounce Satan and his evil works. The first four words of the Apostle's Creed say it all. 'I believe in God…' There is so much power and grace in these words that they cannot be captured on a page; they cannot be explained to those who refuse to believe. You have heard about the stories of Christmases past, and so it goes with Easter. However, Easter carries its own newness as it comes in the spring; the Earth and Nature are awakening again, the animals are rising from their winter sleep, the breezes and sun rays are fairer and brighter. This is indicative of the awakening of the human spirit upon the occasion of Easter. It is symbolic of the end of the suffering of men and the reward that awaits them once they have endured the battle. My children, I have given you many high-toned messages about Easter throughout the years, and I bid you to remember some of them when you reflect upon this day. We have a great deal to ponder when we consider what Easter means to those who believe in their hearts in the fullness of the Lord's Absolution. It is about renewal and recommitment; it refers to the overflowing jubilation that one feels when he has been liberated from the incarcerating chains of human sin and brought to the mountaintop of redemption.

I ask you today to believe Me when I tell you that the conditions in the world are no worse than in centuries and generations past. They are simply a different kind of unseemliness. There have always been tragedies, wars, natural disasters, desecration and unholiness. You are only now hearing about what is happening in your day as though everything that occurred before you were born never took place. The fact is, you are seeing some rather opportune changes around the world that are making way for the success of the Holy Gospel. I hope you consider what it means to have participated in this Age of Grace, in this period in history when I have spoken to so many seers and hearers in so many nations, in so many locations. You have seen My appearances and apparitions dismissed as coincidence and fanaticism, but never mind those comments. You have heard about the new definition of the term 'cult' used pejoratively because it is associated with darkness and alarmism. There will be many more words that you will hear, many attempts to explain-away what the Holy Spirit has done, to ignore the signs that God has placed along the road on which all are traveling in any direction but toward the Cross. Especially on Easter, be joyful that Jesus is getting their attention. Know deep in your hearts that the peace and compassion of Easter will touch them once they have tasted their share of the Cross. There are songs and speeches aplenty waiting for them at the end of their journey. Indeed, you have written some of the lyrics and strains for these songs and speeches. You still harbor many more in your hearts that you will commit to the page in future times. It is My distinct privilege to tell Jesus that you have come to Him through Me, that His recognition of you as My adopted children on Good Friday has borne incalculable fruits for the betterment of the world. This is what we do together; it has been My mission throughout the ages and during the most stressful times for mortal man. We march onward through the thickets to the Triumph of My Immaculate Heart in which you are deeply seeded. Thank you for your willingness to give your lives for the conversion of the lost, and thank you for responding to My call.

My Special one, it is particularly My pleasure to greet you and your brother today as I appear around the globe to offer My blessing to the millions who have been loyal to Jesus. Each of you have your own means of honoring Him during the Easter Triduum as you do during other celebrations of the year. Yours have been special this time because you watched all three hours of the Holy Father's service to the Church in Rome. You and your brother received his Papal blessing along with all who appointed themselves to witness the Holy Saturday events. You said later in the evening that it was a good day. I echo this sentiment with all the fervor I can muster. Your brother continues to be assailed by horrendous evil attacks that are real in nature to him, not unlike the Saints you have mentioned. He will simply do the best he can. *"How can they be mitigated?"* How can what be mitigated? *"How can he be delivered from these things?"* By recanting and renouncing everything he has done over the past twenty years. This is never going to happen. *"He will never deny you."* It is so gracious of you to comfort him when he is enduring these demonic attacks. He is doing the best he can. He prays a great deal more than before, and he depends on your prayers as well. You know that it is only through the grace of God that he will prevail over these attacks. You must always remind him to take life one day at a time. Why? Because this will allow him to endure these attacks as individualized events. You have seen that life's dailiness has been a blessing for many souls who focus only on any given day's problems. If they do not, it would be too overwhelming for them. There will be periods during the year when your brother will not be bothered by these attacks at all. He knows what he has to do. It is obvious that your love for him is as overwhelming as Jesus' Love. I cannot tell you how much you are honored in Heaven for this. The key component of this year is to allow your Bishop to continue the discernment process of your books and messages, and this is the reason your brother is under such attack. I have told you this before. Again, I ask you both to not focus on the end of the year or anything the Bishop might do or say, but to live your lives simply, one day at a time. Take whatever comes in those measurable doses about which I speak. And, as Saint Pio once said, strive to be happy; pray and do not worry. There will be good days and ones that are not as good. This is the way of life for every soul on Earth. You and your brother are no exception. Do you understand how much you are loved? *"Yes."* It must be something that you internalize to an infinite degree. God loves you, Jesus loves you, and I love you. All of us pour-out this love upon you and the whole world through the power of the Holy Spirit. There is endless grace and bounty in these things for all who believe. Thank you for your heartfelt prayers for all who are far from God, for the ones who are suffering, for the lonely and afraid, and for the infirm and homebound. And, especially thank you for praying for the welfare of the unborn. Please enjoy the Light of Easter!"

Saturday, April 30, 2011
2:25 p.m.

> "We often search for words to describe our dilemmas, ways to express how we feel about the condition of the world's soul – if it has one, so that we can find a means to inspire it, touch it, heal it, and comfort it. This is really what is missing among the nations. We are never wholly shed of sorrow because many of us have not completely opened to Our Lord's Resurrection. Our years are more about process than consummation. It is how we get to the destination that matters most, whether we make the right decisions that determine how fruitfully we live. Let there be no mistake; life is no vacation, but it need not be a toilsome experience in futility. We have credentials and principles inherent to all those who believe in God, and we can invoke them spontaneously at any moment, whenever circumstances demand it."
>
> William L. Roth

"Now, My dear little sons, your Mother has come to bless you and pray with you for every reason you have spoken about. You are in the battle that is determining who shall inherit the Fruits of Heaven, and whom shall be cast into Hell. We are skillfully reciting our prayers with focus, knowing upon whom the Lord is shining His Divine Light in places that have heretofore never known Him. I ask you today to remember that the cultivation of the Earth into the likeness of Heaven is an arduous process, one filled with many snares that Satan has set in your path. We are here again today to celebrate the Easter Resurrection of Jesus for another year, as you know that it is perpetually celebrated both in Heaven and Earth throughout the year and all eternity. Today, My Immaculate Heart is dwelling on the many who have recently entered the Church sacramentally, who have converted from other religions, some of whom have come to the Church after having practiced no religion at all. My Special son, you have mentioned them recently in your daily conversations with your brother and in your prayers because you know the importance of their faith, that it must be strong and be nourished by the love and dedication of all who surround them. You are also painfully aware that some who have been lifelong parishioners are leaving the faith because of the disciplines required in remaining true to the teachings of the Church. They meet other people who lure them away from the Holy Eucharist, some by infatuation and matrimony outside the Roman Catholic Church. I join in your concern for them, and I add My prayers to yours and your brother's that they will return to the fold. There will be a grand and glorious celebration upon the beatification of Pope John Paul II because he has been so admired by the faithful around the world. He has inspired many new vocations and led people from all walks of life, all thoughts and intentions, with various backgrounds and education to the Holy Eucharist. He has inspired the young to remain strong in their faith when others have attempted to take them down dark secular avenues. And most of all, Pope John Paul the Great has delivered millions of men, women and children to the warm embrace of My Immaculate Heart, inspiring them to pray the Holy Rosary faithfully every day.

I also wish to say today that your Bishop here in the Springfield Diocese continues to be the warrior whom you have come to know. He is aware of the significance of My role in this Diocese, and he has great devotion to Me as the Mother of the Church. I ask you to pray for all Bishops everywhere, that they will be strong and dutiful in completing their charge in their various locations, leading their flocks with sincerity and holiness. You can see that this is a crucial time for the Church when you read your Bishop's recent editorial column in the diocesan newspaper. Imagine what it must be like for Pope Benedict XVI to see the world in such turmoil, with such destructive secular forces attempting to inhibit the mission of the Church. He is also aware as painfully as you that there have been untold numbers who have wandered astray, taken away from the Sacraments by the lure of other influences. We pray that all who see this Pope will recognize that his is a significant Pontificate for these perilous times. Consider all the wars that are occurring around the globe that hardly anyone mentions. There is still fighting in the Middle East where Americans and others are guarding and dying. Some of the nations of Africa are coming completely unraveled. The two Koreas are fighting again, and the natural disasters that made such headlines in Haiti and Japan are still taking a toll on the residents there. Indeed, there are myriads of places for which the prayers of the faithful are needed – I am not telling you anything new. I am only asking you and your brother to join Me. The Lord God does not deign that people should suffer needlessly. You have known this for decades. You have excellent vision and perspective about what such suffering does. It has not come yet to you in ways that it has others, but you are still aware of what it means. We in the Church are rightfully concerned that those who suffer are incapable of placing it into perspective in the ways the Church teaches. You and your Bishop are correct when you say that suffering is not punishment for sin. Jesus expunged that punishment on the Cross. Human suffering is the opposite of punishment; it is the elevation and dignifying of all who have decided for God, for the many who have yet to make that decision, and for those who are themselves weighing the burdens of the Cross in their daily lives. Please remember that God loves you. He sends His Spirit every day to remind you. Here again, when I say you, I am referring to humanity entire.

    I wish to speak again about the demonic attacks that are happening to your brother by the visions and circumstances he is undergoing. Yes, they are like those endured by Saint Pio, but your brother is being transported to places where someone without Saint Pio's faith can barely understand. Your brother is far from a theologian. He does not comprehend all the dimensions of the devil's work the way someone like Saint Pio did. This is why it is so frightening to him. Saint Pio was himself terrified by what he experienced, even in the massiveness of his faith. Your brother is simply placed into a state of shock because he has never seen anything like this before. These are real and tangible visions and trans-locations that he is undergoing. They are real. They are real in every sense he has. They are the devil's work in the physical realms, and they have the force to incapacitate someone. Thus far, your brother has not succumbed to this kind of reaction. It is imperative that your brother try to repeat what you say to him as often as he can, that it is in some way converting lost sinners and purifying the world. Your part in this is as important as his. You are his guide and counselor. You are his spiritual hero. I cannot say how many more of these reparative events there will be, but I recently told you they would occur many times a week. Your brother has been reluctant to tell you about many of them because he fears that he is becoming a burden upon you. You surely can see why he feels this way. After all, he believes that he is supposed to be some strong-hearted, courageous, self-assertive, confident individual who never becomes flapped in any condition or circumstance. You know better, and I know better. These are different times for the reasons I gave you regarding the progress of your work in this diocese. Your part of this cross is to simply be your brother's brother, his friend and confidante in every way you have shown him before."

Sunday, May 8, 2011
8:40 a.m.

"We see every day the paradox of Our Lady's urgent calling to be more enduring and to encounter the days of life one at a time, while simultaneously being mindful of the purpose of them all. The constancy in what we do rests in the diversified ways we examine and compare ourselves with Christ Jesus and the Heavenly Father's eternal perfection that has nullified our deep-seated errors. We are drawn-up to Jesus by way of the Cross to all things miraculous and perpetual that we hope to see someday. My hope has always been that we can defer to everything the Lord asks of us, and then we can say that we are worthy of summoning the Angels and Saints upon whose prayers, blessings and intercessions we passionately rely."

William L. Roth

"My calling is for the heart of humanity, My little sons. It is the opening of the future that the Father anticipates for you. I come today in prayer that you remain vigilant against all who would see your work dismissed, and this vigilance is best expressed by simply living in peace. Do not allow the physical world to wear your spirit down when you know of all the irrelevance by which so many other people live. While I have never sinned, I call out to sinners for help in purifying the Earth. This is the secular observation of mother's day, and I once told you that abortions are almost nonexistent on this day. Oh! – that every day would be mother's day! I also call your attention to the fathers who should remain faithful to their wives and children, that they would be good providers and moral examples to their sons and daughters. We pray that all of these things will come true because this is the way the world is brought to purity. This speaks to the difference between responsible spiritualism and fanatical spiritualism. It is responsible to hold true to the mystical gifts that the Lord gives you through the blessings of the Holy Spirit, through the dispensing of the graces that keep your faith alive. This is different from the fanaticism that causes so much violence from other 'beliefs' that purport to be representative of God. I have told you that there is only one God in Three Divine Persons, the God of Abraham, Moses, Isaac and Jacob, and this is God to whom all humanity must eventually reply. My little sons, you were reared in an environment and the institution of the Church of Christianity that taught you the Truth from long ago. Others are born into the error that distracts them from accepting the Son of God as their Savior, and it is to them that I have given reason to convert. It is through the Sacrifice of Jesus that they have been saved, and by no other reason. I have always tried to make this distinction clearly and delicately because the Good News comes shockingly to those who have been hard and fast in other beliefs. I ask you to join Me in praying for their conversion to the Blood of the Cross that has redeemed all men.

    Lessons and teachings are not an end in themselves, but they refer to a greater conclusion about their thesis and purpose. My Special one, this is what you were writing and speaking about at the opening of this message. One cannot reach a destination unless he takes one step at a time, not unlike the days you mention, so that in them, there is a greater goal. No one knows which of these days shall be the last in exile for any one man, and this is why you should focus – you meaning all men, on the day and the tasks at hand. Believe it or not, happiness can grow from this. Patience and enduring are products of living a day at a time. Your rest and leisure are given to you one day at a time; as the hours wane and night falls, you should remember that you always give God the best of your heart. This is the mission of the Church and the hope of all the blessed. Living life moment to moment in peace is a prayer to Jesus that He is welcome amidst the turmoil. It is humanity's summoning invocation of the Hosts of Heaven to infiltrate the material world with everything miraculous it needs to survive. Heated suns and waxing moons do what they do, but it is the inspirited hearts of men that prove that the universe is alive. All the daring in humanity's courage grows from the belief that all things will change for the better, that not every dark shadow harbors a demon, that the new dawns and midday sun rays are indicative of the rejuvenation of the converted soul. I hold you dear to My breast, My Special son, and all who come to Me for prayer, intercession and consolation. I have in My midst all the Angels and Saints about whom grand eloquence has been spoken and you have written. The Kingdom Come referred to in prayers and passages holds all the gifts and pleasures that have been promised, all the fulfillment and contentment that the human heart can imagine. This is why that Kingdom must be brought into this world now. I have repeated often that if this comes true, human souls would not realize their passage from this life into the next. While this seems more figurative than real, I am attempting to describe the intensity of love that makes one feel so wanted, so cherished and nourished, so embraced and consoled. I have always spoken about this love, this supernatural elevation of the mind, heart and spirit that eliminates sadness and eradicates darkness. This is Divine Love brought into the Earth by the Holy Spirit, and I have long asked that My children be open to receive God with outstretched arms. Yes, there are millions upon millions of Americans who are tired. They are weary from the culture of competition and fanaticism. They are tired of the hyped sensationalism that slaps their face every day in the media and people who do not know God. I ask again that you and all My children around the globe do not get caught in this web of lies, in this heightened sense of irrelevance that keeps the Earth embroiled. Be at peace knowing that the Spirit of the Son of Man is alive in you, and you will feel at peace. You will dismiss the alarmism that America is peddling against the innocence of inspirited hearts. This is My message for today. *"Thank you."* This is what I have come to say to you and your brother, and to the larger masses of humanity, their consciousness, that you will touch in future years. I will never leave My children. I cannot say that the Father will not allow certain suffering and losses to continue, but He does indeed give you and all men the strength to go on. Your focus is on the Cross, the Cross that has pardoned and redeemed the whole world. And, the Cross is the source of the Divine Mercy that grants absolution to those who seek that Mercy, that awe-inspiring pardoning that cannot be found anywhere else in Creation. It is defied often in places where punishment seems the only response; in prisons and other places that penalize instead of forgiving. The devil does his worst against impressionable people, against those whose consciences were not founded in the Gospel message from their youth. These are the ones who go on to commit the crimes and do the damage that harms so many others. But, they are redeemable too. You see and hear about these things because this is all the secular world chooses to focus on. They care little about the hundreds of thousands of Christian organizations that foster peace and feed the poor. They drop from their headlines anything redemptive that good people perform in the name of God. They delete from their manuscripts what it means to go the last mile for those who cannot help themselves. We know that there are workers, missionaries, clergy and millions of others whose goodness has descended on the Earth like a mighty shield against the forces of evil, but they are not hailed as heroes in this world. Hear Me now. Someday, they will! This is the Lord's promise to all who believe in Him."

Saturday, May 14, 2011
1:13 p.m.

"Most secularists perceive spirituality as nothing more than a mere effigy, something that at its core contains no real life. They train their eyes only on the avenues and overages that help them garner the fullest material benefit from what they believe. This is not the way of Christianity. We are servants, stewards, custodians, and facilitators of a living Kingdom belonging to the Son of the Blessed Virgin Mary, one that God shares abundantly with those who are courageous enough to defend it. Our lifelong struggles are about spreading the Gospel in the face of everything about humanity that opposes it. This is how we discover the true meaning of life, the reason for our trials, and the rewards that rightly belong to those who seek redemption. Christians are not out of touch with the practical world, but we are careful in discerning what is really worth pursuing."

William L. Roth

"My endearing little sons, it is during these moments that Heaven rejoices, when you see the realities of your faith alongside what all men must do to reach the fruits of Eternal Salvation. Your greatest work in this world is to be confident in your redemption in the Cross through Jesus, and all else will follow. Remember that it is Salvation that calls your soul to the excellence of Divine Love; it is your faith that tells you that everything the Scriptures contain is true. Today, I come calling again to invoke your participation in praying for lost sinners, for all who are suffering for the sake of conversion, and for the unborn who are crying-out for birth in the wombs of their mothers. This is the month of May, and you and all around you recognize the gift of motherhood, of the values and assets of prayer that in turn allow unborn children to see the world as you have known it. We rarely see a mother who will abort her child if enough people reach her heart with earnest prayer. My Special and Chosen ones, you are both still working in your own ways for the propagation of the Holy Gospel through your daily chores, and this is what all men are called to achieve. You labor in the valley while the Father watches you from the tallest summits above. The Holy Spirit lives in you and surrounds you with the Providence of Redemption. See how the Angels have interceded for you! Remember how the Saints have taught! I come to this home where I have always brought My blessings, teachings, lessons and messages because there is peace here. There is joy, faith, conviction, resilience and compassion. You acknowledge the need for prayer because your conscience tells you that the world is not right. This is the way of all who believe in God, all who have for themselves appropriated the faith that is given freely from Him. Heaven rejoices because the Earth is becoming more like the Kingdom to which it is devoted in the Most Sacred Heart of Jesus.

My little ones, I ask you today to ponder all the good you have done, all the gifts you have tendered to the Father and humanity on Earth. You tend to lose sight of all you have done for Him because you are so humble and unassuming; you do not require accolades and laurels that are expected from those who focus only on the secular realms. You have Eternity in your favor, and they have time working against them. Sweet are your hearts and intentions because you mirror the intentions of Jesus for the Church, for all its members, for the parishes around the globe who are needing your prayers. All the priests, nuns, missionaries and other servants of the Lord feast on your intercessions; they are helped in ways that you cannot see. This is also how your works are propagated here in this diocese. There are people worldwide whom I have enlisted to pray for what you have done, what we hope can become of your investment of years. Your thoughts and reflections that are so moving to Jesus will live on throughout the end of the world, and they will heal and console all whose eyes see them and ears hear them. As I have said on many occasions, I did not come to this place for no reason. I speak about these things with hope in My heart, and you live in the realization that great gifts will be bestowed because of your hearts. The most important words I have uttered in all My appearances throughout the generations are prayer and love. The first is a function of the latter. We know; we have always known that God summons prayer from His creatures. He has proven it time and again. Jesus prayed deeply and from the heart while He lived on Earth. He taught the Apostles and disciples how to pray. He enlists all who have hands to touch to reach out into the world with the Good News of His Kingdom, of the New Covenant that has forever amended the lives and purposes of those who believe. My Special son, I recently heard you praying for nonbelievers in such a way that they would envy you if they knew what you and your brother and all Christians know. They do not yet know what they are missing, but they someday will. All will eventually realize what it means to embrace the Cross and the Kingdom that has brought such forgiveness to those who are laden with sin. Do you remember what your brother told you were his beliefs of the most prominent statement in the Bible? He said that the Spirit of the Lord is upon you. You have been sent to help the poor and heal the brokenhearted. And, you responded that surely the Salvation of the soul must live in this. You are both correct in your speech. You have seen the Coming of the Lord in advance!

Also today, I call on you to be patient with those nonbelievers that you spoke about in your opening narrative. While you have been believers all your lives, millions of others have not. They have not yet tasted the sweetness of redemptive suffering, but they will. No one escapes this life without that flavor on their lips. It is welcomed by those who believe because they are united with the Sacrifice of Jesus on the Cross. They identify with what this kind of suffering means. It is more than just aching and weeping; it is of a much higher accord than what it appears to be for someone far from God. I have not told many in the world that suffering is good – I am saying that it is purposeful for the transformation of humanity from lost sinners into canonized Saints. *(Mankind will surrender humbly and voluntarily to God through faith or endure suffering in order to be separated from the world in order to have faith.)* Saint Paul has said as much. Did it take a miracle for him to believe? Perhaps it did, but it is as great a miracle, even a larger one, when someone converts of their own volition simply by willing it to be true. Saint Paul was summoned in a different way than most modern people convert, but the outcome is the same. The Spirit of Salvation that spoke to Saint Paul is the same Spirit that speaks through you and all who believe. Priests and witnesses from all walks of life who evangelize the Gospel repeat the strains of the Angels who have guided humanity through history's darkest times. Your simple utterances of 'I love you' and 'I will pray for you' are as well-timed and imperative as the voices heard by Saint Joseph in the night. How many souls have awakened to their newfound faith because of the vigilance of people like Blessed John Paul the Great! These are the kinds of miracles that God seeks from mortal men. This is the power of The Word. It is found not only in turning water into wine or raising someone from the dead. The most awesome miracle in Creation is when someone chooses for God, when they disavow their wicked ways and decide for the Father in Heaven. And, while this seems simple enough, you have seen how difficult it can be. You and your brother and all who have accepted your portion of the Cross have tried to speak-out about the Kingdom of God in ways that have shaken the very foundation of the Earth on which you live. And yet, many have done little more than shrug their shoulders and walk away. They have stood staring at you with perplexed looks on their faces. This is the intensity of the opposition that the Holy Spirit has faced for 2,000 years. You and the modern Church are in good company when you see so much animosity leveled against your faith.

I do not tell you these things to bring you despair. I do not wish for you to have any darkness of heart. I ask you to live in the same hope that has kept millions of Christians before you at peace. Indeed, millions and billions. There is a direct course for the Salvation of men to be awakened to everything the Lord wants them to know, and this is through shock and awe. This shock and awe comes a moment at a time, a revelation at a time, when someone least expects it, when they are going about their daily routine and a flash of light cuts through the darkness. It is sometimes when a child is born or one is lost. It can be something they see in Nature or other simple men. The point I am making is that it all adds up. Even though these things are dispensed through time, and even as they are all seemingly incalculable, they pale when placed alongside the shock and awe in your twelve deposited works. There are centuries and millennia of shocking events that are recorded in your books from the past twenty years. Thus, you see the deception of time. Imagine someone presenting your books to you twenty years ago. Consider what you would do. The world has never seen anything like this before! And, this is what your Bishop is discerning. It is the reason Satan is attacking your brother with such relentless evil. It is the origin of the blessings that will come into the Earth like the great deluge when all who have eyes and ears see and listen. This is why I have come to you. It has required the past two decades of you and your brother's lives. It has come at the expense of your own joys, at the cost of keeping you here praying with Me instead of frolicking in the park. I wish for you to remember, especially of your prologues and prefaces, that humanity will take a turn. The world will take heed of what the Mother of God has to say, and they will take another look at My other Marian shrines. Please do not lose sight of this hope because the Holy Spirit has implanted it within you."

Saturday, May 21, 2011
1:53 p.m.

"Everything we yearn for; the good fortune we desire, and whatever we hold-out for comes through the same hope springing forth from the faith of our fathers, knowing that deep inside our best kept secrets is the recipe for fulfillment that God has implanted there. We will never see or capture it

without Him. Without the love that comes from On High, we would be too shortsighted to envision the grandest of what life can be. We might become giants among men in all other ways, but if we fail to clothe ourselves in the raiment of the Father's saintly blessing, we will never shine like Jesus Christ. Instead of being stepping stones into Paradise, we will remain like scattered grains of sand, idle to the universe, with no wisdom or grace to foster a better world. Is this what the heirs of our Lord's Resurrection foresee? I don't think so. Christians expect far greater substance out of life than simple mortality, much more than the fiery arches of offensive weapons or the grim images of such things as school book depositories and hundred-year floods."

William L. Roth

"Like sounding the clarion and ringing the bells, your hearts are willing to celebrate your immortality in Jesus' Most Sacred Heart, in the bounty of His Crucifixion, and in the Wisdom that has assured you that human redemption is true. I have come to pray with you again on this beautiful day in May 2011 because the Lord has sent Me. I am with you both; you are worthy of the blessings that have come to you through the years. I speak today in strains of joy because the Holy Spirit is still enlightening the faithful about remaining true to the Church in your time, about living for Jesus hour by hour. Your prayers are particularly welcome because you know what the Lord wants. If you consider the fruits that the earth has borne your breadlines, you must also remember what has grown from your faith. I have said that humanity's pathway to Heaven is not always strewn with flowers. There will be dark and soily days. We have indeed been through many of them together. However, I ask My children the world over to never lose sight of the gladness you have discovered in your openness to God. Yes, this has always been the thesis of My messages around the world. If you consider what graces are accorded the Church, you must never forget that the Holy Eucharist is the summit of those signs. It is your connection with Jesus that cannot be garnered any other way. I wish for you to accept with deep awareness that the centuries-old Sacraments are the purification of lost humanity; they are the blessings that have brought good men to become even better men; they have cultivated in men of ill will the holiness they need to come to Heaven. Here, you have learned that anyone is capable of knowing the God of Abraham. Your lives are complete in Him, My Special son, just as you have written at the fore of My message today.

You have seen that I have given you personally many sacred images, many lines about how the world ought to be, even after December 28, 2008. It is My intention for you to realize that I have done this for My other messengers as well. Even those in Medjugorje to whom I have appeared, those who I advised would see Me only on their birthday and other observations thereafter; even they are as close to Me as they ever were. I have said to them that they would see Me or hear My voice on a lesser number of days in the same way that you have told America that My messages to them ended on the last Sunday of 2008. In other words, I am sharing the bounty of My Immaculate Heart with all who have confirmed their faith in Jesus and agreed to record My messages to the world. I once told you that there would one day be no need for faith, and I clarified it to reaffirm that it would be after Jesus' Second Coming. There are other kinds of faith that blossom from your primal religious faith. These are reflective of your hopes, which are fruits of that same faith, in that you see inside your hearts and minds the way the world is supposed to become according to the Holy Gospel. Faith in itself is a living being, not separate from you, but within you, just as your soul is a living spirit. My Special son, you and your brother and all who believe in God inherited this Life of Faith because you have all submitted your will to the Father. You have known this for a very long time. I am saying here today that those who decline to submit their will to Him must be persuaded; they must cast off their penchant for logical arguments in favor of unseeable beliefs in the context of the mission of the Church. You can say that you believe something, and any action that proves that belief comprises a product of that faith. Faith is the seed; it is the catalyst that leads to discernable action by those who have accepted the Cross. Thus, you see the transformation from cause into effect. Outside and inside of time, faith is a valuable asset because it reconfirms after they die everything men have always practiced. Faith is the confirming element of the Salvation of the human soul before and after it is delivered from the flesh. Why? Because those who accept Jesus here in exile recognize Him when they see His Holy Face, and He assuredly knows them. While this may seem to be an elementary perception of what occurs, millions of people on Earth have never drawn the connection between living with faith and waiting until they die to decide. Is it too late for them? You have learned through the Church and in My messages that it is not, but this does not imply that anyone should wait. I could go on about the preliminary and Final Judgement, but you already know what they are.

You may not be aware that priests and other clergy do not look at everyone they meet on the street or elsewhere through the perception of whether these people have given their lives to God. Perhaps they should, but they do not. On the other hand, if they did so, they would be spending so much time analyzing the motivations of other human beings that they would have little other time for prayer and the practical aspects of their vocations. They minister to their flocks the best they can and allow the Lord to decide whether these people are fully converted. Here again, this is a process of the unseen world, but the actions of those who are converted are uniquely different from those who are not. This is where I have arrived at the crux of My message today. How do you suppose Jesus looks upon politicians and others who claim to be Roman Catholic, but who support abortion 'rights' and other immoral liberal agendas? You rightly cite your senator as an example of one of these people. The answer is this. They are undeserving of the Sacraments of the Church because they are ignoring the Gospel Truth. I am not saying that they will be condemned, for surely God will employ the fruits of others' suffering to make reparation for the politicians' error. However, these same politicians are reducing the intensity of the immortal joy that they, and the others that they lead astray, will receive. Do you remember that we once spoke of the levels of Heaven? It is not certain that the fullness of eternity will remain hierarchical this way because the mission of the Church, the suffering of the Church-Militant, is still underway. This again is another purpose of the element of time. I have said these things to impress upon you that there is more reason for prayer and the actions that accompany faith than simply making the world a better place. You and all the faithful are literally shaping the timeless nature of the Kingdom of God. You are making room for more Saints, calling out through your petitions for Saint Joseph the Carpenter to add more rooms to the Father's House. You have also been told that some of the particulars of human redemption include an enlightenment that can come only after someone sees the Face of God. While this is factually true, all aspects of your Salvation can be garnered inside the heart. This is the sacred vision that you wrote about earlier today. I have said that one can become so holy here on Earth that they would not realize their passage from this life into the next. So, what is the difference? It is simply this – I will use Saint Padre Pio as an example. Once he crossed over into the beauty of Heaven, his flesh was not a burden anymore. He was not burdened by its weight against the Earth or the force of gravity upon it. This is the way of everyone who enters the Land of

Promise. But, he took the vision that the Holy Spirit gave him while he was a priest on Earth to Heaven with him. Everyone who is saved does this as well. This is the reason why Saints are said to be alive in Heaven and on Earth.

We have discussed in various conversations what it means to refine and align this vision according to the condition of the human heart. People like the Catholic, pro-abortion politicians have sold out their hearts to the devil even before they surrendered their principles of Catholicism. They do this for the reasons you already know – power, wealth, influence, recognition and all the rest. They are in no way making the world a better place when they turn away from the teachings of the Church. In fact, they become its enemies in disguise. They claim to uphold their Profession of Faith while practicing the opposite. And, this is one of the reasons why there is so much suffering around the globe. Here again, you have learned nothing new. Therefore, when someone asks you why there is such suffering of the innocents and those who have done no harm, you may feel free to tell them that sinners like your senator have placed these people on the Cross. These politicians are the hypocrites who do as much harm and practice as much malevolence as someone who rejects the Church altogether. You have My permission to say that I have told you that these politicians and others are to blame. This is what I have come to tell you today."

Saturday, May 28, 2011
2:01 p.m.
(terrible storms today)

"*We have learned that it is possible to become overly introspective, to be too self-examining about our own humanity, disallowing our heartstrings to sound unscripted melodies. We must try instead to live according to the Gospel message without expelling the spontaneity from our everyday lives. Even though we are yet exiled from the presence of the Father, we are not solitarily confined. We have inherited a freedom that most people have never even conceived. We are at liberty to presume how vast God's Kingdom can become. We are free to harvest our victories at will and build our dreams on foundations as huge as thunderheads. We have the birthright to reclaim our heritage from the opportunists who are slowly trying to steal it. And we have every reason to believe that we will win the watershed battles against the evil that is devouring this world, because our Roman Catholic faith is poised to destroy it like lighted dynamite inside a glass jar.*"

William L. Roth

"Yes, My Special one, I have pierced the storm clouds and have landed safely here in this place. What a wonderful sense of humor you have! Truth is, I have really always been here. Like the Saints, I am in Heaven and on Earth. Your writing to preface today's message is some of the most visionary you have ever penned. It gives humanity a lot to think about; it even gives God a lot to think about! Your words have come to you through His Spirit of Love and Wisdom. You are at liberty to presume how massive His earthly Kingdom can become. This you do through your faith and trust that the lost will be converted. It is a product and function of your willingness to believe that good will conquer evil, that love will vanquish hatred, and that the Light will chase away the darkness. These things are happening now because of the faithful, because so many are keeping their promises to Jesus they made the moment they were baptized. Today, I come eager to share with you and your brother My happiness and visionary peace, the way that all My children should live. You live generally and specifically for the purpose of enhancing the Kingdom about which we have spoken here today, not to add to that Glory, but to reveal and spread it to those who are incapable of seeing it for themselves. You know the contrast between winning and losing. The world of competition has made it clear. As strange as it may seem, there is no certain key to winning the battle for souls in the context of black and white. Being redeemed in the Holy Cross is that clear, but the degree to which each person comes to know God during their lives is not as clear. People enter and exit various stages of trust and belief. They have doubts that dissipate and then return again. They accept suffering with open arms, and then they begin to question its sublime efficacy. This is the way of mortal beings. While no one on Earth is perfect, this is the direction that everyone must travel. When Jesus said that all sinners should become perfect as He is perfect, He meant that all should come to Him, to lift Him up, to adore and cherish the Cross; and in this, they shall find perfection. In other words, if those lost in sin will take the first step away from sin, Jesus will lift them into His arms and carry them the rest of the way. You have known that this is true.

The point I am making about the turning of the human heart away from sin is positioned in that part of the personal will that makes the soul see right from wrong. This cannot be achieved if someone is fixed in doubt and distraction. It cannot be attained if the soul is not rendered blameless through the Sacraments of the Church. When you write your opening chapters of your memoirs, you are and will invest a great deal of time speaking about your innocence, the innocence of humanity at large, and how that innocence is exploited by the secular void. This implies, and you are quite correct, that innocence is inherent in young children when they are born, when they are growing into their adolescent years. But, what happens to them? They are changed by the characteristics of their environment, by other people who would see them live another way. Their innocence is slaughtered like a helpless lamb and tossed aside into the darkness. You and My other children must make clear to humanity that this same innocence can be resurrected and returned to the person that lost it, much the same way that Jesus was raised from the dead at Easter. You see, innocence is ageless. It is not affected by the element of time. In other words, it is lost by individuals to their particular lives of guilt, but it does not lose its substance as the pure condition of the human heart and soul. They simply become separated. Heaven is filled with innocence. There is no guilt there. Jesus was born to retrieve the lost innocence of the exiled world and restore it to those who properly own it. I am making this point today because nearly everyone on Earth is unaware of it. They believe that once innocence is lost, it is dead in the grave. However, it is not. It is simply waiting in suspension until it is returned to its rightful owner. This is more than just imagery or poetic form; it is the truth as sure as I am speaking it.

There are timely implications that accompany this concept. What else does it mean to retrieve one's lost innocence? It means that the burdens of time itself are reversed. Victims are healed and dignity is restored. Divisions are eliminated and darkness is lifted. Spiritual insight is again given venue. The New Covenant Gospel becomes a better way of life. This is what conversion is for. The Holy Cross becomes a real, true and tangible fact in the conscience of those who have given their lives and souls to Jesus. Humanity is capable of 'touching' Divine Love through the heart, spirit, and in the faith that comes from the Father. Living in accordance with the Commandments and Beatitudes becomes the new norm. Sacrifice, holiness, prayer and peace are internalized in ways that are never before known. This is what My messages around the globe throughout the generations have tried to make clear. Are people listening? Will My appearances, messages, apparitions and locutions change anything before the end of the world? The answer is an affirmative 'yes' because My purposes here and elsewhere have been to preface the Return of Jesus in Glory. I am ushering Him a second time in the same way that My Fiat welcomed Him at the Annunciation. And, you must remember the role of the Angels in all this. I have said this to you and your brother before. Without the assistance of the Angels, there would be no Morning Star deposit of works for your Bishop and the Church to pore over. Without the Angels, we would not have known to flee into the safety of Egypt. It is the Angels who are your advocates, as much as the Holy Spirit dispatches them, because they pray for you and guide you. They uphold your works in grand style before and beyond the created world. They sail, fly and soar high above the clouds and come into your bedrooms at night. They sing to your souls in ways that only your heart and subconsciousness know. I bring them with Me when I come here, wherever I go around the globe, to pray in gladness for the many who are given to My Son. We remind the Lord what blessings you are to the Church when you foster forgiveness between enemies, when peace pacts are signed, when little children are conceived, and when someone makes the case for Christianity in some romantic way. There is an exchange that occurs between Heaven and Earth that multiplies the graces accorded to those who love Jesus when a person tells someone else that he loves them. Why? Because it is only through the Sacred Heart of Jesus that something like this can be said. There is no end to the ways that this prospect can be described to the world, through the beauty of Nature, in the harmonies of songs, the inspirations that make people write and speak the lofty strains of human Salvation, and in the mystical ways that charismatic Christians become one with the Spirit of the Father. I am pleased and overwhelmed that you and your brother, and all My worldwide messengers, are maintaining your patience while the world is being converted the way I have outlaid here today. I have told you that there is urgency in this process that you must encounter with patience. I am not double-speaking when I tell you this; I am only reminding you of the many paradoxes of your faith. It is true that chastity and purity, absence of the flesh, and the destruction of lust are the only ways to be fully united with Heaven. God is filled with charity and hope, with plans for the fulfillment of everything that humanity is supposed to become. This is what it means to be Creator of all things good. And, this is the reason why abortion is such a grotesque mortal sin. It is the opposite of everything that God believes. There are other examples of human thought and action that represent the antithesis of what the Father wishes His people to do. They are all the product of humanity's distance from Him; it is about their pride reigning over their moral discipline, about hatred manifesting further evil where prayerfulness should prevail."

Saturday, June 4, 2011
12:56 p.m.

"If it is possible for a Saint to be charming, let it be said that the Mother of Jesus is the incarnation of charm par excellence. Our Lady surpasses so many dimensions of humanity and motherhood personified that She seems miraculous Herself. Nowhere have I seen another mother listen so attentively to her children's concerns. The Blessed Virgin looks us straight in the heart with Her welcoming eyes and mystical gaze, peering deep into our souls; and She speaks not just about the culture of the exiled world, but about the beauty beyond the celestial skies. We are absorbed by Her compassion for those who are lonely and the millions who suffer in reflection of Our Lord on the Cross. And, it is through Our Lady's endearing command and exquisite poise that we understand the holiness of God in human form. After all, besides Her Son, Mary is the only other sinless person born into the physical realms."

William L. Roth

"My heavens, what adoring words you have written, My Special one! Thank you and your brother for your devotion, consecration and veneration, for your faith and trust, and for the love you have accorded the Angels and Saints, to Jesus in His infancy and maturity, and to the Roman Catholic Church. We have arrived at the month of June 2011 where many things are happening in the world, most of them expected, some less anticipated, and a great many more manifestations of the Will of God that come in excruciating ways. I wish for you to remember that everything the Father allows and condones is for the conversion of the lost. He has given you the Most Blessed Trinity, the thrice-blessing of Himself to aid in your understanding of the framework of Heaven and the Salvation in Jesus on the Cross through whom all are redeemed. This is a special time to be devoted to the Sacred Heart of Jesus because His Divine Mercy is being poured out all over the world. Through the incalculable acts of Christian heroism by the clergy and lay-people alike, My Son is encouraged. He is aware of the sacrifices and suffering that you referred to in the writing for your memoir. Let it never be said that Jesus Christ is unaware of everything that His people do on behalf of the spiritual conversion of those who do not know Him. There is warmth in Jesus' Most Sacred Heart, and His Love emits the Light of Wisdom required by those who are ignorant of the Truth. We are taking advantage of this time together to reveal to Jesus and to exiled humanity that we are fighting for that cause of Love; we are praying that the Father will realize that His creatures are worthy of His pardon. I assure you that we shan't cease our prayers until all who will enter Heaven someday have been awakened to their future course. It is for all these reasons that I am a happy Mother, that I come to you and your brother today for the purposes that the Father has in mind. It is not that He has nothing better to do. He has been watching and assessing the conditions in the world since He first positioned it in space; and but for the rogue will of its inhabitants, the Glory of Heaven would already be reflected by the Earth below.

You are building in intensity toward your fullest understanding of the maturity of the Church, and it is time that makes this true. You and your brother, and most all the Bishops, and everyone who is devoted to My Immaculate Heart can already see what I came to know from whence I was but a child. The temporal world cannot contain the jubilation that is known to those who love God. There are no constraints or hand-binding parameters that would prohibit the inspired soul from searching for the land beyond the stars. Your hope, all humanity's hope is this promise. The entire fulfillment of a human life is encapsulated in the understanding that life truly begins here in this exile and comes to fruition only after the soul has entered the gates of Paradise. In other words, the years during which men live on Earth take them like stair steps to complete oneness with the Creator of those men and the overseer of the years. It is in this life in the mortal world that you and all others can appreciate the perfection that Jesus has been teaching in mind, Body and Spirit. I have said that when someone thinks about the righteousness of God, it is God infusing into them the Wisdom of His Truth. There are multiple forms in which this Wisdom is dispensed, through the teachings of intelligent priests, the beauty of Nature, the innocence of children, the visions and images that come to the open-hearted from the vaults of Heaven, and in the seemingly coincidental ways that daily life unfolds. There are signs and wonders aplenty that prove that the Lord is with you. He has manifested His own grace and patience in ways that most people will never comprehend. He spreads the rains and offers the sunshine to speak to the heart of those who kneel and pray. He has handed humanity Salvation for the taking because He realizes that you are worthy of a more glorious fate. He positioned the destiny of eternal redemption before you like a flash of lightning cutting through the darkness because the soul becomes even more hungry for knowledge than does the body require food. This is why I have come calling through the decades and generations, imploring My children to feast on Him, search for Him, emulate Him, and welcome Him. There is no eloquence that can quite capture the miracle of these things, and nothing in any universe can negate them.

I told you that we would be speaking about the Sacred Heart of Jesus during this month that is so dedicated to its sweetness. Does judgment come from there? Yes, in certain measures, but the fullness of His forgiveness is through the Love that lives in His Heart. The Most Sacred Heart of Jesus is the vessel in which the vindication of lost humanity comes to pass. It is not that the innocent are pardoned for something they have not done, but that they are remade into the innocence that I spoke about before. God redeems everything in the converted soul that is redeemable and wipes the rest completely out of mortal and immortal existence. There has never been something born out of forgiveness that ever died in vengeance. I wish for you to remember this.

Let there be no mistake in what I am saying here. The events of this past week that took place in the local courthouse are directly from the bowels of Hell. There is no such thing as the union between two people of the same sex. This is despicable and ruinous; it gives young people the wrong impression about the purpose of their gender. It validates the indefensible. It brings shame upon a land that professes to believe in the Christian Gospel. And, it was signed into law by a Roman Catholic governor. You already know that this is why suffering continues; it goes on to open the eyes of the blind, those who will not see what the Lord wants them to envision with their eyes of faith. We pray for all who are committing these atrocious acts, not that they will be destroyed, but that they will be enlightened by the power of the Father to put them in their place, to raise them from their dungeon of darkness, to wrest them from the grip of the devil, to reclaim them from the clutches of the world's secular evil. Thank you and all who are praying for humanity to awaken from their slumber, from their indifference and error, from their outright rejection of the teachings of the Church.

I have yet many lofty speeches and inspiring words to say about the Son of Man. I have reams of inspiring poems to dictate to those who will receive them. I have memories of a Man-God whose own father took him under his wing with adoration and affection – the one Saint Joseph who would have given life and limb to see His stepchild succeed. I have seen with My own eyes,

My Special son, in the same way that you wrote about to open this message, a world filled with such awesome human potential that it would stretch the mind. I have heard words of tremendous valor coming from those thought to be too timid and afraid to utter them. I have seen violinists wielding sabers of war. I have heard piano players shout-out marching orders to millions of men. I have seen ballet dancers taking the first charge on the battlefield. I have seen blood shed so copiously that it made the Messiah weep in gratitude. I have walked among the dead and soared above the resurrected. It is to these things that we dedicate ourselves, My Special one. These are the reasons why we shall never concede. High on the mountaintops? Yes, we are there. Deep into the valleys? Yes, our spirits have been there too. And, most people live somewhere in between, just shy of the greatness to which we would ask them to aspire. Our mission has always been to lift the oppressed from under their burdens, to slay the wicked and advise the uninformed. The good news, My Special and Chosen sons, is that we will not fail! We will take charge of the last hill and raise the flag of Salvation at the summit of the world! We will watch the breath of God cause it to flap in the breezes of His preordained forgiveness. I seek of you today to remember all I have said when you believe that life is getting you down, when things are not as they should be, when you hear another person say that they want to give up. Thank you for hearing what I came to share with you on this hot summer afternoon."

Saturday, June 11, 2011
1:04 p.m.

"Another key benefit of practicing Catholicism is being able to see life beyond the parameters of time and space, to circumvent corners, barriers and obstacles that cannot be easily overcome by those outside the Church. With this insight, we discover what was previously unknown about the framework of the world; we have the capacity to embrace everything conceivably good about humanity because Jesus the Messianic King helps us look beyond our faults, failures, and weaknesses with the same sacred keenness awaiting us in Heaven. What else can we see around those corners? Surely it is retracing our footsteps so as to straighten crooked paths, reestablishing our connection with hopes that slipped away, and reviving memories that lost their sheen through the coarseness of the years. Many people walk through life while straddling, kicking, gouging and tinkering around the edges of the greatest

possibilities known to man, but they never quite get there because they refuse to accept the Savior who makes us whole inside Himself."

William L. Roth

"My dear little sons, you have come to another juncture in your heavenly messages that represents your determination to stay the course, to walk with the Angels along the path that helps you see the reasons I have come. The meditation that you have written for today is as beautiful as anything I have ever seen, read or heard in the centuries-long existence of the Church. You can see that the Father has dictated it to humanity from the center of your heart through the same Holy Spirit that created the Church at Pentecost. You are aware that the faults, failures and weaknesses about which you speak are completely overcome by your faith in Jesus. Were it not for the suffering and sacrifices that accompany The Faith, the world would scarcely be converted to Salvation in the Cross. Without this faith, what would be humanity's justification for suffering? How would the world of exiled men prioritize and categorize the great tragedies that befall them on the Earth? The essence is that suffering and sacrifice are the two pillars that uphold the imperatives of the Church in the Passion and Crucifixion of My Son, like Saints Peter and Paul, and all the Saints. You have spoken about the towering reverence that they all had and still have for the Faith Church on Earth, and their pity for the Poor Souls in Purgatory, and their presence in the Church Triumphant right now. They have transcended all the phases of human thought and growth; they have come into Heaven where men and women who have lived and died in Jesus have been raised in Him. I ask all creatures through your thoughtful writings and memoirs to remember that the transition that we have discussed through the years, the passing from indifference to unbridled commitment to God, is a function of the devotion and dedication of the human heart to anticipating unexpected things. Who would have thought that your brother would have called you from Beardstown in the night? He was the least to expect it, while you did not seem as surprised. And, the reason is because you have always been favored toward receiving the gifts of the Holy Spirit as a life-long Roman Catholic. You have always embraced miracles, holy mysticism, and deep charismatic meditation because of your birth into the Church, not having been converted from another one. Here is the point I am making. We have discussed and you have written that fully four-fifths of the world's population is non-Catholic. They are far from contemplative thought, from miracles, from embracing all the Seven Sacraments, from knowing that the Lord can and will utilize every avenue imaginable to reach those distant from Him. He proved this from the beginning when Jesus chose His First Apostles. They were not deeply holy men who yearned to take upon themselves the burden of following the Christ. Far from it. And yet, look what they did. They went to their own martyrdom in defense of their Savior because they not only sensed the urgency of His message, but that what they decided to do in their day would have repercussions until the end of the world. Indeed, it is through the Apostolic Church that human Salvation has come! It is from their obedience, their deference to the Messiah whom you spoke about earlier today, their loyalty to the Chosen One that so many graces have come. You and your brother are representatives of this same commitment to God; you too are His advocates and carriers of the Gospel message. And, you will also suffer the same persecution that they once endured; all who stand-up for Roman Catholicism are subject to this fate. I am telling you this because Jesus in My Arms wants to thank you. The warmth and radiance of genuine gratitude that He offers you and your brother, and all who follow Him, is not unlike the glowing sun rays touching the faces of all believers. If God were not a Father of gratitude, He would not be much of a Father at all. He is more thankful for His flock on Earth than anyone might ever be of any achievement they have made in this life or planned for the next.

Thus, we ponder and contemplate what this day, this June 11, 2011 will accomplish to change the constitution of the world. Surely it will have the sacred benefit of reflecting the Love of God into the most distressed corners of the world. Yes, our prayers right this moment are doing that. And, perhaps this day will be one upon which mothers everywhere give birth to their children whom Satan did not kill in the womb. Thousands and millions more will be led away from temptation because the Faith Church on Earth continues to believe. Rosaries are being prayed and Masses offered. All the goodness that those with vocations espoused when they took their vows still lives in them; it remains in them, and they are emitting and sharing those promises in service to the Church. They bow their heads and pray, lift them with hope, speak the Truth with clarity, reunite the separated, console the brokenhearted, and give vision to the blind in the world who refuse to see Jesus for who He is, for what He has to offer them that makes the difference between condemnation and Eternal Redemption. So many have asked how a faith this simple can be so complex. Why are there millions of pages written by theologians about the Death of One Man and His Resurrection? Because the implications, the facts and certitudes that accompany His Holy Sacrifice and Resurrection from the Dead are so imperative, so huge and beneficial to the exiled mortal soul. I recently said that the first four words of the Apostles Creed are evidence enough that the human heart has been converted to this Redemption. While we know this to be true, how do we account for all the thoughts and actions that earthly people have every day? What occurs during the lives of men that helps them constantly compare their experiences in the world with what the New Covenant teaches? The world is not large enough to contain all the books to discuss this. Therefore, something must be said. Spiritual enlightenment must begin somewhere, and it was initiated upon the occasion of the Annunciation of the Archangel Gabriel. Of course it began with Moses and the Old Covenant prophets, but the true enlightenment about the transition of the human soul from the physical world into the Father's House began at the beginning of the Messianic Age. The New Covenant Gospel is, therefore, the Word, the Beginning and the End, the Alpha and the Omega, the culmination of all comprehensible stories about what happens when people die. You have seen; all men have seen that it is according to the way those people lived. You have lived in Jesus as have all the Saints before you. The Popes, Bishops and all the clergy who have served the Church in truth and dignity have seen even before they have died their own happy destiny. This does not make living in exile any easier, but it surely allows the believer to witness with faith in the heart what Jesus has done for them, what He has prepared for them, what they can expect as reward for that faith."

Saturday, June 18, 2011
4:04 p.m.

"O' Lord, you are loyal to our well-being; you are our health and shield, our comfort and peace, our beatific assurance. We call upon you every hour for guidance and protection. We ask that you ratify our prayers in your love; we seek your encouragement when we are in doubt. We urge you to enter the exiled world with justice during these difficult times. Tend to those who are discounted and dejected. Console the afflicted. Heal the infirm. Shine your everlasting brilliance upon the dreariness that besets us from taking charge over our enemies with the tenacity of the Saints. Jesus,

you are the hero of the Cross, and this is why we come to you. We will surely fail without you. We cannot carry the burdens of this life without the strength we gain from you. It is in this confidence that we are disposed to your blessings, and we ask that you touch us with your grace through the whole of the ages. Amen."

William L. Roth

"My dear children, would Heaven not be remiss if the Lord did not dispense to you another blessing for your loving hearts and good works? Thus, I am here today to do so. I am with you in mind and spirit to help you pray for the awful condition of the souls of your lost brothers and sisters. We have a great deal to be thankful for because we hold one another dear in the Most Sacred Heart of My Son. We have Love and the totality of the Glory from which Divine Love is emitted. We share a mutual vision for the way the world ought to become because I have seen the Kingdom of Heaven as its Queen Mother, and you are seeing bountifully around you its Fruits in your fellow Christians, visionaries, missionaries and the ordinary servants of the Cross around the globe. Thank you for remembering to pray for the Poor Souls in Purgatory and all whom you have mentioned in your prayer here today. I hope you remember that Jesus hears you before you even utter the syllables of your petitions. God knows your desires. He speaks through you about what should be said to those who are in need, to the many who hold out in opposition to the doctrines of the Church. Today, I also ask you to pray for the many innocent priests who are persecuted and ostracized because of the insecurities of some local Bishops. They have become paranoiac because they, themselves, have been routinely mocked and criticized for allegedly concealing the indiscretions of those under their authority. They have cowered to the pressure of secular forces who take them into courts of law with unfounded charges. It is true that some Bishops believe that it is easier to remove a member of the clergy than deal with the charges head-on. It would seem that they have more to do than address these distractions. As Mother of the Church, I do not condone what some clergy have done, but I also believe that the innocent should be defended at all costs. Hence, we lift our prayers to Christ Jesus to safeguard the entire Universal Church against the wrongdoings that are perpetrated against it almost every day.

Also today, I ask you to welcome the peace that the Holy Spirit has implanted in your hearts. Peace yearns to reside in your hearts! It is natural for the human heart to be receptive to the peace and confidence given from the Father in Heaven. I have told you many times that the human heart is the vessel into which heavenly Wisdom and Virtue are deposited. You live by the heart through good times and difficult times as well. There is nothing wrong with immersing your thoughts in the sacred knowledge that permeates your heart from the mind of God. The Holy Spirit delivers this to you in abundance when you are in prayer. This is the message that you must forward to your brothers and sisters. Thank you for being support for each other during these times. The Church has prevailed through many difficult ages, especially during its worst persecution, and it will forever stand tall against its detractors. Remember that you are not only living in the Church, but the Church lives inside you. You find direction and counsel there; you satisfy your curiosities about the Lord's motivations by lending yourselves to the Traditions of the Church. I have said that Jesus will never depart from your presence, no matter what the future brings. It is in this power that you are made stronger. Through sickness and health, through sunlight and darkness, and through sweetness and bitterness, the Catholic Church is humanity's source of strength because of the Grace of the Holy Sacraments. The Lord cherishes your admiration of His Word and your participation in building-up His Kingdom in the physical world. It is not a selfish act to pray for yourselves when you ask Jesus to touch the lives of your friends, and your enemies too. I have dictated many messages here, and thousands more in Medjugorje and My other holy shrines. Humanity is slowly awakening to My call because of the 'gift of conscience' that is given to those who believe. Where you shall go from here is a blessed place because it is the Will of the Father that you become conquerors in His Son. Let there be no mistake about it. The Earth rests on surer footing because Jesus has sent Me here to speak, to teach and lead, and to beckon and bless. Please be at peace knowing that My purposes have always been benign, that I pledge to intercede before Jesus for your deepest desires and noblest causes."

Sunday, June 26, 2011

"Have we ever stopped to think about the co-dependency that we share with the Church Triumphant in Heaven? It seems rather contradictory, really, that anyone whose soul lives in Paradise could actually yearn for our inclusion and integration in what is already their glorious experience in perpetual bliss. The

whole matter comes down to what the Saints desire as their concept of Heaven. If it includes living eternally alongside someone in particular, surely the Father through the Son will provide for them. After all, this is what it means to have the intercession of the Communion of Saints. Their prayers mean just that. It is what they deserve, indeed their right, to have us next to them as they concelebrate the timelessness of the heavenly skies. For what vibrance would the Faith Church on Earth have if not for the Church Triumphant? We are converted by the Holy Spirit through the gift of human faith, and we are redeemed when that same faith leads us to accept our final redemption when it comes. This faith allows us to see the Blood of Jesus on the Altar from the Cross, and it provides living proof in our hearts that the promises of Christianity are true. All we need do is believe and profess. This is the essence of being commissioned through the Roman Catholic Church to be chosen and elected, to be fully reliant on Our Lord's Resurrection that we cannot yet see to restore our life. We know that this is true because our hearts of faith are filled with the sublime Truth proclaimed by the New Covenant, and the Holy Gospel lives in and through us by virtue of the presence of Jesus inside us both spiritually and sacramentally. The boiling pot simmers down to reveal the unity of the Church here on Earth, the Church Suffering in Purgatory, and the Church beyond the gateway of Glory. Christians have attested to this fact for over twenty centuries."

William L. Roth

Saturday, July 2, 2011
1:42 p.m.

"My dear beautiful children, we have come together again to unite in the Love of the Holy Spirit and bring Light to the nations. You must remember that all conversion is manifested through the glorious sacrifices of the Faith Church on Earth. Every gift of grace given to the Son of Man grows the righteousness in the seed of faith that Jesus has planted on the Earth. My dear sons, we will do whatever we properly can to communicate our love in the realms of the exiled world. There will someday be no need for physical sight or mechanical motion when we share together the complete perfection of your redemption in Jesus. Remember that eyesight and vision are not necessarily the same. Eyesight is mechanical action and vision is spiritual wisdom. Nothing has happened to impede your vision. Today, I have come to speak about the mountainous events that must occur for humanity to overcome their own error. My Special son, you have spoken about it well with your cousin Michael who visited you here today. The Roman Catholic Church is taller than any earthly summit, wiser than any sage, more momentous than any other historical event, more filled with divinity than anything else conceivable, and built on the foundation of Truth as defined by the Son of God. What does this mean? Surely you know that the Church is far larger than the collective lives of all who have comprised it. It is the culmination of the Will of God for mortal people still in the flesh in the exiled realms. Jesus has said that you can be one in Him while still living on Earth. Therefore, you have become so by your faith and trust; you have inherited from Him that great courage and vision about which I speak. I ask you and your brother to always remember that the Will of God for His people, for His Church, for all believers in the Sacred Word, reflects your future that was created upon your Baptism. You answered affirmatively when questioned about your loyalty to the Most Blessed Trinity. You profess your faith in the Sacraments of the Church. Can you now see that these Sacraments are enshrined in the Wounds of Jesus on the Cross? Can you imagine how they were first borne by the Son of God and passed along to you? The whole matter is encompassed by the need to convert lost sinners to Christianity, and not just any Christianity, but the Original Apostolic Church, the Catholic Church, the Universal Church, the reason for the faith of men. You are all touched by this Church in the ways you know and through means that you cannot readily see. My presence here today is evidence of these extraordinary blessings. Even in your most weary moments, I ask you to never concede that you do not have the power to change the world. When you are most exhausted, this is when your words speak their loudest. When you lay flat on your back, after fighting your worst battles, your victories stand their tallest. When you clasp your hands one with the other in deep contemplation, you are reminding the Father that you know who He is. You are telling Creation that you have only begun to fight. And O' how God and His Creation will respond! It seems not to come in the moment; there are other influences standing in your way. But, in the grand scale of the proliferation of God's Holy Kingdom, they will come nonetheless. Human life issues every man a challenge to stand and withstand all that is faced through life with the valor of the Saints, propagated by appropriate prayer, so that wisdom and knowledge become more important to mortal men than food and water. This is the seeking of genius that drives humanity to invent and reinvent itself through every new age. The power and presence of faith personified by holy Christians is the root of righteousness grown deep within the soul. I have spoken for generations to the broken and the hailed about the reorientation required to set the world aright. You know more than most that I speak about hope even though I have seen beyond its need. Why? Because I am with My children to help bend and reshape the course of future events so that certain other events can be averted. I also pray when you pray! I yearn for the love of My adopted children. I seek the same humility in other men that you desire. At times, I even ache in the absence of righteous men. And now, the proverbial question – What is a Mother to do? I have calmed and consoled, taught and led, blessed and comforted, and scolded and reprimanded. I have brought forth miracles and prophecies. I have asked My Son to grant the answers to your prayers. It is all according to the Will of the Father. Here we are at another seeming crossroad where tradition and modernism intersect. The perversions about which you speak will never diminish the strength of the Original Apostolic Church. No mortal man alive or none yet to be born will ever have the power to dilute the authority of the Roman Catholic Church. The Holy Spirit cannot be divided. The Most Blessed Trinity can never be disassembled. The grace of God can never be lessened. As I asked before, what does all this mean? It confirms that you, your brother, your friends in faith, the collective family of Roman Catholicism and all who believe in the God of Abraham will win at the last. Deeper than any ocean, farther than east, west, north and south, it is beyond these limits. It is farther than anything imaginable that your victories will rise. Satan tries his best; evil does its worst, and yet, the children of the Immaculate Conception never cower. You raise your swords in the image of the Christ, bearing the Scepter of the Salvation of man. You are eager to emulate this power while still here in the heated battle. Therefore, My message today is that you rest with a peaceful heart, realizing that your share of the Triumph of My Immaculate Heart is assured. No persecution or ostracizing of the holy men and women who have fought for human conversion goes unnoticed by God. He tempers His response through the Divine Mercy of His Son. It is here that the compassion of Heaven is most fruitful. This is the substance of My message today. I promise I will return and speak to you and your brother through every means we can possibly employ. Thank you for your prayers for those who have crossed over into death, for the diseased and impoverished, for the end of abortion, and for those who have sacrificed so much for the Glory of the Church. Please be happy. Please be confident that Jesus is with you and your brother through your whole lives."

Sunday, July 10, 2011
9:12 a.m.

"My holy and blessed sons, you are truly beginning to suffer for the good of this cause. I come here today with the Lord's thanksgiving for your willingness to accept your share of the Cross for the conversion of lost sinners. Here we have met a juncture in time when all good men and women should realize that their destiny in God, warehoused within humanity, has always been the ability to emulate Jesus' life with prayerfulness and determination. I have said many times that there would be difficult hours, months and even years for those chosen to share in the suffering of Jesus on the Cross. These gifts to God have been far and wide dispensed around the world to those faithful to Him. Think about this, My children. You surely realize that there is Glory yet to come for all who are given to the conversion of the lost. Today, it is My honor to appear among you again to pray for their souls, for the conversion of their hearts, purity in their lives, and good will among their peoples. Knowing that there is only one true path to redemption, you would not bargain away your portion of Jesus' suffering for any reason. Why be thankful for these things? Because it means the difference between righteousness and impiety, peace and war, justice and inequity, and Salvation and condemnation. The Lord does not expect for you to understand His motivations in all ways. Remember that you walk by faith and not by sight. Your sacrifices to the Church are magnified intensely by God's blessings upon your lives. Today, I ask you to pray for the millions who are lost in sin. It is their will that must be employed to bring them to the foot of the Cross. We indeed pray that they will give themselves to Jesus by the power and intercession of the Holy Spirit. It is true that humanity is broken in incalculable ways. Each person has his weaknesses. There are flaws deep in every man, but they are overcome by your identification with the perfection of the Kingdom of God. Most excellent men are aware of their fate, and more aware of their destiny to which they dedicate their lives. I seek more than an earthly dedication, but a divinely inspired consecration to the Sacred Heart of My Son. For many, this is the most difficult task they will ever pursue. They have long roads to travel. They have more gifts than they realize. We must ask them to share these gifts with keen intuition with those who seemingly have none. The world is large, filled with diverse opinions, multitudes of actions, countless events, and broad social perspectives; and yet, they must all become centered in the mission of the

Church. As the Mother of humanity, I am vested with the authority to take My children in hand and lead them to the Cross. I take them to the place where I witnessed the Salvation of the world come into being. Remember how painful the Crucifixion was for all who knew the Son of Man. We listened to His words of wisdom, we heard His dying gasps, we saw His courageous determination, and we believed that He would prevail. This is the same faith and conviction that every Christian must know of themselves. This is a hearty way to live in Jesus. It is moving toward full communion with His Passion and Holy Sacrifice that has not only changed the world, but redirected its course toward the Eternal Kingdom. This speaks to many questions asked by many who have served the Messiah with courage. What can one poor soul do to effect such change in the span of one life? How do my prayers influence the Will of God from such a lowly place where I live? My children, it is precisely from this remoteness that the outer expansion of Christianity is magnified. The Savior of humanity was born onto the Earth in this same simplicity, this same innocence, so that the world would know that all goodness comes from the littleness inside every man. Reclaiming this innocence is the mission of those who are living in exile. You have been given all the templates and blueprints necessary for this task. While Christianity is universal, it is spread by the ingenuity of the individual heart. You cannot expect to know all of them in the course of your lives, but I promise that they are there. There are millions of them, countless souls just like you, who wish for a better world. They pray for the focus of the collective human heart to be on the Holy Sacrifice that has brought the world to eternal forgiveness. Jesus would have it no other way. I have asked My children throughout the centuries to allow Jesus to touch them with His miracles, with His vision and compassion, and with His suffering, for it is in this that you will attain the glory that you seek. Now it is to these missions that all who live are called. It is not always an audible voice. There are signs and wonders aplenty. As the Mother of humanity, and as I have said – I pine, yearn and pray that you will listen to Me.

I ask you to keep your hearts alive and aloft in the peace of the Holy Spirit. Please do not become embittered by the burdens of this life. It is imperative that you remember that holy men and women are praying for you from On High. Call upon them, enlist their assistance, and most importantly, remember what they suffered. Heaven surrounds and engulfs you. Your own strength is a valued asset. And, the power of the Cross supports your hearts. There are better days to come. The Church itself, missionaries abroad, visionaries and seers, priests and religious are all at this time under intense and focused attack by Satan's evil legions. My Special son, you and your brother are suffering but a small part of this massive onslaught against the Mystical Body of Jesus. If you think in terms of Jesus' Agony in the Garden, you will know that it is perfectly human to have questions. It is not unholy to ask why. Turn to prayer. Always turn to prayer, and the answers will come. My Special son, are you still happy that you have chosen this course of life? *"There isn't any other life that matters."* Then, you feel a sense of fulfillment? *"Only when I think about the end of time, not now."* Where then is your gladness for today? *"I have to place it in my health and ability to go on."* You indeed have these blessings where so many others do not. The gifts of the Holy Spirit will keep your heart at peace. Follow these gifts with your heart and your thoughts will give you rest. I ask you again to pray for the priests who are undergoing such stress while fulfilling their vocations. Remember the imprisoned and incarcerated, those who are abused, the hungry and homeless, and refugees who are fleeing from wars. Consider what it means for family members to be killed and divided. Ponder the plight of those who have endured natural disasters and their resulting ravaging diseases. Ask Jesus to heal and touch the lives of the afflicted, those born with birth defects, and mothers who are contemplating aborting their children. There are certain priorities about which humanity must pray, and these are certainly among them. Thank you for praying as I have asked."

Sunday, July 17, 2011
4:15 p.m.

"My precious little children, you look around the world for answers to the questions that are asked inside each human heart. You have found them in your own faith and in the love that God is freely giving you. Yes, Jesus is dispensing ample messages to warn His people of the impending chastisements that can be avoided. I have told you on many occasions that to live in the image of Jesus will bring the peace and pardon that humanity desires. You have the answer. Therefore, let us not cease praying for the awakening of the human family to this same faith about which I have centered the purpose of your life. Today, it is My joy to pronounce approval upon your thoughts and actions that will mitigate many sins around the globe. You have the power, indeed you have the authority through the petitions available to you to grant this broken world a reprieve from the destruction that would otherwise come. This is a joy that cannot be rescinded because you realize that the Divine Mercy of Jesus is irrevocable. It is a fruit of His Holy Sacrifice, one that is sweet to the taste for those who accept Him. Let us be aware of all who are in need of spiritual conversion in our prayers. Ours is the highest calling because we can determine whether lost sinners eventually believe or continue to live in darkness. I ask you to be perseverant in your prayers with Me. The Lord will not forsake the prayers of His people. Millions more will be taken to the foot of the Cross. Jesus' Ancient Sacrifice is as powerful today as it was in the beginning, and it is to this power that the Church is drawn. I have every reason to believe that My children whom I adopted on Good Friday will respond. My Special son, I come to you briefly today along with your brother to bless your lives in the apparent suffering that you are undergoing. The designs of God are always built upon and focused toward the Cross. Please remember that it is through the Cross that the Paschal Joy of Easter comes.

I wish to address the messages that you and others have seen, dictated by Christ Jesus, to seers in distant lands. They are not meant to strike fear or manifest anxiety in those with strong faith. The content of those messages, as all others through history, is contingent upon the response of those to whom they are directed. I have said this throughout the centuries, especially in Fatima and Lourdes, in Medjugorje and Akita. Jesus is saying that humanity decides what will occur in the future in the same way that humanity determines the thickness of the veil. You have said in many places; you have written quite eloquently about this matter, that prayer to God is the best means to shape the course of human events. This is also the way it was in the beginning, and shall be through the end of time. The fact remains true that God depends upon His chosen flock, His righteous ones, to reach and convert those who are unholy. This is a process that takes time, that is marked by enduring perseverance because there are so many distractions and detractors. I need not tell you how many people are tethered more to the world than the Kingdom of God. You are aware of the purpose of suffering, of the introduction of new and innovative ways that the people of the Church can approach and enlighten the lost. Even more than your deposit of Marian manuscripts have the capacity to change the landscape of world history, simple prayer from the heart from all who believe in Jesus through the gifts of the Holy Spirit will alleviate the dangers and deadliness spoken about in the messages of Europe. Here again, Jesus does not wish to instill fear in those who have already accepted Him. By all means, most who claim a share of His Kingdom welcome Earth-cleansing manifestations. It would appear that you and your brother are among them, and rightfully so. With few exceptions, I have given you messages of hope and amendment, lessons needing to be learned by the millions who will then come to the Cross. I have rarely spoken of destructive chastisements because I believe in this hope; I foresee the amendments that must come. This is the way I have taught you to live. This has been the thesis of My apparitions from centuries ago. If it were only for punishment that the future exists, I would not need to appear. My messages would be redundant, and with little beatific meaning. It is the Mercy of Jesus that has caused Me to appear. Why? Because the world has the capacity to change, and it is those to whom My messages are given who must spread the word. You and your brother have done your part. You have given Me your lives. You have handed Jesus the keys to your hearts. You have presented to your Bishop the intentions that I have drawn to your attention. Does this mean that your mission is complete? Absolutely not! Your heart and that of your brother is filled with brilliant reflections and meditations that must be presented to humanity. They come to you and thereby from you, through the Wisdom of the Holy Spirit whose genius shall never die. I know that you welcome everything your Savior wants humanity to learn, as much as He teaches His Mystical Body about the Father's Kingdom through the daily homilies of His priests. You see that you are instruments in His hands with which He plays-out the Sacred Mysteries of human redemption. There is great joy in this. Of course, there is tremendous laboring and patience required, but you must accept in peace that this is the resolute necessity that will eventually unite all peoples, races, institutions and societies into one flock beneath My Son's guiding hand. Those who live by true faith will have no anxiety. Remember the words of Saint Padre Pio – pray, hope and do not worry. He never said that this would be easy. To not worry means to realize that prayerful petitions in fact do have power. It means to accept one's portion of the Cross. It means to believe in the compassion overflowing from Jesus' Most Sacred Heart. To not worry is not a concession or attitude of defeat. It means to embrace the Will of the Father who knows what is best for His Church. To not worry means to walk with confidence throughout one's life while knowing that the Holy Spirit is your compass to the Cross, and the Cross is your compass to Heaven. Let Me repeat your brother's metaphor here today. While seated on the ledges of history with your feet dangling in the past, see below you the fathoms of goodness that believers have left in their wake. You and your brother are like them. The Bishops and priests reflect the best actions and contributions of the Saints. Anyone who receives the power of the Holy Spirit with an open mind and heart, with arms stretched wide, has the wherewithal to defeat any enemy of his faith. Nothing in the world can defeat the Holy Spirit. The Spirit of God can never be muted, altered or amended when received in its original form, either with oratory or by manuscript. The Will of God is simply His Will. And, as you have seen in earlier times, His Will is made clear by those who receive Jesus' words in faith and trust. It is daily prayer through which God's Will is made manifest."

Sunday, July 24, 2011
3:04 p.m.

"Blessed are you, My dear little children, for remaining persistent in your prayers and efforts to change the world into the realms of true righteousness that lives and thrives within your hearts. You cannot yet know how well you are effecting these changes by your suffering – by all you have and will continue to give Jesus as the future unfolds. I only ask that whatever else comes, you do not lose hope. Never lose sight of your goals, those of the Church, the ones that will alter the course of the future when time and the Will of God place them into being. I wish I could convince you that these are some of the most productive days and years you have ever lived. You see such a stark contrast in the way I have described the Earth in the context of Jesus' Kingdom and the way you see it now. Please do not lose heart! I have told you throughout the years about the opposition. I have described in detail how My children are hated and despised. These are the times for which the world has been waiting to clarify what Jesus taught during His earthly ministry because there are so many new ways that human conduct can be assessed. You see the rapidity in which world conditions can be evaluated because you have reached an age of swift communication. This is an asset for reaching the millions who have yet to hear the Good News, but it is also a liability in the process of attempting to stem the spread of evil works. Today, it is My honor and gladness to secure your oath, that you will proceed with your daily works in light of everything that tries to block and impede your progress. There is such opposition to everything I have said to you in over twenty years. Look at the enemies of your faith! My Special son, you have said that those enemies would be more easy to recognize as these modern days unfold. You are now seen as having been a prophet! There is ample time to reach and convert the millions who must turn to the Church for help, for holiness and wisdom, for grace and Salvation. It is indeed our intent to pray that all of this will come, that it will be part of the immediate future and not far in the distance. Jesus has said that the world is groaning in pain. The Holy Spirit has been the comfort of those who are agonizing for the advancement of the teachings of the Church. I have asked My messengers worldwide to maintain your poise and composure in the face of the horrible struggles that have come. There is such indignity and ugliness, such destruction and desecration. However, the opposition to the teachings of My Jesus has always been this way; this opening century has brought nothing new, this third millennium does not offer anything that has not been seen before. I have attempted to focus My messages greatly around those I have given in the hills of Medjugorje. I have not meant to instill fear in the hearts of the faithful. I have not told of gruesome events to come. I have appeared there and in this home as the Queen of Peace and Love because I still believe that this is the way that the success of the Church's mission will be won. Of course, there will be wars and holocausts. There is no question that holiness is under assault. I have simply told humanity for thirty years in Medjugorje and twenty years to you and your brother that those who are faithful to the Holy Gospel need not get entangled in the hype. Remain confident of who you are. Remember the genius that has lived in you for so many years. This is what I have sought from all My seers and hearers since I first appeared here on Earth after My Heavenly Coronation. The faith you practice is simple, but the battles are complicated and intense. Satan is trying to distract My children into battling issues that are not truly related to the Christian conversion of men. Yes, this is his own way of creating diversions, of making the fight between good and evil more about the divisions between men than fighting against him. It is the theory of triangulation on a spiritual level. Whatever battles become the most heated are the ones that receive the most attention. I have said this before – if all men would gather under the Cross in opposition to everything that opposes the New Covenant Gospel, the lines would be clarified even more.

I come to you as a happy Mother today. I know that this is difficult to believe, given everything you see and hear in the world. I am happy for the reasons you already know. Everything I have told you in the past is coming to pass. I have said that the battalions and companies of Christian Saints would come to the aid of those fighting for righteousness. This is happening now.

I have also promised that there would be clear skirmishes and outright fights between believers and nonbelievers, and this is occurring too. I have always sought consistency from My children. I wish for you and your brother to always remember this. The word is 'consistency.' Another word I ask you to remember is commitment. These are like the two pillars of Saints Peter and Paul. Consistency and commitment. What does this mean for the future? You must be consistent in the intensity of your commitment of faith. You and your brother have lived long enough to see that time changes most everything worldly, that it brings great and tremendous confusion to those who are not fasted in the teachings of the Church. There is fluidity in secular cultures. Personal beliefs change according to the direction of the winds. There is no true consistency or commitment in those who are not standing on the solid ground of the Roman Catholic Church. This is what My messages have always proclaimed. It is what your writings have asserted and confirmed. There is time for My messages to you and your brother to reach all who must hear them, even if amid the other unfolding events that have been prophesied to other visionaries and locutionists. I have come to America as the Morning Star because your friends who live in this country must know what the Father wills for their nation. The United States was given progress not simply to make its citizens comfortable. Indeed, America itself has been inhabited by Europeans and millions of others from different foreign origins to prove that all can be one under a singular sky. The cause about which I speak is of the Christian Gospel that will eventually consume the world and cast the remainder aside.

Therefore, I come here seeking your confidence. This is the third word for today. Consistency, commitment and confidence. And, this confidence need not take a defensive tone. Confidence is never a product of being overly defensive because defensiveness is routinely a product of not being confident. The Martyrs were confident enough in their faith that they were unafraid to die for the Church. The Saints were chided, ridiculed, ostracized and persecuted for their confidence in faith. And, what you and your brother must come to know is that these same Saints thought nothing about it. For them, it was business as usual. It came with the territory of granting asylum to the Holy Spirit in the depths of their hearts. It is American secularism that has attempted to persuade anyone from any walk that it is a travesty to be made uncomfortable. They believe that it is a grave injustice to be told that someone is doing something contrary to the teachings of the Church. They have created so many victims that one might wonder who are the perpetrators! This is part of the false divisions that I spoke about earlier, some of the distractions and infighting that take the world's focus away from the battles against evil. You have learned through the years that one cannot follow Jesus without being insulted. It is impossible to provide for the poor without sacrificing the self. It is impossible to shed light unless that same light comes from within. It is all fairly and ironically logical when someone thinks about it. Jesus came to serve and not to be served. However, He also is the Master in whom He wishes all to reside. You and I know this to be possible. All Christians throughout the ages have proven that it can be done. When I say that it is logical, I mean that it is spiritually and theologically practical on a basis that sustains the worthiness of your faith."

Saturday, July 30, 2011
3:04 p.m.

"My dear little sons, I pronounce upon you this auspicious day the favor of the Lord who sends His blessings. You are aware that He is utilizing your sacrifices in and through the Church by the Providence inherent in Him for the conversion of the wicked and the cultivation of His vineyard in which so many Saints before you have labored. As I come to you again today, I implore you to remember in your prayers all My intentions for My children worldwide, especially that they will capture and maintain the purity of heart that I have spoken about in Medjugorje. I will indeed expound upon it there again. You know of the purity of Holy Love because you have lived it for many decades. You have in your faith kept your baptismal promises to Jesus, expanding your knowledge of righteousness and holiness by emerging into the world with authentic trust and faith in Him. It is always My honor to address the two of you through My messages that I have offered you for so long. Have I not told you that My own conviction, My own commitment to you has been foretold in other places around the globe? Thus, I am providing you with My own presence as I have similarly accompanied many before you along the walk of faith, through the travails of life, in your most needy hours, that you will know that you are not motherless in your journey toward the rewards of Heaven. Today, you have seen that there are untold other intentions that must be brought to the Altar, to Jesus' attention as if He did not already know, to God the Father who lives and reigns above you. It is more than an association that you share with them, it is a unity of seamless dedication to which you have devoted your lives. It does not seem possible that you can be so united with the Lord through your exile, through the veil that precludes mortal souls from seeing the Glory of Heaven. I have said that it is done so primarily through the facets of your heart and in your state of grace through the Sacrifice of Jesus on the Cross. Your impulse is to replicate His compassion for others in what you have come to accept as your own redemption. This is likewise the profits of your belief in His Resurrection from the Tomb. You receive these things, these blessings and wonders, because you have chosen to believe; they did not come in advance of the gift of your heart to Jesus. I have called your attention to the billions of souls who have lived-out their lives in this faith before you because it gives you reason to know that all humanity is collected and unified through it. One of My earliest messages told you about the bay in which the Mystical Body of Jesus is formed and cleansed. All of My messages have resounded the unity of the world beneath the Cross and inside Jesus' Most Sacred Heart. However, given the fractured and splintered nature of nations at this point in time, it would appear nearly impossible that such spiritual cohesion in the Christian Gospel will ever come to pass. You have become aware that all things are possible with God, and this unification of all nations and peoples is salient among them. If it were not, Jesus would have never entered the exiled Earth from the start. And, He came to convert and redeem all sinners, regardless of their status, no matter what they have previously been taught, and notwithstanding their animosity against the Church at this time. Jesus is one of the most hopeful human beings who ever lived. This is what He also asks of those who believe in Him.

What must God do to convince your brothers and sisters that the Holy Cross is the key to surviving the throes of death? How can the Father more clearly state that they must live by faith before seeing the values of their judgement firsthand? How can the world believe in the Messiah without having first placed their hands in His Sacred Wounds? By recognizing His presence in the brokenness of others. He is deeply imbedded in the starving and physically suffering. His Spirit lives in those who agonize for His sake. He is especially present to the meek, to the ones who serve His Church in remote geographic locations. The purpose of the Church to which I refer is to garner greater dependence upon Jesus by those who are living by that faith and not by sight. What would be the benefit of this sight before a soul has had the opportunity to imagine its length and breadth through the teachings of the Church? This is what the Sacraments bring to those who worthily receive them. They offer vision, wisdom, consolation, foresight and strength for all who are consecrated to the New Covenant through their own baptism and the daily practice that it brings. Promises are more than mere words. They are greater than secular social contracts that keep men from warring for inordinate reasons. Promises define the man; they give him reason to pursue virtue and righteousness. Promises measure the conscience of the souls who make them; they open the passageway for the accomplishment of all that is good. Sacred promises are the vows that are taken by human beings bound for Salvation. My Special and Chosen ones, you have made and lived-out your promises to the Son of Man through everything you have given Him in your lives. You have fulfilled your vows made when you were baptized by remaining obedient to the call of the Holy Spirit in you to adhere to the mandates of the Gospel and accept your share of suffering. This indeed makes you like the billions before you whom I have mentioned in that you will be likewise rewarded with the gift of Eternal Life. My Special son, there is no putting into words what Jesus sees in this world in terms of those who accept their share of His Passion and Sacrifice. It is not His intention to appear by apparition to everyone who endures these things and say that they should recognize rejection and persecution for what they are. It should be obvious by now that they are what they are. Although the Father has made provisions to communicate His Will and intentions through such hearers as you and your brother, He expects that His people will allow His Paraclete to infuse deific knowledge into their hearts as they live their daily lives. You must remember that these are the souls who will receive intense accolades upon the culmination of their term in exile, equally and commensurate with the messengers who have faithfully discharged the duties to which they were called in supernatural ways. Everyone is blessed with his assigned mission in life that advances the goals of the Church. You have seen this time and again when you and My other children seem amazed by how so many simple people can accomplish so much goodness with such sparse resources. It is incumbent on the whole Church to recognize what it means to be united in all ways with those who are searching for answers and challenging the secular void to do better in complying with the mandates of the Father. He presides over Creation through the Most Blessed Trinity, and this is the reason why all who believe in Him listen for His responses with actionable and visual spiritual intelligence. You have spoken along these lines in your writings, so I am not telling you anything new. I also wish to thank you and your brother for maintaining a spirit of friendship with your former

Bishop who has grateful memories of your love and support. He does in fact remember imparting His Apostolic Blessing on the very room in which I am now speaking. Also, it is apparent that you and your brother have the capacity to place certain inequities in proper perspective so you do not allow them to be a burden upon your hearts. Everything you do along these lines permits you to be more closely united with the suffering of Jesus, and they will lead to your sharing in the bounty of His Glorious Resurrection. I have heard from many others that they do not mind undergoing this kind of torment if the Lord would once in a while offer a glimmer of His Glory! It is present in your hopes, in your determination and consistency, in your knowledge that all things are passing toward the joyful morning when the Son of the Most High shall come again. *"How long will Timmy be tormented by Satan with such horrors? I feel sorry for him."* It is simply something that the Father has handed your brother. Different people have different crosses to bear. I am praying and interceding according to the Will of God. No one knows better than Me what it means to see innocent souls suffer for the conversion of the wretched. Thank you for having such compassion for what your brother has been undergoing. I ask you to reach-out in prayer on behalf of all who have given their lives to the conversion of lost sinners, wherever they are located in the world, whatever their role in the mission of the Church. I hope that you and your brother see that there is true happiness in this life. It is not all about suffering, rejection, doubt and isolation. It is about the eminent victory of Christian Salvation that you are helping the King of kings spread across this broken world."

Sunday, August 7, 2011
1:57 p.m.

"Good afternoon, My dear children, and welcome to the comfort of My Immaculate Heart. It is My honor and pleasure to speak to you on this special day, dedicated as always to the conversion of the world. I am here representing all the Hosts of Heaven, the Most Blessed Trinity, the beauty of ethereal nature, and the promises upon which you have built your spiritual faith. You have been told that the Lord is filled with Mercy for those who repent, for earthly sinners who recognize the error of their ways and ask Him for forgiveness. It is to this blessing that I have always spoken; it is this fact that reigns supreme over all other pursuits of humanity on Earth. Therefore, I ask that you not be disconcerted when My adopted children are led to this conversion by events and opportunities that do not seem to fit into any given circumstance. I have said the world over that Jesus knows what He is doing, and what He allows touches the hearts of the millions seeking to receive His compassion. Divine Love has been described in many ways in the Sacred Scriptures, most evocatively about sacrifice. Please remember that My Son's Holy Sacrifice is the thesis of your faith; it is the essence of what redeemable men and women believe. My Special son, I know that you are wondering what to make of all My messages from January 2009 to the present. I have dictated them to you and your brother so you can continue your journey of enlightenment about the condition of the world, what Jesus sees as He looks upon it, and how Heaven influences all that is just and good in the temporal realms. You are aware that the battle between goodness and evil rages on horribly every day. Love has already defeated hatred, and I have told you that the latter is breathing its last; evil is in its final throes. This may seem difficult to believe for those who are savoring the eternal victory that you have gained in Jesus' Crucifixion and Resurrection. This is the reason I have spoken to you about conviction and consistency. Back to your memoirs. They need not read like a storybook. They need not be a chronology of what you have done in your life. They should be comprised of essays, paragraphs and phrases to inform humanity who God is. Even though your memoirs will always be about you, they must ultimately lead to your relationship with Jesus through My intercession, the power of the Holy Spirit, your interaction with the Christian giants of history, many whom you have known, and to the witness that you and your brother are giving humanity by everything you have done in deference to the Salvation of man. I realize that you have already composed many pages of your first memoir, and they are wonderful content. The connection that you must always draw, every reference and implication, must emphasize that human beings must submit and surrender to the power of Christ Jesus in the shaping of the future here in the material realms. The blueprint for this has always been the New Covenant by which you have lived all your mortal years. There are no other rules for your memoirs. You can pen them as you wish, illuminate whatever you believe will touch the hardest of hearts with stories and discussions about the presence of God in the lives of those who have responded to His call. Here, and in this, you will have plenty to say."

Sunday, August 14, 2011
4:00 p.m.

> *"Humanity will never be able to justify before Jesus Christ our neglect in upholding the sacred mandates He gave us from the Mount of Olives and Crucifixion Hill. There is no pragmatic or philosophical reason for our having allowed society and the Earth to deteriorate into such a depraved condition. We might make frail attempts to explain-away our passivity in the wake of the onslaught against our unborn children by saying that we could not take-on city hall. However, I am convinced that Our Lord would have us forthrightly take down city hall with all the brainpower and righteousness we can muster to restore the world's order of love and dignity of life that the Father commands. God would support any dynamic that would better enforce His ordinances before a people who have brazenly shunned them for thousands of years. This is what I see occurring in the not too distant future; for there is coming a reckoning so massive that it will be too large to grasp within the confines of the rational human mind."*
>
> William L. Roth

"My little sons, the world does not yet realize the immensity of the Love of God for His creatures, His living and breathing beings who are representative of His generative power. You know that those surrounding you now, all the little people and lauded ones, all the souls who compose Jesus' Mystical Body, are called into the service of the Church in their individual ways. We have watched and listened for their response because we know that it will come, just as sure as Jesus will come again in Glory. I have spoken about the ability of humanity to bring into being that righteousness to which Jesus has drawn you because you have the capacity by virtue of your faith in Him. Is this not really what you and your brother's memoirs are saying? You speak about the accomplishment and implementation of everything that is possible through Jesus' Sacrifice and Resurrection. And, this is done on the Earth by sinners through a sinless Savior. It has been asked if Jesus ever sinned. It is a legitimate question, one that almost everyone who has accepted and followed Him has asked. It is legitimate because Jesus is like all the peoples of the Earth in every way except sin. This leads to a veritable landslide of discussion topics about how someone could be similar in nature to every other person on the globe, even though those people are so radically different. It is about the soul. It is about conduct over appearance. It is about possessing and actualizing the wisdom of the ages that has healed divisions and mended broken relationships. This similarity is healing, uniting, reuniting, converting and embracing. When we have spoken through the years about the 'oneness' of the Church, this is what we mean, and such is not the case with secularism. The latter highlights and emphasizes diversity and pluralism. Secularism is a concept of belief that perfect Truth is dependent upon whom you ask for a definition. This is the reason why secularism is such an enemy of the Church; rarely do any secular beliefs or practices align with the teachings of Christ Jesus.

You have seen messages around the globe that speak about random atrocities, genocide, the felling of world leaders, violence and social unrest, chastisement and catastrophic events of all kinds and proportions. Indeed, many of them will come. This does not mean that God does not love His Creation; by all means, He is trying to reorient the exiled world toward the issues and ordinances that truly matter. If He did this in a peaceful way, the conscience and cohesion of humanity would not be stirred. If He attempted to touch lost sinners through some kind of softness or levity, those He is trying to reach would simply say that His overtures are kind gestures, and would otherwise smile and turn away laughing. The destiny of the human soul is more crucial than that. You and your brother have lived long enough to realize that most all memories held close by human beings are about certain tragedies that seem to divide time into poignant segments. Such things as world wars and plagues will never be forgotten by the generations involved or those who follow. However, how many people are speaking with any sense of history about the Fatima Miracle of the Sun? The answer is that they are hardly speaking of it at all. Does this imply that terror and suffering are the only way the Lord can reach His creatures? Certainly not, but it seems that the will of those creatures directs their attention away from the gravity of human sin and the effects of their error. Millions of people maintain that God is meanspirited toward those living on the Earth, but He is only responding to their own indifference with power that they will long remember. It has been said by such writers as Emerson that Nature does not like to be observed, that every time a man figures out Nature's essence is an accident. This need not be the way that humanity approaches their relationship with the Son of God. He welcomes examination. He implores lost sinners to scrutinize the Holy Gospel. Then, if they should thereafter determine the value and content of His Will, this is no accident. This is the mutual exchange between Heaven and Earth.

You are living in a time that is rarer than the first generations. You are seeing the consequences of twenty centuries of Christianity taken to be serious food for thought by those who believe. You are also seeing billions of people who, due to the availability of advanced communications, know the teachings of Jesus Christ, but who reject them anyway because they are at such odds through the secularism that I have mentioned. In other words, they cannot focus their vision on the Promise because they do not know Him who has made the Promise. They need to realize that not everything passes into history. Many images, mandates and events are timeless. Such is the New Covenant Gospel. The Truth of the Cross will outlive everyone who was and will be given the breath of life. The absolute joy of the Resurrection cannot be dimmed in the hearts of those who believe. This is the stability of life that must be known in the thoughts and actions of all the world. This is the stability that calms the storms, both literally and figuratively, that makes all other problems disappear. This is the stability of the new sunrise, fair weather and cool breezes, of comfort and consolation, and of fairness and reconciliation. The key concept is 'stability.' Thus, you have known this for decades, and you have lived-out this purpose since you were a young boy. If there is instability in someone's life, it is because they have not adapted to life in a world with the absolute Truth of Jesus Christ as their guide. This seems elementary to you, but it is not as clear to those who are distracted by rampant secularism. And, this comes and goes with whomever is speaking or who is being spoken about. For example, the current United States president gives only casual reference to Christianity because he has found fame, power and fortune in secular elitism. This problem goes all the way through the seats of government and houses of representatives nationally and in all the states. The Lord realizes that organized people require structured governments, but not ones that make the belief in and action of prayer to the God of Abraham an exception to common personal freedom.

I wish to thank you for spending so many days with your brother. He so needs you! I need you! Jesus and the heavens need you! You and your brother are admired and smiled upon by all the Hosts of Heaven. There has never been any question in your mind about this. It is not that God does not care about your welfare when you fight your battles. It is not about Satan having all the weapons. It is definitely not about always deferring to those who are corrupt when times come to make decisions that affect so many others in either welcome or unwelcome ways. It is about the Holy Sacrifice of Jesus on the Cross, about everything that rests inside it, around it, through it, and because of it. You win when you realize that certain issues do not matter. You carry the banner of victory when you attest to the judgement and conduct of the Saints before you. It is about ownership, the eternal possession of grace and power that will slay and defy everything about this world that seems in opposition to your plans. Ownership implies proprietorship, and there are huge implications that accompany it. You must have the drive to persevere against those who believe that defeating you and your brother to be the most important thing they will ever do. Ownership means that your brother must learn to not take for granted the sufferings he is having, but that he can overcome them by addressing the way he responds. It is not a sin to be afraid. It is not a signature of weakness to be exhausted. This is what it means to enter the arena with courage, for without fear, there is no need for courage. It means that the whole world of Christians, My adopted children, should become so holy that anything unholy rolls off them like raindrops from a brass steeple. This is where vision plays its most important part. Having said what I have said, I do not mean to suggest that any of this is easy. There is true discomfort, weariness, despair and mourning in being a Christian. This was built into the Faith of the Gospel from the beginning. We shall address more of this subject in depth in the future. *"It still seems like individual Christians don't have any power to retake and change the world, except to suffer them. There is no one that walks around like Jesus and the Apostles, striking the lightning of supernatural power, of raising people from their sickbeds or their tombs, or anything that pierces this dismissive mind-set to where they are put on notice that the Kingdom of God is at hand. The leaders of the Church are asleep, and it seems that our only option is to wait for disasters to wake everybody up. It's different when Peter dropped two people in their tracks for lying to the Holy Spirit and sent them to the throne of God, striking that fear into the community, and telling them why. People mock God because they haven't seen that power in centuries."* My son, the answer to your assertion is not difficult to understand. God is waiting to give the power about which you speak to the community of believers who hail Him in modern times in the multitudes. In the multitudes! He wants cohesion between Christians who will all stand with acclamation and declare that the Earth belongs to Him. *"They will if they saw that power again. They will follow the word of the person who displays it. If you had someone who had the power to command any supernatural act at their will, millions would change overnight."* The Mystical Body of Christ is the person about whom you are speaking. *"Their individual human wills have them scattered and blind."* Yes. Why do you think I have been speaking to you and your brother for so many years? To unite them into that one voice, speaking and thundering everything you have affirmed today in this room. This is not a complicated matter. 'That all shall be one in Him.' This is where the power to address and redress all the problems you have cited today rests. There is only one Messiah, and His Mystical Body is living here in this world. If a billion Roman Catholics united in a single voice, you would hear the Son of Man speak through their unity with clarity and direction. Thy Kingdom Come implies that everyone is living and breathing-in the Savior of the world, and because of Him. Now, does this mean that you have to wait until this total accord occurs until those miracles about which you speak come into being? Certainly not. The Lord will provide the miracles about which you have spoken, and over which you have wept. You will see this happen with dispatch, but I ask you and your brother to continue your own work without placing all your expectations in those future times. You have work to do on a day-to-day basis. I truly appreciate the sentiments that you have expressed today. And, Jesus has heard you as well. What you have proclaimed is a unique prayer to which My Son will respond. *"I just wish the people at my workplace, and all the different places I have seen, were as terrified of what the power of God would do next as those people who stood before Peter, and those people who were struck-down for lying. Then, they will try to be good because there will be consequences; man will not change until there are verifiable consequences. That's just how humans are. They have been inflicting consequences on humanity for centuries, and Christianity must now be able to stand-up and inflict the consequences."* It shall be done as you ask because this is your prayer. The whole Church has offered the prayer you have given today for Justice to come to the Earth. Yes, being a Roman Catholic Christian means having the wholesome spiritual vision that you are exhibiting now."

Saturday, August 20, 2011
7:16 p.m.

"If scientists could prove the existence of God, spirituality would be reduced to a hypothetical laboratory experiment, devoid of the mysticism that humanity needs to elevate us from the depths of the common and ordinary. God reveals Himself to the Earth on His own terms; we will never discover His identity in a test tube or petri dish. The Father is uncontainable, but His Spirit can be isolated inside the human heart as a

knowable and approachable conceiver of Creation. This must begin with the desire to in fact search for Him and sense the need for reaching out for wisdom beyond our years that cannot be divulged anywhere else. Our forefathers would have given life, fortune, and limb to have been able to see for only a moment what awaited them beyond their lives; when in fact, we already know what they yearned to see. It is found in professing our religious conviction in the revelations of the Messianic message, for this is how we are touched in unprecedented ways by supernatural powers beyond our own realms. If we give ourselves to Christ Jesus to every imaginable degree, we will embark upon the journey that will take us to the beatific heights heralded in the Scriptures. It is obvious that no theoretical equation will ever be this transcending."

William L. Roth

"This is the writing that will alter the course of human events, My children. Your vision and eloquence are fruits of your faith in God, your association with everything that is of God, and your awareness that God precedes every created thing. You have for so long remained faithful to Him because you wish to go to Heaven someday. And, you desire that all your brothers and sisters will go to Heaven with you to join all who have passed before. My little sons, I wish I could convince you that the struggles of mortal life are worth the fight. Indeed, many Saints before you fought with great internal difficulty believing this to be true. There are so many calamities and tragedies, they thought, for the Lord to have very much interest in the plight of the exiled. I have told and taught you that most of the misfortune that mankind faces is manifested by himself, by not turning to the Father when it would be justly prudent. Jesus will not forsake those who trust deeply in His capacity to lead them by the heart to the holiness and righteousness that brings such joy to the human spirit. If I were to suggest to many people here on Earth that most of the suffering is caused by those who suffer, they might hear My words with disdain. I am not speaking about the kind of suffering like Jesus and His followers endured and still endure, I am talking about the suffering that comes when people refuse to live prayerfully, when they are reckless and steeped in sin. I am speaking about suffering that comes when the human heart is more attuned to the distractions of worldliness than the Kingdom of Love. You have seen, My little sons, that those who walk with care and compassion are received with gentleness, for this is inherent to the heart of those who yearn to live in peace. And, there are likewise different kinds of pain. Some pain is mental and other is physical. Pain is a great discipliner of the human soul and conscience. Pain integrates the knowledge of Heaven with the perils of the Earth. And yet, pain can also drive souls to question the degrees to which the Father is engaged with His people. 'Why would God let this happen to me?' This is the question that suffering people are prone to ask.

My little ones, there is no need to search for rhyme or reason. These are such glorious times for humanity! There is so much that was once held secret that is being revealed, so many facts and circumstances that will awaken the sleeping hearts among you! I am pleased and elated that God has chosen to dispense such revelatory messages worldwide as He is doing during these crucial days of the Earth. When you hear the words, '...let not your heart be troubled...' you must remember that there is intense converting power in the passing of these days. If you will only take the time to ponder it, you will notice that a great many issues I spoke about in My messages to you from 1991 through 2008 are being addressed by the Church at this time. The millions of Christians who inhabit the Earth are finally understanding the significance of the teachings of the Church and the power of the Cross. This makes Me very happy! It is never an exercise in futility when the world's population, at least those who believe in God, ask what He is doing! What is He up to now? This is what they want to know. And, the answer to this question is that He is responding to the thoughts and actions of His faithful flock on Earth. He is answering the prayers of the Roman Catholic Pontiff, and He is directing all who will be saved into that fateful place where they are confronted by those who will not be saved. The battles between goodness and evil have always been the same. It would appear that there is great loss being sustained by the Church, and there are certainly countless Martyrs along the way. However, these glorious sacrifices are never in vain. All that is given to the Glory of God and the Kingdom of Heaven is utilized in these battles to destroy everything that opposes the Salvation of man. You must convince My other children that this is true. It is clear that you will be successful in this! Therefore, I am giving My support to your work and encouragement for your hearts. You know all about the injustices in the United States and around the globe. You know about the unfairness in the distribution of wealth and the cruelty that is heaped upon workers and employees who are simply trying to feed their families. You are aware of the grotesque and obscene costs of food and clothing, medical care and everything else needed to ensure the dignity of the human person. These are passing issues, but there is no doubt that they are significant to the millions who must suffice them. I ask for the world's continuing prayers for the alleviation of suffering that comes from the greed and neglect of unholy people. As for the other suffering that arises from disease and other illness, pray for healing and for the Will of God to be done. After all, this remains a world affixed to the dangers, unfairness and haughtiness of those who despise the worshipers of the Cross. There is safety and harbor in the faith you have been given, in the trust you place in Jesus, and in your confidence that all will end in victory for the blessed. We have walked the paths of Wisdom and discretion together in different centuries. We have seen the same openness to the Holy Spirit by the friends of the Church. Even as the young pray for the world with Pope Benedict XVI in Madrid during these days, there are millions of others who need to pray. They will do so if they see the need, if they become aware that it is their petitions that can make a difference in bringing peace, hope and justice to a world so broken by the grossness of sin. My Special one, thank you and your brother for permitting Me to come speak to you on this pretty summer evening."

Saturday, August 27, 2011
1:39 p.m.

"Blessed are they whose homes are filled with peace, whose families are touched by righteous grace that comes from the heart of the Father in ways inexplicable and beyond the logic of men, for the universal sharing of love, capable of dismantling the Earth and reassembling it again."

William L. Roth

"Holy days, My children! What a wonderful quotation you have composed for today's message, My Special one! So simply profound and unequivocally true! By the designs you have given Jesus, and through the architecture of your heart united with your brother, you are continuing to broadly touch the universe and heal the soul of humankind. If I have yet to make it abundantly clear, these are the means through which the Wisdom of the Holy Spirit is imparted, transmitted and transferred to the world. I come to you in elation and happiness because you and your brother are still praying for all that must come, every avenue and all the scenarios that will convert lost sinners and change what must be changed. It is the faith by which you live that serves as the catalyst for all these things. I am in Heaven and on Earth, and I assure you that the whole of Creation and everything beyond it hears the prayers of the Church. While you may not see it firsthand, there are lives being amended by the sacrifices of the faithful. And, to be sure, this is not done by such prophesies that you have seen in recent messages elsewhere around the world, it is accomplished by living precisely as you and My other children are approaching the cultivation of the material world. You do not and have never shared messages of doom and gloom; and although we have declared the Imminent Reckoning, you have not given advance notice of something called The Warning because you have lived not unlike the Saints of old. You realize that bringing holiness and goodness into the lives and hearts of sinners is a process of small steps and thoughtful reflections. This is the reason you have never surrendered your desire to see the journey through. It is in your nature to accept what is offered from the hands of the Lord in His time. You are willing to plant the seeds of hope in the appropriate places, and nurture and cultivate them so they will grow like spires into the nighttime skies. Quietly, the Roman Catholic Church has gone about its work of determining the outcome of all human events, not by bombastic fanfare or summary judgements portending the wholesale destruction of the Earth. You and your brother, and all My faithful children, have been like carpenters who drive every nail meticulously, measuring and fitting, eyeing and protracting. This is the life that Jesus expects of His disciples. There will surely be time-dividing events come in the near future, and it is those like you and your brother who must speak with calming voices, giving assurance that the Kingdom of God is growing on the Earth exactly as it should. The maturity of your graceful knowledge, your poise and confidence, and all the experience you have had with Me are the sources of your composure. The Holy Spirit in your heart is the genesis for all this. Divine Love is your energy; your determination to see the Church victorious is your focus, and your daily petitions are the implications that God notes for the completion of His Plan.

  I speak to you and your brother today in both broad and specific terms about this energy, about the drives and impulses that keep you at peace inside the Sacred Heart of My Son. If anyone ever asks how you have come to know so much about the Savior of the world, tell them that you learned it from Me. Say that I directed you to the Holy Gospel, the New Covenant, as the Matriarch of the Church and the Mother of the Redeemer. Give your honest assessment of what the world means to Me in the ways I have always described it to you, how it presently exists, and the innovative changes that must come. I have told you many times that the spiritual life of the Church is not a science, it is a movement that began in the heart of the first Apostles at the behest of Christ Jesus, Himself. Many have asked how the first Apostles could have known that Jesus was the Messiah when they did not have the benefit of the Paraclete yet inside their hearts and consciences. What do you suppose you should say to them? *"The personification of the Holy Spirit was directly in front of them."* This speaks to the Mystery of the Most Blessed Trinity. Was the Holy Spirit then born of My Womb upon Jesus' Nativity in Bethlehem? *"Yes."* And, was God likewise born that glorious night? *"Yes."* He was born unto Man of Himself in Perpetual Light for which there is no beginning. There has never been an instant before, during or after history when God did not exist, yet He was born into the world the first time in His Only Begotten Son. I birthed the Son and the Most Blessed Trinity concurrently to humanity in the night at Bethlehem. It was the simultaneous profusion of the Divine that was living in My Womb since the Annunciation, given birth and venue to heal and convert the Earth and its human inhabitants, and to judge their worthiness in and outside of time. Again, I say that it is all about energy – sacred energy, popular energy, the kind of energy that makes the sun rise in the morning and little children yearn for their parents at night. This is the energy of curiosity that makes men fly into outer-space, look into microscopes to search for the origins of life, wonder what their brothers are thinking, and will-into-being a happiness and fulfillment that only true faith can supply. This sacred energy fosters the fruits of victory over death and light conquering the darkness. It makes men stand before throngs with mightiness in their words and proclaim that humanity is better than what they have been. The sacred energy about which I speak gives life to hopes, facility to everything possible under the sun having to do with love, and reason for the decisions and actions that move the collective conscience of men toward the Cross of Salvation. Notice that I have not spoken here of arithmetic methods or mind-numbing calculations. I have referred to a process of creating and releasing energy in ways that forge righteousness into being, that grows it, shares it, and saturates the hamlets and ghettos of the world with high expectations that justice is nigh.

    I am not unmindful that everything I have spoken about today is of a framework that requires the profession of faith spoken about in the Church through the teachings of Jesus' earliest words. You and your brother realize that no length of time can reverse the Will of God for the redemption of His people. When the Church says that the Grace of Heaven is timeless, humanity can be certain that this is precisely the case. Sacred energy is as timeless as Paradise itself; it is fixed and permanent in this world and the next. Indeed, Popes, Bishops and clergy throughout the ages have pondered the workings of this sacred energy, that it is the effect of the Holy Spirit that fills books with Truth, that opens eyes blinded by centuries of hatred, that holds fast to the very crux of goodness that Jesus brought the world from the Manger. This energy of the Holy Spirit is the honesty of God forthright, given to men in servings small enough to ingest and large enough to never exhaust. It is like a roaring wind blowing across the lands and prairies of the human heart in such a way that the hearts who feel it gain a sense for the possible; everything is possible with God. And, it is this sacred energy that makes all Christians live-out their lives realizing that, no matter what happens at any point in time, the Lord God in Heaven is always there. He knows what is best when men wring their hands in confusion. He heralds the best of all possible lives before those who believe in Him. It does not have to make sense for now because so many of His followers are still between hammer-swings. Others are reaching for tools; and still more are viewing and evaluating what must be done next. This is why there are ebbs and flows in life, why it often seems stagnant and at times so overwhelming. Life with the sacred energy of God's Love has a discernible melody and audible harmony. It has grain and texture, fullness and lightness – and most of all, it has purpose."

Monday, September 5, 2011
12:46 p.m.

"It would seem that the important issues in human life are clarity and direction, perspective, values and beliefs, identification and association. These are indicators of the inward aspects of the individual, but they do not address the condition of the soul. Everything that permeates the designs of man on a sensitivity scale fosters our self-actualization and sufficiency, but the most critical decision we will ever make is how we will judge ourselves before the Father who created us. What do we use as criteria? It is not always as difficult as it appears. All we need is for the Holy Spirit to give us the proper rhymes and reasons, clefs and registers, and we will sing with such dimensions that we will begin to wonder who we really are. How we

vocalize these strains is the essential element telling whether we have truly lived or just existed. It has a sweet cadence too, like a child's hand rustling through a jar of jelly beans, or someone reaching into a paper bag of carpentry nails, getting ready to hammer down a sheet of plywood. There is something about hearing the rolling and rattling that is like music to human ears."

William L. Roth

"My little sons, while the rest of the world is flailing about as though lost in space or burdened pushing boulders uphill, you are at peace with Saint Joseph and Me in the Love of Jesus, the Providence of God, and the Wisdom of the Holy Spirit. I cannot state too many times that it is in this peace that you must always live, forever discovering your meaning in life, and purifying your thoughts. You are made perfect in your faith because faith is the pristine gift of the Father to those who are open to receive Him. Today, I bring you the elevation of the grace to which all men are called, to look upward and outward into the softness of the Divine and Sacred Heart of Jesus. My Special son, your writing at the beginning of this message is again profound; it exhibits a vision of the simplicity of the mysteries of life that few take time to enjoy. Yes, the judgement of God is firm, and His purposes reflect the commands that He has dispensed to the Earth for thousands of years. You must remember that there is tremendous militance shown even in some of Jesus' messages to the world, those elsewhere as the Church is trying to survive in lands with growing secularism. I have said to My seers and hearers that Jesus is a patient Lord, but I have not addressed the factual degree of His patience's thickness or thinness. There are levels and ranges of patience that humanity practices, and you must remember that Jesus is a Man. He is subject to the pleas for Mercy by those who are only now coming to know Him. He is as persuadable as any other man because His Heart is touched by sincerity and repentance. He knows the qualities and characteristics of men who attempt to amend His judgements by their ardent desires to change for the better, but He also recognizes those who attempt to seek His favor with insincerity. Throughout the ages, servants have sought the approval of their masters, but they have not always employed the proper approach. When someone asks Jesus for aid, it must always be done with a firm purpose of faith in the Blessed Trinity; it must be through authentic belief that the Father in Heaven is equally as impressionable as the Son. Neither seeks the tears of the faithful if they are not joyful ones. It is the world that makes men sad. I have for centuries attempted to enlighten the Church about confidence, but it eludes them because of their daily battles with the devil. Prayer is always the answer. Some do not believe in prayer; others know about it, but claim that it has no true power. The power they are seeking is God, Himself, and prayer is the way to communicate with Him. Every time the record of someone having passed-away appears in the public news, friends and cohorts say that they will pray for the surviving family members. While this is rightly what they should do, they never say they would pray for them before the death. Is this really what it takes to make prayer come? You have seen it over and over again; the heart-touching conduct of humanity ordinarily comes only when there is something to mourn. On the contrary, I have spoken about the gladness, the utter ecstasy of the Salvation of the whole world, and only few bother to heed My call for thanksgiving prayers. I am not complaining here, I am only making an observation. I must assure you and your brother that our prayers together to Jesus are worthwhile, and they make-up for the many prayers that are left unsaid, the greatest waste in the world. I have spoken on every continent of the Earth about the deficits and overages that need to be ameliorated. There is little common sense about the extremeness of the offenses of sinful men against the dignity of the Church. Indeed, there is no sense at all; the world simply believes that the Catholic Church is fodder for ridicule and criticism because nobody will fight back. But, you fought back! I am duly and justly proud of you for standing upright in defense of the priests of the Church. I must tell you that Jesus is blessing you for your proclamations, for your courage and upright heart. Never mind what repercussions might come. I only ask that you be at peace knowing that you are a warrior for God in ways that you do not even know. Be confident in your actions, and forget about what might happen. Do not make anything greater of this than what it is. (*I was recently near a group of individuals at my workplace who began jesting and mocking the priests of the Catholic Church as abusers. I began to peacefully explain, as to a group of friends, how their wholesale mockery was unjust in light of the actual facts. At that point, the most aggressive of the individuals, who happened to be a Protestant, walked across the room, got within twelve inches from my face and snarled in rage how they all should get the death penalty. I did not flinch as I stared him in the eyes and told him that he was nothing more than an anti-Catholic bigot.*)

Also today, I bring you the promise of intercessory prayers from Blessed Teresa of Calcutta, and you and your brother must know that her alliance with

Pope John Paul the Great means holy things for you. This tandem of Saints is overseeing the condition of the Earth with sorrow, but also with hope and promise. They are basking in Eternal Light in full view of the Face of the Father and inside the arms of Jesus. As you are prone to say, '...think about it.' You and your brother are suffering the pains of being Christian in an atheistic world, just as millions more around you are doing. This does not imply that you do not have power. You are seated in the most powerful place in Creation – in the Love of Jesus Christ as He inhabits you, manifests greatness in and through you, and touches the lost through your lives of good works. It is all right to wonder what might happen to the other millions who do not believe in the Cross because such pondering is the substance of converting prayer. I have said that the greatest power in the world is in your communication with the Hosts of Heaven. I am here with you today as proof. I came to you and your brother in 1991 because of the status of your own faith, your decision to offer your lives and human will to Jesus, and the sentiments you hold for the many who have served the Church in generations past. You and your brother believed in the conversion and redemption of humanity when others refused. You held hope in your hearts and the burdens of the world in your hands. You walked in the Light of Truth when too many of your friends tread the dangerous darkness of sin and error. I have said that I came to you not because you were worthy, but this does not mean that you were not worthy. You have loved Me and cherished My messages for over twenty years. You have held the Cross high before humanity and dared anyone else to live so sacrificially, to die so willingly, and to seek the blessings of the Father so publicly. You have lived in trust and prudence, with your eyes on the business of the days and the promises of the future. This is the way that I have called all My children to espouse the faith that you have been given, not only through your Baptism, but through your openness to God that led to your Baptism in the first place. Even as infant children, little souls yearn for someone to take them to the Sacrament of Baptism, even before they are old enough to realize where they are. This is the timelessness and agelessness of the human soul that instinctively knows that it must be washed clean of original sin.

Thank you for helping your brother complete his college paper. It is true that he does not believe much of the content of the document, but he must play the game of the secular university for now; it is what they expect, even when they know themselves that some of their students are speaking only what must be heard. It is all so irrelevant! It is steeped in secular correctness, a movement toward the bland and meaningless, an attempt to make a point about a matter that has no substance at all. And, not only is it irrelevant, it is such a distraction. It takes people away from time spent praying and pondering what God will do next. They even have a poll for this! When they are distant from Him, they blame Him for the vacuum. They cannot see that it is their own indifference, their own callousness, their faulty viewpoints that keep them from knowing Him better. These are among the things for which I pray because they must someday judge themselves before the Father through the Sacrifice of the Son. I am aware of your continuing writing, the pretty phrases that make you cry, the emotion that will touch the hearts of those who see it. This does not come to you lightly. You are open to receive the inspiration of Jesus in your writings because, as I have said, you believe in Him in ways not known to the rest of the world. Thank you and your brother for your years of service, for fighting the good fight and keeping the faith. You are proving that the dead will rise again from their graves."

Saturday, September 10, 2011
1:41 p.m.

"We know that mortal life has exhaustible texture, that it can be rough or smooth; sometimes intense, gutting, craggy, cruel and unseemly, and even suffocating and overbearing; but most people do not know how to touch or view it with any sense of understanding what to look for. Fortunately for us, everything we will ever need to know about Christianity is that we can walk as believers before seeing, making our way beyond the most startling moments, perilous threats, thunderous valleys, deepest forests, and darkest nights to arrive safely in our eternal homeland, to turn back the years and defy the ages; ultimately discovering that our eyesight was perfect all along."

William L. Roth

"Good afternoon, My beautiful sons. It is My pleasure to be here with you among the Hosts of Heaven who have attended Me, to assist in the intercession and intervention that humanity needs to be drawn into the Holy Light of the Love of God. My Special son, you are obviously aware of the immaculate writing that you have placed on the page for your memoir. Your writings are visionary because you can see through the eyes of faith to which you refer. You realize that Creation is not a void or vacuum, especially due to the presence of the Lord, and that the Father breathes life into every creature because of the Love I am speaking about. He has created nothing that is meant to be lifeless, even the earthen soil and rocks and mountains. They have life by virtue of being framed into existence through His perfect designs. I am speaking about a world that is pneumatic, that is filled with spirit, filled with the miraculous substance of God's creative genius. He has never been without this power because He is perpetual. Every thought of the Father should be framed in the context of this permanence – this perpetuity that reigns supreme over every other conceivable thing, every other thought or framework. When you speak about the craggy surfaces of life, or that it is unseemly, or perhaps unwieldy, you are using words that describe life on the Earth not as it should be, but what it is like because of human sin. The world Jesus is trying to build is inhabited by a humanity that shines brilliantly in His Glory, that is obedient to the Will of the Father that has fashioned the globe from its beginning. Remember that billions of years mean nothing to Him. They have no effect on what God has done or will do hereafter because His Glory is about a succession of events that are not affected by time. It is true that succeeding events implies the passage of time, but the succession about which I am speaking consists of the terms 'succeeding' and 'concurrent' or 'simultaneous' being paradoxically synonymous. This means that events are eclipsed by other events such that eternity is one glorious streaming permanence of Eternal Light. This Light can travel, but it need not travel to reach anything that is of Creation or beyond it. I have given you this type of image before, speaking about the overlapping of timely human events that comprise one eternal moment.

We join our prayers and thoughts at the behest of the Blessed Trinity because the world of men is still in turmoil. There is tremendous unfairness and indecency, horrific and treacherous danger and filth. We have discussed these things in depth, and many of My messages to other seers reflect what I have said here. You can doubtlessly see the power in your writings and what they will mean for the enlightenment of the whole world in due time. You are a precious creature to Me, to Jesus and Saint Joseph, to God the Father, to the Angels and Saints and everything about the history of the world that ever reflected the goodness and holiness inherent in your faith. Your brother is seen this same way, as are all who invest their lives and purposes in the teachings of the Church. Those who are loyal and obedient to Jesus are humongous in number; they are unstoppable, unflappable, fearless and visionary. However, this is not something that they have claimed of their own accord; it was given to them through the Love of God. While My children on all the continents seem shocked by every new depravity and degradation, it is not necessary to see them this way. You should expect that Satan and his demonic legions will throw everything evil they possibly can against Christians who are living-out their faith. It has been this way since the beginning, and it is ongoing to this day. You and your brother see things well; you utilize the perspectives I have taught because you have tasted victory before. You are My children who live innocent lives in Jesus, and you are at the same time mature in knowing where the perils lie. In other words, Satan does not seem to surprise you concerning what he is liable to do next. He is all about abusing power and authority, about spreading prideful corruption any place he can. He is about impurity and desecration, disloyalty and a stench of death and darkness that only he can effect. I ask you and your brother and all My children to remain on guard against him, to not grant him any avenues with which he can harm you. If you live prayerfully, your Guardian Angels will succeed."

Sunday, September 18, 2011
1:37 p.m.

"Our Lord's call to suffering must be something of greater value than all the gold and precious metals on earth, more healing than any salving balm, more tasteful to the palate than a thousand sweet confections, more capable of slaying the evils surrounding us than a glistening saber's edge, and more brilliant than a million magnifications of the glaring midday sun. So why is humanity so afraid? What makes men so reticent, fearful, and resentful when summoned to bear their crosses? What are we worried about? The fact is, we are perpetuating the defeat of Satan through the same redemptive agony that took our crucified Lord to say on the Cross that the whole created world, its final legacy, and whatever else might come were finished."

William L. Roth

"My dear little sons, you are always creating ways to help others, finding new avenues to lift people up, always giving and never taking. This is the admirable divinity in you that has brought such distinction to your life's legacies thus far; it is the reason you are so blessed and cherished by the Father in Heaven. You know by now that you are attacked by Satan's evil legions because you possess this glorious goodness. Evil forces work most egregiously against those who are doing the most good to advance the Lord's Kingdom on Earth. You will be pleased to know that your service and gifts matter, your sacrifices are helping convert the lost and change lives into holier estates. I have come to share with you the sentiments of Jesus as you work every day for Him. His thoughts are spread throughout Creation in the New Covenant Gospel, and you hold them in your hearts for the life and nourishment of your faith. I wish you well in everything you set out to accomplish in His name. It was the same for Saint Joseph and Myself as we were rearing the Child Jesus. There were difficult circumstances and awkward conditions because we intended to shape the life of the Anointed Savior in the fruits of our own love for God. This was never an easy prospect for us, and this exists yet today in the exiled world. I wish to tell you something that you must remember for future reference. I was never exiled from Heaven. I was not one of the Earth's exiles. I had no reference to the sin that plagued other men because I was born without sin. Yes, indeed, I knew it. I could sense it in My Immaculate Heart from whence I was a young maiden of Joachim and Anne. It is true that the Spirit of God was in and upon Me. His favor rested on Me as this same favor was bestowed upon Jesus. Hence, this begs the question of what it means to have the conscience and consciousness of a sinless creature inside a world that is gripped by sin. The answer is that, from My vantage point, the world itself was not exiled from Heaven either by virtue of My flawless beatific vision. The world became sin because of the sinful nature of Adam and Eve. In other words, you are looking every day at the innate aspects of perfection through the works and beauties of Nature, through the growth and development and changes that time brings to the created world. By all means, you have seen what sinful man has done to the pristine attributes of the Earth! The point I am making is that I am a sinless Woman who walked without sin, who spread the perfection of My Immaculate Heart and Soul across the lands far and wide. I offered humanity the most powerful prayers they ever heard until the coming of age of My Son.

    Here, we are discussing the potentials and possibilities inherent to the conversion of sinners to the Cross. I have said that holiness becomes you. When you are perfected through Jesus as He prescribed in the Scriptures, you open your eyes to a new world inside the old world in which you were first born. Yes, you are born again into the New World of the Love of God in your heart once you accept everything the Church has to say. The New World about which I speak has already eclipsed the old world in every way that it can evolve because Old Adam has died and was raised again in the Messiah. You doubtlessly perceive this in the way of many theologians who attempt to place the events of human redemption in the context of time, and you are correct in doing so. However, many of them are yet unaware of the eclipse about which I am speaking because they cannot see it with their eyes. They believe that the eclipse will come only upon the Return of Jesus in Glory. Here again, it is both because Eternity has already consumed the material universe. It is true that God can have things both ways. He has said it time and again in the Holy Scriptures. Admonish your brother at the same time you remove the wooden plank from your own eye. Pray in private so as not to be like the hypocrites, but go onto the rooftops to proclaim the intensity of your faith. These seem like contradictions because they must both be done. It is in this that My Son's messages also appear to be contradictory, when they are actually consistent in their substantive content. Be proud of everything that makes you one with Jesus, but remember that pride is what forced the downfall of man. This goes on and on. Therefore, you know that the Crucifixion of Jesus and His Paschal Resurrection are concurrently in place for the whole of history and all the ages, even though they were separate timely events. If it sounds to you as though I am engaging in doublespeak, please forgive Me and see your lives as I do. I am simply giving you other reasons why mortal men and women refuse to believe the messages that are given around the globe. More about My life on the Earth and that of Saint Joseph. I was called 'Woman' by Jesus only when we were in the company of others because He wanted the whole world to realize that I am the perfect incarnation of what women were supposed to be. He in fact referred to Me as 'Mother' and 'Mama' when we were in private, and sometimes 'My Maternal Love' and 'Helper of all Souls.' We walked with mutual admiration because We are the Immaculate and Sacred Hearts who have for centuries watched over and protected those who believe in the God of Abraham. Jesus came to Me with His injuries sustained as a Child, and thereby came to Me for compassion when He received His Sacred Wounds that redeemed the world of men. It was always the same; I gave Him the same comfort that I was accorded by Saint Joseph and the intercessory Angels who deigned to reside in our presence.

My Special son, the world was as unsightly in our day as the one you are seeing right now. The same sins were being committed, the same desecrations were going on, the same indifference and ugliness. There has not been a new or revised definition of 'sin' from our day to the one you are living now. The subtle and radical acts of hatred that happen in this new century occurred during the century in which we lived. I was particularly aware of what this meant for us because, as I have said, I perceived the exiled Earth through the eyes of a sinless Woman. This was not only a manifestation of My Immaculate Conception, but because My love for humanity was, and still remains, so strong. The latter is what I wish all My children to aspire to attain. Your Baptism and Jesus' Crucifixion have removed any signs of sin from mortal men, so there is nothing to impede your vision of what Divine Love should be. It is as natural as breathing fresh air and looking out in wonder at the marvels that the Kingdom of God has wrought. Human spiritual perfection is an achievable goal because you have been given the framework to achieve it through the Son I bore, through the wise teachings He gave His flock, through the Saints who have lived and died since then, and through the Holy Spirit reigning even as we speak in the depths of your faith. Indeed, Jesus referred to Me as Mother with the same emphasis and devotion that He spoke so righteously from the Cross, asking Saint John to look not only at the Woman, but to John's Mother. This is when the personal and private relationship between the Mother and the Crucified Son became the public revelation of human Salvation; it was the moment when all men were saved and the entire body of humanity was given an eternally living Matriarch. This Crucifixion was a publicly manifested tragedy that saved the lost; and our union, yours and Mine, and all the citizens of the world became consummated by the Man-God with the power to pronounce it good.

I lived both for the moment and with the eternal expanse of Heaven in My mind and Heart for the entirety of My life. I knew that there would be a glorious tragedy come to us, that would be fatal to the Son of My Womb and raise the rest of humanity from The Fall. It was an exercise in contradiction to know that My own Flesh and Blood would die, even though He was innocent, for everyone else who bore guilt. The pure would be Crucified to redeem the impure. I speak of the irony and contradictions that I referred to at the opening of this message. And, when people become Christians to capture the promised eternal joy, they are bombarded with so much evil and hatred that you would think they are the faithless ones. Here exists the irony as well.

There is hope for all Christians who have oathed their lives to Jesus. It resides not just in the promises of the future or in the Afterlife. The hope is in the realization that you understand the power of your prayers, especially the Holy Rosary. It is in your newly-acquired wisdom of knowing right from wrong, and what this means to God who is looking on from His Heavenly Throne. This hope has made teachers of men who would otherwise have lived privately in abject ignorance. It is the shining of the Light of Truth in the darkness of the world in ways that cannot be effected through any other venue. You have in your hands the ability to reach the lost and downtrodden, the broken and the poor, the lame and diseased because you have the power of prayer in your heart to reshape Creation into the likeness of Heaven itself. I am not saying that you can each and every time amend the Will of the Father, but you have the capacity to tell Him what you believe He should do out of love for His creatures, for the good of the Church, and for the cause of unity and compassion in the exiled realms. My Special son, most all of the sadness that you feel sometimes is caused by the hardness of other hearts. It is caused by coldness and selfishness, and by blindness and greed. It is a function of crass human pride instead of mutually shared righteousness. While everything I have told you today is true, you must remember that it is possible for Christians to be joyful in patience because you have accorded yourselves the opportunity and willingness to live as Jesus has asked. Happiness comes in this form; it is based in your awareness that you have lived the human excellence that He has asked since He spoke His first words."

Saturday, September 24, 2011
2:17 p.m.

"Sometimes the winds of change blow more placidly upon us, with a divine air of sophistication to their breeze; and this is when we are saturated with peace within and without, felt so coolly and gently that they could almost lift us entirely whole to the sovereignty of the altars. Even as the Holy Spirit speaks volumes in poignance and urgency at times, there are moments when we realize that the Lord dispenses His calmness with ease. And in this, we no longer wonder what human emotions are for. What must be said about our holiness is that even in our most excruciating hours, we painted the prettiest pictures of redemption in our hearts; we applied our rarest innovations against the strains of daily life, and we won our place

beside Jesus Christ by a landslide and a mile. Remembering this high architecture is how we force our anxieties into the farthest voids and bring to surface the love and trust that are most worthy of our faith."

William L. Roth

"Now comes the Mother of souls to pray with you and for you, to ask your assistance in profiting the Church with the blessings Jesus will bring when we gather so humbly together. My Special and Chosen ones, I am the Immaculate Conception. I am Mary, the Mother of God. I am your Lady of Perpetual Help, your Eternal Queen of Peace, Queen of Love, the Holy Mother of all humanity. It is My honor to be here with you today because you remain so receptive to My messages; you welcome My presence with open arms and prayerful hearts. You must be sure to help the world to know that I have assisted in the opening of the spiritual eyes of My children; and more than that, I have helped focus them on the real issues that need to be seen. These spiritual eyes blink only when one takes his sight away from Heaven in the here and now. These eyes weep when they see Jesus' suffering, and they glow in the Light of His Resurrection. I am with you, My Special son, and with your brother not only because I love you, for I would love you profoundly if I had never uttered a word to you, but because the Earth is still in need of the knowledge about redemption, meaning that this knowledge has a greater purpose than to simply help suffering people through their days. We are on a mission that began when I said 'YES' to the Archangel Gabriel. This seems a long time ago, does it not? The holiness of humanity is made manifest in Jesus; it grows fuller because you are fed Wisdom and righteousness in every gift He brings. This is why we must pray together silently here in this blessed place, or any other location in which we pray, because it will be equally as blessed. History has shown that the most effective disciples of the Church were those who surrendered themselves to the persecution that comes from the secular void. They proved that winning the faith is more than a sublime implication of future intent, but an ever-present action leading to the cultivation of the Earth, weeding-out evil and indifference, planting seeds of goodness, and remaining in God's vineyard to nourish the fruit of converted souls as they grow in the direction of the Crucifixion.

I am blessed to be here, and you are blessed because you have the willingness to remain with Me beside the Manger, the Cross, and the Tomb.

You and all My messengers are like fertile ground, deep and rich in love, prepared to be filled with the seed of souls, excellently inspired to commit to Heaven all who have been given the gift of life. This mission of holy love becomes you! I have appeared around the globe in many places, saying the same things, offering the same promises, exalting the same principles, and requesting the same petitions. We think of the many who have lost loved-ones in accidents and by disease, those who have died from starvation and neglect, and we remember the brokenhearted and depressed. It is more than fate that makes other men those who are so oppressed; it is the constitution of the world brought by decisions that do not comport with the teachings of the Church. Many people make many other people suffer. And, we know that our prayers to Jesus and the Father through the power of the Holy Spirit helps ameliorate these things. We know that exceptional people do exceptional things! This is right where you and your brother come in. It is where all peoples in every land who are consecrated to My Immaculate Heart do their best work for God. There is no retreating for them! There are no concessions, no regrets, no second-guessing. There is no looking back over one's shoulders to see who might have been offended by the Truth with which Jesus is purifying the Earth. There is no guilt in those who have reprimanded sinners in ways that hurt those sinners' feelings. All that exists is goodness that shall prevail until the end of time! Think about history and the record of all the annals to have come since the world was first positioned in space. What inside or about it matters if not to glorify the Kingdom of Heaven? It has nothing to do with mothers' pride for their sons and daughters who sing songs about subjects having nothing to do with human Salvation. There is no relevance to someone who finishes a race if that person does not do it for the glory of God. I pray every day that you will maintain your peaceful relationship with your family and friends. It would be easier to remain secluded here in this home, away from the seeming distractions that occur on a regular basis. However, your face alone bears the holiness of Heaven. When people see you, they see the Son, just as they saw the Father in the Son. You and your brother have been accorded special lives here in this world because you have been so obedient. I only ask that you remember how special you are, not in an egotistic way, but in such a way that you always and forever see yourselves inside the Sacred Heart of My Son. There is no better resting place this side of Heaven. As I say, I have come only briefly today because these are the days of the fall that you love to see. I will continue telling you about My life on Earth in the future, and about the awesome plans that Jesus has to more deeply touch the people in your midst. Thank you for sharing your time with your family, for keeping and maintaining contact with all who call you their friend. We pray for the end of abortion, for the ceasing of war, and for the opening of the hearts and consciences of the millions who are looking another way."

Saturday, October 1, 2011
1:39 p.m.

"It is true that Christian moral piety consigns us to the utter pursuit of spiritual holiness, and most of us are still tapering ourselves away from the manipulations of the world while growing in our appreciation for the Church. It is said that humankind cannot achieve complete oneness with Heaven while living exiled on Earth, but the Holy Mother tells us differently. Our Lady says that we can manifest the kind of genuine love and charity that prepares us for redemption while we live these very days and hours. The only thing holding us back from believing this is our own self-doubt about the princely value of the human soul. Our faith must become like wildfires too vast to extinguish, cascades of wisdom for the parched curiosity of men, and whirlwinds to expel the stale pride of the billions of unbelievers around the globe. Our flesh may be waning as we speak, but our eternal spirits are ever-growing, ever-reaching, ever-striving for this higher form of life."

William L. Roth

"Here we have come together, My children, to speak about all you have learned about the redemption of humanity, all that you know and realize, all your hearts tell you about true goodness in the world, and all you will share with your brothers and sisters before time is through. You live in the Church as a spiritual creation, not a collection of buildings or some material contraption, but humanity en masse given to God through His Messianic Son. You can see that it is His intention to try the best He knows how to dismantle your anxieties, allay your fears, stop the movements that distract humanity from accepting the Cross, and encapsulate you inside the Wisdom that has become the reason for your lives. It is My privilege to facilitate this process in accordance with the role I have played as Handmaid of the Lord, your Immaculate Mother, your Holy Intercessor, and your next best advocate beside the Holy Spirit, Himself. It all comes down to opening oneself to the peace of God coming to you through the knowledge that He dispenses in the signs and wonders of the Church. You are collectively the Church here and now. You are one with humanity who believes in the God of Abraham. I will ask you to recall when you were peaceful in times past, and why this came to be. It is because you were more focused on practicing the peace of the Holy Spirit than recognizing it as an option. There have been countless; and I mean countless, messages that yet remain in My Immaculate Heart that I have been unable to dispense to humanity because those to whom I wished to speak would not prioritize what they perceived as problems as not being problems at all. Humanity creates issues and distractions because they believe that it is '...something to do.' I wish to speak now more about My life on Earth during the years of Jesus' adolescence, and how He viewed His life through the eyes of God Incarnate on the Earth. You must remember that Jesus is the supreme example of human genius mixed with the divinity of God. In other words, human genius can be equated with the Sacred Divine when it is utilized to examine the world in the context of redemptive grace. This is what we have been doing together with your brother for more than 20 years. We have been asking and answering questions about which matters are notably important enough to address, which are sufficiently imperative that they have a bearing on the judgement of the collective souls of men. Some of the questions have been obvious and rhetorical, like what makes some people behave badly, while others are exemplary of perfect piety. Other questions are not as clear cut, such as what makes one homily better than another. It would seem that there are quantitative questions about how many prayers are spoken or lives converted, and qualitative questions about what shades of gray or white someone might be living in compliance with the Gospel, depending on their perception of right and wrong.

My little children, this is the touchstone that Jesus employed when He encountered His friends and companions when He lived as an adolescent child, and I knew that this was the case. It was My role as His Mother to assist Him by listening to His reflections about those He met. You may not find it surprising to know that Jesus was not a popular child any more than He was on the day He was crucified. Right has always been right, and wrong has always been wrong. Jesus was always capable of knowing the hearts of other people, especially those who expressed friendship with Him, but who behaved in ways contrary to His beliefs. He spoke in ways that would change their consciences, amend their thoughts and actions to bring them into compliance with what the Father wanted them to do. The day will break when all Jesus' disciples time will come. Miracles are living in you now. This is the reason His first Apostles could work miracles of conversion and healing; it was their time. Anyone who holds and cherishes the Holy Spirit within them has the capacity to perform certain miracles vested in them by the Father in Heaven. This does not imply that everyone should walk around the world wondering what their miraculous works might be. It is the suffering of the soul that breeds the capacity to perform miracles. This is the paradox involved. You know that Jesus had the capacity to heal Himself in every way. If He were to be injured, He could have instantly removed the pain. If He tripped and skinned His knee, He could have reversed time and it would have never happened. When He was crucified, He could have inverted the world and placed every one of His crucifiers on crosses instead. The fact is, He chose to suffer the pain of injury, either accidental or deliberate, because that is the effect of Divine Incarnation. He could have chosen which afflictions to heal and others that He would not. He could have left Lazarus inside the tomb, and the world would have known no different. But, why did Jesus bring him out? To dispel any notion that the Divine Love that was living in Him could not perform the greatest miracle of all, that of raising the dead from their graves. This was the precursor to what He has done for all humanity. And, the world was desperate when Jesus performed His greatest miracles, nearly as desperate as today. Yes, there will be signs and wonders come the end of time, and the Book of Revelation speaks of fateful events at the opening of the final annals of the world, its cultivation and conclusion. My Special and Chosen sons, you live an admirable and decisive faith that shows humanity what being human and divine really means. This is what Popes do as well. You tell the truth, preach the Gospel, leave your mark on the history of the Church, pay homage to the Most Blessed Trinity, give alms, and do all the other things that evangelize and glorify Jesus on Earth as He lives in Heaven. The essence of My message today is that I was aware of things to come concerning the conversion of humanity because I was inspirited with this wisdom at the Annunciation. The Second and Third Person of the Holy Trinity lived with Saint Joseph and Me throughout His life; and therefore did God the Father. I watched and fostered. I taught My neighbors about their friendship with God through My Jewish faith, leaving open the door for them to accept the redemption that would come through the Fruit of My Womb."

Friday, October 7, 2011
Feast of the Most Holy Rosary
3:03 p.m.

"We conduct a constant interchange with our own sense of conscious awareness and our environment, the ecosystem, our neighbors and friends, the transcontinental mass of humanity, inorganic nature, the vile crassness of our partisan affairs, the forces of stagnation and change, our historical connection to the past, the uncertain future, and everything else that shapes, impacts, and influences our opinions, the way we present ourselves, our key impulses and reactions, and how we perceive the frameworks and values of everyday life. Surely we can find some time for God, the Master of Truth, who watches the universe sovereignly and yet from within, waiting for us to accord Jesus the Lord our fullest attention and purge ourselves of the rest."

William L. Roth

"These are the words from the Holy Spirit speaking directly through your heart, My Special one. As it has been said, you are a remarkable man who shares your love for Jesus with steady emphasis and direction. You know where Jesus has been and still remains; this is where you are now and shall forever be. I come today to share My thoughts and prayers with you about everything you included in your introductory remarks. I ask you and your brother to remain calm through all that is ongoing during the present days, weeks and months. It is imperative that you find ways to remain peaceful in the midst of the horrific commotion and destruction that are occurring around the world and here in your own country. You can see how Satan has infiltrated the city in which you live with his thugs and minions, his evildoers who have in mind the undoing of the peace and holiness that we have built here together. Today, I wish to continue My message that I began last week about living with Saint Joseph and Jesus on Earth as Jesus was growing in stature. My emphasis today is upon His calling on Me as His Mother for spiritual support, for guidance that only a Mother can provide. Jesus possessed all the wisdom required to succeed as His sinless self in a world filled with sinners. He was aware of anything I might say or do that would assist and influence Him. He knew that I was the incarnation of that Motherhood. I was physically visible to Him and in His immediate company. We shared our thoughts and feelings impressionably because we were two perfect creatures in locations that gave us the opportunity to convey our emotions and concerns in the way of ordinary people. Jesus came to Me to ask about the conditions of the community, not that He did not know, but so that He could hear My impressions impact His ears as if spoken by the Father. I remain the Seat of Wisdom, the intercessor who has perfect knowledge of the way humanity and the world ought to become. I told Jesus on many occasions that there is much competition for power on Earth. It is even worse in these modern times. Jesus was not perplexed by the sins of other men, but He was surely disappointed because the Father had dispensed through Moses and the prophets sufficient means for men to remain pure and insightful about preserving one's innocence. The concept of living in contravention to the Old Testament seemed foreign to Jesus, although He understood the forces of temptation. Many were the hours when The Holy Family would sit outdoors in the evening beneath the nighttime skies and ask the Father to ensure that His Will would be done according to the Scriptures. We were aware that Jesus was the fulfillment of those Scriptures in the Person of the New Covenant. Jesus was the Incarnate Gospel, the Word, the Prince and King who would conquer evil and establish on Earth the Kingdom of Heaven that the Father put into place. He would vanquish the enemies of the redemption of lost sinners and create the pathway for their deliverance into the New Jerusalem.

My message today is about a young Man who knew who He was from the moment He was born of My Womb. He knew that He was the King of the world in a newborn baby boy. He realized that He had been placed in a physical body, a flesh framework that looked like every other man. And, this created a challenge for Him that was unknown to others, even as He chose His Apostles. After all, one would think that the Messiah from Heaven would walk in midair, glow in the dark, speak in refrains that would bring the wayward to their knees, and light up the night with flares of fire emitting from His fingertips. However, this is not the way the Son of Man would impress upon the exiled world that He was indeed the Savior whom He claimed to be. He came to inspire faith and build a Kingdom on a foundation of sacrificial love, not on the spectacles that one might see at an Armistice Day parade. He exuded a dutiful and stately peace that revealed to humanity the Grace of God, the determination of Heaven to renew the Earth through My Son in painstaking ways. One must remember that Jesus could have ended the world as everyone knew it on the day of His Ascension. However, there were billions more people yet to be born, those who were forced into exile by the sins of Adam and Eve. A Church needed to be founded through the power of the Holy Spirit that would purify and enlighten these creatures, all. Jesus knew that He would return to Earth in three distinct forms before the existence of the Earth would be permanently changed. He would descend as the Holy Spirit upon the Church and into the hearts of the faithful. He would feed humanity in His Eucharistic Sacrament. And, He will come again to judge the living and the dead. He knew that His Kingdom would have no end. These are among the crucial thoughts that passed through Jesus' consciousness on Holy Thursday and Good Friday. If My Son had declined the Father's Will and chose to come down from the Cross, the Kingdom of Heaven would not have extended to the Earth. He chose to remain on the Cross until He delivered His spirit and every other soul to the Father so that all Creation, seen and unseen, would be united at the feet of the God who fashioned it. He was dreading the suffering, for sure, but He was more determined to succeed because of His love. Jesus pondered not what He would do, for His Will was completely aligned with the Father who lived in Him. He pondered what the soul of every man, woman and child would suffer if they refused the Sacrifice He endured that day. He knew where they would go if they turned their backs on His Sacrifice of Love. The Crucifixion! This was the only way that the future of humanity would have a happy ending.

    I saw the signs of this commitment in Jesus' eyes when He was a young boy. I saw His determination that appeared to be more like hope than anything else. He was always dreaming about ways that all souls would be touched, all hearts would be opened to receive and accept what He would endure after He reached the age of 33 years. Theologians, Popes and mystics have for centuries laid their thoughts along these lines, and they all came to the same conclusion. The Crucifixion of Jesus Christ had to occur. The Sorrowful Passion, the Agony in the Garden, the Scourging at the Pillar, the Crowning with Thorns, the Carrying of the Cross, and the Crucifixion itself was the Father's way of installing the pearls and diamonds of redeemed human souls into the priceless Kingdom that would live beyond this world. These souls could not be stolen. They could not be given to Heaven for free. They could not sneak into Paradise in the pitch of the night. No indeed, a price had to be paid by the Victim on the Cross. It was suitable that God in human flesh would appear on the Earth to redeem broken humanity for every reason they were created good in the first place. He came to lend the opportunity for men to exercise their own volition for sinlessness this time, not for pride or esteeming oneself as having equality with God. This is the volition that Jesus thought about as a young boy and young Man – 'How do I bend their will in the direction of love?' This is the question that He kept asking Himself, and one that He asked Me as well. The Crucifixion was both the logical and illogical answer to His question. It was such an irrational thought that it had to be true. My Special son, if one searches for reason in this, they will find it in the consciences of those who choose for Jesus, who see Him the way you and your brother do. Without enlisting the faith required to believe what the Holy Gospel says, there is no such thing as reason, divine or otherwise. Reason and mysticism are copartners in the conversion of the world, for it is through this conversion that the will of humanity is given to the Messiah. This is not the same thing as 'choice' as though one might decide to bake either an apple or cherry pie. Once the Holy Spirit enters the heart, the decisions are made by the Spirit, not by man. Did Saint Paul not say that he would be emptied-out, and that it was not for him to live, but that Jesus would live through him? This means that Jesus made the choice because Saint Paul and all others like him, including you and your brother and all Christians, got out of the way. For you to live is Christ."

Saturday, October 15, 2011
1:57 p.m.

"Educators and psychologists often speak about the abstracts of human contemplation, those things we dwell upon randomly when our mind seems to wander or we lack clear focus in our perceptive thinking. It is during these moments when we are open to the influx of external forces as though our guard is let down. However, this is not always the case. Our personal identity and true innocence are best revealed when we set aside even temporarily our cognitive shields, at least long enough for the Holy Spirit to infiltrate what is ordinarily our impermeable state of being. This does not imply that we should not be aware of evil influences around us, but be open enough to accept what truth is being revealed from outside this world. There still seems to be some question as to whether we see human life with our eyes or through our eyes, or both, and so it is with our religious faith. Moreover, do we look for raw confidence in other men, a kind sense of understanding, intelligent emotion, courageous insight, or a composite of these things?

Whatever makes-up our random reflections should include our flexibility to be receptive to God's overtures in the wake of our own assertive disposition. Only in this way will we recognize the difference between thieves and givers, gargoyles and flowers, fact and fiction, and love and hatred."

William L. Roth

"The brilliance of your personal reflections amazes even the most thoughtful theologians who have already joined the ranks of the Saints in Heaven, My Special son. *"Thank you Mama."* You write these resounding images by living in accordance with Jesus' own dictates and proclamations to the material world. This is also where the romantic strains of your new song lyrics are pouring from; it is because you are aligned with the Spirit of Love in the Sacred Heart of My Son. I have come today to bring you the Peace of Heaven and speak to you about the decades of My life again. I wish to speak about My own youth and adolescence as a young Jewish girl. There are a great many facets to My life that have never been revealed because I am not the focus of the Salvation of humanity; this is reserved for Jesus, the Savior of the world. You will see in time, however, that just as the Archangel Gabriel came to Me to announce the Immaculate Conception of Jesus, I am foreshadowing the Second Coming as well. You must remember that I was likewise aware of My sinless nature as a child. I knew that there was no sin in Me. All the talk about a poor helpless Maiden who walked about in ignorance of Her identity is sheer nonsense. I possessed the innocence, and I was absolutely aware of who I was from the moment I first perceived the configuration of the Earth. In other words, I knew My stainless soul was living in an environment that was inhabited by sinners. Please do not misunderstand. I am not being condescending here. There are certain personality traits, ways of perceiving human life, frameworks by which to make decisions, and attitudes of prayer possessed by Jesus and Myself that were once missing from every other human being. Since Jesus' Life, Death and Resurrection, billions of people have acquired these gifts. Always remember that they are fruits and reflections of spiritual faith. They can neither be invoked nor appropriated by anyone alive or beyond the grave without the seed of faith to first nourish them into maturity. It is all about the faith that Jesus came to instill. And, faith itself is a foundation. It supports your hopes and dreams, it fosters the clarity of your beliefs, it hones your practical skills, and it establishes a sensitivity in your heart to everything that Sacred Love implies. I knew of this faith, love and hope when I was a young girl. I attended My friends and acquaintances much the same way as Jesus, although the boys and girls were routinely apart. We read the Old Testament Scriptures, offered up our sacrifices, tended to the chores at home, prayed at the Temple, and asked for joy and happiness to be abundant in our everyday lives. Are these not what humanity seeks to this day? Therefore, you are privy to the way I was reared in a community of people who did not have a rapid sense of communication. Prayer was our life, and I knew that the future would require much more prayer because it was the only way that the world I witnessed had a chance of surviving. How did I know? Because I viewed it much in the same way that you are seeing the world in your day.

My personality was meek and yet confident; and I had a comfortably-aching need inside Me that I knew only the Lord could suffice. It was like a constant hunger for the future. It was an anticipation building-up in Me that foretold the Annunciation of the Archangel Gabriel. It is true that the Angel came unexpectedly, just as it has been said, but I knew that a Divine Intervention was imminent. This is how Jesus will come in Glory to redeem the Earth. The voice of the Spirit of God came to Me many times when I was a young girl, just as the Angels spoke to Saint Joseph in the night. I was comforted and guided, given signal graces and signs, and taken to places through visions and insights where no one else had gone. There was an absolute readiness in My Womb for the Incarnate Son of Man that began when the time approached. I saw the world through the lens of this anticipation for what seemed to be an extended period of time. I saw it much like you and your brother see it now. I asked silent questions about why certain devastation had come into so many people's lives. I felt as though the Lord God of Israel could do more to alleviate the pains and suffering of the people in exile. I read and reread the warnings in the Psalms about what would happen to those who scorned the power of God, who rejected Him and persecuted those who believed in Him. There is no doubt that I look now in hindsight with the feeling that I was more accepting of His Holy Will than many of My friends. However, God and Saint Joseph never allowed Me to be persecuted. I was treated with dignity and gentleness, with respect and care. It was not until Jesus went missing and found in the Temple that I began to realize that I would suffer too. These are some of the sentiments that describe My young life in anticipation of the Annunciation. It was as though I felt a need inside that could only be satisfied by the gift of blessing that the Archangel would foretell. I carried this feeling until I was visited, and I shared with My cousin Elizabeth the greatness that was implanted in Me, both through My own state of perfection and the Incarnate Flesh of the Son of the Most High. I have much more to share with you about this subject at a later time if you ask Me about it someday."

Saturday, October 22, 2011
3:05 p.m.

"Zestful living means that we have learned to overcome our anxieties and emotions through our unabridged trust in what we know Jesus Christ is capable of doing. He can turn the whole world upside down by snapping His fingers, but He wants our footsteps to ramp-up the beat. Our communication with Heaven is humanity's rosin on the bow of everlasting life and the means by which our thoughts and prayers are attuned to the mind of God. All we have to do is look around at the moral depravity of this world to realize that the good Lord Jesus must be the most patient individual who ever lived. I am beginning to wonder, however, whether that patience has finally worn thin. We as Christians should not minimize or trivialize what this might portend for an unsuspecting humanity and the exiled Church."

William L. Roth

"My dearly beloved children, you are receivers of My messages so that the world might be made upright in My Grace. Have you ever wondered why humanity has been saved by the Blood of a Man instead of a woman or some organic creature who is gender neutral? The answer is because man was created first, and in the image of God. And, it is through this same primordial fashioning that Jesus was begotten, not made, one in Being with the Father. The Incarnate Son was born of the Womb of a Woman, thereby establishing the holy entity of the child and mother joined forever as the population of the world would grow. However, it is for this reason that so many worldly women refuse the Blood of the Cross. What does this mean? What are the implications of this? That humanity comes by faith through the Holy Spirit present in mother and father, sister and brother; and it is the father and brother who lead in faith as did Saint Joseph and all the great Princes of the Church.

The feminineness of women is where man reaches the nurturing spirit of My own reflection. We have spoken about the role of patriarch and matriarch in the human family before, but not in the context of sacrifice for the redemption of lost souls. It is clear that Martyrs have been made from both genders, and for the same reason. However, billions of souls have throughout the ages wondered why a Man would be crucified; why does the collective female gender have to worship and praise and adore a Savior who is a Man? This is what they ask. My Special one, I will give you an opportunity to respond to this question. *"So that they can find the emptiness to be worthy to bear children."* This is absolutely true, but there is more. The primal nature of humanity rests in its beginning in Adam. Was it not Adam who was first given life? Then, Eve was created next. This is the simple answer. It is the male who was first created so that the seed of life could await the fertile ground. The fertile ground came subsequent to the seed of life. Hence, God the Father is the sower of the seed of religious faith in the fertile ground of open human hearts. The human heart is the receptacle of the seed of religious faith. In other words, why would there be a need for fertile soil if there were nothing to plant there?

The point I am making is that the seed must be in the possession of the sower. This is clearly logical. It is the sower who deposits the seed in the fertile ground. The Father is the sower of all good seeds, and He has been throughout the entire timelessness of His existence. He had no beginning, and He will have no ending. You have heard the expression that the grand show is eternal when looking at the sunrise because it is always daybreak somewhere. This is the same principle as applied to the Will of the Lord God to perpetuate life on Earth and elsewhere in Creation. Now, He sees what is happening amid the nations during these modern times. And, His patience has been nearly exhausted. This does not mean that He does not love humanity anymore; indeed, He still loves His creatures and followers as intensely as ever. You must be careful in your writing not to say that God loves humanity now more than He ever did. That would be factually inaccurate. The intensity of His Love cannot be measured or weighed, and it therefore cannot change. When considering the point about worldly females not accepting the Crucifixion of a Man for their eternal Salvation, this says volumes about their viewpoint in the context of redemption. They have not yet grasped the meaning of the primal role of Man in the creation and completion of the world. This is a sorrowful state of affairs for the gender who bears children for the sake of the multiplication of the species of creatures in whom Jesus has invested so much trust. What kind of being would have her unborn progeny physically stripped from the haven of her womb? What kind of evil has led to this? The answer is the same as when Eve confessed that the serpent caused her to fall. The serpent is still consuming the flesh of the unborn descendants of Eve, but the serpent cannot have their souls. This discussion can be taken much further. What did Adam say to God when he was asked why he ate from the tree? *"The woman gave it to me."* Does this not therefore imply that the serpent used the woman to corrupt the man? *"Yes."* This also means that the man was not strong enough to disavow his own weakness and reject the temptation. This has not changed to this day. Therefore, in order for men on Earth not to be tempted in the way of Adam, what must be done? All the female descendants of Eve must not take the course that she did. In other words, the women of today's world must take a lesson from Eve, recognize their own identity as females in this world, and stop trying to tempt modern men into violating the commands of God. And yet, two-thirds have rejected the lessons that should have been learned in the Old Testament Scriptures about Adam and Eve. They claim that they are self-liberated because they own the power of autonomy from man and their liberation from the Father who blamed them for the fall of Adam.

    This seems to be quite a paradox for them, does it not? The Lord God responded by saying that it was the weakness of Adam that caused the fall of all humanity. Therefore, giving-in to the temptation was worse than the party doing the tempting. This is key for the current condition of the world. It is not that humanity is tempted that is most egregious, it is that humanity surrenders to the temptation. This is why the 'Our Father' asks that God not allow those who pray to be led into temptation. Why? Because the fight against it is simply much too difficult. I have told you that it is not natural for humanity to sin. Therefore, it takes extra thought and action for men and women to defy the teachings of God. But, humans are prone to sin because of the faith required to believe that it is wrong, and because of the atmosphere of the exiled world that provides numerous occasions to sin. So, where is the fight in all this? It rests in the recognition of Christians to know what is right from what is wrong. There is darkness and light. There is goodness and evil. So, how are all these things connected in some main theme? It is this – The seed of everything good cannot produce a fruit that is bad. God the Father has poured His seed of righteousness over the Earth because He knows that there is fertile ground, naturally fertile ground because He makes it so through the

Sacraments of the Church and the Sacrifice of His Son. The Crucifixion began when the serpent first approached Eve. Therefore, in the absence of the discipline and piety of Adam, in the wake of Adam's weakness to deny the temptation that was put before him, a Man of Truth instead of lies had to redeem everyone from that moment forward. It was Jesus who has stepped forward to reverse the damage inflicted by Adam when Adam refused to reject the temptation he faced. This is the reason the redemption of both males and females fell upon a Man instead of a woman. It was the New Adam who rejected the temptations of the serpent and washed-away Old Adam's error. Thus, the first and the last come full circle. Our perfect God created man and woman who made themselves imperfect, and the perfect Son restored the sinless nature of the man and woman. This is unequivocal proof that Jesus Christ is a Man from the first. He is the Father, the Son and the Holy Spirit in the Second Person of the Blessed Trinity. Women who reject this, who say that they do not need a 'man' to get to Heaven, are falling victim to the lies of the same serpent who corrupted Adam and Eve in the Garden of Eden. I have made this as clear as possible. I am trying to clarify the roles and responsibility of men and women in the world to foster the growth of holiness for these present times. Women must become stronger creatures to not concede to the temptations of the devil, and men must not concede to the coercion of unholy women. This does not imply that the devil does not tempt men directly without the influence of women. The human heart and soul must be sown to the Spirit, not the flesh."

Sunday, October 30, 2011
1:18 p.m.

"It is becoming increasingly apparent that secular Americans mistake peacefulness and quietude for idleness and non-productivity; and they equate prayerful meditation with psychosomatic illusion. However, their opinions are not in agreement with the facts. In truth, our Christian faith creates a spiritual buffer-zone separating us from the obscene fallout of the material world. This is what makes our redemption in the Cross so fruitful, reassuring, restorative, and meaningful. It makes our environment one that reflects the confidence to which Our Lady refers. The identity we have found in Jesus comes from our awareness that the Holy Spirit changes our entire constitution and makes us more enduring creatures than we ever

thought possible." William L. Roth

"You are indeed enduring little creatures in the Sacred Heart of My Son, and endearing ones too. My Special and Chosen ones, it is always My honor to be in your company while you pray for the conversion of lost sinners. I know that those who are consecrated to My Immaculate Heart want to know when these kinds of prayers will no longer be required. Let us hope along with our prayers that it will not take until such time that the Son of Man returns in Glory. The beauty that I find here after all these years is stunning – your dedication to the Church, your vision for what prayerfulness means, your desire to fight the good fight for the Salvation of the world, and the innovative ways that you offer yourselves and your lives for the spreading of the Holy Gospel message. In this, My Special son, you and your brother have distinguished yourselves among the ranking members of the Church. You are esteemed because of your service to God. This is a truth that I beg you to never forget. The same Holy Spirit who forms My words also fashions yours. It is My duty to reassure you that we have done so much to advance the calling of God through My messages here. Those who are unaware of this are being opened to receive the graces that will enhance their consciousness. This is what led the little monk to find your first diary in his hometown library. I directed him to it. Thank you for your generosity in sending him a copy without charge. It will help perfect his soul. We are making progress every day in these sorts of things; they are simply beyond your sight. You must realize how shocking things such as My supernatural intercession are to those who have never heard of them before. What is good and remarkable is that you appear to everyone to be stable in every personal and psychological way. You are not eccentric or overindulgent in your discussion of what I came here to do. You are stable in your thoughts and actions, and this lends credence to your claims that I have come to you so long ago. The Father in Heaven extends His gratitude and congratulations for your stability, your steadfastness, the simplicity in which you live, and your hope for the future that has never receded. You have learned these things from Me and the ideals that you have espoused as a Roman Catholic Christian.

Today, I have come to speak to you about the means by which My children are grounded in other ways that serve to positively influence your role in the maintenance of the Church. The first point is that you are all excellent judges of right and wrong. You have the capacity to know what God wishes

His people to become within the spacial and time-consuming confines of the physical world. You have learned what morality means because you have attended the Holy Sacrifice of the Mass, read the Sacred Scriptures, heeded the advice of the Doctors of the Church, witnessed the sacrifices of the Saints, and welcomed whatever newness and revelatory occurrences that you have encountered every day. You are as a result of these things more resilient than you have ever been. Why? Because you have never been more wise than you are at this moment. The years have been profitable for you in this regard. You have utilized your experiences, your suffering and toils, to categorize human thought and actions into your vision of life on Earth. This is how everyone learns right from wrong. Second, you have shared your new knowledge through the venues that have been made available to you through your own judgements about how effective your faith can be. You hold a grasp on the technologies and your knowledge of the culture in which you live to determine when and where to act. You have become diplomatic in your delivery and concise in your speech and writings. My Special one, this is called 'maturity' in its most essential form. And, it facilitates the propagation of the Messianic message to the unknowing. Truly, these are not always specific or conscious decisions that you are making; they come to you through the power of the Holy Spirit in your heart. This means that they are natural to your psychological consciousness. Jesus said that you need not wonder what you will say in times of persecution, that the Holy Spirit would give you the text of whatever you will need to say. Do you remember this commendation? *"Yes."* And, it implies that you are, as Saint Francis suggests, an instrument of the Lord's peace in every place and time. This leads to the third of My points today. You are proactive and evangelistic in your possession of The Faith. It is a power that is rightfully yours to wield; this is the case with all Roman Catholic Christians. It is all about relevance in the themes that Jesus has taught since He was born of My Womb. Even the mere suggestion that God the Father could be born into a world filled with sinners gives the impression that He deigns to make humanity a better lot. If this were not possible, He would have never come."

Saturday, November 5, 2011
3:13 p.m.

"Never think you are alone. Listen to the music in your heart."
Said to vocal contestant Sungbong Choi in South Korea, 2011

obstructed power, strength, energy, force or exertion creates pressure

Transactional vs. Transformational Faith

"Valiantly you face the enemies of Divine Love, and with finesse do you dismiss the temptations that would draw you away from the Cross. My special children, you have within you the radiance that shines across the universe, widely gathering the souls of men into communion with God. I wish for you to remember that you have not entered a business partnership with the Lord; you do not wish to exchange something of value for His greater good. Indeed, you are of transformational faith, one that changes Creation through your prayers. You likewise receive blessings and graces seemingly without merit; they come to you because you are loved. There are no receipts to be held for anything you give to God here in this life. Whatever good you do is His work in and through you. Hence, you see that your spiritual faith is not transactional, it is transformational. You will see many writings discussing the difference between the two from others who have lived, from those who are still reviewing what it means to be transformed. My Special son, you have seen at the beginning of this message certain terms that describe outward action or motion, such things as power, strength, energy and force. These things often seem without origin, and they also appear to be perpetual. You learned years ago that when these things are impeded, they create pressure from the backflow. Pressure can be defined as a given force per unit. This is what human actions are like, good and bad. These pressure points are what you deal with every day, what everyone alive has to face during their waking and sometimes sleeping hours. They are dilemmas for many people, outright obstacles and impediments to others, and prohibitive roadblocks to millions more. It is when these obstructions are removed or overcome that you feel the release of pressure. This pressure about which I speak can come in many forms and feelings, many emotions and calculations. Pain and sorrow are indicative of this pressure. So is unexpected grief. However, pressure can come in the form of a competitive spirit when someone is about to win a contest or vanquish an enemy. There is pressure and there are pressure points all around the world, inside the home, in the cities and nations, and even inside the human heart and mind. The point I would like to make about this matter is not that the existence of pressure is the problem, but how that pressure affects persons and societies that is important. Relieving pressure can come in the form of feeding, clothing and housing the poor. It can be manifested by bringing justice to the unjust. The other side is that sometimes there comes the need to create or intensify pressure. This is when you are convincing someone else to do the right thing, to desist from pursuing an unworthy goal, or admonishing someone who is about to harm someone else. These are the examples of good pressure. *(Bad pressure - trying to incite people to an unworthy goal in opposition to the Gospel, such as instigating a riot.)*

You just spoke to your friend about the pressure of being cast aside by his female friend. You have felt this pressure before. Your brother has likewise felt it in his lifetime. This is negative, counterproductive pressure that tends to diminish the dignity of the human person. It is offset by your own positive pressure, by putting things in perspective, by turning the tables on the offenders by refusing to let your dignity go. It is these feelings that Jesus has sensed most intensely during these times. He often feels violated and betrayed by millions of people around the globe. Imagine the pain He felt on Good Friday, and that He knew in advance that so many would refuse to accept His Love. This hurt Him as badly as His physical Wounds themselves. These are among the reasons that I am still speaking to you and your brother. It is because the Father knows that you will spend your lives telling the world about the Truth of human sacrifice and prayerfulness. Through these two things, you create positive pressure points and eliminate negative ones. You build levees to capture sufficient water to quench the spiritual thirst of lost sinners. You likewise destroy dams that drown innocent victims in the depths of their predators' lies. It is the latter that is extremely important in these modern days. There is stagnancy abounding across America and around the globe. We are working a prayer at a time to create an atmosphere of movement, motion toward the Cross, in the direction of redemption, for the good of the Church. You and your brother, and the billions of other Christians throughout the past 2,000 years, have seen these obstructions in your hearts, and you have tried to do something, anything that would alleviate them. You have softened the pangs and pains of life for countless sufferers through your prayers, litanies and petitions. I am only telling you this so you will know the true essence of why you are alive, the reason you have been accorded the kindnesses of Jesus in whom you have found your own identity. When someone asks your name; if anyone wants to know who you are, you are silently telling them that you are Jesus' vessel on the Earth, and your mission is to advocate for the Salvation of unconverted sinners. When you say the words 'Bill Roth,' this is what you are saying. When Jesus sees and hears you, when you are pronouncing your name before all other men, Heaven hears you say 'Jesus' disciple.' This is your name. When you announce your earthly profession, you are saying 'converter of sinners.' No matter what a man or woman does for self-sustenance or to feed and house their children, their names are always 'servant of God.' This is how Jesus knows you. It is not by your level of handiwork in a given profession, it is through the lens of your own faith and the degree to which you strive for the coming of His Kingdom. We have spoken in intense detail about this kind of vision in earlier times. The Third Person of the Trinity, the Advocate gives you the power, energy, force and exertion to create enough pressure to draw all men to God. This is your primal insight, the way you perceive human life in the flesh. This power gives you the ability to reign over your own feelings and emotions, to control your temper, give sound advice, move others to tears of joy, and recognize the presence of Jesus in other people.

  This brings Me to the young Korean boy who sang so prettily in the vocal contest. You and all who have witnessed this event have been moved to weeping because you are happy for the boy, you are joyful that he had his moment before the world. You recognized the innocence of the Christ Child in him and the talents of Christ the King. These seemingly disunited forces are present in all who come forward like young Sung; and while this is important to know, it is more important that you understand why you know that Jesus is hidden in people like the young Korean boy. You have come to a crucial point of comprehension of the divine purposes of God. When the human mind grasps the presence of the Holy Spirit inside another man, that mind is in unison with the creative Love of God. This is why you wept when you saw the video. It is the reason why 10-million other people wept as well. This certain feeling of absolute unity with the mind of God creates an internal dynamic in the human heart that is larger than the parameters of the soul. It creates a positive, love-filled pressure point that becomes released in the way one would breach a levee. The parable of young Sung has wide and varying implications. Why? Because of the way he grew up. I have often heard you describe someone as having a Cinderella story. This means that success comes to them from out of the blue, on a somewhat miraculous scale. It is where divinity and opportunity meet. It is where love and action coalesce. There are but few of these moments in life because there are so few Cinderellas alive. The poor rarely believe that they will be anything greater than paupers. The unread are thought to have no means to the archives of the greatest histories of the world. Their works will always lay in anonymity. They never believe that the miracle will come to them. I have taught you differently. I have said that the Father is a God of miracles, the Maker of Justice, the Creator of Purity and the Restorer of Innocence. He does these things when He pleases because His sovereign wisdom and vision permit Him to know what is best in every circumstance. Thus, if the weaker soldier somehow does not prevail, there is a reason somewhere not yet known. And, it is what the victor does with his triumph that matters most. If he shares his joy in an inclusive way; if he stands tall for the meek and helpless, if he lifts-up those who have no other way, then he is indeed a worthy champion. This is the example that Jesus has taught. Therefore, when so many millions of eyes saw the face and fruitfulness of Sungbong Choi, they saw one who was brought from a suffering past. As you see, he was told that he is never alone, and that he had never been alone. He was simply waiting for the glory of his day. Whatever suffering arose, the pains and deficits he felt, were all wiped clean by the acclamation of those he touched with the fruits of his life. Here is the thesis of this message. Can richness come from poverty? Yes. Can joy come from sadness? Yes. Can Eternal Life come from Sacrifice? Yes, indeed, and it has already come. Irony abounds. This is the substance of what I have come to tell you and your brother today. I hope you have enjoyed it. I ask you to pray for all who are being persecuted for their faith in Jesus. And, please pray for all the Poor Souls in Purgatory and the many who are contemplating taking the lives of the children in their wombs."

Friday, November 11, 2011
11-11-11
2:54 p.m.

"When the world seems inconceivably vague and hard, when the clarity of our thoughts blurs into confusion and beyond recognition, when the cold shroud of uncertainty creeps upon us for no apparent reason, we must remain footed in the serenity of the Cross. The crassness of human life

cannot dim the sheen of God's stardom that still comforts our forbears from generations past. We are told that Jesus Christ stands beside us and simultaneously within us. How malleable we must become! All we need to do is focus our eyes on the heart, turning our attention to the keystone truth that has laid-claim to our meandering lives. This is the presence that prolongs the daylight and soothes the night! This is Jesus who has spread the undying sureness of Divine Love across the annals of modern men. This is the Savior who has raised our souls to the stature of royalty before the grand parade of the ages."

William L. Roth

"My Special son, that is one of the prettiest reflections I have ever heard. Your heart is indeed finely attuned to the Providence of God and the pious strains of the Holy Spirit. Jesus is deeply embedded in your heart. I have come today to say hello to you and your brother, to offer the peace of God in your lives, and to bless you with My Motherly affections. It would appear that you are both doing well in your prayerful lives, in that which Jesus has given you to do. Neither of you is yet an old man. You have sufficient physical strength and cognitive acumen to continue your work together. I thank you for your efforts to remain safe from harm and do whatever you must accomplish to maintain your good reputation here on Earth. You have been told repetitively that Jesus loves you without cessation and that the miracle of His Birth is always with you. He came into the Earth as a little Child and ascended into Heaven with that same innocent heart. He did not let the events of His life affect His trust in those who loved Him. He never denied those who came to Him with contrite hearts, and this is also the same today. I know that you are pleased with all your works and charities that you have given humanity during your years among the societies that are still growing in faith. You and your brother have been good teachers and friends to the simple and suffering ones, those who are looking for spiritual guidance, and the many who are consecrated to My Immaculate Heart. I am your miracle for this day in history. Please remember that My love for you is unfathomable to the minds of men. It is imperative that everyone call on My intercession because I speak directly to the Son of Man in Heaven. I see and touch Him. I give Him consolation as He sees such a corrupt and indifferent world. I am His Mother who does everything for humanity that I do for Jesus.

The winter will soon arrive, and the cold winds will come. The snows will be hearty, but beautiful. There is something kind in the offing that will bring solace to those who place their hopes in Jesus. It is a sign of satisfaction and inner-peace that will allow the faithful to know that they have always been on the fertile ground. It is a unique time in history for you to see what is ongoing around the nations and here in your country as well. I only ask that you and your brother continue to be peaceful here, that you pray well for all My intentions, and that you exercise and rest in ways that do not strain your feelings. It is true that time goes quickly for those who are focused on their chores and duties, and this is not always a negative thing. You have My assurance that the Angels and Saints are trained on the success of the Church-Militant, everyone who struggles chiefly for the conversion of sinners and the preservation of unborn human life. It is an excelling gift that you have given Father Ted who has his own challenges in the land where he has chosen to work in the vineyard of the Lord. I know that you remember Father Ted and all the missionaries and foreign workers in your daily petitions. You are seeing in your country the positive and negative effects of democracy unfolding again. While it is a draining process for those involved, it is not something that must be ignored. The will of free people must be done. I join in your prayers that your leaders do more to serve the poor and protect the innocent. The crimes that are being revealed are not even the beginning of what is occurring all over the world. The evils of Satan are oppressing the poor and raining fires of hatred on the lovable innocents that it is almost too grotesque to explain. Some have asked why Jesus does not intervene more promptly to end these things. The answer is that He is trying. He is asking His faithful people around the globe to be the catalysts that will bring this much-needed change. It is through prayers such as yours that Heaven will succeed. You must remember that you and your brother must take precautions that are not necessarily needed by people who lead other lives. If you give Satan the opportunity to protract his evil, he will do it. Please provide your Guardian Angels the conditions under which you can be best protected. These are perilous times for those who are close to Jesus and Me. Your brother was correct when he said that it would be improper for either of you to walk alone around the blocks of your neighborhood. There are thieves, robbers, kidnappers, shooters and wild animals that Satan can use to injure you or worse. I simply ask you and your brother not to worry. Keep your faith alive and be happy. These are some strangely unique times of great opportunity for the Church in America and around the world. You can see from the turmoil in the nations that the time is ripe for the Master of the house to make His presence known. The question that comes to mind is how many innocent victims will suffer before the errant thugs who are causing all the violence and unrest are brought to their knees. It is truly a fight between good and evil, about the clash of cultures that will yield the final face of human life before the Return of the Son of Man. The events you are seeing unfold during these times could have ramifications that would last 500 more years if Jesus does not return in Glory before then. Hence, it is about ripeness, readiness and steadfastness. The world is growing-on, but are the chosen disciples of Jesus prepared to engage the fight with faithful vision? Thank you again for receiving Me in this beautiful place where you and your brother have grown so much like Jesus over the years. I ask you to remember to pray for all My intentions, and I shall pray for yours as well. All the Church Triumphant is cheering for the Faith Church on Earth."

Sunday, November 20, 2011
1:52 p.m.

"We are schooled in the sacred principles of religious virtuousness by the way we present ourselves as Roman Catholic Christians and what we can glean from others about our personification of the Gospel transcripts. This is the impeccable proof of our orthodox faith. We feel a mutual companionship with other Christians in our supposition that they have been branded by the same suffering that first begot the purification of the world. What a thought! We have discovered even more common ground with Jesus Christ. Certain people are specifically chosen to endure pain and torment so that other people can live beyond the immortal horizon. Here, we humbly submit that we are as deserving of the same victorious blessings that Our Lord heaped upon the believing Apostles during His brief ministerial mission on Earth. This is the inimitable wonder of the Crucifixion and Resurrection, and this is what we live for every time we wake in the morning with as much Christological fervor as that which accompanied us to sleep the night before."

William L. Roth

"Today, My little ones, I come to you with a heart filled with joy because the seasons of the climate of God are all becoming one. We have in this place brought tremendous healing to the world because of our prayers. One might not recognize it, but humanity is much more whole because of the relationship that we have enjoyed. My prayers are united with yours for the further healing and purification of your brothers and sisters, especially those who have yet to make their full professions of faith and their seamless unity with God. This is the conversion for which we have always prayed. Yes, today is a day of joy and happiness for the Mother of God because you have not left Me; you have not strayed from My Motherly guidance at all. I have come to you for so many years to speak about righteousness that will restore lost hope and fill empty hearts with meaning. My presence here is the reality of God in human and spiritual form. I am the same Lady to whom the Archangel Gabriel came in much the same way that I am speaking to you now. I have indeed spoken about righteousness and Divine Love, but I have also told you about wrongness. I have spoken about the awful 'wrong-ism' that exists in the material world, the error that only few are willing to address. I am not speaking just about the wrongness that you see in the news every day, but that which is wrong in the individual heart. Its basis is unconfessed sin; it is a manifestation of humanity's reluctance to choose the good and decent path, the holy path, the Way and the Truth whom all must follow to Heaven. There are many events that are the result of wrong-headedness, but there are also untold sins that arise from wrong-heartedness. It is to the heart that I have always spoken because this is where the Spirit of Jesus lives; it is where total perfection feeds the thought of the mind so that each person can live in purity and discretion. My Special son, it is clear to Me that your work with your brother is on course; you are still doing what you were asked to do. You are not biding your time, waiting for some other door to open. You are working diligently every day as you pray for the Second Coming of Jesus.

I ask you to think about all the people around the globe who would envy the way the citizens of the United States spend their lives. You still have upward mobility and ease of life here in America. I am not suggesting that your country is as spiritually secure as it ought to be. In fact, you know that there is widespread corruption and impurity here in the States, just as there is in other underdeveloped countries. It is all about the conscience, the spiritual conscience of mortal men and women according to the mandates of the Church. There are compounds and serums for many illnesses, but there is only one gift that can purify the hearts of men. It is love. You have known this for all your years, and you have practiced it well. There comes a time when everyone must make their own judgement about how deeply they will be devoted to God. Imagine a warrior on a battlefield who has been knocked unconscious, face-down on the ground. Now, when he regains consciousness, he will raise his head as much as he can, and then he will do one of two things, or a combination of both. He will either call for help or rise on his own and resume his pursuit of the battle. On the other hand, he could do both. The combination of enjoining the Spirit of God and the determined human will is what is needed to bring harmony, holiness and justice to this war-weary world. Humanity has been incapacitated by its own egoism, its own belief that the human will is enough. We both realize that this is not true. The Holy Spirit and the human spirit were always meant to be one. There has always existed the desire of the Father to be united and reunited with His human creatures in the Light of Heaven. This is what makes the Church so important to Him. It is the reason why the Church Triumphant has never loosed its grip on the Faith Church Militant and the Church Suffering in Purgatory. The reaches for new Saints are far ones at times, but the momentum and the direction are always there. The draw never recedes. The desire for unification never wanes. It can be likened to the inversion of a plant. The roots for the growth of the Faith Church are in Heaven. This is why the world appears upside down. The Church-Militant has in its grasp the seed of its own future, and this is as it was meant to be. You must realize that this is the reason that I have come to you in such joy today. I realize what lies in the offing. I have seen the flashes of light that have come from this place where you live, here in this home. I have seen the holy fires that you and your brother have lit that are only now growing into larger blazes. You must trust Me and know that I am telling the truth. I have been praying that you and your brother will not begin wearing your feelings on your sleeves. You are both much older than you were when we began, and you are unwilling to be spoken to as if you were not as advanced in age. I have asked you to be My little children, and this means that you should not be offended when one or the other of you speaks out of turn. At this point in time, there is reason to believe that you and your brother will remain peaceful brothers as long as you live. I have prayed for this to always be true. Please exercise your human will to help Me ensure that the two of you remain united for Jesus and Me. How can I expect the world to live My messages if the messengers themselves will not live them? I am asking for your prayers, that you support your brother in the ways of the Angels, that you hold in your heart the remembrance that your brother has loved you more than anyone else on Earth. I am not foretelling any disastrous events that might come, I am only asking you and your brother to realize that you are both in Satan's line of fire. It is especially more true now than ever before. Satan will attempt to injure, harm, divide, desecrate and dissolve everything you have ever done and stood for. Please do not be naive about what he may do next. I am pleased that you are singing songs, writing lyrics, playing tunes and sharing the content of your heart on the page and in musical form. The writing that you provided for today's message is some of your best, but it is no match for the lovely lyrics that you write for your songs. The Spirit of Love helps you compose these things."

Sunday, November 27, 2011
2:14 p.m.

"*Love has no underside, no dark side, no pitchy slogans, no infatuations, no ulterior motivations, and no selfish whims. Love is not a pastime for fame seekers or self-indulgent profiteers. Human love is all about consecration and devotion, prudence, truth, compassion, holiness, and service. Love requires the company of a sympathetic heart and blameless mind. Love in the way of eternal redemption means little if not imparted to forgive one's enemies. Absolution is love's companion, its other self, its mirrored reflection in the physical world. Love without sacrifice is but a hollow shell, a mantlepiece, an idle instrument, a blurry image. Love is the definition of human perfection in heraldic form, the lifeline we cling to when we are submerged in pain.*"

William L. Roth

"Indeed, I love you, My dear little children. Wherever you travel in this life, I shall be with you. The Love of Jesus the Savior is wrapped around your lives and souls. He infiltrates your hearts with Wisdom and kindness allotted to humanity as in the olden days. You have with you now all the assistance you will ever require to see the Truth clearly, to know when to act and when to refrain, to comprehend the wholesome edification of the spirited mind in the themes of righteousness. Today, I bring with Me the peace of God to dwell here in this place because you are worthy of His blessings. The Dove of Peace rests comfortably here. Your innocence is comforting to Jesus, and your holiness is tremendous solace for the burdens He still carries over the condition of the world. When I bring you these blessings from Heaven, I blanket your lives in grace, in the healing and magnifying resolution that you take into the world when you encounter your families and friends. Even still, I see you as children, as sons who are in need of My constant intercession. While Jesus makes you heroes among men, I make you see well His gratitude for living your faith. You have been told that faith is a gift from the Father; and this is true, but the human heart must welcome this gift with an acceptance of all the trials and burdens that accompany your faith. You have seen in today's age nearly everything conceivable that can insult and desecrate the holy gifts from the Lord's hands. Whatever is sacred to you, whatever you deem cherishable because it reminds you of the Son of Man, you will be ridiculed for this. You will see the wretched attacks of Satan against your most comforting goals, against your most noble moments that reveal the Light of the Cross to other men. Even in all this, My little sons, you are defeating the enemies of the redemption of lost sinners. By all means, you are hastening the demise of evil when you are burdened by the calling of your faith. This is why this age and these times are so critical to the Church. You can literally feel the communion of hearts and minds that pray for you, and you for them. You can sense the power of the Church from bygone ages praying for you. Your consciousness is aware of all the advocates that assist your lives during the present hours. This is why you must remember your dignity in this lineage. Never forget that you are especially chosen for the mission you were assigned when you first came of age, when you attained an inclination that Divine Reason would eventually call on you for help.

    I have been speaking in recent weeks about the unseen workings of the Holy Spirit throughout Creation, in and around the precincts far and wide that are important for the accomplishment of pious works. I have included in My revelations the events that are occurring in your own diocese, and those that are lent to the development of the manifestations that will awaken those who are slumbering in sin. This is the ultimate calling of the ages, My children. To stir the indifferent from their wicked ways is an order that must be filled at all costs, and this is why you are seeing such cascades of messages around the globe from Jesus and the Father, and also from Myself. We have absolutely not left humanity orphaned, but fully incorporated into the sustenance that keeps the Holy Family united in love. It is the Will of God that makes this true. It is the compliant Hearts of Jesus and Me, and the honorable heart of Saint Joseph, that provides ample Light for the world to see its way clear to the gateway of Salvation. Hence, I wish you peace from the Holy Family, from all that has been given to you in word and deed from Heaven because of our love for you. My Special son, you are certainly not moving away from your work for Me in any measure. You must remember that I have told you that you never will. You are dedicated to Me in ways that even you have never brought to mind. Why? Because the sacred discipline of your apostleship is embedded in the very fiber of your life and conscience. We are all thankful that the Lord has made you and your brother this way. The fruits of your service to the Church are sweet and bountiful; they are delectable to the taste; they are available to anyone who desires to know God. I must repeat that you stand tall; you have grown in the knowledge of God and His Wisdom. You have been elevated in your awareness of the purposes that are delineated in the Sacred Scriptures, the good and the bad, because humanity will look to you and your legacy on its journey into His presence. This makes you and your brother more than simple men, but spiritual giants of the Christological Kingdom that has upended the globe and brought tremendous cultivation where it is required. We have spoken about the centuries and epochs, the generations and decades that make-up the years of the lives of men. Everything we have done together has transcended these things for the Glory of God."

Sunday, December 4, 2011
3:10 p.m.

"*There is a visible resolution to the obscure aspects of human thought and action that are clarified by focusing on what makes us think. We have a grip on everything we have done and desire to do when we take into account the internal framework in which human intelligence is formed. It comes from our receptivity to the wisdom of God. This is the way we foster revolutionary change and purge toxicity from our homes, villages, and neighborhoods. It is also how we barge through the doorway of everyone who hates us and demand respect for the Messianic King whose Cross and golden Scepter will bear our souls to the cherished succor of the endless ages. It is in this vein that we should prepare for that great moment. We must journey carefully, respond openly, listen keenly, right ourselves smartly, pray devoutly, and hope beyond the constellations that all the blessings we seek will come in our day.*"

William L. Roth

"It is with tremendous joy and admiration that I have come to pray with you today, My children. It is the elation of My Immaculate Heart that you see human life so prayerfully and gratefully, and that you stand firm in your confidence that the work you are accomplishing will be effective in defeating the enemies of the Cross. These enemies are real and forceful; they are cagey and terrifying, and they are on the prowl to harm innocent souls everywhere. Therefore, it is imperative for you to remember that you are loved beyond all measure. I realize that you have difficult days and tiresome hours, and I am with you through all of them. I ask Jesus to help you adhere to the blessings that He has given you through the gifts of patience and perseverance. Can you not tell that He is with you? Do you not know that My Son can reverse the effects of time and bring happiness to all the nations? What this means is not that the sins of evil men are not egregious. Neither does it imply that bad things do not happen to good people. What it does mean is that good people triumph over the evil works of Satan through the same faith that good people manifest perfect divinity in an extremely dark world. God the Father and Jesus the Son are within you through the power of the Holy Spirit. They have inspirited you in somewhat the same way that Jesus became Incarnate in the physical world. The Holy Spirit infiltrates you. Sacred Love devours you to help you walk the righteous path in the same way that Jonah was taken in. You surely must see the reciprocity in what I am saying. And, it is about this Love that I have always spoken. It is about this Love that our work has been focused. Never mind the spiritual weaklings that live in your midst and around the world who are too blinded by their own persuasions to recognize the hand of God in the greater good. You are living by the sacred architecture that first fashioned Creation, that deigned to call humanity to the highest powers ever known. This is still the Father's call. It is His summons to those who will hear. It is His mandate to men who will listen. It is His order to the many who must respond. It is for these reasons that all our work is worth the cost; it is truly worthy of the effort that the two of you have already invested.

Yes, it is a gray day outside on this December afternoon. The overcast skies will give-way to the sunshine again very soon, and you will feel that brilliance of light as do your souls sense the holiness and righteousness of God beaming upon you now. My little sons, nobody ever said that being Christian is easy. I defy anyone to locate such a passage in the Bible. The Sacred Scriptures also contain only vague references to what will come when you most expect that the end must be near. It would seem that the rioting and treachery would indicate that end to be already upon you. You see life as a series of precursors to eventful times that are in the offing, but that cannot change who you are. They indeed should not affect your present identity at all. You are good and decent people who have always kept your faith intact, always depended on your trust in Jesus to face every new day. This is why you are already seen as victors and champions far above those gray skies about which I speak, and in quarters far and wide that you have not yet seen. You have been charitable to the poor, sympathetic with the suffering, one in mind and body with The Christ, and willing to walk through perilous corridors and along thunderous shores to arrive at your destination in Jesus' Most Sacred Heart before you shutter your eyes in sleep every night. There is peace in both of you that you have not yet tapped. There is visionary genius already growing at the pit of your minds. There are stars and endless moons, light and reflection, innovation and instincts that hold you fast to the Cross and set you free in the Paschal Resurrection. When you consider what Advent means as we speak, you realize that it infers a period of waiting. Waiting for what? It obviously means the wait for the anniversary of Jesus' Birth, but it also means something utterly profound for the anticipating world. Advent in the context of the Messianic Nativity means that you are prayerfully awaiting the Eve of Joy that you have so often spoken about. However, in a greater sense, it implies the Advent of the Second Coming that you live the whole liturgical year. This is not only the joyful hope in which you wait for the Lord, but also the timely conversion of the whole of humanity to the faith by which you have lived. You are waiting for the arrival of all living beings at the doorstep of Eternity by committing themselves to living their lives in accordance with the Gospel. There are prodigal sons and daughters wandering the nations all across the world. There are eager fathers waiting for them too, fatted calves waiting to be slaughtered, arms opened-wide to receive the home-comers, and sunlit rays ready to shine on the entire procession. It is true that the Return of the Son of Man is nigh, but newborns are being given to mothers and fathers because Love still creates life. Humanity continues to live right. Families and friends remain bonded to one another through the goodness that has come down through the centuries since the ancient days. It is in this sense that the world is one, that the passing ages do not really matter. It is the future that is most important to you now, and the present that you stand upon like a platform to serve Jesus and His Kingdom with courage and vigor.

You see, I am trying to impress upon you the immeasurable level of joy that I have in My Immaculate Heart about how precious you are, how special and unique, how grand and eloquent. I have made you this way because you have been obedient to Me and Jesus in all ways and all times. There is newer life for all the world that can come only when hearts are opened-wide, only when men and women search for true meaning beyond their back porch swings or around the dinner table. This life is discovered in the sacred love that is human love, a love that is founded upon the Divine Love that reigns supremely over all. This is not conjecture or supposition, it is an indisputable fact. Just as sure as you are alive, you must expect that all hearts and minds will come to this. Everyone given to death will be preserved for life by the Man on the Cross. This is the Christian message that you have both known for more decades than you might have wished to be passed by now. It is the march of Creation, the grand alluring of redemptive seniority that is claiming you in mind, body and soul. And, I adore you for this, My children. I offer you My congratulations for the way your lives are unfolding. I extend My gratitude for the excellence that you have embraced and the character with which you are carrying your burdens. It is said that '...there comes a time.' This is true for most everything on the mortal Earth. It is time that My Son's Church embrace My messages without reticence wherever I have given them. I have approached Jesus with your petitions in conjunction with My own intentions. There are such pitiable people and living conditions all around the globe for which we must continue to pray."

Sunday, December 11, 2011
3:25 p.m.

"We think of eternal salvation as more than something that happens to us beyond death; it is a tangible institution in the here and now. In this sense, salvation is a preeminent domain beyond this world at the same time it is an ongoing redemptive process. Salvation is a synonym for our new reality at the moment we are taken into Paradise. Therefore, salvation is simultaneously a place, an event, and a description of a place and event. Another transcending word in our vocabulary is love, through which God reveals His desire to take us into His presence through the Crucifixion and Paschal Resurrection of His Messianic Son. Let it henceforth be forever told. We can offer ourselves to Jesus like snapping our fingers together. And we can flourish in His grace as though waking from our sleep."

William L. Roth

"My little children, it is in the strains such as you have spoken here that the Lord finds such consolation because He realizes that you are not only attuned to His Will, but that you are sharing it with the entire world. It is sufficient that you obey the tenets of the Sacred Scriptures, but it is extraordinarily supernatural that you convey to humanity the sentiments of God who wrote them. I have come to you today with great joy. It is to the domain of perfection that humanity is taken when everyone participates in the sacrifices required to purify those who are yet lacking in the knowledge and wisdom of redemption. I bring you the wholesome blessings that keep your hearts abreast of the facts by which you live. It is factual that you are embraced and warmed by the Holy Light whereby you can sense your unity with Jesus as you walk through the world with Him. It is equally factual that you respond with intense compliance when God seeks from you the actions and prayers that make reparation for the evils attacking the Church and the deficits of the sinners who are causing them. Your introductory reflection is reminiscent of the writings of the Saints in that they pursued their daily chores while deeply imbedded in the immediacy of the moment; and at the same time, they subconsciously remained focused on their reward in Heaven with the Father. It is imperative that you remember that the Salvation of broken humanity took place prior to the Ascension of Jesus into Heaven. Thus, the Crucifixion is one of the Sorrowful mysteries, and the Ascension is a Glorious one. I have made this clear because it is important for you to make known that the Holy Spirit was crucified as well, and this is what happens every time someone rejects or impugns the Lord's intercessions from Heaven. In other words, when Jesus is betrayed by someone, the Holy Paraclete feels the same betrayal. This makes these offenses against the Most Blessed Trinity resonate throughout Creation, and this is the reason we are addressing the matter through the parameters of the entirety of the universe. There can be no division between the Father and the Son and the Holy Spirit. One might ask how a spirit can be crucified. The answer is that the Holy Spirit is the Living Truth to which all men are summoned, deposited in Jesus on the Cross. Mortal flesh will fade away, and souls will be uniquely woven to the Kingdom of God by their unity with the Holy Spirit. Hence, you know Heaven to be a spiritual Paradise. It is imperative for Christians to remember this, or they will not have appreciation for the resurrection of the body that has been willed at the end of time. It is not a dichotomy, but a parallel line beside which bygone souls repose until the moment when the Return of Jesus in Glory combines all thought and action into one glorious domain. Men live in exile through lines and symbols, but you will live infinite dimensions upon the Second Coming of Jesus.

It is important for humanity to know what Jesus sees when He looks upon human actions. My Son observes what His disciples and followers are doing for Him while they live on Earth. I wish for My children to remember that small acts of kindness are mammoth overtures to the Father in Heaven. This is how a race horse can run like a tremendous machine. It is how a 'Little Child Can Guide Them.' It is how the fullest framework of one's holding another person precious can be expressed by a flower or sweetheart ring. Conversely, errors and omissions are diminished by the prayers of Jesus' brothers and sisters on Earth. This is the origin of the word 'beloved.' Someone who is united with God to the extent that they sacrifice themselves to share the virtues of human sanctity are beloved in His sight. There is a difference in being loved and beloved. Here, you see another way to clarify what it means to be acceptable in God's sight. It is important to remember that the beloved are blessed. This is the essence of the Sermon on the Mount. Jesus loves all sinners, and He holds beloved all who reject sin and follow Him. My Special son, can you not see why I am so elated that you have remained with Me for so many years? To whom else could I offer My timely lessons and teachings? The friendship of yourself and your brother, your unity and holy contributions to the conversion of lost sinners have made this possible. Thank you for your prayers that are making the Earth a better place. There is pardon and forgiveness for everyone! I wish the whole world knew what you know to the depths of your soul – that inside every man, woman and child is the potential to be the perfect likeness of the Christ Child and the King of the World. You have never lost sight of this hope. You have never stopped believing in miracles. Your focus has remained on the future of the Earth that includes triumphs and exhilarating moments that make humanity believe that the miracles of the ages are coming upon you now."

Sunday, December 18, 2011
3:07 p.m.

"We must be careful to never allow any stain of hatred to infiltrate our hearts. Hatred is a mortal sin. Not only does hatred reveal to humanity that we are an enemy of redemption, but that we are incapable of aspiring to the perfection of Jesus Christ. Hatred eats away at our soul like a

parasite, like a gargantuan monster devouring what is left of our conscience. Anyone who hates his brother confirms that he does not want to go to Heaven. Those who espouse hatred are themselves indicted by the very virtuousness they reject. It is only by seeing life through the lens of complete love that we recognize how evil hatred is. Love is freedom, while hatred is incarceration. Love is sweet and warm, but hatred is bitter and cold. Let there be no mistake that it is possible to detest the actions of other men without hating their souls. Hatred is the ultimate act of depravity. We must never allow ourselves to become ensnared in the hatred that shrouds the human spirit from seeing the resurrection of life that comes through love and forgiveness."

William L. Roth

"Faith, My children, is your way of seeing what has yet to take shape in visible form; it is your means of touching the Lord's Kingdom with your heart long before your soul becomes eternally redeemed there. These are indeed happy days, pleasing days, important hours, crucial times and evocative moments that prove that everything you have invested in Jesus' Holy Name will reap the fruit not only that He desires of the Earth, but the fruits that you seek from Him in Heaven. The distinction you have found in Him is profoundly indescribable to others around you because it has so many facets. There is obvious beauty and brilliance in your new identity that Jesus forged on the Cross, but there is also kind intelligence and charisma. You are now creatures who have taken-on the form of the sacred divine that humanity was always meant to espouse. Every year at this time, you celebrate what it means for God to come to the Earth in His Only Begotten Son, birthed to sinners by Myself, the Sinless Maiden. This is truly a miracle for the world. Even the concept of the Nativity never grows old because it contains so many beatific dimensions that it takes years and decades for ordinary men to understand. And yet, it is simple. It speaks to the ability of the Blessed Trinity to exist and persist inside and outside of time, in the physical and spiritual realms, in the mind and the heart, and in the Church here in exile, the Church Suffering in Purgatory, and the Church Triumphant in Paradise. When a man thinks about conceiving something, about the beginning, the opening, the genesis of anything that is good, he is prone to wonder from where true goodness originates. In order for a man to do good, he must first be good. This is the simultaneous existence of doing and being, of being and doing. This process has a recognizable face in that humanity feels inside what a smile or a frown looks like. When humanity thinks about goodness in the context of action, it cannot be fully comprehended without the same humanity embracing the framework of all that is good, which is God. The same can be said of people who are bad, who do bad things. These are the ones who partner with and practice evil with God's adversary, the devil. All men and women of sound reason have the capacity to know the difference. The conscience makes this clear.

Today, I have come to pray with you for everything you have seen that you know to be good. And, I have come to pray with you for the eradication of the things that are not good. Does the elimination of all that is not good mean that the world is then filled with goodness? Not necessarily. The absence of evil is indifference. Where there is no goodness or no discernible evil, there is only a void, a vacuum not unlike the realms of outer-space. The goodness that is so important to human beings can only be prevalent when they actively pursue and personify the goodness of God. This is done not only by identifying with Jesus, but personifying Him in all that He says and does. The Living Spirit of Jesus Christ is who speaks through faithful Christians. He becomes the nucleus of His own disciples, their spirit that establishes the full means for propagating the Holy Gospel in the here and now. Jesus is not only this, He is also the begetting of the newness of life in those who have converted to the Cross. Why? Because as the Holy Spirit, the Son of Man can be anywhere He wishes to be. This is the essence and the meaning of a spirit. There are no parameters that can confine God the Holy Spirit. There are no barriers or partitions that can hold Him back from permeating and inspiring. The Principles of Truth can be taken anywhere in Creation that God wants them to go, into the human heart and mind, atop the mountains, beneath the seas, and in all other sites and locations that He deigns to travel. The Holy Spirit reigns in churches and prisons, in dungeons and aboard airplanes, in little children and stately old men. It is by the power of the Holy Spirit that you are capable of understanding the words I am saying now. All of this is a gift to you, My little sons. It is a gift because the Lord asks you to keep giving for Him – offer His Wisdom and presence through your own lives to the rest of the world.

My Special son, had you in the beginning of My messages pondered the fact that I would speak to you long into the span of two decades? *"No."* Do you realize that I have done so because you and your brother have been so loyal to Me? *"Yes."* And what has this loyalty meant for the Church, for the whole of humankind, for the Glory of the Cross? That all of it is true. Your life could never have been given this long to something based on error. *"I know that to be true."* It is imperative that you ponder the proportions of all this. It, in itself, is almost as dimensional as the Incarnation that I spoke about earlier today. The past twenty years have required your own blameless faith, your own vision and foresight about what the future might bring. It has demanded your capacity for hard work and perseverance. There are millions upon millions of people who have lived-out their lives committed to things of far lesser importance. The import of your life with your brother is not only that you have created a foundation upon which millions of others can base their trust in Jesus and affinity for Me, but that you have made the most of your years in this place, in this time, during this age of doubt and destruction, of evil and indifference. You have drawn deadlines in space and time and dared the devil to cross them. You have challenged humanity to do better by God, to hold deep to their breasts the remembrance of what redemption should mean to them. You have highlighted the stark contrasts between darkness and light, between goodness and evil works. When people say, '...therein lies the proof of the Holy Spirit,' they are speaking of Christians like you and your brother who have remained together for so long. You have discarded other meanings about life and influences from doubters that have nothing to do with where your heart is trained. You have attested that God cannot be impugned, that your dignity is intact even when you are being insulted and assailed. This is what the glory of apostleship is all about. It is what God sees. It is the boundless benevolence of your dignified existence that will transcend this life and fill Eternity with joy. I say again, it is what God sees that matters most. Yes, He sees the suffering in the world, and it matters to Him. Thus, I have come again today to pray with you for the end of abortion; it is never too late. I have come into your presence because I feel welcome here. I feel loved and admired. I feel appreciated and adored. I feel embraced and venerated. This is what keeps Me so quietly in your midst when you call 'Hail Mary.' This is the genesis of My fullest gratitude for your endearing faith in My Son. I will tell you that I am as much in love with you as ever, and as evermore I shall be. During this week that will take you to the Eve of Joy, I am still the same Mother who nurtured you from the beginning of your life. I am the Woman who has reciprocally admired you. I am the Queen who is humbled that you have chosen to remain faithful to Me."

Saturday, December 24, 2011
10:17 a.m.

"It is surely true that the Nativity of Jesus Christ is also a testament to the love and faith of the Fair Maiden who gave Him birth, Our Lady of the New Covenant whose grace and energy have capsized humanity's pride. We are drowning in our own nakedness and being rescued by Her blessings, while She continues teaching us the ways of God, coaxing us to change, soliciting our prayers, inspiring our meditations, and admonishing our wrongdoings. The Blessed Virgin Mary must have knelt beside the Bethlehem manger with peace in Her Immaculate Heart, knowing that the Incarnation of the Son of Man made Her likewise the perfect servant as the Savior whom She bore. Mary is the Sacred Vessel whose intercession has made all the difference in the identity of Heaven as we shall see it in Eternity. Her converting kindness in this world and the next has elicited the Divine Mercy of Jesus to delve deeply inside His own Wounds to find forgiveness for our sins. While Jesus is the bravest Man who ever lived, the Mother who kneeled beside Him in prayer and stood by Him during His most painful hours is the most perseverant of any woman, the longest-suffering and most enduring of them all. And we owe Her our lives here and beyond our exile as much as we accept the Crucifixion of Her Son for the remission of our sinfulness."

William L. Roth

"The Eve of Joy has arrived once again! I bring with me My prayers and promises of future prayers, My humble wishes of good will for all humanity, and the blessings and gifts that My Son has given Me to hand to you. My little sons, your love for humanity is indeed authentic and priceless. You are the image and likeness of Jesus when you offer your loyalties to those who serve Him and who believe in Him. I have said that you do not yet realize the glory of these moments because you are suffering tiredness and distraction. It is clear that you are one with the Father because of this suffering and because of the seemingly endless labors here in your exile on behalf of His Kingdom. I have through the years asked you to have peaceful hearts and listening ears, to know with the fullness of trust that you are walking the path that Jesus has blazed for you. The observation of Jesus' Nativity is a time when families take a look at this Feast in the Church, but they look toward one another as well. Neighbors and friends offer their own gifts and blessings, their good tidings and charities; and this is the reason you are able to comprehend the enduring definition of mutual love. It is not wrong to offer material gifts for Christmas, but it is incorrect to assume that these gifts are a substitute for the love that must be shared the whole year through. Remember that the Child Jesus did not shun the gifts of the Wise Men, even though they were more than just representations of homage. The gifts portended something to come, a particular event that would occur in the life of this Little King. This is also how humanity should look at gift-giving on the occasion of Christmas. These gifts should be seen as earnest deposits, representations of the promise of the fullness of life and love from parent to child, child to parent, friend to friend, and neighbor to neighbor. Long has been the tradition that goods and services are ways to show one's dedication and allegiance to someone else, but they must always be in the context of a loving relationship.

My Special son, you and your brother have both given yourselves to God and your fellow human beings in ways that are much too large to measure. It is imperative that you know how greatly you are admired by the Lord God in Heaven and My Messianic Son. This admiration is another dimension of the Divine Love in which you are wrapped to keep you warm in the coldness of the physical world. You have seen the steep mountains and cavernous valleys that Christians must scale and travel to reach the Promised Land. If not for the sinful indifference of those who do not believe in the Gospel Covenant, your journey would not be as difficult. It is true that anything that takes a great deal of time and effort seems to be more worthwhile because the rewards are always more grand. Would it be appropriate for God to hand Heaven to lost sinners on a silver platter with tasty garnish? Let us look at the record of ways the great Saints have served in His vineyard for the answer to this question. They knew that the perfection of the High Kingdom was worth their sacrifices. They were aware that a goal that elevated the Cross would require a battle that was always uphill. It seems that the enemies of the Church always have the upper hand. In reality, however, this is not true. You have yourself said that no one in 2,000 years has been able to destroy the Catholic Church. My goodness – think about the forces that have been thrust against the Church during all those centuries; and yet the Church still stands upright and undaunted. It has always been comprised of sinners who have done the right thing. The Church is the Mystical Body of Jesus; and therefore, the Crucifixion was not just God's way of redeeming the whole of humanity, but consecrating humanity to Himself. He did so many great acts by His Crucifixion that it is almost too intense to ponder. He lifted humanity from the soil on the ground, washed humanity in the perfect Blood of His veins, raised His humanity by His Resurrection as if to be putting on His vestments, and will return to Heaven after His Second Coming with humanity aboard His shoulders, fully absolved. And yet, He is the very humanity that He is bearing to the City of Light. It is all about Jesus. Just as the world became the Cross, the whole of humanity that has accepted Him as their Savior will reside in Him, through Him and with Him. He has already become one with you!

This all began at the Annunciation, and it became visually apparent by the Messiah in My Womb. I walked as a pregnant Mother around the temporal spaces of the exiled world, carrying the Victim who would set free and pay the ransom for everyone else walking there and those who would eventually walk there as well. And, on the night when this Holy Child was born, the Earth could barely contain Him. He was born of My Womb and lay next to Me in a Manger like a saber of light cutting through the darkness. This Light began to grow in meaning for all who would come to Him, for everyone He would later approach, for writers and theologians to celebrate, for the centuries to extol, for priests to consecrate, for Popes to imitate, for the Saints to evangelize, and for all men to adore and worship as the Father would require. We have the brilliance and genius of all Creation and through the fullness of time with us, My children. A Woman who lived with humanity 2,000 years ago gave birth to the Son of the same God who created both the world and the time in which the Earth is fixed. A priceless birth came into being on this night so long ago, and no one has ever been able to devalue what the Lord God has done. Jesus is the star and the gem; He is the cache of Salvation to which many others have aspired but been unable to attain. He is the war chest and arsenal who has defeated Satan and his evil legions because He has come from God as God. And, at the center of all this joy is the same focus that we have spoken about time after time. It is the legitimacy of the practice of humanity to become like Jesus in your day and time. You have it right. The Church has it right. All the Popes and Martyrs have had it right. However, those who have doubts, those who have failed to believe, those who have been too cowardly to practice the profession of Sacred Love have always had it wrong. It is the difference between being an intentional hero and an accidental one. Those who know in advance what they stand for and will die for already own the tenor of greatness that the Father is searching for in them. It is their direct will to walk into the line of fire. However, the billions who have come upon their faith in Jesus by the example of those giants about whom I speak are heroes as well. Yes, they may have come by their greatness by accident, but at least they did not turn away. They did not abandon their duties. They did not hand their swords to someone else. They did not dodge the flaming arrows. These are the heroic acts that all faithful Christians are performing when they suffer for the sake of the Church. It is all in the intent of the heart and fastness of the mind. It is in the courage that makes ordinary people do extraordinary things. In the final analysis, it is through this determination that common men become heroes and conquerors in the Cross! I have been speaking about the ripples of hope that were born with Jesus on the Eve of Joy that grew into massive moments of victory on the battlefields of life. The Little Prince became the King of the World. It is all about process and procedure, about principle and promise. From this night so long ago grew the inspiration of the Catholic Church whose beginning was conceived of My Womb because I have forever loved God and the humanity He created. I knew on that Holy Night that the world was given a Savior whom they could see with their eyes. These are the strains that I wish would resound from the pulpits of the Church tonight. Someday they will, and those who shall lift them must begin to ponder what they will say sooner rather than later. It may not be true that your generation will still be here on Earth when My Son returns, but again it may be – I do not know. However, I am apprised as I have told you many times before that the ages are quickly ripening. My children are being prepared for the grand photograph that I have spoken about, and they are being poised for change. This has come through suffering and testing of the human will. The endurance of those who believe in Jesus has been put under fire. What is the integrity of this mettle? This is for humanity to decide. This is the essence of the Holy Gospel and the meaning of My messages here and around the globe. Humanity must choose to do good. I ask you to pray for all families, for everyone who is estranged, for the poor and elderly, for those who have nothing to eat, for the many who are sleeping in the streets, and especially for the children in their mothers' wombs. These are unique times, special times, even as dark as it seems. We are close to the Return of the King! He will reenter His Kingdom soon."

The Final Colossus
In Battle Array
AD 2012

Monday, January 2, 2012
1:25 p.m.

"There is nothing quite so rewarding as an accomplishment that revolves around the coming of our dreams, or a visionary beginning, or the permeating melodies of new worlds conquered and friendships renewed. There is nothing more satisfying than opening someone else's eyes, softening hard feelings, soothing aching wounds, declaring an end to war, hitting the highest notes, treading where no one has walked, or restoring lost faith. There is little that can take us to eternal happiness than the things we achieve in the name of redeeming grace. These are the designs and purposes that make us who we are in Jesus and Jesus in us. These are the intricacies of the excellence we have found in His Paschal Resurrection. This is the conclusion of the book of life's mysteries where everything unknown to man is fully revealed."

William L. Roth

"Now, My blessed little sons, I have the honor of speaking to you about the benefits of faith that you have realized above and beyond millions of others in this world. We are continuing to take our mission to the material world where the battles between goodness and evil rage like wildfires in the night. We pray that the Lord God will intervene in the particular ways that He knows will propagate His Kingdom for the inclusion of all souls who are worthy of His Mercy. You must remember that Jesus is Mercy Incarnate, and that when earthly sinners call on Him, He will offer His Mercy as the God-Man. My Special son, when I say to you and your brother that you are blessed, I am speaking not only about your relationship with God and Myself, but about your connection with the Church Triumphant in your day. It is true that you are praying for the intercession of the Saints. The Lord God and the Saints hear you. And not only that, they hear the call of the poor and disadvantaged. What this means is that you are an intercessor for the poor on the Earth as well. You must believe Me when I say to you that this is one of the most important matters regarding your life as a Christian that I have thus far been unable to impress on My children. I have said in Medjugorje that everyone must become active in their allegiance to their faith, that it is not enough just to say that one agrees with the teachings of the Church. Here again, we cite the consistency between being active and proactive. I have for centuries appeared here in the world to tell My children about Jesus' Divine Love so they will accept this Love before it is too late for them to convert. I have spoken volumes to you and your brother about the facility of human potential. When it goes unrealized, it is as though it never existed at all. This potential is like a seed planted in the hearts of believers by the Holy Spirit. While you and your brother have no difficulty understanding what I have said throughout the years, millions more have not a clue about what being a proactive Christian means. It has little to do with working in the parish to promote bingo games and other such social events. However, it has everything to do with asking oneself why bingo games and trivia nights are more important than conducting Marian cenacles in these same parishes. It would seem that there is a diffuse definition of the priorities of the life of a child of Mary. You have told your brothers and sisters on many occasions that the plight of the suffering should be deposited into the compassion of My Most Immaculate Heart.

    I open this year 2012 with My reassurance that I will be with you and all My children throughout and beyond the conclusion of time. It is the reason I have given My life to the redemption of men. While there is no greater love than that which Jesus shared with condemned sinners than to be crucified to save them, the love that I share with humanity is to prepare everyone for the reception of the Fruits of the Crucifixion during this life here in your exile. You are seeing that there are awesome and wondrous events occurring around the globe that portend what God will soon accomplish to conscript and absolve those who have been His from the start. I do not mean to imply that this conscription means that they are taken to His Grace against their will like a soldier is drafted into the military. The type of conscripting that I am referring to is that good and decent men and women move closer to the City of Heaven every day they profess their allegiance to the Church. They cannot see this process with their eyes, even though they can feel it in their hearts. In this sense, they are led to the Glorious Kingdom by the hand of the Father as though He is actually touching their souls. This is a conscription because it is done by God behind the veil. It must be made clear that a human soul is aware when that person is not attuned to the Will of God. People who are bound for Heaven already know it. Those who are condemning themselves by their lives of evil can already sense their separation from God. This is what mortal sin does. The point I am making is that this precludes someone from living a hellish life here in this world and expecting a miracle in the end. If this miracle comes, it will be because that soul who lived a hellish life emits the proper contrition and says the appropriate words of confession to convince the Most Holy Trinity that the world had them deceived all along. Their next step here would be Purgatory. There are untold ways that a person can exhibit due contrition, and the most important way is to lay their lives alongside the Saints and proclaim that they failed to mirror their bravery. I intend to speak to you this year about the pleasantries that Jesus has left you, has left all humanity, in the wake of His Ascension. There is sufficient beauty in what Jesus has taught and told to keep your hearts fulfilled for thousands of years. What the Church is trying to do is help men on the Earth actually outlive themselves. The Holy Spirit is deepening and broadening the deposit of human wisdom that will allow all in the world to comprehend what it means to accept their share of the Cross. Why the Cross? Because the Cross precedes the Paschal Resurrection. The Church would be incomplete without the Easter Mysteries that have brought such joy and eternity to the minds, hearts and souls of ordinary men. They are spoken about as being Mysteries because they have so many dimensions that no one can take them in. It is believing without seeing that proffers such grace into the created world. It is faith greater than that of the Martyrs that helps humanity to be elevated in stature to see in advance what the true meaning of Salvation is."

Saturday, January 7, 2012
3:37 p.m.

"Lord, let the healing balm of your holiness come upon us during these crucial times. Let the ages resound your victories. Let the love in our hearts become the antidote for your tears. Amen."

William L. Roth

"The loveliness of this hour is too grand to describe, so I will simply say that you are the nourishment that Jesus needs to suffice His hunger for righteousness in this world. It is clear that He senses your love for Heaven that you describe in your prayers, and this is reflected in the peace that He gives you. My dear little sons, we shall pray until all souls have turned to Him for this peace, for the absolution that all people require to eventually see and accept themselves the way they are known to Him. In many ways, it is a matter of the relationship between perception and perspective, knowing what to see and when to look. The perfect wisdom in human thought is recognizing the sequence of events that deliver you to a vision of transparency about what really matters in the world. This involves discarding some long-held assumptions that perhaps matter here in this life, but that are not so important in the grander purview of immortality. My Special son, if someone is lost in a dark cave somewhere, and they have in their possession only a candle, a match, a ream of paper and an oil lamp, which do they light first? Indeed, the match. This means that you have the primordial vision required to touch the essential context of the truth that God desires the whole of humanity to see. Only a couple in a hundred people would not be stumped by this question. Why? Because the origin of their thought patterns, the veritable essence of their own inquisitive contemplation has been supplanted by the distractions and networks of the meticulous world. When Jesus thought and spoke about broader themes in the material world, His ministry reflected that one essential element that threaded them all together. It is the same foundation of simple truth that led you to respond accurately to My question of someone in a dark cave today. There are no hidden agendas in Heaven. There are no trick questions, no deeply mathematical or philosophical conclusions. One cannot assign a value to the gift of human redemption. When it is said that Jesus paid the cost, it is also known that the price was an immeasurable sum. There are many gifts that are incalculable, invaluable and too great to be appraised. There are no estimations that can capture the totality of the infinity of what they mean to humanity in the here and now. This is how the Father sees your lives and prayers against the backdrop of the secular void. It is not unlike the apparatus on your video camera that allows you to focus on one particular item in a scene while other items in the background remain blurry to the sight. The Holy Spirit in the human heart is also like this; the heart is the filter that reminds the spirit what is simply too precious to ignore. We have spoken before about the various priorities by which men in the world live, which ones are worthy of life and treasure, and which are better left ignored.

You are seeing that the new year 2012 is bringing many great gifts to the Church, especially the upcoming installation of new Cardinals in Rome. When this happens, it is the Vicar's assertion that the power and legacy of the Church will continue long after he is gone. This is the Lord's way of sustaining His holy electorate so that the mission of the Church proceeds. You have also heard testimonies from people who have said they converted to the Roman Catholic Church because of the piety and compassion of Pope Benedict XVI when he visited the site of the September 11, 2001 terror attacks. He brought such consolation that day! His heart was filled with such love! His face beamed with the comfort of God! He listened to the mourners there; he held their faces in his hands, he bound in Heaven what he bound here on Earth. This was his pronouncement that no evil attacks could ever darken the brightness of shared human love in times of sorrow. The whole world saw My Pope that day beaming with the divinity of the Messiah as on the day of His Resurrection. This is what it means to share the power of the Papacy with a world starving for the intervention of their God. Every time someone sets eyes on the Holy Father from Rome, they see in the flesh the dignity of God in Heaven walking in the material world. The point I am making is that the Pope is the example that all men and women should seek. I have spoken about constancy and sequencing when referring to the Pontiff of the Roman Catholic Church. The succession of Popes is proof that the Holy Spirit moves from one heart to the next, from a collective College of Cardinals to a single Vicar of Christ. This is not plurality, it is unity. This process of shared wisdom from On High is indicative of the Holy Spirit to maintain the consistency of the Church from its inception to the Second Coming. Can you tell Me whether the first Pope Saint Peter was elected? *"He was chosen by Jesus."* Yes, Saint Peter was chosen by Jesus by the power of the Holy Spirit, and this goes on yet today. It is Jesus through the intercession of Saint Peter who has chosen every Pope since. We share in the eloquence of their homilies and the promises from their lips about the Kingdom of God for all the world to hear. We recognize the Providence of the Father in their actions, in their bulls and edicts, in their decrees and commendations. This is reason for the whole of humanity to celebrate on bended knee and folded hands that God has so loved the world.

It is My intention to ask My Son to heal and herald all who will receive Him through the power of His Word. I have never conceded a sinner to the netherworld. It is they who have placed themselves there. I have reached-out to My children with emphasis and sincerity, heart in hand, with truth and wisdom, fairness and empathy. I have tried to seek in My children their desire to lend their will to the Will of the Father because He knows what is best for them. You and your brother and all My messengers have been My advocates for them. You have said your prayers and offered your petitions for the many who are unaware of their stations in this life. When I tell you that Jesus is forever grateful, I am saying that His gratitude will never die. What Jesus has given to the world cannot be taken away. When He says that a person belongs to Him, this state of grace is irrevocable. No matter what this same person may do the rest of his life, he will be purified and made whole again. This is the commitment of the Holy Cross. It is the magnitude of the forgiveness that humankind has found there. This is the reason that I speak to you still. There will be moments in the future when you will be reminded of days like today. There will be times when you will wonder what you might say to lift an aching soul back to dignity once again. They could perhaps ask you what the Mother of God has to say about a particular instance. And, lo' and behold (look and behold), you will remember a sentence or two from one of My messages just like this one to ignite the fire in their hearts. They will be conflicted by the debate between the candle, the paper and the lamp, and you will remind them of the only essential element that matters. You will match their innocence with God's genius. You will turn their eyes back to the beginning, back to the genesis of all that matters in the eyes of the Father. He sees them there in those dark caves and dungeons. He sees them in prison cells and on death row. The same primordial truth by which you have lived will come to them because you will be there through your presence and in your prayers. If perhaps only one opportunity comes to you or your brother in the future to cause a light to flicker in another heart by what I have said in My messages since December 28, 2008, then it will have all been worthwhile. Besides that, it is the joy of My Holy Being to come pray with you."

Sunday, January 15, 2012
2:08 p.m.

"The Christian conversion of the human person is not like searing it with a fiery brand or affixing an embossment to the surface of the soul, but actually dismantling and reconstructing the entire constitution of our spiritual identity. The Roman Catholic Catechism describes a radical reorientation that occurs the moment the mind and heart are consecrated to Jesus Christ, so much so that the old self is supplanted by the divine framework of our new irreducible nature. We often speak about the fibers of our being as though we are made of divisible components comprising the essence of the self. This may be true for our physical body, but our soul cannot be diluted or dissected this way. We either belong to God wholeheartedly or not at all. There can be no fractures or fissures in our commitment to redemption if we expect the Lord to resurrect us when we

die. The human soul does not enter Heaven in phases. Hence, our conversion to the Cross and dedication to the Church consist of our willingness to be remade as though to be born again, shedding our original birth like crawling out of a shell. The whole concept of fullness is made of this because the Holy Spirit fills us to overflowing with the grace and peace of our Eucharistic King."

William L. Roth

"My beloved sons, many are the times when Jesus intervenes for you before the Father, and even more often do I ask Jesus on your behalf to bless you as He did in the days of old, when He wrapped His arms around the Apostles, reaffirmed their deeds, augmented their prayers and dignified their lives. We are here in this place for the same reason, that all humanity will be likewise blessed as the Apostles were blessed, that the undertakings of men will be ratified in the Blood of the Lamb, that the vision and actions acquired by mortal men in exile will replicate those of Jesus in His time and eternity. These are the petitions that you give to My Son, that we lay upon His nail-scarred Hands, that we utter to Him humbly and brilliantly with the conversion of the world on our lips. My sons, the whole matter of accepting Christianity is surely about your own redemption, but it is also about guiding and assisting others to the Cross as well. And going to the Cross means more than just looking at it, more than internalizing what Jesus did on the Cross to save the world. It is also about adopting the Cross as a way of life, imagining what Jesus thought and how He felt on the day He died. There are so many false dichotomies drawn by sinful men, false choices that seem to lure other people away from The Faith. They suggest that religion is a matter for weak-minded individuals who have no anchor other than their spiritual lives. I have said here in this home that their spiritual lives are their anchor. To what are good men tethered that make them marksmen for the Son of Man? What steadies their hands and sharpens their eyesight? It is the power of the Holy Spirit in them. Your faith is also about the power of persuasion. All of your books and writings have been about persuading your brothers and sisters to accept Jesus as their Savior, to invoke the mission of the Church as their reason for life. You have likewise tried to dissuade your brothers and sisters from following errant courses, to admonish them in areas where their opinions and actions run contrary to the teachings of the Gospel. But see here! Is not dissuasion the same as persuasion? When you dissuade someone from doing something, you are persuading them to do something else. Thus, it is all about persuasion. The dichotomy drawn between persuasion and dissuasion is another false one. It is all about leadership by teaching and example. This is the reason Jesus speaks so often in the Bible about what to do. He highlights the holier life, the course of righteousness, the journey of the narrow path. There is little in the Sacred Scriptures about what other paths have to offer. Jesus focuses on what should be done, and this is His power of dissuasion to keep His followers and disciples on the holy course. You will notice that this has also been the particular path of My messages to you. I have asked humanity through your Diary and Anthologies to walk upright and with sound faith that Jesus is leading them. I have declined to dwell on what will happen if they do otherwise because we live in hope that they will heed My call. Therefore, we pray today in that direction and to that end. I would not have come to you if there were some sort of predestination that humanity would fall and never rise again. The Resurrection has allowed the people of the Earth to live and change as they will, in real time, creating a new history for eternity to record. What I am saying is that Jesus proclaimed 'It is finished' from the Cross according to the prayers that He knew were forthcoming. We are committing into time and eternity that very finishing according to the response of the faithful and the souls who are only now converting. This is what it means to belong to the Living Church. Human life is a constant struggle, it would seem, against the obstacles and distractions that attempt to lead sincere Christians away from the tasks to which they have been assigned. It is the work of the devil. When someone goes astray and takes an errant course, it is like someone holding their breath. Their very life, the very function of their spiritual being begins to suffocate and become immobile and paralyzed. This is the ancient origin of the metaphor that someone is 'feeling blue.' Their happiness is stifled because they cannot see beyond the darkness that is strangling their lives of fresh air.

Now, you have come into 2012 where you are continuing to work for Jesus, just as you have for so many years passed. I keep telling you both that Jesus will bless you if you live in trustful peace, if you offer yourselves and your lives as a sacrifice for the conversion of the lost. This is the commitment that Jesus seeks of all who love Him. I am not saying that there are predetermined results based upon what you do and say, or that by offering a given number of litanies, a certain outcome will evolve. God does not work that way. However, He does recognize the intent of the heart and the commitment of the spirit. It is not that God cannot commend anything into factual being that He pleases, but that He asks His people to do their own work. He asks humanity to be activists and participants in the completion of the world. Everyone who has come before you who embraced the Church, its teachings, and its mission has done this. This is the reason that I have given you the names of so many Saints in your Anthologies that have not been canonized by the Church. You can imagine how many Saints have acquired the gift of Salvation who have never been named, given the fact that there have been some 80 billion souls live and die in the centuries that have passed. And, it is not a matter of how many of them there are, but that they are now one collective body. They have been united in death in ways that they could not have imagined when they walked the Earth in the flesh. The point I am making is that there could have been 80 trillion or 8,000 trillion souls instead of 80 billion; the resultant effect is the same. Their unity is the key factor of My discussion. This is a unity that began here on the Earth where you are now, where you and your brother share the same social atmosphere and physical environment with everyone else alive. The genius that I have spoken about for the past 21 years is in your recognition that you and your brother are not alone in this. There is seamless divinity in the cause of all holy men. There is light and life in the hearts of all who are given to the Cross, comprised of flickers and embers and outright sky-leaping flames. This is the gem in the night that the Saints see from Heaven. It is where Jesus stoops to warm His Hands. It is where the Angels are lured like fireflies to a flame.

    If you think about human life in this context, you begin to share a newer vision about birth, life and eternal passing. You begin to garner a better sense for seeing the passing of the soul from this world into the next as a natural event. However, the gladness and joy that accompanies the passing need not wait until then. If not for the sins of other men – the ignorance of atheists, the greed of capitalist thieves, the impurity of those who reject the Cross, and the outright hatred of the enemies of the Church, you would realize this happiness already. When I say 'you,' I am speaking of humanity at large. Hence, My message to you and your brother today is about realizing the greatness of the way you are living. Comprehend the difference you have made. Anticipate the reaction of the Lord for what you will do in the future. Be at peace inside knowing that anyone who stirs fears or spreads darkness here in this life has already been rebuked. They have done it to themselves. When the Holy Scriptures suggest that God's justice is swift, it means that the vengeance of the Father has already been exacted. It is a mathematical certainty. Those who love Jesus will see this in due time. I again ask you and your brother to pray for the errant and haughty ones, for the people who are leading innocent souls astray and exploiting them for their own personal gain. The whole matter comes down to the destruction of the pride that is deeply seated in those who believe that they will never have to answer for their sins. The Truth of the Final Judgement is bold and raw. None can hide from the decisions rendered by Jesus and the Father about the tides of history and the men who caused them to flow."

Wednesday, January 18, 2012
CPM 260 - University of Illinois, Springfield

"When I say that our organization is religious oriented and faith-based, I am suggesting that we have been given little voice in the public policy development process because we live in a pluralistic, relativist and secular humanist society. In other words, the policy issues most important to our organization would serve to reconstruct and reorient the content and effectiveness of our public laws to reflect the way we believe the world ought to be. Let there be no mistake. We do in fact communicate with our congressmen and legislators about certain poverty matters as food and housing assistance, hoping they will provide sufficient funding for the less-fortunate. However, we are precluded from taking political positions about private matters that revolve around a moral constituency that protects and defends unborn human life. The secular world will simply not listen to us, claiming that certain courts and jurisdictions have issued predetermined judgments about what we perceive to be radical injustices. We are not allowed to hire canon lawyers to put forth our case in front of legislative committees, not because it is against the law, but because the respective congressional and General Assembly leaders will not give us the time of day. We can approach them wearing other hats, speaking about other matters, referencing lesser evils than those we prefer to discuss. Sadly, this is only a portion of the problems we face when redressing the intense inequities that must be resolved here in central Illinois."

Timothy Parsons-Heather

Sunday, January 22, 2012
39th Anniversary of Roe v. Wade
2:53 p.m.

"These are the days when the blessings of the heavens come to you because you are receptive to them; your hearts are wide opened to ask for the intervention of the Lord as you have been inspired to petition since you were young boys. Today, I have come with another installment of God's response. I am completely aware of the tawdriness of life here in the United States and the actions that tend to lead lost souls even farther away from their ultimate conversion. You know what the concept of temporary setbacks entails and all the reasons why people have not yet listened. However, their hunger for Salvation is nearing its peak, and their curiosity about their origin is laying heavily on their minds. It must be made clear not only by you and all My messengers worldwide that their patience is worth the wait, but that the more they strive to reach the holiness that will satisfy their hunger, the larger their feast will be. My little ones, the family of humanity is aching because of the bruises and contusions that have been inflicted upon the world by the egregiousness of its own error. The etiology of many ills is founded in the lack of love of the world for the Messiah who has come to redeem it. Please do not be dismayed. This lack of love need not be seen as any legitimate reason for losing hope for the way the world will come to an end. There are multitudinous ways that Jesus can convert those who have not yet given their lives and souls to Him.

Hence, we speak about intervention, intercession, receptivity, response, and spiritual awareness in the same framework as though they are simultaneous actions. Outside of time, they are. You and your brother have been working on the petitionary phase of this process along with the rest of the Faith-Church on Earth. How many times have I told My children throughout the ages that your efforts are not in vain? You have lived long enough to see that prayers are indeed answered. People will eventually listen. Change inevitably comes. And, it is not so much that the people in exile receive the precise answer from Heaven that they might believe to be most important, but that God does respond in the way that best reveals the mystical aspects of His Kingdom alongside the way the final days of this world will unfold. This represents both the intersection and parallel lines inherent in the relationship between the Father and His children that sets-forth the beauty and architecture of the final times to which all souls are imminently drawn. This is the environment and beatific condition in which all ages are reconciled with God through Jesus, the same Son of Man who lived and served among men on Earth, and the same Son of Man who shall come to judge the living and the dead. This should be cause for intense peace and satisfaction for the Faith-Church because it exemplifies the realization of everything you have always held to be true in the vision of redemption in your hearts. Therefore, not only are there parallels and intersections, but there is concurrent stillness and movement as well. We have spoken before about the issue of multiple dimensions of the life of humankind as being not unlike overlaid templates. This is how many acts and ages can be perceived as though all time is one. It is the way the Crucifixion can be the Holy Sacrifice of the Mass so many centuries from Good Friday. It is the way you are born and also on the pathway to absolution in the Blood of the Cross as though it were all done at the very moment of your Baptism. You are born and born again in the same lifetime. These are the impressions that I have had difficulty making clear in My appearances and messages across the ages. I have tried in so many ways. It is not that My messengers have failed, but that the distractions of lost sinners have been that grotesque. The implications of My asking Saint Bernadette to soil her face at the Grotto seems counterintuitive to what the Mother of Jesus would pursue. Why did I ask her to do so? So that the doorway between Heaven and Earth would open wide enough to admit even the most skeptical among you. This breaks through barriers and inhibitions that could in no other way be breached.

This is also the origin of the irony of Jesus being crucified so that all men can live eternally. It describes the seeming contradiction that exists between the Commandment that says 'Thou Shalt Not Kill' and the fact that the violation of that Commandment by the soldiers who put Jesus to death redeemed the entire human race. The point I am making is that God reserves the right to erect and relocate the parameters inside where all exiled men live, and He does as He chooses when determining how and when He allows certain people to actually see these boundaries with the vision of their souls. You and your brother are two such seers who have not only been privy to the location of these lines, but you have also been shown in no uncertain terms the actual reason they exist. No stain shall be permitted beyond the veil, and nothing as pure as the essence of Paradise shall ever be allowed to fall into the hands of the devil. I am pleased and overwhelmed to tell you about this because it accords Me the opportunity to open your eyes even more about the origin of My joy. All in all, the world has a happy ending. Even more than that, this same happiness can be moved backward from the last day of the Earth and into the lives of the people who are living on the surface of the globe right now. There is so much imminence and inevitability that I cannot help from being overwhelmed with this joy. The souls in Purgatory will never endure the fires of Hell. The penitent shall be forgiven and raised on the last day. The sinners who have already rejected the Cross and will never accept Jesus as their Salvation will be cast into the flaming Abyss where they belong. This is also fitting for the choices they have made. Even as evil as Satan is, as difficult as it is to resist his temptations, human beings on the Earth have the power and opportunity to tell him 'no.' There is sufficient grace and enlightenment flowing down from Heaven every second of the day to preclude the satanic works of the devil from leading another soul astray. People sin because they choose to sin. They fall to temptation because they will not invoke the power of their own faith.

It is in these themes of Christological thought that humanity will find their reason for life. It is in the infusion of the Holy Spirit into their hearts that they find the strength and wisdom to resist the influences of the secular domain. As you have written in your memoir and many other places in your recorded works, the cultivation of the Earth and the conversion of unwary men rests in their desire to satisfy their hunger for righteousness here in this time and in their own way. God has provided the impulses and venues through which all men can be found by the Son of Man as though He has suddenly seen them drifting at sea in a lifeboat from a shipwreck. We remember this when we pray for the end of abortion that was legalized in the United States thirty-nine years ago today. I completely understand you and your brother's belief that the end of abortion now would do little to reverse the tides of time and save the 60 million U.S. children who have already lost their mortal lives to the doctors and abortionists who killed them. However, the parameters that God has set are larger than such thinking. He will indeed give these aborted children plenteous life, the whole of the decades they were expected to receive, even if the material world never admits that their decision to abort these children was wrong. This is all the Lord wants from His creatures on Earth.. He wants an admission that they have been wrong. He wants confession to pour from their lips, and He will saturate those same lips with celebratory wine. God asks for the opportunity to say that He accepts their repentance in exchange for the Crucifixion of His Only Begotten Son. Then, He will turn back time, make the necessary amendments, and give His sinful flock the means to correct their own errors. Yes – All the Father wants is the day to arrive when every soul He ever gave life will say that He was right and they were wrong. He could even begin Creation anew from the days of Genesis if He wanted, revising the way time and history have unfolded, and have His way as though watching a scripted motion picture that has a completely different plot. While this is not likely to happen, He would do so if He pleased. It is for all these reasons that we pray and have hope."

Friday, January 27, 2012
CPM 310 - University of Illinois, Springfield

"Whether it comes to cultural competence in the workplace, developing a strategic plan, engaging the external community, building effective partnerships, underscoring organizational ethics and values, engaging employees, developing sound advocacy plans, or doing veritably anything else having to do with public sector management and leadership, it is imperative for the people in charge to have a clear focus and operational grasp on the capabilities and characteristics of everyone involved. This may seem like a tall order for a profession that rarely places emphasis on the bottom line. After all, does it not seem that taxpayer dollars are inexhaustible? In order to administer the various programs and projects to which we have dedicated our most dependable expertise, we must realize that it is people that make these things happen. There are personalities to engage, talents to excavate, ideas to sustain, lessons to apply, and solutions to generate. My experience in the CPM Program has not only assisted my technical knowledge in accomplishing these worthy goals, but has given me a more comprehensive awareness of the great responsibilities we have taken on. If each of us as public sector leaders and supervisors remembers this fact, then we will have effectively succeeded in putting a recognizable human face on the blank stare of public management. It is for this reason that we must never turn back."

Timothy Parsons-Heather

Sunday, January 29, 2012
3:21 p.m.

"Now, My children, the Mother of the Lord has come here in your midst to assist your prayers for everything wrong. I have also come to thank you for everything you are doing right. Correctness does not always imply propriety because the definition of goodness varies from one culture to another. My Son insists that He be known as the standard by which all goodness is measured, and that the Cross is the means by which all societies come to know the meaning of sacrifice. Thank you for allowing Me to pray again with you. It is good and right for Me to do so, and for all the reasons you understand and have always understood about the meaning and purpose of prayer. Today, you are seeing Creation in a state of change, sometimes up-heaved, with brief periods of tranquility, and an unwieldy drive toward the indifferent. I have said that it is not normal for God's creatures to be indifferent because people are born with curiousness, and they are prone to make judgements about what is happening to them. This is also the case in matters having to do with the spiritual conversion of the heart. I have also told you that children are born with a propensity to know what love is from its foundation in Heaven, descended upon the world, and seated and ingrained in the consciousness and lives of those who pray. We must never let them believe that anything that they have come to know about living the Holy Gospel is in vain. Whatever else we do here in this land before I see you in Heaven, we must ensure that we have made clear to the masses that there is always hope and new beginnings in Jesus. There is always a movement toward the Resurrection even before the death of the body.

The exiled world needs to remember how powerfully the Roman Catholic Church emphasizes the gift of the Holy Eucharist and the Sorrowful Crucifixion from which it comes. It is preceded by the words of Jesus calling all to partake of Him at the Last Supper. Surely we have the capacity as the Mother of God and His creatures on Earth to attest to the fact that miracles can come in the form of transformation and transubstantiation. We do this because we cannot help it. We do this when we ponder the fate of the world that would come if not for the Sacrifice of My Son. Indeed, we do this when we pray for everyone alive to be aware. My Special son, how many times can I tell you that I am bubbling-over with joy that you and your brother are living as you are? In response to the question as to how much more you will give Jesus here in this life, I know that you are saying 'everything.' This not only implies that you are determined to rest perpetually in Him someday, it says outright that you have begun to do so now. The peace and movement that you realize from within come from Him; they are fruits and products of what He is still saying to those who believe. Your movement has always been that of the elder Saints who preceded you in this life, especially your predecessor Pontiffs and the many Mystics and Martyrs who lived their lives so well. I speak of fruits and products because they are the blessings you are returning to God, even as He has been bountifully blessing the Church for over 2,000 years. There is yet determination in your eyes. There is transcending vision in your sight. You and your brother have good days and bad days; this is the way of human life. You respect the desire of other men to grow into the people that Jesus wills to embrace with His aura of divinity. You are not offended or depressed by those who disagree with your testaments about the meaning of redemptive love. I wish I could make clear through these words, through these sentiments and examples, what it means for you and the whole Church to stay the course. It is not as though I come into every household every morning and say that it is time to get up and go again. I appear to those who will have Me, and to those who pray the Rosary. It is not a visionary appearance, it is a spiritual one where each person knows that I am there. You have felt this presence along with those same Popes whom I just mentioned. I have said on prior occasions that you must imagine what your life looks like through Jesus' eyes. It is obvious that you have been making tremendous strides in your daily prayers in leading lost sinners to the Cross. You can feel it in your heart and sense the movement in your thoughts. This makes every day that you and all My other children live imperative for the cultivation and conversion of humanity that is strewn across the Earth.

We have spoken in past years about deeply spiritual contemplation and about practical things too. It is also spiritually practical to think about what the Church must be doing during this second decade of the Twenty-First Century. When you have such thoughts in mind, it is a prayer for the priests and other religious. You are infinitely aware of how grotesquely the servants of God have been accosted and attacked throughout the ages. They are being impugned and maligned as much today. They are being martyred both spiritually and corporeally. They are being marched toward their deaths by the evil legions who believe they have gained a foothold against the salvation of the world. I have said that we will meet them where they are going in due time. We will make the case for the conversion of their hearts and souls, and it will be at that critical time that we shall see their response. I must say that there are people who are not as apt to be as receptive as you and I. They seem embittered because others are not changing now, that they are not reversing themselves in their tracks and joining the ranks of the warriors for the Cross. You and I know, however, that the final battle will supercede everything they believe about the influence of the element of time. Time is important now, but it never has the last word. If there were a prescription for disaster when it comes to the judgement of humanity, it is in the belief of those closest to the Church that there is no way to reverse the awful effects of time. We are certain about what we already know; every soul in the Church Triumphant is equally as certain. And, we are doubly sure about the power of the Crucifixion to remake time and space in the way that the early members of the Church always believed. I feel sorry not only for the sinners who will awaken to such a stark reality on the last day, but also those who live and work for Jesus here and now who are unsure of the irrevocable power of His Sacrifice. Without this certainty, My Special son, no one can live with the intensity they deserve. They cannot anticipate their share in the Resurrection with the immeasurable gladness they should have. You and I agree on this issue among all other things.

It would appear as though your brother is about ten days away from completing his CPM studies. There is no question that your brother is tired-out from being a student for so many years, but he keeps thinking of you and Me. He continuously reminds himself what Jesus went through on His way to the Crucifixion. Your brother places himself inside the Holy Sacrifice as though he were affixed to the other side of the Cross. This does not make him superhuman. It simply says that he still has fight left in him. You gave your brother intense dignity on the occasion of his birthday on Friday, as you do every day. This is not all about him; it is not all about you. It is about what both of you do. It is about Jesus looking down from Heaven seeing two soldiers who have never retreated from the fight, even when that fight was against enemies who were coming at you from atop a hill. Your vigilance, your sacrifices and love, your perpetual holiness, and your persistence are the seeds of a victory coming to you so humongous that you will scarcely be able to take it in. We have examined many things and discussed countless issues about the pressures of the world, and how you and your brother are avoiding these pressures by the way you live. Those who seek to have the kind of hope you espouse must ultimately realize that Christians have the power of discernment about what is worthy of pursuit. You can make a difference in the secular arena by taking your spiritual intelligence into the world. I pray that you will never relent in your realization that nothing can bother you unless you let it. Can you see how happy I am that you have lived for so long in the lineage of the Saints? I ask you to always remember that I have said this. I beseech you to always bear in mind that you and your brother and all servants of Jesus have been warriors for God on the battlefield where goodness is defeating evil. You are not only Children of the Cross; you not only see the Cross and understand the Cross, the Holy Cross has become an innate part of you. The Crucifixion lives inside you now. And, the Resurrection will lift you into eternal joy through this same power."

Sunday, February 5, 2012
1:23 p.m.

"The way we protect our world, conduct our affairs, embrace our friends, confirm our beliefs, structure our values, perform our duties, teach our children, and shoulder our weapons says more about who we are than our own modest impressions of the way history ought to be. There are no such things as factions or fissures in the Kingdom overflowing with unconditional love. We are led to absolution not by the northern star, but by a whole host of New Covenant luminaries guiding us through the night. Hail O' Risen Christ! Greet us with joy come the morning dawn!"

William L. Roth

"With powerful intercessory graces, I speak to you now in whose presence I never depart. It is clear that you have listened to Jesus' call to fill the empty void of the physical world with your love. I am pleased that you have responded to My call in ways unknown to many visionaries. Your faith, persistence and consistent joy have made My own joy more complete. When I ask the whole of humanity to do as I have requested of you, they often hesitate; they often turn their heads away as if to desire not to have Me. Why? Because they do not feel as though their Redeemer is listening to them. Millions more do not even believe in Him. My Special son, do you realize the unimaginable dimensions of what you have written to begin our message today? *"Whenever you open someone's thoughts to their own dreams of the way history ought to be, it opens-up hopes and happiness for the things they used to think about only when they were children."* Yes, and I have spoken in years past about bending history backward until it laps over itself. This is where the present reconfigures the past in ways that only those dreamers can assume. These modest impressions imply that good men, common men assume that their actions and lives will be examined by historians and new generations to determine the depth, value and workability of what has been done before them. A motion picture about creatures from outer-space once spoke about making 'future history.' This is a contradiction in terms, but it implies that something can be done now to rewrite what has not yet been committed to the page. Conversely, everything that has been written can be expunged and supplanted by a new history that might or should have come. This is the power of God, the impact of the Holy Spirit on Creation, that emanates from the altars of the Church. The altars are not idle between Holy Masses. They stand like grand statues, like receptive plateaus supporting the graces falling to the Earth from Heaven, not unlike you can physically see raindrops impacting a stone. These graces come upon the altars between Masses, and when the Mass finally comes, they hold themselves near. They are recommissioned and re-ratified by the Son of Man who is Sacrificed there. He tells them from earlier times to come into the world today as it was in the olden days. These graces come in the form of healing, wisdom, freedom, nourishment and delivery. They augment faith and love in ways that are not seen with the physical eyes. This is why the sacred altars should never be desecrated. And, it is important for you to know that these same graces come to those who pray in their homes, in the great fields and meadows where they speak to God, in hospitals and nursing homes, and in private residences where children are at play. They are like radiant shoots of light bomb-shelling the darkness of the world with the Glory of the Father's Truth. I have attempted to apprise humanity about these graces with only little impact. Why? Because they are as invisible as the Holy Spirit, Himself. It is clearly the effect that is seen by those who believe. You can see only the effects of the Sacraments of Baptism and all the rest, but they are literally true. They are not invisible to the heart. And, this is why you believe in them. It is the same reason that everyone who has ever moved their body in the direction of holiness feels these graces on the inside. I wish for humanity to remember that whatever you tell them about these graces is true. It is a great year for America and the world. I am bearing My intercession and wise messages to humanity everywhere because we have every reason to believe that they will ultimately respond."

Sunday, February 12, 2012
2:53 p.m.

"When a person says that something is farther than a country mile or faster than a New York minute, they intentionally make pseudo-assertions that a given distance is relative or time passes at different speeds depending on the location. We hear these kinds of false comparisons every day. This is the way people justify such wrongs as abortion and contraception. They say that they cannot afford to raise a child on their income, ignoring the fact that there are millions of willing families waiting to adopt and feed them. They buy into the evil pretense that just because they cannot support a child, the child must die. Birth control is another example. Instead of relying on the beatific conscience, that of corporeal chastity, they turn to illicit mechanical and chemical methods to nullify their responsibility to apply sound moral standards. Such are acts of slothful, faithless, selfish individuals who refuse to listen for themselves to what God would have them do."

William L. Roth

"You are well groomed and smartly developed in the themes of righteousness to which all men are called to engage. My little sons, I wish you well on this cold February day when you are both suffering the effects of a virus. You know that these are passing, cleansing things that must be endured and worn through. I come to you today more happy than in recent times. I see the Roman Catholic Church through the Bishops fighting for morality in the face of tremendous opposition. This, My Special son, is what makes your reflections so relevant. I pray that the Bishops will indeed be this strong in other measures regarding your government and president. These officials do not have holiness in mind; they have power and expedience in mind. They have closed hearts and greedy motivations. My sons, when you see such wrongs as the United States executive branch demanding Catholic institutions to provide so-called birth control to their employees, you are seeing the kind of America that I soundly reprimanded in My messages to the world from 1991 through 2008. It is a source of vindication for your Mother when societies see what I have been passionately denouncing all along. The events of this past week are only one example. As I say, I am more joyous now than in prior times because the Bishops have taken-up the battles to end and ameliorate the conditions that I spoke to you about for 17 years and 10 months. Your prayers and Mine are being answered. It is difficult for people of righteous faith to live in a nation under such secular wickedness because you do not know from where their next attack will come. You have no advance notice of what holy tenet they might try to dismantle tomorrow. You have read many accounts of secularists making an attempt to eliminate Christian piety from the mainstream thoughts of impressionable people everywhere. The answer is that if those who claim to be Roman Catholic do not fight the good fight for the Truth as taught in the Holy Gospel, the Bishops' criticism of secular government will have little effect. I am pleased that more Roman Catholics than ever before are listening and responding. This is the direct result of the prayers of the faithful, especially those who are loyal and devoted to My Immaculate Heart."

Saturday, February 18, 2012
2:27 p.m.

"There is something to be said about the way we play the game and how we adhere to the rules that does not diminish who we are. Straight talk and feistiness are still in vogue, but I have never been one for landing low blows, shin kicking, mudslinging, backbiting, showboating, hypocrisy, distortions or outright lies. Our reputation for true gallantry is always on the line. I can sleep soundly at night because I have a good conscience. Others sleep well because they have no conscience at all."

William L. Roth

"These are auspicious days, My little sons. There are tremendous forces for good aligning against the evil legions who falsely believe that they will find ultimate victory in the battle for lost souls. God is too powerful, and His enemies are too frail. I realize that it oftentimes seems difficult to believe what I am saying because you recognize the highs and lows of your victories in the Cross. It is when your enemies seem their most fierce that they are about to take their hardest fall. And, it is when righteous men appear to be at the cusp of losing that they leap forward into their most joyous triumph. I have told you many stories about these two opposites. The world and Nature are likewise inundated with these themes. Light and darkness. The deserts and the seas. The mountains and the valleys. Miles and millimeters, and on and on.

This is true because there is such stark difference between love and hatred. There seem to be only mundane days, days that have no impact on future times, and little meaning at all. These are lulls only in the human mind, for Creation is forever trekking toward the glorious conclusion of the world you see. It is not in haste that you pursue or await this reckoning. Indeed, it is with steadfast faith and assurance, dignity and poise, and trust and allegiance. Today, I have come to share with you some information about the future that will assist your happiness. When you speak as you did today beginning this message, you reserve your right to be a dignified warrior. You have staked your claim on history as a valiant man, like the great ones before you who not only changed the world and saved entire societies, but who also redefined with courage what it means to become engaged in battle. You have seen that warfare has changed through the centuries because weapons systems have become more fierce and sophisticated. What has not changed, however, is the judgement of well-meaning men who are called into battle to preserve peace and good will, to uphold the virtues of righteousness, and to lay the land for succeeding generations. It must be made clear that they are not all physical battles. Most of the important ones have been struggles about principle and matters of truth. The great debate into which holy men are called pits your wisdom about God against the ignorance of secularism that rejects Him. I must make clear that the physical battles are often more easily won! You have seen this in the writings of the Saints, the archives of encyclicals of the Popes, the anthologies of priests and clergy, and the literal stories that have been handed-down through the ages. This is where the concept of 'legend' finds a divergence in meaning. Legend is generally reserved in the context of the Church to imply something that cannot be proved. You have heard of urban and pious legends before. This is the reason the great Saints who have served and died are not spoken about as being legends. The other side of the meaning of 'legend' is more modern, sometimes interchanged with the concept of 'hero.' The two terms do not mean the same thing. I cite this example because I want you to know that '...things of legend' may not always be statements of fact. Legendary and heroic are not precise synonyms. I am not attempting to parse syllables, but there are many Roman Catholics who do not understand My role in the Church as they should. Many refer to My influence on My Son and the Apostles as legendary. They have no ill intentions when they are speaking this way; they are in fact trying in their own way to elevate Me before humanity. But, the proper words must be said. You have them. You have written them. Your books are filled with them. This makes Me tremendously pleased, and I am confident that it will make you happy in the future as well. Many terms have come and gone; others are simply misused, and you should be prepared to guide and inform your brothers and sisters as circumstances warrant.

Another example is that the early Church spoke about those who venerated Me as belonging to the Cult of the Blessed Virgin Mary. This was quite appropriate for the times, but you obviously see the reason why it cannot be said today. Modern cults have worshiped Satan, claimed allegiance to false prophets, and even committed mass suicide. Hence, the term 'cult' is no longer proper for naming a group that claims consecration to Me. The Blue Army is a better term. The Legion of Mary is another. There are many times when you will hear about the conflict between the users of the early terms and those who know that the transformation of definitions has caused other words to become anachronistic. The reason I am telling you this today is so that you will be confident that you have the proper terms for identifying your Mother in your writings and speeches. You will be practically assaulted by some who are faithful to the Church to return to the usage of the equivocal terms, but you must not defer to their positions. After all, we are trying to lead the remaining 80% of the human race to the Cross, and words like legends and cults do not serve very well. Again, you should be pleased in the future because I have given you multiple titles under which I have appeared as The Morning Star Over America. You can likely see the reason I identified Myself in Lourdes as the Immaculate Conception. In addition, your brother is catching up on his rest. He prays every day for the whole world, and he ponders what each day might bring as it relates to the conversion of the lost. He is aware of the awful tasks at the university over the past 14 months that have now been placed behind him. He has been exhausted by the experience, but the way you prepared him yesterday and took him to the war memorial for his photograph was of the grandest nobility on your part. It reflects on what you and your brother have done together, what the world sees in the aftermath of your having recorded 20 years of messages. There is glory and happiness abounding because of the strength of your friendship over the decades."

Sunday, February 26, 2012
2:03 p.m.

"Guttersnipes and street urchins. Ironic as it sounds, this is what many wealthy people have become these days, not by the measure of their assets, but by their self-imposed spiritual squalor. Millionaires living in mansions and jewelry-clad socialites walking down red velvet runways. They are segregated not only from Heaven, but from the grace of God too. Charitableness has escaped them for no apparent reason; they have no idea what their excesses are heaping on the suffering of the world. It is not as though they are not old enough to know better. Little children are cute when they make mistakes, but self-indulgent adults are expected to make reparation for theirs. This is not to say that there should be no reward for hard work or that we should adopt a socialist approach to governing the commonwealths. It simply means that we should be more 'social like' and not so closefisted in our charities."

William L. Roth

"With the Love of the Father, I have come to pray with you for the conversion of humanity. As important as My messages have always been, this is the imperative purpose of My presence here. Yes, you have seen the worrisome faces and distraught expressions that define the lives of those who are holy, the millions who are seeing secularism attack and assault the tenets of the Church. My little sons, it should be clear to you by now that your spirits should not be held in darkness over this. Your hearts should remain aloft with Me. Your vision should forever be more clear than the awkward lines that have become blurred. I ask you today to preserve your composure and realize that you are both undergoing a happy decompression from months of toils and labors. It is even the measure of the years that are helping you ease your minds, but you do not see things this way. You somehow believe that you must maintain the same cadence that you have in past months and years when your efforts have been at their peak. This is the issue that I told you would come. Please remain with Me in the Truth; speak with self-sympathetic strains of confidence, sureness and peacefulness. Rest your eyes not expecting to open them again to some kind of strange horror that you have never seen before. Listen for the melodies of prayer coming from the Angels and Saints; let them intercept your consciousness as you allow your souls to relax. You have nothing to be afraid of. God the Father is commanding His Glory around the globe because of the fruits of your love. I ask you to look once more at the gifts you have been given. There are ruts only where you choose to find them. I pray that you will listen to My call. I beg you to summon within you the joy that I have in Me. There are few flower-strewn pathways on the road to Paradise, but you have in this nation been given a smooth existence, free from rampant disease and warring in the streets. You have electric power and running, potable water. You have access to the best medical care on the face of the Earth. You have been given hope by the Holy Spirit in your hearts. You are free to travel and learn, to adhere to your sacred principles in public and in private. Your family members are well, your neighbors are benign, the cloak of grace that shields you from the buffets of the devil is light and comfortable. My words today have nothing to do with reprimand, but a heartfelt plea for you to reconsider the way you are perceiving your lives.

My Special son, human sin is the reason for your despondence. This is a time of Lent, and I ask you to join Me in praying that this will change. It is the same around the globe. There are some people who are simply not comfortable to be around. Some are overbearing, others are spiritually blind, and more and more have little consideration for what they are causing others to suffer. I have no gentle words for them today. I only ask that you do not permit them to cause you any torment. Please depend on Me. Lift your heart to Me, and I will help you feel happy again. And, please remember those in jail-houses and all who are being held against their will. It is significant that all the people of the Church, the faithful who are far and wide, all who believe in God realize that being locked in jail cells is more about punishment than amending someone's conduct. Can there really be rehabilitation in this? Does it not cause someone to become even more bitter? I am present all around the world. The Church reigns supreme on every continent and in all the nations. Why? Because the Holy Spirit subsists inside the human heart. Some people believe otherwise. You have seen this through the years, the people who left your prayer group here who believed that miracles can be found only in the mountains near Denver, Colorado or the shrine of Medjugorje. I have been left incapable of the proper words to describe how curious this makes Me feel. The Crucifixion was a worldwide gift that happened in the Holy Land. The whole world became the Cross on Good Friday. Thus, the Church has arrived again in the annual Season of Lent. You and your brother are doing fine in your sacrifices for God. Your years of labors and kind hope for the conversion of the lost are awesome gifts being laid at the foot of the Cross. Look at what you have done for humanity, My Special son! Consider all the years, all the chores, all the sorrows and loneliness, all the prayers and Rosaries said! Imagine all the souls who will come home to God because of the miracle of your books, no matter what any Bishop decides to do. Healed souls, converted hearts! Human beings taken into the Light of Salvation forever! There is no seed of despondence in this. There is no darkness, no apprehension, not even a sliver of regret. Please see these present hours the way I am seeing them. I know that it is not easy for you. Let the years unfold. Let the times, as brief as they may be, come upon the unsuspecting world while you confidently and peacefully do your work here at home. Yes, let God be God. Watch in awe and appreciation that something is finally being done. Let your boyhood heart take you to thoughts of ultimate triumph, of the justification of everything the Lord will eventually claim, and the rejection of everything He already despises.

The Lord God is more merciful than you know! And, it is to Him that we must always defer. The sovereign genius that fashioned Creation and all the creatures too, His Only Begotten Son, Myself and Saint Joseph and all the Saints, the billions who have preceded you in exile, all the animals and fishes; the air, seas and skies – everything you can imagine in the span of human consciousness – all this is wrapped inside God's Providence, and it is unfolding before you now. People pray with Me because they realize that I will intercede. It is true. I do just that. And, I ask every day in Medjugorje and around the world for the Church to trust what I have been saying. God knows and sees and hears everything and every word. He deals with the defiance of the human will every day. He trusts that the prayers of the faithful will more strongly call upon Him. This is what He is waiting for. This is the reason it seems as though evil is running rampant around the globe as if to take it over. God is waiting for the unanimity of the human race to come collectively to Him through the Cross, and life will begin to turn around. He has tried nearly everything conceivable to pierce both intelligent and ignorant minds. He utilizes Nature, messages about doom and destruction, flowers and rain, sunshine, tragedy, celebration, evolution and outright miracles. Humanity is being held in the clutches of its own indifference, its own pride and arrogance, its materialism and relativism, but these are not permanent bonds. They are passing things; they are expiring more rapidly every day. You know that spools of thread run out more quickly upon each turn of the spool. The same can be said of the exhausting of the world. Every day unravels another turn, and this perpetuates the defeat of evil even more auspiciously. This can be a year of grand occasions and unprecedented joy if only My children will adhere to My call for confidence. Hear Me now! I am aware of the daily grind that you speak about. I understand the alarm clock sounding every morning. The idea of 'going to make the doughnuts' is not foreign to Me. But, as has been said, you are being deceived by the element of time. Please see the passing of the days for what they are, but remain invested in them. Do not let them pass by as though they do not matter. Create peace in your heart by refusing to surrender to the darkness of the Earth. Never cede an inch of your life to the devil. You were created for ethereal joy! What some people call the 'circle of life' is merely their recollection of what should have come in a new generation that was so embraced in the past. Know that the Saints and Martyrs before you looked at the same world with discomfort, disgust and disdain. Now, however, even as they have come to Heaven, they would not have lived life on Earth that way. They do not know it now because there are no regrets in Heaven. I am asking that you do not look for darkness in the motivations of others. These are among the things you should write about in your memoir because such success would drive such a death-striking blow into Satan that the world would be taken by surprise. These are the depths, heights and degrees to which you and your brother are going to create an atmosphere of holiness in your age."

Sunday, March 4, 2012
1:28 p.m.

"Lord, let the depths of our suffering lead the world to greater light. Let humanity's sacrifices make us whole. Let decent men vanquish the evil ones. Let fairness prevail over injustice. Implant in us the distinction of accepting your miracles. May peace and good will be our final legacy."

William L. Roth

"Today, My children, I come to prevail upon your presence to hear Me speak of the affinity that the Lord holds for you in His tremendous love for all Creation. We must not desist in doing our part to reach lost sinners. We should remember that this is in our hands; it is the duty of the Church to manifest clearly the Good News of redemption to all who do not yet know God. My Special son, My love for you and your brother is overwhelming; it is incapable of being measured. I do not think like other women. I do not have the burdens of their possessions. I come here because I need your help in reaching those who should turn their hearts and hands to their Mother who loves them. Thank you for assisting Me. I have always blessed you and your brother for staying strong in this journey of life, even when you have not known in advance the turns and stumbling blocks that have taken you unexpected ways. I beg you to remember that you are much stronger than you believe. You have good hearts, intense faith, clear vision, lasting courage and humble intentions. You must begin to think more highly of your ways. Today, I am here to resound your prayers to Jesus, to amplify and augment them, to accompany them to the heights of Glory to which you have directed them. There are so many ways that God is misunderstood by those who do not see as you and your brother see. He is viewed as a Lording Master who does not touch the hearts of men in the way they have imagined. The fact is, He wants to live inside those hearts, but He is forced to compete for space alongside so many other human interests. It would seem that He is not a priority even to some who are faithful to the Church. It is our duty, yours and Mine, your brothers and sisters, and all who are loyal to Jesus to pray for them, to ask God the Father to descend upon the Earth in unprecedented ways. I know that I do not speak often enough about His boundless beauty. I keep dwelling on the deficits of the mortal human conscience because I want you and your brother to be prepared for those who will attack you. It is these lessons that will make you ready, that will help you pre-fashion your answers to some very difficult questions. I have told you only portions of what will come in the future because every time I speak generously with a messenger, Satan hones in on that future in an attempt to corrupt it. He is trying to make My statements false. Jesus wants you to live your days in faith like everyone else. What would life be worth without its happy surprises? No one can stop My Marian movement as The Morning Star Over America. You must trust that what I am saying is true. I am not inclined to tell you what will occur because you are given the gift of life one day at a time. This is as it should be. Happy surprises cannot come if the Mother of God keeps preempting them with revelations of My own. My Special son, I wish I could tell you how much you are admired in Heaven. You have advanced the Salvation of souls who would have known Jesus no other way. You have emptied your own life of its early beginning and taken upon yourself the yoke of a Saint. I am not telling you these things just to bolster your self-impression. I am saying them because they are true. Everything you would have wanted in this life will come in the next. I have asked you and your brother to live soundly in your lives the confidence that you have gained from the Holy Spirit. There are no two people in the world who are doing this better than you. There is so much to be hopeful about; so much has been accomplished, so many doors opened, so many hearts and souls that will be born again and live anew because of your faith in God and response to Me.

There are so many deceptions that Satan uses to try to bring My children to tears. He wants humanity to believe that God is not there, not responding to your prayers. He wants you to assume that we have no power in bringing his evil acts to an end. This is why they have such ferocity now. There is an end. Satan has been defeated. He is taking his final swings on his way down. The Catholic Church is being assaulted because it is blameless in the spreading of the New Covenant. This is the way it has always been – nothing new under the sun. This is why I ask My messengers and humanity worldwide not to panic. If it were any other way, Jesus would have already intervened. The Gospel of faith remains strong. The Church remains upright; the journey of conversion is still on course. I ask that you believe that if it were otherwise, I would have taken other action to preserve the dignity of My beloved Church. I always ask the Father to bring Saint Michael the Archangel to bear upon anyone who dares to utter a crooked word. These are lines and strains of hope for you because I wish for you to share them with humanity. If ever there were a time for hopefulness, it is now. It is a moment during which you must realize that God is poised to strike. He does not do so because He knows that humanity that belongs to Him will lift themselves from the earthen floor and stand tall again. How many heroes on the battlefield have done this before? How many were taken by the hand and lifted by someone else? It is the former that everyone remembers most."

Saturday, March 10, 2012
1:58 p.m.

"Jesus is the procurer of our wisdom and the fashioner of our courage. He comes to us bearing the hallmark of all the lifetimes that will providentially conclude in Him. The chastity of the soul is our ultimate signpost whereupon is conferred our redemption as Christ himself has inscribed His Crucifixion on the breastplate of our hearts. If ever we dare question this fact, let it be only to reassess what more we should do. Why not pray with more passion? Why not believe that there are statelier measures than the changing of the seasons? Why not see each new day as a gateway to the exculpation of our faults by which we defer to the Kingdom of God? Why not downplay our desires in favor of His? Why not become ourselves a new humanity?"

William L. Roth

"My goodness, My Special son, this is one of your most awesome writings. Statelier measures than the changing of the seasons. What an amazing thought. You and your brother have been brought by God's grace to believe in what you have written, to imagine the romance of the spiritual life that has been with you for decades. I thought about these same preponderances when I walked the Earth, considering what might preclude and prevent those around whom I lived from straying from the majestic poise that they knew in God. Can you imagine what it was like knowing that the one Savior of humanity was My Incarnate Son? It often takes generations for this kind of awareness to be handed down to the masses. Every person must come to know this in their own way. How could the Mother of God in turn rear His Son in the created world without traveling to the Earth's four corners to proclaim what would eventually come? We had the miracles. Saint Joseph and I possessed the determination. However, it would have taken miracles of proportions yet unmatched to have set foot on every continent that was inhabited by people. We remained in the land where Jesus was born, and then to a nearby nation to escape the slaughter, and back again to finish the world the way it would eventually be known. I looked with human eyes on a Divine Man who would grant the immortality of all men to come. This Man was left to purify a globe of sinners that still goes on today. Hence, like you and your brother and the whole Church, our mission was more than what we did and said in our time. The true benefit of the gift of Jesus to humanity reigns yet within you. This is why Christianity was modern at the moment of Pentecost, indeed at the hour of the Nativity. You are celebrating birthdays today all around your country for those whose birth is March 10. What does this imply in the grander scale of human thought? It means that there is a recollection of the gift of life in the hope that future lives will mean more. Birthdays are about history and reflection, about understanding that your exile need not be just a place of preparation. This is the reason I have said worldwide that it is possible to pass from this life into the next and not recognize the change. It is wholly a spiritual transformation, the relocation of the soul. This prompts the discussion that Saint Joseph and I had on a number of occasions, and it was answered by Jesus when His time arrived. Is it possible for a soul to reside in Heaven and on Earth simultaneously? The answer is that this occurs after the shedding of the flesh. Souls in Heaven have access to the beauty of the world as their reward.

When Saint Joseph and I spoke about these ethereal matters, we concluded that the Lord God chose us to be Jesus' parents because of what we could already do, not what we had the potential to do, but what we could forthrightly manifest in the nurturing and embracing of His Son. The Son was born sinless to a sinless Mother, an Immaculate Mother; and I am the only one. His perpetual vigil over those who belong to Him and the Church is constantly composed of new souls. We have spoken about the daily deliverance of souls into Heaven and millions more who are conceived in the womb. The changing of the seasons is something that speaks directly to the genuineness of one's religious faith. If someone were to assign a value to different levels of faith, he would discover that the holiest regions of the world are located in places where the seasons constantly change. There is vibrancy, viability and flexibility in people who must adapt to the changing environment. Darkness and cold weather give way to fairer days, warmth and sunshine. This is a metaphor for what occurs in the spiritual life of Jesus' followers. And, where are the people residing who do not hold to the tenets of the Christian Gospel? In desert places with the blazing sun and sandy terrains. This is likewise a parable because these people have never taken root in the God of Abraham. The changing of the seasons means the conversion of the human soul, the stateliest measure possible in the life of a man or woman. Nothing else on Earth rivals this beauty and power. This is the reason you and your brother's lives have born so much fruit. It is also the reason you often wonder what will come next. It is about the prospect of new life and the hope that is represented by the blossoming of all things newborn. Buds on the trees are replicas of this. So are flowers breaking through the soil. And equally emphatic of this is a baby's cry. They are all expressions of new life and the chance that future days will be better for these seeds. I assure you that Jesus' birth was the beginning of the end of human stagnancy in all things beatific. He was raised and spoke the Father's Word as the Father's Son. He did not just carry out the Will of the Father, He personified it. Mount Tabor has never been the same. Golgotha has likewise been transformed. And, these are exemplary of the renovation of the human heart and soul, its renewal and rejuvenation in the Spirit of God in Heaven. When your friends and peers, even those who despise you, speak about the constancy of dull emotions and nothing new under the sun, they do not speak about them the way I do. I recently used the phrase 'nothing new under the sun' to describe the way men approach daily life, but it can be seen in larger parameters than this. What is new is that time and the elements of human evolution in spacial quarters are always changing. This is a newness to which most men devote no attention. It was not this way in Joseph-the-carpenter's home. We knew what holy meant because we exuded holiness. We did not need to take it in. This is the reason our household was universally different from all others that would exist in the created world. Our home was the light shining on the hill, but it was rarely seen as such. We did not need any candles to see in the dark. The Son of Man was light for our eyes and our warmth in the night."

Sunday, March 18, 2012
2:44 p.m.

"Christ Jesus, valor of Martyrs, we pray that you grace your flock with dignity and comfort those who are persecuted for your Church. Encourage the doubtful to seek their way into your Kingdom. Make human hearts the wellspring of your holiness the world over. Give paupers dominion over their lives, and make us mentors to wayward sinners who look for direction in their final journey toward your heavenly dawn."

William L. Roth

"We have come this far in our prayers because you have been willing to forfeit your earthly exile in favor of God and not for yourselves. I wish to make clear that the prayers we recite are never hollow. Prayer is not a vacuous exercise. You can be assured that the Father will come to you wholly and confidently to convince you that He is always listening. His Will is fashioned around what will best convert the lost sinners whom you have mentioned in your opening prayer today. My Special son, no one has spoken about Me the way you do. They mention Me in passing; they tell others about the pretty woman who birthed the Son of Man, but they do not speak about My unbridled ability to seek the best of all worlds for those who accept the intercession that I offer. We speak about unimaginable things because they are realized in your consecration to My Most Immaculate Heart and to the Sacred Heart of Jesus. I wish to remind you that you are loved immeasurably, that you are admired by the Holy Family and the Father and the Holy Spirit. There are no secrets to this. You and My children worldwide are aware that we are constantly battling against those who do not believe us. We realize the onslaught of attacks against the Church as being the work of the devil. No one can point to a place in Christological history when the Church has been weakened or its power to usher the Kingdom of Love into the world diminished. Jesus would never allow it. It is also through history that you have seen the lives of the blessed and venerated, of the Saints who have done the work of redemption around the globe. This goes on yet today. I have desires that cannot be captured in words about what My children must do to receive the blessings, signs, graces and wonders that will make them feel as though they are connected to eternity. It is not about building empires or becoming famous among the nations. It is in leading lives of simple truth based on faith, sacrifice and service. It is in remembering that the Perfect Man born of My Womb did not arrive to the sound of reporting trumpets or caroling choirs. The Angels did sing indeed, but mortal men were still unaware. A certain kind of indifference toward the Nativity of Jesus is being foisted upon the modern world that must be reversed by everything miraculous that disbelieving men refuse to see. I have mentioned that Fatima was to be one of these signs and miracles, as well as the Mexico Shrine of Guadalupe. Grace abounds in all these things; you simply must believe that the Holy Spirit is working in places that you cannot yet see.

Even as the Catholic Church celebrates Lent, there are some who are still engrossed in materialism and hoarding possessions. They are being changed by the workings of the contemporary Church that is deeply fasted in the sacrifices and self-denial that Jesus taught on His journey into the desert. You will always have in your hearts the affinity for My Son's determination not to concede to the temptations that He faced. It was more than stubbornness. It was also more than the power that He knew that He could wield at any time. It was His time to remind Satan that food and power are not the keys to the eternal identity of the human soul. Such things are passing; they are important in the survival of the body, but not imperative in the permeation of the soul through the veil of human exile into the presence of God. My Special son, all the Apostles and the incalculable number of disciples and servants of the Cross have said through the centuries that secular settings made them feel as though they already have one foot through the veil into that presence about which I speak. You have recently mentioned this. It is not so much that they and yourself passed any further from your station here on Earth into the paramount enlightenment of Heaven, but that Heaven is coming to you. This has been the way of all the Saints. I speak about permeation as though it is some sort of distance to travel, but you know that it is more a condition or a station. This is how you can go to Heaven and not realize your passage from this life. Heaven can exist in the highest elevations of the House of the Father and here on the Earth as well. And it does. The point I am making is that there are no mistakes or missteps in Heaven. This means that it is possible for mortal men and women here in this life to be perfected in thought and action before they deliver their spirits to Jesus. This is not difficult to imagine. You have also seen with your own eyes and heard with your ears visions and sounds that are so filled with eternal beauty that your thoughts cannot process their dimensions. This is the way of the sun flat-lighting the trees on your journey through the country last evening. You saw it in the shape and color of the clouds, in their formation and intensity, the way in which they were perfectly situated in the foreground of the setting sun. You knew that you were seeing precursors of the beauty of Heaven here in this life. It does not require a great deal of faith to believe what you have seen. On the other hand, secular humanity does not employ this primal faith. Secular faith is derived from the 'maybe, just in case' viewpoint that says that they will assume certain immortal things to be true. It is the concept of hedging. This is no faith at all; it is simply a concession that they do not have the answers. Contrastingly, you and all who accept the Blood of the Cross already have answers to questions that have yet to be posed. You understand the logic in the seeming illogical fashioning of human conversion and Salvation of humanity through the death of one Man. It required a grotesque Crucifixion filled with immeasurable grace to ratify the pardoning of the whole human race. Beauty came from this ugliness. Life came from this death. Immortality has come from this mortality. It is when you combine these points and counterpoints that you begin to know how God sees things. There are contrasts and comparisons, congruencies and contradictions, and a demanding requirement of the Church to recognize what measure of each is present in the Testament of Truth. For example, could you imagine a scenario where someone would not appreciate the vast beauty of the clouds and sunset that you saw last evening? It happens to those who cannot see, the blind and the sightless, but it is also a metaphor for what seeing men and women will encounter upon their transition from this life into the next. If they believe as I have implored them to believe, they will see it vividly now. They will not be blind or sightless; they will be capable of seeing the purposes of God the way you and your brother see them, in much the same way you were awed by the setting of the sun – like a horizon afire that you once wrote about in a prestigious book.

This is likewise how I lived My life on Earth with Saint Joseph in the awesome task of rearing the Son of Man. He showed us a different sunset every evening. They came from His Most Sacred Heart. We saw rainbows and flowers in our hearts and thoughts to rival the imminent bursting of the Earth in the romantic blast announcing the return of Jesus to end the ages. We saw cascades and waterfalls in the middle of the desert. We saw healings and conversions, the rejuvenation of the exhausted, the inspiring of the doubtful, the speaking of the mute, and the hearing of the deaf – all these things the same way you viewed the lovely sunset last night. Jesus taught all in His midst that if they would see the handiwork of God in these simple gifts, they would realize in time what Peter, James and John came to know. I am pleased to see that humanity is becoming prepared in many cases not because of their own volition, but because they have nowhere else to turn than God. Millions of them are already physically spent and spiritually exasperated. They have seen with their hearts what they cannot yet see with their eyes. This is pious progress; it is the movement of the world toward the final blessing that will blanket the Earth in peace. There are gifts awaiting those who are so exhausted and exasperated. Peace will soon abound. However, silence will not arrive until the last of the tolling bells has pealed. This will be a ringing of both joy and sorrow, of old passings and new beginnings, of births and deaths, and of slumbers and awakenings. Cultures and times will come of age in these new occurrences that will amend the way people look at their lives and the mission of the Church. And all of this is good, right down to the last man slain! This is righteous work and pious sacrifice. It is meaningful change and overdue transition. This is what you and I, your brother and all the rest are waiting for; and it need not be a sedentary pause. We are accomplishing our goals along the way. I wish for you and your bother to know that I stand beside you in joy and assurance that you are filled with the Holy Spirit and determined to live in peace, far from the ravages of secular academia and the evil-prone agendas of those who teach them. Your brother correctly described his instructor's word 'choice' in the matter of abortion when he said that the term is straight from the jowls of Satan. More Christians should have the opportunity to say this same thing to lost sinners who refuse to defend the sanctity of unborn human life."

Sunday, March 25, 2012
Feast of the Annunciation
3:09 p.m.

posture – physical, mental or spiritual position, attitude or tendency

preference – tactical, theoretical or practical advantage given to something over other alternatives

disposition – predominant or prevailing condition of one's spirits, natural mental and emotional outlook or mood

"Now, dear children, it is My privilege to pray with you that the Lord will look favorably upon the world as He has in past years when all who believe in Him invoke His Holy Name. You see three terms at the beginning of this message that relate to the condition of humanity, that speak to the willingness of Christians to prepare for the Glorious Second Coming of Jesus. One's posture is determined by his disposition to prefer a holy life, to seek God in His entirety as the Father, Son and Holy Spirit. I will leave it to you to broaden your discussion about the relevance of these terms as you ponder your first memoir. I wish to reinforce the point that preferences are contingent upon someone's knowledge about the Will of God. This determines their disposition to accept and believe in miracles, which in turn aligns their posture with that Will so that the Earth is made like Heaven. You can see a process that begins in the prayers that I have been seeking from the world since the Annunciation of the Lord. My Special and Chosen sons, I realize that you receive My messages in a tenor of holiness, and I also know that you are curious not only about the substance of My messages, but also their larger meaning over the passing of time. You are also curious as to the reason why the Angels make statements that seem to be rescinded over the course of days, weeks and months. It is all about prayer. The catalyst for change has always been prayer. It makes both beatific and logical sense that God would issue statements and set conditions that are alterable based upon His interaction with people on Earth. If this were untrue, He would not ask the Faith Church to pray. There is no great mystery in My saying to you something that can change with manifest abruption. We have spoken about this concept before. Most all manifest abruptions are gifts, signs and blessings. Even reversals and counter-reversals are created by the manifest abruptions that I have earlier told you about. I also am aware that this gives people a mistaken sense that what was previously said may have been untrue. This is not the case at all. It is entirely based on the Lord's hearing and responding to the prayers of the faithful and the Angels and Saints. My Special one, do you remember the ledger of names that I gave you of the Angels who come to you? There are hundreds of them. These Angels ask God to make way for the propagation of My messages around the globe. This has been true for centuries. And, the Church Triumphant intercedes for you because you call on them as well, especially your daily recitation of the Holy Rosary. It is because of this that the Angels approach your brother to apprise him of more blessings, opportunities and venues to spread My messages by what the two of you do every day.

    My Special son, I decline to offer messages to those who will not comply with My requests. This has never been the case with you and your brother, and Jesus has asked Me to relate that you must continue to be strong. He suffered the equivalent of hundreds of years of sorrow, pain, stress and pressure during His 33 years on Earth. Even as He is a sinless Man, He knows the depths of pain and sorrow that every person endures. You have in your presence today this same Christ whom I bore and reared, who I taught and from whom I learned, who has assigned dignity to those who believe in Him with their whole hearts. It would seem as though there are still many Americans and others around the globe who do not understand the vastness of Jesus' Holy Love. They fail to recognize the intensity with which He desires mortal men to accept His death on the Cross for the expiation of human sin. It is as though the whole concept of love is foreign to millions of people because they do not lead sacrificial lives. We know that the battle for righteousness is not an endless endeavor. Therefore, My message today is to ask you and your brother not to be dismayed by what you see in the news, at your workplace or anywhere else. I ask all My children to do the same, but many have hardened their hearts. They have decided on their own that this is the hour for God to act in the ways that Jesus has written. They create time lines for the future that will leave out millions of lost souls in the Divine Plan of Salvation. They are mandating and calculating. It is instead the Lord's Will that must be done. Please know that you and your brother are doing your part in the Lord's vineyard. My messages to you will have their intended effect, or Jesus would not have asked Me to dictate them. My Special and Chosen ones, I ask you to pray for your brothers and sisters who do not understand the providence of human redemption. It begins with purifying and cultivating the Earth. This is the reason you are seeing the stark content of certain messages in other parts of the world. I need your help to ask your brother-and-sister visionaries to invoke their patience by praying for them. Imagine what it was like in olden days when My messengers wrote with pen in hand, using quills, and even by writing on clay slates. All those messages did precisely what Jesus wanted them to do. When He declared on Good Friday that everything was finished, He was also speaking of the messages that I would give humanity through the present hour. He spoke on that day about the message you are receiving at this moment. Yes, I need your help because I too draw on the strength of My children the way you turn to Me. This is what I mean when I say that you are predisposed to complete openness to everything the Lord would have you do. You have made clear your posture and preferences about the final meeting between Heaven and Earth. Jesus needs the assistance of every breathing creature on the Earth who believes in Him. Please accept My gratitude for staying the course with your brother, while so many have wandered astray. Your vision is clear. All that is happening now, everything you have endured, all you can possibly imagine is moving directly into the redemptive ending about which I have spoken today."

Palm Sunday, April 1, 2012
2:33 p.m.

"To celebrate kindness and grace, the spirit of peace and the letter of the law, for the expungement of sins, chastity of the flesh, the purification of the soul and the advancement of wisdom: these are the things that make humanity whole, that pave the way for joy, for the truth to be told, and for righteousness to inundate the nations."

William L. Roth

"Your writing is so pretty, My Special one. Imagine it engraved in stone at the shores of a nation or the facade of a building erected in memory of the millions who have kept the faith. These are the reasons I keep returning here where you and your brother live. It is because you have the vision and values that reflect the Kingdom of God, and you share them with humanity around the world and beyond the ages. It is imperative that you remember that there is a dialogue being established between yourselves and the Father that is encrypted in your lives, prayers and actions. This dialogue is unique to you and your brother, like mileposts that are erected along the highway of your years that will ultimately be joined into one place where throngs will gather in awe to examine the portrait of your lives. You cannot yet see this final picture because you are still taking strokes, applying your witness and wisdom to what you want to say to Jesus and His disciples, to the masses and their kings, to those who have long worked silently to propagate holiness wherever it must take root. You think greatly about the same imaginings that have drawn Me here to this exiled world, speaking and encouraging, comforting and enlightening. There are dark crevasses and hidden corners that must be exposed, all of them like the billions of hidden places beneath the skies and seas, and beyond other worlds. We must expose them to the Salvation that has kept you and Me and your brother working and struggling for so long. They must come to know Jesus as you know Him, to feel as He has felt throughout the centuries. He often feels as though His Holy Sacrifice has been deposited into history as would any other event. He yearns to be called with intensity to resolve the world's problems, to bring healing and pardon to those who ask. Remember that there can be no distance between the Will of the Father and the Will of the Son, that theirs is the same Providence. What Jesus sees of humanity can be amended by what the Father chooses to reveal. This is what prayer is for. Therefore, I have come seeking you and your brother to do what you do best – to love God unconditionally. Many others still refuse; they do not understand; they do not take the time; they would rather become absorbed by the material world where they do not have to engage their spiritual conscience or concern themselves with what lies far into the Afterlife. You have known for decades that holy people make up for what is lacking in those who do not know God. This is what Jesus' life and Crucifixion reveal. You are strong because the Holy Spirit is invincible within you. My Special son, I wish to tell you and your brother that even though Heaven is beyond the bonds of time and space, there is a certain momentum there. This is the movement of the Mystical Body of Christ from this world into the next. I have said that everything in this world that is worthy of redemption will exist in Heaven. You will see many of the same holy relics and hear the same strains of pious eloquence when you stand on the streets of gold. What will be absent is the pall of depression that falls into good people's lives. Also missing will be the endless repetition of the days and the repeating charges that the Church has not done enough. And, there are also precious gems in Heaven, ones that echo the beatific ecstasy that you and your brothers and sisters have sought since you were born from the womb. Your souls have known to hunger for the Sacred Divine by which you are now being fed.

Jesus is the Sacred Meal that has brought this transition to the millions who have preceded this generation on the globe. Truth is uncontainable, and yet Truth was Incarnate in Christ Jesus as one Man, born of My Womb. This is the same reason that your hopes and dreams must be as infinite as everything beyond the stars and above the heavens. I cannot make you happy in this life, but you can. Humanity has at its disposal the power to overcome every act of ill will and every hint of darkness. This is the joy of the Resurrection. Just because other people will not listen or they refuse to comply does not mean that any Christian's efforts are in vain. God sees them and writes them down in the eternal record. He keeps count of the grand and ethereal sentiments that you share with people who scarcely believe what you have said and written. Your Morning Star Over America diary will fall onto their consciences like a humongous boulder from the skies. I am not speaking terms that cannot be understood. The whole impact of your lives is saved in the context of the Popes, Bishops and priests who have lived and died for the same conversion of man. As you recite the Holy Rosary, you dictate before the exiled world your proclamation that every soul is worthy to be saved. When you become frustrated by what you see as obstinance in other men, this is the Son of Man working through you to reassure them that in the future they will change. This is not a threat. It is not anything portending damnation at all. It is the Good News for which they have waited the whole of their lives. It is the good measure that will vanquish every inch of unsavory thought and action that would stain their minds with guilt. Therefore, My message today to you and your brother is one of hope that is based on facts. This may sound contradictory, but you must remember that all things work for good for those who believe in God. What is this love about which I speak? How can this be true love when the world of man seems so upside down? Because the Crucifixion of Jesus is mightier than anything that opposes it. Jesus' life on the Earth was lived in assurance that His Second Coming would find millions of souls having walked in His footsteps. His Light is so brilliant that it has lasted through the ages. This is the Light that you and your brother have shined for lost sinners. It is also your brilliance, your own assurance, your hope and consolation that these repeating days will culminate in the Triumph of My Most Immaculate Heart. Father Gobbi discovered this on his own; he knew it before he died. Saint Pio suffered his own obedience into being because he placed it into the Crucifixion of Jesus during every Mass. He shed his blood in the likeness of the Son of God because he was united heart, mind, soul and body with the Redeemer whom he served. This is the same Saint who is so close to you. He knew at the moment of his affliction that My messages would come to someone passed from another mother's womb on that same day.

There is Providence in all this, and planning and justice. The inequities of the world are no match for these miracles. The sunrises yet to come and the sunsets following them are like a drumming cadence that leads to the fulfillment of everything you would like the Earth to become. Jesus hears the pining of your heart. He knows how you feel spiritually, physically and emotionally. He is aware of the burdens that come to those who are tethered to the Will of God. And, if I can come into this home and muster your spirit to rise, I will do it. If I can visit here and tell you that God has planned a victory that rivals the grandest ever to be celebrated in the history of all histories, then I will say it. If I could place your heart aboard all the rocket ships that have ever been launched into the heavens above, then I will bid you a good flight. If there are flowers or waterfalls that will take your spirit to the destiny I am describing, I will give them to you. If there is any happiness, any joy, perseverance or contentment in your hopes that Jesus can provide for you, then I beseech you to turn your face to the skies with arching confidence because the sacred hour will soon arrive. So, I will tell you today what I have been saying to all My Marian messengers around the globe on this Palm Sunday into Holy Week – do not surrender to the duplicities of the devil. Never allow Satan to prick your heart or wear down your desire to see this journey through. Never mind his deceptions and trickery. Do not give him the pleasure of believing that he has any force or power over you whatsoever. This is the young confidence that keeps you going strong. It is an adolescent joy that made Jesus play with His friends in the dooryard and not care what problems arose. It is the same hope that makes little children laugh and middle schoolers drive lifelike automobiles toward checkered flags across finish lines. It is the appreciation for what God has done and is about to accomplish through those who believe in Him. Men do not get tired because they wear out. They become exhausted because they refuse to see the beauty of one day – this day, this hour, this moment. They decline to recognize that the stairs they are climbing are taking them higher than most constellations will ever go. There are indeed rough patches on these stairs for sure, loud storms and turbulence. There is danger and peril, sadness and suffering. There is plight and plundering, and blasphemy too. But, men are going to new heights anyway. They are taking their greatest strides, rising above the fray, keeping their eyes trained on the summit, and trusting that I will never loosen My grip on their hands. I promise above all other oaths that I love you beyond anything you can imagine. You know this to be true. This is reason enough for humanity to go on. It is what makes people like you and your brother embark time and again on praying for the world to change. It is the reason the aged Pontiff travels to distant lands, carrying the Word of Salvation with him. These people trust; they trust without seeing. They believe that there are ovations aplenty to be heard once the trumpet of the ages is sounded. I will be there too, as I have said. I will be the Lady holding the Child as you pass by in your chariot. We will enter together the Land of the Living and close the door on the past so tightly behind us that no one will be able to crack it. These are My wishes and sentiments for today."

Holy Saturday, April 7, 2012
2:45 p.m.

"Forgiveness lets the mind rest, the heart sing, and the soul rejoice."

"The honor of speaking to you during these prayerful hours is a distinction that I shall never forget, My children. I have been calling the world to unite in preparation for the Second Coming of Jesus in the same way that His believers anticipated His Resurrection from the Tomb. There will come a day when wild creatures will wander the world looking for the collective soul of humanity, and the Holy Spirit will tell them that humanity is not there; they have been raised, just as Jesus said. Today, we ponder the fate of lost sinners with the hope that they will convert to the Cross. We applaud the speakers and ministers who call them to this new life, to redemption and the forgiveness about which you have spoken at the opening of this message. The entirety of this faith is in advance of the reunion between deceased and living loved-ones, of the renewal of the face of the Earth spoken about in the Scriptures, of the New World that will supplant the old one. We have the best of intentions and holy ways to describe to wayward sinners the future they will inherit, the promise that has been made. But, the only issue they worry about is suffering – not suffering in the way of sacrificial love, but suffering that poverty brings. They are reluctant to be poor so that others can be enriched by the fruits of the Earth. They fear suffering the indignity that comes from falling into commonness. They are terrified at living life in the way of the Son of Man because He teaches them self-sacrifice. My little sons, some of your brothers and sisters do not pray because they seem to hear no one at the end of the line. They are so used to speaking and audibly hearing a response. Who would believe that there is an answer in the silence? How can earthly life be lived in privilege if others keep the profits of material exchange? But, when seen clearly, this privilege is about having access to redemptive grace and receiving the blessings that accompany it. Men are taught that action prompts reaction. They learn at the last that this is not what eternal teaching is for. It is about giving and not counting the cost, fighting and not knowing the outcome, walking without measuring the distance, and forgiving without expecting to be pardoned. The whole energy of the Christian heart must be directed toward these things and away from self-satisfaction. The reward is in knowing that honor and Salvation are yours. The satisfaction is in realizing that Christ Jesus adorns you with power unknown to those who reject Him. I understand that these things are subject to the influences of time and opportunity, but holy men create these opportunities at the proper moments. This is what the song is about where the rejuvenated man stops his brother from leaping off the bridge into a watery death below. It is about hearing the Word of God in the eloquence of mortal men. It is about sitting quietly amid the beauty of Nature and realizing that the Father is present there with you. (*Our Lady was apparently referring to the country music song "Moments" performed by Emerson Drive.*)

So the world today waits in joyful hope for the Coming of the Lord. The agents and representatives of the heavens advocate for your wisdom and patience. Creative love flows from above into the hearts and lives of those courageous enough to believe. All darkness and deceit are exposed and vanquished by the will of Christians to fight the good fight against the questionable attributes of life. Being on constant vigil means living peacefully, not with anxiety, and in a state of prayerfulness that this day and all tomorrows have already been conquered in the Sacred Heart of Jesus. We witness today all the architectures of the Church, both spiritual and physical, standing like sentinels in the night. We see Bishops and priests who are honing their homilies for the Paschal Resurrection. And, they will be grand; they will be pretty too! But, they will fall short of truly capturing what really happened when Jesus rose from the Tomb. Why? Because words do not suffice. They will speak in tongues and languages that will build platforms and frameworks upon which the Holy Spirit will infiltrate every believing heart with the capacity to understand. Easter is the recurring preparation, the annual practice for what the human soul will see when all is said and done. Jesus the King has in His arms the future of all the world. He has planned a special gift for each soul who has come to Him, and they are as innumerable as the birds that fall from the sky. This is the King who has not changed His mind about dying, but chose to live again. How many earthly kings can do this? How many can replicate His holiness, His intense desire to seat the worst sinners in the world at His dinner table? How many kings in exile have the power to cast out demons and bring nations to their knees without firing a shot or flinging a single arrow? How many worldly kings have said to God that it is all about His Will and not theirs? This is the origin of the concept of Savior. Savior means the one who has suffered in your place. Savior means the Man who has spared humanity from the wrath of God. It is possible for good men and women to understand this gift because it is through the Savior that Salvation comes. Every soul born into the world has the capacity to see this far. My Special son, you and your brother have given so much to the Kingdom of God that it cannot be weighed. I ask you to realize what you have done, as modestly as you wish, but to know that you have made a difference that only few in the history of the world have done. God did not send His people into the world to become rich. He did not dispatch them to practice the art of profiteering. He has sent His people around the globe to teach the Gospel by word and deed. This is what you and your brother are doing. Just as Saint Pio has said, the years will come to you as they did for him. You are still young, but you will someday see what he was saying, what has come to all your predecessors. This portends greatness and renewal. The future holds years and decades, even an eternity of unity with the Passion of Jesus for everyone who has been claimed by the Father. They are the blessed ones, the fortunate ones, the chosen ones upon whose shoulders the sanctification of humanity rests. There will be gladness for the weeping, light piercing the darkness, miraculous visions overcoming blindness, and peace in the face of calamity. Please remember that I am with you and all My children through the length and breadth of days. I am the mentor of the Teacher and the inspiration of all the inspired. I birthed the same Holy Spirit who proclaimed the Conception in My Womb. I celebrated the Salvation of the world before it ever occurred. This is what you mean when you say that the heart sings and the soul rejoices. I pray that Easter helps you realize how blessed you are in this life, what gifts God has given to America, and how far humanity has come in accepting the absolution that rightly belongs to them."

Sunday, April 15, 2012
Divine Mercy Sunday
9:16 a.m.

"If peace comes naturally, men will be rewarded supernaturally. If peace comes in the aftermath of war, is it compromised by the spoils? Probably not. Sometimes defending righteousness on the battlefield is sufficient evidence that your enemies are the only ones without reason."

William L. Roth

"I come this lovely Sunday morning to give you My blessing and remind you of the deeply-held admiration that I have for you. Jesus is in fact dispensing His Divine Mercy on the world in ways that millions have never recognized. How do I know? Because He has not reduced the exiled world to a cinder. He has spared humanity the devastation that it would require to annihilate the wayward sinners among you. This comes from the days of old when My Son was asked what would become of those who still spurn the Gospel. Today is more than a special day for this reason, but because you are at the eve of the birthday of the Holy Father. You are blessed with true guidance and leadership by one who is informed about the future I have told. My desire over these days is more than the conversion of men, but that this conversion will lead to discernable action so that poor people will be lifted from their poverty; unborn children will be preserved into birth, the servants of God will be heeded when they speak, and the masses will take to their knees in thanksgiving for their Salvation. I am happy today, My little ones. You may find this curious due to the intense impiety around the globe. But, I am happy because unholiness cannot prevail over the future or eternity itself. I tell you often that human life is a struggle, but it is one worth waging because you have already won. These hours and days are the approach to the great reckoning predicted in the Scriptures. You walk on streets and hear the sound of voices that echo this fact every day. If not for the Seven Deadly Sins, My Son Jesus would not have allotted the world more time to change. These are too crucial to ignore, too indicting to permit the world to be finally judged as it is. Let us remain one in the Most Blessed Trinity as we wait out those who are still ignorant about their responsibilities in Creation. What has been soiled must become cleansed. What has been exploited must be made new. What has been killed must be resurrected, at least those worthy of God's eternal blessing. My Special one, you have seen by your writing that nothing in you has been lost. You are still the conduit for the Holy Spirit to teach the world about the Church. Your heart is still capable of rendering essays and reflections that are worthy of the Saints and Doctors of the Church. This will never leave you. It cannot. It has become ingrained in your spiritual fiber and has become the center of your being. This is the way of all good men, everyone who belongs to Christ Jesus, all who have found their way from the darkness of this world into the Light of Eternal Glory. You were destined for this from your conception.

I wish for you and your brother to know that I remain indebted to you for your loyalty to Me, for your veneration of the Cross, and for your consecration to My Immaculate Heart and Jesus' Most Sacred Heart. No days shall pass without a recognition in Heaven that you belong to us. You have within you the piety that should spill across these lands as though they are overcome by floods from the seas. I tell you these things not to open a doorway through which boasting may enter, but because you must come to the realization of your station in life. Your tiredness is the same tiredness that comes upon the Pope, the Bishops, all the clergy, and lay persons everywhere who are lifting up the Cross before the nations. A man once said here in this home that he has never seen anything so opposed. This is disheartening in itself. All those whom I have just mentioned have discovered at the last that their despondence has been misplaced. They should have been rejoicing all along. They should have had loftier hopes and keener vision. They should still recognize that ultimate justice resides in your thoughts and prayers about the defeat of your enemies. This is surely what your opening quotation today is all about. Therefore, as Jesus offers The Divine Mercy to those who ask, remember the intercession of Saint Faustina and all who have accustomed themselves to the way of the Cross. Does confession come before pardon? Absolutely. Does repentance precede forgiveness? There is no doubt. And, does suffering lead to the atonement of sin? History has proven this to be true.

There is a mystical sense of progression here. There is charity and destiny, enterprise and reward. If we speak about human interaction as the marketplace of ideas, then we must surely demand that the whole share of the market be about the purification of the world. It must be about reversing the tides of error, the rejection of sin, and the renewal of the baptismal vows that remind each Christian what it means to avoid sin and avoid whatever leads them to sin. It is true that one cannot control the kinds of temptation they will face, but they have absolute power to turn away from those temptations. To deny Satan is to be supernatural and superhuman in the flesh. To reject sin means to be not only like the Son of Man, but to coopt His Kingdom in the depths of the human heart. To renounce the errors of secularism means to justify any medium for spreading the Gospel of Redemption around the globe. My Special son, history is replete with examples of the victory of love over the tyranny of hatred. You and your brother have participated in these battles. You have developed tactics that have countered the schemes of Satan. You have blocked his progress on multiple fronts. You have made headway against the secular humanism that is devouring America. These are the fruits of your allegiance to God and your awareness that your prayers do matter in changing the world. Never forget that the free will of men can be the greatest obstacle to the conversion of the heart. There is a false sense of freedom in these men and women that the new millennium has given them license to entirely change the configuration of their individual and collective identities. They see the coming of the new century as recognition by God that they are doing things His way. They feel legitimized because they have not yet been struck down in their tracks. They are delusional – they have not the slightest inkling about the motivations of their Maker. This is the reason we are working to advance the Kingdom of the Father. Again I say, we have already won, and they need to know it. Their vision needs to be extended to the last day of their lives so they will realize that their animosity toward the Church is in vain. They must comprehend the peril in which they have placed themselves. I do not envy them for the lessons they will learn, but I do envy them for being rescued from their destruction in time to know the Truth. I have said that those who will serve the Lord most fruitfully are those who have the farthest distance to travel into His good graces. These are the souls who will not simply say, 'I should have known better,' they will say, 'Oh, dear God! I should have known better!' This makes the future a propitious time. It makes the effect of our work all the more sweet. Thus, I have made way for humanity to receive The Divine Mercy of Jesus every day of the world. My mercy upon My children is My Crucified Son. Thank you and your brother for everything you do to aid the mission of the Church. You are restful inside, even when your bodies seem tired."

Saturday, April 21, 2012
1:42 p.m.

Seize the day, savor the moment.

"My children, it is appropriate that you remain with Me in prayer for the conversion of the world. Your vision is clear, and your consciences are clearer. Today, to celebrate your friendship, I wish to speak about the proverbial seizing of the day and savoring the moment, not that eternity does not matter, but that you will realize precisely how special these days are. Each moment, you must know that you are embraced by the same grace that has edified the world in the themes of redemption. I wish not that you look always to the future that is in many ways uncertain because you do not yet know what prayers will be said to avert disasters and mitigate the errors that are keeping your brothers and sisters embroiled in disagreements and encased in darkness. Please never forget that I have said over and again that prayer changes the present and reshapes the future. It amends the past and makes reparation for people's mistakes. All in all, you are given a good life in this country beneath My Holy Mantle. There are blessings and benefits to life in a nation that is under the Patroness of the Americas. Please remember, My sons, that you have come this far by this grace and these prayers. This is what it means to seize the day. Savoring the moment means that you are capable of issuing to your own consciousness an awareness that the times of your lives are building blocks and stepping stones to the finality that you seek in Jesus, to the new beginnings about which I have spoken for so long. The gifts that have been brought at My hands signify that these days matter in the larger framework of your experiences. My Special son, when you write by the minute and hour the way you have been organizing your thoughts in your memoir, you are reflecting seconds and minutes at a time. This is the way you were meant to live. I am not suggesting that you should lose sight of the Glory in the offing, but embrace and accept the newness of each day. This is how Jesus was raised because this is what He asked of Myself and Saint Joseph. Even in His adolescence, Jesus called us to live with Him peacefully and deliberately. He did not implore us to dwell on the future because He knew even at that young age the power of prayer. It was in Him that the world would know redemption and purification, born of a Jewish Mother, bound for the Sacrifice and Resurrection that have redeemed the lost. This is what it means to replicate the victory of the Cross, that you and your brother and all humanity will find within you the joy to realize that no evil can withstand the judgement of the years. I ask you to pray for lost sinners because they cannot help themselves; they are too blinded by their own ignorance and animosity against the Church. This is similarly good reason for you to keep your sights on this day, what happens during the hours that you see Creation with your eyes and listen with your ears. The Lord God will commend your triumph over these years if you live through Him one day at a time. There are horizons aplenty for good reason. They are metaphors for realizing that what lies between them must be addressed, the good and the bad, and that you must set your sights on the blessings and difficulties that you face. The greatest Saints who ever lived gave themselves to the essence of the moment, even as they knew that eternity loomed brilliantly beyond their mortal years. This is where permanent peace in the heart can be procured from the swiftly passing ages.

Outside these doors is a world that is welcoming and yet callous. It is filled with innocence and exploitation. It calculates advantages against these innocent souls because it is not vigilant against the forces of the devil. There is insufficient prayer; there is too much greed; there are too few willing to sacrifice their comfort for the comfort of others, and there is an entirely contradictory view of human life to that summoned by the Gospel of the Lord. We knew centuries ago that this was the case, that it would continue to be the case all the way up to today. We knew that there would be greed and impurity, that there would be desecration of holy relics and the impugning of the sacred. This is the way of the world, but it need not be inevitable or insurmountable. I often speak to you about how happy I am to be here because it reminds Me of Heaven when I see the way you live. I am taken to places in My thoughts that harken to the times when we prayed with Jesus when He was a young boy. You are making this difference with your prayers as well. You are reshaping the outside world by what you have done here in this home. Its wood, plaster, bricks and mortar are insufficient evidence of what has actually occurred within these walls. I have consulted with you many times about what you should believe about the power you have wielded on behalf of Jesus. I pray that you do not permit your enemies' words to discourage you or make you believe that they have any influence in the mind of God. They are your enemies for a reason. They cannot even bring themselves to believe that the Lord would be born of a Virgin, let alone that this same Virgin would appear around the globe and reaffirm what the Incarnation was about. We have reflected many times about Jesus' Nativity, ministry, betrayal, Passion, suffering and Death. We have spoken about the boundless parameters of His Resurrection with such glorious overtones that it is almost too much to take in. When you ponder all you have been given, I ask that you consider how this process has affected you. You have been the recipients of pious grace – this is the most important part of our exchange. You are the vessels into whom Jesus has poured His Sacred Wisdom. You have been willing; you have cast aside your self-preferences in favor of the conversion of the world. You have wrapped your arms around the mission of the Church as though you began it yourselves. You have elevated the Holy Cross, venerated the Saints, defended the Faith, walked with your brothers twain, suffered as the Lamb, and still you hold your heads aloft. You carry yourselves with humble dignity and poise. You refuse to allow your enemies to win. You will continue to do this if you remember to seize the day by savoring the moment. Life is a collection of memories captured in repetitive days, but no two of them are exactly alike. These moments are unique; they each represent new blessings and challenges that you approach with the Spirit of the Father and the Spirit of the Son residing vibrantly within you. This is the message that I share with you today. I know that you feel confident that the whole of your years will culminate in the Triumph of My Immaculate Heart. I am simply asking you to live one day at a time. We shall soon see what Jesus does with the prayers and sacrifices of the Church. My Special son, the fruits will not come if there is no sacrifice by those who hear My messages."

Sunday, April 29, 2012
9:39 a.m.

"...(and) when the Son of Man looks lastly upon this world with eyes so fragrant and convincing, we will realize beyond any shadow that His gaze has validated our faith, that we have echoed the arpeggio of the ages that magnify our redemption in ways more replete than the heavens. Therefore, if we defy every obstacle and speel every mountain that stands between us and that faith, we will not only win the battle, we will enshrine the victory itself."

William L. Roth

"My little sons, the tumultuous world cannot hold back the joy that has come through the Resurrection of Jesus, and you cannot escape the grasp of the hands of Salvation holding you now. It is good that you have in you the awareness that has changed the course of history. I remind you that the record of your lives is already that catalyst. You in effect need to do no more, but you will anyway. You will thankfully keep working for the Kingdom of God; you will build upon your past successes so the future will be fuller for everyone on Earth. There is no question that suffering abounds in human life. Sinners make it this way. However, the joy about which I speak is more than simply overcoming sin. It is about what occurs beyond this life, what resides in your hearts and minds that is already eternally here. There is no such thing as material prosperity to those who are close to God. Humanity must work toward the richness of the spirit, the human spirit that is vast in generosity and self-sacrifice. One who has a generous spirit does not surround himself with comfort. What would the Saints say to the two Texan ministers you saw on the television this morning? 'Sell what you have and give to the poor.' You see people every day who pluck certain passages from the Bible that 'permit' them to prosper in disproportionate ways. I would ask what these two married preachers will say about the end of abortion in their stadium presentation. This is a means by which to assess the Christianity in their hearts. What will they say about missionary work in foreign lands like soon-to-be Saint Father Ted Hochstatter? How can they justify wearing pearls and diamonds in front of millions of people who cannot afford to put bread on their tables? We are aware; we know the truth. We are not hypocrites. You have seen their kind before. They protest against the sacrifices that will make them holy for the rest of their days. They are no different from abortionists themselves. My little sons, I remind you often about the joy that I offer My suffering children. Saint Pio speaks about envying those who are broken in the name of Jesus. What would Saint Pio say to the two Texans if they walked into Mass? Their hypocrisy knows no bounds. The kind of hypocrisy they are committing is the worst kind of blasphemy. They would do better to have their tongues cut out and fed to the dogs. Fear not the truth that this Mother speaks. I am praying that anyone who is far from the realization that Christianity is a religion of self-sacrifice comes to know their own record of error. I also have spoken about the record of history; and as you know, history is a subset of the fullness of Eternity. History may be changed, but Eternity rarely will be. We must remember to pray for those who refuse to learn this difference. Time can be reversed, as can the course of human events. However, the Judgement of a soul is permanent. We are in the midst of shaping these crucial moments by our prayers. I have said that it is not necessary that anyone believe that he needs to conquer the devil. Jesus has already done so. What needs to be done is for everyone on Earth to accept and magnify the Crucifixion that has annihilated the forces of evil around the world. Those who have not done so are being used by Satan to recite his final words and perpetuate his dying acts. This is what you are seeing during these times. Satan has no power; he can only use force. He utilizes sinners who cannot conquer their own temptations to steal the future of the innocent. This is also why we pray.

And, we pray so those who are reckless will be careful. We pray for the best exercise of Christian talents to be extended to the far corners of the globe. This means applying the Works of Mercy, admonishing the wicked, enlightening the ignorant, and uplifting the poor. This cannot be done if members of the Church look only inwardly to themselves. My little sons, you have seen in My Medjugorje messages that I have called the Saint James parish and the whole of humanity to recognize their station in this life. The Father wants His children to come to Jesus through Me in the same way that He sent Jesus into Creation through Me. I am the same humble Maiden that I was in those days. I have power within Me that can destroy any obstacle to the faith of unholy men. It was given to Me by the same Holy Spirit that descended upon the Apostles at Pentecost. This kind of power is natural to those who accept the Cross of Redemption. This kind of power makes weak men strong and the obtuse upright. This is the kind of power that makes you patient and enduring while the will of all peoples everywhere is being lent to the Father in Heaven. No sinner can be saved against his own volition. This is the point that must be made. My Special son, it is a good day during an auspicious time in this home and around the world. Why? Because we are together speaking about the logical conclusion to an illogical world. It makes sense that the devilish shall be slain, that the unrepentant will perish. For all I have said about the absence of pragmatism in the themes of righteousness, these things make sense. One reaps what he sows, and then come the miracles! Enter The Divine Mercy! How can love be true love without this forgiveness? After all, human redemption is more than a mere transaction between the Father and the acceptance of His people. A transactional approach to the Salvation of humanity implies that there is no trust. It suggests that everything must be committed to the page. If this were the case, there would be no need for miracles. Supernatural manifestations would not suffice. I am speaking about spreading a Living Gospel that makes room for tall utterances and wide expectations. The New Covenant is not just a record of what occurred centuries ago, but what continues to be true today. And, as you are aware that the Gospel cannot be changed; it is fixed by the Holy Spirit and engraved in the teachings of the Church, God the Father makes it current by providing new manifestations every day. If this were untrue, why would I appear around the globe over the centuries to remind My children of this? I have come as a miracle to pronounce new miracles. We are together fulfilling another phase of earlier miracles that are making such a difference in these times. I will announce later this year specific actions that you and your brother can take to proceed with the propagation of My messages to your lost brothers and sisters. We will employ every venue of communication, every mode available, every friend and adviser, and every moment of the day and night to reach those who must be touched. This is the reason you must have joy. It is in these moments we are speaking together, in the hours of every new day, in all the immediacy of time, and in your realization that you are living the purposes of Jesus as you see the world and your vicinity with such hope and inspiration. I simply ask you to remember that Divine Love is your constant companion here and now, tomorrow and next week, next year and for all eternity to come. I offer My messages to you because I love you! And, thank you for taking such good care of your brother. He is deeply devoted to you and Me because of the strength of your faith."

Sunday, May 6, 2012
8:59 a.m.

"Jesus, give us the insight to see through the perils of this life and the deceptions of our enemies so that we will forever train our focus on your Kingdom through the Sacrifice by which our embattled souls are saved. We ask this through Christ Our Lord. Amen."

William L. Roth

"Let the joyful bells peal the presence of the Holy Spirit here in this place and around the world, for the Paraclete of Salvation has given Wisdom to the Church. My little children, I reign inside and outside of time as your love and consecrations are alive always and everywhere. I have never answered your question from November 1991 when you asked whether I have ever danced. I have indeed. I have lived the jubilation that has come forth from the divinity of the Father into My life. I have been assured of the redemption of the entire human race through the Crucifixion of My Son. Even as sorrowful as I was on Good Friday, that sorrow was turned into dancing because Jesus' death was overcome by the Glory of God. It is the same for all who come to Jesus for Salvation. You have known this since you were babes. Your hearts and souls have lived this Truth. You have shared your witness about what I have told you in all the years and through the timelessness of My apparitions and locutions. There is joy in knowing that one has participated in the conversion and deliverance of humanity from the throes of sin to the perfection of holiness. This is the same joy that the Angels have brought into the Lord's earthly Kingdom like dewdrops on the morning blades. You must remember,

My little sons, everything I have told you about the awakening of the world. There will be dark days and bright days, sorrow and rejoicing, and all the other storied contrasts that I have mentioned through the years. It is a part of the experience of 'going' to God, to stand firm in one's conviction for God here on Earth. It is part of the parameters that are seeable in the infinity of His Kingdom. One knows what the deepest sadness feels like, and someone knows what it means to stand at the apex of joy. These are defining descriptions; they are like east and west, locations that are spiritual but not physical. Nonetheless, they assist in the description of a Kingdom so vast that it cannot be taken in on the Earth without the fullest reciprocity between the Lord and His people. I have said that God always gives His limitless best. It is the responsibility of humanity not to match that infinity, but to give to Jesus and His Church every portion that can be mustered in prayer and fortitude for the advancement of the Gospel. My little sons, you have both done these things well. If you consider yourselves fortunate to have been hearing My words for so long, your messages are about hope and love, about the pleasance of My intercession and the Mercy of God, rather than about constant suffering and premonitions of chastisements. We have brought into this world the promise of peace that was given to Christians of old.

Even though the Father sees your spirits more clearly than you can even see your flesh, you must realize the beauty that you extol. God sees in the human person such divine potential that it is difficult to place into words. Divine potential. What does this mean? It means that the Father is pleased by His creatures simply because He created us. He gave us life and being. The Love of God has nurtured us from our mothers' wombs and given us direction in the righteousness bred into our faith. There can be no denying the Love of God that you see in the innocence of little children and the wisdom of the learned. This, My Special son, is why your writings that you read to your brother yesterday afternoon are so filled with truth. During those times when you believe that your written pages are too filled with negativity, then write about the way life ought to be. Incorporate into those pages thoughts and images about what would exist if the conditions you are describing were not there. This will balance and offset the seeming drumbeat of negativity that concerns you in your manuscript. There are plenty of hopeful thoughts to cite because there are few truly in existence here in America. You speak and write about a nation that is devouring itself through impurity, selfishness, secular indifference and bombastic speech. There is such division in the United States of America that it seems strange to call it a nation. I seek from you the ability to see beyond all this trouble and write about the peace of Jesus through the lessons you have learned from Me. This is what you did in 'Supernal Chambers' extremely well. These texts and those images will not be left behind. Humanity will be required to hear every word I have said to you and your brother before the closing of the ages. I simply ask that you do not dwell on 'when' the world will end, but how. The latter is what you and your brother have been addressing since you first laid eyes on each other decades ago. I was there with you, as I have said to you both many times. And, I will be with you always as will Jesus until the end, all the way through the stoppage of mortal time and into the eternity that has already begun at the center of your hearts. There is such suffering and turmoil that has consumed humanity that they are often blinded to the beauty about which I am speaking. However, this is not singly a facet of your age. If you had seen the world during the largest two Twentieth Century wars, you would have thought that Creation could not have lasted another day.

My Special son, your first memoir harkens to My warnings to humanity in Fatima and Lourdes. Have people listened? There is sparse evidence, but those who have taken heed have made up for the indifference of the rest. This is the reason one man in one place can effect the change that will completely reverse the tides of the Earth. You have seen and read about it many times over. And, you are correct in your thoughts. It could not have been done without the grace of God that you have prayed about so profoundly in your opening invocation to our message today. Leaps and bounds. This is what occurs simultaneous to small steps. As the Church makes its way to the gate of Heaven one day at a time, I am picking My children up as you see a mother lifting a child by the arms and swinging him forward and setting him back down on his feet again. All these things happen beyond the sight of mortal men, but they are not outside your imagining. I have brought into the world the capacity to see Salvation unfold in the same way as the first Apostles and disciples. I have allowed you to see what it means to have stood at the trial and refrained from shouting 'Crucify Him' without being told to get behind Jesus. You have been advised and apprised, enlightened, inspirited and delivered to an awareness that cannot be procured from any other source. And best of all, you have accepted. You have proclaimed yourselves up to the task, and you have proven it by your lives. You have personified the faith of the early Church by your actions and proclamations. Souls can hear the melodies of redemption above any other sound inside or outside the universe. Thank you for realizing that I birthed that Message into the Flesh because this places you high and above the billions who refuse to listen. My Special son, you make Me so happy when you allow Me to speak to you because I am eager to share what the Father would like all Creation to know. He desires the perfection of every man, woman and child. He asks from those who are distracted to cast away whatever blinds them and look at the Cross. One cannot see the Resurrection of Christ Jesus without first looking through the Cross. You and your brother have known this all your lives. Thank you for supporting your brother in his academic work. You are the warmth of his soul and the foundation beneath his feet. This is the legacy of your lives for millions more. You have chosen the path that will bend the course of history and change the outcome of the created world."

Saturday, May 12, 2012
3:15 p.m.

Think, dear Lord, about what we think.
See our pain with the glow of your eyes.
Bring us back from the troubled brink.
Safeguard our faith below the dark skies.
Upon your sea crest, we shall never sink.
Healed by your Sacrifice, together we rise.

William L. Roth

"Well shared is our love, My little sons. We are unified in the Sacred Heart where you find yourselves shielded from the buffets and snares of earthly dangers. Thank you for being persistent in your works and prayers because God hears them. He responds in ways that you can see and others that are invisible to the eye. For My part, I come to you again with elevated spirits, and you are aware of the reasons. You know that I admire My children who are serving and searching, who are sowing and reaping the harvest of converted souls for Jesus. There is no means by which to measure your worth before the Lord because you have surpassed the boundaries of your own existence and transcended the parameters in which ordinary men are enclosed. Yes, you are seeing and reading messages elsewhere around the globe that speak of untold suffering. But, this must not give you reason to believe that conditions will not change. Most of the messages you are hearing are preceded by an unwritten warning that says, 'If humanity does not change, then...' and the identified possibilities of the warning continue. We have spoken about consequences before, both immediate and eventual ones. When they occur is of small concern because they do not have to be inevitable. My Special son, you and your brother have seen many lives restored to purity; health has been given anew, eyes have been opened wide, and dark corners have been lighted by the suffering of innocents. This is the Church that has embarked on the transformation of the world, each and every one, singly and collectively. You are both also aware of the imperative works of each day that are amassed in the treasury of Heaven for the Lord to dispense in His good time. The prayers that you and all the faithful offer each day are representative of the blueprints and templates by which the finality of the Earth is still being fashioned. When looked upon from abroad, the United States appears to be a place of constant infighting and negativism. Authors worldwide have lamented over the greed, division and backbiting that have become a staple of the American culture. This is the environment in which the Catholic Church has been forced to work. Do you know with what success the Church would touch the hearts of lost sinners if those same sinners were not made so cynical and doubtful by secular societies? It is beyond unfortunate that the Church must not only fight against its own enemies, but must also face the blather of the enemies of common decency as well. It is all about the competition for souls between God and the devil.

Your memoir is going well – it is utterly fine. The Holy Spirit assists your writing, and when you feel a vacuum in your thoughts, it is because your mind needs to rest. There is no schedule on which you and your brother are required to work other than the mandates that you are placing on yourselves. I ask that you do not put your work for Jesus in such constraints. Be at peace knowing the contributions you have made. Whatever you compose and share in the future in terms of memoirs and other reflections are a simple way to place your life and future in a frame of reference that will give impulse and energy to those who read and hear them. What I am suggesting is that the evangelizing that you have embedded in your prior works is ample. You may now think and write more reflectively as a means of providing the world spiritual support. Your brother was correct when he said that it is difficult to write about the realities of the world in laudable terms when 99% of what you see and hear looks like the distraction and destruction of the devil. You are sensing the difficulty through your experiences that many priests and homilists have in keeping a positive tone to their messages. Think about most every homily that the Popes in Rome have given through the ages. They have been consistently clarifying the Truth or admonishing someone because others tend to ignore what is actually occurring. It is the responsibility of Christian evangelists to tell humanity without being judgmental what God has done and what He is apt to do, what the earthly world looks like compared to the promises of Heaven, and how human beings should conduct themselves in contrast to the actual behavior of men. I know that there is little felicity in these things. Look at My messages over the past generations and centuries. Indeed, think about them. Did I come into the exiled world to tell humanity that everything is fine? Did I appear at Fatima and Lourdes to reveal that God is pleased? I came bearing the news that there will be certain consequences if men and women do nothing to reverse the terrible course of human deportment. This does not imply that you must relate everything in this same tone. I have given you messages that are clearly different. I have spoken rarely about what parts of the Earth will be set afire by the vengeance of the Father, and which will ultimately be spared. I have come to you and your brother as the Queen of Love and the Morning Star Over America because I knew that you would share My new hope. I knew that you had optimistic hearts that would not concede to the sarcasm of the world. This is an extremely difficult task, but I know that you are doing well. All the impulses and worldly opinions that you are hearing come from origins that do not pray for peace in your country or elsewhere around the globe. It is easy for you and your brother to be impacted by this misery, and I am asking you to continue to resist. Americans everywhere take life too seriously because they are often trying to collect their wealth, uplift themselves in stature over their neighbors, compete for the right to boast about their talents and possessions, and become isolated from places where they might otherwise do the most good for the poor.

  My Special son, I ask the same questions as you. How many more holy relics and doctrines will be desecrated and impugned? How much more evil will be allowed to prosper? This is the reason I am still speaking to seers and hearers around the globe. All is not lost; there is still time, it is not as bad as you assume. Hence, we have the opportunity to access the holiness of indifferent people and turn them against their own lack of initiative. Remember that it has been said that evil people are the scourge of the Earth, but those who remain indifferent are only mild degrees better. Thank you for everything you are doing to help your brother in every way, in giving him food and shelter, being his companion, assisting in the completion of his studies, and listening to his concerns about life. It is a gift to God and the world that you are making so many sacrifices toward the Triumph of My Immaculate Heart. It is imperative that you see beyond the difficulties you face and realize that your victory has already been won. Life is one great process of turning the heads of humanity in the direction of the Cross from which this victory comes. We have shared today another pleasant message about peace and hope. It is My desire that all for whom we pray will live as confidently as you and your brother. Please pray for all mothers who are heavy with children, that they will allow their babies in their wombs to be born into this world."

Saturday, May 19, 2012
2:28 p.m.

Mother and Son, Heart to Heart
Ref. – Message January 25, 2009

"Now, I return to the placidness of this sacred home where you occupy the world for the conversion of lost sinners. My little sons, the shrine about which I speak is always within you. The role of messenger and seer goes where you go; it remains with you because it is your hearts that live for Jesus. It is similar to a vocation because the identity of messenger is a bestowing of grace upon you, and it is always in you. I have told you on many occasions that your home is a sacred place, but only because you continue to live here. I ask that you welcome My words today about one of the conversations that Jesus and I had when He was in His adolescence about His Kingship among the peoples, about His conveyance of approval upon those who were loyal to Him, and about what everything He was born to accomplish was with Him upon His conception in My Womb. I am giving this message as another installment of My January 25, 2009 promise to tell you what our lives were like in those days before His ministry began. You first must realize that as Jesus' Mother, I was also His disciple. Jesus belonged to Me in Body and Spirit, and I belonged to Him in all ways a person can be lent. The role of Motherhood for Me was accorded by God in ways more sacred than others because I was born without sin. My Holy Wisdom came from within. My eternal perfection was bestowed upon Me from the beginning. I tell you this so you will realize that Jesus knew Me the way the Church teaches to this day. Imagine the truth that Jesus on Earth was equally the Father, and He was the Son of the Father and Son of the Virgin. He was not given to Me like someone might claim an infant whose role in the world is unknown. We understood His mission. I reminded Him often of the Divine Mercy as He was learning to walk. I watched in awe at this Child-God. It was not unlike knowing in advance that a young foal just rising to its feet was none other than the great Secretariat. I had immense respect for what these feet would do, where they would travel, the ground they would bless, and the wounds they would suffer. I spoke to Jesus the little Christ, and He looked upon Me with supernal affection for admiring Him so. Yes, we spoke about the centuries to come. We foresaw all the wars and births, all the great cities and nations to be built, the artifacts and spaceships. We knew about discoveries in the arts, sciences and medicine. And, through everything we were advantaged to foresee, we prayed that the world would not forget the integration of love into daily human life. We asked Heaven to invoke a special blessing on the pure and virgin. What you have seen during your lifetimes and through the record of history does not mean that our prayers were not answered, but that they were ratified. God chose to protect untold numbers of sinners through the faith and charities of the Roman Catholic Church. He laid in the hands of the Popes the right to pronounce what should be done in the east and west and north and south for the Glory of His Kingdom and the Covenant of His Son. Heaven has handed to humanity through My miraculous messages a map to the Holy Gospel that cannot be discovered anywhere else. It is through My advocacy that the world has come to see its own error and to turn to the Divine Mercy of My Son. And, when Jesus and I spoke of these things in ancient days, we were reminded of the Love of God that is universally and irrevocably present in this world and the next. We were proof – we were God's witnesses! And, we remain together Heart-to-Heart so all in the world can stand upon us as if we were two feet. We had in those early years sorrowful thoughts about the suffering of men, and yet we were joyful about the victories they would eventually know. The fear that the Church would in any way be brought down or dissolved never crossed our minds because the Church is eternal. You have the sacred presence of Jesus here in this life both now and forever. Jesus has been enshrined in your hearts. He has commissioned you to prosper and worship the Kingdom of God. This is the reason that I knew these things, that the Church was born of Me; the Head of the Church was My sinless Child, the Holy Spirit was conceived in Me, the Glory of the Father was imbedded there too, and the redemption of the entire human race had found its origin within My Most Immaculate Womb. This means that the Will of God took refuge in Me. Within My Womb, the Wisdom of Truth was given venue to take on the sins of the world and expunge them forever.

Let Me say again – Jesus knew these things the moment He was begotten and before His Spirit and Body were placed inside Me. This is the reason He was begotten, not made. Jesus knew everything I have told you because His soul was inspired by the capacity of My love to touch Him in the way of no other creature. We became the fore and aft of the Great Ship Redemption. We gave honor and respect to each other, and we talked about the Sacred Mysteries to be fulfilled for which both of us had to prepare. And, when we placed these thoughts before the backdrop of the redemption of lost humanity, we were prone to hear the thunder of reconciliation breaking overhead. It was not a fearsome thunder, but the awesome sound of confession from the Church. It was as though there were a thousand Clydesdales stampeding across our roof, ones that were on a mission, ones that were heading-up the battalions of warriors who were fighting for the Cross. Their presence was in advance of the great Saints of the Resurrection and the Archangels that hovered above them. They foreshadowed a prescience on the Earth that the New Covenant had arrived, and with this would come the New World too. Jesus and I heard these clapping hooves and thought about the future ages into which they would eventually march. They were bearing years, decades and generations of Providence that would bequeath to each new century the awareness of men that this world is not their final resting place. Jesus would refer to their manes flapping in the winds as we thought about the resplendent peace they would bring to all who believed in Him. 'Mother, it is through you and I that all we are seeing and everything yet to come will be fulfilled.' These are among the reflections and observations of the adolescent Son of Man. And, I would tell Him that this was true because we were one in the purpose of human Salvation. It was upon these conversations that I reflected during the crucial moments of Jesus' life, during His ministry, and when His time had come to suffer and die. I once told you that when the sun set on Good Friday, My Heart went with it. This does not mean that My Immaculate Heart was any less with humanity. Just as I am today in Heaven and on Earth, I was on Earth and in Heaven that day as well. Unlike mortal sinners, I could see the intentions of God unfolding before My eyes. I knew that nothing in Creation or beyond it would ever drive a wedge between My Immaculate Heart and the Most Sacred Heart of Jesus. No sorrows would erase our compassion for the world; no swords would drive us back, no thoughts of suffering would steal our joy of knowing that our lives and legacies would never be in vain. These are the thoughts that I will leave you with today, My children, and there will be many more in the months to come. My Special one, I ask that you and your brother place your lives and impressions in the context of Jesus' life and Crucifixion. Remember what He said about forgiveness and having the wisdom to know when to strike and when to relent. His Holy Sacrifice is within you to give you peace. I ask you to never forget about what I have said about poise and self-control, about retaining your stature when others try to tear you down. You are children of the Mother of God! Think about all the blessings this brings and the effects it has on the exiled world. You have gained through Me vision and knowledge, foresight, courage, spiritual acumen, charity, gentleness and perseverance. You are children of the Blessed Virgin Mary! If anyone asks who you are, tell them that this is what I said."

Sunday, May 27, 2012
2:38 p.m.

The Difference between Conception and Construction

"Here we have assembled in prayer, in dedication to the Kingdom of Love from where I come, in honor of Jesus' wholesome life and Sorrowful Crucifixion, and in triumph because humanity has been raised by His Resurrection. My dear sons, it is not that the world will not be redeemed that I have come speaking to you, but precisely because it has already been redeemed that I come to pray with you. If you think of the kindling of spirits kept warm by the fires of light coming from within and without, you will recognize that there is awesome Providence in everything I have said. There are timely miracles in everything you believe, and there is rest and satisfaction in your consecration to the Gospel through which souls are converted. You see at the opening of My words a dichotomy between conception and construction because it is amidst the artwork of Creation that the sharing of love is formed. Someone's early and final actions are products of the conception of his reflections, divine and otherwise; and what he makes of these reflections is the construction of his life's work and his legacy before men. This leads to the prospect that many conceptions have never come into being because their foundations were never laid. This is the case for those who have yet to turn their hearts to Jesus. There are good people around the world, but this does not mean that they are constructing goodness. Some see idle indifference and the lack of evil as a seed of goodness, but you learned fifteen years ago that goodness must be an active manifestation. All human goodness has been conceived by the Father, but some earthly 'good' is the byproduct of the absence of malevolence. This is the reason Jesus calls His disciples to commitment, to active participation in propagating His Paradisial Kingdom. You have been told that faith must be accompanied by good works, and the opposite is also true. Good works absent faith are only one-dimensional; they are the reaction of simple people to complex problems that require far more depth and spiritual function. This is the reason you are seeing such opposition against the Roman Catholic Church and dissension within its ranks. If a person does not fight for the preservation of unborn life, but this same person feeds the poor, he is simply doing good acts. Righteousness on the other hand must be transcending and farseeing in that the Will of God must shape the conscience of the believer. This is the conception that I am describing. Whatever constructs are born of this beginning are evidence of the conception of the human heart, inspired by the Divine Love of God. Men build airplanes and skyscrapers not to glorify or advance the Kingdom of God, although these things can be utilized to do so. The glorification about which I am speaking rests in the conception, in the blueprints and architectures that begin in the heart and soul. This has been the thesis of My Medjugorje messages since they began in June 1981. There are millions of pilgrims who still do not understand.

It is possible that conceiving something and constructing it can occur simultaneously. Here, we have the essence of prayer from the heart. If there is no prayer from the heart, there can be no construction because the words are ill-conceived; they are hollow and meaningless. I have just given you the sub-thesis of My Medjugorje messages. There are many reasons that My children do not conform to what I have taught there in the past 31 years. It is mostly that they are taken in by all the commotion. They become enthralled in the spectacle that has overcome My Marian shrine because they are unaware of the sacrifices to which they are called. It is not just a place to take a vacation. The point I am making is that there are thousands of 'little' Medjugorjes all around the world, and this is why I have been telling My seers and all who believe in the messages to conceive compliance with My messages inside their hearts, and they will constructively live them out. I am providing the conception, but it is My children who must build on them to advance the Kingdom of Salvation about which I am speaking. You have heard a simple message from Me two days ago in Medjugorje because I do not want My words to overwhelm the simplicity of what I have told you today. I see as many cameras there as Rosaries. While it is not wrong to procure images of this holy village, some pilgrims are prone to return home and resume their old lives being absorbed in the pictures instead of taking up their Rosaries. I indeed bless all the pictures that are taken in Medjugorje, and I bless even more fervently the petitions of the pilgrims who pray there and at home upon their return. The difference in the two is that the photographs may be iconic in nature, but the prayers are the life-changing elements that humanity needs to convert. It is the same when you see the phenomenon of statues shedding blood and tears. The prayers of the faithful are the conception of these signs that God is listening, that He has built His Kingdom on their foundation of faith. This is the construction of the stairs that will pave the way for millions to climb out of the dungeons of sin and despair. My dear children, I know that the two of you understand what I am saying, but it is like a foreign language to those who see God as separate from their inner-being. The truth is, the Holy Spirit must be allowed to assimilate their lives into the Will of God, and it is on His behalf that humanity must act. It is not for My children to live, but for Jesus to live in you.

    My Special son, I have happily wept seeing your wondrous work on your books as you are forging another medium for the world to read and hear My messages. I am so proud of you and comforted by you. I admire you as you are living the brilliance of the Saints and Martyrs. And even in this, you take the time to read your brother's homework so there will be no errors. You pray keenly and divinely in the likeness of the holiest Popes. You share your knowledge with anyone who asks. You are charitable to the poor and unfortunate. You take care of your brother as well as Jesus, Himself. Where can My words travel that can describe the ultimate perfection by which you live? Your thoughts and actions are the prayers that are inducing Jesus to offer His Divine Mercy to the wicked. And, I must say that your brother is trying to work as hard as he can on what we have together asked him to do, even as he is very tired from going to school. You have heard him speak of the hideous expectations that professors require and the controversial subjects he is asked to address. They are guilty of issuing so many contradictory requirements that your brother often does not know which way to turn. This will be the way of it when he meets on Tuesday with the 'doctors' of philosophy. Please do not worry; he can handle them with ease. They lack his poise and confidence; they are unaware of his stature before the heavens and his ability to avoid being ensnared by their contrivances. The summer has come and you and your brother must be sure to avoid situations where you might be adversely affected by the heat and humidity. All in all, things are going well for both of you. I know that you and your brother pray for your country and the vice and animosity in which it is entangled. As Patroness of the Americas, imagine what I feel when I see such things as that which your Bishop addressed in his episcopal column last week. I am proud of you for staying the course and not surrendering your desire to complement what I have come into the world to do. Thank you for responding to My call. I will speak to you again at the opening of the month of the Sacred Heart of Jesus."

Saturday, June 2, 2012
2:51 p.m.

"Dear Lord Jesus, place within the circumference of your care all who are broken and alone, the outcast and ostracized, those castigated for teaching your Word, and the millions who are in their last agony in reparation for the sins of the unconverted. We hold in our hearts the grace of your Crucifixion through which all human endeavors are sanctified. The restitution owed for the transgressions of men has been paid by you, and we are liberated from the culpability of Adam by our imitation of your love. Give us the fleetfootedness to shine your torchlight into the darkness, and make of us whatever glorifies your holy name. We ask this through Christ our Lord. Amen."

William L. Roth

"Amen. May all we pray for in the name of Jesus come to pass for humanity in abundance, especially that love in the way of redemption be shared worldwide without end, throughout time and into eternity. My little sons, how can I begin on this day to reflect about what you mean to Me? It is surely to convert lost sinners and strengthen the spirit of the Church that I came to you long ago, but mostly to be with you in voice, figure and example so you can live peacefully as Jesus' image on Earth. My rejoicing takes many forms for the fruits of your hearts, and My Immaculate Heart takes particular comfort in knowing that you raise such prayers as your invocation this afternoon to Jesus and the Father in Heaven from the center of your hearts. Indeed, My messages have been informative and have accorded you the opportunity of attaining new insights about the ways of God. You have learned that Jesus is a merciful King who summons respect from the world and requires charity and humility from those who serve His Kingdom. You have been told multiple times that Jesus became Man not to be served, but to serve the poor, disheartened, the rejected, the ill and weak, and those who are searching for the spiritual conscience that will focus their eyes on Heaven. Jesus came to serve. Is this what kings do? It certainly is true of benevolent ones. We spoke last week about the Holy Spirit coming into the world with power, and we refer today to the Most Blessed Trinity that is empowered by the Lord's Spirit to make Creation like Heaven itself. We also have discussed the fact that this is more a process than an event. There are monumental milestones and crucial occasions during this process, but the 'event' is the culmination of all the hours, alms, prayers, blessings and transitions that man makes on the journey of cultivating and harvesting this earthly exile in preparation for the conclusion of the ages. I remind all to whom I speak that this is not a conclusion in the way that such events are known to ordinary men. The conclusion spoken about in the Gospels is one that simultaneously commences the resurrection of the dead and the grand reorientation of all living things into the Glory to which the righteous are already bound. We cannot overstate now or during any epoch what this means for the disciples of God.

It is to address the properties and elements of this transition that I first came into the world centuries ago beyond My Assumption so that My children would know Me as Mother. I have been telling My children for centuries to be prepared. And, the most casual observers and even the keen ones have asked, 'prepared for what?' It is the 'what' that I have spoken about more than the 'when.' 'What' must be the reason good men breathe, the reason they rise in the morning and toil beneath the shining sun. It must be the reason they study to comprehend the willingness of their forebears to comply with what Jesus taught. And, it is for this 'what' that so many have died, have laid-down their lives as Saints and Martyrs, have sacrificed their years so selflessly that others might share in the dignity afforded them from the Cross. Even My usage of 'what' is lacking to describe the efficacy of these gifts and challenges because the Salvation of man cannot be reduced to a single term. Two words suffice the miracles better – Crucifixion and Resurrection. It is said that Jesus shall come to judge the living and the dead. Judgement is therefore the proper action subsequent to the Sacred Mysteries on which the deliverance of men has been stationed. All beatific reason is fashioned upon what Jesus thinks about those who profess to believe in Him. Hence, the Kingdom of Glory becomes fuller in the action of Judgement. The Salvation of man is fulfilled in this Judgement. This is the point I am making. The Crucifixion of Jesus capitalizes the purpose of the Judgement of the human soul because God said to humanity on Good Friday that unless all who wish to see His Glorious Face accept this Sacrifice, this Judgement shall not come with joy. It is not that humanity is crucified in the flesh that they are redeemed, but that the soul must be sanctified so the Will of the Father can prevail. This is the bleeding of the world that you do not see with the physical eye. I speak about worldly prophets and principals who have wisely served the ages with words and testaments that have alleviated suffering and averted wars. These worthy people have tried their best to enlighten the lost in the midst of tremendous opposition. Put plainly, they have all become Saints, but so have those who made mistakes because of the temptations of the devil. They fell and rose up once more while promising to never fall again, though some did. The latter of these regained their spiritual composure and their stature in Jesus because they asked again and again for absolution. It is those who never ask that remain in the cold. It is the ones who cannot bring themselves to invoke the forgiveness of the King who go on to die languishing deaths of guilt and self-pity.

My dear little sons, you speak about the conclusion of the ages with accuracy, but you must focus your attention on what happens before that. This you are doing well. It seems a paradox to keep your eyes trained on the Glory in the offing and the particulars of what life brings you every day. You escape this paradox by not worrying when Jesus will bring Justice to the wretched, but by what means He will do it. Instant annihilation is much too benign for them. Why? Because they must know well in advance of their downfall what they did wrong. They must see with their own eyes what depravation they heaped upon others, what suffering they have caused, what lacking they have imposed. They must be parched and stood next to the quenching spring without opportunity to satisfy their thirst. They must be deprived of food for days and weeks and be drawn to the aromas of the Final Banquet, knowing that these finest tastes will never touch their palates. They must be shown what it is like to walk in the darkness amid mine shafts galore with wind gusts breaking at their feet. They must touch fire and ice with hands that cannot tell the difference. They are to be exposed to all the promises they can imagine, only to discover that all of them are in vain. Thus, you see the secular void in pain, misery and torment, in appalling indifference, in ignorance and unlordly, defiling pride. Why? Because the story will not be complete until the final scene has played. The rains cannot cleanse what lies below them until the world hears the final splash. A saber is not a saber until it is removed from its sheath. Arrows cannot fly forever. Boulders cannot roll downhill beyond their aptness to descend. Starlings cannot remain aloft without the approval of their God. My dear sons, there is Providence in all these things. There is mastery and mystery, too. Let us live forward on Earth and in Heaven, watching and praying for the 'what' that you mentioned in your opening prayer today. It is all forever good; it is providential and profoundly cultivating – world without end indeed!"

Sunday, June 10, 2012
9:21 a.m.

The Difference between Faith and Belief

"My endearing little children, I come to this exquisite place to bring you My sacred love in the way of the Father and the Son. My Special one, please allow your brother to retrieve the glass candle stand from the basement. Thank you. Now, please put the blue candle to your right on the candle stand. It is on the second shelf of the table. Thank you. Now, please light it. Thank you. Let us light this candle going into the future, and new candles when this one expires. I come today to speak about the reason we have done this. My message today will have many mystical overtones that enhance the reasons that you have been given faith by God. This is, in fact, the first point. Faith is a gift from the Father. Belief is something that is decided by someone who chooses to accept and exercise that faith. Belief is a product and manifestation of human volition. Faith is the communion of the Holy Spirit and the hearts of humankind. Belief is the cognitive acceptance of faith, and it is this cognition based on faith that translates spiritual love into recognizable action.

People with faith are eligible to tell the world that what they believe has been validated by God. On the other hand, people who say that they believe in God but who do not practice faith, as faith is defined in the Holy Gospel and the Catholic Catechism, are liars and hypocrites. This describes Roman Catholic politicians who accept abortion as legitimate public policy, for example. Anyone who holds office of public or private domain that exemplifies or wields power over those who are learning about personal and public morality has the responsibility to speak and act according to their faith, not just what they 'believe' about their faith. The teachings of the Church cannot be misinterpreted to advance one's standing in the public sphere or improve others' perception about what kind of person he is. Trusting in God and serving His Kingdom is not about stature, it is about measure. The difference in stature and measure is that the focus of stature is on the person, and the focus of measure is on the device being used to measure. Hence, it is not about what 'I' have done, but what others are able to see by what you have said or shown them. Therefore, the second contrast between faith and belief is that faith always extends outward by extolling the teaching instead of the person providing the lesson. The obvious exception is that Jesus is the lesson and the teacher, and equal emphasis should be placed on the Holy Gospel and the Second Person of the Most Blessed Trinity whose life and teachings are celebrated there. Indeed, this second contrast delineates the difference between faith and belief in that those who teach the Gospel do not proclaim the text of their speech and writings to be of their own making, but from origins garnered throughout the history of Messianic human redemption. A third distinction between faith and belief is that faith is timeless and immutable. The faith you have inherited is the same faith that was given to the Apostles by Jesus and every disciple who has prayed for that faith since the beginning of the Church. Beliefs, on the other hand, are amendable. Beliefs can evolve over time, and they often do. Beliefs are subject to life conditions and the view of the world of the people who practice their beliefs. Faith is consequential to the imminent conclusion of the material world, but beliefs will never escape the world's confines. Faith is the father of mystical courage; beliefs and the children of that courage spread into new groups and societies to coopt listeners and seers to that original Faith. Faith is the mission; beliefs are the objectives employed to accomplish the mission. Faith is the mountain, the base of all immortal things, and beliefs are the sounding board for sharing that faith with those with different beliefs. There is only one true, completed Faith in Creation, and that is the Gospel of the New Covenant, divinely secured in the bosom of the Roman Catholic Church. All other orientations are false beliefs that have no bearing on the future of humanity or how individual believers can affect the Will of God to amend the course of history. Jesus Christ is the Master of Faith and the King of all who believe in Him. This indicates the reciprocity between God and man, between Heaven and the human heart. Faith and belief are inseparable only in the context of Jesus Christ.

My Special one, I am providing sufficient evidence that faith and belief are topics worthy of discussion in your public speeches and writings. *"Yes, I like it."* Therefore, when someone approaches you and says that they do not have to believe what you tell them about My messages, or even the teachings of the Church for that matter, you can draw the distinction that you are speaking from your God-given faith, and they are denying what you are saying based on their callous indifference. Those who 'believe' other than what the Church teaches are denying their own eternity. Like children, they refuse to eat the nourishment that will sustain their spiritual lives, and they will die an unprovided death and be lost into the abyss for the ages long hereafter. If they would feed on faith instead of their own beliefs, they would grow, learn, prosper and prevail beyond the end of the world without need of anything more. Faith is a giant redwood tree that stands over and shades them. Faith is the lighthouse that guides them to the shore. Belief is that the giant redwood has characteristics that are inexplicable to them, while faith informs them that the Father put it there. Faith is the internal framework of moral conscience that comes from the Wisdom of Heaven; belief is doing something only because it seems like the right thing to do, or that their forbears did it that way, or because they will be the first to do something in the way of no one else. Faith is the flag pole, belief is the flag. The flag will be nothing more than a rag on the ground without the pole. The pole is the often overlooked foundation that provides elevation and awareness to the flag. The pole is the standard to which the belief is tethered that gives definition to its existence. Flags are meant to be on poles. You can see the broad implications of this discussion everywhere you look. 'I have faith that the car will not quit, so I believe I will drive it on a 1,000 mile trip.' Faith is the furnishing of the fires of conviction, and beliefs are consumed by that faith to make one's actions come true. It is endless, on and on. The Lord God responds to whatever you offer in His name. Faith tells us that He sees the candle you just lit. Belief says that He will be equally looking at it through your eyes. All the parameters of existence and dimension are transcended by the distinction between faith and belief. Now, I will give you the most important reason that I have discussed this today. The secular world and non-Christians see Messianic Salvation as though it were a belief instead of the Universal Faith. This is one of the greatest stumbling blocks for those who are still waiting for great signs from God before accepting what the Scriptures teach. They are looking for something more believable instead. This is what has led to the whole gamut of detractors of the Church and its enemies who have tried for twenty centuries to bring the Church down. The Catholic Church cannot be felled; it is a manifest impossibility. No man or group of humanity has the power to bring extinction to the Apostolic Church. It is not only like trying to put out a burning skyscraper with a thimble of water, there is not even any water to be found. The roots of the Catholic Church are located at the feet of the Throne of God. Mortal men cannot reach them. Men on Earth are not even as large as ants beneath the soil. They cannot singly ascribe for themselves even a self-identity or recognize themselves as self-evident creatures alongside the Glory of the Roman Catholic Church. I am speaking about a Church of Faith that 'believes' in what it is doing. This is the Kingship belief that is fed by the Faith of One God, given to those who accept Him. The Roman Catholic Church is embedded in the foundation of the whole created universe, and it is upon Saint Peter that the Church has been stationed. No organic or inorganic creation has the power to deny the existence, propagation, progress or eternal consistency of the Roman Catholic Church.

The Catholic Church is more crucial to the survival of man than all the aspects of nature and the world combined. It is clear that this is the Faith to which wise men turn during their waking hours. It is food for the soul that keeps its future in Heaven from dying. The Catholic Church is the origin of the whole world's elegance and eloquence, its majesty and authenticity. The Church is the glittering sequine in all the heavens in which the planet Earth is only a subpart. God sees the Roman Catholic Church suspended in space before He sees the world. God sees righteousness brought forth in faithful people before He sees the plight of the poor! Look around and you will see ample evidence of this. Indeed, God sees the faith you practice in everything you do for Me, for the Church on Earth, for your brothers and sisters, and even your accidental blessings of other men in the same way you might inspect a diamond the size of the Moon. Thus, I have come today to give you an introduction to what you have already learned about the providential majesty of the Roman Catholic Church. Why? Because you have an understanding between the faith of Jesus' disciples and the believers who stray in other ways. It is true that Christian faith and believing in that faith are united in one place. However, belief without Christian faith has no place. It is irrelevant and inconsequential. Faith has made all the difference in your life with your brother. It is the reason you have shared your sacrifice. It is the genesis of all your books. Faith is the seed of your growth in wisdom and the things of perfection, and you have done well; you have followed the Light and inhaled the scent of Salvation from whence you were a young child. My Special son, I hope you have enjoyed what I came to tell you today. *"Could you explain to me how someone's conscience fits into the discussion when people say that they are allowed to follow their conscience?"* Indeed, if their conscience is not based on the Gospel and the teachings of the Church, they have no conscience. They are calling on a resource that is not truly there. If they say that they are following their conscience by committing to something that is against the teachings of Jesus Christ, they are actually channeling their own will, not the Will of God. It is this simple. *"And, their will can be in the possession of the Antichrist who will dictate it?"* My Special son, if someone believes in or practices or teaches something contrary to the Kingdom of God, they are already under the influence of the Antichrist. That was a very good question. Are there any more? *"No, thank you."* I am deeply touched and consoled by your new song about the willow's cry. Congratulations on such a beautiful aesthetic work! *"Thank you."* Let us remember the prayers of the faithful to Jesus' Sacred Heart in this holy month dedicated to Him."

Saturday, June 16, 2012
2:40 p.m.

The Personification of Beatific Love

"My dear little sons, I have been waiting the whole of human history to give you this message today. I have been sent by the God of our fathers to invoke His Name through the endless power of the Holy Spirit. Yes. Today I have come to speak about the personification of beatific love. This means that the Love of God can live in the hearts and minds of earthly sinners. I am not speaking about sinners who perpetually break the rules and commit the worst sins of impurity and blasphemy against His Holy Word. I am telling you about people who are living on Earth that are prone to sin, but who do not fall to temptation, and who avoid the occasion of sin. When Jesus told the Apostles and disciples that each one should be perfect as He is perfect, He was speaking to those whom He recognized as sinners. This made them unlike Himself who was incapable of sin. This is the same thing as a diamond telling a rock to shine with facets as awesome as its own. This means that what the Father determines to be perfection is what defines the perfection of man. If heretics refuse to repent and are ultimately slain in the end by the righteous at the command of God, it is a perfect act. Saint Joan of Arc, too, was a sacrificial witness to the perfect righteousness of God. Begetting children is a perfect act. Rebuking one's enemies and forging peace pacts are perfect acts of beatific love. The personification of this love is what the enlightenment of the spiritual conscience is about. There does not have to be context and relevance for beatific love to live in the material world because it is irrevocably capable of existing on its own, for its own reward, for its own glory. Then, there is the man, any human or any soul who is given to the Truth. There exists both inside and outside of time the essence of 'man' that makes him simultaneous. I am saying that it makes him something that describes something else. In this, man is material and the eloquence of material, flesh that lives-out the prudence of the Father's Will in every possible way. We have seen and spoken about these men and women many times through the years. They are called Saints! My little sons, you have reached this personification of beatific love because you have internalized the meaning and excellence of redemptive sacrifice. The waves and echoes of your perfection ripple through time in ways that you cannot yet see. In the overall image of what human beings are meant to be and supposed to accomplish, you have forged a discernable pattern of that perfection. Why am I telling you this? Because you must begin to see yourselves as venerable 'beings' in the eyes of God which will help you stop taking seriously what cold-hearted sinners think about you. Worldly beings and creatures are selfish; they are stubborn in their error, they are consumed by pride, and they are unwilling to share the pardon and forgiveness that they require from those they offend. Therefore, when we speak about the personification of beatific love, we include the excellence about which I speak, about which you have read in the Sacred Scriptures and spoken of yourselves. Do you remember some of the strains? 'If there is any excellence.' This is a question posed in the Word of the Lord. The answer is that there is indeed excellence. It is there because of all the reasons I have outlined so far today, and for more and better reasons than these. There is excellence because the Father has placed in your hands the tools to create divine excellence in ways that have not yet been defined by lexicons or lines of purpose. Excellence, like beatific love, is whatever the Father says makes His Kingdom complete. When He says that people shine, He is not speaking about light reflecting off their skin. He refers to the awesome softness of the spirit and kindness of heart that is of old, tendered to humanity by the Martyrs who laid down their lives, by the Saints who served and suffered, by the children of those who knew only to raise children as their means of glorifying His Kingdom on Earth. Shining implies that there is some essential light that reflects from the surface of these souls. The emphasis of life, the determination to satisfy righteous curiosity, the drive to discover the Teacher of Salvation – all of these are facets from which this essential light is reflected and repeated. When good men speak highly of creatures for whom the Lord has died, they are telling of the eternal greatness that has captivated the world throughout all times and places. I have said that Jesus died to save good men and those prone to commit evil acts. It is your commission to tell the good ones that they cannot live in silence just because their eternal reward is imminent. There is such thing as retrofitting the human spirit with the conscience of the Gospel, and this is what sharing the Word of God is all about. It is indeed about feeding the poor and tending to the needs of those who are lacking, but it is even more about telling these souls the reasons why. In this way, saying 'thank you' also means saying 'I love you.' And, it means that saying 'you are welcome' also means saying 'I love you.' Fashioning for human fate a future of victory gives living beings a purpose for rising in the morning beneath the guiding hand of God. If you see these things in other people, you are seeing wise innocence. You are seeing mature beginnings in little hearts that are too tender to hate. This is what makes people like your nephews see you as contributors to the conversion and salvation of lost sinners. There are millions of nephews and nieces around the globe. I see them committing to tremendous goals that resound the power and innocence of the adolescent Christ. I have witnessed their kindness and bravery in single swipes of genius. They are here and all around, and they will make a difference in the world before their mortal years are through.

    I also have said that there is a sense of urgency in what I have told you through the years. Your prayers and patience will provide sufficient action and thoroughness to suffice this urgency. If the Son of Man does not return before you are taken to Heaven, please know that you and your brother have established a record to be followed by the Faith-Church until He does. You have built a sky-scraping castle here on the ground where your forbears have tread and your successors will walk. You have painted pictures of beatific love across the skies where the Morning Star is poised, night and day, through good times and bad, through floods and droughts, through the wailing of men and their ecstatic joy. This is the reason people like your little nephew is reaching-out on his own, far advanced of his years, to conquer material things so he will be prepared to be victorious in the spiritual realms. They are like you, My Special son, in that they will never forget the sweet taste of victory through the bitterness of the years. (*There was a recent news item where a school administrator thought it was appropriate to assail a class of graduating students during their commencement ceremony, telling them they were nobody special, because he believed they had already been coddled too much and the world would not treat them as such.*) By all means, if I were standing before that class of graduating children, I would never have told them that they are not special. I would have said that inside each of you lives the heart of a lion that is calling-out to be fed. I would say that your commencement apparel becomes you. It is fitting that you are decked in dignity for the lessons you have learned, for fighting the good fight, for finishing the race. I would tell them that you are special because you are the legitimate heirs of a God-given Truth that must be shared in all ways and to all nations. Speaking in first person, I would say that you have inside you seeds that were planted there not the first day you attended school, but the very moment you inherited the breath of life. You have lives that will be lived-out in the world and before a humanity that is broken, and you must help good men fix it. You must take all the wisdom that you have gleaned from your experiences here and build on it; make humongous righteous mountains out of simple 'good will' mole hills. You must change the world and the destiny of humanity! You must chart the course by which your own children will travel the worthy path of human achievement, if that achievement makes the world a better place. You must not agree with other men just for the sake of harmony, but you must foster harmony when that agreement upholds the principles of Truth. You must blaze new trails and pore-over the workings of your predecessors to blend in your own lives a fitting way of life that takes all with whom you work toward the horizon beyond which your reward and redemption lies. You must stare into the sun with eyes peeled, and emit this same light into the night with the bequeathal you have gained. Yes, My little sons, I would tell them that the personification of beatific love is the most important mission they will ever attempt because it is all about the renewal of the self. It is about identifying with the same genius that created the universe and the prodigies that replicated it for the advancement of human excellence. These are not just hollow words; they are words that the material world seems too busy to hear. These are sentiments that will make a difference in who succeeds and who does not. 'Yes' is the answer to the question you are thinking. I will in fact before the end of time appear to all My children simultaneously to tell them that My Incarnate Son will presently return. I will introduce Him as more than the miracle worker whom they have been told about in writing and the spoken word. I will remind them that their victories in Him are the only true ones that matter. I will share with them the same sense of anticipation by which we lived on Holy Saturday and in anticipation of Pentecost. Salvation history has proved that God can only speak the Truth. The Truth is this – Christ Jesus is waiting, all right. He is poised and prepared for entrance into His earthly Kingdom with Justice and Judgement. Please, if you are standing in the Light of the Crucifixion, do not be afraid! Woe to them, however, if they cower in the shadows. The Second Coming of Jesus Christ will be like a massive flood that will flush-out all peoples everywhere, the good and bad, the timid and courageous, the meek and mighty. This return of the King will be about making moral goodness the reason for the creation of man. It will be about giving valor to the timid and preparedness for the meek. My Special son, I have more to say in the future about this matter, about the personification of beatific love. *"Thank you, Mama."* I only desire for you to remember how awesome you are to Me and in the presence of God. I am with you in all the suffering you endure. I ask that you ignore what others say about you. Refer again to the quote of Saint Fulton Sheen from your bedroom dresser."

"Jealousy is the tribute that mediocrity pays to genius."
Archbishop Fulton J. Sheen

Sunday, June 24, 2012
1:27 p.m.

Medjugorje: Making life an image instead of a blur.
Part One

"These are the years hence, My little sons, that Jesus spoke about while walking the Earth Incarnate, and these are the ages that have begotten the arrival of the vast cultivation of His vineyard. I ask that you remember every day why you were called to Medjugorje because it is My messages that you are living. You are sustained by the graces that you receive week to week and month after month here in the United States. You have considered what this means for the history of the world. All the acts of the Church and decisions of the Hierarchy are being placed into perspective these days, and this is the reason I ask you not to form your conclusions too far in advance. I speak about the measures of conscience by which holy people live so your reflection of these measures can become the stepping stones for your brothers and sisters to travel holier paths. And, from the foundation of the world, I intended to come into your home on this Medjugorje anniversary to speak about maintaining an image of the life you have taken-on in these times. Your mission and objectives are fashioned by whatever you affirm in Jesus' likeness. Yes, you are born in the image and likeness of God, not in the image and likeness of a blur. I have spoken to you about the peaceful parameters that engulf those who are devoted to the Father. This is the way He wants you to live. Your mission is to pursue the prayers in your hearts that open other lives to this same peace. As I have said on many occasions, you are doing this well. You do not need a course correction; you need not alter your direction in any way. This is what 'stay the course' implies. So, what does it mean to distinguish an image from a blur? The image about which I speak relates to the spiritual perfection to which I often refer, but it also includes your own intuitive thoughts and imaginings about how the exiled world should unfold. It is like unfurling a flag for display in honor of a distinguished nation. One does not unfurl a flag like shaking a rug. Revealing the future is a matter based on the conditions of the past and present. Indeed, there are no properties of a 'blur' in this whatsoever. In the early days of 1991, I spoke to you about the concept of motion. We spoke about wisdom coming from the heart shaping the thoughts of the mind. We were revealing a preexisting image of what your

Marian works entail today. There was never any hint of mechanical urgency in what we were doing. There was no rapid race toward a finish line. There was nothing that led you to believe that you must sacrifice your peace or pursue quick results in the way you have lived. You learned from Me that some life pursuits have nothing to do with propagating the Kingdom of Salvation.

When we place these things in reflection of My Medjugorje messages, you see the elementary way that I have spoken to the children there and the millions of pilgrims who have traveled there to pray. Massive numbers of them are still trying to evaluate the fact that I would appear in the world at all, let alone what I might say. This is the reason My Medjugorje messages have been so simple. Their intent has been more a process than an event. Moreover, there have been over thirty years of births and conversions that have occurred since this day in 1981. The mere fact that birth and life comprise a succession has made it necessary for Me to speak to humanity in Medjugorje in periodic and structured installments. The whole idea of a 'blur' arises when anyone inside or outside the Church decides that God's timing is inadequate, that they would not conduct the affairs of His Kingdom the way He does. When the human will and the Divine Will of God are at odds, it is the latter that always prevails. And, this causes the spinning and commotion in the lives of men who are adamant about following their own way of thinking. When mortal men turn on a light switch, a light is supposed to come on. When God the Father turns on a light switch, the light is seen only by those willing to see. My Special son, you said earlier today, just hours before I gave you this message that was fashioned into history at the foundation of the world, that life is sometimes just a blur. This means that you are living in 'accourse' with God. You have preempted your life's events by the attachment of your soul to the Love of God, united at the foundation of Creation. You authenticated your union with Jesus through your Baptism with water by the power of the Holy Spirit. Like millions of others, you did not turn on a light that was not already glowing, you just made it brighter. This is what I have been trying to do for humanity in Medjugorje since June 24, 1981. No one who has traveled there to pray has told Jesus that it was anything other than His Will that should be done. Their lives are measured according to Jesus' life, teachings, admonishments, and by His Passion, Death and Resurrection. The image of human life is clarified in Medjugorje, and the 'blur' is removed. If your brothers and sisters would consider what I have told you today as the reason for their pilgrimages to Medjugorje instead of elevating their self-view of the legitimacy of their faith, the world would be converted by now. I am not saying that these pilgrimages are not meant to evaluate and strengthen one's faith, I am saying that once this has been done, this should be the image to which others are drawn. What happens instead? Most pilgrims return to their previous lives as though their travels to pray at the Saint James Church were just something to do. Rather than seeing their pilgrimage as a life-altering event, they reverse course, they impede the process, and they compartmentalize their renewed inspiration under the 'that's nice' category. Millions have come to the conclusion that there are no real Earth-shattering events to have come from My appearances at Medjugorje, and that there will be none in their lifetime. This is precisely the train of thought that has caused so many to turn away when they ponder what My messages are all about. They refuse to see the image of holiness that the Lord places in their hearts, and they return to the blurry commotion that I have mentioned today. We should reenforce the fact worldwide that this image is not necessarily a snapshot in time. This is not what I mean at all. The image is multi-dimensional, vibrant and breathing; and it bears all the authority and majesty of the Living Will of God in visible and spiritual form. Humanity is on a high-speed train trying to read a billboard alongside the tracks that says 'I Am the Truth and the Life.' But, by the time most people focus on this image, their motion has caused it to become an illegible blur. My Medjugorje messages through the years have been meant to slow them down. This is working to a degree, but not enough to be relevant in the grand scope of human affairs. Not enough people have listened. Too many who have listened have forgotten what they heard. Millions more have allowed what they heard to be drowned-out by their immersion in the secular void. You know that the ramifications of this have been terrible, and the implications of their indifference have brought troubled circumstances in nations everywhere, along with tremendous opposition to the mission of the Church."

Wednesday, July 4, 2012
9:29 a.m.

Medjugorje: Making life an image instead of a blur.
Part Two

"My loving sons, your freedom in the United States allows you to publicly proclaim your faith in God, and your faith in God is what makes your nation free. We have come together again in recognition and celebration of the liberating Gospel that I have been evangelizing throughout the ages because humanity remains in such great need. There are not only wars and massacres, but the gruesome torture of everything that is holy by thugs and nonbelievers. We spoke before about My Medjugorje messages and what they mean for the world. You know that a message is not transmitted until the receiver understands its meaning. There is meaning in My messages not only in Medjugorje and here in your home, but in the expressions of My love that remain unspoken. No one has ever asked Me whether I offer prayers on behalf of humanity to Jesus in audible words. Of course I speak audibly to Jesus, and He responds with equal volume. We pronounce the words of conversion to the world from our lips, and they are heard with ears given to the betterment of all who are exiled. Our words are enlightening and comforting; they are advising and uplifting. My little sons, you also know that My Medjugorje messages are simple. They are spoken, translated and transmitted to people from all different languages and origins because the Word of Truth is universal to all souls. I am again with you today to share My Immaculate Heart because I too wish you to know that you have already spoken in audible words to humanity about their conversion and redemption through the eloquent strains of your books. I have transferred sacred knowledge to the world about Heaven and the Angels and Saints in refrains that have not been heretofore told. I ask that you not compare My messages to you with others on this basis, but My messages to you have the same purpose; they are intended to yield the same result. My Special son, do you remember My prescriptions for the conversion of humanity that I spoke about in Medjugorje? Peace, prayer, penance, fasting, forgiveness, confession and so on. And, this does not just mean fasting from food, but from pleasures and distractions that keep the soul from uniting with the Spirit of the Lord. It is no secret that millions of pilgrims who return home from Medjugorje keep these promises, but millions more do not. They have gone dormant in the awakening they inherited in the Medjugorje hills. And, the reason is the same that causes the people of the United States to ignore the teachings of the Church. There is yet no singly recognized messenger in America to keep humanity focused on the mission of the Church because of the freedom to be relativist and pluralist. You do not live in a theocracy, but a secular cauldron of distractions and illusions.

Do you remember Sister Lucia? She wrote more than a dozen times that My messages to the little children contained one word more than others. One would surmise that the word would be 'prayer,' or perhaps penance or self-denial. However, with great surprise, Sister Lucia said that the word most pronounced in My messages to the children was patience. The word 'patience' implies that something is not yet finished. The crop is not quite ripe for harvest. The fullest light of dawn remains a little more time away. Patience implies that someone somewhere is dragging their feet, even if it seems to be God. You can imagine how many times I have used the word 'patience' in My Medjugorje messages. For 31 years! Let Me tell you the true meaning of patience. There can be no doubt in what I am about to say. Patience in the context of My messages means that I have not yet completed the fullness of My teachings. It means that the Holy Crown of Salvation has been cast and polished, waiting for the Mystical Body of Jesus to be fully united in the Church-Triumphant. Patience means that the whole world and the Heavenly Universe have paused to admire the Glory of this Crown long enough for the timely ending and the final days of the old Earth to arrive. Patience means that there is healing going on. It means that the echo of the first cries of Jesus in the Manger are only now reaching the ears of the last to be born. Patience means that walking through the darkness of mortal life is worth the wait for the visible joy that everyone will see in the Light of Heaven. Patience means that the Second Coming of Jesus Christ will supercede most everything new that is being fashioned on Earth today. All the new trees and old tombstones will be much the way they are when Jesus comes again. And, while you recognize My messages elsewhere around the globe, I do not wish to instill fear in those who hear Me. God the Father and Jesus the Son do not market in fear. They are simply saying that serious circumstances can foster serious consequences. On the other hand, love begets love; holiness begets holiness, and peace begets lasting peace. This is the essence of My Medjugorje messages that have yet to be interpreted by modern theologians in the Church. Many of them are preoccupied in trying to determine whether the Mother of Jesus Christ would even speak to humanity every day for 31 years. They prayed for this miracle, and now they cannot believe that it has come. Such is not the case with you and your brother, with millions more who remain loyal to Me. I owe you a tremendous debt of gratitude for everything you have done for Jesus, for Me and for the conversion of the world. As I keep telling My Medjugorje seers and hearers at the appointed times, there are few days left to wonder what the future might bring. Of course there will be a final battle for souls! Of course there will be wreckage and carnage! The true victors in Jesus would have it no other way. And, even as the Crucifixion has redeemed the whole history and super-history of humankind, God will allow all who have claimed the Blood of His Son to witness His vengeance upon those who reject Him. How this will be carried out is according to how many more are converted before the end of the world. There will be children who are only days old upon the Return of the King. Many will be still in the womb. Some will be in the process of being born when they are taken into the House of the Lord. So, what is an example of the vengeance of God? Every unrepentant mother who has ever aborted a child will undergo the labor pains of motherhood, multiplied a thousand times for every year their child would have lived. Another example will be the torture of the torturers whose pain no death can alleviate. It will end when God says that it is time. These are acts of sacred vengeance, and these two terms used consecutively are not a contradiction. It leads to teaching lost sinners that forgiveness is a grace. And, it is by this grace that I have come, that Jesus was born providentially in the Flesh, that the Father has dispensed His Mercy upon the penitent. This is the grace by which those who ask for absolution in the Blood of the Cross will receive it. These are the true messages of Medjugorje!"

Sunday, July 8, 2012
9:26 a.m.

The Homeostasis of Creation

hypostatic: something that stands under and supports; the underlying or essential part of anything, as distinguished from attributes; substance, essence or essential principle; one of the three real and distinct subsistences in the one substance of God.

homeostasis: the tendency of a system, the physiological system of higher animals, to maintain interior stability, owing to the coordinated response of its parts to any disruptive situation or stimulus.

"Thank you, My lovely sons, for your willingness to remain in prayer with Me. I am amazed that so many around you have given-up the fight. My Special son, please take the dictionary from behind you and turn to page 633. You will find there one of the terms at the opening of My message this morning. What does its definition say? *"People want to have interior peace."* So you are familiar with this word? *"I am familiar with the concept."* Homeostasis is the capacity for something to maintain a sense of equilibrium. Would this be correct? *"Yes."* You are an intelligent Doctor of the Church in waiting, and you know how this phenomenon applies to the architecture of the world. Let us further examine this term against the backdrop of history. This is where exiled humanity recognizes the hand of God in earthly life, where the Father has touched the universe in ways that could not have come by happenstance. Men engage in activities that grow the stability of the world, but also some that only diminish it. As a Doctor of the Church, you know that growing the stability of the world means making policies, positions, laws and actions that constructively unify peoples and nations. These are such things as shared sacrifices and commodities, making peace, healing and comforting, and seeing truth in the Word of God. What are some destabilizing forces? *"Selfishness of the rich hoarding their wealth, naked aggression, hatred, discrimination and oppression."* Yes, all of these things. What needs to be done by world leaders is the fostering of communities in which stabilizing factors outweigh, diminish and eliminate those that cause division and instability. The issue that keeps this from happening is that there are so many world views; there are so many deep chasms between the way people think and behave. I told you recently that peace begets peace. It is also true that war begets war because no one remembers which acts are offensive and which are defensive. They lose track of how much vengeance has been exacted and who started the fight. All they know is that it becomes natural to shoot and kill somebody, and to prevail and die on the battlefield. War becomes the new mode of nations that refuse to embrace the consistency of human unity beneath the hand of God.

When you spoke the definition of 'homeostasis' a few moments ago, did you sense anything that refers to an initiator of homeostasis? Is there a catalyst for it, or does it occur naturally based on the characteristics of the system? *"Well, it is related to the psychological systems of higher animals, which means our relationship to the heart and soul."* Indeed, you are correct to assign homeostasis to the heart and soul. This is the orientation to which all men should be drawn. But, why must it be attributed only to higher animals? Or does it need to be? *"No, it would probably apply to animals and their instincts too."* Yes, you are correct again. Let us therefore think about homeostasis within the framework of Creation itself – all that you see, and everything that humanity encounters in the environment as well as the body, mind and soul. Does it apply there as well? *"Yes."* This is what humanity refuses to learn. The application of homeostasis must be examined in the context of hypostasis. By its definition, you know that God through Jesus is the hypostatic support of humankind and the created world. Does it not therefore seem logical that homeostasis is a product of hypostasis? *"Yes."* This idea has never been adequately shared in the history of man. There has never been the connection because many theologians believe that hypostasis and homeostasis are contradictory terms. They believe that the latter is a common effect of being created, but not a blessing from God the Creator. And, this is the missing link in their teachings about what God wants. Oh yes! There are many implications to this connection. Most of all, it proves that the Father is always working in Creation from inside and outside its parameters. Birds and fishes seek homeostasis, and they remain in the air and beneath the waters. Fires are quenched by floods. Heights are counterbalanced by depths. The point I am making is that the homeostasis of the human soul is to find its relocation in the Church-Triumphant. And, this is procured by the soul's belief in and acceptance of its hypostatic union with Jesus Christ. Remember that you are a Doctor of the Church; you have the capacity to view this clearly. And, you also understand the fact that theologians are reluctant to draw this connection because they refuse to believe that exiled souls have any form of beatific power. We know better. We comprehend the connection between the enlightened human spirit and its destiny before the Throne of God. This is the appropriate application of the human will. This is the awareness by men that they can follow their own destiny that has been ordained by Jesus on the Cross. They either accept it or reject it. The conclusion is that this human 'judgement' precedes the Lord's Judgement about the finality of the existence of the soul. Is the soul allowed perpetual life in Heaven or plunged into the bowels of Hell? Humanity has the ability to make its own choice. Therefore, if we ponder what it means to seek homeostasis or equilibrium in this life, does this life not infer that everything that stabilizes tends toward Glory, and everything that destabilizes tends toward condemnation? The correct response from those who know the difference between life and death is an affirmative one. As I say, there are broad implications in this discussion that could fill chapters and books. I do not intend for you to do so, but it is something that you might incorporate somewhere. The whole basis evolves from the fact that God and humanity are meeting in the here and now. It is the same concept that we once discussed about speaking and hearing as opposed to speaking and 'listening.' A man often hears things to which he pays no attention; he does not listen for any particular meaning. Aircraft fly overhead, dogs bark, the breezes blow, and frogs chirp in midnight swamps with sounds that go mostly unnoticed. Is there homeostasis in this? There is to the extent that if all these machines and creatures fell silent, the background sounds would be gone and the ears of men would seek new fashions of awareness. It is all a matter of adaptation. This is the reason unconverted men must 'adapt' to the call of God to become holy creatures, to be changed and purified in such a way that His hypostatic grace becomes the new norm encompassing their lives. And in doing so, there becomes a magnified spiritual homeostasis between Heaven and Earth. Thank you for allowing Me to discuss this with you today."

Sunday, July 15, 2012
1:16 p.m.

Subliminal Absorption

"My little sons, this is My favorite time when I travel the world teaching and comforting My children. Whenever I appear in this home, it is the highlight of My Motherhood. This is because you are here laboring in the Lord's vineyard that is being cultivated by your prayers and good works. My Special one, I have come speaking to you and your brother about the infusion of holiness and the Spirit of God into the human person – mind, heart and soul. This is not a process of appropriation or acquisition, but an absorption by the children of God of His Wisdom and Spirit, the acceptance of His Will in the physical realms. Humanity cannot be holy without God, and they cannot become holy without Jesus. It is by absorption that the Spirit of the Lord comes to rest within you. Appropriation implies power to demand something of someone else. People appropriate funds; they appropriate attitudes and positions that are not theirs to own. Some people appropriate rights over others that they do not possess. In other words, someone cannot approach Jesus and demand that He give them certain gifts or make them righteous without due sacrifice and obedience. This leads to the second concept – acquisition. This applies to something that is taken without specific purpose, or purposes that serve only the party doing the acquiring. The fact remains that there should be no material gain in someone's relationship with God. No one can issue a decree that tells God to hand over something by a specified time. This is what acquisition means. Hence, you can see why acquisition also does not apply. Absorption is the best way to describe the infusion of the human heart with the truth, wisdom and peace of God. And, this absorption is subliminal because you cannot always tell when it is happening. Appropriation and acquisition can be identified according to certain times and measures, but absorption of the spirit cannot. Why? Because subliminal absorption toward the perfection of humanity has the capacity to be as infinite as Heaven itself – it is a simple concept with supernatural implications. It is another means of expressing the immeasurable authority of the Church and the Kingdom of Heaven in terms that sinners can understand. Yes, you have seen the writings of theologians who parse words in complicated ways. You have researched some of these subjects after My previous messages.

You know that many theologians' works are more complex than they need to be. They often have their subscribers threading needles and jumping through hoops. While I appreciate their constancy in analyzing the relationship between God and man and Heaven and Earth, they could more easily convert lost sinners to the Cross using simpler speech.

You have seen through the years that My messages are not complicated. Changing someone's heart from ruthlessness to righteousness is not always something that can be yielded from complex theses. Most theologians write manuscripts meant to keep converted men and women involved, to increase their curiosity to learn more about the Afterlife, and to give them philosophical reasons to remain faithful to the Church. But, My simple messages do the same thing. Mathematicians, scholars and practitioners are usually too preoccupied with numbers and theories to be doing the work of the devil. I am not saying that they are holy as they might be, but most of them are doing no harm. We are instead trying to convert the coldly calculating sinners who are taking advantage of the ignorant, who are draining honest people of their monies, who put pride and prejudice before sincere piety, and who care not what the end of their lives will bring. We focus on converting people who are leading innocent children down errant paths and exploiting them for material gain and corporeal wickedness. These are the sinners who need to hear messages of simple holiness. They would never take time to ingest the writings of the Doctors of the Church. As I have said, you have the capacity to serve as their practical Doctor of the Church; and as this kind of Doctor, you can reach the simplest among you. This is the subliminal absorption of the righteousness of Heaven into the human heart. Some theologians would dismiss it as infantile, but I want you and your brother to know that this is how the Lord perceives your service in His Kingdom. Do you realize in what high esteem and excellence you are held before the Throne of the Father? *"I want to be held that way there. I would be grieved if I caused there to be any sadness to the Trinity."* It is imperative that you recognize the efforts of the Catholic Bishops as they endure the assaults of secular governments. It is happening just as I have said. I will offer another message in the future to teach you more about the infusion of the Holy Spirit."

Saturday, July 21, 2012
2:06 p.m.

Three Moral Majors of Roman Catholicism
Part One

Monopolist for Redemptive Revelation

"Bounteous blessings I bring to you today, My little sons, as you stand upright in Jesus for the conversion of the world. There are graces seen and unseen cascading into the material realms from Heaven because you are praying to lift up the poor. I ask you to remain steadfast in your belief that I have given you My messages for so many years because they will make a difference in shaping the present world and the New World to come. I wish to speak to you today about the first of Three Moral Majors that can only be procured and provided by the Roman Catholic Church. When I am finished describing and discussing these eternal components, you will understand why it is imperative that we wait for lost souls to convert. While it is obvious that the concentricity of the Church is important, and the Seven Sacraments are imperative for the purification and preservation of the human soul, they are not among the Three Moral Majors that I wish to discuss. I am not saying that they are not moral imperatives, I am simply saying that there are three other majors to which I wish to focus your attention. The first of the Three Moral Majors of the Roman Catholic Church is that the Church is pursuing a Monopoly of Salvation in the exiled world. The Apostolic Church alone is the Monopolist for Redemptive Revelation. The Roman Catholic Church is the only entity commissioned by Christ to pursue a Monopoly of Salvation in the exiled world. There is no other savior than Jesus Christ. The Savior is Jesus Christ. Jesus Christ founded the Original Apostolic Church on Saint Peter the Rock, and this Rock cannot be protested against. Jesus commissioned the First Apostles to indeed make apostles and disciples of all men and nations. Jesus told His disciples to work for the unification of all peoples in Him through His Crucifixion and Resurrection. He told Peter the Foundation of the Church to teach, preach and apprise in His Holy Name. There was only one Saint Peter. There has been only one recognized successor living at a time since the original Rock of the Church. Saint Peter and the power of the Papacy has lived in each successor, handed-down through the ages by the invocation of the Holy Spirit.

Hence, the term 'Monopoly' implies that all sinners must be reconciled with God through the Apostolic Church headed by Saint Peter and his successors to the exclusion of all other faiths and beliefs. Now, there is much more to this than the simple framework of the Hierarchy comprising the consistency of the Catholic Church through the epochs of time. Inherent in this one Church is the superstructure of all immortal 'being.' Those who stray from the Church lose touch with the Immortal Being of God. Those who wander into other beliefs or into none at all are not fed by the Seven Sacraments, and they are therefore starved for Truth. Hence, I have told you the difference between evangelicals and evangelizers. Belonging to the Roman Catholic Church implies that you are the sacred property of God. The Catholic Church does not belong to its people, the people belong to the Church. And, while there are stringent properties and responsibilities inherent in this ownership, it also means that the members of the Roman Catholic Church simultaneously belong to God. Heaven is your spiritual inheritance, so you claim ownership of Heaven as you are concurrently repatriated to the side of the Father. This is indeed a beatific Monopoly. The Father and the Son have effectively set-out into the world through the Incarnate Being of Jesus and the invincible power of the Holy Spirit to claim all living creatures for the Will of the Father.

Let us see what this Monopoly implicates for the future of men. It certainly implies that anyone who denies this Monopoly is destined for Hell. And, those who would vainly attempt to compete with this Monopoly are committing blasphemy, and they are also destined for Hell. Anyone who would claim equal divinity with the Savior of the World without first engaging and living His Commandments and Gospel is materially and spiritually separated from the Kingdom to Come. Ministers and preachers whose edicts and decrees lead the innocent away from the Truth, the Way and the Life are destined for Hell. There is no bargaining or negotiating with God that could cause or bring Him to change His mind about His Monopoly of Messianic Salvation to make it instead some humanistic fraternity of pluralism where everyone is admitted to Paradise because they were nice to their friends. This is not what Jesus' life was about at all. No human person in body or spirit has the power to dissect or dilute the Lord's intention to deliver His Original Church intact into His presence upon the Final Judgment of Jesus Christ. The Catholic Church has by the sovereign power invested into its prayers the right to claim lost souls for Heaven and dispense eternal Absolution upon those who repent. The Monopoly of the Roman Catholic Church implies that the

Church stands in the fullness of grace and light beyond the horizons of mortality with Jesus Christ at the Victory of the completion of the world. This sacred Monopoly permits the Church to unilaterally mandate both theory and practical thought and conduct for those who profess to believe. The Roman Catholic Church can expel anyone who teaches or lives in ways that contradict the teachings of Jesus Christ, and it is not a sign of lack of mercy to do so. The Roman Catholic Church can invoke the intercession of the Angels and Saints in ways unknown to those who do not accept its tenets, and these Angels and Saints will respond. Yes, the Roman Catholic Church is a Monopoly in the physical realms working for the unification of all men in the Afterlife, without regret or apology, responsible to no other power or principalities, answerable to no secular governments, and designed and destined to remain unified here and now and in the Church Triumphant for the multiplication of the eternal ages. The Church will never surrender to any other origin; it does not only not have the desire to do so, it does not have the capacity to surrender to any other dominion. Men and women who profess allegiance to the Roman Catholic Church take an oath to be the Lord's agents and representatives here in this life. This is not a license, it is a commission that is capable of withstanding the onslaught expected from all enemies, adversaries and detractors. While the Holy Spirit can speak through non-members of the Church, this same Holy Spirit will bring all to whom sacred knowledge is given to the foot of the Cross where the Original Catholic Apostolic Church is stationed and sanctioned. Let Me repeat that this is a Monopoly. There are no other limbs or branches, no subcategories, elements or sects, no other entities whatsoever that could be visualized or imagined as being complementary to the unity of the Church. The Catholic Church is one, and there are no others. It is imperative for all mankind to realize that it is through these things that the Church has prevailed for 2,000 years. Although made-up of sinners, the Church has completed a perfect mission. Its purpose is to refine those who call themselves Catholic and convert all who do not.

Therefore, the Monopoly of the Roman Catholic Church will deliver the Mystical Body of Jesus to the presence of the Father as itself. Just like the Transfiguration on Mount Tabor, Jesus is glorifying humanity through Himself, and humanity is elevated and perfected in Him, as Him. I ask for all who will eventually hear these words, My little sons, to dare not speak harshly about the Roman Catholic Church or those who have been commanded to defend its honor. I declare that miracles will be wrought at the invocation of the evangelizers, and you will see miracles of transformation abound in this life and the next. And yet, there is hell to come. There are bloodbaths and agonies in the future of man. There are annihilations and outright onslaughts. The Monopoly of the Roman Catholic Church will be unfazed. The Church will not be deterred. The faithful will keep their faces to the wind. You and all who are Saints now and Saints in your new lives will never lose sight of the grand Light of Redemptive Love. There will be snarls and growls from those who refuse to believe. They will plead with you and call themselves victims of the devil, but if they do not change according to your words, they will remain the devil's victims with no compassion from you. You must have no mercy on those who refuse to fight against the very evil that has them in its grasp. They have been given both the will and willpower to escape the influences of Satan and choose to accept the salvific balm of Christ's Love. My little sons, the Monopoly of the Roman Catholic Church gives eyesight and vision to those who will see. It grants Eternal Life. Everything else is just an illusion. All other enticements are the work of Lucifer. While I have not taught you anything here today that you do not already know, I hope that I have given you another way to describe to lost sinners how utterly lost they are. They have not only abandoned God, they are betraying themselves. My Special son, do you have anything to discuss with Me today, or any questions? *"I'm anxious to hear the other two."* Well, we do not have time today, but we will get there. I will provide the other two during our next two messages. Please allow Me to mention something that I am unsure whether you understand. It is not clear to you how grand is your favor before Jesus for taking such good care of your brother. I cannot overstate this. I cannot repeat it too often. Like you, he is still working to make headway against the perils and evils of the world so that Jesus can more readily claim souls that will eventually be His. I simply ask you and your brother to take life one day at a time, living simply and intelligently, with peace and wisdom. Be careful where and when you travel; live according to the habits and themes that will preserve your health and safety. And, while it is necessary to look toward your self-preservation, it is not urgent to believe that your country is headed into an immediate state of anarchy. You will see more signs, clearer signs than you are seeing now."

Sunday, July 29, 2012
3:04 p.m.

Three Moral Majors of Roman Catholicism
Part Two

Custodian and Steward of Apostolic Faith

"My dear little sons, we speak of duty and honor as inseparable tenets of the Christian conscience because they are like legs upholding the ladder of ascendance upon which you grow in faith. Even young children learn what they mean from their brothers and elders so as to instill this discipline in them from a very young age. If a person is given responsibility, it implies that he is trusted to carry out the mission to which he has been assigned. This is how Jesus, the Head of the Church, became Incarnate in this world to commission His own followers. He has entrusted in your care the responsibility of transferring the knowledge of the Gospel through the ages, that it arrives back in His beatific library in Heaven intact and fully honored. The Roman Catholic Church has always been the Custodian and Steward of Apostolic Faith to which generations and centuries have dedicated their lives and the substance of their being. Taking custody. This implies taking control by power vested and applied from the Great High Priest on His behalf while He remains there with you. Thus, what does control mean? The control leads to the stewardship. To be a good steward implies that you handle something carefully and thoughtfully, respectfully and with a firm conscience toward preservation. And, in order to do this, your stewardship must always be comprised of deference to the Head of the Church. Through the power of the Holy Spirit in your hearts, Christ Jesus serves the Church as its Master. There is no doubt that there have also been different opinions about the composition of the Apostolic Faith. There have even been contrasting definitions. The Apostolic Faith embodies the conceptual definition of the role of the Roman Catholic Church. It is both action and description. Here, you comprehend the meaning of custody and stewardship in both theological and practical terms. While the Catholic Church is the Monopolist that preserves the integrity and defends the dignity of the teachings of Jesus Christ, the Church also holds in its own hands the responsibility for never allowing itself to be assaulted or denigrated by any outside forces. It cannot surrender its supernal monopolist authority to the democratic whims of any cohort of sinners or other manipulative totalitarians. Hence, the Church is its own shield against the wickedness and snares of the devil because the Church in all three forms is the Mystical Body of its Head. Now that I have outlined the premise for custodial leadership and dignified stewardship, it is important to place this premise in the context of time and space. This is indeed where the free will of pious men applies its own strength and vision, its own version of sacrificial love in the parameters of the Earth. This is what makes humanity's free will a force for good. This free will need not be a hindrance to the conversion of the wicked and the ferreting-out of those who would do it good from those who would do it harm. Therefore, custodial leadership and dignified stewardship can only be procured through allegiance to the Cross and the firm affirmation of the Resurrection of Jesus from the Tomb. It is through these two keys that the lockbox of redemption is made open to those pining to get in. It is this custodial power that Jesus handed Saint Peter when He declared that the Church would be stationed on him. Jesus knew that Peter, even though Peter had denied Him in the moment, would be a worthy custodian and steward for those times and these times. Saint Peter was a sinner. All the Popes have been sinners. But, their conviction in and proclamation of matters of faith and morals have always been infallible. This same infallibility of holy love is transferable to all who believe. All become custodians and stewards of the Apostolic Faith simply by practicing and believing in the tenets of the Church.

  The distinction I am making is that the custodial leadership and dignified stewardship of the Apostolic Faith is not concentrated in anyone who is not Roman Catholic or in those who are not in harmony with the Roman Catholic Pope. It is head-centered as much as the Salvation of the whole of the world is head-centered. I say this not in the sense of intellectual scope, but by Apostolic scope in the lineage of the Saints. Jesus Christ is the Head of the Church in this world and the next, and the Pope of the Roman Catholic Church is the custodian and steward of the Apostolic Faith here in this life, dispatched and transmitted to all who are obedient to the Pope. This makes little popes of all who believe in the Roman Catholic Papacy. This is how a new Pope can be culled even from the ranks of the male laity. It could not be done otherwise. The Great High Priest, Jesus Christ, reserves the right to commission any man He pleases to serve as maintainer of the faith of many in a world of many. Please think about it in these terms. Jesus made Apostles of lay men. He ordained them as Bishops upon the utterance of His Word. And,

He continues to instill in all who believe in Him the same genuine desire to uphold the tenets of His Gospel with equal measure. What can be seen of this power? One great example is Saint Francis of Assisi. Saint Francis made a leader of himself by importing into his life the mission of the Church and tendering his own free will as a servant of the masses. This was done through his acceptance of the Will of God that supplanted his own. He grasped a share of the Apostleship of the Popes in his day and laid down a record of piety and humility that has been unmatched by all but a few. This, My little sons, is also the record you are making of your own lives in your time. You have become custodians and stewards of the Apostolic Faith as members of the Roman Catholic Church. This could not occur if you lacked commitment. It would not happen if you chose to piecemeal your faith in Jesus according to the whims of other things. Like Saint Francis, you have given your lives to Jesus altogether, to the point that others look at you in awe, but do not tell you to your face. This is your appropriation of the power of your own faith to be a force for good in the modern world, and it is proof that you are exhibiting Jesus' mandate that His disciples should go out into the world two-by-two and teach and preach the Holy Gospel with confidence. The point I am making is that when people hand their will over to God, they will be led by the Wisdom of the Holy Spirit instead of their own prerogatives for the way life ought to be lived. This offsets the fact that people are sinners, and it is the way that the Pontiff can be infallible in the faith and morality of the Church, indeed of human life entire. The fact that humanity is imperfect is irrelevant here because all men and women are in the process of being perfected in Jesus, the Head of the Church. It is as though you become aware of the true power of your Baptism and the Sacrament of Confession by seeing for yourself that you have been set free from sin, then living the new perfection that you have inherited. Here again, this is power that can only be appropriated by practicing Roman Catholic people. Why? Because the custody and stewardship of the Apostolic Faith has been deposited there. It is the Christological cornerstone of the Monopolist nature of the Catholic Church, described and applied in operational terms. My Special son, this completes My description of the second of the Moral Majors that I began describing last week. Do you have any questions about it? *"No, it makes sense, thank you."*

Saturday, August 4, 2012
12:54 p.m.

Three Moral Majors of Roman Catholicism
Part Three

Vessel and Visionary of Theological Truth

"My Immaculate Heart is deeply filled with eternal triumphalism when I come to speak with you because you inspire happiness in Me. You must realize, My Special one, that you bring Me elation because you are so admiring of My Son and affectionate toward Me. The consecrations you and your brother have taken to follow the teachings of the Church, and the dignity of Jesus' Sacred Heart and My Immaculate Heart, set you aside as among the most dignified in the exiled world. Your faith encompasses not only what the Catholic Church believes, but everything you believe that complements its mission, its mystical grace, and its everlasting joy. Therefore, I come today to speak about the Roman Catholic Church as the Vessel and Visionary of Theological Truth. My little son, even as I have told you that the first two Moral Majors are not complicated to understand, neither is the third, although it contains all the attributes of this trinity combined, and therefore is simultaneously comprised of the first and second Moral Majors. It is not unlike the Most Blessed Trinity itself standing alone as one deific poise, as the Godhead is concurrently comprised of three distinct parts. Having said these things, you can imagine that Theological Truth is inclusive of the Church's Monopolist role and its role as Custodian and Steward. The Vessel and Visionary of Theological Truth is the Church's overall mission. Every facet of contact between God and man, and Heaven and Earth, is harbored in and protected by its existence, its perpetual existence. Its connection to the higher plateaus and infinite ages begins here for you and all the faithful. Morever, it is not practical to divide the Church's composition as Vessel and Visionary as though they are somehow exclusive of each other. This vision comes from the Deposit of Wisdom that has been granted by the Father through the Son, and the Church receives this Wisdom as His Vessel. This is one of the reasons that the Vatican is referred to as the Holy See. This is the Visionary aspect of the Church under the leadership of the Pope, who is the Vicar of Christ. Now, it is clear that I could speak for hours about theology here today, but this is not the point. The fact that the Theological Truth has been deposited into the Roman Catholic Church, and only the Church, is the point I am making. There are countless implications to this definitive proclamation. People will ask whether the Holy Spirit works through Protestant denominations, and whether their faith and good works are in alignment with the Eternal Father. The answer is that prayer and good works come through the suffering of the Roman Catholic Church. God inspires prayers in those who pray because He sees in Heaven the sacrifices of the Catholic Church. Good works can be done by people of faith and those who practice no faith, but the Spirit that is initiating those works is being called upon them in answer to the prayers and penances intoned by the Catholic Church. And having said this, it is clear that those who possess the Apostolic Faith can commend themselves to intercession before God for the accomplishment of conversion and good works, knowing that their duties and sacrifices are founded in and resultant from their identification with Jesus on the Cross. Hence, the terms Vessel and Visionary are reserved as two-pillared descriptions of the Theology of the Roman Catholic Church. The latter flows from the first at the same time they are each interchangeable. You see how this is difficult for Me to describe in the same way that the Most Blessed Trinity is not easy to describe. It is also necessary to make clear that the Catholic Church is the genesis of exemplary action in the way of Jesus for all humanity, and those of other denominations who act likewise are repeating the example of the Original Apostolic Church. They are merely imitators of the original. You see that one is the sound of grace, and the other its echo. The reason I have not drawn these kinds of distinctions in My other messages to the world is because I do not want to drive others away who would be offended at the thought of their faith in Jesus not appearing authentic. Remember that I am trying to draw all men to the Holy Eucharist. One does not set out to increase someone's faith by telling them that the power of their faith judgement is wrong, but it must not deter any true evangelizer from annunciating the Truth that sent Jesus to the Cross. They have simply been misled by their forbears, and have taken upon themselves the cloak of pride in their families' legacies. Indeed, when these people see others with no faith at all following the teachings of the Roman Catholic Church, they will be more inclined to convert, themselves. Notice that I am not saying that non-Catholics who believe in God and pray every day are bad people; they are simply misled about beatific truth that Satan has been working day and night for millennia to obscure. This is the reason they must begin to think of Jesus'

Original Church as the Universal Church under the guidance of one Vicar. If they would rouse themselves from the protesting platitudes which define their environment and their doctrine, then study this in the context of the whole world, they will begin to see. History will teach them. The writings of the Saints will instruct them. The Angels will hover before and above them to advocate for their assimilation into the Catholic Church where they will be pronounced on Earth and in Heaven as participants in and recipients of the Faith that Jesus ordained upon His Resurrection, Ascension and Pentecost. Jesus told His Apostles and disciples that they were and had become the Vessels for all that would be known about Salvation in the Cross. He asked them to 'see' as He sees Creation, and to transform this vision into discernable action, based on the Theological Truth enshrined within the Church that He commissioned in an Upper Room filled with fire.

Hence, you see that it is obvious that there is only one Faith. There may be other beliefs, but only one Faith. And, this Faith is based upon and grown from the Theological Truth that has been deposited in the Roman Catholic Church by the Holy Spirit. This is an irrevocable Moral Major that humanity-entire must come to know. And, as you can see through your empirical lives, your lives of experience and interaction, humanity is yet sorely divided; the world is not attuned to what I am telling you today. You have heard the term 'vessel' before. You have heard such titles as 'singular vessel' and 'vessel of sacred knowledge.' This is the thesis of the existence of man's awareness that the Lord wants to save the souls of lost sinners. He wishes to fill up men's lives with heavenly purpose instead of secular effects. God mandates from His Throne that all who know and accept Him turn to His Son for this guidance. Other implications include the fact that generations of detractors are going to be difficult to dismiss. However, it is more a disposition than a dismissal, a screening-in process rather than screening-out. It is about welcoming rather than ostracizing. Imagine if someone came to you and said that another seer said they heard from God that the Roman Catholic Church is an imposter, or a harlot. You would rebuke them and call them the devil in an instant. This is the same way that it is horribly difficult to pry Protestants and those of other religions from their positions outside the Church. In their exiled human perception, everyone is conscripted in darkness; no one has the Light; no one has authority; no Vessel of Truth exists, no entity possesses legitimacy. They do not even trust one another. If they would look for legitimacy in what the Catholic Church is saying by the power of the Holy Spirit, they would find that I am this legitimacy. My miraculous intercession is their Sign. I am the Mother of God, the Universal Mediatrix who birthed the Church of human Salvation in the Second Person of the Trinity for the whole word. This gives Me the standing, authority, Wisdom, presence and desire to set the record straight. I cannot be opposed because I have never come into the world as a prophet. I have never claimed to be the Messiah because I am not, and neither is any other man than the Man whom I bore. Enemies of the Roman Catholic Church everywhere believe that the Lord God can speak only through a man. I am the exception that they cannot ignore. How does this make Me different from all previous female seers and visionaries? I am not a sinner. I have never sinned, and I gave birth to the sinless Messiah as a perpetual Virgin Myself. There are no other women who can claim this distinction. There is but one Mother of God, and it is this Mother who is speaking to you now. Yes, Vessel and Visionary of Theological Truth. This is the Patriarchy of the Roman Catholic Church, given to the exiled world in the image and likeness of God the Father, the Divine Patriarch, the Master and Creator, the Father of the Alpha and the Omega. My Special son, I have concluded My discussion about the Third Moral Major of the Roman Catholic Church. Do you have any questions about what I have said? *"No. I understand everything you have said."* I am grateful that you have taken into account the first two Moral Majors, and you may fashion their presentation as you see fit. As I have said, it is My indescribable joy to speak to you about matters that will strengthen your resolve to defend the Church and arm you with facts to uphold the premises that you make to the physical world. August 2012 has come, and you and your brother are doing well. I again thank you for taking such good care of him. He has made decisions and framed his workload to continue his schooling, and you realize that none of this would be possible without you. I will give you some specific actions to take toward the dispensing of My messages later in the fall. It is not something that you need to dwell upon until I mention it again. Thank you for the intensity of your faith, your kindness to those around you, and the sincerity of your love."

Sunday, August 12, 2012
1:33 p.m.

The Sacred Amalgam

"Lest you stray too far from your peaceful hearts, My dear little sons, please stop worrying so much. I have come today to bring you comfort and wisdom. I have come to tell you about Jesus! You are not afraid of what tomorrow will bring because you trust in Him, and you know that His Providence has provided for the cultivation of the far corners of the globe from inside the bounty of your hearts. I have spoken to you the past three weeks about the configuration of your faith in this world, and the presence of holiness that you possess and espouse. I have spoken about your mission, about your alliance with God to bring to humanity all that will make things right. Everyone who has come into His presence through death has told Him when asked that the most intense impression they had about life on Earth is the battle between love and hatred. Love is the presence and actualization of the Father on Earth and in Heaven, and hatred is manifested by those who reject Him. This is why it is a lie to say that there is love at the foundation of same-sex marriage. There is only hatred manifested by those who reject the language of life in such a willful way. The language of Creation speaks volumes about its Maker. There is no actualization of the Father in same-sex marriage or any other homosexual union. Therefore, it is imperative that the Will of God and the will of mortal men become one through the process of conversion. Does this imply that they are originally separate? Is it possible that baptized Christians can exercise their will in contradiction to the Will of the Father? The answer is yes, and this is the product of either intentional or unintentional thoughts, impulses and actions. There is nothing wrong or sinful about questioning the motivations of God, but this is not the best use of your faith. There is no doubt or question in faith. Hence, you see that questions about the Lord's motivations are more based in ascending levels of faith than in right and wrong. If you trust that God knows what He is doing; if you defer to His Sacred Will even when you do not understand, then your faith will be strong. Notice, My Special son, that I am not speaking about you and your brother in particular here today, but about humanity in general. And, it is often difficult to remember everything you are supposed to do in various situations, and this is why the Holy Spirit guides you; this is the reason the Holy Spirit will give you the words to say when your time has come in accordance with the Holy Scriptures. Sometimes the answers you seek lie in hidden places; sometimes they are more obvious. We have discussed many times over the overpowering, cleansing, clarifying and redeeming purpose of human suffering. It indeed ratifies humanity's trust in the Father when accepted in faith. The suffering of the Son and the suffering of His Mystical Body are one in the same Sacrifice. And, other matters are not as clear while simultaneously being prepared for clarity. This is the process of life in the exiled world. Human beings are creatures of insight, habit, judgement, renewal, expectation and culmination. Each of you has drives that capture your attention every day, and these drives assist you in pursuing purposeful living. It is a Sacred Amalgam when humanity does not always seek answers or justification for earthly events that transpire at any given time. You will discover in your research a definition for 'amalgam' that includes the element of mercury, but this does not apply to what I am saying here. I am speaking about a spiritual amalgam that ties the love between God and men into one prenatal and postnatal unit on Earth and in Heaven. Men are born, and then born again. They die and are resurrected. These blessings are given through the amalgam of human faith and the reciprocal faith that God shares with those who believe in Him. This concept of 'amalgam' has so many dimensions that they can scarcely be described. The Sacraments of the Church are a manifestation of this salvific Sacred Amalgam. God offers the Sacraments, and faithful men on Earth recognize them as such. The Holy Eucharist even brings the spiritual and physical Communion between Jesus Himself and worthy communicants. The Sacrament of Marriage is an amalgam of two hearts, minds and lives into one holy union. You can see that these apply in all the Sacraments. And, the Sacred Amalgam is especially present when someone offers another person forgiveness because this is the Spirit of Jesus acting through them. Forgiveness can only come from God! Satan never forgives; and if he says he does, he is again lying. Blessing a meal is another example of the amalgam of God and His people."

Saturday, August 18, 2012
10:09 a.m.

Gilding Creation and the Pollination of Humanity

"My little sons, it is My delight to pray in your midst for your petitions and ask Jesus to bless you. You are making tremendous headway in the conversion of the world and the defeat of the enemies of the Church. You have learned about 'gilding' in the context of making holy everything about you to be like gold. This does not mean that the inside of the heart is already golden, but the presence of the human person, the presentation of the human person, reveals a side of the world that is willing to try. When something is gilded, it is covered with a sheen of brightness and beauty, but this beauty must begin to come from within. This means that the Holy Spirit must infiltrate the human heart from its very core and fertilize the soul with righteousness. Holiness must be deposited within the being of humanity by God, and this is why all who believe in Him, and even those who do not, must open themselves to everything that Heaven provides. And, as I have told you in recent weeks, this means accepting whatever comes, even in the face of suffering. My Special son, I am saying that to be gilded is to be given the appearance of perfection. This does not mean that someone should be gilded and remain unsightly inside. The gilding of Creation must come from inside the hearts of men. And, in order to inherit this restorative presence, the human heart must be willing to be impregnated and grow in the wisdom and knowledge of Sacred Truth. It is somewhat like pollinating a flower. All around you, this is happening – but it is unseen because it is a spiritual blessing. The conversion of human hearts and the purification of souls is accomplished because of the deference of man to the Will of God. Let us imagine what fruits this has borne. All the greatest leaders and visionaries surrendered themselves this way to the Father. The beauty of Nature, the animals, and the invisible attributes of peace and hope originate from the willingness of God to bless His Creation. The Father thrives on being worshiped. He signifies His sovereign Providence to the needy when He realizes that He is loved in return. Indeed, Jesus the Son of Man is the Living Being of the Father in the exiled world, and His Conception in My Womb was fashioned by the desire of the Father to be reunited with His people. This speaks to the ill-conceived notion that some profess that since humanity is exiled from Heaven, then Heaven and all its Hosts must surely be exiled from Earth as well. This is simply not the case. Everything in Heaven is love to its core, not just gilded on the outside. Therefore, in order for the Earth to be like Heaven, the deep sacredness of Divine Love must replace the hollow center of the fallen nature of man. It is obvious that you know this story well enough to understand what I am saying. Do you have any issues to discuss today? *"Thank you for speaking to me for so long."* You are welcome. I am elated that you have allowed Me to be here! I am pleased that My children are obeying where I have spoken; the needs of the world are great. And, I am happy that so many righteous people are fighting to defend the sanctity of life and the preservation of marriage. There is teaching, learning and sharing happening all around the globe."

Sunday, August 26, 2012
2:17 p.m.

The Providential Godhead
Civilization and Anarchy

"My two little sons, as you know, I come here because I love you, and with the hope that the love we share will change the world. My children, there will never be any exhausting of My willpower to convert lost sinners. It is what I live for. There is no running out of prayers; there is no such thing as the post-reign of the Queen of Heaven. I speak to you to assure you that your lives are blessed in Jesus, to remind you that I am with you as I am with all humanity. The fact that I am still speaking to you is reason for you to believe that the world is still changing, still growing and becoming better. There is Providence in everything good that comes to men, and the Blessed Trinity in One Godhead presides over this transformation. My Special son, you have indeed studied for decades the contrast of civilization over anarchy. The latter means that there is no central control by government over a society or region. Civilizations can likewise exist without invoking the presence and power of God, but they all eventually devolve into anarchy because there is no moral framework to keep them alive. The reason I have brought this concept to your attention is to give you yet another subject to ponder for your speaking and writing. Can you tell Me any nation or region in the world whose government is comprised of Christianity? *"Not that I can think of."* Of course, we except the Vatican State from this discussion, but you are precisely correct. Does it stand possible, therefore, that Jesus did not come onto the Earth to establish a world government? *"Yes."* This is the Will of the God of Abraham. The Lord has chosen His disciples and apostles to work in His earthly vineyard that serve His Kingdom, not His nation, but His Kingdom. And, this Kingdom is one that is seen and unseen. It is seen by the products of the virtues by which Christians live and survive. It is replicated from the Most Blessed Trinity in that the invisible Father is the Maker of Creation; the Son of Man is the Savior of the world in that He was crucified Incarnate on the Earth. And, the Holy Spirit presides over the pious cultivation of the world and the sustenance of the unseen Kingdom where the Church Triumphant rejoices. The Godhead is present in all these gifts, and civilization and anarchy represent the fight that is ongoing on Earth to prepare the Faith Church for the End of Time. Hence, can one presume that civilization must precede the Second Coming of Jesus? *"Yes."* But, this civilization must be a fruit of the Kingdom of Jesus that has already begun here on Earth. Where there is no welcoming of the Holy Spirit, there cannot be a 'just' civilization; there can only be anarchy. This also presumes that no nation on the Earth is rightly civilized because they do not honor the authority of the Pope in Rome whom Jesus would see as the leader of the exiled world. As a result, there is anarchy in every nation. And, you can see the gruesome effects of this anarchy especially in the United States by all the sins and depravity that are devouring the dead consciences of public leaders and private wealth-holders. The whole debate about the condition of the United States revolves around what to do in a nation that refuses to bow to the wishes of the Holy Father in Rome.

Never mind the concept of democracy. Democracy is a term substituted for secular societies that deplore coming into alignment with the teachings of the Church. And, never mind Democrats and Republicans. These two terms stand-in for whatever other words could describe two sides that are battling for the most wealth. Which thief can capture the most profits in a capitalist society? This is what such partisan distinctions mean. And, socialism is also a failure because everyone starves at the same time. The Holy Gospel of Christianity is the rightful structure of human global government because it is based on sacrificial love and benevolent leadership. It is based on recognizing and actualizing the Christian definition of gender and family responsibility. If women obeyed their husbands, and if husbands treated their wives as prescribed in the Scriptures, there would be no need for an equal rights amendment, affirmative action or any pressure for equity in wages. Women would remain at home raising the children they instead aborted, and men would be winning the bread for their families as the honored heads of their households. The point I am making is that the 'civilization' called the Western world has fallen away from the march toward Truth to which the Americas have been called by Me, their Patroness Saint. They call this freedom. They refer to this as progress. They are invoking the vision of the founders of the United States to secure irreverent rights that they were never intended to hold, much in the same way that sinners have exploited the Second Vatican Council to lead more liberal lives. You are seeing the desecration of the meaning of solemn documents, a rewriting of history in secular and religious terms. Now, it is clear that Satan and his legions have caused this, but Jesus has laid the foundation for a world to subsist under His guidance that can lead to the avoidance of sin and prompt men and women to perform their duties according to the Bible and the Catechism of the Catholic Church. This is why you correctly refer to relativism and pluralism as the downfall of the stability of civilized societies. They are indeed secular forces, fed by the indifference of the ignorant and the outright evil works of those who refuse to pray for religious faith. Is it possible, therefore, to conclude that civilization and anarchy are separated by only a thin line? The answer is yes. It is the same as someone saying that agony and ecstacy are equally close. Sadness and joy are divided only by one's perception about what makes them happy or sad. And, this is how the worst sinners and persecutors of the Church can become its greatest Saints. There is hope for everyone. There are roads to Damascus spread all over the globe. Hence, we have discussed today another topic that you might consider broaching for those who are dedicated only to themselves and pledged solely to secular states. Their vision is blinded by their refusal to invoke the 'power' of the Kingdom of God. They are walking in darkness and do not know it because they have never availed themselves the opportunity to bask in His Divine Light. Where they see civilization, God sees them struggling in anarchy. The Providential Godhead is the fullest measure of human freedom ever laid before the eyes of the world.

Thank you for allowing Me to share this with you today. I wish for you to know that I come to be with you and your brother for reasons far more endearing than to just be your teacher. I am the Lovely Mother who cares for your hearts. I hold Jesus in My Arms and am poised in gladness for His Easter Resurrection. Thank you for your kinship in Jesus, for your reverence and dedication, and for your untiring efforts to persevere during the days of your life. As you have seen most recently, Jesus answered our prayers as we joined in asking Him to address the life and times of Pietra Giganti. Her life has been eternalized, and her time has come. Our sweet Pietra entered Heaven the moment her last breath left her lifeless in her bed. She is now in Heaven and on Earth. I have said that the Lord replicates the joy and successes of men. Here where you live and serve, there are glorious accomplishments occurring every day. On August 28, 1972 your brother walked into a college classroom the very first time. He will do so again 40 years later to the day when he goes to the campus on Tuesday. I wish you could see with your eyes all the greatness you and your brother have composed for Jesus since you were called to be His disciples from your youth. It is something that you will see in time and be humbled by your gifts to the Godhead about whom I have spoken today. We espouse perfection in the New Jerusalem, and you and your brother are practicing it now."

Saturday, September 1, 2012
12:56 p.m.

The Didactic Consciousness
Moral Instruction

"My beloved little children, the word 'didactic' is an adjective that means a letter or epistle that instructs others in moral Truth. A didactic letter is sometimes formal and oftentimes informal, but they both try to persuade and enlighten the receiver about living according to the Gospel, according to the teachings of Jesus. Now that I have explained this for you, I wish to attach the term 'didactic' to the word 'consciousness.' The latter is the state of the understanding of the person on his place in Creation, the way he sees his participation in the world according to measures of existence and purpose. Therefore, a didactic consciousness is the condition of the human person along the lines of knowing moral Truth and instructing himself and others about the parameters of mortal Truth. I have introduced another term to you today so you will have more ways to describe what the Lord is seeking in exiled men when the cultivating events of the future begin to unfold. You have heard of the radical reorientation of the human person to the tenets of faith, an openness to the Will of God to establish His Kingdom here on Earth. This radical reorientation transforms physical beings from finite temporal perceptions to infinite spiritual ones. The point I am making is that no one is truly conscious unless they are aware of the morality prescribed by Jesus as their way of life, their purpose and mission of life, and their destiny for the whole of their years. My Special son, you and your brother, and all who hold to the teachings of Jesus, have this didactic consciousness by virtue of your baptism in the Church, your allegiance to the Cross, and your consecration to My Immaculate Heart and the Most Sacred Heart of Jesus. You are commissioned and ordained to teach and preach, enlighten, reprimand, console, bless and underscore the benefits of Christianity in the same way as anyone who holds a vocation. I have said that moral instruction is instinctive to the didactic consciousness because there is no morality if the person is not self-aware that he exists there. You also must know that the didactic 'conscience' is a product of the didactic consciousness. One cannot have a conscience until he is first self-aware. This is a rather simple context in which you can lay your faith alongside that of your forbears and the first Apostles and early disciples. By the power of the Holy Spirit, you have inherited this consciousness and its accompanying conscience. Everything you have ever done since you attained the age of reason has been accomplished through your didactic consciousness, every morning that you have awakened, the decisions you have made about your private life and your public image, the ways you approach friends and strangers, your unity with those who also believe, and the sureness about your state of holiness with which you retire for your sleep. You and your brother, and all Christians, have practiced to the best of your awareness the Faith to which your souls have been given. God knows this consciousness because He has implanted it within you, and He has assimilated your identity and intentions into the fullness of the Church Triumphant already, before you have departed the material world. Another reason that I have introduced you to the concept of the didactic consciousness is because its presence is another criteria by which the Church discerns private revelations. Those who have read your books and seen My Morning Star messages have in fact conceded that you and your brother possess the didactic consciousness, which is generally reserved for apparitions that are already approved. This is a major event for our work. Now, you may write and speak more about this concept in the future as it applies to your preferences and situations where you believe it to be relevant. With this in mind, please know that it has always been to this state of your consciousness that I have always spoken and appealed. Your response and obedience are its fruits. Your charity on behalf of Jesus in this world has grown from your self-awareness that you have power with God and here in this life because you believe what the Bible says. Many Doctors of the Church have said that they wished that their didactic consciousness could have grown by immeasurable dimensions during their earthly exile; and they did the best they could, but they were not hearing messages directly from Me. The Holy Spirit was their Wisdom and guidance, and this was sufficient for their contributions to the Faith and the betterment of the world that existed before they were born. This is a supernatural dynamic that comes to and overwhelms all who relinquish their self-will to a sacrificial will that spreads the Holy Gospel and prospers the Kingdom of God. I must assure you that I realize the difficulty of this process. I am aware that your secular brothers and sisters are utterly separated from even the slightest comprehension of what I am saying. They are asleep in sin, and as such, they have no consciousness other than the allures of materialism, lust and all the other perils of the world. They are 'sleep walking' through life as though they have trained their eyes on a massive billboard somewhere, and you and I can see them staring at it as if to be mesmerized or in a trance. This is their state of not yet being converted to the power of the Cross and the enlightenment that they should share by accepting the Crucifixion and the Resurrection of Jesus from the Tomb. You once watched a television program, indeed more than one, where certain actors and characters were walking around amidst other people, but they could not be seen. This is the same principle. Those who are not converted cannot see what is right before their eyes because, as you have said, they are closed-minded about faith, and refuse to believe in miracles. This is rapidly changing for all the reasons about which you already know.

Therefore, My message to you and your brother this week comes to this – know that you are aware, that you are also self-aware, that you know right from wrong and peace from anarchy because you have lived in the good graces of the Lord. For billions of people around the globe, they would fall faint in joy hearing this from the Mother of God. I tell you this not only because it is true, but because it reaffirms the way you and your brother have lived and the panoramic purpose that has become the substance of your days. However, I also restate that you are free to go outside and play any time you wish. Your work for Jesus is sufficient. I will stand by you and support you in anything you wish to do, as long as it is a prayerful venture. I have said this to you many times. Even though the world is in turmoil, it is peaceful here in this home. It is holy in your hearts. It is quiet in your souls. The growth of the Kingdom of God in and around you is astounding; it is wholesome and unique, it is timely and reassuring. I am with you, and I hear every Hail Mary that you utter. I bless you, and I bless those for whom you pray. We wait in joyful hope for the Coming of the Lord. Please remember to pray for all priests at home and abroad, for missionaries and servants, for children in the womb, for the end of euthanasia, and for all who are lonely and afraid. You and your brother have been working and serving side-by-side for a very long time! Yours is a blessed life, a worthy life that you are living. Jesus knows the sacrifices you have made. He is aware of your commitment and perseverance. Do not fear being proud of who you are and feeling a deep sense of accomplishment about your didactic consciousness. Listen always to your didactic conscience."

Saturday, September 8, 2012
Nativity of the Virgin Mary
2:57 p.m.

"Dear Lord, maker of all good things, redeem us from our weaknesses; bring your mighty consolation into this world with vigor; give us the blessings warranted by our faith in you. Unleash your mighty powers across our land and damn the devil's works. Behold in us the desire to be one in you, to take upon ourselves the burdens you prescribe, to clarify our comprehension of your Gospel and make it triumph in our day. Accept our humble prayers and plant in them the trueness of your Spirit, that all the world will succumb to the Glory of your Sacrifice and awaken at your door. We ask this through Christ Our Lord. Amen."

William L. Roth

"My Special son, this is a stunningly beautiful prayer. Jesus holds it in His hands and in His Most Sacred Heart because you pray so beautifully and sacredly. I have come today speaking about the Love of God and His kindness and empathy, about His openness to His people, His command over the Earth; and I speak about the Providence upon which I have focused the past several weeks. I too pray as you pray! I have requested from Jesus the gifts yet untold that He will bring to humanity because I know that My children are capable of conquering all that stands in the way of unconverted souls. It is therefore with joy that I continue here, even as your Bishop is keeping his word in reading My messages. He is a voracious reader; he loves to be touched by the writings of others to allow his vision to be expanded beyond what he has already learned. My lessons and teachings are not difficult to understand. Your Morning Star Over America has not brought portents of gloom and doom, but of hope and reorientation. I have foretold the demise of the enemies of the Church and the fate of those who reject Salvation, but I have been reluctant to speak in strains that you are seeing in other messages. You and your brother are instruments of peace; you are children of the Queen of Peace, the Queen of Love. The future will hold what the effects of human prayer will bring. Where there is prayer from the heart, sins and wrongdoings will be mitigated. If you consider your decades of dedication to the Church and the immensity of your sacrifices, you will see as Jesus sees. You will know what it means to have a pure heart that you own, that you have owned all your life. I pity those who will see the record of your years against their own lives, those who will wonder why they did not respond to the call of the Mother of God. I once asked My children to walk softly on the ground. What does this mean? Does it imply that you must always be meek and unspoken? Not at all. Walking softly implies that you can take the higher ground in the battles against the enemies of the Cross. You can defeat them with your charities, with your refusal to become loosened from your foundation of peace. This is what Jesus meant when He said that the Holy Spirit will always give His disciples the proper words to say. Christians who are speechless must learn to recognize the reason they are speechless; it is not always to remain silent so the peace of the Holy Spirit can remain. Speechless in the context of the secular world often means dumbfounded, and this certainly does not apply to those who preach the Holy Gospel. Off with the old, and on with the new! This is the reclamation of the material world by the spiritual realms that bring harmony and stability to global regions ravaged by corruption and war. I have not brought you a lesson today. I simply desired to come speak about My Sacred Love and give you assurance that your lives continue to be blessed. I seek in you the vision that others are lacking because you share it in your writings, with those to whom you speak, in your thoughts and contemplations, and in your future plans. You know that there are good days and bad days along this path. There are vile miscreants and outright wicked villains who are trying to keep the Church from succeeding in its mission. They have failed; they will continue to fail. I ask you to join Me with your holy sight to fashion more prayers like the one you offered today.

When you speak about your transformation into a miraculous state of mind, you base your thoughts in your Medjugorje pilgrimages, and rightly so. However, the first miracle that was accorded to you as a young boy remains with you today. It is your honest innocence. It is your gift to humanity and the Church. Where would I have gone? To whom would I have turned with your brother if you had not taken him in? Where would your Marian works be now? The answer is that they would be caught somewhere between Heaven and Earth, not pressed into Creation. You and your brother have manifested their production through your faith so that they can be placed in the hands of those who need them. My graces and your time have not been in vain. Your efforts and dedication will garner their intended results. It is for these reasons that you must remain steadfast in joy, not in apprehension or discouragement, but in the realization that you have factually accomplished everything I have asked. You have a holy and placid life here in this place, lacking the noise and commotion that exist elsewhere around your city and in the world. You make Me happy. You make Me trust that the confidence we share in the maturity of your brothers and sisters' faith will eventually come to pass. This is all Jesus asks. He did not send Me to weaken the faith of those who believe what I have had to say. You once said that miracles do not dilute faith, they make it stronger. This is the reason Jesus performed miracles. His love is so intense. Therefore, I speak to you with supernatural grace, fondness and appreciation for your lives. I have eternal vision that sees where you are going and where you have been. I understand the plight of the poor and your prayers that eradicate their poverty. You also know that Jesus is as concerned with converting the well-to-do as aiding the lives of the poor. Why? Because the latter already belong to Him. Do you have something to tell Me, My Special son? *"I wanted to wish you happy birthday. We are honoring you in the Church today!"* Yes, you and your brother have honored My birth today and every day – always do you give Me the feelings of fulfillment that lead to your eternity with Me in Heaven. You have said that time passes quickly, and this is why I ask you to live peacefully. If you do not, you will not realize the vast blessings you are accorded. I will speak to you again before your next birthday! Our birthdays are very close together, and you will someday see that we are the same age. I ask that you rest and remain peaceful of mind and heart. Thank you for praying for the Holy Father in Rome and for all unborn children in the womb."

Sunday, September 16, 2012
5:02 p.m.

"Lord God of the Saints, hear our pleas for help. Let your sovereignty reign over the travesties of this world. Wipe the sweat from the brow of our exile, and make peace inundate our lives. We offer our honest confessions in exchange for your forgiveness; please render us your aid. As we witness the destruction of this world's unholy places, grant us the strength to trust you in all times and seasons. May we become acclimated to your Holy Will as your Kingdom spreads across our tortured domain. Help us be strong in the image of your Son, and grant us the awareness that we are seamlessly united in you. We ask this through Christ Our Lord. Amen."

William L. Roth

"My dear little children, your loveliness surpasses the ageless beauty of Creation because you live perpetually in the Lord's Divine Love. It is clear that you are being vexed and tormented by Satan because you are doing so much good. My Special one, I have trust in you and your brother to overcome the forces of evil that are attempting to stop your progress. It has been the same for all souls who belong to Jesus since they first accepted Him in faith. You are seeing what following the Cross implies, and you have seen what it means in both radical and practical terms. If you remember what you have written in the forewords and prologues to your books, especially your anthologies, you will live with clearer perspective. I simply ask you to remember that the future is bright. The journey for Jesus' Kingdom is long and difficult; it is filled with obstacles and calamities, but you will win the fight. What happens along the way is converting souls; this is nothing new to you. What fruits you bear for the Kingdom of the Blessed will be sweet to others like you. They need to be nourished by your faith; they are craving the mastery of today's living saints. The latter include you and your brother because you are pure and far more enduring than Satan. You are determined to make Jesus' wishes come true. You will see the last gasps of Satan before your eyes. Your fingerprints are among those on the saber that finally does him in. My Special son, I wish there were more words that I could issue that would convince peoples in your homeland and far abroad that the newness of the Gospel remains. It will never die; the Word has been raised and will never suffer death again. I wish that I could bring them to an enlightenment so profound that they would fall on their own swords in contrition. I wish they would surrender their wills to the Will of the Father today, before the horrible events to come. I wish that Jesus and the Father did not have to speak so ominously around the globe. And, I wish that all who claim to belong to God lived like you and your brother. Yes, you sometimes become disappointed to the degree of approaching bitterness. It is not wrong for you to despise hatred. It is not a sin to desire the destruction of the enemies of the Cross. It is not unholy to imagine those who have rejected the teachings of the Church kneeling down before Jesus, begging His forgiveness. And, it is not beyond the realms of possibility that His followers will bend to speak into their ears at that time, saying that they should have listened when the opportunity arose. There will be no recriminations because the logic of cause and effect will no longer apply. Only the future will matter. Only the heartiness of eternity will be of concern. I am like you and your brother, like all My children who have been faithful to God. I have thought about what goes through the minds of those who die and see the immensity of their sins. I have wondered why they allow themselves to be put in such a place. Were the Gospel tenets not enough? Did Jesus' Spirit not appeal to their sense of self-survival? Were the lures and temptations of the world too great that they could not invoke the majesty of the Church? All of these questions are answered when each soul judges his life before the Light of the Crucifixion. Some of them are like souls in foreign lands. They look around themselves with trepidation in their eyes. They hear their own self-assurance creaking from beneath their consciousness like a wharf being devoured by the seas. They jolt inside and shudder; they look to the suffering of the Messiah on the Cross and wonder how His Divine Mercy could ever come to them.

    My Special son, Jesus will show them the times when they handed a glass of water to a thirsty child. He will reveal to them their own childhood innocence and explain to them why it was lost. He will speak about everything mitigating, all things that made them reluctant to fall in love with Heaven, anything that lets them see themselves beneath the blanket of His Providence. You are seeing the destruction of those who have not accepted the Cross. They are causing havoc worldwide, across the face of Africa and in the Asian nations too. They are like animals out in the wild, starved because they are not being fed the truth. They are madmen in search of an asylum; they are untethered from rhyme and reason, they are hidden from the true light of day. We are not surprised, you and I, about what we are seeing around the world. We are not perplexed to find that those who reject the God of the Nativity are living in such unrest. It suits them. They wear their disbelief like epaulettes on their shoulders, and they are utterly deluded about the purpose of human life. They will someday see what they prescribed for themselves, only darkness and hellfire that is incapable of producing any light. They will see their own mocking of the Vicar of the Church, and they will wonder how they could have been so blind. I have asked you to pray for them, but not to pity them. And, I have described many motives of those who refuse the Cross. There are tens-of-thousands of them. There are cults and sects of nonbelievers who are destined for the same sad end. Is the Divine Mercy of Jesus sufficient for them? It is they who must decide. Thank you for hearing Me today, for holding your strength against the wickedness that you have seen in your day. And, thank you for being patient. Pray for your coworkers who are as exhausted as yourself, and for those whose marriages are failing. Peace abounds in this home because you and your brother do not retreat from the work you have been given. You know the distance that must be traveled, the challenge of the days, the joy awaiting to emerge in you, and the rest that you will deserve. Choose wisely to remain at peace of heart and mind. Live with confidence that you are in control of your days. Never defer to the cynicism to which you are drawn because you are not a disparaging people. Thank you also for praying with Me and remaining united with your brother. I will be with you again on your birthday! I love you. Goodnight."

Sunday, September 23, 2012
Saint Pio (Pius) of Pietrelcina
8:54 a.m.

Laughter and Thunder

"Now, here we have joined our hearts in the Providence that has redeemed the ages and the humanity that has brought such calamity to them. My little sons, you have arrived at the autumn of 2012, and we know what this means for the future. I promise that you are stronger than you believe; you are determined to see the Triumph of My Immaculate Heart realized in your day – and these are not false hopes. Everything that you expect from God is knowable and seeable in your hearts right now, and they are occurring with ferocity in other realms and provinces. If you concern yourselves with linear time; if you worry about the reconciliation of Heaven and Earth coming into full witness during your mortal years, you are missing the point. I have opened today with a mention of the great Saint Pio. I need not remind you how relevant Saint Pio's life and experiences are in your lives. What you need to internalize even more, however, is his approach to life both inside and beside the priesthood. He would be heartily laughing and giddily witnessing the events of this new millennium if he were on Earth today because these years and moments are filled with the fullness of the promises of the End Times. Imagine living in his cell and being attacked spiritually and physically by Satan. Imagine writing letters to his friends and parishioners about his dark thoughts and horrific pains. He knew what God knew. He was aware that all that was happening to him was for the purification of humanity. Never once did he lay his head on his pillow and think that he was enduring the agonies of mortality in vain. He never felt sorry for himself. He never thought life to be unfair. He did not worry about spreading the spoils of war. He gave everything to God the same way you are giving. And, this is what makes you like Padre Pio. If you think about it, what agonies you have seen in this life have been plentiful evidence that you have already prevailed against them. You have seen the shortcomings and putrid acts of evil people, and they have not impressed you. They have left you looking beyond their effects. In fact, your strength of imagining and faith in the Church have you standing tall above your enemies' throes; you have within you the presence and willpower that will complete your lives in joy. I wish I could say this about everyone, but it is not the case with most others. I have given you the same vision that brought the Apostles to be martyred. I do not want you to be physically martyred, but your spiritual martyrdom in defense of the Gospel is a radical certainty. Proceed through these months and years in the confidence that you have already collected the victory that Jesus has assured. My Special son, your monologue two weeks ago has not fallen on deaf ears. You are commended for speaking the strains that have been raised by Saint Thomas Aquinas, Saint Ambrose, Saint Benedict and other Doctors of the Church. They all refrained the same vision and espoused the same belief that their work seemed fruitless to change or convert the secular masses. Hear Me now. The fact that you harbor such sentiments about the Church and the Will of God is what spurs Jesus to delve more deeply into His cache of miracles. He once asked the Father, 'Where are the people who care whether I give miracles or not?' He still wants to know who dares approach Him and ask Him to deploy His supernatural powers against the evils of the world. You have this courage. And, it is not courage as though you would face some kind of retribution for broaching the subject; your courage comes in the fact that you know that if Jesus responds, all those miracles will be ridiculed and rejected by the enemies of your faith. These are the same enemies that have laid waste to innocent people on all continents because the followers of the Gospel would not pray more devoutly to the Man on the Cross. When you do this, and when you laugh in the face of persecution, Jesus believes that you really care.

I once told you about the phenomenon of the electricity that comes during rainstorms, that these charges cause thunder, and the sound waves from thunder cause more rain to fall. Do you remember? *"Yes."* Your testimony two weeks ago is the same as this thunder. When you broach the subject that you would do more if you were the Lord, this induces Him to know that He has finally touched someone who cares enough about this world to change it. This must be laid alongside the power of human suffering for the sanctification of the lost, but there is a point where Jesus says adequate reparation has been made and sufficient blessings have been requisitioned. I am saying that there is a constant exchange between these two elements that Saint Pio knew about. His response was the one that is often employed by the greatest disciples of the Messianic Kingdom. He laughed in the face of danger; he was impish when others were sarcastic. His humor was disarming for those filled with cynicism. Yes, you say that he was given miracles that helped others believe in his gifts. He carried the Stigmata for 50 years. He was capable of bilocation and reading hearts and minds. But, these were not powers that made any more difference than any other person's willingness to succeed. Saint Pio's supernatural abilities were his crutch! They allowed him to navigate through life with a compass and instruments. They were certainly not his blessings. He suffered for them deeply and profoundly. Always remember that mystical gifts come through the diminishment of the flesh, often in excruciating ways, as you and your brother have experienced. Please believe Me when I say that everyone who lives with faith in things yet unseen are the true miracle workers. It does not require the Wounds of Christ to get others to follow you. It takes true piety and fierce wherewithal. It requires affirming relentlessly against all opposition what you have seen and heard from the Mother of God. It requires prudent patience and an awareness that justice and righteousness are true and real, that if not for time, all this would have already befallen those who are making such a mockery of discreet human life. Time, time, time. Everyone is worried about time. Let us not delude ourselves. Evil acts on the physical Earth are causing real pain and suffering on specific days in time. We all know that this is true. But, enduring and securing victory over these acts is the perfect reflection of Jesus on the Cross. You know that Jesus' Passion and Crucifixion occurred inside a single day. And, you know that He was raised from the Tomb on the third. What does this say about the patterns of God's good thinking? It says that the world of Christians is being crucified in the likeness of Jesus right now. The Church is being assaulted, maligned, beaten and all the rest. However, the Son of Man has already been raised, and this same Paschal Resurrection is simultaneously celebrating the resurrection of the perfected human soul. You are becoming perfect creatures living in an imperfect world in breaking bodies. This is your time in the Tomb. Hence, you are being persecuted and crucified inside a world that has been poised for the gate of Heaven since that first Easter. This knowledge was the source of Padre Pio's strength and perseverance in his cell and wherever he went. It was his way of knowing with definitive proof that everything written in the Holy Gospel is true. It played out before him and in spite of everything else that tempted him to not believe. If you live in a dungeon all your life and are suddenly raised to the summit of a mountain, what do you believe when you look back on those earlier years? That the vision from the mountaintop was inevitably true. And, once that moment arrives, it is often difficult to return your thoughts to those darker times with as much intensity as they originally possessed. The awe and joy of the final victory are simply too overwhelming to allow any negativism in.

This is where you are going; it is where Padre Pio knew that he was going, and it is why he laughed. Like millions of other Christians, his laughter was the thunder that sent waves of belief into the continents, waves that brought the shedding of joyful tears for countless souls who needed just one sign that God was on their side. They thought that if someone marked with the Crucifixion who was beaten beyond all imagination in the middle of the night, that if someone whose letters and missives spoke about the darkness in his soul and the agony in his heart could muster a laugh, then what would keep them from doing so as well? My Special son, I speak about these things and bring softer tones not because I am trying to distract you from your own pain. I am not trying to diminish the intensity of the world's suffering. The point I am making is that the conversion of lost sinners is not like spending a dollar for a loaf of bread, then spending two dollars for two loaves the same size. Suffering in the image of Jesus means pouring out everything you have without counting what is being received in return. God is the judge not only of the worthiness of your suffering, but of how merciful He must be toward those who continue to disbelieve. When you look at a crucifix and see the likeness of Jesus there, you should remember that He thought of the same questions as you. He wondered whether there would be sufficient time for everyone to take hold, for all sinners to accept what He had given humanity in exchange for their sins. We now know the answer. Time was not a sufficient factor – it never has been. And, how do we know? Because some sinners have already been cast into Hell. Time did not matter for them. And, all the emphasis that one wants to place on the element of time can matter or not matter based upon the response of those sinners to the Divine Mercy of Jesus. We are still waiting for passengers to be boarded on the airplane that you wrote about. And yet, if time somehow morphed into eternity, there are people who would never believe; it is all according to the will of exiled men. So, what is God supposed to do? He gives humanity the gift of self-direction, self-determination, and even self-destruction – the will to practice what they believe. And still, those who would know Him refuse to listen. This is the truthful origin of the most gruesome sins in the world. This is what caused the fall of Adam and Eve.

What I am saying is that the sublimeness of humanity needs to be heralded. It needs to be sounded from the summits of mountains and the valleys between them. What is good about humanity is that they have the power to choose rightly. This is what Padre Pio knew. It is the reason he did not disengage his vocation. How easily he could have retreated into isolation! After all, there existed another person bearing the Stigmata who was not a priest. But, he allowed his good fortune to choose rightly, to choose smartly and self-sacrificially that ultimately prevailed. Every time he heard it thunder in the skies overhead, he would laugh. He laughed because he knew that the world and humanity were in transition. He laughed because he knew that God was there, that Nature was responding to His Will, that water would fall where people were thirsty, that plants and crops would grow, that change would happen, that the skies would clear and rainbows likely appear. These were not only metaphors for his persistence, they were his way of writing inside his heart and for the ensuing ages that God's Kingdom consists of these things. They were the songs of his peace; they were his way of seeing his unity in God while God visited the Earth. And, it brought him to say and write so many inexplicable strains to those around him whom he congratulated for suffering the torments of human life. He actually told people that he envied them for their suffering! Now, that is an amazing thought! – so unified with Jesus, so efficient in forethought, so willing to see the imposition of his difficulties as stepping stones to a holier world. And, God said it was good. Padre Pio received graces even more. Hundreds of thousands of sinners went to confession. Jesus Christ and Padre Pio figuratively clinked their champagne glasses together in a toast of unity because humanity on Earth and God in Paradise were dutifully engaged. They were so romantically prepared to conquer the evils of the Earth, so determined to be friends that it would take the death of them both to prove it. They are now together in Heaven; they were resurrected by the Love of God. Yes, they laughed to keep from crying. They reached out to prevent themselves from becoming hermits. They looked into each other's eyes the same way that you and your brother will someday peer into the eyes of your Savior and tell Him that He did everything right. Hell took over the entire world, and the Kingdom of Love annihilated it. This is what you will say. This is what Padre Pio is telling humanity today. 'Pray, hope and don't worry – I will be waiting for my spiritual children at the gate of Paradise.' He is indeed waiting to greet the new Saints not with 'I told you so...,' but with '...thank you for not giving up.'"

Sunday, September 30, 2012
3:38 p.m.

"Heavenly Father, through your infinite wisdom, grant us the blessing of your peace throughout our lives. Hone our spiritual vision with a sense of comprehension of the abounding presence of your Will. Through knowledge and servitude, let us realize beyond hesitation that our every gift to others is a prayer to you. All in all, make us the people whom you always wanted us to be, and grant humanity the grace and dignity that preserves the holiness for which your Son was crucified. Our Lady of Perpetual Help, always remain at our side. We ask this through Christ Our Lord. Amen."

William L. Roth

"My sacred little sons, My presence here is indicative of your determination to thrive in the holiness about which you speak. You are infinite in this sense, and you are permanent and indispensable in the Lord's divine plan. As you pray with Me now, consider everything we are doing to address the deficits of the exiled world. We are making-up for what others will not accomplish in their lives because they consistently refuse to communicate with Heaven. I have asked you to be proud in a righteous way of all you have given to God because this is the record you will see in the final synopsis of life. You see far into the hearts of those who must come to their own realization of what the Kingdom of God means. This is their calling into perpetuity, and all the issues that must come before they are granted their bearings in that perpetuity must be addressed before they will comprehend its meaning. We have shared our joy of love, our collection of prayers and works that have already impacted the outcome of all these things. My Special son, I have come to you in honor of your faith and holiness. I want you to know the limitlessness in which you are loved. I want you to remember that the world is meant for preparation and reparation. You have always understood this fact. You are watching another presidential election in America come, and it will go on and away just as quickly. I have said that no matter who is chosen, they will fall short of satisfying the mandates of the Holy Gospel. I am happy that you have the opportunity to participate in public elections due to the insights and sacrifices of your American predecessors. Your brother stated it correctly when he asked what kind of people want to wade into the wastewater of Washington politics. I watch the proceedings with interest because it gives a chance for the American people to see how out of touch their government has become. Most private citizens live simple lives, lives of sustenance and maintenance. You would not recognize this kind of orientation in the people in public office if you were unaware what to look for in them. They have become cynical and detached; many are power mongers and pathological liars. Hence, I wish not to remain in this vein of thinking very long because even the Mother of God is capable of detesting what they do! I am like you. You are like Me. We look around the globe and see the fighting and infighting, the murders and political executions. We know about the violence and vengeance that have defined the global landscape. However, I also see the holy acts that are pushing the perpetrators into the dust. I see the sacrifices and humongous contributions to the mission of the Church by unknown people in remote places. When these people rise, they will not be able to be held back. They are the collective weapon of mass-destruction that will unleash holy triumph over the evils of this world. If you placed a dot on the surface of the globe where each of these people live, you could see from outer-space that these countless dots, when connected, create a framework that will place the enemies of the Cross in chains. You are part of this network that is seeable to God from the realms just above the Earth. Jesus has placed it there with your help. It is a network of wisdom and grace, healing and unification. I am telling you that the coalition of these manifestations will occur in your lifetime. Also, I continue to be aware of the plight of little children at the hands of abusers and molesters, and these little victims are playing a part in the suffering of humanity. I offer you now My holy blessing. Thank you for your prayers. I love you. Goodnight."

Saturday, October 6, 2012
9:59 a.m.

"Masterful God, with divine reason we acclaim your holy name and dedicate this world to the Scepter of your Providence. Cleanse and remake us in your likeness. Deepen the furrows of our sacrifices that your Will might be embedded in our being. Help us become creatures of the light, willing to shed the darkness of our exile. Absolve us of our sinfulness and lift our hearts into the infinity of your love. Remember those who have died and restore them to everlasting life. Hear our petitions in union with your Immaculate Mother, and grant us the humility exemplified by her life. We ask this through Christ Our Lord. Amen."

William L. Roth

"And, the Mother of God stands with you too! I bring today My outpouring of accolades for your righteous lives because this is what the God of your fathers desires. Would it be too much for the Matriarch of the Church to bring into Creation even more adulation for everything you are doing for the refinement of humankind? It is clear that My children do not receive the recognition they deserve for cleansing the Earth of the dirtiness that secularism has wrought. It is not that the recognition is lacking from Heaven, but from ordinary people everywhere who do nothing themselves but criticize others who do. It is equally clear that the mountainous gifts and praises already coming from the New Jerusalem are inundating the world in ways that cannot yet be seen. They are showering down upon the servants of the Cross like gentle rains, and their impact is felt by the satisfaction inside the human soul. I cannot overstate what this means for the future. Every person who has visited

Medjugorje has taken home with them an inflection of righteousness that they cannot see. It is like a pious infusion of good will and holiness that will always be with them. And, they can spread this holiness to others just by being around them when they go back to their cities and workplaces. Jesus has injected His Will into His people. This is not a culmination, but a new beginning. Souls will soon stir like babes waking from their sleep. They will sound the truthful strains of olden times through the new corridors of the Earth. All the goodness of the centuries will rise at once. Light will shine, and explosions will occur. The flash of divine awareness that God has promised the Church will be obvious to all who believe and to those who have never tried. My Special son, these things will occur in your lifetime. What you wrote in support of your Bishop is absolutely correct. His statements and positions about those who pander to evil are true. There is a place in Gehenna for everyone who supports, fosters, performs and suborns abortion whether it is the doctors, politicians, the courts, judges or people who visit and vote for them. This is no idle threat, and its ramifications will be seen in time for those who are guilty to run to your Bishop and thank him for his heroic voice. Why is this the case? Because Jesus saw your recent letter in support of your Bishop as a prayer. It makes no difference who else sees it for now; someday all will see. The power of your letter has become the urgency in the Sacred Heart of Jesus to respond to you. This is how prayer works. Therefore, I have come today to bring My heartfelt gratitude for your faith and loyalty. I thank you for taking such good care of your brother. I thank you for resting when you are tired. I thank you for remembering the poor and downtrodden in your morning prayers. It is clear that you are preparing the way for the grand entrance of the Son of Man into His Kingdom with unprecedented joy. I realize that you are doing everything in your power to persuade Jesus to have Mercy on His enemies. I am as well. And, as you see the poise of the world, know that it is positioned for all the manifestations that I have spoken about this morning. It is a good day; these are auspicious times. I only ask that you protect yourself when you are driving and traveling. Remember that the flu and cold season has just arrived. Be at peace in your heart, despite the antagonism at your workplace. This is a time of transition in America and around the world, and it is one with eternal consequences. We are making the most of it by what we are doing now."

Sunday, October 14, 2012
9:03 a.m.

Love is Handsome, Grace is Beautiful

"With holy gratitude, I come to pray with you in the vibrancy of your faith. I ask that you remember what a great gift this is for the world. We ask the Father in whose presence I stand to bless you in all ways, in all perfection and assembling. Today, I ask you to pray for all who are conceiving children and birthing them, for all who have adopted children, and especially for children who are in need of guardians and mentors – Christian mentors. Jesus is the Savior of humanity, and Jesus is the Mentor of Christians so that you may realize the depths and heights of His Truth in the exile of man. I wish for you to know that there is a distinction to God, that He is both handsome and beautiful. Yes, He is handsome through Jesus, and He is beautiful through Me. What does this mean? What is it like to be handsome? First, it means that God is generous. It means that He approaches the world through an amalgam of consolation and fruition. The Father stands above the created Earth and kneels down to it, not in deference, but in pity and compassion. The Lord knows what every person will eventually discover. He knows that the whole preeminence of your religious faith was formed from the start of all the universes. Your faith was given to you from the days of Genesis. I ask you to remember the Father for this handsomeness, for His prayer-inducing Will by which the Church has lived. God also provides for His people in the gifts that await you, in the anticipation of the human heart that His Providence is overwhelming you. There are crooked lines on Earth, but smoothness in the Most Sacred Heart of Jesus. There are paramount imperatives that He seeks from those whom He has redeemed. It is here that you discover the identity of the Christian soul. This Providence says that souls bound for Salvation cannot fail. There will be glad times and joyful days. There will be toils and setbacks. There will be triumphs and defeats. But, there will be ultimate victory. My Special and Chosen sons, you have accepted this course, and you are charting new courses for those following you. These things are accomplished by the virtue of your very being. The essence of your identity before the Cross and before the Seat of Wisdom is defined by this tremendous greatness in you. I ask that you look at yourselves through the lens of this sacredness. You have been created in the image and likeness of God. You have manifested His mandates. You have deferred to His Gospel. You have bowed before His Scepter. You have forged new beginnings at home and abroad, and brought them to His right hand. And, why have you done so? Because you know that God is handsome, that He draws all creatures to His power, that it is in Him that humanity has inherited the future. The Father waits for the eyes of all to look at Him, to envision His splendor and authority. You are directing your brothers and sisters' focus toward Him; and for this, you will see the grandness of your own elevation.

Our handsome God redeems His creatures through Grace. I assure you that this Grace is the initial beauty in which I was created. I am dispatched from Heaven to summon all seers and hearers to take up their crosses for the cause of human redemption in the Blood of My Son. It is through this Grace that My children are awakened. It is time to be immersed in the Baptismal waters and in the Blood of the Lamb! This is My call to My children. It is a beautiful chant from a beautiful Grace that is intrinsic to God and the Mother of the Son. It should be remembered in the context of the conversation between Heaven and Earth, the Lord to Moses, the Angels of Enlightenment, the Archangel Gabriel, the Intercessory Saints, and all who speak and relate to the cultivation of the Father's vineyard with strains of sweet revelation. The graceful are accompanied through the exiled world by the handsomeness of God. It is all beautiful. The destination is imminent for all who hope for change, all who are dedicated to the Church and consecrated to Jesus' Sacred Heart and My Immaculate Heart. Look at the grand scales and portions of change that have already come. My dear little sons, millions of people wonder how the Mother of God could come to this world with any semblance of joy. I do so because you are here! I come every day and all night long in appreciation that so many are living-out their faith in Jesus. How could a Mother who sees all things given to the Holy Cross not be filled with joy? All the tragedies and calamities on Earth are caused by lost sinners who do not join in this joy. I assure you that we have accomplished more in the past fifteen minutes toward fulfilling the Will of God than some people will yield in their entire lifetime. This is what we do here; it is our prayer and works of holiness. Every second that ticks from the clock ratifies that you are living for Jesus! You have perpetuated an environment of welcoming for the Son of Man to return. You are casting out demons with your prayers; you are healing and providing. And in this, you are handsome too! You are standing strong in the Light of Wisdom for all the world to see. You are hailing the heavens to visit you here, to heed your call to manifest change where amendments must be made. You are filled with the favor of Holy Love that you are spreading across these lands and beyond your sight where the Blessed Trinity reigns. Hence, My message today is a blessing for you. It is My way of reminding you that the Lord God stands with you and beside you. His Spirit is implanted within you. And, My Special son, you are making the most of My intercession and your prefaces to My weekly messages by compiling a thoughtful manuscript to stake claims on behalf of God. These hours that you spend are like those of the Doctors of the Church. Please reflect upon your work as the righteous beauty, the grace that dignifies the sacrifices of the Church and the Crucifixion of Jesus on the Cross. You are seeing time getting on these days for many people you have known who are coming now to Heaven. Some are your age, and some are younger. As I have said on many occasions – for everyone in every place, there comes a time. These are meant to be fruitful weeks and months that you and your brother are living, and you are assuredly doing your part. You are asked to rest all you can, to see that you do not become exhausted mentally or physically from your workplace. You can do this if you lighten your heart about what you allow to bother you. These matters are sustainable because you have the Holy Spirit working within you. It is important for you to recognize the hand of God where you see it, and pray in thanksgiving for the blessings that He brings."

Sunday, October 21, 2012
2:53.p.m.

Perfect.

"My little children, when autumn comes, you are prone to lend your thoughts to the grand parade of seasons that have heretofore come and gone; you are touched by the meaning of it all. You are welcoming of the memories that have made you feel a sense of unity with Nature and time, with God and His beauty, and with His peace and passion. As backward as it sounds, it is not the springtime that reminds most people of the awakening of the Earth, but the harvests of autumn. This is a time when the maturity of the world seems its fullest. It is the time when the planted seeds are reaped. Autumn is where your hearts are headed, but you must work in the springtime fields to get there. You must endure the heated summertime battles of human cultivation. Today, I have come to tell you that it will be all seasons upon the return of Christ Jesus because His universal awareness implanted in all who believe transcends any one moment in time. I have said that you have prayed in the likeness of the Saints. You have imparted to your brothers and sisters the hallmarks of Salvation. You have been the incarnation of spiritual and physical sacrifice. And, all this makes you perfect. You have written your hearts into justice by pouring-out your souls before men. You have wrought the pardon of sinners; you have ushered the light into the darkness, and you have taken the lost by the hand to travel with you into the valleys of redemption. My Special and Chosen sons, I come to you today in intense joy. I realize that the world is still brawling and bubbling; it is still creaking under the strain of human error. Animus against the Cross is everywhere, and this means that the stream of human mortality is about to run uphill. Nothing contrary to the Truth of the Gospel has an afterlife. Everything that stands in opposition to the Cross has been slain. Anti-Christian philosophies are already bleeding to death. Heresy is hanging by a thread, hoping the thread will never break. The Catholic Church is in joyful agony in the image of its King. Conversion is ongoing; awareness is overcoming ignorance, commitment is defeating indifference, love is conquering hatred, warmth is vanquishing coldheartedness. The sun rays of the Lord's favor are piercing the paleness of the Earth like daggers. Societies have been born, and most have died. Civilizations have run their course. Believers are being vindicated. The righteous are racing toward the finish line with the baton of victory in their hand. These are all signs of the harvest of the world. And, they are perfect. Now, the Church is naming new Saints poised beside the Saints of old. The Mass is the redemption of the hell-bound, the Sacraments are food for the unconverted. When you see from the other side of life what I have told you today, you will know that you have understood it all along. Therefore, it matters not what injustices appear to be insurmountable. The lives of the Martyrs will be saved after all. Your dreams of past years will be realized before they shall ever cross your slumbering eyes again. And, do you know the reason why? Because they are perfect.

I once spoke of your absolution from God as though it were an undeserved manifestation. And yet, this may still seem the case, but what is worthy of His graces? The Father does not ask for all that much! Battles and holocausts are surely not the cure. It may indeed require battlefields and bloodbaths; and if it does, they will be perfect. All in the name of the Son of Man! You are sacred children. You are given to the Wisdom of the centuries.

Your legacies belong to the ages, and your future belongs to the Messiah. If you search for peace and cannot find it, perhaps it is lost in the shadows of your perception. Could it be possible that you have planted your faith so deeply in the sacrifices of the Christian life that your hopes are also there in the furrows? If this is true, do not despair, the harvest will come. This is the message that you are giving humanity. This is the hope that you have handed to your Bishop. This is what he sees; it is what the Angels tell the world. I speak about reaping and weeping, about getting tired and resting again. I imply that one must pass through the gauntlet before basking in the glorious Son. We know what we have seen! Your time here has been preceded by your own good intentions. Your service to the Child of Bethlehem is worthy of esteem. Your willpower and staying power have upheld your drive when others would have you fall into disbelief. Like all those masters who have stayed the course without faltering, you have been there too. Do you know why? Because you are perfect. I have spoken about the renewal of the human domain. You have written about Jesus wiping His vineyard clean. We have laughed and wept together about the same eternal joy. And, we have never parted from one another or departed from that vision inside you that makes you confident of your life's mission. Those who have begotten children have done the work of God. Those who have not begotten children have inherited His Kingdom before others shall see its undimmable sheen. Vocations and consecrations are consuming the material world. The flames of holy love are glowing everywhere. And, My Special son, do you know why? Because they are perfect. Your souls are blessed; your years are filled with honor, you have dignified your births; you have uplifted the reason Jesus was commissioned here in the earthly realms. This is the message that I hope you will place in your writing and expand upon it. Tell your brothers and sisters and your friends and enemies that the Mother of God has not forsaken the oath that I made on Good Friday. I will stand beside My children beyond the final day of the world. I will be here and there as well. I will pursue the conversion of lost sinners, and I will invoke the Cross to defend them. There is resonance in everything I say. There is melody and harmony, cadence and timbre. I simply want you to know that the course of events that seems unavoidable every day is oftentimes more irrelevant than mentionable. Find the grace in the days ahead! It is there. It is not an insurmountable prospect to filter from all the noise and jargon the voice of the Holy Spirit speaking through the years. You know, My Special son, that this has always been My gift to you and your fellow human beings. My arms never tire holding the Little King. My eyes never grow weary looking at My children rising to their feet. The intensity of My Motherhood is never dimmed by those who do not obey. Their concessions will come. Their drive will opt toward the direction of Salvation. This too is the reason I am able to come here with joy, to remind you that the great battles of the world have come and gone, and the last one will be of the truest consequence. When you are asked to lift-up your hearts during Holy Mass in the context of the mission of the Church, and in everyday life, this means to tender your unlighted candles to the Light of Love. I ask that you and your brother remember to share this joy that I have spoken about today. I have said through all My messages of the past two decades that these years would come. I have spoken about breaking hearts and dwindling fears. I have said that death and destruction would sever lives and consciences. All this has come true. You are getting on in the world that is moving by the hour closer to the Return of the Son of Man in Glory. And, this is why I have asked you to live each hour of the day one moment at a time. Understand the greater message of human deliverance, but keep your eyes and heart focused on the tasks at hand. The Lord will bless you when you do. Please pray for the brokenhearted and those suffering for the conversion of the lost. Saint Pietra Giganti is interceding for you and your brother, and good tidings are coming your way."

Sunday, October 28, 2012
12:40 p.m.

Common Depths and Decisive Moments

"Such beauty resides here in this place, My little sons. Yes, I have spoken to you nearly four years privately, and I intend to continue My messages as long as the Lord allows. You have grown as much in wisdom and enlightenment in the past four years as you have in the first years. And, the reason? Because you love Me. It is the simplicity of authenticity of your sacred love that keeps Me coming here, returning to depend on your faith, asking that you remember in your prayers all the lost souls we are trying to reach. I am speaking today about common depths and decisive moments. These are two terms you may wish to speak about in the future, two concepts that you may tell the world that I spoke about in My messages. Common depths simply means that all Christians are called to equal sacrifice; and this is the utter denial of the self and surrender to the Will of God. It is the measure of these depths that determines the reciprocal heights that those for whom you pray are raised. Yes, it is the image of the trees on the surface of the water. And, decisive moments are created by these common depths. Decisive moments are those times when you take advantage of private and social circumstances to advance the Gospel message and refer to the content of your books. Creation has been filled with decisive moments that have lasted months and years, and at times only a few seconds. This begs the question about the difference between a moment and an event. The difference lies in another similar word, 'momentum.' Momentum is the collection of consecutive decisive moments seen across chasms of time. You have been living this momentum for decades. I ask you today to also remember that those who deny the Cross and reject the Gospel have no momentum either way. They are imbedded in their own lack of faith. They move neither forward nor backward. It is for the reorientation of these people that I have come to the Earth for centuries, to awaken them and call them to Christian awareness. How many times must the Mother of God ask Her children to pray and fast, do penance, pray the Rosary, and perform the Spiritual and Corporal Acts of Mercy? Until all men come to realize that all these elements are in their power. Common depths. The equal realization by the whole of humanity that the world is broken. Humanity has a soft underbelly that leaves it open to the predators and assailants from beneath. I have asked My children during every age to remember this, to know that it is not just what people see that matters, but what constitutes the underside and inside of Christians that must be considered. My apparitions and appearances are obviously not new. I have even been seen in more than one location on Earth before I was ever assumed into Heaven. I had the gift of bi-location in the way of many Saints and seers before they died. My apparitions are the same. I am in Heaven right now. I am on Earth at this moment as well, and in as many places at once as My Son wishes Me to be.

My little sons, the concept of common depths unites you with the Church of bygone ages and all those who comprised it. You can feel these depths when you pray and oftentimes as you are walking and seeing the world about you. Common depths does not imply a negative circumstance; it does not always have a negative connotation. It unites you with Jesus' whole earthly life and His Passion and Crucifixion. Common depths allow you to know what Jesus felt when He went for the keys and came back again during the first Easter Triduum. Common depths help you comprehend the sadness of others;

they assist in your sympathetic identification with those who mourn. You say the right things at the right times to comfort and console the dying and grieving, and these are the origins of decisive moments that change those hearts that are begging to understand the Will of God. It is here that you are one with the Messiah; you are His emissaries and ambassadors. You are dispatched by the Holy Spirit to bring Good News to the poor and heal the brokenhearted. And, these are among the reasons that I have told you many times that I admire you. It would have been more comfortable for you to have pursued more worldly lives. You could have allowed the Kingdom of God to come to Earth without you; and it would have come even so. However, this same Kingdom is now more inclusive of souls who would not have known. This Kingdom is more whole than it would have otherwise been. Make no mistake about it; there are fewer condemned souls for the fires of Hell to consume as a result of your faith and years of hard work. My Special son, you may remember the saying that has been often spoken, 'Keep the Faith.' It is used as a street slogan and a pep call to commit the uncommitted to certain movements and causes. I have never lost sight of what it has meant to the Church and the secular world. Keep the Faith. This has been the battle cry of Christians for hundreds of years. Walk hand-in-hand to the common depths that elevate the Son of God before all men. What you are thinking is true. There will eventually be one final decisive moment. As humanity prepares for that time, we continue to pray and realize in advance that it will be one of tremendous joy. The burning of useless secular 'shrines' and the destruction of archaic social institutions will foster a time of tremendous celebration for those who believe in Jesus Christ. Walls of opposition will fall in clouds of dust, and the sun will shine from behind. The din will be heard; the rustling of ages-long Christian traditions will be seen standing again from beneath the centuries of modern human indifference. The Resurrection of Jesus foretold all these things. You and your brother will deal with practical and pragmatic matters as long as you live. This is part of life. But, there can be tremendous victories in these practical realms. Behind them all will be your confidence of the world to come, your ever-living surety that you have given your lives and years to God for every reason that could be manifested through the teachings of the Church. It is all about this, My Special one. It matters not what your detractors say or who moves from one continent to another. Neither does it matter who holds the greatest wealth or the highest office in the land. What matters is that good and decent men like you and your brother build upon what Jesus has given this world. You build it in your hearts and by your prayers; you build it by hoping that everything you have implanted into the consciousness of other men will bloom like giant redwood trees. Never mind the mustard seed for now! I am speaking about your spark of fire, about your inexhaustible vision through which God Himself is viewing the condition of His earthly vineyard. You and your brother are seeing for Him as though you were satellites in outer-space, relaying messages about intent and content. He listens to your evaluations of why men do certain things and why others do something else. He accepts your interpretation of what must be done, and when. This is the power of your prayers. The Father takes all this into account because He loves you, and He lays your perceptions and requests alongside the Divine Mercy of Jesus when He decides what to Will and allow. It is this struggle that has been ongoing for thousands of years. And, believe it or not, it is not a struggle about opposing viewpoints. It is a means by which the Father exacts His justice against those who will not comply. It is about the power of the Crucifixion to forgive them. How great Thou art! This means that the Holy Sacrifice of the Mass is the living and breathing evidence that the Lord's power to pardon the guilty is now and shall forever be intact. Will He forgive sinners *after* the Second Coming of Jesus in Glory? Yes, by all means, yes. But, the measure by which He forgives will be determined by that last gasp of men as they have the choice to accept the Cross or condemn themselves to eternal death. You and I know that this is the decisive moment that will alter the course of eternity. Please remember to invoke the intercession of all the Saints and pray for all souls this week. I will join your prayers to Jesus."

Saturday, November 3, 2012
1:31 p.m.

"Every song begins in the middle of a melody whose opening strains have yet to be written."

"My dear little children, these are the glorious hours that have meant so much to the Kingdom of God and the conversion of the lost souls about whom I have been speaking in Medjugorje and elsewhere. I remind you of the Gospel Covenant to which your faith is given. I wanted to come speak to you because of the virtuous life you and your brother have accorded My Son. This is beneficial to the Church and for everyone who will hear the resounding voice of your Bishop in the future. I am foretelling times to come that you have anticipated, but this will be more burdensome for you and your brother than you could have believed. You have fulfilled your responsibilities to the Church; your future of Salvation has been assured. What needs to occur in the near future is the recapturing of your confidence that My plan continues to be on course. I have said here in this place and around the globe that cultivation consists of many forms, many components, elements and dimensions. This requires a vision for all My children that is inclusive of the wishes of Jesus to be gentle, even with the most disdainful souls. You have seen them; you are still seeing them, and their identities will become more distinct than ever before. It is true that people in the Church will persecute you for what you have done for Me. Remember that it was the Church itself that martyred Saint Joan of Arc! This means that you must be strong in the face of your adversarial acquaintances. Why? Because some of these people have established a record of friendship with the Church and distinction among the masses. You and your brother have become very tired. I ask that you both take some time as you are planning tomorrow to set your minds at ease. We must get through this together for My mission to succeed. You are seeing the unfolding of the Triumph of My Immaculate Heart in ways that are heartening to God. He has placed such emphasis on My Grace! Even the great Saint of Communication, Saint Gabriel, is chanting the strains of joy! He has seen all your books and other writings. Saint Gabriel has been the inspiration for your holy insights; Gabriel has assisted you in compiling your works and messages, your prologues, prefaces, and prayers. These times are revealing the marvelous fruits of what we have done for God here on the Earth! And, you must remember that the deliverance of the millions whom I have tried to convert through My global messages is ongoing; it is a certainty that they will remain in the ranks of those who will fight until their last breath for the dignity of the Church. However, there are so many questions and incongruities abounding around the world. As you say, many people and leaders of large flocks have decided that they do not require the intercession of the Mother of God. Please tell Me, should I remain among them nonetheless? Should I attempt to communicate with someone who will not listen to Me? Am I throwing My paradisial messages for humanity before the swine? *"I hope not."* When Jesus sees no reference to His Mother during the Holy Sacrifice of the Mass and in prayer groups, how do these Catholics differ from the Protestant sects? *"They have been taught to be that way since Vatican II."* And, you have seen that an entire generation of Catholics has been born to supplant the previous generations that have died. This new generation is shorn of the devotion that was once held for Me, for the Holy Rosary, the Marian Litanies, and the prayers to the Archangels. You must realize that My messages here and around the world are recalling the conscience of Catholics to these traditional themes. It is only by doing this will Roman Catholics remain faithful to the Pope. It is only in this that they will return their focus to the conservative principles by which the Church has survived for twenty centuries. We have spoken about liberalness before, all its relativism and proneness to turn away from the true Faith that has been the focal point of orientation to God. This is why these are happy times!

These trends and persuasions are dying because they bear no righteous fruit. This is likewise the reason your books are with your Bishop. Consider the revelatory urgencies that I have invoked in My Morning Star Over America messages. Imagine yourself in his shoes! My messages that your Bishop and others are reading unfurl a whole new meaning of life for those responsible for the propagation of Christianity and the preservation of the Church. I have said what you repeated in your video to your Bishop in My messages – themes and frameworks that can provide the restructuring of the modern world around the institutions of the Church, away from the diluted morality of secular humanism. Everything that lures people away from holiness is addressed in My messages here and in Medjugorje. The things I said at Fatima and Lourdes are surely good beginnings and sound foundations for what is happening now.

My Special son, this is why I have hope that is larger than the sun and just as brilliantly bright. It does not take a perspective from Heaven to know that this is true. Anyone who is aligned with the content of the Gospels knows that there exists here in this time and place an architecture of inherent justice that is breaking past the dawn. You and your brother and like-minded people are the fortunate ones who know this in advance. Yes indeed, there will be high leaders in the Church and secular governments who will wonder why they sold out to greedy sources, who did not stay the course in honor of the Cross, who have foregone their mission in favor of self-elevation and self-aggrandizement. Why invoke the Most Blessed Trinity if the human heart does not see fit to respond? This question is unique to My Morning Star messages. I have placed a massive conscience-examining inquiry before the Church and before the world about what the true intentions and motivations of modern Catholics really are. Your brother's student friend even said at the campus that the greatest opposition to My messages will come from other Catholics. Imagine that! These people do not oppose My messages because they are too conservative to believe, but because if they believe, they will be required to abandon their casual druthers. I have been fighting against this paradox since before you were born. I have begged and admonished My children at every turn. I have tried miracles and cures. I have drawn on the most impassioned principles of those who choose the ways of Christianity, and most of them have said that the chapters and verses of the Bible are sufficient. My answer is that they are correct; everything they need to get to Heaven is there. But, what about the cultivation of this world? Jesus performed miracles when He tread these lands for the same reasons that I am performing them now. And, many people believed Him! Those who did not saw fit to take Him to the Cross. This same Crucifixion is ongoing as those to whom I am speaking are crucifying My Immaculate Heart. I cannot redeem anyone through My sorrows, but their persecution of My Queenship can keep them from being converted. These are among the reasons that I keep coming to you. All your works and words have made clear that the Mother of Jesus Christ should not be ignored. And, whether you choose to believe it as too good to be true or not, this is what the Catholic Church is finally coming to know. You are correct. The Bishops confer among themselves behind closed doors to share their thoughts and discern what to do. They are coming to the conclusion that My Immaculate Heart is the answer. They are seeing that I am more than an Advocate for the Church before their Savior. Again I say, this is all good news. There is grand excellence occurring out of sight of your senses that will elate you and your brother when you finally come to see it. The road of life is as long and arduous as people choose to make it based on their life's choices, who they marry, who their friends are, where they live and work, what their habits become, what they wear and drive, where they travel, and all the rest. The Lord God should not be blamed when something goes wrong during these human discernments and decisions. I have given you a great many things to think about, but mostly that you should try to keep your thoughts aloft where they belong."

Sunday, November 11, 2012
9:29 a.m.

Signology: Peace, Joy and Brotherhood

"Now, My dear little sons, you understand the power in congruence with the Cross; you realize that purity is as begotten as the Son; you share in the Glory that has destined humanity for Salvation. I come in tremendous joy today that we have reached such summits in the conversion of lost souls. Like the beating of a heart, you do not see this with your eyes. You cannot tally the number of converts. You scarcely have access to the acts and desires of those who have come to know their Savior. You are hearing the sound of the winds blowing where they will. The brightness overhead is more than the sun. Arriving through the driving force of those winds and beneath the solar brilliance are sacred signs of peace, joy and brotherhood. Would God permit the winds to blow somewhere that His Providence would be missing? Would He allow the sun to shine on a land without promise? Of course not. I have spoken about a bright and shining hope in My prior messages because they are aglow in the prayers of the faithful. Christianity is not just about duty, service and obeying. It is about touching and feeling – the two are not the same. One cannot feel anything until after the touching occurs, either spiritually or physically. I have told you about process in My previous messages as well, about how the sequence of events is as important as the individual events themselves. Hence, Grace has come from Heaven to teach the world about redemption. The Sacrifice of Mount Calvary forged it into being. The Resurrection of the Messiah raised all mankind from death. Yes, the Crucifixion erased all human sin, and the Resurrection wiped away the ravages of mortality. Here you see the sequence in the parameters of time. The word I have issued at the beginning of this message is 'signology.' This means that there are identifiable revelations in the absolution of men, and they are embedded in your levels of faith. The more you believe, the more you see. The more you serve, the more you know. Knowledge comes to those who serve. When peace, joy, and brotherhood intersect at the crux of this equation, you arrive at the plateau of understanding, and the world stops spinning. Surely it is true that the benefit of religious faith is to further the self-identity of those who believe. What does this mean? It means that the constancy of God takes root in the inconstancy of the mortal being. The identity of a mortal man is supplanted by the being of Christ Jesus. Once this happens, peace and joy become the feet upon which brotherhood stands. There is no such thing as a depressed Christian. There is no such thing as a Christian without hope. This is the reason, My Special son, that I have come with such confidence to you and your brother. What we have done here together will affect the world and the ages precisely as I have been telling you for almost 22 years. We can speak of signs and wonders all day, and they have reciprocal importance at any given moment. However, they are not the source of the revelations about which I speak, they are their products. The source of the signology is your willingness to believe, your decision to stay the course, and the vision you have gained from decades of faith and laboring in God's vineyard.

You and your brother are among the chosen elect who not only live here, but bear the self-awareness about the reasons why. We know that it all began with Adam who was redeemed by the New Adam. This New Adam placed into the hands of all the faithful descendants of Adam this fixture of inevitability, the redemption of the world. When I speak of Grace, I foretell the Sacred Will that has brought it down from Heaven. The Will of the Father sows every seed of goodness that will ever be harvested. They have fully grown from the soil of Creation, and are ripe for the harvest now. The fullness of the vineyard has been realized, and the pruning is being commenced. This is the harvest that continues to remove the weeds before the final harvest day arrives. I ask that you and your brother and all My children remember that you have been given a gift that will last beyond the closure of the ages. You have inside you the Church. You have within you the Truth. You have told and have been told the stories of the Gospel that are living out their realms. When you look into the faces of your friends and strangers you have yet to meet, you see only the outside, only the facade of what hollowness lives inside. It is our mission to fill this void with an awareness of God that is living in you now. It will come; it is happening; the process cannot be stopped. The infiltration of the Holy Spirit into the hearts and minds of His people is an irreversible force. This is the source of the peace and joy that serve as bookends for the brotherhood that I have described. There is no doubting the troubles and suffering that plague mortal men. There is no question that evil is making its mark. But, these plagues and evils are mortal, and the faith and truth of converted men are eternal. This is why I carry hope in My arms in the person of Jesus Christ. It is the reason I will not leave My children unaware of the grace in which they are living."

Sunday, November 18, 2012
9:03 a.m.

Eternal Sweetness

"Jubilation always accompanies Me here, My little ones, because I know that the Lord cannot fail from His purview within your hearts. It is forever the joy of Heaven to be wrapped in your care, to come from the ethereal realms to seek your assistance in converting the world. I know that you live for these times when I speak to you, but you should realize that it is not the moments when I am speaking that matter most. Here, we are taking account of what the days and years mean to you. When you live-out your lives, you are making it happen. You are brandishing Truth; you are finishing the work that Jesus spoke about on the Cross. You are completing the mission of the predecessors of Pope Benedict XVI whose mortality ended their reigns. My little sons, I will be careful in My speech today because I wish not to offend you. It seems that you have gotten yourselves caught up in the commotion of the world that I have asked you to avoid. How? You are allowing the physical domain to determine your thoughts. You are permitting sinners who do not know God to make you angry and cynical. Your voices and the content of your conversations exhibit disdain and vitriol. Your expressions are replete with frustration. These are not attributes of the children of the Mother of God. What has happened to your simplicity in Me? I wonder where it went? Why all this crass sarcasm and unpeaceful chatter? It makes Me extremely sad to believe that you have disregarded My call for peace of mind and heart. I have not taught you this way. I have asked you to perceive the exiled world as a place of darkness, and that you are supposed to bring it light. My children, are you not listening? We are moving into a year that matters greatly to My intercession throughout the past 32 years, and Jesus has asked Me to give this message today in this holy place. Please be clear about what I am saying. When a seer becomes embittered because humanity is not changing, he is betraying the Holy Spirit by his lack of inner peace. I am not saying that he is committing blasphemy, I am saying that he is violating his oath as a messenger of God's peace. My Special and Chosen ones, please do not join them. I am not speaking with admonishing tones. I am begging you to change. I rarely fall to My knees while pleading for someone to listen to Me, but I will do so if you require. I only ask that you cast-away the cynicism by which you live. There is no peace in it. If bitterness is to be your lasting legacy, then all your books have been written for some other reason. This is why I have come seeking your help. I want to know what I can do to turn your hearts and minds back to the Eternal Sweetness that you felt on February 22, 1991. Those were the hours and days when you were so receptive to everything I said about what would come 20 years hence. I warned you about not becoming cynical. I asked you to remain at peace. I pleaded with you to see the world for what it is, and not become caught up in its negativity. You told Me that it would not occur, but I knew then that I would be giving you this message now. I ask that you do not travel the path of darkness by thinking you have done something wrong. You have done nothing wrong. You have been tempted by evil to become cynical, and you have had a difficult time overcoming it. This is nothing for which you need forgiveness or anything that you must confess. It is simply a matter of fact in the lives of mortal men. It is an effect of living in your exile. It is a product of being around so many arrogant people who believe they can manipulate you and trod you down before they deem you worthy of a decent salary and a day's pay. You are victims of the greatest cynicism known to man – secularism. It is true that you must engage the secular void for your sustenance, but it is not true that it must change who you are.

Eternal Sweetness commends you to the Peace of the Holy Spirit, not because it is your last bastion, but because Peace is the only state in which holy people should live. Looking beyond the hubris of other men means that you understand the brevity of their force; you know that they have no real power. They have only their temporary vaunted self-image by which they make decisions that help them feel esteemed. I am one with you, My little sons! I pray for the future of My messages here. I seek your compassion for My Immaculate Heart! And, I know that you will tender your compassion because you love Me. Your messages from My Wisdom are the center of your lives; they have become the origin of your joy. And, I have promised that all I have said to you will reach the ears of the sinners who need it. It is a question of when. Therefore, please pray that all My messengers will abandon their hopelessness. You see the importance of being good messengers and examples of the Word of the Prince of Peace! I am not weeping over this. I am not embittered. I am simply asking you to respond. I have known that life has its way of pulling the heartstrings of My messengers at times, but I am unprepared for the abandonment of peaceful self-confidence that has occurred with many of them. My Special son, you and your brother are on that path, and I am trying to reverse it. I am simply saying that this is not the way My messengers should live. This is not the perception I wish to portray. I ask you to focus on the concept of Eternal Sweetness because it implies that you have kept above the fray. It means that you are willing to be the little child with your little friend sitting next to you who first responded to Me in February 1991. There is nothing you can do about growing older and more mature, but there is something you can do about how to get there. This does not imply that you will be less informed about the strangeness and perils of the exiled world. It does not mean that you will be subject to extra abuse or exploitation. It simply suggests that you will fight the battle without becoming embittered. You are happy warriors who belong to the Kingdom of Love inside you. Feed on this love, and do not surrender to the darkness against which you are fighting.

Now, before I close, I must say that I realize that I have run the risk today of making you believe that you should make some radical reorientation of who you are. I do not mean this at all. I am not asking you to check your thoughts every five minutes to ensure that you do not say something negative. I am not referring to this kind of attitude examination. I am simply asking that you and your brother refrain from internalizing the secular commotion. You do not have to make a value judgement about everything you see or hear on the news or about your country. Laugh when you can, and be stern when you must. I am not going to be hovering above you with a clipboard in My hands to make sure that you and your brother do not slip up, so please do not make this issue more than it is. It is a simple, matter-of-fact culture of not taking yourselves down the road of cynicism. Your health and longevity depend on your perceptions of life, and I need you to remain peaceful and happy for the work we have set out to do. I can accomplish little here on the Earth without the help of My children. Thank you for being My holy ones, My children who turn away from bitterness and sarcasm. You are My children who espouse Messianic Peace, and strive for the Kingdom of Eternal Sweetness. Thank you for praying for those who are lost in sin, for mothers contemplating abortion, and for the end of disease and famine. You would be shocked to visit the precincts in New York and New Jersey and see the plight of the people living there. You just simply would not believe your eyes. I ask that you remember that everything I have told you today has been from the bounty of My Most Immaculate Love."

Sunday, November 25, 2012
1:27 p.m.

The Saber

"Now, we reassemble to the delight of the Holy of Holies to pray not only for the potential of mortal men to convert, but for their transference into the high holiness from which they can see the remainder of the years. My little sons, you should remember that you are held in great esteem for fostering the venue through which so many of My messages have come. The last decade of the 20th century was elevated by the miracles that have come through your love for Jesus. I ask you to remember that the last thing you did for God in the previous century was to help lead your brothers and sisters to the Cross. Now, you have made this your legacy as we are speaking through the first decade of the new millennium and into the second. The Lord has issued His plenteous Mercy upon lost sinners because you have prayed that they might be spared. You have asked for and received pardon for the contrite and a period of grace for those who have yet to repent before the Son of Man. Do you not realize in what stead this places you before the Father? These are not simple words to make you feel worthy, they are facts that cannot be expunged from the ages. Here, we have manifested the reprieve that so many sinners have sought until they can at last learn the lessons of Christianity. Millions more have been brought to Medjugorje because they have been intrigued by the scent of your pilgrimages there. You bear the distinction of having returned to the United States and wrought the venue through which the Holy Spirit can infiltrate millions of other lives. I cannot place into words what this means for the future, and for eternity too. Together, we have shaped the events that will determine the architecture of the remnants of the Earth for the Angels and Saints to inherit. Your prayers, and the very prayers you are offering now, have been the difference between darkness and light. Your envisionment of what eternity should hold is truly making that infinity come to pass. Now, your passage into another Advent season means that the Incarnate Word through the Holy Spirit resides in you still. It is a matter of record that you have repeatedly made your life's profession the advancement of His Kingdom, and yours is the future to behold. The future about which I speak is between your hands and petitions; it rests in your solidarity with the Will of God to make all things holy through the Sacrifice that has indeed wiped His vineyard clean. If you were to see it now, you would realize that ten states of disruption and destruction have been narrowed to four. The one they call Sandy was calmed by the Savior. I assure you that there would have been ten billion abortions by now if not for the prayers of the faithful. The Lord oftentimes has difficulty fighting against the will of humans who care not that Heaven even exists. Their view of paradise is living however they please. Their release from the pressures of life is the convenience that comes with their irresponsibility.

You see today that I have begun My message with "the Saber." What does this mean? It is true that men have lived and died at the edge of the sword for centuries, but this is not the saber about which I am speaking. I am speaking metaphorically about the saber as a reference to the Cross. Even though men have lived and died by the Cross, the emphasis is not so much on self-defense or self-preservation as it is on the propagation of the unseen realms. When you see the Cross, you recognize its physical resemblance to a saber. It is as though the Lord has hold of the hilt, pushing it into the ground. Indeed, it is the reverse. God will pull the Cross from the Earth and supplant it with the Scepter of Jesus Christ. And, the Messiah will be here holding it in His hands. The saber is a sign of power; its simple appearance implies that force is being used. What is the force of the Cross? The death of Satan. We have spoken about the power of the Cross in all ways possible and to incalculable degrees of righteousness that have cracked the hard hearts of mortal men. The Cross is the saber that has lanced the world like a boil to allow the poison to escape, and the poison is being drained like the fathoms from the seas. The Saber. Strong and confident. Filled with audacity. Determined and defiant. Never relenting against its purpose. The Cross. Strong and confident. Filled with audacity. Determined and defiant. Never relenting against its purpose. The Cross is emblematic of the redemption of the whole human race; the Saber is indicative of the slain human will. If My children will come to Me as you say, My Special son, they will understand. I have said during My 2012 messages to you and your brother that the Bishops are coming closer and closer to realizing that they cannot succeed in their vocations or the mission of the Church without My intercession. They cannot draw the world's attention to the Holy Cross without the Mother who stood beneath it. This is the reason I asked Saint John to pray until the end of time for the conversion of My children. Humanity was represented by him. I ask all My Christians to pray along with Saint John and all the Saints for this to happen. On the Cross is the Man from Galilee. On the Cross is His Sacred Blood. On the Saber is the future of humanity. On the Saber is the blood of the Martyrs. Why would the Father remove the Cross from the groaning Earth? Because its inhabitants must see the Providence that placed it there. Do you remember what Simon Peter did when Jesus was arrested, and what Jesus said in return, when He said that it must come to pass that He should die? *"Peter drew his sword."* This was in fact Peter's denial. Jesus replied that the Will of the Father should be done. Do you remember? Simon Peter said that his Savior should not be slain. And, what did Jesus say about that? *"He told him to put away his sword."* And why did Jesus say that? *"Because He had to complete His Sacrifice."* Yes, and was not Jesus saying that it was His Crucifixion and His alone that would redeem the whole of humanity? *"Yes."* Hence, the sword, the saber became the Cross that slays the entire composite of evil works that began in the Garden of Eden. The Saber would assemble a Church to carry-out His apostolic mission.

My Special son, the image of a saber always implies the presence of blood. This is what swords do. The image of the Cross always denotes the shedding of Jesus' Blood. This is what the Son of Man did. I wish to discount some of the speech about Jesus turning Himself over to the executioners from a position of weakness. There is a movement afoot to attempt to disprove that Jesus is the Savior and King of the world because no savior or king would allow himself to be crucified. The image of Jesus being nailed to the Cross appears to be one of helplessness. Indeed, I have told you about Jesus' Last Step in a message many years ago. His obedience to the Father was emitted from His realization that the excavation of the eternity of all humanity from the ruins of damnation depended on His Love. He grew-up in a household whose father plied his skills using a hammer and nails. How fitting that this should be the way He remembered with sanctity the constructive beatification of the world that He saw in Saint Joseph's carpentry. Do you understand? *"Yes."* The thoughts of Jesus being nailed to the Cross were like the strains I have given you today about the Cross and the Saber. God the Father and Jesus the Son can command through the Cross that demons and evildoers be defeated through its power. This power is available to mortal men. The more religious leaders ignore My apparitions, the more apparitions I make manifest. They can stomp on Heaven's flowers all they want, but they will never stop their flourishing. These are all good signs of auspicious things that make the future worthy of beholding and the present worth enduring."

Sunday, December 2, 2012
9:49 a.m.

"Jesus, give us your guardian Spirit. Grant us the perseverance to prevail against our enemies who ridicule us for what we believe. Soften their hearts to the grandeur of your Kingdom; open their eyes to the tenderness of your love. We are freed by your embrace and captivated by your holiness. Let us savor every moment your providence endows; and may every living creature defer to your judgment as your Crucifixion summons us into your presence. We ask this through Christ Our Lord. Amen."

William L. Roth

"Amen, indeed. My dear little sons, it is through My Son's Love that we have gathered in prayer for the conversion of lost sinners. This has been our purpose since your births. If the world will follow Me, I will lead the whole of humanity through the darkness with the Light of My Torch. Today, I ask your prayers for all whom you have known, the hundreds and thousands whose lives were lived with hope and imagining, with deliverance from evil because of your prayers. We must remember them, My sacred little sons, because they will in turn ask the Father to bless and forgive everyone they have known. When you ponder your families, your schoolmates and playground friends, the companions with whom you have sported and studied; they all possess individual qualities that made them unique. This will never change. Even as they are one in the collective conscience of Christianity, they have their own characteristics that make them who they are. This is the way of the Lord. I am pondering what else I could have done to reach them in accordance with the Will of God. And, it is not so much that there was anything lacking in My efforts and the Father's summons, but what each person to whom we have come did in response. Some saw the signs and chose to call them coincidences. Others hardened their hearts. Millions have attributed miracles from Heaven to daydreams and delusions. I promise that Heaven has tried with overwhelming emphasis to reach every living being on Earth, to awaken them to the dawn of the Living Christ, to perpetuate in them a desire for the supernatural, to feed their hearts Eternal Wisdom, and to lift them above the tragedies and travails of everyday life. Humanity's presence in the world is called 'exile' for a reason. My little sons, you must impress upon the nations that the physical realms in which you live and breathe every day are not the home of resurrected men. You will all die here where you have lived, but you do not belong to this world. I am not asking you to become disengaged from the temporalness of life. I am not suggesting that you should become hermits or uncomfortable in your own skin. I am simply saying that if you do not view the crassness of secular life through the lens of this transcending vision, you will never be happy as members of the Church. Everything by which you live and in which you believe is a function of your capacity to rise above the darkness and see reality for what it really is. This is the definition of the sanctity of human foresight.

My Special son, I veritably trust everything that you say and do. I pursue your reactions to world situations because your response is a prayer to God. You do not live by ideologies or self-adulation; this is not who you are. You have acquired a practical combination of logic, pragmatism, spiritualism and miraculous charm. This is what I have sought of all the Saints. And yes, the life that Father Ted has chosen is one of tremendous sacrifice and service, but each person has his or her own gifts to hand Jesus in the manger, on the Cross, and upon entering the Church Triumphant. You know where the devil does his work; you can see it in the gruesome conditions of places like Kenya and Nigeria. This is not something new. If you had placed your hands in those of Mother Teresa as a Roman Catholic priest, and looked into her eyes as she commended you to a life of poverty serving the poorest of the poor, you would have responded with as much sacrificial fervor as Father Ted. The point I am making is that you need not compare his frame of service with your own as though he is giving something greater. You and your brother are dealing with precisely the same kinds of evil, but in a different context. You will become as great Saints as Father Ted and all other foreign missionaries. When people place themselves in the false dichotomy of making assumptions about who is serving Jesus better, let the Lord judge it for Himself. Roman Catholic priests are called to a higher standard because of who they are; they willingly choose the gifts and sacrifices they tender to the Kingdom of God. They have taken on crosses to which they have declared oaths; secular people bear crosses that are heaped upon them as pious lay-persons. While I have consistently in My Medjugorje messages asked for prayers for these shepherds, it is for this reason; that they have chosen their way of life, and they deserve the prayers of the rest of the world. It would not be prudent for someone to make comparisons and draw contrasts about whom is the better servant. The life you surrendered, the future you could have had and all the rest is what is important to God. I am simply saying that the devil will torment anyone working on behalf of Christianity with false impressions about their life's work. Some who even boast of their service are doing just the opposite. Anyone who tells the world on national televison that Christianity is not a religion, but merely a philosophy, is under the influence of Satan.

So, I have spoken Myself here today about My unity with your life with your brother. This is a sacred place; you are sacred people. Your Bishop continues to discern; you continue your daily chores at your workplace, your brother continues his studying and learning, and all the citizens of Heaven and Earth who are relevant in the redemption of humanity continue their respective roles. Life goes on happily to most of these souls because they know the outcome of the exile of man. No one should dismiss the suffering of the poor; no one should take anything away from their grieving and mourning. However, you have probably noticed by now that most of the great tragedies inflicted upon people, especially here in America, are self-induced. Too much recklessness, too many lives lacking prayer, too much drinking and carousing, too little caring about self-preservation and the protection and well-being of others. Too many crimes of passion and neglect. Too little emphasis on righteousness; and yes as your brother says, too much selfishness. One would tend to believe that the more things change, the more they stay the same. This is what makes your prayer opening our message today so revealing. 'Let us savor every moment your providence endows.' I have never heard such eloquence in one prayer to God. You are saying that humanity must pursue the righteous life, to feed on the holiness of My Son, to awaken to the newness of the religious realms, and to stand in confidence against those who chide you for standing strong in your faith. This is the genesis of the title of 'Saint.' Making Father Ted a Saint is going to be easy. Making Saints of many others whose gifts and sacrifices are only now being developed and divulged will be the true test of the Divine Mercy of Jesus. Heaping forgiveness on those who are creating the conditions in foreign lands and here in the United States that make innocent people suffer is the true exercise of the power of the Cross. You emit this light and this power by the way you live and pray. All faithful Catholics do. Taking your brother by the heart 35-years ago this Christmas Eve to Holy Mass will stand-out as one of the greatest gifts to humanity ever recorded in the history of the world. Look where we have come from there. The eternal emphasis of a thousand Father Teds resides in that one night of prayer. Therefore, I ask for your sureness that all is well with Me. I know what I have seen. I certainly am disappointed about the way other people live. I become disheartened by their indifference to the call of the Cross. They are more ignorant than malevolent. None of My children know enough about hatred to hate. They are more or less victims of hatred; they were raised that way and are simply imitating what they have internalized. Hatred can be imprinted in little children to make them grow into absolute villains, but they are only living-out the doing of Satan as his instruments. It is all the spirit of the devil working through them. Inside every evil-acting person is a little child begging to come out. Thank you for your voluminous prayers. It is proper that you remember all who are suffering for the Faith, and the victims of wars and natural disasters."

Sunday, December 9, 2012
10:19 a.m.

"Lord God, Father of spirituality fulfilled, prepare for us a thanksgiving feast by which we may be nourished in your grace and blessings. Give us the poise to face suffering with courage. Make us your victors in the world's last throes. Hand us the keys to your promises, that we can conquer your enemies, flush them out, storm against their wickedness, and reorient their focus upon the glory of the Cross. Instill in humanity the desire to remain forever in the palaces of your Kingdom, and let no man walk away unsure of his destiny in you. We ask this through Christ Our Lord. Amen."

William L. Roth

Woodwinds

"Synchronized and syncopated, you are attuned with the Love of God. Here, you have realized the purpose of your lives; you are bringing forth new beginnings for the world. My little sons, outwardly and inside, the Holy Spirit is remaking the identity of mortal men in ways that will last forever. This is what we have been doing together because all that is not of God must be supplanted by everything that comes to fulfillment in Him. There are preachers and homilists proclaiming this transformation all around the globe today to millions who yet do not understand what they are saying. It is only by lifting-up the Cross as the standard of life that the whole Mystical Body will comprehend the Gospel of human redemption. At last, I have come to tell you that there are movements and initiatives afoot that will lead to My success in places where the Spirit of God has never been allowed access. This is the power of the prayers of the faithful. And in doing this, we can share here in this land and in Heaven from where I come the happiness of knowing that lost sinners are being found. For them, it has become a matter of perception. When someone thinks of the word 'faithful,' they know that it is an adjective describing someone, or in the case you just saw on television, a pet dog. Only Catholics consider the word 'faithful' to be a noun. We speak about the faithful all the time. The reason for the larger sense of the word is because it has been written in the Scripture that the Earth should be filled with the faithful faithful. We are seeing the realization of the action of love, the sharing and unification of love, becoming a personified replica of itself. Hence, the action of loving becomes a discernable entity. This is a mirror of the Incarnation of My Son. The Spirit became Flesh. The active Love of God became a visible being. My Special son, do you understand? *"Yes."* This is what the magnification of the holiness of Jesus has always been about. He said to humanity that all should share His love, and be His love. The designs about which I speak are paralleled by converted men and women, and children too, when they set aside their own volition and permit the Holy Spirit to become their identity.

Please remember that human identity is drawn toward the implementation of the revelations of God. We must be sure to pray for all who yield to their willful misidentification of who they perceive themselves to be. It becomes a matter of commodity and convenience, a way to disavow the sacrifices that the Lord commends when those who are struggling inside look only at themselves instead of outwardly toward the greater good for their suffering. I have spoken more than a few times about a grand number of identities that compose collective humanity, and this is what I am saying. All kinds of identities imply that there is mutual agreement between the different gifts that men and women bring to the Altar and before the world. Do you remember that the body has many parts? *"Yes."* All identities are sacred when they are oriented toward the purification of wayward sinners. And, when someone foregoes their own comfort and pleasures, they are giving to God their own thanksgiving for the Crucifixion of His Son. I have said that each person is like an instrument in the hands of the Father. He is a multi-talented and expert musician in the strains of righteousness. He loves to hear His instruments play the frameworks of His Will. The most natural to Him are those of human nature, the same human nature that celebrates the holiness about which I have been speaking. This is the human nature that is made from the blessings and graces from Heaven that are so plentiful to those who seek them. In the earliest years, most instruments were carved from wood; hence they had the name of woodwinds. Wood is a natural element of the created world. Men took that Nature and fashioned instruments that sounded music that has consoled the human heart and soul for centuries. This is the same principle of humanity taking the Gospel of the Lord and making it in themselves a symphony fit for Christ the King. The cycle becomes complete. The Lord gives humanity the Wisdom to transform His own Kingdom into a gift for Himself. If one looks at human salvation this way, it makes even greater sense that God became Incarnate in His own begotten Son. Remember that Jesus was not made; He was begotten. The term 'made' implies that there previously existed some unrecognizable form that was transformed into something different; it implies that disparate ingredients are combined into a wholly new product. Jesus was begotten in the image of God, and you know that this follows in the Sacred Scriptures. Begotten implies that a single Man was sent to Earth as One Person, the Second, in the Most Blessed Trinity. The point I am making is that this is what the Father procures from the new inception of every man, hewn into a renewed creature once spiritual conversion occurs. Therefore, Christians are not made; they are begotten. Do you understand? *"I understand."*

    This is an extremely important prospect because secular humans believe that something must be combined with their current identity to make them Christian. However, the truth is that their identity must be set aside, and that identity supplanted by their oneness with Christ Jesus. I am not saying that their identity is destroyed. Again, they retain all the attributes that glorify the Kingdom of Salvation, and Jesus decides what instruments they will be. Jesus chooses what part of the body they become. The whole debate about human identity must conclude in the Gospel of the Cross. Everyone must utilize their natural identity to glorify God through obeying His Commandments and entering the New Life through His Crucified Son. They must become like the woodwinds. Thus, I have completed My message for today, on the day that your brother's father Thomas turns 98 earth-years old. I can tell you where he is right now. He is everywhere and anywhere he pleases to be. He is in the heights above and the valleys beneath your feet. He is living colors and heart-touching sounds. He is speaking to the souls of the great composers, the Popes, the presidents, the common people, the shepherds, the laborers, the farmers, doctors and priests, all who have come to dine with the God of their fathers. This is the bliss; this is the tremendous and undescribable power of the Salvation of the redeemed human soul. Thomas is rewriting the history of the world with the Blood of Jesus Christ. And, so it is. With gladness and purview, he bids you hello. Even as I ask you to pray for many blessings every week, and through all the years that I have been speaking to you, please remember that I am praying for you as well. The Saints are praying for you, and the Church Triumphant is living within you!"

Sunday, December 16, 2012
12:37 p.m.

BVM – Human Thought Continuum and Pendulum Theory

"My dear little sons, Jesus did not Will that the children would die at the Connecticut elementary school; it was the work of Satan and the way young people are warehoused to learn. The evil acts of murderers are the direct result of America's rejection of Jesus. It is a product of the atrocity of abortion. It is the result of a lack of prayer. No one should blame God for the sins of humanity. My Special son, you are correct in saying that these things occur because mortal men refuse to hand over their will to the Father. They see My presence and ignore it. They have the Gospel at their hands, and will not reach for it. They are loved beyond all telling by the Kingdom of God, but they reject Him. There is no great mystery in these things. Today, I wish to speak to you and your brother about the cognitive processes of mortal men that keep them incarcerated in lives of indifference. This is a simple concept with a complicated name. It is natural to know that all people residing on Earth live in linear time. And as a result, their sights and conclusions are also linear. Their perceptions and pursuits are equally as linear. This is a line, a continuum imposed upon people on Earth because of the construct of time. I am speaking about a phenomenon that can be compared to a thermometer laying on its side. This is what time looks like to men in exile. However, the temperature on the thermometer keeps going higher and higher, and it never goes down. Hence, the linear thought patterns of men are like the mercury inside a thermometer. This is the first part of My discussion. There are two motions simultaneously at play. The entire composite of human thought, the thermometer, is affixed to a pendulum that swings back and forth in physical space. Humans think about something, hand it to a new generation, and the new generation amends and affects it according to its own views. This is the earthly concept that makes for one image and likeness of humanity, common to all other generations. All men know that those before them were men who, through the evolution of the ages, bequeathed to their successors everything they could pass. There has always been the idea of thought being a pendulum in the created world by philosophers and educators. This is not the point I wish to make. What I am saying is that the thought of humankind is like a passenger on that pendulum; so even though thought does not reverse itself in passing generations, it is set back anyway because of its position on the pendulum. Do you understand? *"So far."* I have made the point I wish to make. What am I saying to you? *"That people's thoughts, and collective civil thoughts, recede and come back at different points in time."* Yes, and most of these thoughts are limited to the conditions of the world and the constraints that human life places on the consciousness. I have given you an idea that describes this because I want My children to know that they have not fashioned anything new that has not been considered before them. It is the same principle that Jesus was thinking when speaking about the Tower of Babel. Those who are unaware of their past believe that they are creating models and concepts for the first time. They believe that they are universal and regenerative. However, they do not understand what the examinations of life entail any more than they can speak a foreign language. They are babbling about things they do not know.

So, if you speak about a human thought continuum and pendulum theory, you are saying that the minds of men are wholly limited unless they are tethered to the sublime eternal. Life and mortality keep pushing them backward like the reverse swing of a pendulum. Do you see? *"Yes."* The issue becomes, therefore, how to become free from this helpless condition and respond to the divine instincts given to mortal men by the power of the Holy Spirit. One of the writers you have seen compared this helpless nature of humanity to pushing a river. We all know that this is not possible without the supernatural presence of God's holy grace. Here is the essence of what I am saying. The rigidness of human life is not the composure of the exile of man; it is a place of preparation. Exile does not imply punishment, it fosters cultivation. Motion as though one is playing on a swing or rocking in a cradle does not permit room for expansion beyond the distance of the swinging or the arch of the rocking. You have personal knowledge that it is possible for the miraculous to overcome these tethers of mortality. And, this is what all mortal human beings will eventually know before they recognize that eternal salvation can be inherited from the Cross. It is all about miracles that happen every day. These miracles are having to fight against the enemies of the Church, especially the secularism that has been so damaging to the faith of millions. Satan is a secular devil. The righteousness of God is the social and psychological 'normal' of those who belong to Him. The collision between these two opposites began in the Garden of Eden, and the fight has been raging ever since. Every time a generation gets closer to finding their redemption in the Messiah, the secular forces act like a pendulum and reverse their progress again. It is much like an automobile being taken upstream on a ferry. There are many implications to this concept. I will allow you to ponder it in the future to decide whether it is something you would like to share with the rest of the world or retain as knowledge for yourself. You and your brother have matured in your faith to the degree that you are like many theologians before you. It is in your nature to be united with Jesus through the Church and within My intercession so that such communication comes easily for you."

Sunday, December 23, 2012
3:26 p.m.

The Incarnation of Jesus Christ

"My little sons, we delve deeply into the hearts of God's children, and soar highly to take them to Him. Surely you realize that the miracle of My messages will flourish equally as far and wide. I offer My tremendous gratitude for your faithfulness through the years and across the decades before. Goodness and Mercy shall follow you all the days of your lives. We have come within hours of the celebration of the Eve of Joy with great promise for the creatures of the world, for the citizens of Earth who place their hopes in Jesus. There is no reason to believe that your lives of labor have ever been in vain. Imagine a priest sitting in a rectory somewhere after having served another year in the Lord's vineyard. His holiness and peacefulness intact, he imagines the life he would have otherwise led. And, he contemplates all the earthly fathers who bounce their children on their knees, the ones who see their offspring play and grow, who move forward in life to be fate-changers themselves. These fathers of children are doing the work of Jesus by going forth and multiplying, but they are not fused together with the Holy Spirit the same way as priests who work for God. My Special son, you and your brother have acquired the acclaim of some of the most holy gentlemen to have walked the Earth. Your children are the souls you are conceiving into the freedom of Salvation by your pious service and prayers. I ask you to consider the reciprocity about which I have spoken on prior occasions. The Father places souls on the Earth in exile at the behest of mothers and fathers' matrimonial love, while you and your brother lead these souls back home into the Light of Paradise because of your communion with the Holy Spirit of Truth. The whole of Creation will someday see you this way, as the workers who gave more than the harvest required, as the children of God who remained at His side to pray rather than running about the nation-side frolicking in secularism and materialism. Can you see how the years are rushing away? This is your blessing! And, it is also the ratification of your birth as humanity's advocates in your mission as Saints and Saint-makers. Those who dare do this are aware of the brutal forces that oppose the holiness of the Church. You are in this state of grace because you have been chosen by Me. It was ordained upon your birth and placed into being when you opened your eyes to the depth of suffering around the globe. This conscience has accompanied you through the decades as your connection to the Divine Domain of the Father in Heaven. You must realize your stead before the Hosts and in the eyes of the Angels, to the benefit of the ages and the joy of the Saints. Now, you can likewise imagine the Lord looking at His Creation from beyond the stars and knowing that Moses had prefigured the world with the message of the coming Messiah. All the nations wondered how their Savior might come. They prepared their castles and boardwalks for this most auspicious hour. They made plans to hail Him with welcoming trumpets and songs. They warned their progeny that Moses had prophesied the closing of the ages at a moment's notice from then. They clad themselves in boastfulness that the Messiah would finally come to them, a King of kings, they said. Now, you know that this King arrived on the wings of righteousness as the faith-dweller and seat of holiness. You discovered that the King of the world came as the Prince of Peace; the Son of God would be the Son of Man! Greatness itself was deposited in this world upon the Nativity of Jesus Christ, the whole composite of human excellence in one innocuous Child. Sinless and perfect. Humble and delightful. This is the Son whom I knew to be conceived in My Womb by the gift of the Holy Spirit. I never once believed that I was unworthy or unfit for Motherhood as the Matriarch of the Church and the Mother of Jesus Christ. I had foresight and vision that surpassed all human understanding, even to this day. Why? Because the good Lord created Me that way. I was the Vessel who would carry the Salvation of humanity into the land of exiled men. Whether anyone chooses to downplay My role, station or power, I have within Me the capacity to deliver any soul who ever breathed mortal life to the Cross and baptize him in the Blood of My Crucified Son. We have knowledge, you and I, that others yet do not own. We have what they all want; it will be their big surprise. You and I bear the dignity of the lifeless in our hands; we give it to them every time we pray. We have the fortunes that will excavate paupers from beneath the rubble of humanity's greed. We have hands that will remove the blinders from the eyes of those who refuse to see the truth. We have the ability to reshape the surface of the globe, to make mountains tremble, to rise the oceans' floors to the highest arches in the skies. We can bring eagles to cry and babies pronounce the eloquence of the universe's ingenious strains. We can dress the Martyrs in their hooded gowns, and make them Doctors of the Church. Yes, My Special son, we do all these things because we belong to God. We are abounding in goodness and purity, consistent with the Sacred Love that said in the beginning that there shall be eternal light. This is why I ask you to remember that it is as if no time has passed since I first came speaking to you. I am the same Virgin of virgins, the same Queen of Love, the same Mother of Perpetual Help who has been watching over My children since Creation groaned its first labored pains beneath the burden of humanity's sins.

These are the rhymes and rhythms that must come-to-be in all human hearts so they will claim their identities in Jesus, and reclaim their place on the road to Paradise. Beyond the parameters of the world that you and your brother have always known lies the perpetual state of Divine Truth to which you shall someday return. You have been lent and leased to this earthly domain so the truth can prevail, can propagate and manifest a cultured and purified existence. The Earth has borrowed you from your station in God's parlor, just as Jesus was sent into the world to claim it from the Cross. As you were incarnated here, My Son was likewise given to the Flesh. He kept this Flesh pure. He gave His life for the redemption of the lost. He became the compass with which all who are searching for the reason for life will find it. And, when

He ascended into Heaven according to Scripture, He placed this holy commission in you and all who are obedient to the Church. He vested you with piety by virtue of your profession of faith. He created geniuses of you with the Wisdom of the Holy Spirit. This is the reason we are speaking to each other today. You have become like Jesus, and you have become like Me. You know right from wrong because your earthly mother and father communicated to you the teachings of the Roman Catholic Church, even before you reached the age of reason. You have made the best of their effort; you have dignified their desires to make you like Jesus, and you have succeeded in the mission of maturing in the Faith that has saved billions of souls. I have told you about happy endings, but the conclusion of the ages is rightfully the final new beginning. Imagine what I just said, the 'final new.' There would be only one Son of God, Son of Man. He is the first, the last and the perpetual state of goodness to whom those in the dark world would turn for elevation to the heights of righteousness. And thus, it is so, for sure. There are two sinless people who have walked these lands of yours – Jesus Christ and Myself, the Mother of exiled men. We became one upon My birth, and we have never been severed from each other. These are the melodies and Glory Hallelujahs that must be raised on the Eve of Joy tomorrow. I implore you and your brother to remember the perception that Jesus sees of you, still one and together for His Kingdom here in this place. Peter and Paul, Cosmas and Damian, William and Timothy, and all the 72 who trekked far and wide to make disciples of the nations and bread-makers for those who are hungry for life in the Sacred Word of Absolution.

    When the Lord places a soul into its mother's womb, it means that His joy is complete from the days of old. It means that there is still potential for the renewal of the Earth through the helplessness of every newborn child. It means that He desires the world to have its babes in the woods and children on the playground when the Son of Man returns. He places into the care of everyone walking the paths of their forbears the progeny that will shape their lives in years to come. It means that God still trusts broken humanity with His most fragile creatures, despite all evidence to the contrary. Therefore, I share this Christmas message with you and your brother in confidence that you will see your way clear to embracing the holiness in yourselves. Be aware of your stature in Heaven, your place in the Church, your poise before the horizon that will soon break to the last day of the world. I have undescribable admiration for your lives, for your chastity, for your daily prayers, and for your determination to not let the world get you down. Yes, Jesus brought His baptismal gown to the Father unstained because He was incapable of sin. And, you and your brother will bring your baptismal gowns to Jesus equally as immaculate through the Sacraments He has ordained. And, when He comes again, go out and greet Him with your hands held high to the skies. Give Him tomorrow evening the same hearts that you will bear on that day, the same signs of jubilance, the same determination to deliver to Him all the souls for whom we have prayed through the years. Jesus came to the Earth through Me so humanity would go to Him through Me. We do not make assumptions about something so grave as the fight between the salvation or condemnation of a mortal soul. But, with this in mind, we are assured beyond any doubt that your commitment to the Father will succeed. When counting the number of souls who will make it there, let us simply say that their Salvation is a celebrated sum. Let us pray that 2013 becomes everything that you ever wanted a new year to be. I am asking My Son to ensure your happiness and good health and longevity. We have already won, you know, and we will assuredly win again. Thank you for taking such good care of your brother. You know that he is getting older, but you are not quite there. I wanted to say that I am taking your petitions for those who are ill to Jesus, as those prayers coincide with the Will of the Father. Your petitions are a gift to many. You have all the adulation from Heaven that any soul could possibly conceive."

Sunday, December 30, 2012
2:24 p.m.

A New and Glorious Morn

"My children, it is with a bountiful Heart that I come speak with you once more during 2012. And, here you go running through time with swiftness on your heels. Even so, I ask you to not run too quickly. I seek from you a sense of peace that represents your commitment to all you have taken-on during your earthly lives. Peace in the heart cannot survive when you are in constant motion because you lack the perspective that the stillness brings. I have told you many times that humanity has become indoctrinated in the commotion of the world, and this relative movement fools the human spirit about the rapidity of life. You become desensitized to the spinning in which you are oftentimes a part. Indeed, I ask you to be as peace-filled and confident as you have represented the heavens by your messages and through your lives. It is as though you are still kneeling alongside the Manger where the Child Jesus lay. Today, I invite you to remember the stillness of that night. This is the life that I ask you to embrace in 2013. Imagine what this means for all who will come to you! The prayers we have lifted during 2012 have lessened the seriousness of untold numbers of tragedies; and if the whole world were praying with you, they would have been averted altogether. My Special and Chosen ones, here we have come to the midnight of 2012; we have arrived at the dawn of AD 2013. I am here with you inside of time and beyond the physical realms as your Mother, building your faith in God to trust that His Will is the purpose for your actions. How do you know the intricacies and parameters of His Will? It comes to you by inspiration from the Paraclete, from the Advocate who grows your wisdom of the Eternal Kingdom. I have said that suffering in this world comes from sinful men, either by their direct error and unholy acts, or by the necessity to mitigate human sin by joining in the Glory of the Cross. It would seem at times that one is difficult to identify from the other. Nonetheless, we have come together in this place to the New and Glorious Morn of humanity in the Earth's physical arena and spiritual potential. I assure you that the Lord is prevailing over the sins of men because the sun still rises and sets, babes still reach upward for their fathers, the birds sing and rivers run, and men conduct the affairs of states and nations. It always seems that the words 'Happy New Year' are hollow commendations to friends and strangers alike because mankind seems so helpless to determine the future that way. What precisely is happiness? Does it imply that the volition of men should supercede the Will of God? Does it mean that the wealthy should prosper at the expense of the poor? This certainly makes some people happy. Perhaps no one really knows what happiness means until they have a clear perception of sadness with which to compare it. It is relative to many people in many places; it is inconsistent and incomparable in various lives and communities. However, A New and Glorious Morn can only mean one thing to all peoples. It means that there is universal and worldwide acceptance of the Gospel of Christianity as the reason for life and the purpose of dying. If this does not occur, it is impossible that 2013 can become a happy new year. People tend to compartmentalize their losses and failures when they do not know what to do. Others see their suffering during moments or hours rather than days and months because it frames their lives into more doable doses. These are admirable focal points because they restructure and restrengthen their levels of faith. Trust in God. What does this mean? It simply means that prayerful communication with the Rosary and through the Litanies is never in vain. It is the life of the Christian soul to know that the Father is listening.

Hence, My little children, the New and Glorious Morn sung about in the ancient melody gives rise to new hope, the kind of hope that I can have inside My Immaculate Heart, even though I have seen the culmination of human events. In fact, I have hope in the conversion of sinners by virtue of seeing the culmination. Why would I come here if this were untrue? Why would the world be brawling? Why would the Father not simply put it to rest and end all suffering? Because the management of righteousness on Earth requires the participation of exiled souls. This is the reason the Christ Child was born; it is the reason that the Holy Spirit remains here to inform and cultivate, to heal and bless, and to inspire and resolve. All this work is done inside the human heart. The civility of the conscience of the Christian is a product of this inspiration. So, it is not so much the emphasis on the passing years that matters most, but what happens during their tenure. My Special one, you said it correctly. Everything that ails the world and burdens humanity could be ended in five minutes if it were the Will of God. But, He does not want to do it alone. He pines for the participation of His Church. He yearns for the genius of His people to remake and remold, to soften and cure. This is not a solitary God that we honor. He is sovereign but not isolationist. He wants to have that relationship with His people that you have often written about. Jesus is both human and divine!

This is My message for today. I bring you news of great joy that the Lord is with you still. He will never abandon you; the Holy Spirit will remain in and beside us through the endlessness of eternity. I promise that as you have lived, you shall continue to live inside the blessings of Jesus throughout the years to come and the infinity yonder. I am here. The Blessed Trinity is with you and all men. This is the greatness of the New and Glorious Morn, that the Son of Man has come into your presence for all the reasons you have known for a half-century. Is there any way you can know how much you are loved? Probably not as fully as you would like. I can only tell you about the Promise. It is being fulfilled as men speak. If you saw everything that you will eventually come to know, your spirit would freeze in place from the joy and ecstasy abounding. You would become so still in awe of the majesty of God and the Church that you would not be able to function in a physical sense. My Immaculate Heart is pouring-out this grace to you, as Grace was birthed from

My Womb. Do you remember the most important word that I have ever said in this home? *"Patience."* Indeed, this is the word. Patience is the mainstay of virtuous love. Even as the first Apostles walked the Earth beside the Messiah, their most pronounced question to Him was, 'When?' Now, they have seen that 'when' has always been 'now' back in their day and here in yours. The Eternal Kingdom is flourishing from the olden days and into the future by these present hours. I commend to you the future as you would have it lived in accordance with the prayers of humanity and the Will of the Father to usher-in the final sunrise of the world. I must do the same. I am required to watch and wait, knowing full-well who will act and when they will act in accordance with the Providence described in the Gospels and ratified by the King on the Cross. 'Patience' is not a negative term. Imagine being the Messiah who knew that He would be taken to the Crucifixion. It was this patience that laid the groundwork for the founding of the Church, one day at a time. It is all about the magnification of love through the moments and in the lives of men who will soon gather in the Kingdom of Heaven forever. I promise that this will occur. I pray that you will enter 2013 with the peaceful confidence about which I have spoken here today. A New and Glorious Morn is upon you, and about to unfold before humanity with awesome revelation. Your foresight is prescient. Thank you for sharing Christmas with your family. It was nice seeing you and your brother, along with Saint Augustine, in your hometown parish Church."

www.ingramcontent.com/pod-product-compliance
Lightning Source LLC
Chambersburg PA
CBHW071055230426
43666CB00009B/1715